72nd Volume
2004-2005

The Higley
Lesson Commentary

International Uniform
Lesson Series

Editor
Wesley C. Reagan

Contributing Writers
Ron Durham, Ph.D.
Doug deGraffenried
David Dietzel
H. A. (Peter) Harrington, D.Min.
Tommy W. King, D.Min.

The Higley Lesson Commentary, in this 72nd year of its life, renews its commitment to careful and reverent scholarship, clear and understandable language, practical and insightful application, and interesting and readable writing. We send it to you with a prayer that it will be a powerful resource for you.

Higley Publishing Corporation
P. O. Box 5398
Jacksonville, FL 32247-5398
(800) 842-1093

www.higleycommentary.com

i

FOREWORD

The Higley Lesson Commentary is a compilation of the best insights and illustrations a group of dedicated writers can bring to a study of the Scriptures. Each writer has years of training and experience to bring to a lesson. He studies the Bible to come to an awareness of what the text is actually teaching. Then he thinks about how that can be taught and illustrated so that a Bible student can quickly grasp it.

After coming to an understanding of the text, attention is given to how to apply the principles in modern life. Ways of dealing with problems and frustrations are considered. Here, the matter of motivation is considered. What is it that calls and inspires to a higher level of living? How can we remain focused during times of discouragement? How do we recover from mistakes? How do we hold on to hope?

To realize these objectives, each lesson begins with the text. Then a section called "Focus" states the theme or objective of that particular day's study. "For a Lively Start" is a suggestion about how to capture attention at the beginning of the lesson. Then the "Teaching Outline" shows how the text will be organized for study. The "Verse by Verse" is an exposition or a commentary on the passage being studied. It provides factual information and helps the reader to grasp the meaning of the Scripture itself before going on to a study of how to apply it.

In every lesson an evangelistic emphasis is drawn from the text, and thoughtful comments are made on the "Memory Selection" for the day. "Weekday Problems" portray practical and down-to-earth situations. "This Lesson in Your Life" suggests ways the lesson will be of personal benefit. "Getting the Facts Straight" is a review of some basic questions that have clear answers.

"The Uplift Page" is designed to inspire. Warm-hearted illustrations help people want to do better. In each lesson there is also a boxed "fun" section that is meant to bring brightness to the reader and, on occasion, to give sparkle to his teaching.

To have that array of resources that can be accessed in a short time is an amazing help to those who teach from material based on The Uniform Lesson Series. I am thankful to be a part of this significant teaching ministry and pray that you will be greatly blessed by it.

Wesley C. Reagan, Editor
The Higley Lesson Commentary

PREFACE

GREETINGS
To our friends and fellow-workers in the gospel:

"The Lord gave the Word, great was the company
of those that publish it"—Psalm 68:11

This salutation comes from a trip down memory lane. The greeting adorns volumes 1 (1933) through 16 (1949) of *The Higley Lesson Commentary*, with the quotation from Psalm 68:11 appearing only in the 1941 volume. It is a gentle greeting with a noble ring to it. It seems to light up the area well for this, our 72nd volume.

It is the publishers' desire to tell you of the appreciation we have for the excellent work of the editor and his notable colleagues of contributing writers. I salute them for their help in building a private cathedral where one can be nourished by the fruits of their minds, hearts, and spirits as they offer this remarkable gift, *The Higley Lesson Commentary.* Publishers of biblical literature know, in facing the secular head winds, that there is no assurance of fiscal gain for this type of endeavor. For them, the enterprise is a labor of love. Its reward is bringing Christ to every home that He alone may be glorified.

The long life of *The Higley Lesson Commentary* has been made possible by five devoted publishers over the last 71 years. Those years contain citations that mark a steady decay of moral responsibility in our society. Volumes of earlier years read like summaries of what we see daily with only slightly different adjectives describing the level of turpitude.

Yet the cadence of history flows in soft rhythms for books of spiritual guidance. We have seen in the first generation of this commentary, from 1933 through 1971, a gradual unfolding of the life work of L. H. Higley, the founder of the commentary. Many of those early years were based on the mid-westerner's work from the development of the Epworth Quarterly 100 years ago. Mr. Higley published annual versions of lessons, or "leaves," as he called them, for Bible study. Lesson language at the turn of the century is a rare joy to read. It is hard to lay the beautiful thoughts down.

At the beginning of the commentary's second generation in 1972, the phrase, "Heritage of Trust," was introduced to coin that special inheritance given to us by the Man from Galilee. To this day, the devotional clarity imparted from the contributing writers continues to inspire others to hear the voice of God in their lives. I believe the editor and writers have been, and are, worthy of that trust, a hallmark of *The Higley Lesson Commentary.* With infinite courtesy, we hope that you enjoy this valuable work as we send forth this volume 72 with the same prayer that appeared in volume 1, "that the spiritual inspiration which blesses those who wrote it may be passed on to those who read it."

The Publishers
The Higley Lesson Commentary

FALL QUARTER
The God of Continuing Creation
Created for a Purpose (Lessons 1-4)
God's Creativity Continues (Lessons 5-9)
A New Creation (Lessons 10-13)

WINTER QUARTER
Called to be God's People
God Calls a People (Lessons 1-4)
The Call of Jesus and His Followers (Lessons 5-9)
Whosoever Will—Come! (Lessons 10-13)

SPRING QUARTER
God's Project: Effective Christians
Saved by God (Lessons 1-4)
The Christian Life (Lessons 5-8)
Set Free (Lessons 9-13)

SUMMER QUARTER

Jesus' Life, Teaching, and Ministry

Jesus' Life (Lessons 1-4)
Jesus' Ministry of Teaching (Lessons 5-9)
Jesus' Ministry of Compassion (Lessons 10-13)

The Quest Eternal

For man's unceasing quest for God,
For God's unceasing quest for man,
For records of his love and power
Surrounding life since life began,
    We thank thee, Lord most high.
   . . .

For those great laws the Hebrews made,
Among the greatest ever known,
For early history wise men wrote,
Engraved on parchment, skin, or stone,
    We thank thee, Lord most high.

For those old songs of tuneful verse,
The music of the shepherd king,
For songs the Boy of Nazareth sang,
And still succeeding ages sing,
    We thank thee, Lord most high.

For those most precious books of all,
That show us Jesus Christ, our Lord,
Seen through the eyes of faithful friends,
Who gave their lives to spread his word,
    We thank thee, Lord most high.

—Alice M. Pullen

Unit I. Created for a Purpose

Lesson 1

From the Dust of the Ground

Genesis 2:4-7, 15-24

hese are the generations of the heavens and of the earth when they were created, in the day that the LORD God made the earth and the heavens,

5 And every plant of the field before it was in the earth, and every herb of the field before it grew: for the LORD God had not caused it to rain upon the earth, and there was not a man to till the ground.

6 But there went up a mist from the earth, and watered the whole face of the ground.

7 And the LORD God formed man of the dust of the ground, and breathed into his nostrils the breath of life; and man became a living soul.

15 And the LORD God took the man, and put him into the garden of Eden to dress it and to keep it.16 And the LORD God commanded the man, saying, Of every tree of the garden thou mayest freely eat:

17 But of the tree of the knowledge of good and evil, thou shalt not eat of it: for in the day that thou eatest thereof thou shalt surely die.

18 And the LORD God said, It is not good that the man should be alone; I will make him an help meet for him.

19 And out of the ground the LORD God formed every beast of the field, and every fowl of the air; and brought them unto Adam to see what he would call them: and whatsoever Adam called ev-

ery living creature, that was the name thereof.

20 And Adam gave names to all cattle, and to the fowl of the air, and to every beast of the field; but for Adam there was not found an help meet for him.

21 And the LORD God caused a deep sleep to fall upon Adam and he slept: and he took one of his ribs, and closed up the flesh instead thereof;

22 And the rib, which the LORD God had taken from man, made he a woman, and brought her unto the man.

23 And Adam said, This is now bone of my bones, and flesh of my flesh: she shall be called Woman, because she was taken out of Man.

24 Therefore shall a man leave his father and his mother, and shall cleave unto his wife: and they shall be one flesh.

23 And Adam said, This is now bone of my bones, and flesh of my flesh: she shall be called Woman, because she was taken out of Man.

24 Therefore shall a man leave his father and his mother, and shall cleave unto his wife: and they shall be one flesh.

Memory Selection
Genesis 2:7

Background Scripture
Genesis 2

Devotional Reading
Psalm 150

1

To what do we owe our existence, and what is our purpose on earth? Such questions must not be allowed to be merely abstract and philosophical; we should also give them a practical edge. Especially in trying times, we believers need to know what we're about, staying in touch with God's will for our lives. Thus this first quarter deals with the theme of *Creation*—God's will for us from "in the beginning" to our being a "new creation" in Christ.

The first lesson focuses on how God created us to relate to His world, to each other, and to Himself. Students should emerge from this lesson with a renewed sense of "connectedness," the confidence that God values them as the apex of the created order, and the intention to have healthy relationships with all others, and with this realm that "God so loved."

☜☞

Most members of your group will be familiar with "job descriptions." Begin this lesson by asking them to imagine a job description for Adam and Eve. Statements and contributions might take the form of "Want Ads," such as:

WANTED: Man and woman to care for each other, a garden, and its creatures, and to carry out the wishes of the Gardener.

WANTED: Gardening couple who don't mind being created out of dirt and living outdoors. Ideal conditions. Clothing optional.

WANTED: Man and woman to start a new race of people under the rule of God. Live among friendly plants and animals, eat everything in a garden except the fruit of one tree.

Of course the object of this introduction is to lead into the account of creation that begins in Genesis 2:4.

Teaching Outline

I. Man's Garden Home—4-7

  A. Place without people, 4-6

  B. Enter Adam and Eve, 7

II. Mission and Boundaries—15-18

  A. The gift of work, 15

  B. The gift of boundaries, 16-17

  C. The gift of companionship, 18

III. Managing by Name—19-20

IV. Mates Who Are 'Meet'—21-25

Daily Bible Readings

Mon. Praise the LORD!
    Psalm 148:1-6
Tue. Let the Earth Praise Him!
    Psalm 148:7-13
Wed. God's Good Creation
    Genesis 1:26-31
Thu. God Created Man
    Genesis 2:4-9
Fri. A River-Watered Garden
    Genesis 2:10-14
Sat. Man Placed in the Garden
    Genesis 2:15-20
Sun. A Mate Fit for a Man
    Genesis 2:21-25

Verse by Verse

I. Man's Garden Home—4-7
A. Place without people, 4-6

4 These are the generations of the heavens and of the earth when they were created, in the day that the LORD God made the earth and the heavens,

5 And every plant of the field before it was in the earth, and every herb of the field before it grew: for the LORD God had not caused it to rain upon the earth, and there was not a man to till the ground.

6 But there went up a mist from the earth, and watered the whole face of the ground.

The more familiar account of creation runs from Genesis 1:1–2:3. Now the author presents not so much a second account as one that focuses more specifically on the man and woman who were the crowning act of creation in chapter 1, and their personal relationship with their Creator.

The word "generations" here means "family history," and probably refers to what follows instead of the preceding account. We are not told when the "day" or era was when "God made the earth and the heavens."

Limited space precludes listing the various ways some scientific accounts differ from the timeless and poetic biblical accounts. Suffice it to say that genuine truth is not contradictory.

The author's main purpose reaches beyond science's ability to confirm or deny. It is to show that the Creator-God (Heb. *el*) of chapter 1 is none other than Yahweh, the personal name of the God of the Hebrews. Verse 4 is the first time this personal name appears in Scripture. (In the KJV this name is indicated by capitals-and-small capitals: LORD OR GOD). Now we are assured that creation was not accidental or impersonal, but an act of love by Him whom the Jews call "the Ruler of the Universe."

This love is implied by the note of desolation and loneliness that indicates that creation was not complete since "there was not a man to till the ground." Creation was designed for people to work at keeping it ordered and productive—physically, here, and morally and spiritually in the verses to follow.

B. Enter Adam and Eve, 7

7 And the LORD God formed man of the dust of the ground, and breathed into his nostrils the breath of life; and man became a living soul.

Some scholars believe this language allows for any number of races to have existed before God decided to breathe "the breath of life" into this select man, beginning the truly *human* race. Although most of these races died out (for example, the Neanderthals), some apparently remained and supplied wives for Cain and Abel (see also Gen. 6:2).

The term "living soul" is typical of the ancient Jewish view of persons. We do not so much just *have* a soul, we *are* souls—a body-spirit whole. Although considering persons as "body, soul and spirit" (1 Thess. 5:23) can be useful for focusing on and treating one or another human component, the "holistic" view of persons many think to be a modern discovery is actually assumed in the Old Testament.

At first glance, being made of "dust" (dirt or clay) doesn't seem very complimentary—until we remember that the term "human" is related to *humus*, the rich and nutritious substance necessary for growing things. Whatever our substance of origin, we are to value ourselves and others because we are made in God's image (1:26-27).

II. Mission and Boundaries—15-18

A. The gift of work, 15

15 And the LORD God took the man, and put him into the garden of Eden to dress it and to keep it.

The principle that *work* helps define what it means to be human is clearly established here. Being assigned to "dress" or tend a garden might not sound like a dignified career to modern ears, but it lays down the universal principle that work is honorable, and that caring for the earth is a part of God's will. The term for "keep" can also mean to conserve. This phrase provides important balance to man's having been given "dominion" over creation in 1:28, which has sometimes, though wrongly, been taken to give man the right to treat the environment as he wishes.

B. The gift of boundaries, 16-17

16 And the LORD God commanded the man, saying, Of every tree of the garden thou mayest freely eat:

17 But of the tree of the knowledge of good and evil, thou shalt not eat of it: for in the day that thou eatest thereof thou shalt surely die.

Now the God who commanded creation to emerge from nothing issues a command in the moral sphere. The exact consequence of eating of the fruit of the "tree of knowledge of good and evil" is not clear. It was not bare knowledge of right from wrong, since that would already have to be present in order to know it was wrong to break God's law. Perhaps the meaning is akin to the Old Testament's use of "knowledge" to refer to *intimate union with*, as when it refers to sexual union (4:1).

The promised punishment of *death* for eating of the forbidden fruit probably refers to *spiritual* death, or separation from God, since (1) as yet man had not yet eaten of "the tree of [eternal] life," and (2) physical death seems to have been built into creation from the start, as when plant seeds "die" to produce new life (1:29).

C. The gift of companionship, 18

18 And the LORD God said, It is not good that the man should be alone; I will make him an help meet for him.

Up to this point, each stage of creation has received the divine approval in the form, "It was good" or

4

"very good." The first "ungood" to intrude on the otherwise idyllic scene in Eden is existing alone. This refers to the need to perpetuate the race and the general rule that we all like companionship, rather than applying to every specific instance of single people not having a mate. The "help" for the first man is designed to be "meet" or *fit* for the man—a suitable complement, not a subordinate.

III. Managing by Name—19-20

19 And out of the ground the LORD God formed every beast of the field, and every fowl of the air; and brought them unto Adam to see what he would call them: and whatsoever Adam called every living creature, that was the name thereof.

20 And Adam gave names to all cattle, and to the fowl of the air, and to every beast of the field; but for Adam there was not found an help meet for him.

Ancient societies valued highly the power and privilege of giving names to both animals and children. (The modern phrase in psychological contexts, "To name the tiger is to tame the tiger," illustrates this principle.) As prominent as is the privilege of naming, however, is the poignancy in the last phrase of verse 20; for all the diversity of animal life, none was "meet" for Adam's mate.

IV. Mates Who Are 'Meet'—21-25

21 And the LORD God caused a deep sleep to fall upon Adam and he slept: and he took one of his ribs, and closed up the flesh instead thereof;

22 And the rib, which the LORD God had taken from man, made he a woman, and brought her unto the man.

23 And Adam said, This is now bone of my bones, and flesh of my flesh: she shall be called Woman, because she was taken out of Man.

24 Therefore shall a man leave his father and his mother, and shall cleave unto his wife: and they shall be one flesh.

25 And they were both naked, the man and his wife, and were not ashamed.

Now we can see that the naming of animals was recorded partly as a build-up to the more fulfilling experience of having, and naming, a true partner. Since God made the woman from the man (Heb. *ish*), Adam appropriately names her *ishah*, literally "she-man." The English even bears out this play on words if, as some authorities say, "wo-man" is a contraction of "womb-man."

This, the earliest recorded marriage, states the principle that marriage creates a new and relatively independent entity. Marriages in which the families of origin unduly intrude are proof enough of the wisdom of the classic "leave" and "cleave" statement in verse 24.

Verse 25 shows the pre-fall innocence of the man and woman, who have not yet partaken of the forbidden fruit and connected nudity with shame. It is appropriate that this innocence is associated here with marriage, since that union restores the shameless acceptance of the beauty of the unclothed body.

Evangelistic Emphasis

It is always easy to tell when a person is handling something precious or cheap. When setting the table for a lovely dinner, the fine china is gently but firmly grasped, washed, and returned to the cabinet. Its use reflects everyone's awareness that the dinnerware is not easily replaced, and is worthy of honor.

Something moves deep within us when we become fully aware that we were handcrafted by God like fine china. When we understand the planning, care, and amazingly individual design into which we were all molded, that self-understanding demands we take humble pride in ourselves. To see ourselves as "God's fine china" should change our approach to who we are and our sense of having been created for a purpose.

To see "Handle With Care" stickers all over our own beings, tells us the Creator of all things made us with great honor and worthiness. That awareness alone should give us a whole new understanding of the amazing journey of life.

ഇരു

Memory Selection

The Lord God formed man from the dust of the ground, and breathed into his nostrils the breath of life; and the man became a living being.—*Genesis 2:7*

We are always fascinated when something "comes into being." Children watch wide-eyed as eggs in a robin's nest begin to crack open and tiny babies with mouth agape fill the nest, begging for food. Adults are frozen with amazement watching a cicada shell clinging to a wall split open and a magnificent green summer cicada emerges, with wings that dry by sunrise.

To watch something come into being is a moving experience for just about everyone, but for the person of faith it is especially meaningful because the Hand of God is behind it all. The poetry in the phrase "and breathed into his nostrils the breath of life, and man became a living being" is profound indeed. We who call ourselves Christians see God's Hand in everything, from butterflies to babies, for all things are the products of God's intentional will.

Weekday Problems

A boy was preparing for college, and his parents were fussing with all the things that needed to be accounted for: clothes, finances, books, and whatever a college freshman needs. As a last comment, the father sat the young man down and said, "Now you don't ever forget that you are representing our family. Whenever anyone sees you or watches you, they are seeing an extension of your mother and me. Now you go on to the university and make us proud."

When we learn fully that God has not only made us in His Image, but has sent us into the world specifically to represent His design of wholeness, forgiveness, decency, dignity, and honor, then we are less likely to wind up acting in ways that would embarrass the Lord. When we know that we were intentionally sent into the world with an unbreakable bond to the One who sends us all, our lifestyle and behaviors are changed.

*Are you aware daily that you represent God?

Adam's Lighter Side

The shortest poem in the world is titled "Fleas." It goes:

> Adam
> Had'm.

* * * *

Adam: LORD, I don't think any of these animals is suitable for a mate.

God: Well, I can come up with something better, but it'll cost you an arm and a leg.

Adam: Ouch. What could I get for a rib?

* * * *

I'm sure Adam had his problems, but at least he didn't have to listen to his wife talk about the man she wished she could have married.

* * * *

Physics lesson: The splitting of the Adam gave us Eve, a force which ingenious men in all ages have never gotten under control.

7

There is a great discussion across our land these days as to whether or not we are the product of a random merger of molecules and DNA, or the result of an incredible, designing Holy Spirit, with a plan and a road map for the unfolding of all creation.

Those people who view themselves as just accidental occasions of cosmic synthesis surely must have a frail and weak grip upon their self-respect. In the magnificent play "Death Of A Salesman," Wally is speaking of life after his father died, and how that bond was lost forever. Wally says, "Well, I don't know, ever since Dad died I've just felt sort of temporary about myself." Surely that is the same feeling of someone who does not sense being the product of a loving God.

Christians, on the other hand, see in all things, and especially humans, the intentional design and plan of God, almost as though one were looking on the drawing table of an architect. The designs of nature and the cosmos, the seasons and cycles of life, mountains, patterns of migration and development of a human being, all broadcast a witness that this is the result of a grand intent.

There is something unspeakably amazing when one realizes that every single molecule of creation and its relationship to all other facets of existence was planned, drawn, and set into being no less than Rembrandt slowly fashioned a painting where all the colors are interdependent, and emerge as a priceless portrait. Being a part of a grand plan is deep and moving. Being the result of an incidental accident is a hollow, empty concept.

1. What was the original task of the man when God placed him in the Garden of Eden?
Man was placed in the garden to care for it, and to "till it and keep it." Then and now, we are called to care for the earth.

2. Sensing that Man should not be alone, what was God's first effort to change this situation?
God fashioned all of the creatures and brought them to the man as companions, so that the man would name them.

3. What happened after that ?
It became very clear that while man enjoyed all the wonderful variety of creatures, there was a major emptiness within him, for man needed something more than a beast of the field as a companion.

4. How did God address that need?
He made the man a partner of the same flesh. He created woman, that the two might complement one another and begin the human race.

5. How did God define the role of woman?
God made it clear that the place of woman surpassed that of the man's mother and father. God fully intended for the man and the woman to form a new family and a new union.

6. In addition to wanting the man to have companions in life, why did God allow him to name all the creatures?
For man to name all living things was God's way of letting him begin dominion over them.

7. What is meaning behind woman's being made from the man's ribs?
It is a clear statement that woman will be made of the equal substance of man, and will be a full partner in every measure. It does not, as some have said, indicate woman is subservient to man.

8. What does it mean that God made man from "the dust of the ground?"
It means God formed humankind out of the exact same elements as all the rest of creation was formed, a common theme throughout Genesis. It is a fact that all creatures on earth share common chemical identity.

9. Why did God prohibit man from eating the fruit of The Tree of Knowledge of Good and Evil?
To remind him that man would always be secondary to God, and subject to God's restrictions and guidelines in his life, for his own good.

10. What was the nature of the death that would result from man's eating the forbidden fruit?
It meant sin would separate man from God and that living a sinful life would bring shame and embarrassment.

The story of creation in Genesis 2, and the naming of the creatures, offers a marvelous description of how God intends for all things to work together in harmony.

There is a form of yucca that grows in the arid western plateaus. When that species of yucca blooms, it sends up great stalks piled thickly with ivory white flowers. At the same time, a moth emerges from the ground just in time to fly straight up and pollinate the flowers. The moth does not pollinate any other flowers in the world, and without this moth this species of yucca would rapidly become extinct. So would the moth. The yucca flowers offer nectar and nourishment to the moth. The moth, in turn, lays eggs in the flowers. The eggs drop to the ground and form a pupa. That pupa lies dormant until the next blooming season when it will turn into a moth and the cycle begins again.

The Schomburgkia family of orchids in Central and South America has bulbs known as *pseudobulbs*. A major portion of the pseudobulbs are hollow, and large stinging ants bore into them and make their homes within. The orchid provides a home for the ants, and the ants perform a defense for the orchid. Any attempt to harvest a Schomburgkia orchid or to take it away will be met by an onslaught of defenders.

God has made all things to work together, and any serious student of biology will be aware of the fact that not a single creature is alone and isolated. All things, including humans, are vital, interconnected parts of the earth and the family of creatures that God made. As Chief Seattle once said, "The earth does not belong to us; we belong to the earth." That is so true. In the eyes of God that is very good.

Lesson 2

Beginning Again

Genesis 6:5-8; 7:1-5, 17, 23; 8:14-16; 9:1

And GOD saw that the wicked ness of man was great in the earth, and that every imagination of the thoughts of his heart was only evil continually.

6 And it repented the LORD that he had made man on the earth, and it grieved him at his heart.

7 And the LORD said, I will destroy man whom I have created from the face of the earth; both man, and beast, and the creeping thing, and the fowls of the air; for it repenteth me that I have made them.

8 But Noah found grace in the eyes of the LORD.

7:1 And the LORD said unto Noah, Come thou and all thy house into the ark; for thee have I seen righteous before me in this generation.

2 Of every clean beast thou shalt take to thee by sevens, the male and his female: and of beasts that are not clean by two, the male and his female.

3 Of fowls also of the air by sevens, the male and the female; to keep seed alive upon the face of all the earth.

4 For yet seven days, and I will cause it to rain upon the earth forty days and forty nights; and every living substance that I have made will I destroy from off the face of the earth.

5 And Noah did according unto all that the LORD commanded him.

17 And the flood was forty days upon the earth; and the waters increased, and bare up the ark, and it was lift up above the earth.

23 And every living substance was destroyed which was upon the face of the ground, both man, and cattle, and the creeping things, and the fowl of the heaven; and they were destroyed from the earth: and Noah only remained.

8:14 And in the second month, on the seven and twentieth day of the month, was the earth dried.

15 And God spake unto Noah, saying,

16 Go forth of the ark, thou, and thy wife, and thy sons, and thy sons' wives with thee.

9:1 And God blessed Noah and his sons, and said unto them, Be fruitful, and multiply, and replenish the earth.

Memory Selection
Genesis 9:16
Background Scripture
Genesis 6:5–9:17
Devotional Reading
Genesis 9:8-17

The teacher is well-advised to start preparing for this lesson early in order to have time to read the extensive "Background Scriptures" provided (Gen. 6:5–9:17. This essential background covers the Fall of man, the flood, and the opportunity given to Noah to "begin again."

The impact of this session extends well beyond the facts described in the lesson texts. Since traditional theology views the Fall as the origin of both moral and natural evils, the effects of the "original sin" recorded here reach forward throughout history. Yet the opportunity given to Noah to begin again also provides a positive paradigm of God' willingness to forgive sin and to redeem man from the effects of the Fall. The fresh, new world facing Noah becomes a foretaste of the "new creation" that will be ushered in by Christ.

ഇരു

This lesson's references on the Fall can be effectively introduced by leading a discussion that envisions the opposite—a perfect world. Ask members of your group what the world would be like had sin and its effects never intruded. Encourage specifics, not just generalities. It's more helpful to mention not having to deal with cancer in a perfect world than just saying "We wouldn't have any troubles."

On the other hand, note how God's superior power over evil enables good to emerge even from a fallen world. Who knows how many heroic deeds highlighting man's love for each other have been prompted by the very evils Satan sought to use to destroy love? What other "arks" like Noah's ship of salvation have resulted from the threat of floods of evil of various sorts?

Teaching Outline	*Daily Bible Readings*	
I. Degenerate World—Gen. 6:5-8	Mon.	Great Wickedness *Genesis 6:5-12*
A. God's grief, 5-6	Tue.	'Build the Ark' Genesis 6:13-22
B. God's plan, 7-8		
II. Destruction and Deliverance— 7:1-5, 17, 23	Wed.	Entering the Ark *Genesis 7:1-16*
A. Provision for animals, 1-3	Thu.	The Flood Strikes *Genesis 7:17–8:5*
B. The flood, 4-5		
C. Effects of the flood, 17, 23	Fri.	Noah Leaves the Ark *Genesis 8:6-19*
III. Days of Beginning Again—8:14-16, 9:1	Sat.	God Blesses Noah *Genesis 8:20–9:7*
A. Emerging from the ark, 8:14-16	Sun.	God's New Covenant *Genesis 9:8-17*
B. Blessings and commission, 9:1		

Verse by Verse

I. Degenerate World—Gen. 6:5-8

A. God's grief, 5-6

5 And GOD saw that the wickedness of man was great in the earth, and that every imagination of the thoughts of his heart was only evil continually.

6 And it repented the LORD that he had made man on the earth, and it grieved him at his heart.

Science speaks of "entropy"—the fact that the universe seems to be running out of energy. A similar process seems to have taken over God's *moral* creation between Genesis 1 and 6. At first "It was very good." Then Adam and Eve disobeyed God. Their son Cain killed his brother Abel. People in general imagined evil instead of good. At creation God had continually pronounced the world "very good." Now it has become so bad that God has to intervene to arrest the process of decline.

To say that God "repented" refers not to His having done wrong, but, in keeping with the literal meaning of the word, that He "changed His mind" or had regrets about the way people had abused the gift of free will He had given them. Note that the predominant emotion God has as He looks at sinful people is not wrath, but grief.

B. God's plan, 7-8

7 And the LORD said, I will destroy man whom I have created from the face of the earth; both man, and beast, and the creeping thing, and the fowls of the air; for it repenteth me that I have made them.

8 But Noah found grace in the eyes of the LORD.

The use of the word "man" in verse 7 is expanded to include all life. Evil has become so rampant that God will wipe the entire slate clean. This plan is usually taken as a horrible sign of God's judgment and wrath. In fact, we have no way of knowing what diseases had accompanied the sinful behavior. The Flood will destroy such ills, purifying the environment—showing both God's judgment and grace.

This grace is extended in a special way to one Noah and his family. Although this "election" is based on grace, Scripture does note that Noah walked with God and was an exception to the general sinfulness that pervaded the earth (6:9). The name "Noah" means "comfort" or "rest"; and his comforting role in rebuilding the earth's population is in direct fulfillment of the prophecy of his father Lamech that Noah would "comfort us concerning our work and toil of our hands" (5:29).

II. Destruction and Deliverance— 7:1-5, 17, 23

A. Provision for animals, 1-3

1 And the LORD said unto Noah,

13

Come thou and all thy house into the ark; for thee have I seen righteous before me in this generation.

2 Of every clean beast thou shalt take to thee by sevens, the male and his female: and of beasts that are not clean by two, the male and his female.

3 Of fowls also of the air by sevens, the male and the female; to keep seed alive upon the face of all the earth.

The ark (lit. *chest*—not a ship designed for travel but a huge floatable box for a haven) had been God's prescription for the salvation of Noah and a select group of animals (6:14-22). In those days when the average life-span was so long (Noah's grandfather Methusaleh, lived 969 years according to 5:27), time moved more slowly; and it apparently took Noah 120 years to build this storied ship (6:3).

Although this story has seemed mythical to many, it is interesting to note that many ancient civilizations have a version of a great flood and a great ship—indicating the possibility of a common source and some historical basis for the account. Some researchers also believe that a curious boat-shaped formation sighted in the mountains of northeastern Turkey, as well as a persistent tradition in Iran, provide evidence of the factual nature of Noah's ark.

Note that the tradition of "clean" and "unclean" animals that would become so important in later Jewish tradition is first mentioned here. God wants to save not only pairs of animals to repopulate (or "keep seed alive" for) earth's fauna; He has special interest in preserving the animals that will be used in the worship He prescribes for His people.

B. The flood, 4-5

4 For yet seven days, and I will cause it to rain upon the earth forty days and forty nights; and every living substance that I have made will I destroy from off the face of the earth.

5 And Noah did according unto all that the LORD commanded him.

Again, some scientists say that this is the stuff of myths, while others point to flood stories in many cultures, along with various layers of sediment and fossil sea-life atop mountains, to show the factual nature of an ancient Great Flood. Even believing scientists differ on whether the flood covered the entire earth (as 7:19 seems to indicate), or only "all the earth" known to the ancient author. "Local flood" advocates claim that it is impossible to imagine that earth's environment, orbit, gravitational aspects, and other geophysical traits could have been maintained if water had covered the entire earth. Others note that a supernatural God could certainly have countered such natural problems.

The main point not to be lost in this debate is the fact that the same flood that *destroyed* an earth gone wrong *saved* a man who chose to live right. Through this salvation Noah was enabled to become a "new Adam" and head a new race. In the New Testament, the apostle Peter will note the dual nature of this catastrophic event in discussing baptism (see 1 Pet. 3:20-21).

C. Effects of the flood, 17, 23

17 And the flood was forty days upon the earth; and the waters increased, and bare up the ark, and it was lift up above the earth.

23 And every living substance was destroyed which was upon the face of the ground, both man, and cattle, and the creeping things, and the fowl of the heaven; and they were destroyed from the earth: and Noah only remained alive, and they that were with him in the ark.

Earlier, verse 11 had noted that the source of the Great Flood's waters came not only from unusual rainfall but from the breaking up of great reservoirs of water beneath the earth's surface. The totality of its destructive power is reiterated in verses 21-23; yet in repeating the destruction the author is also showing the potential for a renewed earth.

In a further analogy similar to the one Peter draws, we may note that the story of the Great Flood shows that we are free to place a positive or a negative face on other catastrophes in our lives. The deluge that destroyed all life (except sea life, presumably) on the earth was actually the means of the salvation of Noah and his family and the animals.

III. Days of Beginning Again— 8:14-16, 9:1

A. Emerging from the ark, 8:14-16

14 And in the second month, on the seven and twentieth day of the month, was the earth dried.

15 And God spake unto Noah, saying,

16 Go forth of the ark, thou,
and thy wife, and thy sons, and thy sons' wives with thee.

Noah and his family had entered the ark in "the second month" 97:11), and since they left the ark a year later in the same month we conclude that their sojourn upon the waters lasted a full year. Having been cooped up so long with so many animals, the family must have heard God's "Go forth" with relief. Their departure was preceded by the classic story of the release of a raven and a dove in the tenth month, to see if there were yet any dry land (8:6-12). The imagery is so powerful that a dove bearing an olive branch in its beak is to this day a sign of a peace offering.

B. Blessings and commission, 9:1

1 And God blessed Noah and his sons, and said unto them, Be fruitful, and multiply, and replenish the earth.

With the invitation to depart from the ark, Noah and his family also receive a commission to renew the earth that was destroyed by the flood. No doubt they received this charge not merely as an opportunity to head up a new race of people, but with the determination to do all they can to keep it from degenerating so quickly as it had before the Flood.

Yet we cannot think of these new possibilities without recalling also Noah's later drunkenness (chapter 9), and of the wholesale lapse of his descendants in Babylonia into idolatry—indications that the stubborn imprint of "the Fall" will continue to cling to mankind, and continue to call for further new beginnings and "new creations."

15

Evangelistic Emphasis

At Holy Communion she was a face I hadn't seen before, and she was sobbing uncontrollably. As the bread and cup passed before her, she wrenched a large chunk of the bread and through her sobs gulped down the cup as well.

She later told me that 12 years earlier she had left her husband because she could not take his abusive treatment any more. Yet, despite his conviction on charges of abuse, she still felt guilty about the divorce, and unworthy to take communion. At last, with great courage, she had walked into an unfamiliar church and knelt at the altar. She embraced me while saying, "Thank you, thank you, for sharing the table of Christ."

I told her that Jesus came into the world for healing and wholeness, that her divorce would never separate her from God, and she needed to get on with her life and not look back. She dropped in a year later to tell us that we had been the turning point for putting the pain behind her. God always gives second chances!

ဆာ

Memory Selection

When the bow is in the clouds, I will see it and remember the everlasting covenant between God and every living creature of all flesh that is on the earth. —*Genesis 9:16*

One of our most fundamental needs is to know that we are attached to others, that we are wanted and needed. Most creatures in God's Kingdom cluster together and feel a sense of community.

God's promise of a rainbow in the clouds indicating a permanent and unbreakable bond between God and the creatures of His world is a strong and assuring promise that lies at the very foundation of Christianity. We are told throughout the scriptures that nothing that can separate us from God, not even our own sinfulness. In all of life, there are few feelings, needs, and insecurities that are more totally and completely fulfilled than when we have a firm and unquestionable conviction that we are not alone, and are wanted and loved.

Weekday Problems

During a counseling session the man portrayed his wife as cold, nagging, and indifferent. He portrayed himself as a saintly provider, sacrificing all and receiving nothing in return.

When his wife became a part of the counseling session, she revealed a completely different picture. She described a man who would drink with his friends until the wee hours of the morning, who would gamble away the paycheck, and do little or nothing around the house. He was a man who was more intent on his own pleasures and needs than he was on his family and his children. The truth of her testimony was overwhelming. He had nowhere to hide from his false claims, and he knew it. But, she got out of her chair and hugged him and told him that she loved him anyway and she wanted the man he used to be. With both of them hugging and crying, the meaning of a second chance and the truth of forgiveness filled my office like a lovely perfume.

*When did you give or receive a second chance?

More than You Wanted to Know About Noah

Dad: Son, who was Noah's wife?
Lad: Joan of Ark, of course.

* * * *

Teacher: When Noah began work on the ark, where do you think he hit the first nail?
Student: On the head, I'd guess.

* * * *

Student: What's the difference between Noah's ark and an *archbishop*?
Teacher: Well, one was a high ark, but the other is a hierarch.

* * * *

Noah's sons: Dad, we're going fishing.
Noah: Go easy on the bait, boys. We only have two worms.

* * * *

Q: Who was the greatest financier in the Bible?
A: Noah. He floated his stock while the whole world was in liquidation.

We live in a society that long ago wandered away from any understanding of accountability. Over the years, in a slow, insidious way, we have developed an attitude that tells us our sins were not done by us, our misjudgments were not our fault, but somehow were stimulated and orchestrated by someone or something else. The "blame game" thrives across the land, as we work overtime trying to escape personal responsibility for not living life as God would have us live it.

We are an obese nation, filled with people who overeat. Rather than be accountable for self-restraint, we blame the people who serve the food. We smoke cigarettes for years, knowing that inhaling burning leaves is a horror to the delicate membranes of our lungs and other organs. Then, when the doctor brings us the sad news of cancer, we rail against the cigarette companies for producing this poisonous product. One young man gets drunk, climbs over a barbed wire airport fence, breaks into an airplane and hot wires the ignition. The plane takes off, and then crashes, taking his life. His family sues the airport and the manufacturer of the airplane, rather than deal with his own criminal behavior that cost this life.

Transgression and our own accountability fill the sixth chapter of Genesis. In the eyes of God, we know what is right and wrong, what is good and bad, what is responsible and irresponsible. We know clearly what God expects of us and God has clearly told us that our lives will suffer if we flagrantly disobey Him. There is no room for blaming others for our own willful misdeeds. There is no accounting for our transgressions other than to stand and say "Oh God, forgive me. Make me whole again."

Through it all, like a parent with a wayward child, the punishment and accountability does not mean covenant and love are not present. Indeed, often the greatest expression of covenant is to demand accountability.

18

GETTING THE FACTS STRAIGHT

1. Why did God decide to flood the earth?
Because He had seen too much selfishness and wickedness in the lives of His human creatures.

2. God looked upon man's wickedness with an almost human description. What was it?
God was "grieved" at what man had become, and He was sorry that He had made him.

3. Who was an exception to God's anger and disappointment?
The exception was Noah, who had found favor in God's eyes and was to be used to start the whole process all over again.

4. How did God describe Noah as He prepared to use Noah as a new Genesis for all creation?
God told Noah that He had seen his righteousness.

5. God had already created all living things. Why then, did He instruct Noah to gather mated pairs of everything?
He was so disappointed at what creation had developed into, that He wanted to start all over again to repopulate the earth.

6. Was anything left after the flood had covered the earth?
The scripture says that every living thing that was upon the earth, every creeping thing and every bird of the air, were blotted out. Only Noah, his family, and his creatures were left upon the planet earth.

7. How did God direct Noah to begin the population process again?
He waited until the 27th day of the second month into the flood, when the waters had receded and the earth was dry. Then He told Noah and his family to "be fruitful and multiply upon the earth."

8. Are we to view God as a wrathful and vindictive ruler throughout this story?
No, this story is not unlike a parent who is deeply hurt by the actions of a rebellious child. The parent feels let down and betrayed.

9. What would be an over-arching statement to learn from this account?
In 9:16 God uses the image of a rainbow to declare that, even though He has been deeply wounded by His creation, He is still active and faithful to that which He had created, and will always keep His covenant.

10. What is the significance of the flood lasting 40 days?
For the Hebrew people, names and numbers carried special significance. The number "40" is used throughout the Scriptures as a synonym for a long, long time.

A natural companion for our lesson today is the story of the Prodigal Son in Luke 15.

In this parable, familiar to most Christians, a man's son has squandered his inheritance with immoral living. Yet he comes to his senses and returns home seeking forgiveness. As the father rushes out to greet him, we see a picture much like that of God, who said to Noah:

> *This is the token of the covenant which I make between me and you and every living creature that is with you, for perpetual generations: I do set my bow in the cloud, and it shall be for a token of a covenant betwen me and the earth . . . And I will remember my covenant* (Gen. 9:12-15).

Another similar scripture is in Paul's letter to the Romans when he says that nothing can separate us from the love of God (8:39)." That means that even our own wrongs cannot make God stop loving us.

Someone once said Christianity was a "second chance religion." It is also a third, and fourth, and so on. It is our nature as humans often to take two steps forward and three steps back, to stray afar from God's road map.

Some years ago, I received a phone call from a male voice who said, "Remember me?" I was embarrassed to say, "No," but he then reminded me that he was a troubled teenager in a church I had pastored years before. He had been rude, and outrageous, and delighted in offending everybody. His chances of staying out of prison seemed slim. Now, years after that pastorate, he says, "I've looked you up and want to talk with you. I'm grown, have a college degree, a wife, a child, and a good job. Nobody thought I would amount to anything, and you were the only one that stayed with me through it all. I wanted to find you and tell you that." I was speechless at his testimony. His earlier disgusting behavior had changed to godliness and maturity. It happened because someone else, like today's scripture, maintained a covenant and never gave up on him. After our conversation, I sat with a lump in my throat and a tear in my eye. Today's scriptures flooded over me. Ours is, indeed, a second chance and third chance faith. God does not give up on us. Neither should we give up on each other.

Lesson 3

Power for Deliverance

Exodus 3:1-12

ow Moses kept the flock of Jethro his father in law, the priest of Midian: and he led the flock to the backside of the desert, and came to the mountain of God, even to Horeb.

2 And the angel of the LORD appeared unto him in a flame of fire out of the midst of a bush: and he looked, and, behold, the bush burned with fire, and the bush was not consumed.

3 And Moses said, I will now turn aside, and see this great sight, why the bush is not burnt.

4 And when the LORD saw that he turned aside to see, God called unto him out of the midst of the bush, and said, Moses, Moses. And he said, Here am I.

5 And he said, Draw not nigh hither: put off thy shoes from off thy feet, for the place whereon thou standest is holy ground.

6 Moreover he said, I am the God of thy father, the God of Abraham, the God of Isaac, and the God of Jacob. And Moses hid his face; for he was afraid to look upon God.

7 And the LORD said, I have surely seen the affliction of my people which are in Egypt, and have heard their cry by reason of their taskmasters; for I know their sorrows;

8 And I am come down to deliver them out of the hand of the Egyptians, and to bring them up out of that land unto a good land and a large, unto a land flowing with milk and honey; unto the place of the Canaanites, and the Hittites, and the Amorites, and the Perizzites, and the Hivites, and the Jebusites.

9 Now therefore, behold, the cry of the children of Israel is come unto me: and I have also seen the oppression wherewith the Egyptians oppress them.

10 Come now therefore, and I will send thee unto Pharaoh, that thou mayest bring forth my people the children of Israel out of Egypt.

11 And Moses said unto God, Who am I, that I should go unto Pharaoh, and that I should bring forth the children of Israel out of Egypt?

12 And he said, Certainly I will be with thee; and this shall be a token unto thee, that I have sent thee: When thou hast brought forth the people out of Egypt, ye shall serve God upon this mountain.

Memory Selection
Exodus 3:10

Background Scripture
Exodus 3–4

Devotional Reading
Exodus 3:13-17

The topics of "Creation" and "Re-creation" or renewal in the Bible seems always to be followed by the problem of oppression or slavery—either to sin, as in the days of Noah, or to another nation as in the case of Egypt, in today's lesson. Thus, much of the Bible is about the people God raises up to further His plan *for* liberation, or a "new creation," and *against* the universal tendency for the powerful to enslave the weak.

In keeping with this recurring pattern, *Moses* and his call to lead the Jews to freedom from Egypt is the focus of this session. Many Christians are accustomed to thinking mainly of spiritual slavery. Group discussions can be enlivened by asking whether, and how, civil or political liberty is related to spiritual freedom. Can one exist very long without the other? Are there dangers in relying on civil powers for spiritual freedom?

᠄᠄᠄

Introduce this lesson by noting that the theme of "deliverance" has been implied in the two previous lessons. Remind group members how God used righteous Noah to deliver the human race from decadence. Later, God delivered Abraham from Ur of the Chaldees, making a spe-

cial covenant with him as He had with Noah—one that included the promise that the land of Canaan would be their home.

After journeying there, however, a famine had driven Abraham and his family into Egypt, where his people were eventually enslaved. In keeping with the biblical pattern, Moses is now the man of the hour to carry forward God's thrust toward freedom.

Teaching Outline
I. Fugitive from Egypt—1
II. Confrontation with God—2-12
A. A burning bush, 2-3
B. The voice from the bush, 4-6
C. Commission from God, 7-10
1. Plight and promise, 7-8
2. Plan of deliverance, 9-10
D. Question and reassurance, 11-12

Daily Bible Readings		
Mon.	God Speaks to Moses	*Exodus 3:1-6*
Tue.	Moses Called to Lead	Exodus 3:7-12
Wed.	Instructions to Moses	Exodus 3:13-22
Thu.	Special Powers for Moses	*Exodus 4:1-9*
Fri.	Feelings of Inadequacy	*Exodus 4:10-17*
Sat.	Return to Egypt	*Exodus 4:18-23*
Sun.	Believing in Moses	*Exodus 4:24-31*

Verse by Verse

I. Fugitive from Egypt—1

1 Now Moses kept the flock of Jethro his father in law, the priest of Midian: and he led the flock to the backside of the desert, and came to the mountain of God, even to Horeb.

Introduced earlier in the book of Exodus, Moses was of the tribe of Levi, son of Abraham, whose clan had gone into Egypt to escape a famine some 400 years earlier. His name means "drawn out" (2:10), reflecting his having been taken from the Nile river where his mother had hidden him in a water-tight basket to spare him from Pharaoh's edict to slay all Hebrew male babies. Raised by Pharaoh's daughter, Moses' destiny will also "draw him out" as one of the most prominent leaders in Jewish and Christian history.

Having discovered his Hebrew lineage, Moses had killed an Egyptian slave-master who was mistreating a Hebrew slave. His story is taken up here after he had fled for his life to the desert land of Midian, east of the Dead Sea. Ironically, Moses was related to the Midianites —Midian had been a descendant of Abraham, as had Moses' ancestor Levi. Also ironically, it was a band of Midianites who by taking Joseph into Egypt had contributed to the Jews' migration there (Gen. 37:28). While in Midian, Moses married the daughter of the Midianite Jethro, a priestly prince of the land. "Horeb" probably refers to mountain system that included the peak of Sinai, where God would later deliver the Law to Moses on tables of stone.

II. Confrontation with God—2-12
A. A burning bush, 2-3

2 And the angel of the Lord appeared unto him in a flame of fire out of the midst of a bush: and he looked, and, behold, the bush burned with fire, and the bush was not consumed.

3 And Moses said, I will now turn aside, and see this great sight, why the bush is not burnt.

The famous bush that burned but was not consumed caught Moses' attention. This shrub has been interpreted variously as a bush supernaturally aflame, or one of a species in the area whose bright red flowers made it seem to be afire. It is a mistake to argue the point until the main purpose of its burning appearance is obscured. God chooses the phenomenon to ignite in Moses' heart the flame of freedom and a passion for serving in the role of liberator of his people back in Egypt.

B. The voice from the bush, 4-6

4 And when the Lord saw that he turned aside to see, God called unto him out of the midst of the bush, and said, Moses, Moses. And

23

he said, Here am I.

5 And he said, Draw not nigh hither: put off thy shoes from off thy feet, for the place whereon thou standest is holy ground.

6 Moreover he said, I am the God of thy father, the God of Abraham, the God of Isaac, and the God of Jacob. And Moses hid his face; for he was afraid to look upon God.

Remarkably, despite having been raised in a pagan land, Moses has retained enough of a concept of the true God that he apparently recognizes His voice from the bush. It was suggested in the introductory material that the teacher lead a discussion about whether spiritual freedom can long exist in an oppressive civil context such as slavery. As a matter of fact, many of Abraham's descendants had kept alive the idea of one true God during hundreds of years of Egyptian slavery.

Identifying Himself as the God of Moses' ancestors, God connects with the Jewish history Moses was no doubt taught by his mother, whom Pharaoh's daughter, after finding him in the river-basket, employed to nurse the child. His fear is to be attributed not only to the mystery of a supernatural voice speaking from a burning bush, but because he must have instinctively felt the reason for the later Jewish law that stipulated that looking upon God was a sin punishable by death (Exod. 33:20).

C. Commission from God, 7-10

1. Plight and promise, 7-8

7 And the LORD said, I have surely seen the affliction of my people which are in Egypt, and have heard their cry by reason of their taskmasters; for I know their sorrows;

8 And I am come down to deliver them out of the hand of the Egyptians, and to bring them up out of that land unto a good land and a large, unto a land flowing with milk and honey; unto the place of the Canaanites, and the Hittites, and the Amorites, and the Perizzites, and the Hivites, and the Jebusites.

We learn here that one of God's fundamental concerns is *freedom*. His having heard the cry of His people enslaved in Egypt has become a far-reaching element of human history, planting the seed of freedom and democracy that has characterized the politics of the Judeo-Christian tradition. Unlike the distant and impassive gods of the Greeks and others, Yahweh is emotionally involved with His people: *He hears their cries against injustice.*

This event in the life of Moses is also to be noted as a renewal of the Covenant God made with Father Abraham, when He promised to give the land of Canaan to the Jews for the preservation of a righteous remnant through whom even those peoples conquered by the Jews would one day be blessed (see Gen. 15:18-21).

2. Plan of deliverance, 9-10

9 Now therefore, behold, the cry of the children of Israel is come unto me: and I have also seen the oppression wherewith the

Egyptians oppress them.

10 Come now therefore, and I will send thee unto Pharaoh, that thou mayest bring forth my people the children of Israel out of Egypt.

This concern of God for the plight of His people is now to be translated into a plan for their deliverance—a strategy that would involve Moses as leader of the Jews. We can imagine Moses' shock when God affirms that He will send Moses back to Egypt to bring Israel out of slavery. From his merely human standpoint, his "qualifications" must have seemed limited to having served as a sheepherder in Midian!

D. Question and reassurance, 11-12

11 And Moses said unto God, Who am I, that I should go unto Pharaoh, and that I should bring forth the children of Israel out of Egypt?

12 And he said, Certainly I will be with thee; and this shall be a token unto thee, that I have sent thee: When thou hast brought forth the people out of Egypt, ye shall serve God upon this mountain.

"Who am I?" was a natural response for a man who had been through what Moses had experienced. Although raised in Pharaoh's court, he was now being asked to assume the task of bringing his people out of Egypt—which would have been viewed by Pharaoh as an act of disloyalty or even treason. It would also rob Egypt of the slaves who had contributed so much to their empire-building. And finally, Moses' reluctance is understandable in light of his own kinsmen having rebuffed his attempt to settle their differences (Exod. 2:11-14).

The first "tokens" God used to convince Moses that He would be with him were the horrible plagues that eventually overcame Pharaoh's refusal to let the Israelites follow Moses out of Egypt. Then there was the parting of the waters, signs in the desert such as the guiding cloud and pillar of fire, and food from heaven. All this helped to reassure this giant of a leader that he would be able to respond to God's call. Still, a large measure of faith was required of Moses.

A consistent pattern running through the Old Testament is that the persons God calls for special tasks feel inadequate. David, Isaiah, Amos and others will duplicate Moses' reluctance to take on what would literally be a superhuman task. This remarkably consistent response by those whom God calls for special service remains to this day a factor in the calling of the Church's leaders. One may almost conclude that initial reluctance is a qualification that shows the humility God requires of a leader. Of course when that reluctance assumes a power greater than God's enabling Spirit, it can become false humility.

In the rest of this chapter and on into chapter 4, Moses' understandable questions, doubts, and fears will be expressed. Yet his faith in the presence of fear remains a dissonant but inspirational factor that often guides those who hear God's call to special service today.

Evangelistic Emphasis

Across the world there are millions of churches of all sizes, circumstances, and traditions. One of the main reasons why Christ's Church has now reached every corner of the globe is that the people of God respond to God's own model, to "go into every corner and give witness." Just as God is moving and active in our own lives, so we as believers are moving and active in the lives of the community, of those who are unchurched, and of those who have fallen away. Those individual congregations and those denominations that are growing like weeds are invariably congregations and denominations that place a total priority on being deeply enmeshed within the broader community. Those churches, on the other hand, who sit passively waiting for someone to drop in the front door, are invariably those churches that dwindle and fade. The Exodus model is the model of God's Word being vigorously inserted into the human community.

ഇൻഐ

Memory Selection

I will send you to Pharaoh to bring my people, the Israelites, out of Egypt. —*Exod. 3:10*

Our Faith is unique among all religions, because it involves a certainty that God is active and moving in the world and in our lives. Some of the great religions of the world, such as Buddhism and Hinduism, all have strong believers, but nowhere is the deity of these faiths active and moving in the personal lives of the faithful. One may leave flowers at the feet of a stone Buddha, but those thoroughly informed on Buddhism do not expect the Buddha to be actively ministering in one's life.

Our scripture today reminds us that we do not believe in a passive God, but in a God that is vigorously and actively involved in our lives. Indeed, Christianity began with 12 ordinary people, and has changed the face of the human race as no other faith has ever done, simply because it is a faith based upon a God who is alive and well, and visibly present in every moment of our daily needs, struggles, failures, and aspirations.

Weekday Problems

She was poor, and black, but a longtime employee in the church. She applied for Social Security, to help meet her family needs. The Social Security Office dragged out her application like a subtle statement that she would never qualify. One day we found her crying and discovered her dilemma. To her amazement the entire staff and leadership of that white church—the lawyers, specialists, and members from within it, boldly confronted the Social Security Office. The office was told in blunt terms that this woman was qualified and extremely deserving, and the wheels of justice had better turn soon.

In what has to be some sort of a bureaucratic record, her application sailed through and she began drawing a small check to help out. She could hardly look at those of us on the staff after that without a broad grin and tears of joy at the same time. We had intervened in her life in a healing and redemptive way, just as God intervenes in ours.

*Has God "intervened" in your life? Share the experience.

Reflections on Freedom

God has laid upon man the duty of being free, of safeguarding freedom of spirit, no matter how difficult that may be, or how much sacrifice, and suffering it may require.—*Nicolai Berdayev*

* * * *

Mama had it wrong. *Freedom,* not cleanliness, is next to godliness.—*Anon.*

* * * *

The cause of freedom is the cause of God.—*William Lisle Bowles*

* * * *

Freedom is a need of the soul, and nothing else. It is in striving toward God that the soul strives continually after a condition of freedom. God alone is the inciter and guarantor of freedom. He is the only guarantor.—*Whitaker Chambers*

* * * *

Man is free only in God, the source of his freedom—*Sherwood Eddy*

* * * *

As free, and not using your liberty for a cloak of maliciousness, but as the servants of God.—*1 Peter 2:16*

This Lesson in Your Life

One of the most moving experiences is to observe a person at the end of his rope and watch that individual rise above it in a victorious and self-fulfilling way. Some truly remarkable witnesses of our time are people who have been enslaved to alcohol, drugs or gambling, but who had risen to take control. One of the reasons Alcoholics Anonymous impacts millions is because so many people believe they are helpless in the web of addiction. Through AA's intervention program of 12 steps, taken with like-minded supporters, the addicted climb above the depths of despair, and out of the web.

A strong lesson in this week's scripture is to remember that we all come to a point in our lives when it takes someone or something else to retrieve us back into healthy, wholesome living. Many, however, think that to rise above one's own crisis and do it on his own is a sign of power and self-sufficiency. The truth is we sometimes need an outside strength to motivate us to rise above the bonds that bind us.

The Israelites were certain they were lost forever in slavery and suffering. They feared their cries of help would disappear on the wind. Moses, coming face-to-face with God in the burning bush, was sensitized with challenge and compassion and was sent to liberate His people.

How often are marriages and lives in distress, but the people involved feel embarrassed to seek professional help, fearing it is a sign of weakness. The reality is clear both in secular life and in sacred Scripture. All will eventually need someone to enter and help make them whole again. We who are believers are confident God will always be present in this way. One counselor says, "The wisest among you knows the strongest thing to do is to cry out for help and direction. The weakest among you will be the one who insists 'I need no help. I can do it on my own.'"

Thanks be to God who will not let us "do it on our own."

1. In Exodus 3, the direction of Moses' life changed forever. What was his occupation at that time?
He was a shepherd, tending the flock of his father-in-law Jethro, who was the Chief Priest of Midian.

2. Aside from the obvious paradox of a bush burning that was not consumed, what did that sight say to Moses?
It told him that the rules of physics were not the rules of God, and that a Holy Spirit was present to challenge him, a Spirit that could not be described or explained.

3. God instructed Moses to take his shoes off. What was the significance of that instruction?
Removing shoes is a symbol of ultimate respect, honor, and reverence, just as men remove hats when entering churches.

4. Why did Moses hide his face as he stood in front of the bush?
When we come face-to-face with that which totally transcends our comprehension, it emphasizes how small we are and how great God is. Such was more than Moses could bear, so he hid his face.

5. Other than the fact that God hears they cry of His suffering people, what lesson is there for us from the statement in Exodus 3:7?
One lesson is fundamental to people of faith: God knows us individually, He calls us by name, and every moment of our lives we are known to Him.

6. Why didn't God simply charge into Egypt in all His power and liberate the Israelites Himself?
God has always moved and ministered through ordinary people in ordinary circumstances. From Moses to Paul to Mother Teresa to Abraham Lincoln, and people we never knew.

7. What more did God intend to do for the enslaved Israelites?
He not only wanted them free of pain and slavery, but living in comfort and security. God wants only the best for people who reach out to Him.

8. Other than the burning bush, what does God declare as the next sign in this lesson?
The fact that the people of Israel cried out for freedom, and received it, was proof that a compassionate and divine power was working in their midst.

9. What was the initial response by Moses to the challenge by God?
He attempted to decline, by declaring that he was too insignificant for such a task (just as most of us today would attempt to decline).

10. What finally convinced Moses to accept God's challenge?
It was the promise God made that Moses would not go forth alone, but would be strengthened and guided by God.

Years ago there was a popular song called "Signs, Signs, Everywhere Are Signs." It is commonplace to come to a pivotal point in either marriage, business, society, or other crucial experience and say to someone, "I have seen the signs of this all along." The truth is that few momentous experiences happen in our lives, without earlier indicators of that possible occurrence.

Our lesson reminds us that in the very throes of our affliction and pain, signs are present that God will come to us, if we will but look for them. It is fundamental to people of faith that God wants peace, harmony, and wholeness for His people, and will do everything possible to guarantee that environment. Psalm 121 says, *"He will not let thy foot be moved . . . ."*

Years ago a friend invited me to fly with him in a biplane crop duster. As we raced along the tops of a cotton field, he instructed me to give it more power so the plane would curve upward and over the trees. No matter what I did, however, we were heading for the tree line. My friend yelled in my ear, "Call on it man, call on it!" I jammed the throttle all the way and pulled the stick back to my stomach. The plane roared almost straight up just in time. Later my friend said, "The power is always there, but you've got to be willing to reach for it when you need it."

The signs of God's presence and intent to help have always been there, but we who need Him must not be reluctant to call on that strength. We must be willing to cry out and say, "I have reached the limits of what I can do on my own. Come into my life and set me on the right path."

The Scripture tells us God heard the cries of His people in Egyptian captivity, and quickly began their liberation. Likewise, to this day, I can remember my friend yelling in my ear, "Call on it man! Call on it!"

If you will listen, you can hear God saying the same thing: "Call on Me! Call on Me anytime."

Lesson 4

Becoming God's People

Deuteronomy 29:2-15

*A*nd Moses called unto all Israel, and said unto them, Ye have seen all that the LORD did before your eyes in the land of Egypt unto Pharaoh, and unto all his servants, and unto all his land;

3 The great temptations which thine eyes have seen, the signs, and those great miracles:

4 Yet the LORD hath not given you an heart to perceive, and eyes to see, and ears to hear, unto this day.

5 And I have led you forty years in the wilderness: your clothes are not waxen old upon you, and thy shoe is not waxen old upon thy foot.

6 Ye have not eaten bread, neither have ye drunk wine or strong drink: that ye might know that I am the LORD your God.

7 And when ye came unto this place, Sihon the king of Heshbon, and Og the king of Bashan, came out against us unto battle, and we smote them:

8 And we took their land, and gave it for an inheritance unto the Reubenites, and to the Gadites, and to the half tribe of Manasseh.

9 Keep therefore the words of this covenant, and do them, that ye may prosper in all that ye do.

10 Ye stand this day all of you before the LORD your God; your captains of your tribes, your elders, and your officers, with all the men of Israel,

11 Your little ones, your wives, and thy stranger that is in thy camp, from the hewer of thy wood unto the drawer of thy water:

12 That thou shouldest enter into covenant with the LORD thy God, and into his oath, which the LORD thy God maketh with thee this day:

13 That he may establish thee to day for a people unto himself, and that he may be unto thee a God, as he hath said unto thee, and as he hath sworn unto thy fathers, to Abraham, to Isaac, and to Jacob.

14 Neither with you only do I make this covenant and this oath;

15 But with him that standeth here with us this day before the LORD our God, and also with him that is not here with us this day:

Memory Selection
Deuteronomy 29:12-13

Background Scripture
Deuteronomy 29:1-29

Devotional Reading
Deuteronomy 30:15-20

Moses has led the tribes of Israel out of Egyptian bondage. They were composed not only of descendants of Abraham, but of a "mixed multitude" of races (Exod. 12:38). This diverse group of people have submitted and rebelled, gloried and chafed, under God's leadership through Moses. They are in dire need of a unifying factor before plunging into the task of subduing the land of Canaan God had promised them.

That unifying factor proves to be the Mosaic Covenant. It had already been delivered from Mount Sinai (Exod. 19ff.). "Deuteronomy" means "the second law"; and consists of restating that Covenant and securing the people's promise that they would be faithful to it. This lesson therefore continues the theme of "creation," describing the creation of the people of God.

ଽଠଘ

Ask group members what patriotic acts or celebrations stir their blood and do the most to remind them of their heritage as Americans. Perhaps it is the strains of the national anthem . . . the ritual unfurling of the Stars and Stripes . . . a parade on the Fourth of July . . . a solemn ceremony on Veterans Day . . . a visit to Washington to touring various monuments and view the Constitution.

Note that this lesson is about the event that served this function for ancient Israel. It tells the story of the ratification of the Law of Moses. No other people had been governed by such a rule of both faith and conduct. With the Ten Commandments as its centerpiece, the Law remains to this day a stirring reminder that God chose the children of Israel to be His special people.

Teaching Outline	Daily Bible Readings	
I. Preamble of History—2-8	Mon.	Reminder to Israel *Deuteronomy 29:2-9*
A. Signs of God's favor, 2-3	Tue.	Joining the Covenant *Deuteronomy29:10-15*
B. Need for changed hearts, 4	Wed.	Moses Warns Israel *Deuteronomy 29:16-21*
C. Proof of God's love, 5-8		
II. People Are Charged—9-12	Thu.	Reason for Devastation *Deuteronomy 29:22-29*
A. 'Keep the Covenant!', 9	Fri.	Forgiveness Promised *Deuteronomy 30:1-5*
B. Comprehensive Law, 10-12		
III. Promise of God—13-15	Sat.	Prosperity Promised *Deuteronomy 30:6-10*
A. Keeping faith with Abraham, 13	Sun.	Obey God, Choose Life *Deuteronomy 30:11-20*
B. Extent of the Covenant, 14-15		

Verse by Verse

I. Preamble of History—2-8

A. Signs of God's favor, 2-3

2 And Moses called unto all Israel, and said unto them, Ye have seen all that the LORD did before your eyes in the land of Egypt unto Pharaoh, and unto all his servants, and unto all his land;

3 The great temptations which thine eyes have seen, the signs, and those great miracles:

The first verse of Deuteronomy 29 has the ring of the opening of a final section of what has been a kind of commentary on Yahweh's mighty acts when He redeemed His people Israel out of Egypt. In summing up God's work as a *covenant* (Heb. *b'rith*, as in the modern Jewish group B'nai B'rith, or "Sons of the Covenant"), the author (traditionally Moses himself) borrows a ritual tradition from the desert peoples Israel has met along the way. A great Bedouin chief would promise to protect lesser tribes, in return for obedience and a tax. The agreement was ratified by "cutting a covenant," which involved sharing a meal in which an animal would be cut in pieces, and the parties to the compact would pass between the parts to show their acceptance.

Verses 2-3 provide a brief summary of the events of the last 40 years. Moses emphasizes the miraculous measures which God, in the role of the "great Bedouin chief," has

taken, proving His love for them. They began with the plagues in Egypt that eventually convinced Pharaoh to allow the Jews to leave the land. The people saw with their own eyes God's leadership by fire and cloud, the sustenance of the manna and the quail, and other marvelous rescues from their enemies. They saw Yahweh face down many "temptations," meaning *trials* or tests; and in each case He has shown Himself to be both powerful and loving. What more could be done or said to prove the faithfulness of the God who is here making Israel His own special people?

B. Need for changed hearts, 4

4 Yet the LORD hath not given you an heart to perceive, and eyes to see, and ears to hear, unto this day.

As it turns out, the only other thing that could have been done was to give the people a perceptive and obedient heart. Instead of forcing the people to obey, God has left them with free will, wanting a people who love Him instead of merely dreading Him. But instead of responding in gratitude and obedience, they have been a rebellious people. Here is a call, imbedded in the Law of Moses itself, for a greater willingness to obey on the part of the people, the "lesser" party to the Covenant. This "new heart" would be predicted by the prophet Jeremiah (Jer. 31:31-33), and fulfilled in the gift of the Holy

Spirit after the coming of the Messiah.

C. Proof of God's love, 5-8

5 And I have led you forty years in the wilderness: your clothes are not waxen old upon you, and thy shoe is not waxen old upon thy foot.

6 Ye have not eaten bread, neither have ye drunk wine or strong drink: that ye might know that I am the LORD your God.

7 And when ye came unto this place, Sihon the king of Heshbon, and Og the king of Bashan, came out against us unto battle, and we smote them:

8 And we took their land, and gave it for an inheritance unto the Reubenites, and to the Gadites, and to the half tribe of Manasseh.

Reference to the 40 years in the wilderness of Sinai reminds us that God did not lead the people directly to Canaan, at first in order to harden them for the battles they would face (Exod. 13:17-18), then because of their disobedience (Num. 14:33-34). During the period of the "Wilderness Wanderings," God had miraculously fed them and preserved their clothing (while giving time for the most blatantly rebellious to die out).

"This place" (vs. 7) refers to the east side of the Jordan River, where the tribes paused before crossing into Canaan. There they fought Sihon and Og, and meted out land for the tribes of Reuben, Gad, and the half-tribe of Manasseh. These tribes were composed of cattlemen, so they asked for their portion to come from the grass-covered hills east of the Jordan

(Num. 32). Thus, both in caring for their personal needs and in driving out their enemies before them, God had proved Himself faithful as the "Great Sheik" of the Covenant.

II. People Are Charged—9-12

A. 'Keep the Covenant!', 9

9 Keep therefore the words of this covenant, and do them, that ye may prosper in all that ye do.

With the love and faithfulness of God recalled, it is now time to call the people themselves to enter or "cut" their side of the Covenant. Their part is merely to obey the Great King, and is proportionately much smaller than the King's share of the Covenant. What they were to "keep" included both what has been called the "moral law" of the Law of Moses, and the "ceremonial law," regulating worship and sacrifice.

The promise that the people would "prosper" if they kept Covenant with God is a major theme in Deuteronomy's restating of the Law. Chapters 27-28 recount in detail the blessings issued from Mount Gerizim and the curses from Mount Ebal. Unfortunately, in the minds of many this promise of "reciprocity" was allowed to degenerate into a mechanical "deal," with prosperity as automatic proof of obedience and poverty as proof of wickedness. The righteous and the wicked would not be clearly distinguished until God's final judgment—a concept that would be refined in the New Testament. This misunderstanding of the general rule that the righteous will be blessed and the wicked punished in this life was corrected by Jesus when He insisted that the sun and the rain bless both the just and the unjust (Matt. 5:45).

B. Comprehensive Law, 10-12

10 Ye stand this day all of you before the LORD your God; your captains of your tribes, your elders, and your officers, with all the men of Israel,

11 Your little ones, your wives, and thy stranger that is in thy camp, from the hewer of thy wood unto the drawer of thy water:

12 That thou shouldest enter into covenant with the LORD thy God, and into his oath, which the LORD thy God maketh with thee this day:

These verses show that the Covenant applied to young and old among the Israelites, as well as to the servants who had accompanied them out of Egypt. Although the Law was focused on the blood-descendants of Abraham, throughout the Old Testament exceptions are included to forecast the day when, through Christ, God's rule would be extended over all nations. One of the earliest examples of minorities being included among the Jews is in Exodus 12:38. The theme of inclusion is continued in the story of Rahab the harlot whose deeds were approved by God, and in the inclusion of the Moabite woman Ruth in the ancestry of the Messiah Himself.

III. Promise of God—13-15

A. Keeping faith with Abraham, 13

13 That he may establish thee to day for a people unto himself, and that he may be unto thee a God, as he hath said unto thee, and as he hath sworn unto thy fathers, to Abraham, to Isaac, and to Jacob.

The roles of God, as the Great Shiek, then of the people, cast as the lesser tribes pledging loyalty to Him, have been outlined. The duty of the greater member of the Covenant is to guide and protect His people, while the duty of the lesser members (Israel) is to obey. Moses now calls for the Covenant to be formally ratified, which would be the event that establishes them as "a people unto himself." As Creator, Yahweh governs all nations, but now He has a special "people unto himself" in order to develop a living tradition through whom the Messiah will come.

B. Extent of the Covenant, 14-15

14 Neither with you only do I make this covenant and this oath;

15 But with him that standeth here with us this day before the LORD our God, and also with him that is not here with us this day:

God makes it clear that the solemn Covenant being struck here is to be in effect far into the future, at least until the "new Covenant" of which Jeremiah spoke (Jer. 31:31-33). The *corporate* (as opposed to the merely *individual*) nature of the Covenant is emphasized here. It will apply not only to those who are listening to Moses, but to generations to come.

Throughout the checkered history of the Jews, this principle will sometimes be forgotten. The prophets will provide the impetus for calling for a renewal of the very Covenant God is making with Abraham here.

Evangelistic Emphasis

He was a visitor in church, and said he had been "looking around" for a new place to worship. He finally settled on our church, and then told us something that surprised us all. He said he had come from a church where there was little or no liturgy, and almost never a statement of faith or a creed. In his own words he said, "It was sort of like the beliefs of that other church changed from day to day and they didn't have any roots." He enjoyed very much both the confession of sin, and the various statements of faith that we used, and we explained to him that the church had always been historically in a position to declare what it believed. God's church has since the beginning boldly proclaimed its positions and articles of faith. I will never forget one of his phrases when he smiled and said to me, "It's always good to say over and over again that which you know to be the Truth." In a way, that is exactly what God is telling the Israelites in Deuteronomy.

଼ୠଔ

Memory Selection

Enter into the covenant of the Lord your God,... in order that He may establish you today as His people.—*Deuteronomy 29:12-13*

There is a great difference between a covenant and a contract. In a contract, each is legally bound, with penalty clauses and warnings in case one or the other party defaults. A covenant, on the other hand, is also an agreement, but a sacred agreement wherein the commitment to one another is a transcendent, holy, and deeply heartfelt sense of mutual presence. A contract can be cold, stiff, threatening, and harsh. A covenant is the very essence of holy agreeing. In our lesson today, God expects us to "lock arms with Him," and wholeheartedly enter a sacred agreement that we will always be His, and He will always be ours. Being in covenant with God is to live by God's rules and designs for life, and to always view ourselves as a unique community, built upon principles and standards given and ordained not by humans but a divine creator.

Weekday Problems

Most teenagers, their lives filled with all the latest electronic gadgetry, are blissfully unaware of what it took to build this nation so that a 13-year-old can walk around with $100 shoes and a $200 CD player.

I once insisted that a group of teens from my church go to the National D-Day Museum in New Orleans to spend the day, which they did. They heard the stories of heroism and sacrifice in WWII, and saw many adults old enough to be their grandparents share with them the true meaning of sacrifice. They came back somber, quiet, and with a whole new realization of the world around them.

Sometimes, we just take for granted that the world in which we wake up, the homes that shelter us, the food that feeds us and the relationships that sustain us just popped up like mushrooms in springtime. There is a great danger when we forget who we are and where we have come from.

That is what God wanted of the Israelites: To wake up and understand who sustained them.

*How do we lose sight of our heritage and traditions?

Family Fun

Mom: Judy, I've told you before not to speak when older people are talking. Wait until they stop.
Judy: I've tried, Mom, but they never stop.
* * * *

Father, to daughter outside with a shadowy figure: Sue, what are you doing out there?
Sue: Oh nothing, Dad, just looking at the moon.
Father: Well, it's midnight. Tell the moon it's time to go home.
* * * *

"Daddy, before you married Mommy who told you how to drive?"
* * * *

Neighbor: How do you feel now that your son is in college?
Father: Well, I feel a little like Aaron did in the wilderness: "Behold, I poured in the gold and there came out this calf."

This Lesson in Your Life

We are a people that resemble the hamster in a circular cage. We run, run, run, live at a frantic pace, fall exhausted into bed at night, then start the whole process the next day. Later, when life nears its end, we often wonder what we accomplished.

Our lives are crammed with work, work, work. There are PTA meetings, Scouts, baseball practice, soccer practice, dance lessons, church meetings, Rotary Club, Ladies Auxiliary. Then it's time to dash over to pick up Junior for swimming lessons. It is little wonder that we never have time to see the powerful presence of God all around us.

Today's scripture in Deuteronomy is a wonderful testimony as God reminds the people of Israel that all the wonderful things that happened to them were because He was present and active in their midst. Only now are they beginning to realize that signs, wonders, victories, inherited lands, families, and secure livelihoods occurred because God was there.

The scripture from *Psalm 46, "Be still and know that I am God!"* is another reminder that a life filled with dashing from place to place is a life that will never have pleasure and fulfillment without slowing down, smelling the flowers, and sensing the footprints of God that are all around us. Whenever someone who has renounced the rat race consciously begins to live in a more reverent, measured way, and celebrates each small insignificant moment as a gift from God, he invariably cries out, *"Why have I not done this before! Thanks be to thee oh God for this wonderful, amazing gift of life and all that is within it, which I have in abundance."*

1. What does it mean when Moses said "Your eyes saw . . . but you did not understand?"

It means that Israel had been oblivious to the divine enery behind all that had preserved them in the Wildnerness.

2. What is the significance of the fact that their clothes and sandals did not wear out?

Although their clothes would have fallen apart in their rough lives in the desert, God preserved them even though the people did not realize it.

3. Why did Moses also remind them of the victorious battle with the King of Heshbon and the King of Bashan?

He wanted them to realize that these were not just typical battles, but were part of a broader picture paving the way to the Promised Land.

4. What does Moses mean when he instructs them to "Be careful to do the words of the Covenant?"

When we recite sacred words, promises, and conditions of being, it helps to keep us focused on what is of utmost importance.

5. Why did Moses challenge everyone from the heads of the tribes to the little ones and the "sojourners" or foreigners among them?

He was making it clear that all of them are a family of God together, from the least to the greatest, and that they all have a place in God's plan.

6. Why does God connect this historic Covenant with Abraham, Isaac, and Jacob?

To emphasize that God's Covenant stretches back to their ancestors

7. What is the importance of referring to "him who is not here with us this day"?

The Covenant will last through generations not yet born.

8. Why was God so careful to tell the people "keep . . . the words of this covenant"?

Because covenants, like contracts, are rarely kept unles people are fully aware of their conditions. They are not to be taken on half-heartedly.

9. How did Moses underscore God's presence with the Israelites?

He told them that they had seen it with their own eyes, as if to say to them "this is not ancient history from a book. You have actually lived out your own liberation."

10. Why did Moses emphasize that the people stood, all of them before the Lord on that day? (vs. 10)?

He wanted to emphasize that God was actually in their midst, bonding them together in an unbreakable Covenant.

As founding pastor of a new church, my days were spent raising funds, gathering charter members, and frantically trying to build a new congregation. At the same time, I was being invited to preach numerous revivals, and never said No. Active before the City Council and the Parish Boards, I felt very important in all I did because my days were filled from first light until long after my children were asleep. It is a common and often deadly illusion.

In a crowded parsonage one day, as I stepped in to retrieve some papers, my 12-year old son was drawing at a table, completely surrounded by the Women's Auxiliary meeting. Totally unaware that I was present, one of the ladies asked him if he would grow up to be a minister like his dad. In an amazingly innocent and painful way, he responded "Oh no . . . yuck! I'm never going to be a minister and not have any time to spend with my kids. I'm never going to go to meetings, meetings, meetings, meetings, all the time, all the time."

Every woman in the room became utterly quiet. My boy, still not knowing that I was only a few feet away behind several ladies, turned his comments into a little song, "Meetings, meetings, meetings, meetings, all the time meetings, all the time meetings."

I raced to my office and buried my head on my desk in great sobs of shame and sorrow. My secretary embraced me like a mother and said, "This is your wake up call. There will always be pastors, but there will never be another time for you to be a father than this time. There is a lesson here for you. Don't miss it."

That moment was a turning point in my own life and in my relationship with my children. To this day I frequently remember that moment. As God reminded the Israelites to remember their covenant with Him, I remember the covenant with my children that He gave me.

2 Samuel 7:18-29

Then went king David in, and sat before the LORD, and he said, Who am I, O Lord GOD? and what is my house, that thou hast brought me hitherto?

19 And this was yet a small thing in thy sight, O Lord GOD; but thou hast spoken also of thy servant's house for a great while to come. And is this the manner of man, O Lord GOD?

20 And what can David say more unto thee? for thou, Lord GOD, knowest thy servant.

21 For thy word's sake, and according to thine own heart, hast thou done all these great things, to make thy servant know them.

22 Wherefore thou art great, O LORD God: for there is none like thee, neither is there any God beside thee, according to all that we have heard with our ears.

23 And what one nation in the earth is like thy people, even like Israel, whom God went to redeem for a people to himself, and to make him a name, and to do for you great things and terrible, for thy land, before thy people, which thou redeemedst to thee from Egypt, from the nations and their gods?

24 For thou hast confirmed to thyself thy people Israel to be a people unto thee for ever: and thou, LORD, art become their God.

25 And now, O LORD God, the word that thou hast spoken concerning thy servant, and concerning his house, establish it for ever, and do as thou hast said.

26 And let thy name be magnified for ever, saying, The LORD of hosts is the God over Israel: and let the house of thy servant David be established before thee.

27 For thou, O LORD of hosts, God of Israel, hast revealed to thy servant, saying, I will build thee an house: therefore hath thy servant found in his heart to pray this prayer unto thee.

28 And now, O Lord GOD, thou art that God, and thy words be true, and thou hast promised this goodness unto thy servant:

29 Therefore now let it please thee to bless the house of thy servant, that it may continue for ever before thee: for thou, O Lord GOD, hast spoken it: and with thy blessing let the house of thy servant be blessed for ever.

Memory Selection
2 Samuel 7:16

Background Scripture
2 Samuel 7

Devotional Reading
2 Samuel 7:10-17

Oct. 3

41

Although God "rested" or paused in His creative work after the sixth day of Creation, His creativity endures. We have noticed how He created Covenants with Noah, then with Abraham and Moses. He also created a new way of governance—a system of "judges"—to govern Israel in the early days of their campaign to conquer Canaan. Later He would allow Israel to create a kingship, reserving the right to select the first king, Saul.

Today' lesson focuses on the second king, David—the greatest in a line of rulers fulfilling God promise referred to in this lesson in a remarkable prayer of David. This "covenant-prayer" differs from other kings' claims in its humility. David prays for a dynasty, not for his own glorification, but for God's.

ഇന്ദ്ര

For a "word-association" exercise, tell group members that you are going to say a word that has come to mean many different things throughout history. Ask them to respond with the first idea they associate with that word, to create a collective group concept as background for today's lesson.

Responses might include such words as: *tyranny . . . pomp and ceremony . . . ruthless use and abuse of power . . . power vested in only one person,. . .traditions that pass ruling power to a family member . . . the American Revolution's struggle to replace a king's power with democracy . . . a wise and benevolent king such as Solomon, as opposed to tyrants.* Invite the group to compare and contrast the impression they have of King David's views with their own.

Teaching Outline	Daily Bible Readings	
I. 'Who Am I? Lord?'—18-20	Mon.	God's Steadfast Love *Psalm 86:8-13*
A. A boy among men, 18	Tue.	David Moves the Ark
B. A promised dynasty, 19-20		*2 Samuel 6:1-5*
II. 'Who Are You? Lord?'—21-22	Wed.	The Ark at Jerusalem
A. A ruler's true heart, 21		2 Samuel 6:11-15
B. The one true King, 22	Thu.	God's Message to David
III. 'What of Your People, Lord?'—23-24		2 Samuel 7: 1-9
A. An astounding past, 23	Fri.	God's Covenant with David
B. A relationship with God, 24		*2 Samuel 7:10-17*
IV. 'Bless You Through Me!'—25-29	Sat.	David Prays to God
A. 'Establish my house . . . ,' 25		*2 Samuel 7:18-22*
B. '. . . For Your Name's Sake,' 26-29	Sun.	Seeking God's Blessing
		2 Samuel 7:23-29

Verse by Verse

I. 'Who Am I? Lord?'—18-20
A. A boy among men, 18

8 Then went king David in, and sat before the LORD, and he said, Who am I, O Lord GOD? and what is my house, that thou hast brought me hitherto?

A remarkable series of events, followed by a conversation between God and David with far-reaching results, lies behind this moving and humble self-analysis. When God had told old Samuel to anoint a successor to Saul, he sent him to the house of Jesse, who had several stalwart sons pass in review. God, however, persisted until Jesse admitted that his youngest son was in the field tending to the sheep, no doubt deciding that David was too young to be considered. As we recall, God's choice was in fact David (1 Sam. 16:1-13).

This young king from an unheralded household will justify God's choice by the slaying of the giant Goliath, being crowned king, and growing in power and influence. Eventually the Queen of Sheba would visit and exclaim that the half had not been told of David's wisdom and wealth (1 Kings 10:6-7).

Finding himself dwelling in a palace, while the Wilderness-worn tabernacle was still where the people perceived that God dwelt, David had conceived of building God a most substantial "home," a temple in Jerusalem (2 Sam. 7:1-2). In return, God had promised to build David and his descendants into a "house" or dynasty (2 Sam. 7:11-13). It is in response to this vision of future glory without parallel that David reflects on his humble beginnings.

B. A promised dynasty, 19-20

19 And this was yet a small thing in thy sight, O Lord GOD; but thou hast spoken also of thy servant's house for a great while to come. And is this the manner of man, O Lord GOD?

20 And what can David say more unto thee? for thou, Lord GOD, knowest thy servant.

Promising a prosperous rule for David himself was a marvelous thing, yet a "small thing" in comparison with promising him a dynasty. The first successor to his throne would be his son Solomon, to whom would fall the privilege of building the Temple in Jerusalem that his father David had first envisioned. But in 7:16, God had extended His promise of a Davidic dynasty "forever." The implied answer to the rhetorical question in 19b, "Is this your usual way of dealing with man?" (NIV), is "No! I am uniquely blessed!"

Verse 20 implies that it would be of little use for David to continue to speak of his unworthiness, since God knows his heart. It was this capacity of God for looking into the heart that had guided old Samuel to select David as Israel's future king in the first place (1 Sam. 16:7).

II. 'Who Are You, Lord?'—21-22
A. A ruler's true heart, 21
21 For thy word's sake, and according to thine own heart, hast thou done all these great things, to make thy servant know them.

David proves his capacity for spiritual insight by discerning that God is not promising David a dynasty merely to exalt a man, but for the sake of His own Word. That is, David and his descendants are to be living proof that God's election of Israel was sound. In turn, God seeks not His own glory but the enrichment of all nations, as the people He chose produce a universal Messiah. In short, the concern of a true ruler, divine or human, is for the people he rules, not for self-aggrandizement.

B. The one true King, 22
22 Wherefore thou art great, O LORD God: for there is none like thee, neither is there any God beside thee, according to all that we have heard with our ears.

David addresses an outburst of praise to God as the one true Ruler of the Universe, in gratitude for the promise God has made to him. The skill with which David fashions this brief word of praise recalls the praise-filled Psalms, most of which were written by David.

III. 'What of Your People, Lord?' —23-24
A. An astounding past, 23
23 And what one nation in the earth is like thy people, even like Israel, whom God went to redeem for a people to himself, and to make him a name, and to do for you great things and terrible, for thy land, before thy people, which thou redeemedst to thee from Egypt, from the nations and their gods?

David asks another good rhetorical question when he recalls Israel's journey. God Himself had reminded them that they were of humble origins, and few in number, and that they were rescued for Egypt and destined for greatness not because of their inherent worth or greatness but because of His sheer love (Deut. 7:7-9). Even since Bible days, the story of the Jews has been unique among the nations.

B. A relationship with God, 24
24 For thou hast confirmed to thyself thy people Israel to be a people unto thee for ever: and thou, LORD, art become their God.

Now David centers on one of the most remarkable differences between the God-Israel story and the stories of other nations. While the gods of the nations abused people, even calling for human sacrifice, God and Israel enjoyed a Father-people or *family* relationship. It was to Israel, and to no other nation, that God had revealed His personal name, Yahweh, or the great "I AM" (Exod. 3:14-15). Again, although in their later history some Israelites would boast of this unique relationship, their election was not for their own glorification but as "a light to the nations."

IV. 'Bless You Through Me!'—25-29

A. 'Establish my house . . . ,' 25

25 And now, O Lord God, the word that thou hast spoken concerning thy servant, and concerning his house, establish it for ever, and do as thou hast said.

"The word that thou hast spoken" refers to God's previous promise not only to make David a great king but to extend his dynasty to future generations. This promise becomes a serious problem for Jewish people who cannot accept Jesus as the Messiah, because in fact they have not always been ruled by a descendant of David. In fact, the lack of a king from David's line became a crucial point of contention among the Jews before the time of Christ. Some rabbis were driven to expect a Messiah of more prophetic qualities, such as Elijah; others looked for a "priestly" Messiah who would purify worship.

The only conceivable fulfillment of the promise that David's house would be established "forever" is to (1) assume that the first of the various non-Davidic kings in Israel's later history were symbolically "Davidic" because the *throne*, not the person, furthered the promise; (2) accept the New Testament claim that King David's dynasty was continued in the birth of Jesus. From the beginning of the gospel story, it is Jesus who was acclaimed as "an horn of salvation for us in the house of his servant David" (Luke 1:69).

B. '. . . For Your Name's Sake,' 26-29

26 And let thy name be magnified for ever, saying, The Lord of hosts is the God over Israel: and let the house of thy servant David be established before thee.

27 For thou, O Lord of hosts, God of Israel, hast revealed to thy servant, saying, I will build thee an house: therefore hath thy servant found in his heart to pray this prayer unto thee.

28 And now, O Lord God, thou art that God, and thy words be true, and thou hast promised this goodness unto thy servant:

29 Therefore now let it please thee to bless the house of thy servant, that it may continue for ever before thee: for thou, O Lord God, hast spoken it: and with thy blessing let the house of thy servant be blessed for ever.

The closing words of this remarkable prayer of David reinforce the preceding themes, as follows:

a. Verses 25-26—An appeal for the fulfillment of God's promise that David's heirs would become a dynasty—not for the glory of the kings themselves but in order for God's name to be magnified.

b. Verse 27—The basis for this promise to build *David* a house, or a dynasty, is grounded in God's response to David's stated intent to build *God* a house. It was only because God took the initiative in this promise that David found the courage to pray for its fulfillment.

c. Verses 28-29—David's confidence that God would fulfill this "dynasty promise" is based not on David's worth as a great king within himself, but on the trustworthiness of God's own Word. The promise can therefore be fulfilled only with God's own blessing.

45

Evangelistic Emphasis

She was not a member of our congregation, but we lifted her up as having gone through a long struggle with her mother's death. Her address was distributed to the congregation. Weeks later, she told me she had been astounded at the letters she received from a congregation that was not even her own. People in our church brought her food so she did not have to cook while caring for her dying mother. She said "I'm not even part of this church; so I had to come see you and ask why you did all this for me?"

I explained that when one is a part of God's creation, and has the chance to communicate the support, love, and mercy of Christ anywhere, it matters not what church you are a formal part of. What matters is we fulfill our covenant with God to share His love where that love is needed most. With tears running down her face, she hugged me, then our secretary, and asked if she could come here to worship from time to time. We told her "God's house is your house," and she was welcome anytime.

ഇരു

Memory Selection

Your house and your kingdom shall be made sure forever before me; your throne shall be established forever.—*2 Samuel 7:16*

We are told that our society is deeply rooted in the "me" generation. Everything we do seems to be directed toward "me, myself, and I."

There is something deeply profound when someone acknowledges greatness beyond himself, and majesty in that which he did not create. Our key text today is a lesson of simple, pure, exclamation of wonder. It is a strong affirmation of the majesty of God, based on all that He has done in the past, is doing in the present, and will surely do until the end of time.

All that God is and all that God can do is so much further beyond us that we cannot even comprehend it. Therefore we do as God wants us to do. We stand in praise and astonishment before Him and His creation, anticipating like a child at a birthday party what more lies before us.

Weekday Problems

It is one of the most painful experiences a pastor can have in preparation for the funeral of an adult. You gather the family around and ask them to share those great and momentous chapters of the deceased's life, because now is the time to lift those up and close that book forever.

Sometimes, however, the room is silent. A person has passed after many years on earth and has left nothing behind at all that anyone can recount. It is a chilling experience, a frightening experience.

God intended for us to be participants in revealing His glory and His grace. He intended for our lives to be witnesses to the power of holiness. Whether one lives to be 100 or only 15, a great deal of godliness and beauty can shine through those years if we understand that we are vessels made by God to carry his finest wine.

No, God does not expect us all to be kingdom-makers or famous for great accomplishments. However, it is not too much for Him to ask that the chapters of our lives provide our loved ones with significant memories and revelations of how we allowed God to work through us.

*How would *you* like to be remembered?

*What legacy are you leaving?

David and Christ

David was a shepherd, and Christ a Shepherd; but David of sheep and Christ of souls.

Samuel, a priest, anointed David to be a king; and John as a priest, baptized Christ.

David, anointed to be a King, came not presently to the Kingdom, but was content for a long time to serve Saul; and our Savior, though He was begotten a King from eternity, was content also to serve.

Saul persecuted David, as Herod persecuted Christ.

Absalom, David's son, rose up against his father; and Judas rose up against Christ.

David was anointed by man, but Christ by His Almighty Father.

—Adapted from Henry Vertue, *Christ and the Church, or Parallels*, written in the 17th century.

This Lesson in Your Life

A very frail, elderly gentleman was standing by the Grand Canyon. As the sun rose and the colors and reflections in the canyon changed like a kaleidoscope, his daughter said, "See Daddy! I told you it was like nothing you had ever seen."

Her father looked at her and said in words loud enough for everyone to hear, "I'm glad I lived long enough to see this, and that I could see it with you." Everyone nearby fought back tears.

Standing in awe of God and the majesty of His creation, both in the natural world and human community, is fundamental with believers. There is something very sad and empty when our fast-paced life, so dependent upon gadgets and things, leaves us little time to look around and see the grand plan that we are part of. The old spiritual phrase, "Oh Lord, your sea is so great and my ship is so small!" is not an expression of lostness or imminent peril. It is an expression of awareness that we are part of the great sweep of God's canvas, and that we are aware that it is a good thing to see and be part of. We cannot buy it or earn it; we cannot "archive" it. God made us part of His vast kingdom simply because He loves us so.

In our lesson today, David stands before God, lifts his arms in the air in submission and says, "What more can I say of thee? For thou knowest thy servant O Lord God!" Like the man at the Grand Canyon knowing that He and the earth were made for each other, David knows that God has created him for an extraordinary purpose.

When we know there is a reason for our being, and that we have been created by God to accomplish things no other could ever do, the sense of being commissioned and sent forth can fill an empty heart very quickly.

We all want to know that we are part of something greater than ourselves. When we view our lives like David, or like Paul when he says, "I have run the race and I have kept the faith . . . ," there is a great sense of spiritual fulfillment.

STRAIGHT

1. Why did David "sit before the Lord" and ask why he had been brought thus far?
He was overwhelmed that God had expressed His love for him and would use him in the divine plan.

2. Why did God show David "future generations"?
So David would understand that all generations of people were created and sustained by God and that He would accompany them into the endless future.

3. Why did David assume that God had done all that He had done?
Specifically so that His servants would see it all and know the greatness of God and such majestic creation.

4. Did David feel singled out by God?
Yes! He proclaimed, "Thou, Lord God, knowest thy serevant" (2 Sam. 7:20). We believe that God knows each of us, and calls us by name.

5. In what other ways did David see God's hand across the generations?
In the establishment of the nation of Israel as His chosen people forever.

6. Was David certain that he was standing before the one God?
Yes, for he said, "There is none like thee, neither is there any God besides thee" (vs. 22). David and Israel knew that the one God of creation had created them and would sustain them.

7. David was confident that God had delivered Israel as a people. How was this done?
By doing for them "great and terrible things," and by driving out before His people a nation and its gods, David could see God's fingerprints on every moment of the history of Israel.

8. What effect did David's awe and amazement have upon him?
It gave David courage to speak to God directly and offer prayers that his life in his house would be blessed.

9. What term does David repeatedly use to describe himself?
He uses the term God wants all of us to use: *a servant.* We are not here to stand and gawk at creation, but to minister actively in God's name.

10. David repeatedly refers to God's promise to "build him a house." What does this refer to?
God's promise to build David a house has a dual meaning: a real physical dwelling will be provided, but the larger meaning is that David will head a dynasty of kings, culminating in the Messiah, and that his people will be secured and protected and have a home forever.

49

My wife and I are Scuba divers. In the Cayman Islands we found ourselves on a dive boat with a wonderful dive master named Danny. He was jovial and happy. He and his wife managed the Dive Center where we were staying. Danny was more than a dive master; he was a blessing to be around.

One day I asked him if he had always been a dive master. He and his wife laughed, and he told me that he had reached third in line to be CEO of GTE, Inc. I was stunned as he told me his salary had been in the multiple six-figure range.

I asked why he gave all that up for the relatively low pay of a dive master. He explained that in that job and all that money he was never fulfilled in his soul; never felt he was doing what God had created him to do. He felt like a slave to the corporate world, and owned not a minute of his life for himself.

Finally, while on a rare dive vacation, he realized that God had intended for him to walk a different path. He now spends seven days a week taking divers from over the world to the beautiful clear waters of the Caribbean and introducing them to the magic of God's underwater world. He said that his salary is small, but the peace and fulfillment in his soul are magnified "a million times over."

He showed me his office with boxes upon boxes of letters of appreciation and admiration of divers over the years. He said in all the years with GTE, he never saw a single letter of appreciation. He smiled and said, "It's great to finally do what God always intended for you to do."

In today's scripture, God is making it clear that He is in covenant with all His people, and that He will never leave them. He will protect and guide them forever.

Somewhere I'm sure that God looks upon Danny the dive master, pumps His holy fist in the air in that great symbol of affirmation, and says, "Yes! That's my man, he is a part of my world, and he is doing what I intended him to do."

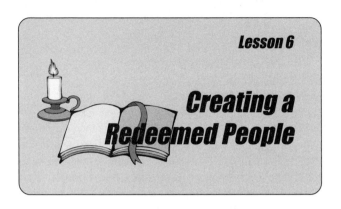

Creating a Redeemed People

Isaiah 43:1-2, 10-13, 18-21

But now thus saith the LORD that created thee, O Jacob, and he that formed thee, O Israel, Fear not: for I have redeemed thee, I have called thee by thy name; thou art mine.

2 When thou passest through the waters, I will be with thee; and through the rivers, they shall not overflow thee: when thou walkest through the fire, thou shalt not be burned; neither shall the flame kindle upon thee.

10 Ye are my witnesses, saith the LORD, and my servant whom I have chosen: that ye may know and believe me, and understand that I am he: before me there was no God formed, neither shall there be after me.

11 I, even I, am the LORD; and beside me there is no saviour.

12 I have declared, and have saved, and I have shewed, when there was no strange god among you: therefore ye are my witnesses, saith the LORD, that I am God.

13 Yea, before the day was I am he; and there is none that can deliver out of my hand: I will work, and who shall let it?

18 Remember ye not the former things, neither consider the things of old.

19 Behold, I will do a new thing; now it shall spring forth; shall ye not know it? I will even make a way in the wilderness, and rivers in the desert.

20 The wild animals honor me, the jackals and the owls, because I provide water in the desert and streams in the wasteland, to give drink to my people, my chosen,

21 the people I formed for myself that they may proclaim my praise.

Memory Selection
Isaiah 43:1
Background Scripture
Isaiah 43
Devotional Reading
Isaiah 42:5-13

51

God's continuing creative power proves literally to be to be a life-saver in this lesson. Since solemnly agreeing to keep God's Covenant, Israel has gone astray. Many in the land, both people and kings, have aped the pagan worship of the cultures around them. They have lapsed into unjust ways, taking advantage of the poor and the helpless for ill-gotten gain. Since they had not kept their part of the Covenant, God sent prophets to warn that a foreign nation, Babylonia, will take Israel into captivity for a 70-year period (see Isa. 39:6).

With chapter 40, however, the book of Isaiah begins to reflect a vision of life beyond captivity. The texts for this lesson affirm that a remnant of the people will be ransomed. Christians see a double meaning to the promise that a Redeemer will come from God to re-create His people.

This lesson can be introduced by discussing what happens in the business world when "covenants" or contracts are broken. Note that when one person defaults on a loan, or when one party to a contract fails to keep the terms of the agreement, the other person is released from his or her own obligations as well, because the contract has been invalidated. Penalties may include fines, forfeiture of property, or imprisonment.

In the case of God's Covenant with His people, only part of this scenario applies. Because Israel broke Covenant with God, He allowed the main body of the people to suffer captivity in Babylon. But out of His superhuman love He chose to fulfill His part of the Covenant by returning a Remnant to the land He had given them. This lesson lays the foundation for this plan.

Teaching Outline	Daily Bible Readings	
	Mon.	The Everlasting God *Isaiah 40:25-31*
I. The Creator's Love—1-2	Tue.	Give Glory to God *Isaiah 42:5-13*
II. Witnesses of the One God—10-13		
A. The servant of the Lord, 10	Wed.	Israel Is Redeemed *Isaiah 43:1-7*
B. The work of the true God, 11-13	Thu.	God Our Savior *Isaiah 43:8-15*
III. A Way in the Wilderness—18-21	Fri.	God Will Bring Salvation *Isaiah 43:16-21*
A. Just as before, 18-19	Sat.	Israel Is Still on Trial *Isaiah 43:22-28*
B. Safety on the way, 20-21	Sun.	God Blesses Israel *Isaiah 44:1-8*

Verse by Verse

I. The Creator's Love—1-2

1 But now thus saith the LORD that created thee, O Jacob, and he that formed thee, O Israel, Fear not: for I have redeemed thee, I have called thee by thy name; thou art mine.

2 When thou passest through the waters, I will be with thee; and through the rivers, they shall not overflow thee: when thou walkest through the fire, thou shalt not be burned; neither shall the flame kindle upon thee.

Why would God need to reassure Israel to "Fear not"? Because for decades He has been threatening them with punishment for breaking His Covenant with them. Prophet after prophet has come to them warning that because their worship has degenerated into idolatry, and because their ethics have sunk to a level no higher than the pagans about them, they would be called to God's bar of justice. With the exception of a few reforms under kings such as Josiah and Hezekiah, these warnings have been ignored.

Meanwhile, God has been watching other events being acted out on the stage of history. Watching the rise of the military might of the Assyrians, God used their armies to defeat the 10 northern tribes of Assyria in 722–721. Later, the prophet Isaiah and others warned that a similar fate would befall the southern kingdom of Judah if it did not repent. Despite some rustlings of reform, both kings and people in general continued to live in disobedience to the Covenant. Since the nation of Babylonia had conquered the Assyrians, this fierce people was the country of choice for God to use to defeat Judah. The final captivity occurred in 586 B.C.

With Israel scattered to the four winds, and their holy city Jerusalem lying in ruins, we can imagine a pious Jew asking, Where is God in all this? Will He forsake His Covenant to be with us forever? To answer such reasonable questions, God inspired Isaiah to peer into the future; and these two verses are a part of what he saw. God will be faithful to His part of the Covenant despite Israel's general faithlessness.

Verse 1 shows why. Unlike Israel, "the party of the second part," God, the party of the first part, is *God,* the Creator. "Thou art mine," He assures the people, even though they have rejected Him.

Verse 2 reminds us that much of biblical prophecy is "right-brained" literature. That is, we must read it in a poetic frame of mind, and not insist on rigid literalism. "When thou passest through the waters, I will be with thee" is a promise that God will preserve a remnant to endure the otherwise "drowning" waters of captivity in Babylon. The promise, of course, is based on the time when God was also with His people as they passed through the waters of the Red Sea. Similarly, God reassures the people that He will protect a remnant when they "walk through the fire" of persecution and imprisonment.

II. Witnesses of the One God—10-13
A. The servant of the Lord, 10

10 Ye are my witnesses, saith the LORD, and my servant whom I have chosen: that ye may know and believe me, and understand that I am he: before me there was no God formed, neither shall there be after me.

The first reason God gave for planning to return a remnant of His people to their land was simply that He is God, not a man (vs. 3). He is above the "tit for tat" mentality that finds many mere mortals retaliating to a hurt, instead of responding in love. Now two more reasons appear: God wants a restored Israel as a *witness* and as a *servant.*

Frequently in Scripture when God would threaten punishment, a prophet would appeal to the testimony it would be to surrounding nations if He proved to be merciful. "Then men will say, 'Surely the righteous still are rewarded; surely there is a God who judges the earth'" (Ps. 58:11). Now God reassures the righteous remnant that He will rescue them so they can be witnesses to the Gentiles that the one true God is a God who keeps covenant.

The terms "servant" and "servant of God" are key words in this section of Isaiah. At times they refer to Cyrus, king of Persia (who by now has conquered Babylon), for serving God in allowing a remnant of the Jews to return. At other times the servant is God's people themselves, as is the case here. They are being rescued not to become a museum piece of God's workmanship, but to be "a light to the nations" and to bring the ultimate "servant," the Messiah, to the Gentiles (see Isa. 42:1-7).

B. The work of the true God, 11-13

11 I, even I, am the LORD; and beside me there is no saviour.

12 I have declared, and have saved, and I have shewed, when there was no strange god among you: therefore ye are my witnesses, saith the LORD, that I am God.

13 Yea, before the day was I am he; and there is none that can deliver out of my hand: I will work, and who shall let it?

Here God explains in further detail just who the redeemed nation will bear witness of. During various periods of their history when they were threatened by their enemies, Israel had turned to Egypt and to other nations in hope that they could be rescued in that way. Here God says that this hope was in vain, since He alone is ultimately the Savior, of both people and nations. In Isaiah 31:1 the prophet had already thundered,

Woe to those who go down to Egypt for help,

who rely on horses,
who trust in the multitude of their chariots
and in the great strength of their horsemen,
but do not look to the Holy One of Israel,
or seek help from the LORD.

In verses 12-13, God has a thinly veiled rebuke for the times Israel had depended on pagan gods for deliverance, forgetting that the nature of the one God precluded any reality in "the gods." Again, it is Isaiah who writes a bitterly humorous and eloquent bit of irony on this topic. He ridicules anyone who would take one end of a log and carve out an idol to which he would bow, then stick the other end of the same log in the fire for heat! (44:9-16).

"Let" in verse 13 has the KJV meaning of "prevent" (see "who can reverse it," in the NIV, and compare 2 Thess.2:7 in the KJV with the NIV).

III. A Way in the Wilderness—18-21

A. Just as before, 18-19

18 Remember ye not the former things, neither consider the things of old.

19 Behold, I will do a new thing; now it shall spring forth; shall ye not know it? I will even make a way in the wilderness, and rivers in the desert.

The prophet had figuratively referred to destructive "waters" in verse 2, recalling for his hearers God's protection when they fled Egypt through the Red Sea. Now he refers to the period of the Wilderness Wanderings when God protected the people for 40 years, seeing to it that they were fed and watered, and that their clothes and sandals did not wear out. This reassuring history becomes the basis for confidence that their fate in Babylon has not escape God's attention, and that he will lead them out through the desert back to the Promised Land.

B. Safety on the way, 20-21

20 The wild animals honor me, the jackals and the owls, because I provide water in the desert and streams in the wasteland, to give drink to my people, my chosen,

21 the people I formed for myself that they may proclaim my praise.

If God is to be true to His promise to return a remnant to the Promised Land from Babylon, He will need to protect them from wild animals and enemies along the way. The literal fulfillment of this poetic passage is seen in the book of Ezra, who led the first wave of returning exiles. On one of the trips back from Babylon through the Fertile Crescent, Ezra declined the king's offer of a protective army, saying "I was ashamed to require of the king a band of soldier and horsemen to help us against the enemy in the way," choosing rather to depend on the protection of the living God (see Ezra 8:21-23).

This protection, Isaiah hints, was grounded in the same fact that led God to allow His people to return in the first place: in His nature as a loving God, not in the nature of a faithless people. He formed Israel out of love, and He will protect them out of the same trait.

Evangelistic Emphasis

He lived near the church for a long time, but only recently joined. He said that the ministry of our church is what he had searched for. He was wealthy, and gave generously, believing that giving is in response to your blessings.

Then, he began to fade and become inactive. Efforts to light a fire under him once more were brushed off quickly. Finally, I made him sit down with me over coffee. I discovered that through some foolish investments he had lost almost all of his income and savings, and was embarrassed that he could not write checks to the church.

I told him his worth to God's Kingdom was not measured in checks, but only in the heart, and that we all make mistakes. Over the weeks, I and many members of the church embraced him with love and support. He later told me this was the first time he had personally felt the power of the biblical term "redemption." While not as monetarily deep as before, his participation was more enthusiastic than ever, and his soul was filled to overflowing.

ℰᎧᏇ

Memory Selection

Do not fear, for I have redeemed you; I have called you by name, you are Mine. —*Isaiah 43:1*

The people of Israel surely must have thought nothing worse could possibly happen to them. They had been conquered, taken into slavery, and spread throughout the entire Eastern world. For all they knew, Babylon and regional cities would be their home until the end of time. Their beloved homeland would become a thing of the past. It was a frightenly devastating condition.

Israel, however, maintained confidence in God's presence. It is a fundamental part of the great story of the history of Israel that even in captivity in foreign lands, they never gave up their certainty that somewhere, sometime, in some way, God would redeem them and bring them home. It is that tenacity that to this day bonds the Jewish people together as nothing else ever could.

Weekday Problems

It is a common experience, when life is filled with difficulties, to feel that you are very alone. One couple in the church was barely holding their nose above water with financial problems, child problems, marital difficulties, and legal issues. They told me they didn't know how they would make it.

Knowing another couple in the church who a few years before had passed through that same kind of stress, I arranged a visit between the four of them. The older couple shared their own frustrations and "at the end of our rope" feelings, then gave witness to the presence of God in their lives that enabled them to handle it and emerge stronger than ever.

Seeing what that confidence did for them, the other couple resolved to cling to God and wade right through their troubles, which they were able to do within a year and a half.

Knowing that you are not alone, and that God will help, makes all the difference in the world.

*Have you felt alone in a difficult situation? From where did you draw strength?

Daffynitions of Love

Love is when two people with their eyes shut can see heaven.

Love is oceans of emotions surrounded by expanses of expenses.

Love may not make the world go 'round, but it certainly makes a lot of people dizzy.

Love is a sweet dream, and marriage is the alarm clock.

Love is blind, and marriage is an eye-opener.

When a girl loves in a breezy manner, the boys soon get wind of it.

Some girls fall head-over-heels in love with a guy, while others go ahead and fall in love with heels.

Love is when you can't kiss a girl unexpectedly . . . only sooner than she thought.

Better to have loved a short man than never to have loved a tall.

The little girl was scared to sleep in a dark room by herself, and she kept crying out for her parents. They came in, soothed their child and assured her all was okay. The child continued to cry out, and the parents continued to come in and offer reassuring affirmations. This went on for some time, until finally the parents told the child "You don't need to worry, we are right down the hall and God is here with you and will protect you. Aren't you pleased God is here with you and will not leave you?"

The little girl then asked "If God is here, where is he?" The parents assured her that while God was in the room, He could not be seen with our eyes like you see most things. There was a long pause, then, the child said innocently, "I'm glad God is here, but I want someone that has some skin on him."

The need for reassurance and security is common to all living things. The understanding of vulnerability is a thread that has always woven its way through every part of God's creation. All manner of fishes, reptiles, mammals, and other creatures immediately search for a secure place to hide as soon as they are born. Security is a natural part of life.

In the wonderful scripture for today's lesson, God, speaking through Isaiah, reassures us (Israel) that ultimate security will be by our side every day throughout our lives. We are reminded that, while it is normal to want reassurance and well being, God has always promised us that security. In verse 13 is that powerful declaration, "I am God, and also hence forth I am He; there is none who can deliver from my hand; I work and who can hinder it?"

This is a statement that there are no powers on earth greater than the all-loving presence of the creator. If God were using human language He would say to us, "Yes, it's all right for you to want someone with 'skin on,' as long as you understand that while you cannot see Me with your eyes, you shall feel totally confident with your heart. And I will always watch over you."

1. How does God personalize His promise of redemption to Israel?"

He says to them "I have called you by name, you are mine." Believers fundamentally cling to the promise that God calls us by name.

2. In addition to naming Israel, God detailed their task on earth. What was it?"

Israel was described as "witnesses for the Lord," as those who could clearly attest to God's power and protective love.

3. In what ways does God assure Israel of His protective presence?

He declares that whether they pass through waters or have to swim rivers or walk through fires, they will not be burned, drowned, or overwhelmed.

4. Why did God say He had chosen Israel as His witnesses?

So that Israel might know and believe in God and understand that the God who has guided them is the one true God.

5. What does God say about His own place in the world?

He says that before Him there was no God nor shall there ever be another God after Him.

6. What was God doing all the while Israel was going through its troubles and difficulties?

God says that He "declared and saved and proclaimed when there was no strange god among you."

7. What does God say about the possibility of other saviors?

God vigorously asserts that "besides Me there is no other savior."

8. Many people and cultures look back to the past. What does God say about that?

God says to let the past fade away and "remember not the former things nor consider the things of old."

9. As Israel looks to the future, what advice does God have?

He says, "He is at work doing a new thing; now it springs forth, do you not perceive it?"

10. How does God define His relationship to Israel in this lesson?

He is the pioneer and the frontrunner; saying, "I will make a way in the wilderness and rivers to flow in the desert. "

When my sister was about 9, my father had invited some couples from his office to dinner in our home for an evening of fellowship. I felt like quite a young man when I was invited to remain in the living room after dinner and visit with them like a "grownup," but my mother had sent my sister on to bed.

At some point during the evening, as we all chatted, my sister came wandering into the living room in her nightgown, rubbing her eyes and looking very sleepy. The conversation stopped, and my mother said, "Well darling, why are you up? I thought you were in your bed sound asleep." Out of my sister's mouth came the substance of a thousand sermons, as she looked around the room and then said, "I just wanted to make sure that you were still here." She then turned and toddled her way back to her bedroom and into her bed.

Part of our task in the Christian church is to live our lives in such an exemplary way that those who see us and know us have no doubt that "We are still here." There are few senses of security more powerful than to actually have confidence that, whether it is your parents on earth or your Father in Heaven, or whoever is in charge of overseeing your life, that entity will not be moved at all.

Some years ago, a young boy was found late at night sitting on a park bench in New York City. Police took him to the station and learned that his mother had left him on the park bench and told him she would be right back, and he should stay there until she came back. The tragic truth in this story is that the mother was in the process of abandoning her son, and she had fled to parts unknown, leaving him fully dressed and with a lunch pail and extra clothes in it. Even though the day had passed and night had fallen, this young boy was so confident and secure in his trust that the One who looked after him, loved him and would hold him in the hollow of her hand, would be back to pick him up and take him home, he was perfectly willing to sit and wait. It was a remarkable example of unshakable trust. It was an example of the exact kind of trust God wants us to have in Him, that what He says He will do, and whatever life brings our way, whether tragedy or triumph, God will be there with us. All we have to do is to be utterly and completely confident in that promise.

Creating a New Covenant

Jeremiah 29:10-14; 31:31-34

For thus saith the LORD, That after seventy years be accomplished at Babylon I will visit you, and perform my good word toward you, in causing you to return to this place.

11 For I know the thoughts that I think toward you, saith the LORD, thoughts of peace, and not of evil, to give you an expected end.

12 Then shall ye call upon me, and ye shall go and pray unto me, and I will hearken unto you.

13 And ye shall seek me, and find me, when ye shall search for me with all your heart.

14 And I will be found of you, saith the LORD: and I will turn away your captivity, and I will gather you from all the nations, and from all the places whither I have driven you, saith the LORD; and I will bring you again into the place whence I caused you to be carried away captive.

31:31 Behold, the days come, saith the LORD, that I will make a new covenant with the house of Israel, and with the house of Judah:

32 Not according to the covenant that I made with their fathers in the day that I took them by the hand to bring them out of the land of Egypt; which my covenant they brake, although I was an husband unto them, saith the LORD.

33 But this shall be the covenant that I will make with the house of Israel; After those days, saith the LORD, I will put my law in their inward parts, and write it in their hearts; and will be their God, and they shall be my people.

34 And they shall teach no more every man his neighbour, and every man his brother, saying, Know the LORD: for they shall all know me, from the least of them unto the greatest of them, saith the LORD; for I will forgive their iniquity, and I will remember their sin no more.

Oct. 17

Memory Selection
Jeremiah 31:33
Background Scripture
Jeremiah 29:1-14; 31:31-34
Devotional Reading
Jeremiah 30:18-22

In our twin themes of *Creation* and *Covenant,* God is proving to be "stubbornly loving" in both arenas. This session focuses on God's willingness to redeem His people from Babylonian captivity even before it occurs. Because of idolatry and other disobedience, the 10 northern tribes of Israel had been taken captive by Assyria in 722-721 B.C. Then the southern two tribes of Judah and Benjamin were captured by Babylon in 586.

Here, however, the prophet Jeremiah, viewing the future from God's perspective, promises that after 70 years God will enable His people to return to the Holy Land. Certainly the disobedient are punished. But God proves to be faithful in his Covenant-love by redeeming a remnant of the people, whose return will once again prove that God's Covenant depends more on His character than on the moral perfection of His people.

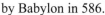

Israel has been behaving like a child; so one way to introduce this lesson is to lead a discussion of how parents can best deal with unruly children. Point out that studies have shown that one constant need of children is to be able to perceive consistently firm boundaries, enforced with love.

Despite consistent signs of God's love, Israel through the years has wavered between faithfulness and idolatry, ethical and unethical behavior. God has alternately allowed foreign nations to conquer them, then, upon the people's reform, blessed the country with prosperity and peace.

In this lesson Jeremiah predicts that God will allow a remnant of the people punished in Babylonian captivity to return. This Divine Parent proves again that His most consistent method of dealing with His children is love.

Teaching Outline	**Daily Bible Readings**	
I. Vision of Rescue—29:10	Mon.	Exiles to Be Restored *Jeremiah 29:10-14*
II. Visualizing God's Love—11-14	Tue.	After Judgment, Freedom *Jeremiah 30:2-9*
A. Plans for peace, 11	Wed.	Abundance and Joy *Jeremiah 30:18-22*
B. Conditions of the Covenant, 12-13	Thu.	God Is Always Faithful *Jeremiah 31:1-6*
C. Promise of rescue, 14	Fri.	Exiles to Return with Joy *Jeremiah 31:7-14*
III. Viewing a New Covenant —31-34	Sat.	God's Restoration *Jeremiah 31:23-30*
A. Old ways, 31-32	Sun.	A New Covenant *Jeremiah 31:31-34*
B. New expectations, 33-34		

Verse by Verse

I. Vision of Rescue—29:10

10 For thus saith the LORD, That after seventy years be accomplished at Babylon I will visit you, and perform my good word toward you, in causing you to return to this place.

Note the historical notes in the "Focus" section for the background of the Captivity. Jeremiah was known as "the weeping prophet" because of the tragic news he bore about Judah's looming defeat by the nation of Babylon, about 136 years after the 10 northern tribes were conquered by Assyria.

Even before the rise of Babylon to prominence, Jeremiah had foreseen its emergence (Jer. 20:4-6). Now, in another remarkable example of inspiration, Jeremiah predicts even the number of years that Babylon would oppress his people (see also 25:11). Also, the oppressor-nation will be held responsible for its own ungodliness, and the prophet predicts its fall as well (25:12).

The "70 years" is only approximate and may be symbolic of two generations, since beginning and ending dates are hard to define, comparing 2 Kings with the Return led by Ezra and Nehemiah. Archeologists, however, have discovered a temple, an altar, and even documents that show a Jewish presence in sixth-century B.C. Babylon (the ruins of which are less than 50 miles southwest of modern-day Baghdad).

II. Visualizing God's Love—11-14

A. Plans for peace, 11

11 For I know the thoughts that I think toward you, saith the LORD, thoughts of peace, and not of evil, to give you an expected end.

It is easy to imagine how a faithful Jew, who was definitely in the minority, might lose heart at the prospect of being carried away from the Land of Promise as a captive of a godless people. Has God abandoned His Covenant-people? Not at all. The Covenant is not a "contract" between two equal parties, each as capable of faithlessness as the other. It is between a consistently faithful God and an unfaithful race; hence "the party of the greater part," God, does not behave faithlessly as does His partner in the Covenant, but has "thoughts of peace." As the NIV completes this moving promise, God "plans to give [His people] hope and a future." No doubt this word from God was also appreciated by the Babylonian powers that be, since it would have contributed to their Jewish captives being relatively quiet and governable.

B. Conditions of the Covenant, 12-13

12 Then shall ye call upon me,

and ye shall go and pray unto me, and I will hearken unto you.

13 And ye shall seek me, and find me, when ye shall search for me with all your heart.

The prophet Jeremiah now moves into a picture of a New Covenant—a change in God's way of dealing with His people. The Old Covenant was not so much "wrong" as it was inadequate; and even this was planned obsolescence. God did not include an eternal sacrifice for sin in the Old Covenant as He will in the New. Other differences will consist more in the people's practice than in a change of God's intent, and in the quality of relationship between God and His people.

For example, God had often promised to hear and respond to prayer in the Old Covenant (see Isa. 58:9). However, when the people would harden their hearts in disobedience, He would turn a deaf ear to their prayer (Jer. 14:11-12). They also often were half-hearted in seeking God, as when they gave Him the worst of their flock as a sacrifice instead of the best (Mal. 1:8). The present promise, therefore, refers not to God's new willingness to hear and answer prayer, but is a prediction of greater sincerity on the part of those who seek Him. The Babylonian captivity will teach them a stern lesson.

C. Promise of rescue, 14

14 And I will be found of you, saith the LORD: and I will turn away your captivity, and I will gather you from all the nations, and from all the places whither I have driven you, saith the LORD; and I will bring you again into the place whence I caused you to be carried away captive.

The experience of "being found" by God was difficult for faithful Jews who had been taken into foreign lands. They could no longer make pilgrimages to the Temple in Jerusalem on feast days. They were dispossessed of the very land God had promised them. No wonder many scholars think that Psalm 137:4 was written during the captivity, for the worshiper laments, "How shall we sing the Lord's song in a strange land?"

Here, however, Jeremiah reassures the captives not only in Babylonia but in Assyria, in Egypt, and other places of "the Dispersion." They will be re-assembled in Judea, and will be able to worship God in the land He had promised their father Abraham so long ago. It is a matter of debate whether this promise was fulfilled in the Return envisioned here by Jeremiah, or includes the modern restoration of worldwide Jewry to the modern nation of Israel.

III. Viewing a New Covenant—31-34
A. Old ways, 31-32

31 Behold, the days come, saith the LORD, that I will make a new covenant with the house of Israel, and with the house of Judah:

32 Not according to the covenant that I made with their fathers in the day that I took them by the hand to bring them out of the land of Egypt; which my covenant they brake, although I was an husband unto them, saith the LORD:

It would be hard to overstate the significance and far-reaching impact of these words predicting a new covenant. It will not only mark the now-familiar distinction Christians observe between the Old Covenant and the New; it is in fact a watershed in the history of religion in general. Most religions, including that of the Jews, stem from a "corporate" relationship between the worshiper and the One who is worshiped. A person is therefore "born into the faith." This was precisely what God intended when He made His Covenant with Abraham and his descendants.,

However, an inherent weakness in such an arrangement has by now become painfully clear. Many Jews began to excuse ungodly behavior on the basis that "I am a member of the Covenant," and therefore exempt from punishment. Jeremiah now foresees a new arrangement in which relating to God will require more individual responsibility.

B. New expectations, 33-34

33 But this shall be the covenant that I will make with the house of Israel; After those days, saith the Lord, I will put my law in their inward parts, and write it in their hearts; and will be their God, and they shall be my people.

34 And they shall teach no more every man his neighbour, and every man his brother, saying, Know the Lord: for they shall all know me, from the least of them unto the greatest of them, saith the Lord; for I will forgive their iniquity, and I will remember their sin no more.

Under Moses' Law, a person became a "child of the Covenant" simply by being born. He inherited a system of laws and religious practices, which he was expected to learn under proper instruction. Jeremiah, however, envisions a time when the rule of God will arise from within a person's heart. Although it will have certain objective content, whether the person who claims to be loyal to it actually "knows the Lord" will be based on his or her inward relationship with Him, rather than decided by comparing behavior with a Lawbook.

Although Jeremiah describes this law as applying to "the house of Israel" even the definition of that phrase will change. The prophet Isaiah is especially known for teaching that this new system of God's rule will be extended to "the nations" (Heb. *goyim*). Moving to the writings of the New Covenant, the apostle Paul will explicitly expand the definition of "Israel" to those who believe as Father Abraham believed, not to those who can trace their birth-line back to him (see Rom. 9:6; Gal. 6:16).

In summary, the new covenant Jeremiah envisions will include more emphasis on personal and "heart-felt" dimension of faith, although God certainly wanted that kind of relationship even under the Old Covenant. God's children will still be incorporated into "the people of God," but the individual, heart-felt dimension of the faith required for peoplehood will be emphasized more under the New Covenant than the Old.

Evangelistic Emphasis

On the signup sheet in the pew, they checked "Desire a conference with minister." Visiting in their home, I discovered they both were carrying their own embarrassing baggage. For years they had been alcoholics, and were now struggling to stay "on the wagon." They were sure the church would not open its doors to people of such weak character, but they thoroughly enjoyed the church and wanted to know what I thought.

They were amazed when I told them their past meant nothing to me, or to God, either. I told them the only thing that matters was their future, and God had promised them a bright future if they would only accept responsibility for it. I assured them their place in my congregation had nothing to do with what used to be, but had everything to do with what we could all be together, with God in the lead. They joined the church the very next Sunday and have been enthusiastic ever since.

ಏಲಙ

Memory Selection

This is the Covenant that I will make with the House of Israel after those days, says the Lord: I will put My law within them, and I will write it on their hearts; and I will be their God, and they will be My people.— *Jeremiah 31:33*

In our lesson today, God makes it once again perfectly clear that He is not in the business of holding transgressions or shortcomings against His people, but only yearns for them to return to Him and seek His face. He is an active and intervening God, declaring that He will "Put His law within them and write it upon their hearts and He will be their God, and they shall be His people."

It is a powerful and remarkable affirmation that the God of all time still wants us and claims us, no matter who we are or what we do. The ball is in our court, and our response is anticipated. He still leaves the door unlocked, the light on, and the sheets on the bed turned back.

Weekday Problems

Even though they had two teenage boys, the wife abruptly decided she did not want to be married anymore, and left. Life was hard following the distribution of community property, but even harder emotionally. The husband was bitter, and struggled to make ends meet and do everything that teenagers required. He built up hatred for his wife, and we all could see it eroding his attitude like rust erodes a pipe.

Then, during the Men's Class one Sunday, someone mentioned that "Refusing to forgive is like drinking rat poison and waiting for the rat to die." A light went on, and he realized that she must make her own peace with God, and that he would forever be separated from God as long as he maintained such a hateful heart. There in the Men's Class, he confessed his alienation from God because of his bitterness, and was forgiven by the class members and assured of God's forgiveness. He then openly professed forgiveness for his wife, though she had not asked for it. Being in Covenant with God sweeps away the corrosive effects of life.

*Have you ever "turned loose" of anger, and become whole again?

Flying with Eagles ... and Turkeys

Passenger to pilot: This is my first airplane flight, and I'm a little afraid. You'll be careful, won't you?

Pilot: Of course. In fact, I intend to be extra careful, since this is my first flight, too.

* * * *

Did you hear about the flight that was so rough that the flight attendant poured the food directly into the sick sacks?

* * * *

Jo: I think the pilots' unions are getting too strong.

Flo: Why's that?

Jo: A pilot won't accept a flight assignment these days if he's already seen the in-flight movie.

* * * *

The jet-age is amazing. Breakfast in New York . . . lunch in Los Angeles . . . dinner in Hong Kong . . . luggage in London.

This Lesson In Your Life

It would not take much of a review of most specialists in the mental health industry to learn the most profound and deeply moving problem in our society: ongoing guilt. We are a society that hears around the clock, through every medium—newspaper, television, radio—that we have failed if we are too tall, too short, too fat, too thin, not educated enough, not enough children or too many children, or not a good enough job. The list goes on and on. One can scarcely move in the morning without hearing or reading something that implies "you ought to be guilty about the way you are _____ (Fill in the blank and you will be accurate, no matter what you write down.)"

When there is crisis in our marriages, in our parental relationships, our decision-making or other arenas of life, our first impulse is to blame ourselves. At no time in history have as many people been applying for spiritual retreats, weekend religious getaways, or extended study opportunities where one can examine one's own life. Society has told us for so long that we should feel guilty about something, and more people than ever are searching their souls, hoping to find God and answers to relieve the sense of implied failure.

Most ministers have long insisted that if you find God, this will be a shield against the pervasive sense of brokenness and failure, because God will fulfill you spiritually and you will not be vulnerable to the message of the world. When people are in Covenant with God, the most amazing transformations take place. In addition to a deep peace and sense of forgiveness reaching into their very beings, the manner in which they conduct every aspect of their lives takes on a more holy direction. The sense of guilt in having fallen short fades into the past, because they have now locked arms with God.

1. God says He will make a new Covenant with Israel, not like the Covenant which was made with Israel's Fathers. What did that mean?
In the previous Covenant, God took Israel by the hand to lead them like children, and they rebelled. In His new Covenant, their hearts will be turned and they will want to be a part of His Kingdom.

2. How does God commit himself in this Covenant?
Like all agreements, God says "I will be their God, and they shall be My people." This is powerful!

3. What did God mean by the phrase "No longer shall each man teach his neighbor and each his brother, saying 'know the Lord.'"?
He meant there would be no need for each one to teach the other anymore, because all will have God's law in their hearts.

4. How did God describe the participants in the new Covenant?
"It will be all people: for they shall all know Me, from the least of them to the greatest."

5. Right up front, God declares His part of the Covenant. What is it?
He is wiping the slate clean. "I will forgive their iniquity, and remember their sin no more."

6. How does God affirm that He is intimately involved in Israel's life?
He says that He has plans for Israel, plans for their welfare and not for evil, to give them a future and a hope.

7. What does God say about His availability to Israel?
He says that when people seek Him with all their hearts, He will be found.

8. God's part of the Covenant includes restoration. How so?
He promises to "restore their fortunes." Their lives will be just as they once were.

9. How is God's new Covenant a "homecoming" ?
God says he is bringing Israel back to its home, from all the nations to which He had exiled them because of their sinfulness.

10. What does God say about Israel's prayers in the new Covenant?
He promises that if Israel calls upon Him, He will hear them all. Never again will He close His ears to Israel.

The great Roman Catholic retreat weekend known as Cursillo has swept the country and its appeal crosses all denominational lines, often under the heading of "Walk to Emmaus." Having been instrumental in bringing Cursillo to the Louisiana Methodist Church, I have found it to be a remarkable blessing of renewal.

A couple in our church were the ultimate picture of the happy, well to do, happy-go-lucky couple. Although I and others had urged them to apply for Cursillo, they always had an excuse, and dismissed it with a phrase such as "Oh, that's not our thing; God has us right where He wants us." This went on for years, until one day they sent an application just to keep us from bothering them anymore. The application was accepted, and the Cursillo alumni community was thrilled. There was nothing they could do, and off they went, smiling on the outside but wishing they really did not have to go.

Upon returning Sunday night they came straight to my house where several of us were in Bible Study. They came into the house, lips quivering, and immediately embraced most of us in the study with bear hugs while tears flowed everywhere. The sense of forgiveness was so heavy at Cursillo, and the feeling of being loved unconditionally was exhibited at every moment. They told us through their tears and laughter that they now were aware that they had been searching for God all their lives, but did not want to let it show. They were carrying guilt about their religious lukewarmness, and about other events and issues in their lives, and never really knew what to do with it. That wonderful, magical experience called Cursillo brought them face-to-face with the holy and forgiving God, and His holy and forgiving people, and this couple were for the first time in their lives feeling cleansed, renewed and "fleshed-out" all over again.

Creating a New Hope

Ezekiel 37:1-14

T he hand of the LORD was upon me, and carried me out in the spirit of the LORD and set me down in the midst of the valley which was full of bones,

2 And caused me to pass by them round about: and, behold, there were very many in the open valley; and, lo, they were very dry.

3 And he said unto me, Son of man, can these bones live? And I answered, O Lord GOD, thou knowest.

4 Again he said unto me, Prophesy upon these bones, and say unto them, O ye dry bones, hear the word of the LORD.

5 Thus saith the Lord GOD unto these bones; Behold, I will cause breath to enter into you, and ye shall live:

6 And I will lay sinews upon you, and will bring up flesh upon you, and cover you with skin, and put breath in you, and ye shall live; and ye shall know that I am the LORD.

7 So I prophesied as I was commanded: and as I prophesied, there was a noise, and behold a shaking, and the bones came together, bone to his bone.

8 And when I beheld, lo, the sinews and the flesh came up upon them, and the skin covered them above: but there was no breath in them.

9 Then said he unto me, Prophesy unto the wind, prophesy, son of man, and say to the wind, Thus saith the Lord GOD; Come from the four winds, O breath, and breathe upon these slain, that they may live.

10 So I prophesied as he commanded me, and the breath came into them, and they lived, and stood up upon their feet, an exceeding great army.

11 Then he said unto me, Son of man, these bones are the whole house of Israel: behold, they say, Our bones are dried, and our hope is lost: we are cut off for our parts.

12 Therefore prophesy and say unto them, Thus saith the Lord GOD; Behold, O my people, I will open your graves, and cause you to come up out of your graves, and bring you into the land of Israel.

13 And ye shall know that I am the LORD, when I have opened your graves, O my people, and brought you up out of your graves,

14 And shall put my spirit in you, and ye shall live, and I shall place you in your own land: then shall ye know that I the LORD have spoken it, and performed it, saith the LORD.

Memory Selection
Ezekiel 37:14

Background Scripture
Ezekiel 37

Devotional Reading
Ezekiel 37:24-28

FOCUS

Ezekiel was a priest, a younger contemporary of Jeremiah. They experienced God's judgment against faithless Israel, the Babylonians' siege against the city of Jerusalem, and the deportations from 604–586.

Yet, in the midst of this national calamity, God granted Ezekiel a vision of a brighter future. He does not soft-pedal the seriousness of Israel's disobedience; but, like Jeremiah, he foresees a time when God will turn the hearts of the people back to Him.

This situation is illustrated in the famous vision of the "Valley of the Dry Bones," in which Israel is portrayed first as disconnected bones left on a field of battle, then as a rejuvenated body in which God's Spirit dwells once again.

ဆင္ဆ

FOR A LIVELY START...

Ask a singer to lead your group in the first verse of the old African-American spiritual, "Dry Bones," inspired by Ezekiel's vision in chapter 37:

Ezekiel connected them dry bones!
Ezekiel connected them dry bones!
Ezekiel connected "Them dry bones!
Now hear the word of the Lord!

The toe bone connected to the (pause) *foot bone.* (Repeat twice, end with *"Now hear the word of the Lord!"*)

The foot bone connected to the . . . *ankle bone.* (Repeat as above.)

The ankle bone connected to the . . . *leg bone.* (Repeat.)

The leg bone connected to the . . . *thigh bone.* (Repeat.)

The thigh bone connected to your hip bone. (Repeat).

The hip bone connected to the . . . *back bone.* (Repeat.)

The back bone connected to the . . . *shoulder bone.* (Repeat.)

The shoulder bone connected to the . . . *neck bone.* (Repeat.)

The neck bone connected to the . . . *head bone.* (Repeat; conclude with *"Now hear the word of the Lord!"*)

Teaching Outline

I. Israel Dead and Scattered—1-2

II. Incisive Issue—3-6
  A. Piercing question, 3
  B. Life-giving power predicted, 4-6

III. Indwelling Spirit of God—7-10
  A. Stage I (external healing), 7-8
  B. Stage II (internal life), 9-10

IV. Interpretation of the Vision—11-14
  A. Sad state of affairs, 11
  B. Israel's "resurrection," 12-14

Daily Bible Readings

Mon.	God's Name Profaned
	Ezekiel 36:16-22
Tue.	New Heart Promised
	Ezekiel 36:23-32
Wed.	The People Shall Know God
	Ezekiel 36:33-38
Thu.	Dry and Scattered Bones
	Ezekiel 37:1-6
Fri.	Life to Enter the Bones
	Ezekiel 37:7-14
Sat.	Nations to Be United
	Ezekiel 37:15-23
Sun.	God's Blessings Promised
	Ezekiel 37:24-28

Verse by Verse

I. Israel Dead and Scattered—1-2
1 The hand of the LORD was upon me, and carried me out in the spirit of the LORD and set me down in the midst of the valley which was full of bones,
2 And caused me to pass by them round about: and, behold, there were very many in the open valley; and, lo, they were very dry.

Although the name of Ezekiel, the priestly-prophet (1:3), means "God will strengthen," this vision and other references in the book show that God will first punish disobedient Israel before strengthening a remnant to return. Ezekiel was among the Jews who were deported from Jerusalem to Babylon, when it invaded Judah (2 Kings 25). He may have witnessed a battle that left a valley filled with literal bones, as the Babylonians overran the holy city.

The location is unimportant, and the vision obviously symbolic. Israel has been disassembled as a skeleton whose flesh and sinews have rotted away, leaving the bones to be scattered by beasts and birds of prey. Although Ezekiel has previously prophesied both the destruction and the restoration of God's people, this vision is unsurpassed in its graphic imagery.

II. Incisive Issue—3-6

A. Piercing question, 3
3 And he said unto me, Son of man, can these bones live? And I answered, O Lord GOD, thou knowest.

This is a standard style of prophecy even in the New Testament, in which God poses a rhetorical question (see Rev. 7:13-14) and the prophet chosen to reveal the vision answers that only God can give its meaning. In the context of the Old Testament, which says very little about a resurrection to life after death, Ezekiel might have been expected to answer "No!" Even speaking symbolically, as the though the question means "Can Israel be restored?" an optimistic reply would be hard, given the continual rebellion of God's people. Yet it is not Ezekiel's task to pronounce judgment, but only to be a vehicle for describing the vision.

B. Life-giving power predicted, 4-6
4 Again he said unto me, Prophesy upon these bones, and say unto them, O ye dry bones, hear the word of the LORD.
5 Thus saith the Lord GOD unto these bones; Behold, I will cause breath to enter into you, and ye shall live:
6 And I will lay sinews upon you,

and will bring up flesh upon you, and cover you with skin, and put breath in you, and ye shall live; and ye shall know that I am the LORD.

As dismal as are Israel's prospects to "come to life," the God of "second chances" charges the prophet to address the lifeless bones with a word of hope. "Ye shall live"—not because of any inherent vitality in Israel itself, but because the God who first created a people for Himself will recreate them by giving them "mouth-to-mouth-resuscitation." As when He created Adam, He will breathe into the dry and scattered bones the breath of life. The flesh and sinews will reappear and reconnect the bones.

The Hebrew word *ruach*, translated "breath" in verse 5, is translated "wind" in verse 9, and "spirit" in verse 14. It literally means "air-in-motion," and is therefore appropriate in all these contexts.

III. Indwelling Spirit of God—7-10
A. Stage I (external healing), 7-8

7 So I prophesied as I was commanded: and as I prophesied, there was a noise, and behold a shaking, and the bones came together, bone to his bone.

8 And when I beheld, lo, the sinews and the flesh came up upon them, and the skin covered them above: but there was no breath in them.

Ezekiel is faithful to the charge to prophesy to the apparently dead bones. The noise and shaking are apparently the result of the "wind" or breath of God sweeping through the valley. However, it is a much more constructive windstorm than a tornado; instead of scattering the bones it pulls them together and supplies the soft tissue necessary for bones to become a body.

Yet something is seriously missing. God's breath has reassembled what appear to be the bodies of the disobedient Israelites destroyed by the Babylonians, but they have no life in them. Stage I of Ezekiel's vision has resulted only in a group of assembled corpses like cadavers in a morgue. At this stage of the drama there are plenty of bodies, but God obviously wants us to ask, "What use can mere corpses be?"

B. Stage II (internal life), 9-10

9 Then said he unto me, Prophesy unto the wind, prophesy, son of man, and say to the wind, Thus saith the Lord GOD; Come from the four winds, O breath, and breathe upon these slain, that they may live.

10 So I prophesied as he commanded me, and the breath came into them, and they lived, and stood up upon their feet, an exceeding great army.

Now the rest of the vision supplies what is so seriously lacking: the enlivening spirit that is the difference between a corpse and a person. The wind of God is summoned from the four corners of the earth, which is both an ancient and a modern way of saying "everywhere." The Jews in fact have been scattered to the land of Magog in the north (38:2), to Egypt in the south, to the east as far as India, and to the islands of the Mediterranean in the west. Now

God's Spirit will reverse this great historical "Diaspora" or dispersion. Even more important is the fact that the bodies that are reunited by God's breath or Spirit are also reanimated with a spirit of their own. We are probably to understand this to mean that the Jews whom God reassembles in Judah will have the "new heart" predicted by Jeremiah (31:33; see also Ezek. 11:19).

IV. Interpretation of the Vision–11-14

A. Sad state of affairs, 11

11 Then he said unto me, Son of man, these bones are the whole house of Israel: behold, they say, Our bones are dried, and our hope is lost: we are cut off for our parts.

Now Ezekiel is given the benefit of a clear explanation of the symbolic act he has witnessed in the vision. The defeat and deportation suffered by Israel has had a deep impact on them, as God intended. They finally realize that the idolatry and injustice to which they had descended was "the death of them," and had cut them off from a relationship with God.

B. Israel's "resurrection," 12-14

12 Therefore prophesy and say unto them, Thus saith the Lord God; Behold, O my people, I will open your graves, and cause you to come up out of your graves, and bring you into the land of Israel.

13 And ye shall know that I am the Lord, when I have opened your graves, O my people, and brought you up out of your graves,

14 And shall put my spirit in you, and ye shall live, and I shall place you in your own land: then shall ye know that I the Lord have spoken it, and performed it, saith the Lord.

Ezekiel is now instructed to reassure God's people that their "graves"—that is, the nations in which they have been taken captive or "buried"—are now to be opened, and that they are to be restored to the holy land. The most notable example of the fulfillment of this prophecy is recorded in the books of Ezra and Nehemiah, who led a return from exile that included the rebuilding of the Temple in Jerusalem.

A difficulty in interpretation arises when we ask about other examples, when deported Jews were allowed to return from the other "corners" of the earth. Three main lines of interpretation have been suggested. (1) Some authorities hold that the return from Persia (which by then had conquered Babylonia) under Ezra and Nehemiah is symbolic of the restoration of all Israel, an implication often established by the Hebrew view of "corporate personality." (2) Others see the fulfillment of this vision in the gathering of Jews "from every nation under heaven" in Acts 2:5, under the preaching of Jesus as the Messiah and the resulting spiritual "Israel," the Church. (3) Still others await a literal fulfillment of the reassembling of Jews from all over the world to the modern land of Israel.

These views have in common the confidence that the God who called His people out of Egypt will also be faithful in His promise to re-create a people for Himself.

75

Evangelistic Emphasis

A delightful family from another Christian tradition began worshiping at our church years ago. Over the months, the family began to meld with the congregation.

Their grandparents, however, who were still a part of the family's previous tradition, were displeased. One day after church, while at lunch with both grandparents, the couple was asked why they didn't return to their lifelong church where "they belonged." Their response carried a thousand sermons.

The husband looked at his mom and his in-laws and said, "We have never felt we belong anywhere more intensely and more wonderfully than we do where we are now. It is not a statement about not liking the tradition we grew up in. It *is* a statement that we have finally found the meaning of religious life as we have always thought it would be." He then told the parents they should be pleased the family was being raised in such an environment.

Soon thereafter, both sets of grandparents began to appear at Family Night Dinners. They all crossed the bridge into wholeness and reconciliation.

ಬಂಡ

Memory Selection

I [shall] put my spirit in you, and ye shall live, and I shall place you in your own land: then shall ye know that I, the LORD, have spoken it, and performed it, saith the LORD.— *Ezekiel 37:14*

Our scripture lesson today reaffirms in a powerful and poetic way the constant theme of God's Word, which jumps at us in the Bible from Genesis to Revelation. That constant theme is reconciliation, the coming together again and resuming a position of wholeness. Over and over again, God makes it clear that he wishes there would never be brokenness between people, between families, between nations and peoples of every kind. Over and over again, God insists that putting "flesh on the bones" of life, and marriages, and parents and children, and every aspect of life is His ultimate goal and design for His kingdom until the end of time, God *will* be in the business of putting flesh on what used to be dry bones.

Weekday Problems

George must have been 6 feet, 5 inches tall and weighed 300 pounds. His number on the offensive line was 76. He terrorized opposing defensemen.

George had a lot of swagger in him, because he was a true Big Man On Campus, and his impact was great. He expected a career in big time football. None of the anticipated college scholarship offers came, however, and George was left with only a high school diploma and grades not good enough to make it into a college without a football scholarship. The swagger was gone, the clout quickly vanished and very soon George went into a nose dive.

He never left the church, however, and at a youth revival, he came forward and accepted Christ. He later testified that all of his previous years had been hollow and empty. He publicly thanked God for "putting His spirit in my life, so that I know how to really live and what life is all about."

The writer of Ezekiel surely looked upon George with a broad smile and a victorious fist pump.

*How can we help youth understand that God wants to occupy first place in their lives?

The Doctor is In ... and Out

Billy: Did you hear about the dentist who married the manicurist?
Willy: No, but I expect you'll tell me.
Billy: Yep. It didn't last. After a month they were fighting tooth and nail.
* * * *

The doctor was struggling financially until he stopped the wheels of his office chair from squeaking. He had invented caster oil!
* * * *

Patient: Doctor, I get the feeling that no one thinks that what I have to say matters at all.
Psychiatrist: So?
* * * *

How many doctors does it take to screw in a light bulb?
It depends on how much health insurance the light bulb has.

This Lesson in Your Life

Someone has reported that America consumes more Prozac for depression than any nation on Earth. It is said that no nation has so many resources and possibilities, yet so many people who feel hopeless and without a future. Surely, to feel there is no hope has to be one of the most deadening feelings possible.

I have a brass paperweight in the form of the lower-case letter "n." Years ago a lovely 27-year-old young woman, a leader of my church, had gone through a painful divorce. Unbeknownst to the rest of us, Nancy had slipped into deep depression.

Late one night her mother called. A shot had been heard, and Nancy's body was found. She left a long letter, explaining her hopelessness, and leaving all her possessions to friends and family. She left the paperweight "n" to me as an "eternal reminder of one of your biggest fans."

The scripture in Ezekiel 37, a passage made into poems, songs, stories, and theatre plays, is a magnificent metaphor for the power of God to take our hopelessness and emptiness and make it into something fruitful. The image of bones (death and hopelessness) fleshing out and breathing and God's affirmation that this is His eternal design for us, is the very heart and soul of our faith. We believe God sustains us and affirms us, and no pit of despair is so deep we cannot rise above it. Most people who attempt suicide, but fail in the attempt, later testify how relieved they are to not have succeeded. They express amazement at having been so deep in despair and are shocked to realize God was extending His hand all along and they just did not see it.

This lesson is clear: as Paul says in Romans 8, "What can separate us from the love of God? . . . nothing!" If we embrace and believe this, dry bones would start rattling and breathing from one country to another and one family to another.

GETTING THE FACTS STRAIGHT

1. God gave Ezekiel a spectacular illustration of His intent to restore life. What did He do?"
He took the prophet to a valley full of dead and scatttered bones, and they all came together and came to life.

2. As if to test Ezekiel's faith, what question did God ask him?
He asked Ezekiel, "Can these bones live?"

3. So many of us, when in an attitude of hopelessness, assume there is no future. What was Ezekiel's answer?
He admitted that God alone would know whether dry bones could be revived. He said, "Oh Lord God, Thou knowest."

4. What command did God give Ezekiel after that?
God commanded Ezekiel to speak to the bones and prophesy before them, saying, "Oh dry bones, hear the Word of the Lord!"

5.God then made clear His intent to Ezekiel. What was that?
He spelled out His intent to have His breath enter the bones, and flesh and muscle and skin and sinew would come upon them, and they would become alive again.

6. What happened right before Ezekiel's eyes following his prophecy to the bones?
The bones began to rattle together and layers of flesh and skin began to cover them. (It must have been an astounding sight!)

7. One thing was missing, however. What was it?
There was no breath in the revived bones.

8. What did God command at that point?
He commanded the breath from the four winds to come upon the bones, and the breath of life entered the dead bones again.

9. What was the interesting explanation of what happened next?
The scriptures say "Breath came into them and they lived and 'stood upon their feet.'"

10. What was the metaphor God used to describe the bones?
He declared that the bones represented the disobedient house of Israel, which as a nation was without hope, cut off, and in despair. But God still loved His people, and He would bring them back to life.

Many of our churches offer wonderful ministries such as Alco-holics Anonymous, and other organizations that help people put flesh on the dry bones of their lives. I always enjoyed sitting in as a guest at such meetings, because you hear so many wonderful testi-monies of lives in despair that have been put together again.

Homer was as fine a member of a congregation as one would want. He was a strong and wealthy business man, shared his wealth with the church, and was a powerful and positive influence on the whole congregation. A couple of years later, while spending an af-ternoon of golf together, he told me his story. He had been wealthy beyond compare, and as arrogant and greedy as he was wealthy. He drank more than anyone, became a bottomed-out drunk with a fam-ily, a business in bankruptcy, and a life totally squandered. He looked at himself often as a dirty, pitiful person and wondered how he could fall so far. He was not a church person, and scoffed at reli-gion, although his now ex-wife and children were faithful each week.

Then one day in a sandwich shop, his ex-wife's pastor sat down and they began to talk. It was a good conversation, affirming God's promise that new life was only one commitment away, one change of heart around the corner. The pastor asked him, "All you need to ask yourself is, 'Do I like what I have become?'" Homer began to cry at what he had become. That very day, he said, he was ready to turn his life around.

Years later, Homer is remarried to his ex-wife, has started a new business that is prospering, and gives credit to God and his Chris-tian friends who never abandoned him. He calls Ezekiel's story of the bones coming alive "the story of Homer."

Lesson 9

Creating a Renewed Trust

Psalm 73:1-3, 12-13, 16-18, 21-26

ruly God is good to Israel, even to such as are of a clean heart.

2 But as for me, my feet were almost gone; my steps had well nigh slipped.

3 For I was envious at the foolish, when I saw the prosperity of the wicked.

12 Behold, these are the ungodly, who prosper in the world; they increase in riches.

13 Verily I have cleansed my heart in vain, and washed my hands in innocence.

16 When I thought to know this, it was too painful for me;

17 Until I went into the sanctuary of God; then understood I their end.

18 Surely thou didst set them in slippery places: thou castedst them down into destruction.

21 Thus my heart was grieved, and I was pricked in my reins.

22 So foolish was I, and ignorant:

I was as a beast before thee.

23 Nevertheless I am continually with thee: thou hast holden me by my right hand.

24 Thou shalt guide me with thy counsel, and afterward receive me to glory.

25 Whom have I in heaven but thee? and there is none upon earth that I desire beside thee.

26 My flesh and my heart faileth: but God is the strength of my heart, and my portion for ever.

Oct. 31

Memory Selection
Psalm 73:26

Background Scripture
Psalm 73

Devotional Reading
Psalm 91:1-10

 Previous lessons on the God of continuing creation have focused on His having created a special Covenant with the children of Abraham. Basic to this "promise-law" was the general rule that obedience to God brings blessings, while disobedience brings punishment (see Deut. 32:1-2, 15). Yet all of God's people occasionally experience tragedy. This may cause them to wonder whether God has abandoned His Covenant.

Psalm 73 portrays the psalmist Asaph asking questions along this line. It has a twin focus: the experience of doubt and anguish, and the healing power of *worship* when answers are few. Point out that since God values honesty, He does not rebuke us for asking such questions. Yet He is still God, and instead of *being* called into question, He is the one who calls us . . . to worship, and in the experience of worship to renew our trust in Him.

Ask group members what questions they ask first when suffering or tragedy strikes. Note that very often our questions include, *Why this? Why me? Why now?* Sometimes we also ask *What have I done to deserve this*? betraying the view that we suffer because we sin. Yet, while God *may* use suffering to discipline us, we also know that since He makes the sun to shine on both the just and the unjust (Matt. 5:45) we cannot always assume that suffering is the result of sin.

Undeserved suffering may even cause us to question the existence and/or goodness of God. Challenge your group to discover in Psalm 73 God's response to this temptation. Does He supply answers, or does He suggest an experience that moves us beyond both questions and answers?

Teaching Outline

I. Confession of Doubt—1-3
  A. The general rule, 1
  B. Result of exceptions, 2-3
II. Crisis of Evidence—12-13
  A. Why do the ungodly prosper? 12
  B. What use is righteousness? 13
III. Call to Worship—16-18
  A. Weighty question, 16
  B. Resolution's setting, 17-18
IV. Confession of Faith—21-26
  A. Anguished questions, 21-22
  B. God's presence assured, 23-26

Daily Bible Readings

Mon.	Sing for Joy to God *Psalm 84:1-17*
Tue.	Trust in God *Psalm 84:8-12*
Wed.	God Is Our Refuge *Psalm 91:1-10*
Thu.	Why Do the Wicked Prosper? Psalm 73:1-9
Fri.	Is Faith in Vain? *Psalm 73:10-14*
Sat.	Temporary Prosperity *Psalm 73:15-20*
Sun.	Renewal of Faith *Psalm 73:21-28*

Verse by Verse

I. Confession of Doubt—1-3
A. The general rule, 1
1 Truly God is good to Israel, even to such as are of a clean heart.

As noted in "Focus," above," God's Covenant with Israel included promises that He would bless them when they obeyed, but curse them for disobedience. The classic and most picturesque portrayal of this common-sense rule is in Deuteronomy 27–28, where blessings for obedience are promised from atop Mount Gerizim, and curses for disobedience are issued from Mount Ebal. Actually, a fundamental presumption running through all major world religions is that doing good wins visible favors from the deity, and doing evil earns obvious punishment.

The common assumption here is that such blessing and punishment would be meted out immediately, or at least in this life. Psalm 73, however (along with its numerically reversed "twin," Psalm 37), faces with head-on honesty the obvious fact that the righteous often suffer unjustly, and the wicked often prosper.

Although it's getting ahead of the lesson to note this, it is important to realize the *general* truth of verse 1. Even in this life, people who do right usually enjoy better health, better relationships, and a better life. This, however, is largely because in God's wisdom, doing right is its own reward. He reserves the right to love and bless the sinner as well: "God's kindness leads you toward repentance" (Rom. 2:4), and to discipline even the righteous. The error is in elevating this general principle to a law that *obligates* God to reward the righteous and punish the wicked in ways believers deem appropriate.

We should be prepared, therefore, to think of the blessings of keeping Covenant with God as a *general* rule, the truth of which may not be revealed until the next life, and subject to exceptions as a Sovereign God deems wise.

B. Result of exceptions, 2-3
2 But as for me, my feet were almost gone; my steps had well nigh slipped.

3 For I was envious at the foolish, when I saw the prosperity of the wicked.

It's only natural to wonder why goodness sometimes seem to go unrewarded, while the wicked seem to garner blessings we thought were reserved for the righteous. The philosopher-educator A. N. Whitehead stated it succinctly: "All simplifications of religious dogma are shipwrecked upon the rock of the problem of evil." It is testimony to the authentic nature of Scripture that honest questions like those which the psalmist has about this problem are a part of God's Word. Yet the fact that he almost slips into the "shipwreck" of unbelief because of the problem indicates that he has not allowed for God's radically free nature. God can supersede exceptions to rules that the psalmist had taken to be "automatic."

The problem here was compounded by the fact that the Old Covenant lacks as clear a statement of rewards in an *after-life* as that contained in the New Covenant Scriptures. One sect of the Jews, the Sadducees, even denied the doctrine of a resurrection (Matt. 22:23). Thus they were limited to looking to rewards and punishments in this life as evidence of proof of the Covenant.

II. Crisis of Evidence—12-13
A. Why do the ungodly prosper? 12
12 Behold, these are the ungodly, who prosper in the world; they increase in riches.

The fact that the ungodly subject themselves to fewer, and lower, ethical standards than the righteous gives them an unfair advantage. They seem to "get away" with lying, subterfuge, and disobeying civil law. For example, an unscrupulous lawyer is hired by a widow to protect her property, and winds up taking it away from her (see Mark 12:40). Instead of being punished, thus proving that

God rules, some prosper from this lack of respect for law. Again, the believer recognizes that the truth of this assertion is limited to this life; in the next life, "they shall have their reward" and the righteous will be vindicated.

B. What use is righteousness? 13
13 Verily I have cleansed my heart in vain, and washed my hands in innocence.

If the belief that the wicked will be punished and the righteous rewarded *in this life* is all we have to go on, the psalmist asks with some justification what good it is to live righteously. Actually, the radically committed believer can answer that living right is its own reward. He does not "cleanse his heart" merely in hope either of riches here or heaven hereafter; but because, like Wilfred Grimsley used to say about eating oatmeal, "it's the right thing to do."

III. Call to Worship—16-18
A. Weighty question, 16
16 When I thought to know this, it was too painful for me;

Innumerable thoughtful people, even scholars, have given up trying to explain why the wicked prosper and the righteous suffer. It is a "painful" question to which Scripture only answers with hints instead of fully-developed arguments. While it is not blameworthy to give up asking the question, the psalmist is building up to appealing for us *not* to give up *believing* because of the problem.

B. Resolution's setting, 17-18
17 Until I went into the sanctuary of God; then understood I

their end.

18 Surely thou didst set them in slippery places: thou castedst them down into destruction.

The "pain" that the psalmist feels is eased not by receiving an intellectual answer to the problem of why the innocent suffer, but by going into the sanctuary, the place of worship. It is in worship focused on the promises of God that we come to understand that the "end" of the prosperous wicked will eventually (after judgment) be seen to be destruction. It was a wise newspaper editor who responded to the question of why an unbelieving farmer's field produced a good harvest, while that of a "good" farmer was poor. Wrote the editor: *God does not make full payment at harvest-time.*

IV. Confession of Faith—21-26
A. Anguished questions, 21-22

21 Thus my heart was grieved, and I was pricked in my reins.

22 So foolish was I, and ignorant: I was as a beast before thee.

As the worshiper looked back on his brush with doubt, and at his assumption that we can tell by a person's well-being whether he is righteous or wicked, he is embarrassed ("pricked in his reins," or spirit). Such simplistic reasoning is little more than at the level of animal instinct. (Even a cow avoids the deliberate "evil" of jumping off a cliff because she knows it will be her downfall!) This confession is an accurate if hardly a flattering description of the sophisticated atheist who uses "the problem of suffering" as an excuse for unbelief. Beasts think

like that, too.

B. God's presence assured, 23-26

23 Nevertheless I am continually with thee: thou hast holden me by my right hand.

24 Thou shalt guide me with thy counsel, and afterward receive me to glory.

25 Whom have I in heaven but thee? and there is none upon earth that I desire beside thee.

26 My flesh and my heart faileth: but God is the strength of my heart, and my portion for ever.

Now the author moves decisively from his position as a questioner and doubter into the full comfort and assurance of a *worshiper*. His questions have not yielded a full range of rational "reasons" for innocent suffering. They have simply been overwhelmed by the greater experience of confessing the majesty and glory of God. The phrase in verse 24, "*Afterward . . . ,*" is a hint of the afterlife with God that will grow into a full-fledged doctrine in the New Covenant.

Even now, however, the experience of worship has overwhelmed the psalmist's questions with love and trust. He has no attorney capable of arguing the law before the bar of God, but he has something (or *Someone*) better: the presence of One who created the Law and the Covenant in the first place. Without that Presence, the psalmist's heart fails because of the impossibility of giving human reasons for unearned suffering. With it, the worshiper is given strength that is greater than his questions.

Evangelistic Emphasis

They were a pair of brothers, but more different than you could imagine. One lived fast and loose, was willing to turn a quick buck even if it meant cheating someone out of his last dollar, and had no scruples. He lived in an enormous home, with boats, cars, and all the accoutrements of wealth. The motto of his life was "anything goes, as long as it provides a buck."

His brother was faithful in all things, but his income was meager and not likely to get better. His family had only the basics. Yet, they were tithers, and the backbone of the church. One day I asked about his brother and to my amazement he openly said, "His brother could have all the goodies in life he wanted, but his brother did not have peace in his soul." He went on to say "I have forgiven him and God will forgive him, but I wouldn't trade places with him for anything in the world." I was blessed by his testimony as he shared how content he was to walk in God's ways and give forgiveness for his own kin who did not.

ΣΟΩ

My flesh and my heart may fail, but God is the strength of my heart and my portion forever.—*Psalm 73:26*

Other than reconciliation, the single greatest word that describes God is "forgiveness." But, as you look closer, forgiveness and reconciliation are all part of the same interaction. It is a foundation of our faith that whenever we have failed, fallen away, or created a violation of God's will, we are always given a chance to make it right and grow through the process.

This scripture strongly underlines a variety of points today, but none as powerful as God's promise of forgiveness. You are not likely to find an act that more completely renews, blesses, and restores a life, a marriage, a relationship, or a world outlook, than forgiveness. Psalm 73 is all about giving and receiving forgiveness with gratitude.

Weekday Problems

A young boy had thrown a rock at another child but missed and broke a window. He was sent home, and his mother angrily ushered him to his room with the warning, "Your father will be home soon, and you're going to catch it." The boy heard his father's car outside, heard the murmurings between his dad and mom, then his father's steps coming up the stairs. The boy shook with fear at the whipping he was about to get. He sat at his desk and closed his eyes tightly. The steps came down the hall, the door opened, and they came across his room to where he sat. The smell of his father's cologne wafted into the air, as he awaited the beating of his life.

Instead of a beating, a strong hand went around his shoulders and his father said "I love you more than I have the ability to tell you. Come on down for supper now, and be careful the next time you pick up a rock." This just might be one of the most perfect examples of forgiveness one could find.

*Why is it hard to forgive?

*Are we a "forgiving people"?

Bigger and Better in Texas?

The Texan being shown around in Australia was unimpressed. "You call those oranges?" he said. "Why, in Texas we have lemons bigger than those."

Then he was shown some large, juicy Australian grapefruit, but was again unimpressed. "In Texas we have oranges are bigger than that!"

Just then a great, grey kangaroo, seven feet tall, crossed the road. "What's *that!*" the Texan exclaimed, finally impressed.

The Aussie calmly replied, "You mean you don't have grasshoppers in Texas?"

* * * *

A guide was showing a Texan the mighty Niagara Falls. "Bet you don't have anything like that in Texas," he said.

"Nope, I reckon we don't. But we got plumbers who can fix it."

* * * *

"My ranch," bragged the Texan, "is so big I can get in my truck on the east side and it takes me three days of hard driving to get to the west side."

"I know what you mean," replied the Missouri stockman. "I used to have a truck like that."

Several years ago Barbara Walters interviewed Bing Crosby for a television special. They spoke about how his children from his first wife were so estranged from him, and Bing stunned the audience when he declared, "There aren't any gray areas of life. It's either right or wrong, good or bad, and they know the difference. If they don't, then I want nothing to do with them."

Barbara asked what would happen if his daughter requested forgiveness after having committed a moral mistake. His response revealed a less familiar side to Bing. He insisted there was no leeway for second chances. He would not speak to her again and "that is all there is to it." No matter how Barbara tried to press him on his rigid approach, he consistently declared he had taught them right from wrong and there were no second chances in the Crosby household.

Wouldn't life be a nightmare if we all had to carry permanently the scars of our errors, sins, and stupidities? We are a people living underneath the love of a God who says, "I made you human, and I know you will make mistakes. Like a father, I will pick you up, dust you off, kiss you, and send you forth with a caution not to do it again."

We will never know how many families and individuals go through life wounded by the scars of rigidity. We will never know how many children grow up as parents who are stern, unyielding, and run their households like drill sergeants because that was all they ever saw or felt as children. We will never know how many marriages, partnerships, or other relationships never had a chance to succeed because one or both refused to offer the most sacred of all gifts, forgiveness.

The writer of Psalm 73 wonderfully expresses a deep gratitude that God's forgiveness will always be present, no matter what. If only we too could do the same for each other.

1. To whom does God show preference, according to the beginning of Psalm 73?
God is declared to be "good to the upright, and to those who are pure in heart."

2. How does the author of Psalm 73 describe his precarious walk at one point in his life?
He declares that he had almost stumbled in his walk with God.

3. How did he almost fall?
By being envious of the wealthy and arrogant.

4. The writer tries to defend his behavior. What does he say?
He felt that his life of innocence was in vain as he looks at those who became wealthy through evil ways.

5. What does the psalmist do about this value conflict?
After trying to understand it on his own, he goes into the sanctuary to seek answers from God.

6. What did the psalmist experience in the sanctuary?
He realized that those who have prospered through evil will experience an eventual crash.

7. What did the psalmist say his behavior had been like?
He declared that when he was bitter in the face of ill-gotten wealth, he behaved like a beast toward God.

8. As his faith becomes stronger and more secure, how does he express this new attitude?
He affirms that God constantly holds him by the right hand and guides him with counsel.

9. As his envy of the rich falls away and his love of God gets stronger, what does the psalmist say?
He declares that he has nothing in heaven but God and that nothing on earth is worth having but God.

10. How does the author finally declare his own weakness and God's relationship to his weakness?
He declares that although his flesh and heart may fail and be weak, God is his portion forever and will never give up on him.

On my first day in that church as pastor, I noticed the congregation eager to see their new leader, but obviously sitting as many pews as possible away from another man. He was surrounded by emptiness. Inquiring about it after church, I was told that he and his wife had taken in foster children, and he had been accused of molesting one of the teenage girls. Even though no solid evidence or legal charges every resulted, the congregation shunned the man. After I settled in, I made an effort to talk to him, and he swore that the mentally-challenged children he and his wife had taken in had never been molested. They had been consistently treated with love and affirmation.

I went to the state and parish authorities and validated his comments. I then went back to congregational leaders and asked why, when there had never been any evidence or charges brought, after an accusation by a 13-year-old with the mental capacity of a five-year-old, the congregation still treated him like a leper. As I continued to go from leader to leader and person to person, a slow realization began to arise that they had in fact been terribly unfair. Little by little, we addressed the matter on a one-to-one basis, and the empty pews around the man began to fill in each Sunday. Without ever formally addressing the situation, it became clear that the matter had been resolved. He was again part of the congregation.

On my last Sunday as I prepared to move to another church, he stood before the pulpit and thanked me for bringing him and the congregation together again, and making him "feel whole." He expressed his forgiveness to the congregation, and one after another, different people rose from their seats and said how ashamed they were of their behavior. Though long past the usual closing time, I watched this remarkable panorama unfolding and was reminded again how forgiveness makes people whole.

Lesson 10

A New Approach

Matthew 5:17-18, 21-22, 27-28, 31-35, 38-39, 43-44

T hink not that I am come to destroy the law, or the prophets: I am not come to destroy, but to fulfil.

18 For verily I say unto you, Till heaven and earth pass, one jot or one tittle shall in no wise pass from the law, till all be fulfilled.

21 Ye have heard that it was said by them of old time, Thou shalt not kill; and whosoever shall kill shall be in danger of the judgment:

22 But I say unto you, That whosoever is angry with his brother without a cause shall be in danger of the judgment: and whosoever shall say to his brother, Raca, shall be in danger of the council: but whosoever shall say, Thou fool, shall be in danger of hell fire.

27 Ye have heard that it was said by them of old time, Thou shalt not commit adultery:

28 But I say unto you, That whosoever looketh on a woman to lust after her hath committed adultery with her already in his heart.

31 It hath been said, Whosoever shall put away his wife, let him give her a writing of divorcement:

32 But I say unto you, That whosoever shall put away his wife, saving for the cause of fornication, causeth her to commit adul-tery: and whosoever shall marry her that is divorced committeth adultery.

33 Again, ye have heard that it hath been said by them of old time, Thou shalt not forswear thyself, but shalt perform unto the Lord thine oaths:

34 But I say unto you, Swear not at all; neither by heaven; for it is God's throne:

35 Nor by the earth; for it is his footstool: neither by Jerusalem; for it is the city of the great King.

38 Ye have heard that it hath been said, An eye for an eye, and a tooth for a tooth:

39 But I say unto you, That ye resist not evil: but whosoever shall smite thee on thy right cheek, turn to him the other also.

43 Ye have heard that it hath been said, Thou shalt love thy neighbour, and hate thine enemy.

44 But I say unto you, Love your enemies, bless them that curse you, do good to them that hate you, and pray for them which despitefully use you, and persecute you;

Nov. 7

Memory Selection
Matthew 5:17
Background Scripture
Matthew 5
Devotional Reading
Matthew 5:1-12

This lesson is on the dramatic fulfillment of the prophecy in Jeremiah 31:31-33, where God promised to give His people a new law, "not according to the covenant I made with [your] fathers." Now, some 500 years later, Jesus of Nazareth, the Messiah, summarizes this New Covenant, or "promise-law."

In many ways, Jesus' commandments will echo those of the Law of Moses. Yet the recurring phrase, "Ye have heard that it was said by them of old time . . . *but I say . . . "* indicates a radical difference as well. That difference can be summarized in a word by the term *spirit*. Many Jews had come to emphasize keeping the letter of the Law. Now Jesus emphasizes its "inwardness." From now on, the spirit of the law, one's attitude, what is in the heart of God's people, will be as important as what they do.

&)CR

Ask group members to give examples of the difference between "the letter" and "the spirit" of the law. One example arises from the "law" or covenant of marriage. It's possible for spouses to remain externally "faithful" to each other while having a cold and distant relationship instead of nourishing a warm and loving spirit of togetherness.

Another example arises from court cases in which an obviously guilty person may escape punishment on a "technicality." Sometimes it seems that external legalities are more important than whether a crime was committed.

Although Jesus' teaching in the Sermon on the Mount must not be used to excuse outward disobedience just because "our heart is in the right place," the difference He draws between mere "legalism" and heartfelt obedience is clear.

Teaching Outline	Daily Bible Readings	
I. The Permanence of Law—17-18	Mon.	True Blessedness *Matthew 5:1-12*
II. Murder and Anger—21-22	Tue.	Obeying God's Will *Matthew 5:13-20*
III. Adultery and Lust—27-28	Wed.	Teaching on Anger *Matthew 5:21-26*
IV. Saying and Doing—31-35	Thu.	On Adultery and Divorce *Matthew 5:27-32*
A. Marriage and divorce, 31-32	Fri.	On Taking Oaths *Matthew 5:33-37*
B. Oaths and deeds, 33-35	Sat.	On Non-Resistance *Matthew 5:38-42*
V. Vengeance and Mercy—38-39	Sun.	On Loving Our Enemies *Matthew 5:43-48*
VI. Hating and Loving—43-44		

Verse by Verse

I. The Permanence of Law—17-18

17 Think not that I am come to destroy the law, or the prophets: I am not come to destroy, but to fulfil.

18 For verily I say unto you, Till heaven and earth pass, one jot or one tittle shall in no wise pass from the law, till all be fulfilled.

In this lesson's selected verses, Jesus delivers part of His famous Sermon on the Mount (Matt. 5–7), much like Moses delivered His Law to the Jews from Mount Sinai. Although the Sermon on the Mount can be considered the core of Jesus' teaching, it is not, as we sometimes hear, a "simplifiedNew Testament." It challenges us to move beyond external act to inner integrity; and that is never "simple." Also, since the Sermon was delivered before Christ's death, it contains nothing about the importance of the Cross in the history of salvation, nothing about salvation by grace through faith, or about the Holy Spirit. Still, no portion of the Scriptures deserves more of our attention and our best efforts to grasp and apply.

Two keys are essential to understanding Jesus' radical statements about "law" in the Sermon on the Mount. One key opens the phrase "law" to reveal that it can refer both to the principle of "law" in general, and to "the Law of Moses" (capitalized in this discussion) in particular.

The other key unlocks the word "fulfill," understanding it to mean "complete" (see Acts 7:30). Thus Jesus is not saying that now that He has come we can live "lawlessly," but that the specifics that made the Law of Moses unique were about to be "filled full"—completed—by his death on the Cross.

The relevance of fundamental laws such as the Ten Commandments—rules that are necessary for people to live together and under God—will never "pass." On the other hand, technical details in the Law of Moses, such as Sabbath-keeping and animal sacrifice, would be "fulfilled" or no longer necessary, since Jesus "canceled the written code, with its regulations . . . nailing it to the cross" (Col. 2:14).

II. Murder and Anger—21-22

21 Ye have heard that it was said by them of old time, Thou shalt not kill; and whosoever shall kill shall be in danger of the judgment:

22 But I say unto you, That whosoever is angry with his brother without a cause shall be in danger of the judgment: and whosoever shall say to his brother, Raca, shall be in danger of the council: but whosoever shall say, Thou fool, shall be in danger of hell fire.

Even the Ten Commandments prove to be subject to reinterpretation by Jesus, who after all is "the Word" through whom Creation, and the Law of Moses, came (John 1:1, 14). Thus it is as Lord of all commandments that Jesus has the authority to contrast what had been taught "by them of old time" with *"But I say . . . ."*

Here His reinterpretation of the Law teaches that it is not enough merely to refrain from murder (the sixth Commandment); neither are we to hate, which is at the root of murder.

This probe into the attitude of heart behind the action will prove typical of Jesus' teaching. In one way, His profound handling of the Commandments can be a relief, such as when a person finds it necessary to kill another to protect his family. In another sense, however, these re-interpretations are actually more challenging than the Law, since they assume that we will keep *both* their external and internal aspects.

III. Adultery and Lust—27-28

27 Ye have heard that it was said by them of old time, Thou shalt not commit adultery:

28 But I say unto you, That whosoever looketh on a woman to lust after her hath committed adultery with her already in his heart.

A movement that would later evolve into "Gnosticism" had already crept into some Jewish circles by Jesus' time. Some teachers of that moment claimed that because a person's *spirit* is the only eternal reality, external actions in "the flesh," such as adultery, were of indifferent moral weight. As noted above, Jesus is not releasing us to commit adultery just because "this is bigger than both of us" or "obviously we're soul mates." He is heightening, not lowering, the moral standard of His followers by making attitude and intent as important a moral arena as outward actions.

IV. Saying and Doing—31-35
A. Marriage and divorce, 31-32

31 It hath been said, Whosoever shall put away his wife, let him give her a writing of divorcement:

32 But I say unto you, That whosoever shall put away his wife, saving for the cause of fornication, causeth her to commit adultery: and whosoever shall marry her that is divorced committeth adultery.

The "writing of divorcement" was a concession made in the Law of Moses (Deut. 24:1). By Jesus' day, divorce was common—and, for men, available as an escape hatch from marriage for the flimsiest of reasons. The fact was that God had always "hated" divorce (Mal. 2:16, NIV); it was only because of the hardness of men's hearts that He allowed it (Matt. 19:8). Thus, too-easy divorce had become a way to "keep the Law" on a superficial level, while violating its intent.

B. Oaths and deeds, 33-35

33 Again, ye have heard that it hath been said by them of old time, Thou shalt not forswear thyself, but shalt perform unto the Lord thine oaths:

34 But I say unto you, Swear not at all; neither by heaven; for it is God's throne:

35 Nor by the earth; for it is his footstool: neither by Jerusalem; for it is the city of the great King.

The oaths and "swearing" of these verses refer first to courts of law, but also probably included the thoughtless profanity that was as common in Jesus' day as ours. Although the Law called for oaths to reinforce some testimony (as in Num. 5:19), Jewish tradition had begun to hold that in some cases a technicality could release (or "forswear") the person from the oath. They had also vastly expanded the kinds of oath one could take, arguing for example, that swearing "by Jerusalem" was not as binding as swearing "by heaven." Jesus calls for a return to the original intent of simply telling the truth, thus not needing to "prop it up" with an oath of debatable weight. The ideal is for personal integrity to give a simple "Yes" the same validity as "By heaven, yes!"

V. Vengeance and Mercy—38-39

38 Ye have heard that it hath been said, An eye for an eye, and a tooth for a tooth:

39 But I say unto you, That ye resist not evil: but whosoever shall smite thee on thy right cheek, turn to him the other also.

Again, the Law *allowed* the practice of the "law of reciprocity," punishing an offender in the way he offended (Lev. 24:20). This allowance, however, had sometimes led to "vigilante justice" in which an injured person took the law into his own hands, often exacting greater pain than he had suffered. Taken on an individual basis as it was originally intended, we can see the justice in the law; but as retaliation spreads it leads to violent societies.

VI. Hating and Loving—43-44

43 Ye have heard that it hath been said, Thou shalt love thy neighbour, and hate thine enemy.

44 But I say unto you, Love your enemies, bless them that curse you, do good to them that hate you, and pray for them which despitefully use you, and persecute you;

Again, it is clear that Jesus is responding here to current Jewish tradition, not the Law of Moses, since the Old Testament never called for hating one's enemy. In fact, Proverbs 25:21 is the source for Paul's counsel on just how to show *love* to one's enemy (Rom. 12:20).

However, especially in the context of conquering the Promised Land, the Jews had been authorized to engage in wholesale slaughter of their enemies. Put together with the natural human tendency to "render evil for evil," Jesus' teaching here on loving one's enemies is radical to say the least.

Arguments persist on whether Jesus meant for the commands to "resist not evil," and "turn-the-other-cheek," to apply only to personal ethics or also to public policy, resulting in anti-war policies and the suspension of such penalties as the death sentence. Some interpreters, noting that Jesus Himself resorted to violence when He cleansed the Temple (John 2:15), hold that all these counsels are ideals we should aim for instead of dogmas we must follow in every situation. Yet throughout history, the courage of a few saints who took Jesus' statement "public" has moved savage levels of living toward civility.

Evangelistic Emphasis

Wherever I am a pastor, I make it clear that members are expected to give active life to their faith. We always try to find a place of ministry for everyone, long term members and brand new disciples.

Years ago, a remarkable book was written entitled *Why Conservative Churches Are Growing.* In that book it clearly illustrated that churches grow when the people are *expected* to follow God's rules about giving, working, teaching, singing, or wherever in the congregational life they can "give wings" to the faith they profess. Many people have joined our church because discipleship is expected of them, and they are not allowed to be just a name on a dotted line somewhere. People need the rules of God and will always respond to them. Many say our churches today are so tilted toward "easiness" and "entertainment" we often bear little resemblance to faith as it was laid before us. People are not seeking an easy path; they are seeking a way to be used by God.

ഇൗൽ

Memory Selection

Do not think that I have come to abolish the law or the prophets; I have not come to abolish, but to fulfill.— *Matthew 5:17*

This, one of the great classic quotations from Jesus, should be required memorization by all believers. Jesus is boldly declaring that while the world at that time was governed by more rules than a computer could count, He had arrived to give those rules meaningfulness and interpretation. He is clearly saying that the rules have a purpose and had a purpose from the beginning of the Jewish state. But, He insists that He as Messiah would be the living, breathing embodiment of *why* those rules were laid down and *how* those rules were to be viewed in the context of daily life. According to Jesus, the rules had only a vague and fuzzy meaning unless interpreted in the light of Himself as the Son of God.

To follow the guidelines for living as God revealed in Jesus is to free us for abundant living, not restrict us with rules for rules' sake only.

Weekday Problems

He sat in my office and told me his family was bankrupt. Though he owned two companies, he was in a terrible bind. As the owner of two corporations, he borrowed more than he could repay. One company's checking account covered bills of another, and vice-versa. They lived extravagantly, with club memberships, fine wines, and expensive cars. Finally, it all collapsed.

We talked about the rules of life, and not spending more than you have, being honest with your spouse and family about your financial condition. We talked about responsible living. We spoke at length on how he might become solvent again, and how to remain so, by following God's rules of planting and harvesting, of sharing and giving, of being faithful to family and honest with everyone. None of these had he done.

Five years later, he emerged, stronger than ever, with only one house, and a sense of gratitude for God's common sense rules.

*Are there fundamental rules for life? What are they?

The Case for Loving Enemies

The fine and noble way to destroy a foe is not to kill him; with kindness you may so change him that he shall cease to be so; then he's slain.—*Aleyn*

* * * *

Heat not a furnace for your foe so hot that it do singe yourself.—*Shakespeare*

* * * *

A merely fallen enemy may rise again, but the reconciled one is truly vanquished.—*Schiller*

* * * *

He who is capable of being a bitter enemy can never possess the necessary virtues that constitute a true friend.—*Fitzosborne*

* * * *

Some men are more beholden to their bitterest enemies than to friends who appear to be sweetness itself. The former frequently tell the truth, but the latter never.—*Cato*

This Lesson in Your Life

Our lesson today is profoundly true for all of us in today's culture, which increasingly says, "I want to do my own thing. I don't want to have to bother with rules and regulations." This sentiment was countered years ago by a popular song with the refrain, "You don't tug on Superman's cape; you don't spit into the wind; you don't rip the mask off the old Lone Ranger, and you don't mess around with Jim!"

Our lives are filled with rules and regulations. All of life is governed by guidelines and directives that are designed to guarantee a safe and fulfilled existence for most of us. God created the entire world and all within it to function according to His established patterns. The natural world is filled with rules and regulations about when trees flower, when crops produce, when creatures migrate during the seasons of the year.

The most extensive rules of all have to do with relationships between people, and their relationships with God. From the very beginning, God has made it clear that our lives will be joyful, free, and fulfilled if we will only live according to His guidelines. Without question, those lives filled with pain, struggle, sin, and anguish are lives where God's way has been thrown aside, and mankind's way has been preferred. Rules are good and good for us. God's rules are *for us*, and not against us.

The riverbanks direct the river's flow to the sea. When the banks or levees fail, floods and damage always occur. When you build a flimsy house in high wind areas, you won't have it long. There are rules and guidelines for everything. God has also given us rules for the care and keeping of our lives, families, souls and our moral strength. And . . . that's good!

STRAIGHT

1. Jesus said that not an iota of the law will pass away until all is accomplished. What did He mean?
He meant that God had delivered His rules, (the Law) out of loving compassion for all of creation and the human community in it, and The Law would never fade away until it reached fulfillment.

2. What was Jesus' instruction about conflict with your brother?
He tells us that our relationship with others is of such great importance that we must not come to the altar until that relationship has been reconciled.

3. How did He expand the commandment against adultery?
Going further than the commandment, (as He always did), Jesus said the act of infidelity was an affront to God, but so was lust.

4. Is there an over-arching theme to Jesus' comments about adultery?
Yes. In addition to condemning infidelity and lusting, Jesus intended for the man-woman relationship to be guided by mutual respect and honor.

5. Why did Jesus deal with divorce so harshly?
In first century Palestine, women could be divorced for little or no reason, and left with children in destitution. Jesus declared that tradition to be unholy.

6. Is there a "background theme" for Jesus' teachings on divorce?
In 1st century Palestine, women were often of little more importance than a piece of property. Jesus insisted this viewpoint was wrong.

7. How did Jesus expand on the ancient "eye-for-an-eye" revenge mentality?
He said that vengeance solves nothing, but reconciliation would solve everything. We are advised to "turn the other cheek" and not strike back.

8. From our scripture today, what is the definition of "swearing"?
In first century Palestine, you swore by calling upon the name of God or another Holy site to add weight to your exclamation. Jesus said we should never use any portion of God's world to strengthen our own promises.

9. What were Jesus' teachings on hate and love?
Growing up in first century Judaism where violence was expected, Jesus admonished us to live otherwise. He urged us to pray for those whom we call our enemies, so reconciliation would come to everyone.

10. What do we learn about Jesus' directive to leave your gift at the altar and return to reconcile with your brother?
To God, reconciliation is of greater priority than going through the motions of worship. It is not acceptable to contribute while holding a grudge.

It is always fascinating to see anyone move from an area of blindness and stubbornness in his life to becoming an awakened person. Life is a continuous journey of learning and growing, which never ends until our lives actually end. There is great truth to the old saying "Be gentle with me, God isn't through with me yet."

In the 1960s a generation emerged that declared rules to be wrong, that you should create your own rules. We watched Woodstock, with thousands engaging in drugs and sexual immorality in the mud in New York. It produced a generation of adults who felt that rules were old, outmoded, and a thing of the past. Faithfulness to one's spouse, faithfulness to God and to God's church, obedience of the civil laws and rules of the community, and the wise use of money and savings to secure a family all vanished in a wave of "rule bashing."

Today, however, the bookstores and libraries are filled with books written by many of that generation. They grew up in pain and anguish to find their marriages gone, their incomes meager or non-existent, and their own children living out the role model of their parents, in defiance of the guidelines by which healthy lives are lived. Most of these books carefully articulate how sorrowful that generation was, and how much rules for living are necessary for us to have a healthy society.

So many of our children chafe at rules of behavior. It is fascinating to see, when they themselves grow up and supervise their own children, how much they realize that being brought up by good rules has meant to their own development. God will never ask you to follow a rule that will not deepen, bless, and make your life better.

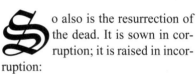

1 Corinthians 15:42-57

So also is the resurrection of the dead. It is sown in corruption; it is raised in incorruption:

43 It is sown in dishonour; it is raised in glory: it is sown in weakness; it is raised in power:

44 It is sown a natural body; it is raised a spiritual body. There is a natural body, and there is a spiritual body.

45 And so it is written, The first man Adam was made a living soul; the last Adam was made a quickening spirit.

46 Howbeit that was not first which is spiritual, but that which is natural; and afterward that which is spiritual.

47 The first man is of the earth, earthy: the second man is the Lord from heaven.

48 As is the earthy, such are they also that are earthy: and as is the heavenly, such are they also that are heavenly.

49 And as we have borne the image of the earthy, we shall also bear the image of the heavenly.

50 Now this I say, brethren, that flesh and blood cannot inherit the kingdom of God; neither doth corruption inherit incorruption.

51 Behold, I shew you a mystery; We shall not all sleep, but we shall all be changed,

52 In a moment, in the twinkling of an eye, at the last trump: for the trumpet shall sound, and the dead shall be raised incorruptible, and we shall be changed.

53 For this corruptible must put on incorruption, and this mortal must put on immortality.

54 So when this corruptible shall have put on incorruption, and this mortal shall have put on immortality, then shall be brought to pass the saying that is written, Death is swallowed up in victory.

55 O death, where is thy sting? O grave, where is thy victory?

56 The sting of death is sin; and the strength of sin is the law.

57 But thanks be to God, which giveth us the victory through our Lord Jesus Christ.

Nov. 14

Memory Selection
1 Corinthians 15:55

Background Scripture
1 Corinthians 15

Devotional Reading
1 Corinthians 15:1-11

Few New Testament writings give such a comprehensive picture of life and thought in the early church as 1 Corinthians. These Christians, most of whom had a pagan background, were full of questions. Today's session focuses on one of the most profound: *What will we be like in the resurrection?*

Sometimes this question arises from those who doubt whether there will really be a resurrection. Paul dealt with this issue in the first half of the letter. Even if we accept the doctrine of life after death, many questions remain. How will we recognize each other after the decaying process in the grave? In our new existence, will we be rid of the pains and deformities of our present bodies? Paul's answer to such questions may defy total understanding, but it shows the strength of his personal faith: *We will receive a new body.*

ഇ൞

Ask group members to respond with the first idea they think of when they hear the word *new.* Responses may include how we *feel* about new things—*fun, different, spontaneous, not boring.* Other responses may include positive ideas such as *opportunity, open door, pathway, ways of thinking,* and *wonder.* However, since the new and unfamiliar can be threatening be prepared also for negative responses such as *fearful, threatening, uncertain.*

Point out that for us to appreciate the new, it must be both *different* from the old, but *connected* to it. If we buy a used car that has more problems than the old buggy, the new is too much like the old to be useful. In today's lesson, Paul connects the fact of our present bodies with the concept of a *new* body, helping us anticipate life with Christ instead of dreading death.

Teaching Outline	Daily Bible Readings

Teaching Outline

I. The New *Opposed* to the Old—42-44

    A. A different state, 42

    B. A superior state, 43-44

II. The New *Compared* with the Old—45-49

    A. God's ordained order, 45-46

    B. Reflecting God's order, 47-49

III. The *Necessity* of the New—50-57

    A. Fit for a spiritual realm, 50-54

    B. Triumph of the spiritual, 55-57

Daily Bible Readings

Mon.	Christ's Resurrection	*1 Corinthians 15:1-11*
Tue.	Doubts about Resurrection	*1 Corinthians 15:12-19*
Wed.	Importance of Christ's Rising	*1 Corinthians 15:20-28*
Thu.	Arguments for Resurrection	*1 Corinthians 15:29-34*
Fri.	A Bodily Resurrection	*1 Corinthians 15:35-41*
Sat.	A Spiritual Body	*1 Corinthians 15:42-50*
Sun.	Confidence in the Resurrection	*1 Corinthians 15:51-58*

Verse by Verse

I. The New *Opposed* to the Old—42-44

A. A different state, 42

42 So also is the resurrection of the dead. It is sown in corruption; it is raised in incorruption:

Paul addresses those who cannot imagine a "substance" so different from their physical body. He has argued that *different* doesn't mean *unreal*. Animals differ from each other, rocks differ from stars, stars differ from each other (vss. 38-41)—yet we believe in the reality of each. Now he applies this line of argument to the resurrected body. If a supernatural God created a "natural" order in which the body decays, why should it be thought impossible for Him to create a supernatural order in which the body does *not* decay? Although the natural body is "sown" in the grave as a seed that decays, faith can well accept a later and non-decaying "sprouting" (see also vss. 36-37).

B. A superior state, 43-44

43 It is sown in dishonour; it is raised in glory: it is sown in weakness; it is raised in power:

44 It is sown a natural body; it is raised a spiritual body. There is a natural body, and there is a spiritual body.

The body that is not subject to decay is not only *different* from this physical body, it is also superior. We honor things that are beautiful, and

that last; but the body that is delivered to the grave is marred by disease, fatal wounds, or old age. Why, then, should the believer dread "trading in" his old-model body that is disfigured and subject to decay for a new-model body that is glorious, powerful, and, like the Spirit, eternal?

Of course the answer is that death is such a radically different experience that it can shake our faith in an after-life. So Paul closes this part of his argument by affirming that the spiritual body in the after-life is as real as the physical body in this life. We do not really know what a "spiritual body" is. We can touch a physical body, and we can tell stories that help us imagine something like a "ghost." Paul boldly combines the two into a single reality. Since he cannot produce a "spiritual body" to be examined, he has not "proved" his point beyond the shadow of a doubt; but he removes obstacles to faith for those who are willing to believe.

II. The New *Compared* with the Old—45-49

A. God's ordained order, 45-46

45 And so it is written, The first man Adam was made a living soul; the last Adam was made a quickening spirit.

46 Howbeit that was not first which is spiritual, but that which is natural; and afterward that

which is spiritual.

As noted in the "Getting Started" section, we rarely accept the new if it is too radically different from the old. We at least want it to connect with previous knowledge and experience. So in these verses Paul compares and contrasts the "natural" and the "spiritual" body. To do this he introduces the concept of Christ as a "second Adam." The first Adam and Jesus were alike in the sense that both were real persons. They are different in that Adam was "made" or created, while, as the Word, (John 1:1, 14) Jesus was Creator.

This compare-and-contrast exercise leaves us optimistic if we reflect on the *order* or sequence of the two Adams described in verse 46. If the sin of the first Adam had *followed* the life-giving sacrifice of Jesus, we would face the after-life not with eager anticipation, but dread. Paul will now elaborate on the significance of this Adam-to-Christ succession.

B. Reflecting God's order, 47-49

47 The first man is of the earth, earthy: the second man is the Lord from heaven.

48 As is the earthy, such are they also that are earthy: and as is the heavenly, such are they also that are heavenly.

49 And as we have borne the image of the earthy, we shall also bear the image of the heavenly.

Since "all have sinned, and come short of the glory of God" (Rom. 3:23), we all bear the imprint of our ancestor Adam. His sin in the Garden, and our subsequent aping of this

tendency, mark us as "earthy" or "earthly" beings. The good news is that if we fashion our lives after Christ as the second Adam, the first Adam's imprint on our souls can be obliterated by the spiritual imprint of Jesus.

III. The *Necessity* of the New—50-57

A. Fit for a spiritual realm, 50-54

50 Now this I say, brethren, that flesh and blood cannot inherit the kingdom of God; neither doth corruption inherit incorruption.

51 Behold, I shew you a mystery; We shall not all sleep, but we shall all be changed,

52 In a moment, in the twinkling of an eye, at the last trump: for the trumpet shall sound, and the dead shall be raised incorruptible, and we shall be changed.

53 For this corruptible must put on incorruption, and this mortal must put on immortality.

54 So when this corruptible shall have put on incorruption, and this mortal shall have put on immortality, then shall be brought to pass the saying that is written, Death is swallowed up in victory.

Paul draws out his argument here in a way that seems lengthy to the modern reader, and to restate some points already made. We must bear in mind, however, that many among the Corinthians doubted the reality of the resurrection; and Paul is determined to counter their skepticism with careful, if repetitive, argument.

Boiled down to its "meat," Paul's argument is that since heaven is a spiritual reality, a spiritual body is necessary to live there. To object to the decay of the physical body, or to death (referred to here by the euphemism "sleep") is to close the door on living in heaven. The argument is similar, if more profound, than the affirmation of the little boy who, while looking for a toy under his bed, asked his mom what the preacher had said about the "dust of the earth." His mother replied that he had said that man was created from that dust, and to that dust he would return. "Well," said the lad, "there's somebody here under my bed that's either coming or going."

Paul is saying that unless our body is subject to corruption, or returning to dust, we're going nowhere. If, however, we accept the decay of the physical body, we can anticipate with joy that somehow that dust will be able to "hear" the trump of God and "put on immortality." As in the vision of Ezekiel, our dead and scattered bones will be brought together, and to life, by the eternal Spirit at the last great Day (see Ezek. 37:1-14).

B. Triumph of the spiritual, 55-57

55 O death, where is thy sting? O grave, where is thy victory?

56 The sting of death is sin; and the strength of sin is the law.

57 But thanks be to God, which giveth us the victory through our Lord Jesus Christ.

Paul concludes his teaching on the reality of the resurrection with an outburst of praise so magnificent that it has appropriately become a defiant word of victory at many a Christian graveside. Verse 55 seems at first merely to quote Hosea 13:14; but when we look at that Old Testament reference we discover that it is only a hope for Israel's deliverance from death that stands shakily on her obedience—which in fact does not materialize. Paul deliberately turns the quotation to a positive affirmation that death's "sting," and the grave's apparent "victory," will be overcome by the resurrection.

Death itself has no inherent "sting" or spiritual trauma. It is part of the natural life-cycle that God created and pronounced "good" in Genesis 1. It was the introduction of *sin* that gave death its tragic dimension of "separation from God." God's temporary provision of the Law could serve as a guide to the faithful, but its emphasis on law-*keeping* or works made it inadequate to provide the grace necessary for salvation. Apart from grace, the Law therefore only strengthened man's sense of sin (Rom. 7:7-9).

This emphasis on works also appealed to the fleshly nature of man, tempting a law-keeper to boast. The death of even the most fastidious law-keeper tended to put the lie to the Law's ability to save; thus Law became an ally to death. However, in the resurrection, grace is shown to triumph over Law, spirit over flesh, and victory over defeat. No wonder Paul closes what began as an argument suitable for debate with a virtual praise-song affirming the Christian's victory, through Christ, over sin, death, and the grave.

Perhaps this is why, at the funerals of Christians, we *sing* more than we debate.

Evangelistic Emphasis

A church in lower Manhattan put an interesting sign on its message board. Located in an area filled with drug users and people living on the edge, the sign read "If you don't like who you are and want to be something different, we can help. Inquire inside." The pastor who put that message out was assuming that some who saw it might respond to an invitation to transformation. He was totally unprepared for what happened next, as waves of prostitutes, drug users, and petty thieves began arriving at the church and inquiring.

They began classes on "Getting your life back together," always leaning upon God's guidance for the process. The leadership of the church was overwhelmed at the response, and assumed it to be a clear statement that we all, from every walk of life, want to be transformed. The pastor told them they could be transformed many times in this life and ultimately and gloriously when this life came to an end. The resurrection for them, as for us, was an electric possibility.

☙❧

Memory Selection

Where, Oh death is your victory? And where, oh death, is your sting?—*Corinthians 15:55*

This quote, paraphrased from the 13ᵗʰ chapter of Hosea, is a profound declaration of confidence in God and the resurrection. Like a child standing on a railroad track looking at an oncoming engine and daring it to keep coming, the believing Christian looks death right in the face and says, "You have no claim on me, my friend! I am part of a higher calling which you cannot touch."

To go through our lives absolutely certain that the end of our life is but a door to a new form of existence that we cannot even imagine, is the fuel that fires the boiler of Christianity around the world. It is the faith that makes us live our lives almost with a faithful and responsible abandon, because we know that in Christ's name we are free from fear, free from eternal death, and free from life being simply transitory.

Weekday Problems

As a hospital chaplain, I found myself in a room with a young man with only a few months to live. He was writing voraciously, page after page, and having helpers and friends stack the papers in neat piles. He told me he wanted to leave something behind, and was writing several books.

One day as we visited, I gently removed the pen from his hand and told him his life was his legacy and God would take him in His hands. I explained to him life did not just end upon death; it only extended into a remarkable arena. I persuaded him to enjoy the months he had left, and the people who loved him, and not shut them out while frantically writing what no one would ever read.

It was Tuesday when I knew he realized this, and put down his pencils and swept his papers to the corner. He visited warmly with an occasional tear, and shared his last months with those who loved him. He was confident in the promise of the resurrection and it showed.

*Who is guiding your life—God or yourself?

Matters of Death and Life

When the woman in the taxi put her hand on the cabbie's shoulder and said "Turn here," he jumped like he was shot. "I'm sorry," said his passenger. "I didn't mean to startle you."

"That's O.K., ma'am," he said. "This is my first day on the job as a taxi driver. I've been driving a hearse for 20 years."

* * * *

Think of how surprising death was to . . .
- The submariner who closed the hatch with a screen door.
- The pilot who, when his helicopter sputtered, hit the eject button.
- The Hindu snake charmer whose cobra turned out to be deaf.
- The stowaway who discovered it was a kamikaze plane.

* * * *

The new minister at the country church thought his head deacon was a bit arrogant, but when he found that an old mule had dropped dead in front of the church, he asked the deacon to haul off the carcass.

"Well, it's your job as a minister to deal with the dead," said the deacon.

"You're right," said the pastor, "but I always like to notify the next of kin."

Several years ago, Peggy Lee recorded a hit song entitled, "Is That All There Is?" The lyrics were depressing and described life, romance, and relationships with a cynical eye. The songwriter looks at the panorama of God's creation, and says, "You mean that's all there is to this business called life?" There are many people who look at life the same way... as something you experience or endure (depending upon your own situation) until finally the darkness closes around you, and that experience or endurance is complete. There are people who don't want to think of tomorrow or plan for the future because their whole existence is *now*. Their need to be fulfilled is now, not tomorrow. There are large numbers of people for whom the only thing in life is what they see, experience, feel, or acquire now.

Our scripture today stands in stark contrast to that view. Paul's letter to the church at Corinth is a powerful reminder that the foundation upon which all of Christianity rests is the promise that life as we know it transitions into a life as we have faith to know it after death.

The truth of the resurrection is a fundamental and irreplaceable doctrine of Christianity. If there were no resurrection, nor any chance to be redeemed and renewed, then the purpose of Christianity would be superfluous and not worth our time. But transformation from one matter to another is God's truth and is all around us. Tiny acorns change into mighty oak trees. A trickle in Minnesota becomes the mighty Mississippi River. A microscopic egg and sperm meet, and years later you have a 6-feet 5-inch football player.

The truth of the resurrection takes transformation one step further, and assures us that we too shall be transformed from one substance to the next, from one being to another, and from one form of existence to yet another through the power of the Risen Christ.

108

1. God makes it clear that there is a distinct difference between the physical and spiritual realm. How is that presented?

With a series of comparisons that what we know on earth is perishable. It shall all be changed to imperishable glory and strength.

2. The scripture says there is a definite sequence in transformation. How so?

The physical must be first and then the spiritual. You cannot have earthliness transformed into spirituality until you first have the earthly and perishable existence.

3. How does that analogy continue concerning the first man, Adam?

The scripture refers to Adam as the first man from the earth, a person of dust (earthliness which is perishable).

4. How do we fit in with this analogy of dust?

We are created out of earthly materials (dust), which will all pass away and vanish. But through faith and the resurrection, we shall be born again "just as the man of heaven" (Jesus).

5. How does this scripture declare this transformation to be absolute?

It is flatly stated that flesh and blood cannot inherit the Kingdom Of God, nor can the perishable inherit the imperishable.

6. What word is used in our lesson to describe the resurrection and transformation?

The word used, which describes why we cannot with our intellectual faculties grasp it, but only through faith, is "mystery."

7. When does this happen?

At the sound of the last trumpet, in the twinkling of an eye.

8. What will happen at that time?

Those who have died in the earthly sense (perishable), shall rise again in a new form that is eternal and imperishable.

9. Where did we first see the quote in 2 Corinthians 15:55, which the scripture refers to as "The saying that is written?"

It first appears out of the mouth of the prophet Hosea in 13:1,14: "O death where are your plagues? Oh Sheol (Hell) where is your destruction?"

10. Do we in our perishable (earthly) nature automatically become transformed into the spiritual nature?

No. The transformation specifically rests upon our faithfulness and our believing, as it says in vs. 53: "For the perishable nature must *put on* the imperishable, and the mortal nature must *put on* immortality."

"We're a resurrection people around here!" That's what the man said. I walked the rows with him as he explained the feast-or-famine nature of big time cotton/soybean farming. He explained how one year you could make more bales and bushels per acre then you ever dreamed, and then have years in which you barely made enough money to keep your home. During all that time you carry hundreds of thousands of dollars of debt for machinery and salaries for your workers. On top of that, you have to raise your children, never knowing if your crop will get out of the ground or not. The previous two years were years that put many farmers into bankruptcy. Dreams were dashed forever, and many young people were told there simply was not going to be a chance for college.

Now, as we walked among cotton plants that were almost six feet tall, bursting with buds, I asked how he could stand that roller coaster life. That was his answer: "We're just resurrection people around here. We die for a long time and suddenly the rains come and we are born again. Just like what you preach about. Whoever you are will ultimately be changed. We know that, and are ready for it and have faith in it."

As long as I live, I don't think I'll ever forget that hard-working, hard-believing, farmer and his self declaration of being "a resurrection people out on the farm." They live for what is coming, and are sure it *is* coming. They are not sure when, but they know it is coming. So they live, work, struggle, try hard, and keep the faith. Then one day, the rains pour down at just the right time.

We all have transformations in our lives, and little "mini-resurrections" all through our days as we are transformed from one state of being to the next, one attitude to the next, sinfulness to wholeness, and then the day arrives when God calls our name and we are truly transformed into another state of being. Praise God!

2 Corinthians 5:11-21

Knowing therefore the terror of the Lord, we persuade men; but we are made manifest unto God; and I trust also are made manifest in your consciences.

12 For we commend not ourselves again unto you, but give you occasion to glory on our behalf, that ye may have somewhat to answer them which glory in appearance, and not in heart.

13 For whether we be beside ourselves, it is to God: or whether we be sober, it is for your cause.

14 For the love of Christ constraineth us; because we thus judge, that if one died for all, then were all dead:

15 And that he died for all, that they which live should not henceforth live unto themselves, but unto him which died for them, and rose again.

16 Wherefore henceforth know we no man after the flesh: yea, though we have known Christ after the flesh, yet now henceforth know we him no more.

17 Therefore if any man be in Christ, he is a new creature: old things are passed away; behold, all things are become new.

18 And all things are of God, who hath reconciled us to himself by Jesus Christ, and hath given to us the ministry of reconciliation;

19 To wit, that God was in Christ, reconciling the world unto himself, not imputing their trespasses unto them; and hath committed unto us the word of reconciliation.

20 Now then we are ambassadors for Christ, as though God did beseech you by us: we pray you in Christ's stead, be ye reconciled to God.

21 For he hath made him to be sin for us, who knew no sin; that we might be made the righteousness of God in him.

Nov. 21

Memory Selection
2 Corinthians 5:17

Background Scripture
2 Corinthians 5:11-21

Devotional Reading
2 Corinthians 4:16–5:5

Sometimes it seems as though all the stories in today's newspaper could have a single headline: "The Need for Reconciliation." There is conflict between Muslims and Christians in several hot spots, between Muslims and Jews in Palestine, Protestants and Catholics in Ireland, blacks and South Koreans in Los Angeles, Anglos and Hispanics in states along the U.S. border with Mexico, husbands and wives, youth and parents . . . . The list goes on.

Thoughtful Christians see a more basic need for reconciliation that feeds such tensions: the need for all to be reconciled to God. If more of us were secure in our relationship with Him, would we be less touchy in our relationships with each other?

Paul also faced the need for Jew and Gentile to be reconciled with each other, and with God. The focus of this lesson is how being *"in Christt"* provides a basis for reconciliation with both God and persons.

ഇ൧

Current events invite a discussion of the need for reconciliation between Christians and Muslims, to introduce this lesson. Ask why animosity exists between these groups.

Some may mention religious differences, feeling that the Muslim faith encourages violence while Christians follow "the Prince of Peace." Some authorities say that poor economic conditions in the Arab world incite jealousy against Americans, who seem to have more than their fair share of world resources. Some feel that America's support of Israel is a problem.

Ask how the teachings of Jesus might impact this situation. Is it too simplistic to say that "Christ is the answer"? How might following Christ's principles lead to reconciliation? What difficulties stand in the way of Arab and Christian peace?

Teaching Outline	Daily Bible Readings	

I. Selfless Motives—11-15
  A. Transparent before God, 11-12
  B. Driven by love, 13-15
II. New Creations—16-17
  A. Transformed view, 16
  B. Newness 'In Christ,' 17
III. Challenging Mission—18-21
  A. Reconciled to God, 18-19a
  B. Ambassadors for Christ, 19b-21
	Mon.
	Tue.
	Wed.
	Thu.
	Fri.
	Sat.
	Sun.
		With Unveiled Face
		  2 Corinthians 3:12-18
		To the Glory of God
		  2 Corinthians 4:1-15
		We Must Live by Faith
		  2 Corinthians 4:16–5:5
		Serve God with Confidence
		  2 Corinthians 5:6-10
		Serving God Faithfully
		  2 Corinthians 5:11-15
		Ministry of Reconciliation
		  2 Corinthians 5:16-21
		Now Is the Day of Salvation
		  2 Corinthians 6:1-10

Verse by Verse

I. Selfless Motives—11-15

A. Transparent before God, 11-12

11 Knowing therefore the terror of the Lord, we persuade men; but we are made manifest unto God; and I trust also are made manifest in your consciences.

12 For we commend not ourselves again unto you, but give you occasion to glory on our behalf, that ye may have somewhat to answer them which glory in appearance, and not in heart.

Some of the apostle Paul's sharpest and most confrontational language has been directed at the Christians in Corinth because of dangerous attitudes and practices there. His rebuke had made some of them "sorry" (7:8). Here he explains that his direct speech arose out of his being driven by "the terror (Grk. *phobos*) of the Lord" to bring them around to his views.

This King James rendering somewhat overstates the original meaning, which speaks, like the Old Testament book of Proverbs, of the *fear* of the Lord. This means awe and reverence more than terror (see Prov. 2:1-5). Here it speaks of Paul's devotion to God and seeing that His will is accomplished among the Corinthians, even at the risk of losing friends. He has not rebuked them to glory in his authority as an apostle, but he cannot apologize for opposing those who glory in *appearing* to follow his counsel while in their hearts remaining unreconciled.

B. Driven by love, 13-15

13 For whether we be beside ourselves, it is to God: or whether we be sober, it is for your cause.

14 For the love of Christ constraineth us; because we thus judge, that if one died for all, then were all dead:

15 And that he died for all, that they which live should not henceforth live unto themselves, but unto him which died for them, and rose again.

Paul's very passion and occasionally explosive outbursts in opposing false doctrine had earned him the accusation among some that he was "beside himself," or insane. He replies that even if he is out of his mind, it is for their benefit.

Ironically, all of God's true prophets were "out of their mind," in the sense that they were sometimes seized by "ecstatic" utterances. For "ecstatic" means literally to stand outside oneself; and the word Paul uses for "beside ourselves" actually gives us our word "ecstasy." Of course in the larger sense this "seizure" is the ultimate *sanity*, since God's message brings us to our right mind.

Paul's true motive is stated in

verse 14: "Christ's love constrains us" (NIV). If all who oppose God, including the rebellious Corinthians are "dead" in sin, and if Christ died to bring them alive spiritually, it is no sign of love to fail to deliver to them the message they need to hear.

II. New Creations—16-17

A. Transformed view, 16

16 Wherefore henceforth know we no man after the flesh: yea, though we have known Christ after the flesh, yet now henceforth know we him no more.

Now Paul explains that he is more concerned about the Corinthians' spiritual health than he is about whether they "like" him in the flesh. In fact, it is this spiritual point of view that enabled Paul to be converted on the road to Damascus, when He was converted from viewing Jesus as being opposed to God's will. After that life-changing experience, Paul is not going to allow the merely human desire to be approved by the Corinthians to prevent him from tending to their deeper, spiritual needs. (The last phrase obviously does not mean that Paul no longer knows Christ, but that he no longer esteems Him in a fleshly way to be an enemy of God.)

B. Newness 'In Christ,' 17

17 Therefore if any man be in Christ, he is a new creature: old things are passed away; behold, all things are become new.

The Corinthians can share this positive view of Christ also, if they will. Turning from their will to His, they would find themselves "in Christ"—a favorite phrase Paul used to describe the secure spiritual place where believers enjoy reconciliation with Christ and others. Being "in Christ" can be compared to being "in the bomb shelter" during an air raid. It is virtually equivalent to being "in the Kingdom." It is such a radical change from being at cross-purposes with God that it can be described as a "new creation." We know something of this experience of "newness" when we have quarreled with a loved one to the point that our relationship feels "dead." Then a breakthrough, perhaps facilitated by mutual forgiveness, gives the relationship a "new lease on life," and we feel released anew to rebuild the feelings that had made us close. The new creation, or "new birth" (John 3:3-5) accomplishes this with both God and His people.

For Paul, Christ not only dwells in believers (Col. 1:27); they dwell in Him. The phrase is especially prominent in the letter to the Ephesians, where it most often refers to the "place" where Jew and Gentile are reconciled. As modern psychologists have discovered, people who feel safe usually feel less fearful, less threatened by what is "outside" their circle of security. One prominent counselor has written that he formerly focused on healing damaged emotions by casting evil spirits from people. Eventually, however, he noticed that this sensational approach brought many back to his office too often for a "supernatural fix." The counselor then adopted the less spectacular but approach of teaching believers *who* they are "in Christ"—with the result that they were enabled to conquer their fears and anxieties with longer-lasting effectiveness.

III. Challenging Mission—18-21

A. Reconciled to God, 18-19a

18 And all things are of God, who hath reconciled us to himself by Jesus Christ, and hath given to us the ministry of reconciliation;

19 To wit, that God was in Christ, reconciling the world unto himself, not imputing their trespasses unto them;

In a monotheistic religion, everything can be traced back to one Being. The Corinthians cannot find salvation by settling their account with Satan, but only with God. It is therefore also God who has provided the means of reconciliation—namely the sacrifice of His Son, Jesus Christ. Note that it is God who gave this way of escape from spiritual death; we did not reconcile ourselves to Him, but He to us. In turn, it is again "in Christ" that we seek reconciliation— not only with God but with others.

In the same breath in which Paul speaks of our being reconciled to Him through Christ, he speaks also of sharing it with others. Reconciliation is not just a prize jewel to be placed in a bank vault or museum; it is a *ministry.*

"Reconciliation" is from a word whose root meant *to change,* or *exchange*, as when, in bookkeeping, the debit and credit accounts are "reconciled" or made to agree with each other. The history of mankind can be written from the viewpoint of man's seeking a way to exchange enmity with God for friendship. Because of sin, we know the need to "balance our account" with Him. Paul says that this cannot be done humanly. It is a transaction made by God, not ourselves; and it was accomplished through Christ's having "credited our account" with *His* righteousness, since ours is not enough.

B. Ambassadors for Christ, 19b-21

19b and hath committed unto us the word of reconciliation.

20 Now then we are ambassadors for Christ, as though God did beseech you by us: we pray you in Christ's stead, be ye reconciled to God.

21 For he hath made him to be sin for us, who knew no sin; that we might be made the righteousness of God in him.

On the road to Damascus, God had committed to Paul the work of sharing this good news that the "balancing of accounts" or reconciliation with God has occurred through Christ. Paul and the other apostles were in that sense "ambassadors," serving in God's diplomatic corps. For the Corinthians to resist this message because of petty grievances against Paul would be for them to decline to accept God's ambassador, which in terms of global politics could be a declaration of war!

Verse 21 closes Paul's plea by reminding us that neither he nor we have the means of making peace with God. It is purely a gift, the sacrifice of the sinless Son of God, that accomplishes reconciliation with Him, and makes it possible for people to be reconciled to each other.

Evangelistic Emphasis

When we moved into the parsonage, our neighbor had misgivings about clergy. He viewed ministers as self-righteous and judgmental.

One day his swimming pool malfunctioned and waves of water swept into our yard, making a quagmire out of everything. Arriving from work, he saw our predicament and assured us he would pay the damage. He was stunned when we said we wanted nothing, because accidents happened. After days of cleaning up, and seeing no anger in us, he began to wonder about his assessment.

Soon afterward, he held a fish fry, and invited us. We accepted, ate heartily, and mingled with the guests with much enjoyment. In a rare moment he later confided he now thought he could see clergy in a different light, and was ashamed of his preconceptions. Belonging to a different church, his wife confided that he had "gone to church again," because he felt better about his pastor.

It was Jesus who said, "Behold… I make all things new again."

ഇരു

Memory Selection

If anyone is in Christ, there is a new creation: everything old has passed away; see, everything has become new!—*2 Corinthians 5:17*

The scripture lesson today reminds us that Jesus Christ is indeed a fork in the road for each of us. Jesus is a line in the sand, a door to be entered, and a day to begin as no other days have begun. If we take the correct fork, or walk through that challenging door, we are promised that our life will begin again as though it had never even been.

This is the miracle of Christianity, that we always have a point at which beginning can take place, no matter how deeply entrenched in our sinfulness and selfishness we are, no matter our age or crusty old traditions. Our scripture tells us that if our life mirrors Christ, we will truly be seen by the rest of the world, and see the world itself with all new eyes. Jesus Christ *is* the dividing line between "what used to be and what can be." Which side of that line we are on depends entirely upon our decision.

Weekday Problems

Doug was a bright young man, raised in the church, but now sporting nose rings, earrings, and every sort of body art. His parents severely disapproved, but assumed he would outgrow it. Unlike many parents who would have been furious, they kept the faith, held to the course, and expressed their love for their son.

One summer Doug worked as a part-time youth director. As he studied the Word with the youth, it became clear to him that he had to get his own journey straightened out. Like John Wesley on Aldersgate Street, Doug's heart was "strangely warmed," and gradually all the buttons and rings came off and out, one-by-one. By September Doug was back to normal because his parents were willing to wipe the slate clean and welcome their son home all over again.

What a wonderful thing it is to have our stupidities not held against us!

*Have you had your "slate wiped clean" by someone else?

*Have you done the same for anyone else?

Speaking of Redemption . . .

A man took on a business proposition that required him to cash in a $5,000 bond; so he called his bank.

"Sir," said the clerk, "is the bond for redemption or conversion"?

After a long pause the man asked, "Am I speaking with someone at the First National Bank or the First Baptist Church?"

* * * *

Q: Why are there so few men with whiskers in heaven?
A: Because most men get in by a close shave.

* * * *

Grandson: Grandpa, why do you read the Bible all day?
Grandpa: Well, son, you might say I'm cramming for my final exams.

* * * *

The prison chaplain, passing through the garment factory, tried to make small talk with one inmate who seemed busily at work. "Sewing?" he asked.

"No," the inmate replied gloomily. "Reaping."

This Lesson in Your Life

It has been said that if you want to see a person's values in life, just glance through his cancelled checks. The truth here is that *something* drives and motivates us all. There is a force within us that determines our direction in life, choices, and values.

There are people whose entire goal in life is to drive to make as much money as possible. There are those who dream of becoming a mother, fireman, lawyer, or doctor. When those dreams are deep within us, that pursuit colors all we are and do, often at the expense of relationships.

In our scripture today there is a fascinating idea in verse 14, "For the love of Christ controls us . . . ." The truth here is that if the love of Jesus Christ is the burning, driving force within us, just as it is for someone to be successful and rich, then our lives will take on such a totally different meaning and aura we would scarcely recognize ourselves.

The key word here is "control." Paul's use of that word is in his own phrase, "In Christ." Both terms mean the same. You cannot have a life that is full and free, with meaning and purpose unless the controlling energy in that life is the love of God and Christ and obedience to His will. Once that has become evident in your life, newness pervades everything that you do. You think differently, you see the world, people, and relationships differently, you begin to see and respect yourself in ways you never dreamed. It is just as if you put on a different set of eyeglasses. You are still looking at the same people, world, office, home, church, and relationships, but you are seeing them in a way you never saw them before. Knowing God and loving Christ, and submitting your entire decision-making existence to Jesus Christ has made you a person utterly unlike the one before.

Praise God for the gift of newness! Praise God that we are only one confession of faith away from seeing the world as we have never seen it before, as new creatures in Christ.

1. Today's scripture describes Paul's overall intent in life. What is it?
To "persuade men," knowing the fear of the Lord. The word "fear" in biblical language is synonymous with standing in awe and respect.

2. How does Paul describe himself and his ministry team to the church of Corinth?
He insists that they are all clearly known by God. There are no secrets or hidden agendas in who Paul is and what he is about. He hopes the Corinthians will know him in the same way.

3. Paul instructs the Corinthians who might be questioning the Christian movement in that era. What does he say?
He commends his ministry to them so they might be able to help those who trust in persons and in power, to trust instead in a holy heart.

4. Why does Paul say he is compassionate for the Corinthian church?
Because the love of God "controls" Paul and his team, and he wants the Corinthians to be controlled by Jesus as well.

5. How does he urge them to change the priority in their lifestyle?
To live no longer for themselves and their own interests, taking pride in human achievement, but in the resurrected Christ.

6. How does Paul say his view of the Corinthians has changed?
He says he no longer views them from a human point of view, but as new spiritual creatures in Christ.

7. Paul draws a line in the sand for the Corinthians about the old and the new. What does he say?
He says the old has passed away, and that when you believe in Jesus, all things are new again.

8. Knowing the Corinthians' tendency to place value in humans, what does Paul say about his message of newness?
That none of this comes through him, but through God who will reconcile Himself to the world in Jesus Christ. This is a "Christ thing" and not a "Paul thing."

9. How does he promise to wipe the slate clean?
He reminds them that their trespasses will not be counted against them. What is past is past.

10. How does Paul urgently appeal to the Corinthians?
He describes himself as an ambassador for Christ, urgently beseeching the Corinthians to accept God's promise of reconciliation and newness.

They were a strong and faithful family within my congregation, and had eagerly anticipated the kind of man their daughter would eventually choose to marry. Their daughter was in her 20s and dated a fellow regularly, but would never bring him to meet them. The reason was that he had a police record. Many years before, he had done some foolish things and spent a short time in jail. He was ashamed of his past, and afraid the knowledge of it would cause her parents to veto their relationship.

Yet he began to attend church with the family on a regular basis, not just a form of manipulation or "making nice," but earnestly seeking the presence of God in his life. Over a period of time, that exact thing happened, as God's spirit moved in him, and he genuinely became a more active participant in the faith community. Through it all, however, the knowledge of his past paralyzed him with fear for his future.

One Sunday, he gave himself to Christ. It was a powerful moment, except for that cloud still hanging over his memory. He wanted to ask for the girl's hand in marriage, but feared her parents would learn of his background and reject him. I told him they were professing Christians, and he had to trust them and God and lay it all on the table.

A week later, with fear and trembling, he did just that, asking for her hand in marriage, and then explaining to them the baggage from his years, how it happened, and how ashamed and mortified he was. The parents reflected on the many years that had passed, his exemplary life, his new birth in Christ, and granted him permission to marry their daughter. The father said that God does not hold our past against us, and they would not either. A 2,000 year old piece of scripture came to reality right there in that living room, just as it does for all of us when we reach out and accept Christ.

Lesson 13

A New Relationship

Ephesians 2:11-21

herefore remember, that ye being in time past Gentiles in the flesh, who are called Uncircumcision by that which is called the Circumcision in the flesh made by hands;

12 That at that time ye were without Christ, being aliens from the commonwealth of Israel, and strangers from the covenants of promise, having no hope, and without God in the world:

13 But now in Christ Jesus ye who sometimes were far off are made nigh by the blood of Christ.

14 For he is our peace, who hath made both one, and hath broken down the middle wall of partition between us;

15 Having abolished in his flesh the enmity, even the law of commandments contained in ordinances; for to make in himself of twain one new man, so making peace;

16 And that he might reconcile both unto God in one body by the cross, having slain the enmity thereby:

17 And came and preached peace to you which were afar off, and to them that were nigh.

18 For through him we both have access by one Spirit unto the Father.

19 Now therefore ye are no more strangers and foreigners, but fellowcitizens with the saints, and of the household of God;

20 And are built upon the foundation of the apostles and prophets, Jesus Christ himself being the chief corner stone;

21 In whom all the building fitly framed together groweth unto an holy temple in the Lord:

Memory Selection
Ephesians 2:19

Background Scripture
Ephesians 2:11-21

Devotional Reading
Ephesians 2:4-10

Nov. 28

In one sense, this lesson can be viewed as the completion of God's plan from the beginning of time—the formation of the "new creation" which would bring together people who had been estranged from God and each other since the expulsion of Adam and Eve from the Garden. The focus is sharpest on the reconciliation of Jew and Gentile; but the scope extends to all people.

In another sense, however, we have only to look about us at the continued strife among races and genders, nations and ethnic groups, even among churches, to see that Paul's vision described here, while real, is not fulfilled. The new creation was inaugurated at the Cross, where Christ's reconciling blood was shed for all. It remains for people to make this godly reality their own, meeting each other at the foot of the Cross (2:21).

೫೧೦೪

Since the reconciliation of Jew and Gentile depends on the Atonement, this session can be introduced by a brief discussion of the sacrifice of Christ on the Cross. Many people were crucified for various reasons in Jesus' day. Why did *His* death alone reconcile estranged people with God, and with each other?

(1) Since sin "kills" the spirit, the Law required "life for life." Thus, animal sacrifices were required under the Law. However, the blood of animals was not effective, so (2) God put forth *Himself* as the sacrifice, in the form of His Son. (3) Of all others crucified, only Christ was a pure and sinless offering, thus fulfilling the Law; and (4) God gave Himself so the *means* of salvation would be an *example* of how the saved should live—in self-sacrifice for others.

Teaching Outline

I. Past Alienation—11-12

II. Present Peace—13-18

    A. Gentiles' acceptance, 13

    B. Means of peace, 14-16

    C. Common need, 17-18

III. Firm Foundation—19-21

    A. For God's household, 19

    B. For God's Temple, 20-22

Daily Bible Readings

Mon.	Grace Through Christ
	Ephesians 1:3-12
Tue.	One in Christ
	Ephesians 4:1-6
Wed.	Growing Together
	Ephesians 4:11-16
Thu.	Alive Together
	Ephesians 2:4-10
Fri.	Once Apart, now Together
	Ephesians 2:11-16
Sat.	No Longer Strangers
	Ephesians 2:17-22
Sun.	Grounded in Love
	Ephesians 3:14-19

Verse by Verse

I. Past Alienation—11-12

11 Wherefore remember, that ye being in time past Gentiles in Christ. Eventually, however, he had to deal with the Jewish bias against Gentiles. Jews haughtily (in a fleshly way, the term "in the flesh" connoting arrogance as well as a physical mark) referred to Gentiles as "the Uncircumcised," while their own status as "the Circumcised" was a boast that they were Abraham's heirs.

However, before Paul can make the case for the inclusion of the Gentiles in the "new Israel," he must show their *need* to be included. Although Gentiles were supposed to be living under God's Covenant with Noah, most had no concept of allegiance to the true God. The fact was that, despite their faults, Jewish communities in general had a higher standard of morality than most pagans. As a whole, they were everything Paul says about them here; and by their rebellion they had placed themselves "without" (NIV "separate from") the circle of those awaiting the Messiah and trying to live holy lives.

II. Present Peace—13-18

A. Gentiles' acceptance, 13

13 But now in Christ Jesus ye who sometimes were far off are made nigh by the blood of Christ.

Having made the "bad news" clear, Paul can now affirm the Good News: despite their general neglect of godliness, Gentiles who had been estranged from God were now made "nigh" or close to Him—not by having reformed their morals but because God had sent His only Son to them to be offered as a sacrifice for their sin. Of course from this point they would be expected to live up to the image of Christ in them; but Christian morality is based on what Christ has done for them, not on what they can do for Him.

B. Means of peace, 14-16

14 For he is our peace, who hath made both one, and hath broken down the middle wall of partition between us;

15 Having abolished in his flesh the enmity, even the law of commandments contained in ordinances; for to make in himself of twain one new man, so making peace;

16 And that he might reconcile both unto God in one body by the cross, having slain the enmity thereby:

Having noted the former distinction between Jew and Gentile, Paul now shows that they have in common the need for the grace of God as shown on the Cross. Jesus' sacrifice has made both Jew and Gentile "one." Just as surely as at the battle of Jericho, "the walls came tumbling down." There is now "neither Jew nor Greek [Gentile], there is neither bond nor free, there is neither male nor female; for ye are all one in Christ Jesus" (Gal. 3:28).

It might be surprising to learn that part of what had kept Jew and Gentile apart was "the law of commandments," or the Law of Moses. In itself, the Law was holy and just (Rom. 7:12). Yet its very holiness made it impossible for unholy people, mere humans, to keep it perfectly. In that sense, therefore, the law was a barrier between persons and God since it was a continuous reminder of their inability to keep it (Rom. 3:20). In Christ, Paul says, that barrier is abolished—referring, as we noted in the previous lesson, not to "law" in principle, as in the universal principles of the Ten Commandments, but to the ritual requirements of the Law of Moses.

By Paul's day, "the Law" was often summarized in one word: the fleshly ordinance of "circumcision" (see again verse 11-12). Therefore it was highly appropriate that the *fulfillment* of the law be brought about in the flesh also—the crucified body of Christ, which was supposed to "slay" or put to death the long-standing enmity between Jew and Gentile.

C. Common need, 17-18

17 And came and preached peace to you which were afar off, and to them that were nigh.

18 For through him we both have access by one Spirit unto the Father.

In counterpoint to the necessity, above, of showing the overall sinfulness of Gentiles, in contrast to the relatively high moral standards of many Jews, Paul now brings the two together under the umbrella of their common need to be brought close to God. "You which were afar off" are the Gentiles, and "them that were nigh (near)" are God's chosen race, the Jews. This distinction is now blurred, however, both because "all have sinned" (Rom. 3:23) and because all can now return to God by the work of Christ.

Because of Paul's Jewishness, we are no doubt to read into his word "peace" something of the rich meaning of the Hebrew *shalom*, which meant not only the absence of warfare but wholeness, health, and relational unity.

The addition here of the work of the Holy Spirit brings together the Trinitarian nature of Christ's sacrifice, which was the work of Father, Son and Holy Spirit. The emphasis, however, is on oneness: *one state*, sinfulness, including both Jew and Gentile, who are brought together by *one sacrifice* of the *one* or only-begotten Son, under the guidance of the one *Spirit,* and according to the sweeping plan of the *one God.* This emphasis makes division within the "temple," or Church, a scandal much more serious than disharmony among people. It actually reflects poorly on the basic Bible doctrine of one God.

III. Firm Foundation—19-21

A. For God' household, 19

19 Now therefore ye are no more strangers and foreigners, but fellowcitizens with the saints, and of the household of God;

Various nations of the world have from the beginning of history made pacts of peace, most of them broken when the self-interest of one or another of the parties to the covenant is threatened. As an educated Jew living under the rule of Rome, Paul would have been well aware of such political attempts at peace. Here, however, he affirms that the peace between Jew and Gentile was won not by an earthly pact but by the victory of the crucified Christ over Satan. He can still describe this peace in political terms such as "citizens"; but it welds people together not in a civil union but in the household of God, the Body of Christ, the Church (see 1:22-23).

God has always had a people or "household." The household referred to here is the chosen race, the Jews, while those who were "strangers" are Gentiles. While the two were, and to some extent still are, strange and foreign to each other, this is not according to God's will. Paul assures Gentiles that they are equal-opportunity citizens with God, in effect forming a new Israel (see Rom. 9:6; Gal. 6:16).

B. For God's Temple, 20-21

20 And are built upon the foun-

dation of the apostles and prophets, Jesus Christ himself being the chief corner stone;

21 In whom all the building fitly framed together groweth unto an holy temple in the Lord:

Again in contrast to political alliances, Paul turns to an architectural metaphor to describe the peace won by Christ. The new Israel, composed of both Jew and Gentile was predicted of old, and accomplished by Jesus. The magnificent "structure" that resulted from their work is described as a "holy temple," the foundation of which is the apostles and prophets, with Jesus Himself as the cornerstone.

Structure such as temples and synagogues in Paul's day were usually constructed of cut stone, with each block cut and shaped on the job to fit seamlessly with those around it. Key to the stability of the walls was a greater stone capable of holding them together. Continuing the imagery of God's people united in a temple, here is the fulfillment of Isaiah's prophecy: "Behold, I lay in Zion for a foundation a stone, a tried stone, a precious corner stone, a sure foundation" (Isa. 28:16).

This symbolism is carried a step further by Peter when he describes Christians as "living stones," built on the foundation Paul describes here (see 1 Pet. 2:5).

Evangelistic Emphasis

They came in after worship had begun. They were dark and oriental, and remained with their two children in the narthex. At worship's end they were gone. Two Sundays later the scene was repeated. The Evangelism Team decided to stay in the narthex as a lookout. They returned and tried to sit in the narthex but our team lovingly brought them into the sanctuary. They were Indonesian, and were not sure how dark, oriental-looking people would be received. They were blessed, however, when the congregation crowded around them, embraced their two daughters and peppered them with questions about life in Indonesia. Then off to the kitchen for Kool-Aid with the girls and extended visiting with the congregation. They told me they sat in the narthex because they "looked so different." There was a day when that would be a justified fear, but thank God that day is mostly gone. Thank God for this congregation that broke down their fears and barriers with Christian love.

ഇഝ

Memory Selection

You are no longer strangers and aliens, but you are citizens with the saints and also members of the household of God.—*Ephesians 2:19*

Today's scripture rings with the idea that "United we stand, divided we fall." It reminds us that there is no possible way for God's kingdom on earth to be present and flourish as long as people are separated from each other, for whatever reason. Paul's eloquent words speak to us of the pain and futility of alienation, and how barriers we erect between each other really tear down any hope of a unified kingdom of God on earth.

The scripture is as much common sense as it is Holy Writ, because nothing will ever be accomplished as long as people are struggling against each other instead of pulling together. Paul reminds us that as we divide ourselves in often a triumphant way we are really separating ourselves from God, grace, and freedom. For all those who find fault with other races and traditions, this scripture stands in bold contrast and denial.

126

Weekday Problems

Early on, like most Christian boys, I had little interaction with Jews. I was well aware of the jokes, taunts, and ugly remarks about Judaism. Then I became close friends with a boy named David Lefkowitz. David and his parents lovingly treated me like one of their own, scolding when necessary, loving and hugging always.

David's father was a Rabbi in my city. As I grew older and heard the bigoted remarks about Jews, I couldn't reconcile the connection between what I heard and the warm family I knew. Then I learned there are those who will create barriers and divisions without ever really knowing the truth of the people on one side or the other. I was blessed by God to know the Lefkowitz family before becoming old enough to be poisoned with bigotry. To this day I have many Jewish friends whom I count as blessings and inspirations in my life. That early relationship with the Lefkowitz family helped to seal me against prejudice.

*Do you witness boldly against stereotyping and bigotry?

Lessons on Lecturing

The lecturer was so dull that everyone in the lecture hall got up and walked out, except one man in the front row. "Well?" said the speaker, "why haven't you walked out, too?"

"I'm the next speaker," he said.

* * * *

Interrupted by the bell signaling the end of the college class, the professor was annoyed to see the students noisily prepared to leave even though he was still speaking. "Just a moment," he said sternly, "I have a few more pearls to cast."

* * * *

A lecturer on astronomy told his audience that the world would probably end in about seven billion years.

"*How long?*" a man in the third row asked nervously.

"Seven billion years," the lecturer answered.

"Thank goodness!" said the man. "For a minute I thought we only had seven *million* years to get ready."

Social researchers long ago identified one of the most powerful needs of the human community: to feel as though we *belong*. People of all ages will do virtually anything to feel wanted and loved. This can often have tragic results, with various cults and sects that exploit this need and rob them of their freedom to choose their own way. We are continually amazed at the number of intelligent people who will throw away everything in order to feel as though they belong.

One of the driving forces behind the need to belong is that our society has created so many ways to tell people they *don't* belong. People of color have long felt there were places from which they were excluded. Each ethnic minority gets the same impression. Teenagers learn very quickly the cruel demands upon them in order for them to have a sense of belonging to a group. Teen suicides have risen dramatically in the past two decades, and invariably the notes left behind speak of despair because "I just never felt as though I belonged anywhere." From one end of the world to the next, in every culture, there are countless ways in which we divide ourselves and build walls between ourselves and others.

Our scripture reminds us that we who call ourselves God's people cannot be a part of the exclusion game. We cannot use our differences in race, heritage, theology, economics, or any other factor as a leverage to divide ourselves from one another. Our lesson makes it very clear that those of us who call ourselves God's people cannot *really* be God's people as long as we are a part of exclusion and division in any way whatsoever. Every time a barrier is brought down, and those on either side embrace one another, God's cheer rolls across Heaven like claps of thunder. And every time someone stands at a door closed in his face, God's tears wash across the land like a driving thunderstorm.

1. Why did Paul refer to the gentiles as the "uncircumcision"?

For the Hebrews, circumcision was one of the key indicators of someone who had been brought into the faithful community.

2. Paul reminds the church at Ephesus that they were once "separated from Christ and alienated from Israel." What did that mean?

In previous years, the people of the church at Ephesus were not believers, and lived in unfaithful and uncircumcised ways, which marked them as outside the kingdom of God.

3. In that previous state, how does Paul describe Ephesus and all others in a similar situation?

They were referred to as "strangers to the covenants of promise, having no hope and without God in the world."

4. Having reminded the Corinthians they once were alienated from God, Paul now switches to the promise. What does he say?

He tells them that the blood of Christ has now brought them from "far off" to "near" to the heart of God.

5. How does He describe Christ to the young church?

As a unifying power, one who breaks down the dividing walls of hostility.

6. To what does the reference to "enmity" refer?

To the Law that had for so long estranged Jew from Gentile, and imperfect people from the Law's perfection. Christ's cross ended this enmity.

7. What does Paul boldly declare that Christ has abolished?

Jesus had ended the rigid code of commandments and ordinances to which the Jews were bound.

8. What does Paul identify as the central symbol of reconciliation in this scripture?

The Cross, as all persons are brought into oneness through the death and resurrection of Christ.

9. How does Paul inject the work of Christ in reconciliation?

He declares that through Jesus Christ we all have access to the Father in Heaven. No longer are we slaves to an ancient set of rules.

10. To what new identity had Christ brought the new believers in Ephesus?

They are referred to as "no longer strangers and sojourners, but now fellow citizens with the saints and members of the household of God."

Unfortunately, my childhood was saturated with the ugly language of racial segregation in the Old South. I heard racial slurs from my parents and friends, and saw the institutionalized exclusion everywhere. Somehow, although I was brought up in that environment, I knew it was wrong, and I continually talked about it with my parents. They thought their son had gone away to a seminary and gotten some new-fangled liberal education. During the turbulent times of desegregation, I marched in Selma, Alabama, with tens of thousands of believers, and it generated an enormous debate within my home. My parents and I continued to argue about exclusionary attitudes and the sin of discrimination and belittling others on the basis of color, economic standing, or educational achievement. This went on for years.

Then one day, after I had become an active pastor, my uncle was visiting in my home and unleashed his usual flow of racial epithets. To my astonishment my mother looked at him and said "Hugh, we don't talk like that in our house, and I would appreciate it if you would refrain."

He was speechless and responded "Since when?" My mother replied that they had given it years of thought and realized anything that divides people is an offense to God and there is no future in being divisive and ugly. My uncle had a crude name for every ethnic group and every circumstance of humanity except himself. After being quiet for a moment he looked at me and smiled and said to my parents, "I guess since you've now got a preacher man for a son that makes all the difference?"

My mother and father nodded and said, "Yes, it does!"

Somewhere in heaven a roar of approval rolled across the clouds, and God uttered a mighty "Yes!" as another pair of His children broke down the barrier and stepped across it for the first time.

Unit I. God Calls a People

Lesson 1

A Call to Follow God

Genesis 11:27–12:9

ow these are the generations of Terah: Terah begat Abram, Nahor, and Haran; and Haran begat Lot.

28 And Haran died before his father Terah in the land of his nativity, in Ur of the Chaldees.

29 And Abram and Nahor took them wives: the name of Abram's wife was Sarai; and the name of Nahor's wife, Milcah, the daughter of Haran, the father of Milcah, and the father of Iscah.

30 But Sarai was barren; she had no child.

31 And Terah took Abram his son, and Lot the son of Haran his son's son, and Sarai his daughter in law, his son Abram's wife; and they went forth with them from Ur of the Chaldees, to go into the land of Canaan; and they came unto Haran, and dwelt there.

32 And the days of Terah were two hundred and five years: and Terah died in Haran.

12:1 Now the LORD had said unto Abram, Get thee out of thy country, and from thy kindred, and from thy father's house, unto a land that I will shew thee:

2 And I will make of thee a great nation, and I will bless thee, and make thy name great; and thou shalt be a blessing:

3 And I will bless them that bless thee, and curse him that curseth thee: and in thee shall all families of the earth be blessed.

4 So Abram departed, as the LORD spoken unto him; and Lot went with him: and Abram was seventy and five years old when he departed out of Haran.

5 And Abram took Sarai his wife, and Lot his brother's son, and all their substance that they had gathered, and the souls that they had gotten in Haran; and they went forth to go into the land of Canaan; and into the land of Canaan they came.

6 And Abram passed through the land unto the place of Sichem, unto the plain of Moreh. And the Canaanite was then in the land.

7 And the LORD appeared unto Abram, and said, Unto thy seed will I give this land: and there builded he an altar unto the LORD, who appeared unto him.

8 And he removed from thence unto a mountain on the east of Bethel, and pitched his tent, having Bethel on the west, and Hai on the east: and there he builded an altar unto the LORD, and called upon the name of the LORD.

9 And Abram journeyed, going on still toward the south.

Memory Selection
Genesis 12:1
Background Scripture
Genesis 11:27–12:9
Devotional Reading
Jeremiah 1:4-10

This lesson is so fundamental to the entire biblical story that it might be called "Salvation History, Chapter 1." For here we first learn the profound truth that "God is love," and that He wants to draw all people into the circle of divine grace.

But where to start? The ancient world had become repopulated after the Great Flood, with people scattering far and wide. Unfortunately they soon forgot about the One God of Noah, and began to worship idols. So God begins by calling a specific family at a specific place: Ur of Chaldea (provide a map). He would nourish and protect the people of Abram, giving them their own land. Eventually this would enable a universal Redeemer to emerge from them. Ironically, it was in blessing one family in a special way that eventually "all families of the earth shall be blessed" (Gen. 12:3).

ഇൻൽ

Our society began with a prejudice against "class" or status. Titles, position, wealth, and prestige became suspect, while the virtues of "the common man" took root. Religiously, anyone who felt he had a special "call" from God was often suspect.

Ask group members how they feel about God's making a special case of Abraham and his descendants. Was it fair for Him to call them to be His "chosen race"? Did God love them more than the Canaanites, whose land He gave Abram's descendants? Point out that this is simply not true. God called a *particular* people to bless people *in general.* Through Abram God would one day bless everyone—elevating "the common man" to a privileged position indeed.

Teaching Outline	Daily Bible Readings	
I. People of the Call—11:27-32	Mon.	God Calls Isaiah
A. Terah of Ur, 27-28		*Isaiah 6:1-8*
B. Two main characters, 29-30	Tue.	God Calls Jeremiah
C. Journey to Haran, 31-32		*Jeremiah 1:4-10*
II. People of the Blessing—12:1-9	Wed.	Jesus Calls Disciples
A. Abram called to Canaan, 1-5		*Luke 5:4-11*
1. Promises to Abram, 2-3	Thu.	God Calls Saul
2. 'To Canaan-Land!,' 4-5		*Acts 9:1-9*
B. Wandering and worshiping, 6-9	Fri.	Abram and Sarai in Canaan
1. Canaanite sites, 6, 8-9		*Genesis 11:27-32*
2. Renewal of the Covenant, 7	Sat.	God Calls Abram
		Genesis 12:1-9
	Sun.	A Covenant with Abram
		Genesis 15:1-6

Verse by Verse

I. People of the Call—11:27-32

A. Terah of Ur, 27-28

27 Now these are the generations of Terah: Terah begat Abram, Nahor, and Haran; and Haran begat Lot.

28 And Haran died before his father Terah in the land of his nativity, in Ur of the Chaldees.

An older King James Version with pronunciation helps will be useful in this lesson, filled as it is with unfamiliar names. Terah, Abram's father, is the 14th-generation descendant of Shem, son of Noah (11:10). This means that he is a "Semite" (Shemite). Note also, however, that Abram's son Ishmael (16:15), widely viewed as the father of the Arab races, was also a descendant of Shem. Thus, despite their centuries-old conflicts, both Jews and Arabs are "Semites," and descendants of Abram. God will expand Abram's name to Abraham, which means "the father of many nations"—which is more appropriate in view of the promises God will make to him (Gen. 17:5).

Most biblical archeologists believe that the ruins of ancient Ur have been discovered in southern Iraq, about 10 miles west of the Euphrates and halfway between modern Baghdad and the Persian Gulf. Abram was apparently born here, when the Sumerians ruled the area about 2,000 B.C. Archeologists have discovered "Ziggurats" or crude pyramids, burial chambers, and other indications that Abram lived in a land of many gods.

B. Two main characters, 29-30

29 And Abram and Nahor took them wives: the name of Abram's wife was Sarai; and the name of Nahor's wife, Milcah, the daughter of Haran, the father of Milcah, and the father of Iscah.

30 But Sarai was barren; she had no child.

Here the Bible begins to focus on Abram and Sarai (later "Sarah," 17:15) as the key figures in God's plan to bless this family destined to become the Jewish race. Later it will be explained that Sarai was Abraham's half-sister (20:12). Although Sumeria had an advanced code of law, it did not forbid such marriages.

The fact that Sarai was barren is mentioned in order for her later miraculous pregnancy (17:17ff.) to have more weight with the reader. In the ancient world it was considered something of a curse for a wife to be childless; yet God chooses

Sarai for His special blessing.

C. Journey to Haran, 31-32

31 And Terah took Abram his son, and Lot the son of Haran his son's son, and Sarai his daughter in law, his son Abram's wife; and they went forth with them from Ur of the Chaldees, to go into the land of Canaan; and they came unto Haran, and dwelt there.

32 And the days of Terah were two hundred and five years: and Terah died in Haran.

Although we are not told why this family went to Haran, scholars believe it was a part of several mass migrations that will later include the "descent into Egypt" of Abraham and his family. Canaan is at the northwest point of the "Fertile Crescent," the cradle of civilization, while Ur is at its southeast point.

Since Haran was the name of one of Terah's sons (who died in Ur), the appearance of the place-name here, some 800 miles northwest of Ur, suggests the possibility that Terah may have named his late son for the land where he was born, and that he and his family are planning to move to Canaan by way of their old family home. This circular route to the north and then back to the southwest enabled them avoid trying to go due west across the great Arabian desert, which would have been fatal.

II. People of the Blessing—12:1-9
A. Abram called to Canaan, 1

1 Now the LORD had said unto Abram, Get thee out of thy country, and from thy kindred, and from thy father's house, unto a land that I will shew thee:

We know from verse 5 that the land to which God calls Abram is Canaan (now generally Palestine). With the voice of God directing the journey, the migration takes on a theological purpose. The ancient writer seems to pile up difficulties that Abram had to overcome to obey the command: he had to leave his kindred and his father's house, and to go to land he could only trust that God would show him. The courage to make the trek to Canaan will become a major definition of faith for the apostle Paul (Gal. 3:6), and for the Hebrew writer as a definition of faith as obedience (Heb. 11:8-9).

1. Promises to Abram, 2-3

2 And I will make of thee a great nation, and I will bless thee, and make thy name great; and thou shalt be a blessing:

3 And I will bless them that bless thee, and curse him that curseth thee: and in thee shall all families of the earth be blessed.

Again, we are not told why, out of all the people living about 2090 B.C., God chose Abram as the recipient of this stunning promise. We can only surmise that (a) Abram was one of the few people living who was not a polytheist, and could therefore still hear the voice of the true God; and (b) God could foresee that Abraham would be a man of obedience in whom this promise would be safe in order to form the people through whom the Savior of the world would eventually come. The fact of God's foreknowledge saves the doctrine of election from being arbitrary and unfair to others.

2. 'To Canaan-Land!,' 4-5

4 So Abram departed, as the LORD spoken unto him; and Lot went with him: and Abram was seventy and five years old when he departed out of Haran.

5 And Abram took Sarai his wife, and Lot his brother's son, and all their substance that they had gathered, and the souls that they had gotten in Haran; and they went forth to go into the land of Canaan; and into the land of Canaan they came.

Lot is Abram's nephew, the son of Abram's brother Haran who had died back in Ur (11:27-28). Abram seems to have taken his nephew under his wing, an arrangement that finally comes apart in a dispute over grazing territory (13:5-12).

Canaan ("merchant") was a crossroads between Egyptian traders in the south and others in the north. It is possible that Phoenicians, Semites, and a variety of other ethnic groups comprised the land God promised to give Abram. There were many more gods than races in the area, with the general term for a god, "El," common to several Canaanite groups.

B. Wandering and worshiping, 6-9

1. Canaanite sites, 6, 8-9

6 And Abram passed through the land unto the place of Sichem, unto the plain of Moreh. And the Canaanite was then in the land.

8 And he removed from thence unto a mountain on the east of Bethel, and pitched his tent, having Bethel on the west, and Hai on the east: and there he builded an altar unto the LORD, and called upon the name of the LORD.

9 And Abram journeyed, going on still toward the south.

Leaving verse 7 to treat apart from these geographical references, we can sketch broadly the route Abram took in Canaan. Sichem (NIV "Shechem") lay between the mountains of Ebal and Gerizim in central Canaan, while Moreh (or "oak," in the NIV) was probably a place of pagan worship.

Bethel, also in central Palestine, was already a place of worship; its name means literally "house of God." It would become more prominent as a worship center later in Israel's history.

2. Renewal of the Covenant, 7

7 And the LORD appeared unto Abram, and said, Unto thy seed will I give this land: and there builded he an altar unto the LORD, who appeared unto him.

More important than these place names is the fact that Abram moves from north to south in the awareness that he is fulfilling God's call. To reinforce this sense of guidance, God appears to him again and renews His promise to give the land of Canaan to Abram's descendants as an inheritance. In response, Abram does the appropriate thing when we are aware of God's presence: he worships.

135

Evangelistic Emphasis

By any standard, Abram was an old man when God told him to "get moving." We can only imagine the angst of trying to explain, pack, and faithfully follow the call of God. Abram traded home cooking and his bed for camp food and a sleeping bag in the wilderness. He ttraded security for God's promise. When God calls us, our life is going to change.

A faith relationship with Jesus means that all things are going to be made new. We are not the same person we once were. God, in Jesus, has called us all to participate in His new creation. We trade the way our lives are for the promise that in Jesus things are going to change. That is great news that things can change. In Jesus, people can change.

The challenge of this good news is that we can't count on being comfortable. Change is the only constant. Participating with God in creation means what you are I are changing even as we are leading others to exchange the old person for the new creation in Christ.

Now the Lord had said unto Abram, Get thee out of thy country, and from thy kindred, and from thy father's house, unto a land that I will show thee.— *Genesis 12:1*

American culture is following the biblical pattern. We are leaving home later. How many of you still have an adult child living at home, or are raising your grandchildren? We Americans are on the move. The average American moves every 5.2 years. You will stay at the same address eight years if you own your home and an average of 2.1 years if you are a renter.

Still, can you imagine being told to leave everything that brings you security? Could you leave your friends, your family, your country and go where God told you to go? Our world is so interconnected; we really don't understand how radical the call of God was. God told Abram to leave *everything* he knew. Could you do that?

We have confidence that if God has called us to a place He is big enough to keep us in that place. We need to have faith big enough to follow God anyplace.

136

Weekday Problems

A.J. stood up in church and announced that after sixteen years he and his family were moving back to their small hometown. He said, "They are getting ready for us. The town has bought a new traffic light. They are in the process of picking out the colors."

The church laughed, but there was sadness in the announcement. We develop friendships and attachments to our church family. When a family departs, our hearts are sad and our prayers are hopeful that God will richly bless them in their new home.

In your faith community is there a way of welcoming new members and visitors? One can only imagine how lonely Abram felt as he left everything he knew in order to follow the call of God to the new land. He was doing what God wanted him to do and there was blessing in that. Even in following God, human beings need human contact. There might be someone in your congregation this very morning who is new to your community and your church. How are you going to make them feel "at home?"

We, like Abram, are all strangers "just passing through." Still we need the comfort and love from a person like you.

Coming Without a Call

The new minister had just begun his sermon. He was a little nervous, and about 10 minutes into his talk his mind went blank. At least he remembered that in seminary he had been taught that if this happens, a speaker can often get going again by repeating his last point. It was worth a try.

"Behold I come quickly," he said. Still his mind was blank. He tried again, then a third time, but nothing came. Then he tried pounding the pulpit while repeating, "Behold I come quickly." The rickety pulpit swayed and the minister fell forward and landed in the lap of a woman in the first row.

"I'm terribly sorry," the minister apologized.

"That's OK," said the woman, "I should have gotten out of the way. You told me three times you were coming."

This Lesson in Your Life

God called Abram when he was 75 years old. That should give most of us hope that it is never too late for God to do something great with our lives. Moses was 80 when he started leading the people of Israel. David lived to a ripe old age. Age, while important for social security, doesn't mean a thing in the economy of God. We can never say that our work on earth is done.

By extension, we can never say that God is done with us. You and I live in an instant society. We put our popcorn and our oatmeal in the microwave, because we can't wait the five minutes it would take to do it on the stovetop. We have "instant messages" on the Internet. We want instant access to all of our accounts. This is an instant world, and we are glad it only took God six days to create it. Tragically we want instant results with our God. We are looking for a program or a Bible study that can relieve our problem or deepen our faith, but we don't want it to "last too long."

Abram was 75 when God called. Abram was 99 when it was announced that he and Sarah would finally have a male child. Ponder the patience it took Abram to follow God obediently for those 24 years. Ponder the faith it took for that old man to wait until he was even older for the promise of God to be fulfilled.

We have a faith relationship with Jesus Christ. Just like the important relationships of our lives, our faith relationship is not built over night. It can't be strengthened in just one revival. Going to church or Sunday school once in a while will not suffice. Faith is a lifestyle that once begun can't be put aside. We fail to see the power of God fulfilled in our lives because we give up, stop short, or think that our time is passed.

There are no instant faith solutions. Remember the lesson of Abraham the next time you are tempted to look for a quick faith fix. Faith in Jesus Christ grows and changes through a lifetime.

1. Who were the children of Terah?
Terah had three sons listed in Genesis 11. The sons were Abram, Nahor, and Haran.

2. What two facts are given about Terah's son Haran?
Haran died before his father Terah, while they were still in Ur. Haran was also the father of Lot.

3. What other interesting information is given in Genesis 11 about the journey of Terah?
Terah had set out from Ur in the Chaldeas to travel to the land of Canaan. For some reason the Bible says that the journey ended with the family settling in Haran.

4. According to Genesis 11, Terah was an old man when he died in Haran, how old was he?
Genesis 11: 32 says that Terah was 205 years old when he died in Haran.

5. Upon the death of Terah, what command did God give to Abram?
Abram was told, "Go from your country and your kindred and your father's house to the land that I will show you."

6. What promise did God give Abram for following this word?
God promised to "make of Abram a great nation, to bless his name, and to make Abram a blessing to others."

7. What details are given about Abram's departure from Haran?
Abram was 75 years old when he left Haran. Abram took his nephew Lot with him on the journey.

8. Once Abram was on the journey and God reaffirmed the call to him, what was Abram's response?
Abram built an altar to the Lord, who had appeared to him. This altar was built at Shechem.

9. From Shechem where did the journey take Abram?
Abram journeyed from Shechem to the area between Bethel and Ai. He was journeying in stages toward the Negev.

10. Once Abram arrived in the area of Bethel and Ai, what two things did he do?
Abram built an altar to the Lord, and he "invoked" the name of the Lord.

When God calls, things change. We don't always see the connection. Perhaps some of the changes in your life are the signs that God has called you for some specific task. There are times when God's instructions don't seem to make sense to us. This is when faith must apply to the situation.

Three examples from the Old Testament will suffice to illustrate this phenomenon. God instructed the prophet Hosea to get married. God even selected the bride. Her name was Gomer. She was a prostitute, and certainly a very popular one. God certainly picked a strange preacher's wife for his preacher Hosea. God was not concerned about what the ladies society would think about the bride of the minister. He wanted to make a point to His people.

God called Moses to lead the Hebrews out of captivity in Egypt. Moses was well equipped for the task. He had been trained in Pharaoh's courts. He had experience in the wilderness watching sheep. Moses had a personal relationship with God. When the Lord told Moses to go debate Pharaoh about the status of the Hebrew slaves, Moses froze. It seems that he suddenly had a speech problem. God listened patiently, then told Aaron to help Moses by serving as his speech coach.

Abraham is our third illustration of how we need faith to obey the call of God. This man was 75 years old, and yet was told he was going to be the FATHER of a great nation. At a time he should have been playing dominoes at the retirement center, Abraham was bouncing a baby on his knee. I have wondered whether, in the intervening years between the promise and the fulfillment, if Abraham reminded God of his advancing age.

When God calls things are going to change in your life. Faith allows us to follow even when we don't understand or appreciate the changes that are happening.

A Call to Lead Faithfully

1 Samuel 16:1-13

nd the LORD said unto Samuel, How long wilt thou mourn for Saul, seeing I have rejected him from reigning over Israel? fill thine horn with oil, and go, I will send thee to Jesse the Bethlehemite: for I have provided me a king among his sons.

2 And Samuel said, How can I go? if Saul hear it, he will kill me. And the LORD said, Take an heifer with thee, and say, I am come to sacrifice to the LORD.

3 And call Jesse to the sacrifice, and I will shew thee what thou shalt do: and thou shalt anoint unto me him whom I name unto thee.

4 And Samuel did that which the LORD spake, and came to Bethlehem. And the elders of the town trembled at his coming, and said, Comest thou peaceably?

5 And he said, Peaceably: I am come to sacrifice unto the LORD: sanctify yourselves, and come with me to the sacrifice. And he sanctified Jesse and his sons, and called them to the sacrifice.

6 And it came to pass, when they were come, that he looked on Eliab, and said, Surely the LORD's anointed is before him.

7 But the LORD said unto Samuel, Look not on his countenance, or on the height of his stature; because I have refused him: for the LORD seeth not as man seeth; for man looketh on the outward appearance, but the LORD looketh on the heart.

8 Then Jesse called Abinadab, and made him pass before Samuel. And he said, Neither hath the LORD chosen this.

9 Then Jesse made Shammah to pass by. And he said, Neither hath the LORD chosen this.

10 Again, Jesse made seven of his sons to pass before Samuel. And Samuel said unto Jesse, The LORD hath not chosen these.

11 And Samuel said unto Jesse, Are here all thy children? And he said, There remaineth yet the youngest, and, behold, he keepeth the sheep. And Samuel said unto Jesse, Send and fetch him: for we will not sit down till he come hither.

12 And he sent, and brought him in. Now he was ruddy, and withal of a beautiful countenance, and goodly to look to. And the LORD said, Arise, anoint him: for this is he.

13 Then Samuel took the horn of oil, and anointed him in the midst of his brethren: and the Spirit of the LORD came upon David from that day forward. So Samuel rose up, and went to Ramah.

Memory Selection
1 Samuel 16:7

Background Scripture
1 Samuel 16:1-13; 2 Samuel 7:8-16

Devotional Reading
2 Samuel 7:18-29

This lesson continues the theme of God's calling His people by focusing on the call of David to succeed King Saul as ruler of Israel. In the first lesson, God' call was for a people. Here, the call is to a person, one whom God calls to serve Him in a special way.

Israel's first king, Saul, had failed both God and the people. After only two years as king, Saul had usurped the authority of the priest-judge Samuel, and had disobeyed God in other ways that showed that the kingship had made him arrogant. Now it is time to seek out a successor; so God sends Samuel to "ratify" the selection God had already made. This lesson shows that the qualities God saw in a potential leader differed from those that Samuel saw, and challenges us to ask how we can look at leader-qualifications from God's point of view.

ಬಂಧ

Ask group members what qualities they look for in political and/or religious leaders. Are external appearances important? Although the first reaction may be No, point out that especially in a day when leaders' pictures are flashed worldwide by television, certain aspects of one's appearance can sway people's thinking.

Then focus on "internal" qualifications. What values do we want leaders to uphold? Do we want them only to represent the views of those who elect them to the post, or to assert their own views? If the answer is "both," how should they determine which should have preference? Point out that just as Samuel needed God's help to recognize David a Saul's successors, so we need to seek God's will when we choose leaders also.

Teaching Outline	Daily Bible Readings	
I. Time for a Change—1-5	Mon.	God Will Protect *Psalm 3*
A. A prince from Jesse's house, 1	Tue.	A Straight Way *Psalm 5:1-8*
B. Sacrifice as a sign, 2-3		
C. Coming in peace, 4-5	Wed.	Our Rock and Fortress *Psalm 18:1-6*
II. Tests that failed—6-10	Thu.	Saul Rejected as King *1 Samuel 15:10-19*
A. Countenance, and stature, 6-7		
B. Others not selected, 8-10	Fri.	Samuel and Jesse's Sons *1 Samuel 16:1-5*
III. The Right Stuff—11-13	Sat.	David Anointed King *1 Samuel 16:6-13*
A. One more candidate, 11-12		
B. David is anointed, 13	Sun.	David in Saul's Court *1 Samuel 16:14-23*

Verse by Verse

I. Time for a Change—1-5

A. A prince from Jesse's house, 1

1 And the LORD said unto Samuel, How long wilt thou mourn for Saul, seeing I have rejected him from reigning over Israel? fill thine horn with oil, and go, I will send thee to Jesse the Bethlehemite: for I have provided me a king among his sons.

Old Samuel was Israel's last judge. When the people clamored for a king instead, Samuel warned that a king would only oppress them (1 Sam. 8:11-18); but God had already determined to let the people have their way. Now it is time to replace him. God sends Samuel to Bethlehem of Judea (Judah) to fulfill the prophecy that leadership in the kingdom "shall not depart from Judah" (Gen. 49:10).

B. Sacrifice as a sign, 2-3

2 And Samuel said, How can I go? if Saul hear it, he will kill me. And the LORD said, Take an heifer with thee, and say, I am come to sacrifice to the LORD.

3 And call Jesse to the sacrifice, and I will shew thee what thou shalt do: and thou shalt anoint unto me him whom I name unto thee.

Saul is so jealous that Samuel fears he will suspect this mission to Bethlehem is to select a successor. So Samuel takes an animal to sacrifice in Bethlehem, since sacrifices were offered at several places (see 9:12), and this one would not be considered exceptional or subversive.

C. Coming in peace, 4-5

4 And Samuel did that which the LORD spake, and came to Bethlehem. And the elders of the town trembled at his coming, and said, Comest thou peaceably?

5 And he said, Peaceably: I am come to sacrifice unto the LORD: sanctify yourselves, and come with me to the sacrifice. And he sanctified Jesse and his sons, and called them to the sacrifice.

Bethlehem's elders knew that chief priests and prophets could as easily visit wrath on the people for disobedience as pronounce blessings on them. Later, the simple act of transporting the holy ark of the Covenant will result in the death of one who touched it (2 Sam. 6:6-7). The elders must have wondered what similar "holy business" Samuel had in their town; but he not only assures them that his mission is peaceful, but invites them, as well as Jesse and his sons, to the sacrifice.

II. Tests that failed—6-10

143

A. Countenance, and stature, 6-7

6 And it came to pass, when they were come, that he looked on Eliab, and said, Surely the LORD's anointed is before him.

7 But the LORD said unto Samuel, Look not on his countenance, or on the height of his stature; because I have refused him: for the LORD seeth not as man seeth; for man looketh on the outward appearance, but the LORD looketh on the heart.

We can imagine that Eliab may have been first in the "reception line" since he was the eldest (17:28), and custom often gave deference to the eldest son. Or he may simply have been the first to catch Samuel's eye because he was tall and handsome. Fortunately, as a prophet as well as a priest and judge, Samuel has access to God's own voice, which quickly reminds him that Elihu's outward qualities are not as important as qualities of the heart, which God can see more easily than persons.

B. Others not selected, 8-10

8 Then Jesse called Abinadab, and made him pass before Samuel. And he said, Neither hath the LORD chosen this.

9 Then Jesse made Shammah to pass by. And he said, Neither hath the LORD chosen this.

10 Again, Jesse made seven of his sons to pass before Samuel. And Samuel said unto Jesse, The LORD hath not chosen these.

One by one, Jesse's other sons are paraded before the king-maker Samuel. We can well imagine that Jesse's experience with these seven sons, such as his knowledge of their values and behavior, or their willingness to work, gave him the understandable expectation that one or another would be chosen for whatever mission Samuel had in mind. Yet one by one they also fail to trigger the approving voice of God in Samuel's mind.

III. The Right Stuff—11-13

A. One more candidate, 11-12

11 And Samuel said unto Jesse, Are here all thy children? And he said, There remaineth yet the youngest, and, behold, he keepeth the sheep. And Samuel said unto Jesse, Send and fetch him: for we will not sit down till he come hither.

12 And he sent, and brought him in. Now he was ruddy, and withal of a beautiful countenance, and goodly to look to. And the LORD said, Arise, anoint him: for this is he.

Perplexed, Samuel asks a natural question about other sons. Yes, as it turns out, there is one more. Perhaps he has not been invited because, as the youngest, he is not significant enough; or because he was too far away with the sheep to be sent for; or because he would have brought to this sacred ceremony the smell of sheep upon him.

However, the sacrificial ceremony included a feast, and Samuel says that it will not begin until this last son is brought to the table; so David is finally summoned. Although, as God has said, He looks on the heart to qualify a person as a leader, David also has external attractions. "Ruddy" probably implies a bronzed complexion, which would have been inescapable as a sheepherder; or possibly red or auburn hair. Although David is only about age 15, or even younger, God finally indicates to Samuel that here is His choice to succeed King Saul.

Anointing with oil was a common way of designating or "ordaining" a special servant of God. The root of this word also gives us the word "Messiah," which is why Jesus will be called "the Christ," or "the Anointed One" (cp. Acts 4:26 in the KJV and the NIV).

B. David is anointed, 13

13 Then Samuel took the horn of oil, and anointed him in the midst of his brethren: and the Spirit of the LORD came upon David from that day forward. So Samuel rose up, and went to Ramah.

We can imagine the range of emotions running through Jesse and his other sons as Samuel anoints David. There must have been feelings of both pride and jealousy as this, the youngest of all, is publicly appointed for some special godly service, the nature of which is a mystery to them.

Old Samuel could have not foreseen the far-reaching effects of the impact of this "call," which was ratified by the Spirit of the Lord. Although we are not told here exactly how this was manifest, the scene recalls the descent of the Spirit in the form of a dove on Jesus at His baptism. Perhaps the Spirit endowed David with unusual physical strength, enabling him to defeat the lions that attacked his flocks, as well as the giant Goliath (see 17:34-37). The Spirit may also have in fact been the power that enabled David, after he succeeded Saul as king, to lead a period of expansion that extended the borders of Israel as never before or since.

The Spirit of the Lord will also play a powerful role in David's life in the area of prophecy. When he flees from one of Saul's spells of jealous rage, he is able to prophesy with a company of prophets by this indwelling Spirit to a degree so powerful that when Saul sends soldiers to capture him, and finally goes himself, they return without David but with his apparently contagious spirit of prophecy! (see 19:18-24).

Finally, the Spirit of the Lord became intimately involved with David in the writing of proverbs and psalms (1 Kings 4:32), many of which are preserved in the book of Psalms. This collection, combined with others by a writer called Asaph, was apparently brought together while Israel was captive in Babylon in the sixth and seventh centuries B.C., and became so important in Israel's worship when the people were allowed to return and rebuild Jerusalem and its Temple, that it became known as "The Hymnbook of the Second Temple."

Evangelistic Emphasis

If you are starting a race of people, select a young man. If you plan on picking a king for the people, you should pick an older man. It is good that God does not listen to human wisdom and understanding before He acts. God called a man to leave his home and to start a nation when he was 75 years old. God chose a king for his people from the youngest of Jesse's sons. God does not judge people and situations the same way we do.

God looks to the heart of a person. This good news has a down side. We tend to judge honest, generous, and wealthy people as being "Christian." Because of their external virtues we assume they have a heart that belongs to Christ. The opposite may as easily be true.

The promise of faith is that when we begin a relationship with Jesus we are given a new heart. In God's kingdom we are never judged by the successes or failures we might have in life. We are judged by whether we have let Christ into our lives or kept Him out.

ॐ

Memory Selection

Look not on his countenance, or on the height of his stature, because I have refused him; for the LORD seeth not as a man seeth; for man looketh on the outward appearance, but the LORD looketh on the heart.—*1 Samuel 16:7*

This verse brings a word of comfort to anyone who has been picked last on the playground, or overlooked because of his or her skin color, or denied an opportunity because he was from the "wrong side of the tracks." The verse is clear that God is not concerned about our Body Mass Index. He is not interested in our pedigree or our income. God is not impressed by our address. God looks to our heart as the source of our character.

The verse has a challenge for us as well. If God does not judge individuals on the basis of externals, should we? We are God-like when we learn to look beyond what is on the outside of a person and see what God sees.

146

Weekday Problems

A boy scout came into a troop meeting with a black eye. "How did you get that black eye?" the troop leader asked.

"I was trying to help an old lady across the street," the scout answered. "But she didn't want to go!"

David was made the leader of Israel at a tender young age. His only experience was leading and tending sheep. Looking at all the things that matter to you and me, David was a poor choice for a leadership role.

In your faith community, how are your leaders selected? Who is leading your Sunday school class? Too often in the church we find the willing and turn them loose with whatever they are willing to do. Of course we have standards to determine who might be willing. They have to have been members of the church forever. They must contribute generously. They can't disturb the way "it has always been done." If they meet our guidelines, they might be worthy of asking if they are willing.

*How many people are we excluding because we don't see them as God does?

Words from the World of Work

Teenager to business tycoon: What's the most important secret of your success?

Tycoon: Work, son, hard work and long hours.

Teen, obviously disappointed: OK, what's the second most important secret?

* * * *

God gives every little bird its food, but He doesn't just throw it into the nest.

* * * *

School counselor: If you work hard in school you'll be able to get an eight-hour-a-day job.

Student: Yeah, and from there maybe I can get to where I own the business and get to work 12 or 14 hours a day like my dad.

One is reminded of the words that Sherlock Holmes is quoted as saying, "My dear Watson, you see, but you do not observe."

How many of us are "seeing" but not really "observing" because we aren't seeing from a spiritual perspective?

We are taught to use our powers of observation and then use common sense to make our evaluations. Common sense is a vague way of determining what God would have us to do. Common sense means that we are being duped.

Think about all the common sense things that have turned out not to have too much sense in them. Common sense would tell us that eating a low fat diet would make us "low fat" people. The last statistics available reported that 60 percent of Americans are overweight. What good is this low fat food doing us? Of course to make something low fat the industry puts sugar into it. Since when have you heard that sugar will make you skinny?

Common sense said that a stock market at 10,000 points would go no place but up. How are your stocks doing now? When a politician answers a question saying, "it's common sense," you are about to be taken. Often people elected to an office leave their common sense at home, in favor of the political process.

When you are being appealed to on the basis of "common sense," mark this down: You are being manipulated! Aside from the fact that Enlightenment notions of "common sense" have been disproved, something even larger is at stake.

Simplistic common sense may constitute the world's most dangerous peerceptual illusion. Common sense is often uncommonly deceptive, and should always be considered with a stern admonition: BEWARE!

God doesn't use common sense. He looks into the heart.

STRAIGHT

1. What did God tell Samuel about the continuation of Saul as the king of Israel?
God told Samuel that He had rejected Saul from being the king of Israel.

2. What instructions did God give to Samuel about anointing another king of Israel?
Samuel was told to fill his horn with oil and go anoint as king a son of Jesse the Bethlehemite.

3. What reservation did Samuel expresss about following the Lord's word?
He said he was afraid that Saul would kill Samuel when he heard that he had anointed someone else to be king.

4. What instructions did the Lord give to Samuel about determining the next king of Israel?
Samuel was to take a heifer for a sacrifice. He was to invite Jesse and his sons to take part in this sacrifice and the Lord would show Samuel the chosen one.

5. What other of Jesse's sons are mentioned as not chosen by the Lord?
The other sons of Jesse who are mentioned in this passage were Eliab, Abinadab, and Shammah.

6. Where was David while Jesse was parading the other brothers before Samuel?
David, the youngest, was out in the field keeping the sheep.

7. How was David described?
He was ruddy, which means a red or freckled complexion, had beautiful eyes, and was handsome.

8. When the Lord commanded Samuel to anoint David, what happened?
David was anointed with oil in the presence of his brothers and the Spirit of the Lord came mightily upon David.

9. What question did David ask as he began the prayer recorded in 2 Samuel?
David said, "Who am I, and what is my house that you have brought me thus far?"

10. What events led up to David praying the prayer recorded in 2 Samuel?
David's prayer came as his reign in Jerusalem was firmly established. His enemies were defeated and the Ark of the Covenant had been returned to Jerusalem.

When God calls, it usually doesn't involve "common sense." We have seen that twice already. God called the old man Abraham to father a nation. He called the young boy David to be the king of a nation. Common sense would dictate that God do something much different. Sometimes our logic leaves us in trouble.

There was a time when I was a bachelor preacher. I had used every paper plate in the house and started using the real dishes. I had collected quite a stack of dishes that needed to be washed. I'm not sure of the wisdom of having a dishwasher in the same house with a bachelor, but I had one.

I dutifully loaded the dishwasher, squeezing every dirty dish I owned into that machine. Proud that I had accomplished that complex task, I looked for the dishwashing detergent. I opened every cabinet in the kitchen. I had no detergent. I had my common sense. Common sense told me that if you washed dishes in the sink with Joy dishwashing liquid, one could certainly wash dishes in the dishwasher with the same liquid. I filled the little cup with dishwashing liquid, turned it to "hyper clean" and went upstairs to read my Bible. I made several discoveries in the next few minutes.

The first discovery was that dishwashing liquid placed in a dishwasher creates voluminous amounts of bubbles. When I walked back into the kitchen I had bubbles at least a foot deep all over the kitchen floor. The second thing I discovered was that it took several cycles to get all of the liquid residue out of the dishwasher. My common sense allowed me to make quite a mess.

I'm glad that God works in His way. Although His calling and direction might not appeal to my common sense, I can trust that He has made a perfect plan for my life. God sees beyond what is to what might be. My response is to follow his direction with faith.

Lesson 3

A Call to Respond

Matthew 1:17-25

So all the generations from Abraham to David are fourteen generations; and from David until the carrying away into Babylon are fourteen generations; and from the carrying away into Babylon unto Christ are fourteen generations.

18 Now the birth of Jesus Christ was on this wise: When as his mother Mary was espoused to Joseph, before they came together, she was found with child of the Holy Ghost.

19 Then Joseph her husband, being a just man, and not willing to make her a publick example, was minded to put her away privily.

20 But while he thought on these things, behold, the angel of the Lord appeared unto him in a dream, saying, Joseph, thou son of David, fear not to take unto thee Mary thy wife: for that which is conceived in her is of the Holy Ghost.

21 And she shall bring forth a son, and thou shalt call his name JESUS: for he shall save his people from their sins.

22 Now all this was done, that it might be fulfilled which was spoken of the Lord by the prophet, saying,

23 Behold, a virgin shall be with child, and shall bring forth a son, and they shall call his name Emmanuel, which being interpreted is, God with us.

24 Then Joseph being raised from sleep did as the angel of the Lord had bidden him, and took unto him his wife:

25 And knew her not till she had brought forth her firstborn son: and he called his name JESUS.

Memory Selection
Matthew 1:24

Background Scripture
Matthew 1

Devotional Reading
Luke 1:26-32

The perennial interest in the story of the birth of Jesus is met in this lesson by retelling "the greatest story ever told" through the eyes of the Gospel writer Matthew. Most birth stories rightly focus on the mother, who must bear the burden of the physical pain along with the incomparable joy of "meeting" the life she has been nurturing within her body for nine months. Matthew, however, also pays special attention to Joseph, Jesus' human "step-father," who was confronted with an unusual emotional crisis, and the question of how to deal with the pregnancy of his unmarried betrothed.

A broader application of this lesson can be made by challenging members of your group to ask themselves how they respond when God calls them in ways that may be unusual or even socially unacceptable.

ഇാരു

One way to introduce this familiar story in a new way is to lead a brief discussion on the group's views of Joseph, Jesus' human father.

Facilitate the discussion by asking such question as: How would Mary have been viewed in the small-town Jewish culture in which she lived when she found herself pregnant but unmarried? What choices would Joseph have been faced with? How might familiarity with the Old Testament Scriptures help this couple? On the other hand, what questions would Old Testament prophecies raise in their minds?

Teaching Outline	Daily Bible Readings
I. Joseph's Challenge—1:17-19	Mon. Our Powerful God *Isaiah 40:3-11*
A. Ancestry, 17	Tue. Sign of Reassurance *Isaiah 7:10-17*
B. Betrothal and pregnancy, 18	
D. Plans for divorce, 19	Wed. An Angel Speaks to Mary *Luke 1:26-38*
II. The Angel's Reassurance—20-21	Thu. Jesus, of Abraham's Seed *Matthew 1:1-6a*
A. 'Fear not!', 20a	
B. Miraculous conception, 20b	Fri. Jesus, David's Descendant *Matthew 1:6b-11*
C. Jesus the Savior, 21	Sat. Jesus' Ancestry Through Joseph *Matthew 1:12-16*
III. 'Emmanuel'—22-23	
IV. Joseph's Obedience—24-25	Sun. Jesus Is Born and Named *Matthew 1:17-25*

Verse by Verse

I. Joseph's Challenge—1:17-19
A. Ancestry, 17

17 So all the generations from Abraham to David are fourteen generations; and from David until the carrying away into Babylon are fourteen generations; and from the carrying away into Babylon unto Christ are fourteen generations.

This verse summarizes Matthew's version of the genealogy of Jesus. It differs from Luke's (Luke 3:23-38) most remarkably in its schematic division of Jesus' ancestors into three groups of 14 "generations." There were more names in Jesus' lineage than Matthew included; but he selectively names them in this way for two reasons. (1) Because three and seven (x 2 = 14) are numbers that signified *completion* in Jewish tradition, and Matthew is concerned to show that the times are completed for the arrival of the Messiah. (2) Matthew groups Jesus' ancestry to emphasize that He is the descendant of "David the king" (v. 6).

Of the several current perceptions of just what kind of Messiah would come, Matthew emphasizes his *kingly* nature. He shows that Jesus fulfills God's promise to David that he would always have an heir on the throne (2 Sam. 7:16).

B. Betrothal and pregnancy, 18

18 Now the birth of Jesus Christ was on this wise: When as his mother Mary was espoused to Joseph, before they came together, she was found with child of the Holy Ghost.

Matthew wastes no time admitting openly that the mother of the Messiah was found pregnant before she married her betrothed, Joseph. His Jewish readers must have felt the full force of the truth that the action of God, not human goodness, is required to bring the Messiah to live among us.

The word translated "espoused" is more accurately translated "pledged to be married" (NIV). This was during the second stage of Jewish marriage tradition of the day, the *betrothal*, which lasted for a year. (The first stage was the *announcement*, and the third the actual *wedding ceremony*.) Matthew is clear that the pregnancy is discovered "before they came together," or had sexual relations.

D. Plans for divorce, 19

19 Then Joseph her husband, being a just man, and not willing to make her a publick example, was minded to put her away privily.

Mary's pre-marital pregnancy gave Joseph the legal right to appear with Mary before a public court and obtained a divorce by pronouncing three times, *"I divorce you!"* Matthew calls Joseph a "just" man for declining to make such a public spectacle out of the divorce, but instead literally to "loosen" or "release" her ("put her away") privately. This shows that the betrothal period in the three-stage Jewish marriage was as legally binding as a marriage. Reading between the lines, since Joseph was "just" enough to save Mary from public embarrassment, we can also imagine that he was saddened at what he considered the necessity to do so.

II. The Angel's Reassurance—20-21

A. 'Fear not!', 20a

20a But while he thought on these things, behold, the angel of the Lord appeared unto him in a dream, saying, Joseph, thou son of David, fear not to take unto thee Mary thy wife:

The angel's first words, "Fear not . . ." challenges Joseph to have the courage to face the inevitable social censure that would come from being the father of a child that an unmarried woman had by someone else. Addressing Joseph as a "son of David" may have had the additional force of showing what an honor it would be for Joseph to be in the Davidic line that brought the Messiah to earth—if he can summon the courage of a King David.

B. Miraculous conception, 20b

20b for that which is conceived in her is of the Holy Ghost.

Another reason Joseph should make Mary his wife is that she has not been a "loose woman"; she is pregnant by the miracle of the virgin birth. Just as "the seed is the Word of God" (Matt. 8:11), which comes through the Spirit, so the seed was planted in Mary's womb by the same Spirit.

This miracle is considered by many to have been predicted in Isaiah 7:14: "Behold a virgin shall conceive, and bear a son." Opponents of this view point out that the Hebrew word *almah* here can mean simply "young woman," whether she is married or not. However, the Septuagint (the earliest Greek translation of the Old Testament), translates *almah* by the word *parthenos,* "chaste" or "virginal," which is also used in Matthew 1:23. Apparently both the translators of the Septuagint and Matthew understood the Isaiah text to be predicting this very event.

C. Jesus the Savior, 21

21 And she shall bring forth a son, and thou shalt call his name JESUS: for he shall save his people from their sins.

The angel proceeds to instruct Joseph as though knowing that he will change his mind about divorcing Mary. She will bear a son which, as surrogate father, Joseph has the authority to name (although at the angel's specific direction; see Luke 2:21). His name "Jesus" appropriately means "savior" or "deliverer." Our spelling comes from the Greek *Iesous*; in Hebrew, He would have been called "Yeshuah," which translates to the English "Joshua." So the

154

Messiah's human name will reflect a previous "deliverer" of Israel—Joshua, the mighty man of war who led Israel during the early days of the Conquest of Canaan. However, the Babe will also have a divine name.

III. 'Emmanuel'—22-23

22 Now all this was done, that it might be fulfilled which was spoken of the Lord by the prophet, saying,

23 Behold, a virgin shall be with child, and shall bring forth a son, and they shall call his name Emmanuel, which being interpreted is, God with us.

Throughout Matthew's Gospel, the author shows a special concern that Jesus' life and teaching be shown to be in direct fulfillment of Old Testament prophecy. Thus, as indicated above, the author supports the claim of the angel that Mary is with child "of the Holy Ghost" by citing Isaiah 7:14.

Here, the emphasis is not so much on the miraculous nature of the birth as on the miraculous nature of the Incarnation. Isaiah, and now Matthew, affirm that the promised Messiah will also be known as Emmanuel; and Matthew obligingly tells his non-Jewish readers that the name means "God with us." It is unfortunate that debates on whether the virgin birth could "really happen" sometimes obscure the equally marvelous claim that God came to earth in the form of her baby. This is the very basis of the Good News. No longer need we feel alone in a universe of chance, or abandoned in times of stress, illness, or strife: *God is with us!*

IV. Joseph's Obedience—24-25

24 Then Joseph being raised from sleep did as the angel of the Lord had bidden him, and took unto him his wife:

25 And knew her not till she had brought forth her firstborn son: and he called his name JESUS.

Now Matthew proceeds to show that another reason for calling Joseph a "just" man is that he simply does what God bids him to do. Against all criticism and misunderstanding, whether from friends or family, he marries the young Mary even though the child she is carrying he is not of his seed.

Verse 25 uses a common biblical "euphemism" (lit. "nice saying"), with Matthew choosing to say that Joseph and Mary did not "know" each other while actually meaning that they did not have sexual union (see the NIV). It is as though Matthew wants the last word in the story to be yet another defiant affirmation against all doubters that the Spirit, not a human being, planted the seed in Mary's womb. He also shows Joseph's obedience in giving the child the human name "Jesus." As God-with-us, He is known as Emmanuel, and as Messiah, or "Christ." Of course the truth must also be maintained that the Savior was not only superhuman, but human—as the early creeds affirmed, both "very God and very man."

Evangelistic Emphasis

We have all shifted into the Christmas mode. Many people right now are facing the impossible task of finishing their Christmas shopping. There are too many names on their list. Other people have little resources to participate in the materialistic side of Christmas. They are finding it impossible to feel good in this time of material excess. If Christmas is judged by the presents under their trees their Christmas is very sparse.

There are all kinds of impossible situations associated with Christmas. Traffic becomes a nightmare at the local Wal Mart. Temporary Christmas employees are no help when trying to shop. The crowds that push and shove really detract from the spirit of "peace on earth."

Christmas seems like an impossible season. It is. It was impossible for a child to be born of a virgin. It was incredible that Joseph married Mary. It was inconceivable that God would come to earth as a fragile baby.

God chose the impossible to remind us that all the "impossibilities" of our lives such as love, forgiveness, and eternal life are *possible* in the person of Jesus.

ഏരജ

Memory Selection

Then Joseph, being raised from sleep, did as the angel of the Lord had bidden him, and took unto him his wife.—*Matthew 1:24*

Maybe we could learn a lesson about making important decisions from this word about Joseph. He had a tough decision to make. His first input was to believe that Mary was carrying a child conceived of the Holy Spirit. His second input was to believe that Mary was not the kind of girl he thought she was. Those were the factors figuring into the decision Joseph had to make. He had to decide whether or not to marry Mary.

Joseph did a wise thing. He decided to "sleep on it."

When faced with crucial decisions that will influence the rest of our lives, we might need to "sleep on it" too. Often God sends clear answers to us if we will learn to wait on Him. Because Joseph took his time in making a decision, he allowed time for the Holy Spirit to guide. What about you? Do you need to "sleep on" a decision you face?

Weekday Problems

Billy was baffled at the behavior of his bride. They began married life happily enough, but recently Sheila was exhibiting some uncharacteristically poor decision-making traits. She was shopping all the time, and running up the credit card bills faster than Billy could keep them paid. She was spending several evenings a week out with the "girls." She was not taking care of her children, those tasks falling to Billy.

Although he was a patient and loving man, Billy found himself at the end of his rope in his pastor's office one day. He confessed that he was angry with Sheila because of how she was behaving. He had confronted her, and pleaded with her. He had taken the credit cards away from her, but she got more. He faced a decision whether his children were better off living in an environment that was hostile, or whether they would be better off raised by him alone. He told his pastor he was ready to decide that very moment. His hesitation was in not knowing what decision would be best for his children.

*If you were Billy's pastor what advice would you give?

*What does the story of Joseph say to people with Billy's problem?

Other 'Christmas Carols'

As fits the holy Christmas birth,
   Be this, good friends, our carol still—
Be peace on earth, be peace on earth,
   To men of gentle will.
                  —William Makepeace Thackeray
                 * * * *

At Christmas play and make good cheer,
For Christmas comes but once a year.
                 —Thomas Tusser
                 * * * *

After all, Christmas is but a big love affair to remove the wrinkles of the year with kindly remembrances.—*John Wanamaker*
                 * * * *

The family, the story, the carol and the gift. These four . . . I do believe that quite a case can be made for a thoroughly enjoyable Christmas . . . using only these four ingredients.—*John D. Tate,* in *The Christian Century*

This Lesson in Your Life

In Christian art, Joseph, when he appeared at all, is often depicted as a very old man, apparently too old to be tempted by the lovely young Mary. But after the Counter Reformation there arose a cult of St. Joseph that resulted in artistic representations of Joseph as a much younger man, as a true member of the "family." Even so, pictures of Joseph holding the Christ child are still quite rare. The only non-baroque representation is Michelangelo's "Doni Tondo." A much later painting by Carl Muller, depicts a toddler-sized Jesus being cuddled by Joseph. But in the vast canvas of religious art, portrayals of Joseph and Jesus are tragically scarce. There is a warning here for our times.

This text is about fathers.

The story starts with our heavenly Father who will do anything, even the impossible, to provide for our safe return back to Him. God sent his son Jesus to be born of a virgin. Jesus is God the Father's gift to humanity. The lesson starts with a loving heavenly Father.

Joseph becomes the adoptive father in the story. He is the man who has to make the tough decisions. He is the man who must listen to the speculation of the busybodies in Nazareth. Joseph is the one that must make a place for the Savior to be born. He is present and active in this story. He is loving and faithful.

The challenge before us is like the religious art depicting Joseph. Too many fathers are absent from their children's lives. That has caused a world of problems today. Even fathers who live in the home are often emotionlly absent. The biblical image of a man as the head of the house is not a right—it is a responsibility. I hope we learn how to be a father, from the pattern of Joseph.

GETTING THE FACTS STRAIGHT

1. Does the genealogy of Jesus have an encouraging word for women?
The genealogy of Jesus lists the names of three women and mentions another woman.

2. What do the three women listed in the genealogy of Jesus seem to have in common?
They were considered outcasts, according to Jewish tradition.

3. What are the three large historical divisions in the genealogy of Jesus?
The first division covered the time from Abraham to David, the second from Solomon to the Babylonian captivity, the third from the exile to the birth of Jesus.

4. What was the relationship between Mary and Joseph at the time of Jesus' birth?
Mary and Joseph were engaged to each other. They were not yet married.

5. When Joseph found out that Mary was pregnant, what was his first impulse?
At first he decided to divorce Mary. He planned to do this privately so the event would not embarrass Mary.

6. What happened to Joseph to make him change his mind about divorce?
He had a dream in which the angel of the Lord appeared to him and gave instructions as to what was happening, and how Joseph was to respond.

7. What was significant about the name "Jesus"?
The name Jesus means "the Lord saves." His named described His reason for coming to earth.

8. According to Matthew, the birth of Jesus fulfilled a prediction made by what prophet?
Jesus' birth was prophesied by Isaiah, in Isaiah 7:14.

9. According to the prophet, what would be the name of the child born to Mary?
His name would be Immanuel, which means "God with us."

10. After Joseph woke from his dream, what did God tell him to do?
Joseph was told to take Mary as his wife. He married her and named the child born to her, Jesus.

In his devotional autobiography, Bishop Woodie W. White compares our culture's dominant image of the Brady Bunch nuclear family with the dominant reality of a nuclear-free family.

"In a scene often repeated in football contests, the ball carrier receives the ball and with good blocking, skillful movement and lightning speed, dashes by opposing players to score a touchdown. Cheers come from the fans and congratulations from teammates. Nearly out of breath, he goes to the sidelines and sits on the bench. The television cameras focus a close-up shot of the hard-breathing hero. He looks directly into the camera, aware that he is the center of attention of millions of television watchers, and raises his hand.

"'Hi, Mom!' he says. Almost never does he say, 'Hi, Dad!' or make an effort to be inclusive by saying, 'Hi, Mom and Dad!'

"'Rarely are songs or poems written about fathers. Frequently portrayed as not too bright or the butt of jokes, they have also a more negative characterization: stern, sometimes tyrannical figure to be feared.

"Unfortunately fathers are absent in many communities."

The Christmas story gives us the example of two loving fathers: God, the heavenly Father who showed His love for us by sending Jesus to be born of Mary, and Joseph, the father who adopted Jesus as his very own son and raised Him right.

Lesson 4

A Call To Hope

Luke 2:22-38

nd when the days of her purification according to the law of Moses were accomplished, they brought him to Jerusalem, to present him to the Lord;

23 (As it is written in the law of the Lord, Every male that openeth the womb shall be called holy to the Lord;)

24 And to offer a sacrifice according to that which is said in the law of the Lord, A pair of turtledoves, or two young pigeons.

25 And, behold, there was a man in Jerusalem, whose name was Simeon; and the same man was just and devout, waiting for the consolation of Israel: and the Holy Ghost was upon him.

26 And it was revealed unto him by the Holy Ghost, that he should not see death, before he had seen the Lord's Christ.

27 And he came by the Spirit into the temple: and when the parents brought in the child Jesus, to do for him after the custom of the law,

28 Then took he him up in his arms, and blessed God, and said,

29 Lord, now lettest thou thy servant depart in peace, according to thy word:

30 For mine eyes have seen thy salvation,

31 Which thou hast prepared before the face of all people;

32 A light to lighten the Gentiles, and the glory of thy people Israel.

33 And Joseph and his mother marvelled at those things which were spoken of him.

34 And Simeon blessed them, and said unto Mary his mother, Behold, this child is set for the fall and rising again of many in Israel; and for a sign which shall be spoken against;

35 (Yea, a sword shall pierce through thy own soul also,) that the thoughts of many hearts may be revealed.

36 And there was one Anna, a prophetess, the daughter of Phanuel, of the tribe of Aser: she was of a great age, and had lived with an husband seven years from her virginity;

37 And she was a widow of about fourscore and four years, which departed not from the temple, but served God with fastings and prayers night and day.

38 And she coming in that instant gave thanks likewise unto the Lord, and spake of him to all them that looked for redemption in Jerusalem.

Memory Selection
Luke 2:30-31

Background Scripture
Luke 2:22-38

Devotional Reading
Psalm 71:1-8

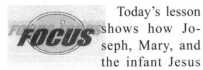

Today's lesson shows how Joseph, Mary, and the infant Jesus took part in an important ritual that provided a fitting transition from the Old Covenant to the New, and signalled boundless hope for the years ahead. (It is essential to remind your class that Jesus was "made under the Law" [Gal. 4:4], and that He lived under it or fulfilled it completely.)

This emphasis also provides a good opportunity for you to discuss the importance of ceremonies and observances in the lives of group members. In the context of the church, baptism and communion are important examples. In the family, we celebrate birthdays, and we mark our nation's birthday with a "ritual" on July 4. For suggestions for leading such a discussion, see the following section.

Lead into this study by inviting group members to imagine the emotion of Joseph and Mary as they took the infant Jesus to the Temple to "present him to the Lord" (Luke 2:22), and to offer the sacrifice required by the Law of Moses. Ask why such ceremonies stir the soul. Although we sometimes hear "rituals" dismissed as referring to dead routine, some are anything but dead. Try telling a loving couple who are celebrating their 50th wedding anniversary that "It's just a cold, dead ritual"! In what other ways do "rites of passage" speak hope to the heart?

What other family, national, or religious ceremonies are important? How can we keep them alive and fresh, avoiding the "dead routine" syndrome? On the other hand, can external ritual actually get in the way of internal dedication?

Teaching Outline	Daily Bible Lessons
I. Sacrifice at the Temple—22-24	Mon. The Lord Is My Hope *Psalm 71:1-8*
II. Simeon Sees the Light—25-32	Tue. Declaring New Things *Isaiah 42:1-9*
A. Promise of a sign, 25-26	Wed. The Birth of Jesus *Luke 2:1-7*
B. Fulfillment of the promise, 27-29	Thu. A Choir of Angels *Luke 2:8-14*
C. A light to the Gentiles, 30-32	Fri. Shepherds See Jesus *Luke 2:15-20*
III. Sign of Hope and of Sorrow—33-35	Sat. Jesus Taken to the Temple *Luke 2:22-26*
IV. Statement from a Prophetess—36-38	Sun. Simeon and Anna's Praise *Luke 2:27-38*

Verse by Verse

I. Sacrifice at the Temple—22-24

22 And when the days of her purification according to the law of Moses were accomplished, they brought him to Jerusalem, to present him to the Lord;

23 (As it is written in the law of the Lord, Every male that openeth the womb shall be called holy to the Lord;)

24 And to offer a sacrifice according to that which is said in the law of the Lord, A pair of turtledoves, or two young pigeons.

As faithful Jews, Joseph and Mary had Jesus given the universal Jewish mark of circumcision after He was eight days old (vs. 21). The scene of His having also been named at this event would later become the basis for "christening" even in many Christian traditions.

Now, Jesus' parents fulfill an additional requirement under the Law of Moses. The firstborn of both people and domesticated animals was to be dedicated to the Lord (Exod. 13:2). This dedication was marked by the sacrifice of a lamb and a turtledove or pigeon, or, for poorer parents, a pair of turtledoves or pigeons (Lev. 12:6-8). Apparently this sacrifice served (a) as a substitute for literally sacrificing the newborn; (b) to symbolize the washing or cleansing of the mother from any disease

in the flow of blood from the birth (see Lev. 12:4); and (c) to symbolize the "death" of any sinfulness that the parents may have associated with the sexual act that produced the child. Unknowingly, Jews making such blood sacrifices also prefigured the ultimate sacrifice, the shedding of the blood of God's only-begotten Son, whom Simeon is now privileged to see with his own eyes.

II. Simeon Sees the Light—25-32

A. Promise of a sign, 25-26

25 And, behold, there was a man in Jerusalem, whose name was Simeon; and the same man was just and devout, waiting for the consolation of Israel: and the Holy Ghost was upon him.

26 And it was revealed unto him by the Holy Ghost, that he should not see death, before he had seen the Lord's Christ.

God apparently arranges for two representatives of the Old Covenant, a prophet and a prophetess, to put their own seal of approval on this scene as providing a true glimpse of the coming of the Messiah. The "consolation of Israel" was a Messianic hope derived from Isaiah 40:1, where Isaiah quotes God as saying "Comfort ye my people."

Simeon's perception that this Child finally signals the Messianic

163

Age is not just speculation. It is the result of the Holy Spirit's constant dwelling in this aged servant of God. The revelation of the significance of the Child is no doubt related to Simeon's being "just and devout," although it was ultimately an act of God's grace—not only for Simeon's benefit but for all time.

B. Fulfillment of the promise, 27-29

27 And he came by the Spirit into the temple: and when the parents brought in the child Jesus, to do for him after the custom of the law,

28 Then took he him up in his arms, and blessed God, and said,

29 Lord, now lettest thou thy servant depart in peace, according to thy word:

Coming to the Temple by the express direction of the Spirit, Simeon meets the Holy Family there. They have come to fulfill "the custom of the law," probably meaning to make the prescribed five-shekel payment (Num. 18:15). Simeon seizes the moment to thank or "bless" God in a praise song that has come to be called the *Nunc Dimittis*, after its opening words in Latin. After being honored with the privilege of seeing the long-awaited Messiah, the faithful old Israelite is ready to move on in peace to the next world.

C. A light to the Gentiles, 30-32

30 For mine eyes have seen thy salvation,

31 Which thou hast prepared before the face of all people;

32 A light to lighten the Gentiles, and the glory of thy people Israel.

Continuing his psalm of praise, Simeon correctly equates the infant Jesus with "salvation" itself. Note that Simeon is not among those Jews whose view of the Messiah was as a purely national liberator to rid the Jews from their oppressors. Instead, in keeping with Isaiah 42:6, He would be "a light to the Gentiles" as well as the "glory of Israel."

III. Sign of Hope and of Sorrow—33-35

33 And Joseph and his mother marvelled at those things which were spoken of him.

34 And Simeon blessed them, and said unto Mary his mother, Behold, this child is set for the fall and rising again of many in Israel; and for a sign which shall be spoken against;

35 (Yea, a sword shall pierce through thy own soul also,) that the thoughts of many hearts may be revealed.

Although Joseph and Mary have been told by angels about the remarkable nature of their child, Simeon's outburst causes them to marvel. It must have been reaffirming for this Child's destiny to be known by such a godly man.

Yet, as history will show, the arrival of the Messiah into the world will not be all sweetness and light. The "fall and rising" of many in Israel may refer to the initial doubt among their leaders, which will lead to Jesus' death on the Cross, followed by the "rise" of faith among many Jews, who were by far the largest ethnic group to become the first followers of the very One who had been crucified.

Even the Messianic prophet Isaiah had predicted that the Coming One would not only be "light" but *judgment* (9:2). The word for "judgment" (*krisis*) gives us our word "crisis"; and we are reminded that it is "critical" to make the right choice when we hear the call of the Messiah to follow Him. Those who refuse are choosing judgment or condemnation, a sword instead of a blessing, a heart-pain not unlike that which Mary will experience as she watches her grown Son mistreated, misunderstood, and finally crucified.

IV. Statement from a Prophetess—36-38

36 And there was one Anna, a prophetess, the daughter of Phanuel, of the tribe of Aser: she was of a great age, and had lived with an husband seven years from her virginity;

37 And she was a widow of about fourscore and four years, which departed not from the temple, but served God with fastings and prayers night and day.

38 And she coming in that instant gave thanks likewise unto the Lord, and spake of him to all them that looked for redemption in Jerusalem.

Now a second verification comes from another aged Jew, Anna, an 80-year-old prophetess who has been a widow for seven years. It is remarkable that she is called a prophetess, since Jewish tradition held that there had been no authentic prophecy since Malachi, and would be none until Elijah returned (Mal. 4:5). Yet here is a "mere female" prophetess preceding Elijah, and adding her Spirit-inspired validation that the infant carried by Joseph and Mary is indeed the Messiah.

Anna was of the tribe of Asher, a rare reference since records of Asherites were lost in the "scattering" and captivity of the Jews. Asher became one of the 10 "lost tribes of Israel" while Judah and Benjamin remained as the two identifiable tribes. Perhaps Anna's tribal heritage is mentioned, while Simeon's is not, to provide documentation against objections to a female prophet.

While Simeon had been ready to breathe his last sigh of relief after being granted the privilege of seeing the infant Messiah, Anna becomes His first evangelist. The Temple where she spent so much time was also a gathering place for the most pious Jews in the area, and those who yearned most earnestly for the redemption associated with the coming Messiah. Did Anna have good news for them!

Assignment for Next Week:

For next week's lesson, group members should bring news clippings that are examples of "good news" from everyday life.

Evangelistic Emphasis

The story of Simeon and Anna is one of patience. It is the story of people whose faith has sustained them through a long and faithful life.

Good news is that Jesus has made salvation possible to all of us through his sacrificial death on the cross. The challenge for us is that we are all in the process of "being saved." Our salvation is completed when we enter into eternity. Until then we are in process. That means that no matter our place, station, or age in life, God is really never finished with us.

Simeon and Anna's continued presence in the temple acknowledged their ever-growing faith relationship with God. They believed in God's promise and God rewarded their belief by letting them experience God's Messiah personally.

What are you still waiting for God to do in your life?

You and I are not completed works until we are perfected in heaven. Until that time we keep growing in our faith relationship with Christ.

⊱⊰

It had been revealed to him by the Holy Spirit that he would not see death before he had seen the Lord's Messiah . . . Anna came, and began to praise God and to speak about the child to all who were looking for the redemption of Jerusalem.— *Luke 2: 26, 38*

Think about all the time you have spent waiting in this past month. You have stood in line in department stores. You have waited to mail or ship packages. Even your fast Internet connection has made you wait because all the sites were busy with Christmas shoppers. Waiting has become a part of the American Christmas shopping tradition. It is the only season that we seem to be the least bit patient. The waiting seems to have a purpose.

Anna and Simeon were faithful in their waiting. They were waiting for the arrival of the Messiah. They had waited their whole lives for one moment in time. Their waiting was honored when both of them saw Jesus.

"Good things come to those that wait." The saying is true in life and one of the truths of our faith.

Weekday Problems

Rosie was in a dither. The preacher had changed the order of worship. First Church had changed pastors every couple of years. It was one of their rituals to find something they didn't like in a pastor and move him along. In all that time of transition, Rosie and the worship committee had managed to protect their sacred order of worship. They had the same ritual since the beginning of time. Now their ritual had changed and Rosie was not going to allow it.

The story is too close to home for too many people in the church. The tension between change and tradition has always been strong. Chaotic change happened when Jesus was born. The census was called for by Augustus. The news of the angel to Mary and Joseph changed their perceptions of each other. The journey to Bethlehem and the subsequent birth of Jesus were stressful for this young couple. These were all big changes.

But Mary and Joseph were following ritual presenting Jesus in the temple.

* Discuss the role of change and the role of ritual in your faith community.

* Where can they support each other, and where are they in tension?

The Blessings of Babies

Will: I'm really worried!

Bill: What's the problem?

Will: Well, my wife read *The Tale of Two Cities* and we had twins. Then she read *The Three Musketeers* and we had triplets. Now she's reading *The Birth of a Nation!*

* * * *

Jack (yawning): Well, it must be time to get up.

Jill (sleepily): Oh, no. How can you tell?

Jack: The baby's finally fallen asleep.

* * * *

The Browns were glad when little Billy was born, but he didn't talk for six years. Then suddenly his first words were "Yuk! This cocoa's no good!"

Stunned, Billy's mom asked, "Why did you wait this long to talk?"

"Because," said Billy, "everything's been OK up to now."

This Lesson in Your Life

The Holy Spirit was active in the early life of Jesus. In the story of Simeon, we learn that the Holy Spirit had revealed that he would not see death until he had seen God's Messiah.

The church needs a fresh encounter with the Holy Spirit. We need to pray that the Holy Spirit would enter into our rituals, breathing new life into our church. Too many Sundays the same thing happens, just different hymns. Maybe we should join in the prayer of a minister friend of mine. He prays, "O Lord, let something happen today that is not printed in the bulletin." The Spirit is ready to enliven our worship and our faith.

Anna and Simeon were involved in the movement of the Spirit because they were properly placed in life. They were in the Temple doing those things they had been called to do. Daily their faithfulness to God kept them moving in His direction. Their faithfulness caused them to be constantly looking for the movement of God's spirit in daily activities. Mary and Joseph were just another simple couple following the Jewish ritual law. From one standpoint, Jesus was another baby. Because Anna and Simeon were in the place they should have been, the Spirit whispered, "He's the one."

That is another clue to feeling the movement of the Spirit. We have to learn to be quiet. Even with all the noise that we make, God still speaks with the "still small voice." A movement of the Holy Spirit is quiet and gentle. It will change the world, maybe even upsetting yours, but the Spirit Himself is quiet, best heard in moments of silence and prayerful mediation.

GETTING THE FACTS STRAIGHT

1. What was the occasion for the presentation of Jesus in the Temple in Jerusalem?
Jesus was being presented for purification according to the Law of Moses. The eldest son was to be dedicated to the Lord.

2. How does the text describe Simeon?
Simeon was a righteous and devout man. He was anticipating the Messiah. He was also filled with the Spirit.

3. What was the promise that the Lord, through the Spirit, made to Simeon?
Simeon would not see death until he had seen the Lord's Messiah.

4. What was unique in what Simeon prophesied about the Messiah?
The child would be a light for the revelation to the gentiles and for the glory of Israel.

5. Part of the blessing of Jesus was a warning to Mary. What was that warning?
Simeon predicted that Jesus would be opposed and would face the sword that would pierce Him, and Mary's soul, too.

6. What was the official role of Anna in the Temple?
Anna was also a prophet in the Temple in Jerusalem.

7. How old was Anna?
The text says she was of great age. She lived with her husband for seven years, then as a widow to the age of 84.

8. How did the prophet Anna spend her time in the Temple?
Anna fasted and prayed day and night.

9. What do you think was happening in Luke 2:38?
Anna was preaching a sermon in Jerusalem about the Messiah who had come.

10. What happened after the encounter with Simeon and Anna?
Joseph returned to Galilee, and nothing was heard of Jesus until He was in Jerusalem again as a boy.

169

A spirituality of delight says "Ah! Ah!" A Zen master once said: "Have you noticed how the pebbles of the road are polished and pure after the rain? And the flowers? No words can describe them. One can only murmur an 'Ah!' of admiration." We should understand the "Ah!" of creation and of life.

How many "Ahs!" have you said lately?

A few "Ahs!" before going to bed is not a bad idea.

Can you imagine Simeon and Anna, after all those years of waiting for the Messiah? I wonder if they said, "Ah!" when they finally saw Him. Sometimes the love of God is so marvelous that words will fail us. These two people had prayed for this day their whole lives, and God's Messiah was a baby. Not only was He a baby—his parents were peasants.

The Temple was the right place to be if one was anticipating the Messiah to come. But to have the Messiah come in such a humble manner. To have the Messiah presented as a helpless baby rather than the military ruler that all had expected, well that was an "Ah!" moment.

Are you looking for Jesus to bring "Ah!" moments into your life? You may have them while watching the sun set. You might have those moments when you are reading a very familiar verse of Scripture and suddenly have your eyes opened to a deeper meaning. "Ah!" moments happen in church when the words of a familiar hymn become your words. These are the great moments of faith. They are not to be dissected, simply experienced.

Jesus Begins His Ministry

Mark 1:14-28

ow after that John was put in prison, Jesus came into Galilee, preaching the gospel of the kingdom of God,

15 And saying, The time is fulfilled, and the kingdom of God is at hand: repent ye, and believe the gospel.

16 Now as he walked by the sea of Galilee, he saw Simon and Andrew his brother casting a net into the sea: for they were fishers.

17 And Jesus said unto them, Come ye after me, and I will make you to become fishers of men.

18 And straightway they forsook their nets, and followed him.

19 And when he had gone a little further thence, he saw James the son of Zebedee, and John his brother, who also were in the ship mending their nets.

20 And straightway he called them: and they left their father Zebedee in the ship with the hired servants, and went after him.

21 And they went into Capernaum; and straightway on the sabbath day he entered into the synagogue, and taught.

22 And they were astonished at his doctrine: for he taught them as one that had authority, and not as the scribes.

23 And there was in their synagogue a man with an unclean spirit; and he cried out,

24 Saying, Let us alone; what have we to do with thee, thou Jesus of Nazareth? art thou come to destroy us? I know thee who thou art, the Holy One of God.

25 And Jesus rebuked him, saying, Hold thy peace, and come out of him.

26 And when the unclean spirit had torn him, and cried with a loud voice, he came out of him.

27 And they were all amazed, insomuch that they questioned among themselves, saying, What thing is this? what new doctrine is this? for with authority commandeth he even the unclean spirits, and they do obey him.

28 And immediately his fame spread abroad throughout all the region round about Galilee.

Memory Selection
Mark 1:17

Background Scripture
Mark 1:14-28

Devotional Reading
Matthew 4:18-25

Mark's Gospel is known for its direct and forceful language emphasizing Jesus' divine power and bold ministry. Mark allows Matthew and Luke to record the beautiful scenes surrounding Jesus' birth and early experiences at the Temple, choosing instead to plunge "immediately" (a favorite word of Mark's) into the work of John the Baptist and the ministry of Jesus.

This lesson focuses on the powerful content of Jesus' first sermons, on the dynamics of calling of His earliest and closest disciples, and on the miraculous work of confronting demons. It's the kind of story that would have appealed most to Romans, who valued action over thought, especially when the divine is seen to be behind the action. Yet moderns also like action narratives, so Mark's approach to Jesus' early work has a timeless appeal.

ഇറ

What kinds of events constitute good news for group members (some of whom, hopefully, brought examples, as assigned.) The story of a little boy's lost dog's being found is good news because we know how it hurts to lose someone or something

we love, as well as the joy of reunion.)

Remind the class that the term "gospel" translates the Greek word *evangellion*, which means "good news." Point out that Mark begins his Gospel with this very word: "The beginning of the *gospel* . . . " (1:1). This indicates that he is interested in driving "to the heart, from the start." What specific *content* will be included in the "news" brought to the world by Jesus?

Teaching Outline

I. Good News About a Kingdom!—14-15

  A. John's imprisonment, 14

  B. 'The Kingdom is at hand!', 15

II. Gathering the First Disciples—16-20

  A. Simon and Andrew, 16-18

  B. James and John, 19-20

III. Going into the Synagogue—21-28

  A. Teaching, 21-22

  B. An exorcism, 23-26

  C. Amazement and fame, 27-28

Daily Bible Readings

Mon.	John Prepares the Way	*Mark 1:1-8*
Tue.	Jesus Prepares for His Work	*Mark 1:9-13*
Wed.	Preaching and Calling Disciples	*Mark 1:14-20*
Thu.	Teaching and a Miracle	*Mark 1:21-28*
Fri.	Jesus Heals the Sick	*Mark 1:29-34*
Sat.	Preaching in Galilee	*Mark 1:35-39*
Sun.	Proclaiming Good News	*Matthew 4:16-25*

Verse by Verse

I. Good News About a Kingdom!—14-15

A. John's imprisonment, 14

14 Now after that John was put in prison, Jesus came into Galilee, preaching the gospel of the kingdom of God,

Matthew's Gospel tells us that John the Baptist was jailed by "Herod the Tetrarch," the son of Herod the Great, Rome's puppet ruler in Judea when Jesus was born (Matt. 14:1-12). John had been so bold as to condemn Herod the Tetrarch's marriage to his sister-in-law, which was illegal under both Jewish and Roman law. This courageous stance cost John his life.

John's execution, unjust though it was, cleared the stage for the drama of Jesus' own work. He began His work near His home in Nazareth, located in "Galilee of the Gentiles" (Matt. 4:15), perhaps to delay the confrontation that would inevitably come with the Jewish-Roman establishment in Jerusalem.

The phrase "the kingdom of God is at hand" is a common summary of Jesus' message. As a descendant of King David, He fulfilled God's promise that there would always be a kingdom with a Davidic king (2 Sam. 7:12-14). Although many would misunderstand His kingdom to consist of territorial claims, it was necessary to use the term to show that Christ's work fulfilled Old Testament Messianic promises, and that it would require submission as to a divine King.

B. 'The Kingdom is at hand!', 15

15 And saying, The time is fulfilled, and the kingdom of God is at hand: repent ye, and believe the gospel.

Like a woman who has been with child for nine months, it was *time* for the "birth" of the Kingdom. The "Roman peace" had suppressed much of the lawlessness in Palestine. New roads facilitated travel, and hence communication. The Greeks had provided a common language more widely usable than Hebrew. Now people could enter the Kingdom simply by obeying the Word of the King—which would eventually open the Kingdom's gates to Gentiles as well as Jews.

II. Gathering the First Disciples—16-20

A. Simon and Andrew, 16-18

16 Now as he walked by the sea of Galilee, he saw Simon and Andrew his brother casting a net into the sea: for they were fishers.

17 And Jesus said unto them, Come ye after me, and I will make

you to become fishers of men.

18 And straightway they forsook their nets, and followed him.

One of the New Covenant miracles often overlooked is the amazing fact that the world was changed by "a few good men"—12 apostles to be precise. Here Mark describes Jesus' first call, which goes out to four ordinary fishermen, two of whom will become members of a cadre closest to Jesus. "Simon" was the given name of Peter, or, in Aramaic, "Cephas" (John 1:42). Simon is the Greek spelling of Simeon, and probably means "hearer," while both Cephas and Peter mean "rock."

Peter's brother Andrew (lit. "manly") was a follower of John the Baptist, and according to John's account brought his brother Peter to Jesus (John 1:40-42). The word for "straightway" in verse 18 is used more than 40 times in Mark, and is sometimes translated "immediately" (as in vss. 12, 28). It may have been an exclamatory word meaning something like "Lo!" (or even, in our vernacular, "Wow!") instead of merely meaning a short time. The "wow factor" here is that both these two fishermen and the next two (vs. 20) were so drawn to Jesus that they risked their livelihood to follow Him in radical commitment.

B. James and John, 19-20

19 And when he had gone a little further thence, he saw James the son of Zebedee, and John his brother, who also were in the ship mending their nets.

20 And straightway he called them: and they left their father Zebedee in the ship with the hired servants, and went after him.

The call of James and John follows so closely the call of Peter and Andrew that it has been speculated that the two sets of brothers were partners in the fishing business. In the complete list of the 12 apostles, Mark says that Jesus gave James and John the surname "Boanerges," probably after an Aramaic word that means "sons of thunder" (3:17). This may refer to their fiery temperament, as indicated when the two brothers threaten to call down fire from heaven to destroy some Samaritans who would not listen to Jesus (Luke 9:51-56).

III. Going into the Synagogue— 21-28

A. Teaching, 21-22

21 And they went into Capernaum; and straightway on the sabbath day he entered into the synagogue, and taught.

22 And they were astonished at his doctrine: for he taught them as one that had authority, and not as the scribes.

True to God's plan, Jesus goes first to a Jewish synagogue to begin His ministry of preaching. As Paul was to be instructed, Jesus was sent to "the Jew first," and only then "to the Greek" (or Gentiles; see Rom. 1:16). Although in the coming years a majority of early Church members would be Gentiles, many Jews also responded to Christ's teaching, and for years attended both synagogue and Christian services.

That Jesus' taught with "authority, and not as the scribes" was because the scribes loved to pose with sophistication the teachings of one rabbi against another, instead of preaching directly from the Old Covenant Scriptures.

B. An exorcism, 23-26

23 And there was in their synagogue a man with an unclean spirit; and he cried out,

24 Saying, Let us alone; what have we to do with thee, thou Jesus of Nazareth? art thou come to destroy us? I know thee who thou art, the Holy One of God.

25 And Jesus rebuked him, saying, Hold thy peace, and come out of him.

26 And when the unclean spirit had torn him, and cried with a loud voice, he came out of him.

Although the term "unclean spirit" (NIV "evil spirit) is singular, it speaks with plural voices in verse 24 (cp. the demon whose name was "Legion" in Mark 5:9). Apparently the demon-possessed man had been worshipping unchallenged at the synagogue until confronted with the Son of God. Since both the demon and Christ are from the spirit-world, the demon knows who Jesus is.

Older interpretations tried to identify demon possession with mere illnesses. Although they are sometimes related in Scripture, something more than a bodily disease has taken over this man. His "disease" is spiritual; and the cause of it actually speaks. In contrast to the ritual of exorcism that would later be developed, Jesus heals the demonic ailment with only "his word," in fulfillment of Messianic prophecy (see Matt. 6:16-18).

Jesus commands the demon to be silent in accordance with Mark's emphasis on what has been called the "Messianic secret," forbidding widespread reports of His work until His and the Father's own time table. Advertising His powers too soon could have brought Jewish and Roman authorities down on Him before He had time to preach sufficiently.

C. Amazement and fame, 27-28

27 And they were all amazed, insomuch that they questioned among themselves, saying, What thing is this? what new doctrine is this? for with authority commandeth he even the unclean spirits, and they do obey him.

28 And immediately his fame spread abroad throughout all the region round about Galilee.

The people are amazed not only because Jesus preached with greater authority than the scribes, but because of His obvious power over the spirit world. Some Jews dabbled in exorcism, as indicated in Acts 19:14-15; but Jesus' act was so much more powerful and simpler that it seemed to be a "new doctrine." Despite Jesus' command for the demon to be silent, His Word and works are so compelling that both demons and disciples are drawn to it with unbridled enthusiasm.

Evangelistic Emphasis

Some people are waking up to a New Year. Even on this second day of the New Year they are feeling the results of too much celebration on New Year's Eve. Those people put 2004 behind them, then toasted 2005 with large quantities of adult beverages. They were up late! They partied hard! Today they are doing what many do on Sunday; they are sleeping it off.

We think it is a sin to party like some do. Perhaps you even resented all the noise that was made welcoming the New Year. You think a hangover is fitting punishment for immature nocturnal imbibing. Maybe you are right!

You know, the very people we think get what they deserve are the people that Jesus has called us to reach. Maybe your New Year's resolution should be to invite some people into your church who don't look and act as respectable as you do. Jesus has called us to fish for people.

We are called to go get them and to let Jesus handle cleaning them up. It is a challenge to us proper Christians and it is the only hope for people without Christ.

ℰℭ

And Jesus said unto them, Come after me and I will make you become fishers or men.—Mark 1: 17

I am a fishing jinx. Preachers are supposed to enjoy fishing. I don't, because I never catch anything. I have gone with professionals on the Bass Master Tour and have shut them out. They say, "Preacher, I don't understand. I always catch fish here." I usually console them by explaining that I'm a jinx. I have never been invited back for a repeat fishing engagement. I will never become an expert fisherman.

Jesus promised that we would always be in the process of becoming fishermen. Making disciples for Jesus is a constant learning process. We are always growing in our understanding of how to invite people to church and how to invite them to Christ. We are called not to *perfect* our craft but to *practice* our craft.

What bait are you using to fish for souls?

Weekday Problems

Kay left home early on Saturday morning to beat the crowds to the Mall. She finally had time to return some of those Christmas gifts that didn't fit or were the wrong color and style. She told her husband Boyd that she would only be gone for a couple of hours.

As the sun set on that Saturday afternoon, Kay turned into the driveway. She hit the release to open the back doors of her SUV. Boyd walked around and saw that the back was filled with plastic bags from every shop in the mall.

"I thought you were going to return things," He said,

"I did," She said,

"What are all these packages?"

"The deals were too good to pass up. Everything I bought was on sale!"

*Do you shop based on price or value?

*Do you think people come to Christ based on "price" or "value"?

*Do you think we have explained that Jesus is a "good deal"?

Too Much of a Good Thing?

Although Jesus' power over demons has a ring of truth, it's a subject that has always been accompanied by superstition and excess. The Jewish historian Josephus claims to have actually seen an exorcism performed in the presence of the Roman General Vespasian and his sons, "in accordance with the methods prescribed by Solomon."

A ring attached to a supposedly magical root was placed under the nostrils of a demon-possessed man. Jewish exorcists, saying a formula over the man, withdrew the ring and root from under the man's nose, and claimed that the demon followed it, and the man was cured.

As proof, the exorcists arranged for a pan of water to be sitting nearby, and when it was somehow spilled they claimed that this was proof that the demon had rather recklessly fled the afflicted man, stumbling over the pan in the process. (Josephus, *Antiquities,* VIII.)

This Lesson in Your Life

Jesus used images and metaphors to communicate eternal truth. He saw two fishermen and used an image they would understand to allow Him to explain what their ministry would be. Jesus used wonderful communication techniques to cause people to understand Him and to follow Him.

This story from Mark is clearly the pattern the church has used to think about our ministry of invitation. We are in the business of inviting people to meet Jesus as their Lord and Savior. We have even made the whole fishing motif an important image for Christian evangelism. What is more important for us to learn in our day is the language of welcome.

The Bible is clear that when we speak in tongues in worship, there must be interpretation. In my denomination we could have an announcement in worship that would say: "The U.M.W. has invited the U.M.M and U.M.Y.F. to co-sponsor a V.I.M. trip to the U.M.C.O.R. depot." Do you know what that means? Unless you have been a United Methodist living in Louisiana for years, you would be confused.

All churches have code language. You are sitting in a Sunday School class. Can you describe what Sunday School is, without using church language? Jesus used the language of the culture to communicate God's love with the culture. Part of what we are called to do is to communicate His message using metaphors and language that make sense to the people with whom we are communicating.

In other words, how do we preach and teach Jesus in a dot.com world?

1. According to the gospel of Mark, when did Jesus begin his public ministry?
After John the Baptizer was arrested, Jesus came from Galilee preaching.

2. What was the essence of Jesus' message?
His message was simple: The time is fulfilled; the Kingdom of God is at hand, therefore repent and believe the gospel.

3. What did Jesus see as He was passing by the sea of Galilee?
Jesus saw two men fishing with nets.

4. What were the names of these two fishermen?
The two fishermen were Simon and his brother Andrew.

5. When Jesus called Simon and Andrew to come with Him, what was their response?
They immediately left their nets and started following Jesus.

6. What other men did Jesus find beside the Sea of Galilee?
James and John, the sons of Zebedee, were working their nets, too. Zebedee was with his two sons. There is also a mention of hired men working with the Zebedee family.

7. What was the response of the Zebedee family to the invitation of Jesus?
James and John immediately put down their nets and followed Jesus. They left their father Zebedee behind with the hired men.

8. What details are given about what happened after Jesus called the Zebedee brothers, and Simon and Andrew?
Jesus went to Capernaum and entered the synagogue on the Sabbath and taught.

9. What was the response of the congregation at Capernaum to the teaching of Jesus?
They were amazed at His teaching, which was unlike the scribes. Jesus taught with authority.

10. What happened in the synagogue as Jesus was teaching that amazed crowd?
A man with an unclean spirit interrupted the services, and Jesus healed the man and told the demon to be silent.

Now it came to pass that a group existed who called themselves fishermen. There were many fish in the waters all around. In fact the whole area was surrounded by streams and lakes filled with fish. The fish were hungry.

Week after week, month after month, and year after year, those who called themselves fishermen met to talk about their call to fish, the abundance of fish, and how they might go about fishing. Year after year they carefully defined what fishing means, defended fishing as an occupation, and declared that fishing was always to be a primary task of fishermen.

The fishermen built large printing houses to publish fishing guides. Presses were kept busy day and night to produce materials solely devoted to fishing methods, equipment and programs, to arrange and encourage meetings, to talk about fishing. A speakers' bureau was also provided to schedule special speakers on the subject of fishing.

After one stirring meeting on "The Necessity of Fishing," one young fellow left the meeting and went fishing. The next day he reported that he had caught two outstanding fish. He was honored for his excellent catch and scheduled to visit all the big meetings possible to tell how he did it. So he quit his fishing in order to have time to tell about the experience to the other fishermen. He was also placed on the Fishermen's General Board as a person having considerable experience.

Imagine how hurt some were when one day a person suggested that those who didn't fish were not really fishermen, no matter how much they claimed to be. The question was, Is a person a fisherman if, year after year he never catches a fish? Is one following, if he isn't fishing?

Jesus Calls Us to Put People First

Mark 2:13-28

And he went forth again by the sea side; and all the multitude resorted unto him, and he taught them.

14 And as he passed by, he saw Levi the son of Alphaeus sitting at the receipt of custom, and said unto him, Follow me. And he arose and followed him.

15 And it came to pass, that, as Jesus sat at meat in his house, many publicans and sinners sat also together with Jesus and his disciples: for there were many, and they followed him.

16 And when the scribes and Pharisees saw him eat with publicans and sinners, they said unto his disciples, How is it that he eateth and drinketh with publicans and sinners?

17 When Jesus heard it, he saith unto them, They that are whole have no need of the physician, but they that are sick: I came not to call the righteous, but sinners to repentance.

18 And the disciples of John and of the Pharisees used to fast: and they come and say unto him, Why do the disciples of John and of the Pharisees fast, but thy disciples fast not?

19 And Jesus said unto them, Can the children of the bridechamber fast, while the bridegroom is with them? as long as they have the bridegroom with them, they cannot fast.

20 But the days will come, when the bridegroom shall be taken away from them, and then shall they fast in those days.

21 No man also seweth a piece of new cloth on an old garment: else the new piece that filled it up taketh away from the old, and the rent is made worse.

22 And no man putteth new wine into old bottles: else the new wine doth burst the bottles, and the wine is spilled, and the bottles will be marred: but new wine must be put into new bottles.

23 And it came to pass, that he went through the corn fields on the sabbath day; and his disciples began, as they went, to pluck the ears of corn.

24 And the Pharisees said unto him, Behold, why do they on the sabbath day that which is not lawful?

25 And he said unto them, Have ye never read what David did, when he had need, and was an hungred, he, and they that were with him?

26 How he went into the house of God in the days of Abiathar the high priest, and did eat the shewbread, which is not lawful to eat but for the priests, and gave also to them which were with him?

27 And he said unto them, The sabbath was made for man, and not man for the sabbath:

28 Therefore the Son of man is Lord also of the sabbath.

Jan. 9

Memory Selection
Mark 2:17

Background Scripture
Mark 2:13-28

Devotional Reading
Ephesians 4:25-32

This lesson focuses on two different ways in which Jesus calls us to challenge tradition. First, He calls Levi (also known as Matthew), a tax collector, to be one of His disciples. Because tax collectors were traditionally hated by the Jews merely because of their occupation, Jesus' acceptance of Matthew challenges us not to make generalizations about people, but to take them as individuals.

The second challenge Jesus issues in this text is against traditional legalistic interpretations of the Law of Moses that ignored people's needs. Jesus' opponents accuse Him of going against two important traditions under the Law—fasting and Sabbath-observance. The way He deals with His critics shows that Jesus calls us to put people before ritual, love above law.

ഇരോ.

Tell your group that you are going to give them an acronym that is often heard in our society, and ask them to respond to it spontaneously to show what they think of first when they hear it. The acronym is: *IRS*. Responses may include: *Aggravating taxes . . . fear of being audited . . . government bullying . . . ignoring complaints . . . being over-taxed.*

Now introduce an imaginary man named "John Jones." Explain that he is an IRS agent whose home burned, and that he and his family "need clothes, personal items, food, bedding—whatever you can spare."

Now how do group members respond to the term "IRS"? Note the difference between our response to a faceless bureaucracy and a *person in need* who happens to work for it? In this lesson Jesus will challenge us to put *people* above stereotypes.

Teaching Outline

I. Persons Over Perception—13-17
  A. Calling a sinner, 13-14
  B. Critics' grumbling, 15-16
  C. Jesus' mission, 17
II. People Over Tradition—18-28
  A. The question of fasting, 18-22
    1. A matter of timing, 18-20
    2. New bottles for new wine, 21-22
  B. The question of the Sabbath, 23-28
    1. Hungry disciples, 23-24
    2. Lord of the Sabbath, 25-28

Daily Bible Readings

Verse by Verse

I. Persons Over Perception—13-17

A. Calling a sinner, 13-14

13 And he went forth again by the sea side; and all the multitude resorted unto him, and he taught them.

14 And as he passed by, he saw Levi the son of Alphaeus sitting at the receipt of custom, and said unto him, Follow me. And he arose and followed him.

Jesus has been ministering in and about Capernaum (2:1), a city on the northwest shore of the Sea of Galilee that Jesus adopted as his home base when He was in the area. Apparently it was on His way to such a "seaside pulpit" that Jesus comes across a tax collector named Levi, in whom He sees the gifts of an apostle. This is as remarkable as His healing miracles, since, sitting at a tax-collection table, Levi would have been despised. "Levi" was apparently another name for Matthew, since Matthew is called a "publican," or a tax collector in Luke 5:27, and a tax collector in Matthew 10:3, while the name "Levi" does not appear. (See also the parallel passage in Matthew 9:9.)

The sorry reputation of tax collectors was usually well-earned. The fact that they were hired by Rome to collect taxes from their Jewish brethren would have been enough to make them hated. Added to that was the fact that Rome allowed them to tack on a high percentage of profit to the base tax, as their own personal income. That Jesus would choose such a person defied popular opinion. He thus leaves an eternal example both of His followers' obligation to avoid making judgmental generalizations from groups to a person, and to reach out to those whose lives have been filled with rejection.

B. Critics' grumbling, 15-16

15 And it came to pass, that, as Jesus sat at meat in his house, many publicans and sinners sat also together with Jesus and his disciples: for there were many, and they followed him.

16 And when the scribes and Pharisees saw him eat with publicans and sinners, they said unto his disciples, How is it that he eateth and drinketh with publicans and sinners?

"His" house probably means the house where he customarily stayed while in Capernaum, rather than one that belonged to him, since Jesus personally lacked a permanent place to sleep (Matt. 8:20). Now His affront in calling a tax collector is multiplied, for apparently several of Matthew's friends join them. Apparently they gather not only for a meal but because they too have decided to follow Jesus.

Sitting together at meal was (and still is in many Middle Eastern cultures) a sign of acceptance and fellowship. Yet here Jesus is found extending just such "table fellowship" to sinners, a word that had by now come to be equivalent to "publican" or tax collector. The scene is ready-made for Jesus' critics to condemn Him. How could He be godly enough to have the authority to forgive sin (as in vs. 5), if He was so willing to associate with ungodly people? This time Jesus does not have to look into their hearts to know their thoughts, since they freely express them loudly enough to be heard (vs. 17).

C. Jesus' mission, 17

17 When Jesus heard it, he saith unto them, They that are whole have no need of the physician, but they that are sick: I came not to call the righteous, but sinners to repentance.

Jesus' answer arises from the heart of His purpose for coming to earth. A modern writer would set off "they that are whole" and "the righteous" in quotation marks, to show that Jesus speaks with irony. His critics have made the mistake of labeling the publicans "sinners," when their judgmentalism makes them the sinners. Jesus' response implies that it is impossible to place ourselves in a position to receive Him until we admit that *we* are the sinners who long to be at table with Jesus.

II. People Over Tradition—18-28

A. The question of fasting, 18-22

1. A matter of timing, 18-20

18 And the disciples of John and of the Pharisees used to fast: and they come and say unto him, Why do the disciples of John and of the Pharisees fast, but thy disciples fast not?

19 And Jesus said unto them, Can the children of the bridechamber fast, while the bridegroom is with them? as long as they have the bridegroom with them, they cannot fast.

20 But the days will come, when the bridegroom shall be taken away from them, and then shall they fast in those days.

In addition to the presupposition that no tax collector could possibly be a follower of the Messiah, many among the crowds who followed Jesus out of curiosity presupposed that if He were really "religious" He would *fast*. Fasting was widely practiced as a sign of putting the spirit's needs above the body's, and as a sign of mourning or grief (as for one's sins on the Day of Atonement). Jesus even assumed His followers would fast, although they were not to look like it! (See Matt. 6:17).

Jesus replies that there would be plenty of time later for them to fast as a sign of mourning after He had been crucified. Now, the disciples should be rejoicing in His presence. Besides, a time is coming when fasting will be placed lower on their list of priorities (see below).

2. New bottles for new wine, 21-22

21 No man also seweth a piece

of new cloth on an old garment: else the new piece that filled it up taketh away from the old, and the rent is made worse.

22 And no man putteth new wine into old bottles: else the new wine doth burst the bottles, and the wine is spilled, and the bottles will be marred: but new wine must be put into new bottles.

Differences in such Jewish traditions as fasting are not the only change ahead. The Messianic Age is a "new garment" (vs. 21) and "new wine" (vs. 22). Unless practices and attitudes change, the fabric of Judaism will tear like an old garment with a new patch, and the "fermentation" of the gospel will split the old wineskins that have become brittle and inflexible. As indirect as His language is, we can be sure the Pharisees would perceive that Jesus is preparing the people for changes—although they could not have imagined the extent or nature of them.

B. The question of the Sabbath, 23-28

1. Hungry disciples, 23-24

23 And it came to pass, that he went through the corn fields on the sabbath day; and his disciples began, as they went, to pluck the ears of corn.

24 And the Pharisees said unto him, Behold, why do they on the sabbath day that which is not lawful?

In addition to not fasting as other Jews did, Jesus and His followers did not practice Sabbath traditions the way others expected them to. Although merely plucking grain as the hungry disciples made their way through the fields could hardly have been properly defined as the kind of "work" the Law prohibited on the Sabbath, Jewish tradition had made it so. Some rabbis even taught that children could not play with sticks in the sand, because the little furrows they made were too much like those made by a plow! The charge that plucking grain "is not lawful" arose from tradition, not the Law.

2. Lord of the Sabbath, 25-28

25 And he said unto them, Have ye never read what David did, when he had need, and was an hungred, he, and they that were with him?

26 How he went into the house of God in the days of Abiathar the high priest, and did eat the shewbread, which is not lawful to eat but for the priests, and gave also to them which were with him?

27 And he said unto them, The sabbath was made for man, and not man for the sabbath:

28 Therefore the Son of man is Lord also of the sabbath.

Jesus' skillful answer uses David, a favorite of the strictest of Jews, to show that human need is of higher priority than religious ritual. The incident He refers to is recorded in 1 Samuel 21:6. Jesus' claim to be "Lord" of the Sabbath would have been taken as scandalous or even blasphemous, and no doubt was remembered by His enemies.

Evangelistic Emphasis

Would you like to join a new group? This group has some tax auditors from the IRS. There are a couple of terrorists in the group. There are one or two shrimpers who tag along. There are some other people who are just not sure of anything. This group will let any of life's rejects join, and they don't ask many questions. The group is looked on with suspicion by the authorities both in government and in religious circles. Would you want to sacrifice your good name to join this group? They promise all sorts of benefits including changing the world.

That is a fair description of the group that Jesus first collected around him. It is a wonder that their Bible studies didn't break out into open and armed conflict. Jesus picked these men because He saw their hearts. He called them not because they were perfect but because He loved them.

The good news for us is that Jesus is still calling misfits and sinners into His kingdom. He doesn't look at what we can do for Him. He calls us because of what He can do for us. It is good to know that everyone belongs in God's family.

80C3

Memory Selection

When Jesus heard it, he saith, . . . I came not to call the righteous but sinners to repentance.—*Mark 2: 17*

As disciples of Jesus we are called to bring healing and health to those who need it.

Some disciples came to see Abba Poemen and said to him, "Tell us, when we see brothers dozing during the sacred office, should we pinch them so they will stay awake?"

The old man said to them, "Actually, if I saw a brother sleeping, I would put his head on my knees and let him rest."

We have all sorts of opportunities to give help to people in the name of Jesus. Listening to someone share a concern and being a friend are such easy ways of ministering the name of Jesus. We are called to those who are lonely and lost. Our calling is the same as our Lord's call to the 12.

Weekday Problems

Mary Hatton walked into First Church. She was unkempt. She was wearing dirty clothing. Mary told wild stories to anyone who would listen. She had been living on the streets for years. In her old age, Social Security had made it possible for her to rent a small apartment near the church. She had decided to come to church because she felt this church might give her a chance. Each Sunday she would sit in the congregation and listen to the sermon. She would leave church each Sunday and tell the minister how much she loved being in church. She had become a fixture at First Church.

One Sunday after everyone left the church, the church lady strolled up to the pastor. "Pastor," she said, "What are you going to do about that bag lady that has been coming to our church?!"

"What do you mean," the pastor asked?

"Are you going to tell her to stop coming? She's spoiling the service for me. She looks bad. She smells bad. She doesn't belong here with us."

*How would you respond to this situation?

Driving Tips

Will: All this talk about "back-seat drivers" is hogwash. I've been driving for 20 years, and I've never heard a word from back there.
Gil: What kind of car do you drive?
Will: A Cadillac . . . hearse.

* * * *

A reckless driver struck another car, but only stuck his head out the window and yelled, "Why don't you watch where you're going?"
"Why?" the other driver yelled back. "Are you coming back?"

* * * *

A guy without insurance was teaching his wife how to drive when the brakes suddenly failed. "I can't stop!" she cried. "What should I do?"
"Brace yourself," said her husband, "and aim at something cheap."

187

This Lesson in Your Life

Tax collectors followed Jesus. They were the most notorious of all the sinners in Palestine in the first century. A tax collector worked for the hated Roman Empire. They bid on their jobs. The prospective tax collector would promise to raise a certain amount of money for the Romans. His salary was made from all the money he collected that was over and above the amount he paid to the Romans. The collection methods varied from bribery and blackmail to brute force. The tax collectors were the most hated of sinners in that time. Could you imagine a tax structure where tax auditors received a proportion of the audit money they collected? Yes, I guess you could.

The Pharisees and other keepers of the truth didn't like the fact that Jesus was having open fellowship with sinners. All sorts of sordid kinds gathered around Him. They seemed to be genuinely happy to be in His presence. It was as though they loved Him and He loved them. The righteous people were mad that Jesus had so many sinner friends.

One can only imagine what chapped the righteous people so much. Perhaps they wanted a supper with Jesus. Maybe they wanted Him to validate their righteous lifestyle. As they listed to Him talk about holiness they would nod in agreement, because in their minds they were holy and righteous. Do you see the problem?

One of the flaws of church life is that we tend to form "holy huddles." That is defined as "us four and no more." We would rather keep people out than invite sinners in. Jesus continues to call us to reach out to the least and the lost. He wants us to make friends with sinners, even IRS tax auditors!

1. As Jesus was beside the Sea of Galilee again, whom did he see and call?
As Jesus walked along he saw Levi, son of Alphaeus.

2. What was Levi doing when Jesus first saw him?
Levi was sitting at his tax booth, collecting taxes for the Romans.

3. Levi the son of Alphaeus is known by another name. What is that name?
The other name most often used for Levi is Matthew.

4. When Jesus saw Levi, he issued an invitation. What was the invitation, and Levi's response?
Jesus told Levi to "Follow me." He got up and followed him.

5. What happened on the evening that Jesus called Levi?
That evening there was a party at Levi's house. Levi invited some tax collectors and sinners. Jesus brought the disciples.

6. Who were some other persons at this party?
A group of people who had been following Jesus were also present. Some Pharisees had also crashed the party.

7. What did the Pharisees see that made them question Jesus' disciples?
The Pharisees noted that Jesus was sitting and dining with sinners and tax collectors.

8. What question did the Pharisees ask Jesus' disciples?
The Pharisees asked the disciples if Jesus knew it was wrong for Him to be eating with such people.

9. What happened next?
Jesus overheard the question asked of the disciples, and He responded to the Pharisees.

10. What was Jesus' response to the Pharisees' question?
Jesus said, "I have come to call not the righteous but sinners."

189

Job hunting.

Levi wasn't looking for a new job, and found one. Often, we can't find a job even when we're looking.

We've all been interviewed for jobs. We've nervously endured those interviews thinking about what *not* to do: Don't bite fingernails. Don't fidget. Don't interrupt. Don't burp. We know we'd disqualify ourselves instantly if we slipped up and did any of these "don'ts."

But the word on the street—that is, on the cyber-street, the information superhighway—is that some applicants are unfamiliar with the concept of interview etiquette. Personnel executives of major American corporations have started swapping stories of the most bizarre and unusual behavior by job seekers.

For example:

A balding candidate abruptly excused himself and returned to the office a few minutes later, wearing a hairpiece.

An applicant "wore a Walkman and said she could listen to me and the music at the same time."

Another stated that, if he were hired, he "would demonstrate his loyalty by having the corporate logo tattooed on his forearm."

One applicant interrupted the interview to phone his therapist for advice on answering specific interview questions.

Jesus has given us all work to do in His Kingdom. Our job is to welcome sinners and point them to the Lord.

No interview necessary!

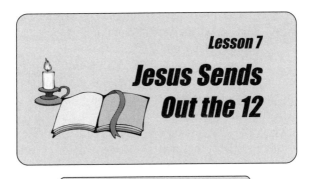

Jesus Sends Out the 12

Mark 3:13-19a; 6:7-13

And he goeth up into a mountain, and calleth unto him whom he would: and they came unto him.

14 And he ordained twelve, that they should be with him, and that he might send them forth to preach,

15 And to have power to heal sicknesses, and to cast out devils:

16 And Simon he surnamed Peter;

17 And James the son of Zebedee, and John the brother of James; and he surnamed them Boanerges, which is, The sons of thunder:

18 And Andrew, and Philip, and Bartholomew, and Matthew, and Thomas, and James the son of Alphaeus, and Thaddaeus, and Simon the Canaanite,

19a And Judas Iscariot, which also betrayed him:

6:7 And he called unto him the twelve, and began to send them forth by two and two; and gave them power over unclean spirits;

8 And commanded them that they should take nothing for their journey,

save a staff only; no scrip, no bread, no money in their purse:

9 But be shod with sandals; and not put on two coats.

10 And he said unto them, In what place soever ye enter into an house, there abide till ye depart from that place.

11 And whosoever shall not receive you, nor hear you, when ye depart thence, shake off the dust under your feet for a testimony against them. Verily I say unto you, It shall be more tolerable for Sodom and Gomorrha in the day of judgment, than for that city.

12 And they went out, and preached that men should repent.

13 And they cast out many devils, and anointed with oil many that were sick, and healed them.

Memory Selection
Mark 3:14

Background Scripture
Mark 3:13-19a; 6:7-13

Devotional Reading
Luke 9:1-6

191

The most brilliant social analyst could not have predicted it: 12 men, most of them unschooled and ordinary, turned the world upside down after sitting at the feet of Jesus for less than three years. This lesson's focus is on the apostles—the men Jesus called, taught, and sent out with His message. Unremarkable at first, they would be immortalized in countless writings, paintings, and sculptures as the 12 apostles.

The listing in today's lesson provides the only glimpse we have of some of the apostles, while others went on to become widely-known for their writings and other forms of leadership in the early Church. Along with the apostle Paul, named to the list as "one born out of due season," they left an indelible mark on history.

₭рс

Ask members of your group what qualities are needed most to be an effective church leader. Should they be effective communicators? Organizational wizards? Motivators and/or dynamic speakers? What kind of training should they have? Does gender matter? Or age? Could a person of one race effectively serve a congregation consisting mostly of members of another race? Should they be married? Must they have an outgoing personality, or could a somewhat scholarly and retiring person serve effectively?

For background, the teacher may want to review the qualifications of elders and deacons listed in 1 Timothy 3:1-13 and Titus 1:5-9. Note the need for diversity of gifts, as indicated in the lists in Romans 12:6-8. Lead into this survey of the 12 apostles, and the impact they made on the world.

Teaching Outline	*Daily Bible Readings*	
I. Appointing the 12—3:13-19	Mon.	Appointing the 12 *Mark 3:13-19a*
A. The concept, 13-15	Tue.	Instructing the 12 *Mark 6:7-13*
B. The men, 16-19	Wed.	Mission of the 12 *Matthew 10:5-15*
II. Planning the Work—6:7-13	Thu.	Authority of the 12 *Luke 9:1-6*
A. Spiritual equipment, 7	Fri.	'Have the Mind of Christ' *Philippians 2:1-11*
B. Serving by faith, 8-10	Sat.	'Press on Toward the Goal' *Philippians 3:12—4:1*
C. Hearers' qualifications, 11	Sun.	'Rejoice in the Lord Always' *Philippians 4:4-9*
III. Working the plan, 12-13		

Verse by Verse

I. Appointing the 12—3:13-19

A. The concept, 13-15

13 And he goeth up into a mountain, and calleth unto him whom he would: and they came unto him.

14 And he ordained twelve, that they should be with him, and that he might send them forth to preach,

15 And to have power to heal sicknesses, and to cast out devils:

Mark 1 and 2 have already recorded Christ's call to some of those in the listing here. The full list of the apostles seems to come at a brief mountainside retreat to ordain those He has already called.

Calling 12 workers no doubt makes the statement that the 12 tribes of Israel are symbolically being reassembled in the work of their Messiah.

Note the five-stage plan that unfolds in verses 14-15. (1) Jesus "ordains," (lit. "makes") the 12, formally appointing them for His special mission. As we will note, the word "apostle" *can* mean simply "one who is sent." However, the word for "ordain" (NIV "appointed") is the same word used to say that God "made" or created the world. Their appointment therefore is endowed with the aura of a creation of God.

(2) The 12 were ordained to *be with* Jesus (vs. 15). He is establishing here a kind of "school" for

apostles, calling them first to be mentored and trained before they are sent out. (3) Only then will they be *sent forth* to do the work Jesus trained them to do. The verb here is *apostello*, confirming that these men are indeed *apostoloi*, or apostles, as Matthew calls them (Matt. 10:2). Matthew also refers to them as *disciples* or "disciplined learners" (Matt. 10:1). While all dedicated followers are properly called "disciples," only the 12 and a few others "sent" on special missions are apostles. (4) Their specific tasks are (4) preaching and (5) healing people of both demonic and physical illnesses.

B. The men, 16-19

16 And Simon he surnamed Peter;

17 And James the son of Zebedee, and John the brother of James; and he surnamed them Boanerges, which is, The sons of thunder:

18 And Andrew, and Philip, and Bartholomew, and Matthew, and Thomas, and James the son of Alphaeus, and Thaddaeus, and Simon the Canaanite,

19a And Judas Iscariot, which also betrayed him:

Simon Peter is mentioned first in each of the New Testament lists of the apostles (Matt. 10; Mark 3; Luke 6; Acts 1), lending some credence to the Roman Catholic tradition that Peter was "first" among the 12. Peter will eventually be arrested, and traditionally remembered for having asked to be crucified upside-down, declining the "honor" of dying as did His Lord.

The next three, the brothers **James and John**, and Peter's brother **Andrew,** formed, with Peter, the quartet of fishermen whom Jesus had already called (Mark 1:16-20). This **James** was martyred by King Herod Agrippa I (Acts 12:1-2), so he could not have been the James who wrote the New Testament letter of James; but his brother **John** is traditionally considered the author of the Gospel and Epistles of John, and Revelation.

Andrew is said to have made the region north of the Black Sea his sector for preaching. For that reason he became the "patron saint" of Russia (as well as Scotland).

Philip seems to have been somewhat slow to believe actively in the power of Jesus. Misunderstanding Jesus' miraculous power to feed 5,000 people, it was Philip who began to calculate the quantity and cost of feeding them (John 6:5-7). Also, Philip apparently did not know what to do when confronted with people who were seeking Jesus, and referred them to Andrew (John 12:21).

Bartholomew is thought by many to be the same as Nathanael (see John 1:45-49), but the evidence is not certain. Tradition holds that Bartholomew worked with Thomas in evangelizing in countries as far away as India. He also, according to tradition, was crucified upside down. We have already met **Matthew,** or Levi, the publican or tax collector. Tradition agrees that he was the author of the Gospel bearing his name.

Most people know **Thomas** as "Doubting Thomas," since he said he could not believe in the risen Lord unless he could see and touch Him (John 20:24-29). In his defense, Thomas had not been present at some of the appearances of Jesus to other disciples. Tradition has Thomas preaching in Persia and in India, where he was said to be martyred. **James the son of Alphaeus** was probably the James known also as "James the less" (or "the younger," NIV), who did not flee so far, when Jesus was arrested, that he could not watch His crucifixion (Mark 15:40).

Thaddaeus was the given name of one Lebbaeus (Matt. 10:3). He was also likely called Judas, since Thaddaeus does not appear in the lists of apostles in Luke and Acts, but a Judas (not Iscariot) does. **Simon the Canaanite** is called "Simon Zelotes ("the Zealot") in Luke 6:15 and Acts 1:13. This identifies him with a revolutionary sect of Jews who advocated the use of force in driving out the Romans.

The inclusion of **Judas Iscariot,** who betrayed Jesus, reminds us that even a direct call from Jesus into His service does not remove free will. Judas is the only apostle not said by tradition to have died a martyr's death. He took his own life in despair over betraying his Lord (Matt. 27:5).

II. Planning the Work—6:7-13

A. Spiritual equipment, 7

7 And he called unto him the twelve, and began to send them forth by two and two; and gave them power over unclean spirits;

It was dangerous to go about the countryside in Palestine unaccompanied. Jesus' pairing of the apostles also provided an extra mind in the intense discussions they would encounter. Their power over "unclean spirits" or demons of course derived from both the Holy Spirit and Jesus' gifting. These spirits sometimes, but not always, were associated with various illnesses.

B. Serving by faith, 8-10

8 And commanded them that they should take nothing for their journey, save a staff only; no scrip, no bread, no money in their purse:

9 But be shod with sandals; and not put on two coats.

10 And he said unto them, In what place soever ye enter into an house, there abide till ye depart from that place.

We have only to reflect on various scandals in the modern Church involving ministers garnering and misusing huge sums of money, to realize the wisdom in Christ's command that the apostles be careful not to give the impression of being in His work for material gain. Unfortunately the King James word "scrip"

might be taken as money, when it actually was a leather bag; money is forbidden later in the sentence. Staying in one place would perhaps help avoid comparisons and jealousy.

C. Hearers' qualifications, 11

11 And whosoever shall not receive you, nor hear you, when ye depart thence, shake off the dust under your feet for a testimony against them. Verily I say unto you, It shall be more tolerable for Sodom and Gomorrah in the day of judgment, than for that city.

Missionaries like the apostles aren't the only ones with responsibility. Those who refuse to hear their message prove themselves unworthy, and the message-bearers are to signify this by shaming them symbolically by shaking the dust from their feet. This admonition seems designed to prevent those Christ sends out from wasting time in debates and quarrels when the real issue is an unwillingness to accept the truth.

III. Working the plan, 12-13

12 And they went out, and preached that men should repent.

13 And they cast out many devils, and anointed with oil many that were sick, and healed them.

The crux of the apostles' mission is *preaching*, which of course includes not only *repentance* but the call to believe in Jesus and commit to *obedience*. The exorcisms and healings grow out of what must be kept central in missionary work: proclaiming the Good News and calling for the disobedient to change their ways.

Evangelistic Emphasis

An Englishman was in the United States for a business visit. As part of the corporate wooing process he was taken to an American football game. (The English play soccer very well, but, as all American fan knows, they wrongly call it "football.") The corporation had selected a cross-state rivalry. This was the game of the year, and they knew their friend from England would be impressed. The game was won by a last-minute field goal. When asked what he thought about the game, the Englishman thought of all defensive and offensive huddles, and said, "too many committee meetings."

Reading the list of the disciples is like reading a roster of a church committee. Their names appear as a simple list several places in the New Testament. The men on this list were not extraordinary. They were simple people.

Yet these simple men from Palestine changed the world.

When you allow God to work through you, the world will be changed. Your world will be changed when Jesus is your Lord. The good news is that he wants to add names to His list of disciples.

৪৩୧

And he appointed twelve, that they should be with him, and that he might send them forth to preach.—*Mark 3:14*

We have come a long way since Jesus sent out the first preachers.

Now we have college and seminaries and a preacher must have an education. Even after he is "educated," he must jump through the hoops for the group that is responsible for his ordination. After ordination, he is required to keep up with continuing education and attend "enrichment" meetings.

In the local church the "preacher" is also the chief cook and bottle washer. He must answer the question, "Who's responsible?" when something isn't in place. He or she must attend all committee meetings and oversee the temporal affairs of the congregation.

I wonder whatever happened to that simple call to preach?

Weekday Problems

Evelyn was the church angel—she was always up in the air about something. This particular Sunday morning, Evelyn had a list of things to discuss with her minister. She wanted to know first of all why more people in the church did not use the library. She thought that a good sermon on reading books might make people use the library more. She was also very concerned about church plans to relocate the prayer garden so that the community would have access to it. She let the minister know in her opinion the community did not need to use "her" prayer garden.

One other thing was on her list. The temperature of the sanctuary bothered her. She sat next to a large stained glass window and she couldn't understand why, with the sun shining into the window, she was warm. She wished that the pastor would be careful when setting the thermostat for the morning worship service. To drive home the point, she gathered some more of her little angels in the hallway to testify about the temperature in the sanctuary.

The minister was exhausted when he finally went into the worship service. His text for the morning was, "And he appointed twelve . . . and sent them out the preach the message."

*Discuss ways your church puts other expectations on your minister.

On Friendship and Trust

A military wife was with her husband on a tour of duty in Puerto Rico. On one occasion she offered freshly made cake to a workman at her house. He started to go outside to eat it, but she inisted that he eat at the table with her and her husband. Since the man had professed an inability to speak English, she and her huband spoke with him in their halting Spanish.

Then, to the woman's great surprise, the workman began to speak fluent English. It turned out that while he knew the language very well, he did not let it be known to Americans whom he has not learned to trust. When he was treated with affection and respect, he became a friend.

This Lesson in Your Life

When you were baptized, that was your call to ministry! Your baptism was your ordination service. You are in the ministry.

Jesus took aside 12 to be close to Him and to learn the spiritual lessons they would need to lead the Church. While they were still in training, Jesus sent them out into the communities to cast out demons and to preach. They were not fully educated in all He wanted them to know. None of them had a formal course in rhetoric. They were simple people preaching a very simple gospel.

The call to preach sounds so "preachy." Yet, when you were baptized you were called to preach! Now before you write out a standard sermon with those three points and a poem, you'd better understand what preaching is. Each time you have a conversation with a person about Jesus you are preaching. Each time you listen lovingly to someone share a prayer need, you are preaching. When you are sharing with someone how God has blessed or changed your life, you are preaching.

Preaching doesn't necessarily involve ascending into a pulpit. Preaching involves living out your faith in Jesus Christ. The best sermons are seen not heard. You preach the great sermons as you live what you say you believe.

The next time you are listening to a really DULL sermon, think about your preaching. Are your words and your deeds pointing people to Jesus Christ?

1. What were the functional duties Jesus gave to the 12 apostles?
They were set aside to be with Him. They were to preach. They had authority to cast out demons.

2. In this listing of the 12, which disciples are listed by multiple names?
Simon is called Peter. The sons of Zebedee who are James and John are called Boanerges.

3. Who is listed last in all of the listings of the apostles?
Judas Iscariot, who betrayed Jesus, is listed last in all of the lists of apostles.

4. What are the names of the men selected to be Jesus' apostles?
The list in Mark is Simon, James, John, Andrew, Phillip, Bartholomew, Matthew, Thomas, James the son of Alphaeus, Thaddaeus, Simon the Cananean, and Judas.

5. How many apostles does Mark list?
There are 12 apostles listed in Mark's Gospel.

6. What do you think is the significance of the number 12?
The number 12 appears to be connected to the 12 tribes of ancient Israel.

7. When Jesus sends the 12 apostles out for their ministry tour how are they sent?
The apostles are sent to preach and to cast out demons. They were sent in pairs.

8. In Mark 6 there is a list of prohibited items for the apostolic ministry, what were they?
The apostles were to take no bread, bag, or money.

9. What were the apostles to do if they were not welcomed into a community?
If they were not received in a community they were to shake the dust off of their feet as a sign against the people there.

10. What were the results of the two-by-two ministry of the apostles?
They cast out many demons and anointed with oil many who were sick, and cured them.

Your words and your deeds preach!

An elderly deacon at the Baptist church in town wore the same suit to church week in and week out, year after year. Some of the more affluent members of the church got together and contributed some funds to buy him a new suit, since the old one was so tattered and worn.

The deacon took the money quietly and without much fanfare. The patrons worried that they had offended him. But since it was a small town, they soon learned that he had gone to the best store in town to buy a new suit, and in the process had enough money left over to buy new shoes, a new shirt, and a new tie to go with the suit.

All the Baptists were waiting for him on Sunday. The faithful old deacon never arrived. Now, certain that they had offended him, the benefactors sent some of the other deacons to his home to see what happened.

When they asked him about his new suit, he admitted that he had bought one. And, he told them, it looked good on him. In fact, he said, although the new suit looked good on him, it didn't look "like him."

Sometimes our good deeds must be followed with words of explanation and expectation, or our lost friends might end up pretending they are someone else!

Jesus Calls for Total Commitment

Mark 8:27-38

And Jesus went out, and his disciples, into the towns of Caesarea Philippi: and by the way he asked his disciples, saying unto them, Whom do men say that I am?

28 And they answered, John the Baptist: but some say, Elias; and others, One of the prophets.

29 And he saith unto them, But whom say ye that I am? And Peter answereth and saith unto him, Thou art the Christ.

30 And he charged them that they should tell no man of him.

31 And he began to teach them, that the Son of man must suffer many things, and be rejected of the elders, and of the chief priests, and scribes, and be killed, and after three days rise again.

32 And he spake that saying openly. And Peter took him, and began to rebuke him.

33 But when he had turned about and looked on his disciples, he rebuked Peter, saying, Get thee behind me, Satan: for thou savourest not the things that be of God, but the things that be of men.

34 And when he had called the people unto him with his disciples also, he said unto them, Whosoever will come after me, let him deny himself, and take up his cross, and follow me.

35 For whosoever will save his life shall lose it; but whosoever shall lose his life for my sake and the gospel's, the same shall save it.

36 For what shall it profit a man, if he shall gain the whole world, and lose his own soul?

37 Or what shall a man give in exchange for his soul?

38 Whosoever therefore shall be ashamed of me and of my words in this adulterous and sinful generation; of him also shall the Son of man be ashamed, when he cometh in the glory of his Father with the holy angels.

Jan. 23

Memory Selection
Mark 8:34

Background Scripture
Mark 8:27-38

Devotional Reading
Mathew 16:24-28

This lesson focuses on Jesus' straightforward statement about the high cost, but equally high reward, of total commitment to Him and His mission. It comes after initial success in drawing crowds who are excited about His miracles. They ask whether this could actually be the Messiah they had hoped for.

Jesus' teaching about His mission reveals that His followers have a different picture of the Messiah they expect. Instead of leading an army that would drive out the hated occupying Roman army, Jesus predicts His death. The apostle Peter is representative of those whose expectations simply cannot be squared with a dying Messiah, who expects others to give their lives, too.

Are we ourselves willing to follow such a Messiah?

ℰℭ

Ask members of your group what it means to "Take up your cross daily." To many believers, this means bearing some burden we can't get rid of, as in *"Well, my mother-in-law is going to move in with us, but that's just a cross I'll have to bear!"*

Explain that originally "bearing one's cross" meant not just patient suffering but "daily death." In today's lesson Jesus predicts not only that He will die, but that He expects His followers to "lose" their own lives as well. Suggest that the meaning of this statements may lie somewhere between that business about the mother-in-law and actually becoming a martyr. Call for open minds that will allow the unfolding of the text itself to amplify and explain the hymn we sing:

Oh there's a cross for everyone,
And there's a cross for me.

Teaching Outline	Daily Bible Readings	
I. The Good Confession—27-30	Mon.	Bread of Life, Eternal Life *John 6:41-51*
A. Views about Jesus, 27-28	Tue.	Christ's 'Flesh and Blood' *John 6:52-59*
B. The disciples' view, 29-30	Wed.	'This Is a Hard Saying' *John 6:60-69*
II. The Goal of Jesus—31-33	Thu.	'Who Do You Say I Am?' *Matthew 16:13-20*
A. The Servant-Son, 31	Fri.	Denying Ourselves *Matthew 16:24-28*
B. Twin rebukes, 32-33	Sat.	'You Are the Messiah!' *Mark 8:27-30*
III. The Glory of Commitment—34-38	Sun.	'Take Up Your Cross, Too' *Mark 8:31-38*
A. Bearing our cross, 34		
B. Finding our lives, 35-37		
C. Shame or glory?, 38		

Verse by Verse

I. The Good Confession—27-30

A. Views about Jesus, 27-28

27 And Jesus went out, and his disciples, into the towns of Caesarea Philippi: and by the way he asked his disciples, saying unto them, Whom do men say that I am?

28 And they answered, John the Baptist: but some say, Elias; and others, One of the prophets.

Jesus' ministry in northern Judea is drawing to a close. With a sure sense of timing, He is preparing to work His way south toward Jerusalem, where He knows that His Messianic claim will not be received as well by the Jewish hierarchy as it has been by the common people (see Mark 12:37). Before he leaves the area, however, He goes to the very northern edge of the Promised Land, to a largely gentile city named for Tiberius Caesar, perhaps because it provides a good setting for Him to affirm that He is a Messiah for the world, not just for the Jews.

Although He knows very well what His followers believe about Him, He asks them so they can clarify their own views in light of the views of others. Various strains of Messianic expectations had grown up among the Jews. Some expected a mighty king in the style of King David. Others held to the divine and powerful "Son of Man" imagery from the book of Daniel and Ezekiel. Some longed for a priestly Messiah to replace the corrupt system of the priesthood. Still others expected a fiery prophet like John the Baptist or even Elijah reborn—the view the disciples report here.

B. The disciples' view, 29-30

29 And he saith unto them, But whom say ye that I am? And Peter answereth and saith unto him, Thou art the Christ.

30 And he charged them that they should tell no man of him.

What counted most for Jesus was the disciples' own view. If they did not accept Him as the Messiah, it would jeopardize His cause after His approaching death in Jerusalem. When the outspoken apostle Peter blurts out the consensus view of the disciples, He uses the Greek word, *christos*, which translates the Jewish title "Messiah." Although, as we shall see, Peter does not understand the role of Messiah, at least he believes in Him firmly; and to some extent he no doubt speaks for the other apostles.

Previously, demons and those Jesus healed had been told not to tell others that Jesus was the Messiah. Now, in verse 20, the disciples themselves are warned that it is too early

203

to broadcast the Good News. For word to spread that Messiah had come may have precipitated an outbreak of Messianic fervor and an uprising against the Romans, resulting in political and social chaos that could cut short Jesus' ministry.

II. The Goal of Jesus—31-33
A. The Servant-Son, 31

1 And he began to teach them, that the Son of man must suffer many things, and be rejected of the elders, and of the chief priests, and scribes, and be killed, and after three days rise again.

Jesus now cuts to the heart of the difference between the diverse views of the people, and the true nature of the Messiah. He *is* the "Son of man," of whom Daniel spoke; but instead of being a power-figure hurling lightning bolts at His enemies, He comes as gentle as a lamb, wanting to be King of our hearts, instead of allowing Himself to be made an earthly king (see John 6:15).

The crowning difference between these two Messianic views is seen in the fact that instead of living to drive out the Romans and restore Israel's political place in the world, Jesus will be killed.

The disciples no doubt had trouble hearing the next words, that He would rise again; for the death of their Messiah would, to them, dash all positive possibilities. Like some today, the lure of an earthly "theocracy" in which the righteous can finally wreak vengeance on the unrighteous had overwhelmed the prophet Isaiah's prediction that the Messiah would be "wounded for our transgression" and "bruised for our iniquities" (Isa. 53:4-5).

B. Twin rebukes, 32-33

32 And he spake that saying openly. And Peter took him, and began to rebuke him.

33 But when he had turned about and looked on his disciples, he rebuked Peter, saying, Get thee behind me, Satan: for thou savourest not the things that be of God, but the things that be of men.

Nowhere is Peter's famed volatility more apparent than in this scene: he who had spoken first and most boldly of Jesus' glorious Messiah-ship is now the first unthinkingly to hurl the words of the very Son of God back in His face. Just as swiftly, Jesus rebukes Peter, and in terms that could hardly be stronger. The Hebrew word *shatan* was not only the name of the Prince of Demons; it had the literal meaning of "adversary." In addressing Peter as "Satan," Jesus warns that opposing His death places one in an "adversarial" role with Him. To try to save the Messiah from the Cross is not "of God."

III. The Glory of Commitment–34-38
A. Bearing our cross, 34

34 And when he had called the people unto him with his disciples also, he said unto them, Whosoever will come after me, let him deny himself, and take up his cross, and follow me.

The next pill prescribed by the Great Physician is equally difficult to swallow. Just as the Messiah must subject His concern for His personal safety to the greater will of God, so must those who dare to follow Him. To "take up (one's) cross" does not mean simply to struggle under a burden, but to be willing to die. Although many among Jesus' followers would, in later centuries, die for the Cause, they are here so caught up in the glory of what they expected to be a joint reign with the Messiah that this saying would be as difficult to accept as Christ's insistence that He would be killed. Taking up one's cross means the daily "crucifixion" of fleshly desires.

B. Finding our lives, 35-37

35 For whosoever will save his life shall lose it; but whosoever shall lose his life for my sake and the gospel's, the same shall save it.

36 For what shall it profit a man, if he shall gain the whole world, and lose his own soul?

37 Or what shall a man give in exchange for his soul?

As challenging as it is to crucify the self, Jesus' next statement shows that selflessness actually meets our deepest need: to be saved. The model for this paradox, of course, is Jesus Himself. Had He refused to lay down His life on the Cross, He would have forfeited His entire mission in life. In a similar way, when His followers fight for control, superiority, and worldly gain, they forfeit all claims for salvation—since salvation comes from following their Master's pattern.

Some scholars think that the famous ICHTHUS or fish that became the symbol of the Christian was developed partly because of the imagery of Christ as the "big fish" followed by a "school" of Christians, the little fish. Here is the Big Fish, Jesus, giving up His life for others. If the little fish decided that they wanted to save their skins instead of living for others, it would be as though the school of fish suddenly reversed course and went in the opposite direction of the Big Fish.

C. Shame or glory?, 38

38 Whosoever therefore shall be ashamed of me and of my words in this adulterous and sinful generation; of him also shall the Son of man be ashamed, when he cometh in the glory of his Father with the holy angels.

Now Jesus puts the clincher on His radical call to discipleship. In a few short months, the disciples will have their loyalty tested when Jesus is arrested. Here Jesus says plainly that they will forfeit their hope of a glorious resurrection if they are shamed by the reality of Jesus' crucifixion. Although all will indeed flee in shame for a moment, they return, wait in Jerusalem for the risen Lord to appear to them (Acts 1), then go to work in His vineyard. In the case of the apostles, tradition holds that all but Judas were martyred. Despite their timidity in the text for today, they will eventually rise to accept the fact that Kingdom-living involves self-giving.

Evangelistic Emphasis

A recent cartoon shows a man worshipfully kneeling at an altar. Instead of the expected symbol, perched on top of this altar is a huge replica of a #1 lottery ball. The man is soulfully closing a just-uttered prayer with the words, "For thine is the kingdom, the power ball, and the glory forever. Amen."

Our culture's growing addiction to gambling is one clear indication of this new and alarming commitment to "success-by-chance." All across America small towns and big cities left with big holes in their local economies are embracing gambling casinos and lottery games as their tickets to salvation.

State-run lottery games are used to fund public education, for we would rather buy a lottery ticket than approve local school budgets.

The good news is that in a world gone crazy, Jesus is still the answer. The confession, "You are the Christ the son of the living God" still brings redemption. Our challenge is to confront the popular paths to salvation with THE WAY. Jesus redefines success as being willing to make a sacrifice. When we give up our human efforts at salvation and trust His sacrifice, we all can know salvation.

ഇാൽ

Memory Selection

Jesus said, Whosoever will come after me, let him deny himself, and take up his cross and follow me.—*Mark 8:34*

Jesus clarifies discipleship in this verse. You don't have to guess at what you must do as a disciple of Jesus. The first step of discipleship is self-denial. Putting aside selfish desires and motives and opening the soul up to Christ is a constant struggle through life.

We are called to take up our cross. This is not something that happens to us as a result of sin or sickness. Taking up the cross is a conscious decision to be involved in our world in ways that are Christ-like.

As we deny self and take up our cross we must follow Jesus. One of the hallmarks of discipleship is obedience. Are you obeying the pattern for discipleship that Jesus gave?

Weekday Problems

Scott was the most spiritual person at First Church, and he was quick to tell everyone so. Each Sunday in worship, his feet were tapping, arms waving, and he was singing at the top of his lungs. His Bible was always with him. It was worn out from all his page turning. Scott loved anything spiritual. He loved talk about spiritual life and especially spiritual warfare. He was always at Bible studies and prayer groups. Scott also loved to talk to others about his spiritual life and how their lives didn't add up quite like his standards would have them.

Scott would be contacted almost every time the Habitat for Humanity coordinator needed help with a house. He was always praying or going to some spiritual training event. He would not teach Sunday school because he liked to go to another church on Sunday to "get more food." Scott would not *do* anything in the church.

He was quick to answer that he was saved by grace through faith. He could never answer the question about "taking up his cross and following Jesus." He said he would have to pray about it.

*Have you known people who were so heavenly-minded they were no earthly good?

Cross Roads

There is no comma after "cross"; the cross is a continuous affair.—*Evert F. Ellis.*

* * * *

No cross, no crown.—*English proverb*

* * * *

The greatest of all crosses is self. If we die in part every day, we shall have but little to do on the last. These little daily deaths will destroy the power of the final dying.—*Fenelon*

* * * *

Though good things answer many good intents,
Crosses do still bring forth the best events.
　　　　　　　　　　—*Robert Herrick, "Crosses"*

* * * *

Carry the cross patiently, and with perfect submission; and in the end it shall carry you.—*Thomas à Kempis*

This Lesson in Your Life

What Jesus said about denying self and taking up the cross flies in the face of some popular theology.

Take healing, for example. The first wrong attitude toward healing is peculiar to the West in recent times. It is the belief that suffering has no rightful place in the world and certainly no place in the redeemed order of things. Such complacency is surely one cause of the spiritual poverty of the Western church. Jesus didn't have that view, nor did the writer to the Hebrews, C.S. Lewis, or John Donne. Suffering has its place and value in this life, no matter how much we yearn for its absence in the New Jerusalem of the next.

Instead of fully understanding and redeeming suffering, praying for its removal but harnessing it to become more Christ-like, we've ignored it and impoverished ourselves, and reduced the opportunities to make practical steps toward softening its inevitable impact.

The second idea is that 's cliché, "instant gratification." We all know the dangers of this, and yet we continually diminish our capacity for perseverance by accepting it. This is especially true when we have minor afflictions. It might be excusable if we actually did anything worthwhile with our lives. Instead, we can't wait for our flu to disappear by the natural healing process God has given us, because it interferes with our TV watching.

Where is the concept of self-denial? Where is the notion of following Christ in the way of suffering? We have lost both in our quest for instant gratification.

1. What information did Jesus seek from His disciples as they traveled through Caesarea Philippi?
Jesus asked His disciples, "Who do the people say that I am?"

2. What was the popular opinion about Jesus according to the disciples?
Some thought Jesus was John the Baptist. Others thought He was Elijah. Still others thought he was one of the prophets.

3. What specific question did Jesus pose to His disciples after hearing about public opinion?
He asked them, "Who do *you* say that I am?"

4. Who answered for the group and what was the essence of his answer?
Peter was the spokesman for the group. He answered, "You are the Christ."

5. What did Jesus tell the disciples they should do with the information about His identity?
Jesus ordered the disciples that they were not to tell anyone about Him.

6. What did Jesus begin to teach the disciples about how the Christ was to be treated?
He taught them that He must undergo much suffering at the hands of the chief priests. He would be killed, and on the third day He would rise again.

7. How did Peter respond to this new insight into the role of the Christ?
Peter took Jesus aside and attempted to correct His theology about the nature of the Christ.

8. How did Jesus respond to Peter's attempt to correct Him?
Jesus rebuked Peter, saying, "Get behind me Satan, for you are setting your mind not on divine things but on human things."

9. What were the conditions that Jesus gave the crowd for discipleship?
The disciple must deny himself, take up his cross, and follow Jesus.

10. What happens to those who are ashamed of Jesus and His words?
"Those who are ashamed of me . . . of them the son of Man will be ashamed when He comes in the glory of His Father."

A magazine publisher installed a new program that was designed to notify subscribers by mail when it was time to renew their subscriptions. One day it went sour, and before anyone realized the miscue, a farmer in Montana received 11,834 letters telling him his subscription had expired. The local postmaster had to hire a special truck to deliver all the letters. After the farmer had read about 200 of them, all exactly alike, he sat down and wrote out a check renewing his subscription. Attached to the check was a note, which read, "I give up. My check is enclosed."

God sends expressions of love to us every day of our lives, but our continued deafness and muteness to these repeated messages keep us from giving up our self-absorbed isolation and self-defeating attitudes.

Could we answer like Simon Peter when asked about who *we* think Jesus is? Could we say, "You are the Christ"? Would we, like Peter, seek to define "messiah" in self-serving ways?

It is time to turn off the television and put aside that newsletter from that world renowned evangelist. It is time to pick up the New Testament and read again for *ourselves* the stories of Jesus!

Jesus Defines True Greatness

Mark 10:32-45

And they were in the way going up to Jerusalem; and Jesus went before them: and they were amazed; and as they followed, they were afraid. And he took again the twelve, and began to tell them what things should happen unto him,

33 Saying, Behold, we go up to Jerusalem; and the Son of man shall be delivered unto the chief priests, and unto the scribes; and they shall condemn him to death, and shall deliver him to the Gentiles:

34 And they shall mock him, and shall scourge him, and shall spit upon him, and shall kill him: and the third day he shall rise again.

35 And James and John, the sons of Zebedee, come unto him, saying, Master, we would that thou shouldest do for us whatsoever we shall desire.

36 And he said unto them, What would ye that I should do for you?

37 They said unto him, Grant unto us that we may sit, one on thy right hand, and the other on thy left hand, in thy glory.

38 But Jesus said unto them, Ye know not what ye ask: can ye drink of the cup that I drink of? and be baptized with the baptism that I am baptized with?

39 And they said unto him, We can. And Jesus said unto them, Ye shall indeed drink of the cup that I drink of; and with the baptism that I am baptized withal shall ye be baptized:

40 But to sit on my right hand and on my left hand is not mine to give; but it shall be given to them for whom it is prepared.

41 And when the ten heard it, they began to be much displeased with James and John.

42 But Jesus called them to him, and saith unto them, Ye know that they which are accounted to rule over the Gentiles exercise lordship over them; and their great ones exercise authority upon them.

43 But so shall it not be among you: but whosoever will be great among you, shall be your minister:

44 And whosoever of you will be the chiefest, shall be servant of all.

45 For even the Son of man came not to be ministered unto, but to minister, and to give his life a ransom for many.

Memory Selection
Mark 10:43b-44

Background Scripture
Mark 10:13-45

Devotional Reading
Matthew 20:20-28

Jan. 30

211

In our last lesson we saw that Jesus' radical definition of the role of the Messiah—to die for others—was resisted by Peter. Surely Jesus' blunt rebuke, "Get thee behind me, Satan!"—would be enough to convince the rest of the disciples that "lording it over" or ruling others did not have a political meaning for Jesus, and that even His disciples must serve others.

Not at all! Here two disciples' request a high post in what they viewed to be the coming earthly kingdom ruled by Jesus. As modern psychology has discovered, we often see and hear what we *want* or *expect* to see or hear. As we reflect on this passage, it will become clear that we too suffer from James and John's presuppositions. We often have the same difficulty learning that to live we must die, and to rule we must serve.

℘℘℘

In this lesson Jesus champions the concept of "servant leadership," which has become a buzz word in both Christian and business circles. Start the class with a discussion that defines the term and includes these ideas:

*A servant leader creates a "culture of service" by **serving**.*

Servant leadership empowers others, helping them develop their own leadership skills.

Servant leadership is not threatened by good ideas from others.

*Servant leadership does **not** mean the abandonment of authority, but the use of authority for the good of others instead of for consolidating one's own authority.*

Servant leadership usually results in more growth than authoritarian leadership.

Teaching Outline

I. The Way Up Is Down—32-34
   A. Jesus' firm resolve, 32
   B. Jesus reveals His fate, 33-34
II. The Rage to Rule—35-41
   A. Lust for a throne, 35-37
   B. The servant-leader, 38-40
   C. Apostles' reaction, 41
III. Leadership As Service, 42-45
   A. Gentiles' example, 42
   B. Christ's example, 43-45

Daily Bible Readings

Mon.	Servant of All
	Mark 9:33-37
Tue.	Surprise for His Hearers
	Mark 10:13-22
Wed.	Perplexed Disciples
	Mark 10:23-27
Thu.	The First Last, the Last First
	Mark 10:28-31
Fri.	Servants Are Greater
	Mark 10:35-45
Sat.	'I Came to Serve'
	Matthew 20:20-28
Sun.	The Exalted to Be Humbled
	Matthew 23:1-12

Verse by Verse

I. The Way Up Is Down—32-34
A. Jesus' firm resolve, 32

32 And they were in the way going up to Jerusalem; and Jesus went before them: and they were amazed; and as they followed, they were afraid. And he took again the twelve, and began to tell them what things should happen unto him,

At this point we are about halfway through the Gospel of Mark, and even earlier (8:31) Jesus has indicated His determination to go from Galilee to Jerusalem, where doom awaits. This proportion has led to Mark's being called "a passion narrative with an extended introduction."

B. Jesus reveals His fate, 33-34

33 Saying, Behold, we go up to Jerusalem; and the Son of man shall be delivered unto the chief priests, and unto the scribes; and they shall condemn him to death, and shall deliver him to the Gentiles:

34 And they shall mock him, and shall scourge him, and shall spit upon him, and shall kill him: and the third day he shall rise again.

"Son of man" is the most frequent phrase Jesus used to refer to Himself. It was a Messianic title that emerges first in the books of Daniel and Ezekiel. Perhaps Jesus favored it because it hinted at both His supernatural power and His humanity. In Mark 9:12 Jesus uses the title to describe the necessity of His suffering for the sins of the world. It is this second meaning of the term that Jesus' disciples have the most difficulty understanding. They have no clue that He must first die in order to be raised to rule.

Jesus would only have to be an astute political observer to be able to predict that He would be arrested and condemned in Jerusalem. His teaching upset both the Jewish and Roman leaders, and it would not be hard to see that He could be charged with sedition. However, it is only His supernatural nature that enabled Him to predict the specifics that he would be mocked and whipped and spat upon, and that He would rise again the third day.

II. The Rage to Rule—35-41
A. Lust for a throne, 35-37

35 And James and John, the sons of Zebedee, come unto him, saying, Master, we would that thou shouldest do for us whatsoever we shall desire.

213

36 And he said unto them, What would ye that I should do for you?

37 They said unto him, Grant unto us that we may sit, one on thy right hand, and the other on thy left hand, in thy glory.

This request illustrates clearly the disciples' lack of understanding of the spiritual nature of Christ's Kingdom. Since they think of the Kingdom as a powerful political entity in which Messiah will rule, they think of leadership in the Kingdom in terms of power and position, too. James and John may also have thought that being members of Christ's most intimate inner circle (9:2) qualified them to have important posts in this Kingdom.

God's "glory" is a frequent Old Testament theme. It often is the "aura" or awesome light that surrounds the invisible God (as in Lev. 9:23). Clearly, James and John's request does not stem from simply wanting to be close to the King of glory. They envision personal glory stemming from posts like that given to Joseph by Pharaoh in Egypt.

In our own times, this kind of request has come from those promoting "dominion theology," in which they propose that believers should infiltrate civil and governmental posts in order to seize ruling power from unbelievers, under the thin guise of the statement that believers will "judge angels" (1 Cor. 6:3), and "rule over many things" if they are faithful "over a few" (Matt. 25:23-

25). Such positions are as obvious an example of the universal lust for power as is James and John's request here, and betray a similar misunderstanding of the Kingdom and the principle of servanthood.

B. The servant-leader, 38-39

38 But Jesus said unto them, Ye know not what ye ask: can ye drink of the cup that I drink of? and be baptized with the baptism that I am baptized with?

39 And they said unto him, We can. And Jesus said unto them, Ye shall indeed drink of the cup that I drink of; and with the baptism that I am baptized withal shall ye be baptized:

40 But to sit on my right hand and on my left hand is not mine to give; but it shall be given to them for whom it is prepared.

The "cup" and the "baptism" Jesus refers to are images of suffering. The cup stands for a drink like the cup of poisonous hemlock that the Greek philosopher Socrates was given to drink, and the baptism is a picture of being "immersed" in suffering. The disciples say they will be up to the task, but it is doubtful that they fully understood that it could mean following Jesus to the death.

Jesus' second response is to assure them that while they will indeed suffer for following Him, He lacks the authority to appoint them to the high posts they requested. Apparently this authority is reserved for the Father. An interesting parallel is in Jesus' statement that only the Father knew the precise time of the end of the world (Matt. 24:36). This submission to the greater knowledge of the Father is itself an example of servant leadership, and is in full agreement with the "rank" Jesus gave up in the Incarnation (see Philip. 2:5:8).

C. Apostles' reaction, 41

41 And when the ten heard it, they began to be much displeased with James and John.

The rest of the disciples grumble about the overt ambition shown by James and John. Yet since they also did not understand the necessity of Christ's death we may wonder if they merely neglected to voice their own ambitions. Jesus' reply to them strengthens this supposition.

III. Leadership As Service, 42-45

A. Gentiles' example, 42

42 But Jesus called them to him, and saith unto them, Ye know that they which are accounted to rule over the Gentiles exercise lordship over them; and their great ones exercise authority upon them.

Beginning the sentence with "but" indicates Jesus' protection of James and John's request, and His perception that all 12 of the apostles need to see the difference between servant leadership and the worldly model. The "high and mighty" model was followed by "Gentiles," He says, using the term to include not just non-Jews but anyone who has the "gentile" spirit of lordship as opposed to servant leadership. As an example at hand, His disciples had only to consider the ruthless leadership of the Romans rulers under whom the Jews suffered.

B. Christ's example, 43-45

43 But so shall it not be among you: but whosoever will be great among you, shall be your minister:

44 And whosoever of you will be the chiefest, shall be servant of all.

45 For even the Son of man came not to be ministered unto, but to minister, and to give his life a ransom for many.

Because of the inspirational "suffering servant" passages of Isaiah 40-55, those who were familiar with Messianic prophecy should have been able to see that He would minister to others instead of insisting on being served Himself.

Now the rich "Son of man" concepts blend the image of divine power in Daniel and Ezekiel with the "ransom" theme of the Old Testament, in which a grain or animal sacrifice would be offered as a substitute for the life of sinners. The implication of course is not that the death of a follower of Christ would be a ransom, but that His supreme sacrifice in death set the tone of the sacrificial life of service to which He calls His followers.

Unfortunately, this remains a lesson that is not easily learned. To be named a leader is for some people an irresistible temptation to pride and an invitation to do precisely what was forbidden in verse 42, which has been paraphrased, "when people get a little power how quickly it goes to their heads" (*The Message*).

Evangelistic Emphasis

America is a nation with a "number one" mentality. We want the best, the brightest, and the biggest. We make assumptions based on this mode of thinking.

A tourist was visiting New York City with his seven-year-old daughter when a man approached to ask for change. The little girl asked what the man wanted.

"He wanted money," her father explained.

The little girl asked why.

"The man is hungry," he said.

His daughter's eyes widened. "They eat *money* in Manhattan?" she asked.

There are also some strange views about money, things, and servanthood in the Church.

The most faithful Christian is often not the wealthiest. The most needy person is often not the poorest. James and John found out that Jesus measures people on a different scale. The greatest in the Kingdom will be servant of all.

ഇന്ദ്ര

Memory Selection

Whosoever would be great among you, shall be your minister; and whosoever of you would be chiefest shall be servant of all.—*Mark 10: 43-44*

Mark it down. Anytime you see a happy family, it is not an accident. Somebody sacrificed. That person sacrificed convenience, comfort, time, power, and the right to make unilateral decisions. There is no success without sacrifice.

We live in the era of the pampered athlete, executive, politician, educator, student, parishioner, preacher, and nation. What has happened to sacrifice? Sacrifice is the sacrament of love.

Putting someone's needs before our own is a form of that sacrament. Perhaps our culture would hear the message of sacrifice clearer than the message of prosperity, if God's people practiced sacrificial living. Some in the church seem to have them confused.

Weekday Problems

Carl Rife tells of being chosen to be the drum major of a new marching band his senior year in high school. "Most of us had absolutely no experience marching in parades," he wrote. "I still remember leading the band down West Market Street in York, Pennsylvania. My basic job was to march in front of the band and every so often blow my whistle in a certain cadence to strike up the band.

"As we were marching down West Market Street for a short time, I heard someone from the crowd who had gathered to watch the parade holler to me, 'Mister, you lost your band.' I sneaked a look back and sure enough, there was the Central High School marching band about three-quarters of a block behind.'"

Leaders in the church sometimes lose their bands, too. Whether it is the Sunday school class we lead or the choir, we can get so caught up in leading that we leave our followers behind?.

*How can we be leaders for Christ and still have the servant attitude that Jesus has called us to have?

The Power and the Glory

Boy Jack: Do you think it's possible to predict the future with cards?

Friend Mack: Sure. My mother can take one look at my report card and predict exactly what will happen when my dad comes home.

* * * *

Demanding customer in a cafe: I want some raw oysters, not too small, not too salty, or too fat. They must be cold, and I want them *right now!*

Waiter: Yes *sir!* And would you like pearls with that?

* * * *

Woman at confession: Bless me, Father, for I have sinned. I can't resist the temptation to sit in front of my mirror two or three hours every day, admiring my beauty. I think I need to confess the sin of pride.

Priest (after peeking): Well, I don't think you need to confess having too much pride, but too much imagination.

This Lesson in Your Life

The church is not in this world to serve and save itself. There are far too many congregations whose only goal is to survive, to keep safe, to form circles that look inward. Missionary discipleship denies that there is any need for the church "just to keep going" if it's not "going" anywhere.

The church has become much too fixated on how to save itself rather than saving the world. The community of faith, the circle of believing disciples, must face the world with its message. The difference between an inward-circle faith and an outward-circle faith is the difference between "Churchianity" and "Christianity."

The number of people parking themselves on a psychiatrist's couch each week, for years on end, testifies to the fact that we all feel ourselves to be endlessly fascinating subjects of attention. There are whole churches that share this self-fixation. What would happen if both individually and as a congregation we shook ourselves out of this self-absorption and began to look for the key to our psychological and spiritual health outside ourselves? Jesus counseled that those who seek to save their lives will lose them. Let us look outside the familiar circle of our own problems, our own concerns, and find healing, wholeness, and health in giving ourselves in service to others.

We will help save both the world and the church as we open our familiar circles outward and start looking at our world differently. Looking to the needs of others will allow those persons to see Christ in us. Isn't that the purpose of being a Christian?

1. As Jesus was walking along the road to Jerusalem, what two responses to what He predicted came from among those in the crowd?
They were amazed and they were afraid at the same time.

2. What did Jesus do as this group traveled toward Jerusalem?
Jesus took the disciples aside and told them again what would happen to Him in Jerusalem.

3. What did Jesus tell the disciples would happen to him in Jerusalem?
He said that He would be condemned to death and handed over to the gentiles. They would mock Him and spit on Him, flog Him and kill Him. After three days He would rise again.

4. After Jesus spoke words about his crucifixion, two disciples came with a question. Who were they?
James and John, the sons of Zebedee, came to Jesus with a request.

5. What request did James and John make of Jesus?
The sons of Zebedee wanted to sit one on the right hand and the other on the left when Jesus came into His Kingdom.

6. In response to their request, Jesus asked a question of them. What was that question?
"Are you able to drink the cup that I drink, or to be baptized with the baptism with which I am baptized?"

7. What did Jesus tell James and John about their request?
He told them that He was not able to grant their request.

8. When the other disciples heard about the request of James and John what was their response?
The 10, when they heard it, were angry with James and John.

9. Jesus talked about the Gentiles and their social structure, what was that structure?
The Gentiles lord it over those they rule, and their great ones are tyrants.

10. What did Jesus tell the disciples about greatness?
Whoever wants to be great must be servant of all, and whoever wishes to be first must be slave of all.

219

A person went into an airport shop and bought a book to read and a package of cookies to eat while waiting to board the plane. The passenger then took a seat in the terminal and opened the book. Immediately the person sitting two seats to her right distracted her from her reading because, incredibly, the man actually was fumbling to open the package of cookies on the seat between them. When he put his hand into the package, extracted a cookie, and ate it, she couldn't believe her eyes. She was so shocked to see a total stranger nonchalantly eating her cookies she didn't know what to do. She didn't want to create a scene, but she wanted her cookies. "No way is he going to eat all my cookies! I'll show him," she thought—and she reached over and removed a cookie from the package and ate it.

Whereupon the man reached out for a second cookie, and ate it. "I'll really show him," she told herself again, as she reached in and ate a second cookie. The man then ate a third cookie and she did likewise. By this time you would have thought the message would have gotten through to this cookie monster, but he still continued eating the cookies and she persisted in eating one for one until all the cookies were gone.

As they boarded the plane, the guerilla warfare continued as each glared at the other with fire blazing in their eyes. Then she took her seat, reached into her purse for a tissue, and there found her still unopened package of cookies!

That is why we become servant of all: ignoring others can lead to foolish behavior.

Lesson 10

Overcoming Grief

Ruth 1:3-8, 14-18

nd Elimelech Naomi's husband died; and she was left, and her two sons.

4 And they took them wives of the women of Moab; the name of the one was Orpah, and the name of the other Ruth: and they dwelled there about ten years.

5 And Mahlon and Chilion died also both of them; and the woman was left of her two sons and her husband.

6 Then she arose with her daughters in law, that she might return from the country of Moab: for she had heard in the country of Moab how that the LORD had visited his people in giving them bread.

7 Wherefore she went forth out of the place where she was, and her two daughters in law with her; and they went on the way to return unto the land of Judah.

8 And Naomi said unto her two daughters in law, Go, return each to her mother's house: the LORD deal kindly with you, as ye have dealt with the dead, and with me.

14 And they lifted up their voice, and wept again: and Orpah kissed her mother in law; but Ruth clave unto her.

15 And she said, Behold, thy sister in law is gone back unto her people, and unto her gods: return thou after thy sister in law.

16 And Ruth said, Intreat me not to leave thee, or to return from following after thee: for whither thou goest, I will go; and where thou lodgest, I will lodge: thy people shall be my people, and thy God my God:

17 Where thou diest, will I die, and there will I be buried: the LORD do so to me, and more also, if ought but death part thee and me.

18 When she saw that she was stedfastly minded to go with her, then she left speaking unto her.

Feb. 6

Memory Selection
Ruth 1:16

Background Scripture
Ruth 1

Devotional Reading
Psalm 31:9-15

Previous lessons in this series have focused on God's call to Abram to become the patriarch of the chosen race, Israel, and on Christ's call to His disciples. In this lesson, the call of God is made very personal. It is the call to every believer to find in Him our source of comfort during times of struggle, pain, and grief.

Most believers know the general invitation of Jesus to "Come unto me, all ye that labour and are heavy laden, and I will give you rest" (Matt. 11:28). Yet somehow it is easier for many of us to acknowledge that *others* might need this Word of comfort, while being unable to confess our own personal need. Be sensitive to the possibility that the story of Naomi's husband's death might be too close to home for some in your group. Try to get across the message that we are all welcome in the comforting arms of Jesus, while not turning the class time into a group counseling session.

Introduce this lesson by recalling the grief of God's people, the Jews, while in captivity. Read Psalm 137:1-4, which reflects these dark times. Invite group members to share times when they have been away from home, perhaps overseas in the military or other situations where loneliness produced its own measure of grief. Note how such experiences are much like that of Naomi, an Israelite who found herself in the land of Moab without financial resources, having lost a husband and two sons. Yet this lesson shows how God used her daughters-in-law to comfort her. We too can be awake to the resources He provides in our own "down" times.

Teaching Outline	**Daily Bible Readings**
I. Alone in a Strange Land—3-5	Mon. Weary with Weeping *Psalm 6:1-7*
A. Death of a husband, 3	Tue. A Sorrowful Life *Psalm 31:9-15*
B. Fate of the sons, 4-5	Wed. Uncomforted Soul *Psalm 77:1-10*
II. Return to a Homeland—6-8, 14-18	Thu. Loss of Family *Ruth 1:1-5*
A. Naomi's plans, 6-8	Fri. 'Return to Your Home' *Ruth 1:6-11*
B. Sisters-in-law part, 14-15	Sat. Orpah Goes, Ruth Stays *Ruth 1:12-17*
C. Ruth's loyalty, 16-18	Sun. Journey to Bethlehem *Ruth 1:18-22*

Verse by Verse

I. Alone in a Strange Land—3-5
A. Death of a husband, 3
3 And Elimelech Naomi's husband died; and she was left, and her two sons.

The book of Ruth was no doubt included in the Old Testament because Ruth became the grandmother of King David, a chief ancestor of the Messiah who was to come. The book is also therefore significant for Christians because, as a Moabite and a gentile, Ruth heralds the inclusion of gentiles in God's Covenant.

Ironically, Elimelech and Ruth had to leave their hometown of Bethlehem because of a famine, even though the name "Bethlehem" means "house of bread."

The land of Moab lay east of Judea, across the Dead Sea. Because an ancient trade route called "The King's Highway" passed through Moab, it was at some times in ancient history a wealthy land, extracting taxes from caravans bearing merchandise to and from Egypt, to the south. It is the site of the discovery, in 1868, of the "Moabite Stone," which describes a battle with Israel (possibly the one also recorded in 2 King 3:4-27), and corroborates the names of some 15 sites mentioned in the Old Testament.

Although the Moabites were descendants of Lot (Gen. 19:37), relations between the two countries were often strained. Moabite leaders went to great lengths to oppose the Israelites' passage through their land during the period of the Wilderness Wanderings (Num. 22-23). Later, Israel was ruled by Moab, for 13 years (Judg. 3:14), and the Moabite Stone referred to above records Israelite slaves working on building projects in Moab at a later date. The tension between the two lands was heightened by the fact that the Moabites worshiped pagan gods.

We know that Naomi was devastated by her husband's death, since after her return to her hometown of Bethlehem she counseled those who tried to comfort her not to call her Naomi, which means "pleasant" or "beautiful," but "Mara," meaning "bitter" (1:20).

B. Fate of the sons, 4-5
4 And they took them wives of the women of Moab; the name of the one was Orpah, and the name of the other Ruth: and they dwelled there about ten years.

5 And Mahlon and Chilion died

also both of them; and the woman was left of her two sons and her husband.

Tensions between Israel and Moab, and the need to keep a pure Israelite line through which the Messiah would come, led to a ban on intermarriage (Ezra 9:1). Yet, as was often the case in emergencies, this ruling was ignored under the pressure of the famine in and around Bethlehem. It was only natural that the sons of Elimelech and Naomi would take wives from among the Moabites, where they lived.

In our day, when so many mature women have job skills and are relatively self-sufficient, the original ominous tone of verse 5 is easily overlooked. In Naomi's day, a widow was usually untrained for working outside the home. Some would go into prostitution after the death of their husband.

II. Return to a Homeland—6-8, 14-18

A. Naomi's plans, 6-8

6 Then she arose with her daughters in law, that she might return from the country of Moab: for she had heard in the country of Moab how that the LORD had visited his people in giving them bread.

7 Wherefore she went forth out of the place where she was, and her two daughters in law with her; and they went on the way to return unto the land of Judah.

8 And Naomi said unto her two daughters in law, Go, return each

to her mother's house: the LORD deal kindly with you, as ye have dealt with the dead, and with me.

We are not told whether Naomi's daughters-in-law accompanied her to the border of Israel out of love and courtesy, or whether they intended to go on to Bethlehem with her—until Naomi had a change of heart. At any rate, Naomi, perhaps realizing that as Moabite women they might not be welcome in Judah, urges them here to return to their own mothers' houses. Note in verse 8 the closeness that these three women felt. They were every bit as much a "family" as are those with father, mother and the U. S. average of 3.2 children; and Naomi's blessing is a prayer that God will deal as kindly with them as they have with her.

B. Sisters-in-law part, 14-15

14 And they lifted up their voice, and wept again: and Orpah kissed her mother in law; but Ruth clave unto her.

15 And she said, Behold, thy sister in law is gone back unto her people, and unto her gods: return thou after thy sister in law.

Another blank the ancient author does not fill in is why Ruth does not return to her home, as her sister-in-law Orpah does. Perhaps she has a closer relationship with Naomi than with her own mother. There may also be a clue in Naomi's statement that Orpah had returned *"unto her gods."* Apparently Ruth had become a believer in the true God of Naomi, and was reluctant to return to her pagan family of origin (see also vss. 16-17, below).

C. Ruth's loyalty, 16-18

16 And Ruth said, Intreat me not to leave thee, or to return from following after thee: for whither thou goest, I will go; and where thou lodgest, I will lodge: thy people shall be my people, and thy God my God:

17 Where thou diest, will I die, and there will I be buried: the LORD do so to me, and more also, if ought but death part thee and me.

18 When she saw that she was stedfastly minded to go with her, then she left speaking unto her.

Although the beautiful language in verse 16 is often heard at weddings, note that its original context is an expression of devotion and loyalty from a daughter-in-law to her mother-in-law. As mentioned above, verse 17 shows that a part of Ruth's loyalty consisted of at least some level of commitment to Naomi's God, Yahweh, which may also have influenced her decision to go on with her back to Bethlehem. Also, as verse 6 said, the family had heard that the famine in Bethlehem had broken, and it is possible that Ruth believes her prospects there would be better than in Moab.

In verses 9-15, Naomi will expand on her willingness for Ruth and Orpah to return to their homes in Moab. She reminds them that, at her age, she would have no more sons for them to marry. She urges them to return even though she knows that this would mean that they will worship the gods of Moab instead of the true God.

This glimpse into the book of Ruth would be incomplete without referring also to "the rest of the story." Ruth gleans in the field of one Boaz, a kinsman of Elimelech, who exercises his right to marry his widowed relative; and, as the story closes, it is recorded that Ruth, as Boaz' wife, was the grandmother of none other than David, who would become king. This is how Ruth's name comes to be included in Matthew's genealogy of Jesus (Matt. 1:5).

This, as well as Ruth's original marriage to a Jew who was one of Naomi's sons, raises the question of how forbidden intermarriages were dealt with among the Jews. The books of Ezra and Nehemiah both note the prevalence of other intermarriages, during the period of the Exile. Ezra leads a painful but faithful reform, and many Jews apparently put away their foreign wives. Yet a forecast of God's acceptance of people other than the Jews is the persistent strain throughout the New Testament of incidents like the marriage of Boaz and Ruth, which were not treated so severely. It is likely that the Captivity, which God allowed His people to undergo because of other areas of disobedience, resulted in a heightened sensitivity against foreign marriages that simply was not a part of the culture in the era of Boaz and Ruth.

Evangelistic Emphasis

Have you ever been stuck behind a truck pulling a "wide-load" mobile home? They are infuriating on the interstate because they slow up traffic. They are dangerous in towns because they don't turn corners well. They are also a symbol for our culture in the last part of this century. Nothing is permanent. Even homes, once called the American dream, have become mobile.

With a mobile society and a disposable culture, the idea of loyalty has almost become foreign to our thinking. The idea of a "company store" is as remote to us as the idea of having a barber administer medical treatment and care. Since people move with such ease and frequency, they no longer feel the need to maintain personal, community, or product loyalty. Ask these mobile people about religion and they will talk to you about "churches that meet their needs."

Many have lost the sense of "rootedness that comes from a sturdy church relationship. On the other hand, God is old-fashioned. He believes in loyalty. He is loyal to us to the end.

ॐ)ॐ

Memory Selection

And Ruth said, Entreat me not to leave thee, or to return from following after thee: for whither thou goest, I will go; and where thou lodgest, I will lodge: thy people shall be my people, and thy God my God.—*Ruth 1: 16*

What did Ruth see in Naomi that caused her to utter this wonderful affirmation of love and loyalty? Think about the power of these words. Ruth is willing to give up everything she knew of life to follow her mother-in-law to another country. She would even give up her pagan religion to have the religion and faith of Naomi.

We are witnesses for Christ even when we are unaware people are watching us. Ruth had watched Naomi deal with all kinds of pain and struggle. Death had been a constant companion on this journey from Bethlehem to Moab. Still, through it all Ruth saw something in her that drew her to Naomi's side. When people look at your life and witness are they drawn to the Christ?

226

Weekday Problems

Marcia sat in the pastor's office in tears. For two years her marriage had been on the rocks. Her husband Paul was not attentive to her. He didn't like the fact they lived in a home owned by Marcia's father. Paul really didn't like the fact that their children appeared to be closer to their maternal grandfather than they were to him.

Paul had told Marcia on many occasions that everything would be better if they would only move from that community. He told his wife that a move would help him at work, and help their family situation. When Marcia hesitated, Paul demanded that she choose him or her father.

"Pastor, I am not comfortable moving," Marcia said. "Paul has changed jobs five times in seven years. He doesn't seem to have any loyalty to his job, or to anything else for that matter. I know I promised to love and cherish him. I just can't make myself believe that moving will make things better between us. What should I do?" she asked.

* How can loyalty overcome problems like Marcia was experiencing?

Pop Q & A Quiz

Q: Why do we have earthquakes?
A: Because Mother Nature sometimes forgets to take her earth control pills.

* * * *

Q: What is a child's favorite way to take his cod liver oil?
A: With a fork.

* * * *

Q: What's the latest entertainment craze that combines swimming pools with the movies?
A: Dive-in theaters.

* * * *

Q: Who was Snow White's brother?
A: Egg White. Get the yolk?

* * * *

Q: What goes Ha Ha Ha Ha Ha Ha, *plop*?
A: Someone who's laughing his head off.

This Lesson in Your Life

The story of Ruth is the story of a God who will not give up on strangers and outcasts. It is the story of a God who provides for His people. It is about a God who loves all humanity and longs to bring them back into his fold. Yet this wonderful story, in which everything works out for the faithful, has an ominous beginning.

"There was a famine in the land." When we read further we discover that the famine affected even those living in Bethlehem. We all know that city as being the city of David and the birthplace of Jesus. The word "Bethlehem" is literally translated "house of bread." That would make a good lesson to talk about the "bread of life" (Jesus) coming from the "house of bread" (Bethlehem). The ominous warning is that there was a famine, even in the "house of bread." In a place that should have been immune from such disasters, one happened.

Famines are serious when they deal with food. We have all watched stories of the starving in Africa and even in this country. I wonder if we are conscious of the other kinds of "famines" that surround us. There is a famine in churches of the Word of God. It is not that God is not speaking to His church. It is that we are not listening for His "still small voice." We rely too much on what others say about God for our beliefs in Him. To illustrate, in many churches this day there will be fewer people in Sunday School than will attend morning worship. Do we really believe we can serve God effectively if we are naive about His Word?

There are other "famines" in our day. How about the lack of serious moral and ethical education in schools? Would you say there is a "famine of hospitality"? What other qualities are missing from our culture?

1. Why does the book of Ruth follow the book of Judges?
The story takes place during the time when the judges ruled the land of Israel (see Ruth 1:1).

2. Give the names of the persons living in Bethlehem who flee to Moab during the famine?
Elimelech and his wife Naomi, plus at least two sons, who were named Mahlon and Chilion.

3. Given that "Mahlon" means "to be sick" and Chilion means "pining" or "failing," what does this indicate about the children?
Both of these boys were probably "sickly." This is further indicated by their early deaths.

4. How long did Mahlon and Chilion live in Moab with their mother and wives?
They lived in Moab for about 10 years (Ruth 1:4).

5. What were the names of the Moabite wives that were taken by Mahlon and Chilion?
The wives were Orpah and Ruth. There is no indication as to who was married to whom.

6. Why did Naomi decide to leave the land of Moab with her daughters-in-law?
She had heard that "the Lord had visited his people," and the famine had been relieved.

7. What indications are given about the age of Naomi when she returned to Bethlehem?
She told Ruth and Orpah that she did not have "any more sons in her womb" and that "I am too old to have a husband" (Ruth 1:11-12).

8. What happened to Orpah?
Orpah traveled part of the way to Bethlehem with Naomi, and even pledged her loyalty to her. However, she eventually turned back to Moab.

9. What pledge did Ruth make to Naomi?
That from now until the time when they were both buried, Ruth would be follow Naomi and be absolutely loyal and obedient to her.

10. What was Noami's prayer and wish for her two daughters-in-law?
She prayed that the Lord would deal kindly with them, and that He would provide them with homes and husbands (Ruth 1: 8-9).

An elderly man was dying in his bed at home. In his agony, the aroma of his favorite food, chocolate chip cookies, drifted up the stairs.

He gathered his remaining strength. He lifted himself from the bed. Slowly he made his way out of the bedroom. With even greater effort, he forced himself down the stairs. With labored breath, he gazed into the kitchen. What he saw made him think he was already in heaven. On the kitchen table were hundreds of his favorite chocolate chip cookies. Mustering one great, final effort, he threw himself toward the table. The wondrous taste of the confection was almost in his mouth. His aged and withered hand made its way to a cookie at the edge of the table.

Suddenly the hand was whacked with a spatula. His wife said, "Stay out of those. They're for your funeral."

We make two big mistakes if we believe that *things* are more important than *people*. Tomorrow is more important than today. Ruth lived a life that showed her daughter-in-law that relationships are most important. She also lived fully each day. Ruth never lamented yesterday nor worried about tomorrow. It was that kind of faithful living that allowed her to endure her struggles.

Overcoming Pride

2 Kings 5:1-5, 9-15a

Now Naaman, captain of the host of the king of Syria, was a great man with his master, and honourable, because by him the LORD had given deliverance unto Syria: he was also a mighty man in valour, but he was a leper.

2 And the Syrians had gone out by companies, and had brought away captive out of the land of Israel a little maid; and she waited on Naaman's wife.

3 And she said unto her mistress, Would God my lord were with the prophet that is in Samaria! for he would recover him of his leprosy.

4 And one went in, and told his lord, saying, Thus and thus said the maid that is of the land of Israel.

5 And the king of Syria said, Go to, go, and I will send a letter unto the king of Israel. And he departed, and took with him ten talents of silver, and six thousand pieces of gold, and ten changes of raiment.

9 So Naaman came with his horses and with his chariot, and stood at the door of the house of Elisha.

10 And Elisha sent a messenger unto him, saying, Go and wash in the Jordan seven times, and thy flesh shall come again to thee, and thou shalt be clean.

11 But Naaman was wroth, and went away, and said, Behold, I thought, He will surely come out to me, and stand, and call on the name of the LORD his God, and strike his hand over the place, and recover the leper.

12 Are not Abana and Pharpar, rivers of Damascus, better than all the waters of Israel? may I not wash in them, and be clean? So he turned and went away in a rage.

13 And his servants came near, and spake unto him, and said, My father, if the prophet had bid thee do some great thing, wouldest thou not have done it? how much rather then, when he saith to thee, Wash, and be clean?

14 Then went he down, and dipped himself seven times in Jordan, according to the saying of the man of God: and his flesh came again like unto the flesh of a little child, and he was clean.

15a And he returned to the man of God, he and all his company, and came, and stood before him: and he said, Behold, now I know that there is no God in all the earth, but in Israel:

Feb. 13

Memory Selection
2 Kings 5:13-14
Background Scripture
2 Kings 5
Devotional Reading
Mark 7:17-23

This series on God's call would be incomplete without looking at *pride,* one of the most frequent obstacles to answering God's call. A classic Old Testament story shows how pride at first prevented one man from accepting God's blessing, and how faithful friends helped him overcome that obstacle.

The story is remarkable because it praises the change from pride to obedience in the life of a man who, to Jewish eyes, had two strikes against him. First, he was a leper; and second, he was a Syrian instead of an Israelite.

If a man with two such impediments is finally praised for his humility and obedience, surely we can triumph over our own pride as well.

಄಄

Retelling the ancient Greek myth of "Icarus and the Golden Wings" is a good way to introduce this lesson on pride. Icarus' father Daedalus was a well-known engineer; but he fell out of favor with Minos, king of Crete; and he and his son were imprisoned in a tower.

Being a craftsman, Daedalus constructed two pairs of wings made of golden feathers, held together with wax. With him, he and his son flew out of the prison—with the warning to Icarus that if he flew too high, the wax would melt. However, overcome with pride, Icarus flew higher and higher. The sun god Sol became jealous, melted the wax on the youth's wings, and Icarus fell to his death in the sea.

Naaman the leper was in a sense given "wings." Would he become "deathly proud," or humbly use them according to God's directions?

Teaching Outline	Daily Bible Readings	
I. Handicapped Captain—1	Mon.	What Defiles a Person *Mark 7:17-23*
II. Hope from a Hebrew maid, 2-5	Tue.	Pride of My Enemies *Psalm 59:10-17*
A. Good news from a captive, 2-3	Wed.	Obstacle of Arrogance *Isaiah 13:9-13*
B. Trying it his way, 4-5	Thu.	Naaman Hopes for a Cure *2 Kings 5:1-5a*
III. Hearing from a Prophet—9-15a		
A. Elisha's instructions, 9-10	Fri.	Elisha's Instructions *2 Kings 5:5b-10*
B. Naaman's pride, 11-12	Sat.	Naaman Is Cured *2 Kings 5:11-14*
C. Reasonable advice, 13	Sun.	Naaman Confesses Faith *2 Kings 5:15-19*
D. Obedience, healing, and faith, 14-15a		

Verse by Verse

I. Handicapped Captain—1

1 Now Naaman, captain of the host of the king of Syria, was a great man with his master, and honourable, because by him the LORD had given deliverance unto Syria: he was also a mighty man in valour, but he was a leper.

This story is nested within the larger account of the prophet Elisha's miraculous work; but the focus shifts from Elisha to a captain in the army of one of Israel's perennial enemies.

Syria is the Greek word for the land the Hebrews called Aram. At the time of this story it was in the same general location as modern Syria, northeast of Israel, although its precise boundaries changed often through the centuries. Its capital, Damascus, is considered by many to be the oldest continuously occupied city in the world.

Old Testament accounts often describe Israel's enemies in a bad light. Even here, the story of Naaman shows God's power over that of the gods of Syria; yet it is remarkable that the hero is a gentile, not a Jew. Naaman must have been a man of unusual moral character and political influence. Otherwise, as a leper, he would have banned from the king's courts and elite society. In-

stead, the admirable words are piled on each other: he is described as a "great man...highly regarded...(and) a valiant soldier" (vs. 1, NIV). Yet all this is almost cancelled by the dread words, "but he was a leper."

The words for leprosy in Scripture may refer to a variety of skin diseases, not exclusively to the horrible disease of leprosy that caused limbs to drop off and the face to be disfigured. Still, none of these diseases was pleasant, and the way the last phrase drops a dark cloud over all the good things that could be said about Naaman, as well as the lengths that his king and servants go to help him, indicate that whatever the specific disease, it was serious.

II. Hope from a Hebrew maid, 2-5
A. Good news from a captive, 2-3

2 And the Syrians had gone out by companies, and had brought away captive out of the land of Israel a little maid; and she waited on Naaman's wife.

3 And she said unto her mistress, Would God my lord were with the prophet that is in Samaria! for he would recover him of his leprosy.

The Jewish girl had been taken captive on one of Syria's many raids on the neighboring nation of Israel. As was often the case with desirable captives, she had the relative good fortune to serve in the household of a high official; although the story invites us to read the account knowing that the positioning of the maid is not "fortune" at all, but God's providence.

In verse 8 we will learn that "the prophet" the maid knows about is Elisha, whose miracles have made him famous. The maid may also have known the story of God's having given the Law-giver and prophet Moses the power to heal his sister Miriam's leprosy (Num. 12:10-14). He was in Samaria because his primary mission was to the northern kingdom of Israel rather than to Judah, in the south.

B. Trying it his way, 4-5

4 And one went in, and told his lord, saying, Thus and thus said the maid that is of the land of Israel.

5 And the king of Syria said, Go to, go, and I will send a letter unto the king of Israel. And he departed, and took with him ten talents of silver, and six thousand pieces of gold, and ten changes of raiment.

The king of Syria at this time was probably Ben Hadad III, who had made a temporary truce with Israel (8:7; but see his cruel siege in 6:24ff.). The king obviously has high regard for his Captain Naaman, since he serves as a go-between to introduce him to the king of Israel. At this time Israel's king was Jehoram (or Joram), who, although sponsoring limited purges of Baal worship, was in the sad list of Israel's evil kings (see 2 Chron. 21).

III. Hearing from a Prophet—9-15a

A. Elisha's instructions, 9-10

9 So Naaman came with his horses and with his chariot, and stood at the door of the house of Elisha.

10 And Elisha sent a messenger unto him, saying, Go and wash in the Jordan seven times, and thy flesh shall come again to thee, and thou shalt be clean.

Naaman expected the prophet at least to come out and greet him and his impressive retinue (see vs. 11). Elisha may have declined to do so out of disdain for this enemy of Israel, or he may have known that Naaman had a deadly skin disease and was simply keeping himself separate, as the Law required (see Lev. 13:45-46). Elisha's messenger, however, is allowed to go out to Naaman and to give him instructions that are an echo of the seven-fold sprinklings the priests of Israel performed over people in the unlikely event they had recovered from leprosy (Lev. 14:7-9). Usually, it was considered that only a miracle could cure the disease.

B. Naaman's pride, 11-12

11 But Naaman was wroth, and went away, and said, Behold, I thought, He will surely come out to me, and stand, and call on the name of the LORD his God, and

strike his hand over the place, and recover the leper.

12 Are not Abana and Pharpar, rivers of Damascus, better than all the waters of Israel? may I not wash in them, and be clean? So he turned and went away in a rage.

Naaman quite correctly sees that the rivers in his homeland are as pure as the Jordan. What he does not see is that obedience to God, not the healing effects of the waters, is at stake here. Naaman has not been shown the honor he thought he deserved as a high official in the Syrian army. He may have condescended to take part in a showy religious ceremony befitting his rank, but bathing in a river was beneath him. This source of his rage is obviously arrogance. He is unwilling to submit to simple commands of the true God.

C. Reasonable advice, 13

13 And his servants came near, and spake unto him, and said, My father, if the prophet had bid thee do some great thing, wouldest thou not have done it? how much rather then, when he saith to thee, Wash, and be clean?

Fortunately for Naaman, his servants are not possessed by such pride. They see through to the essence of Elisha's command, realizing that *obedience* rather than *ritual* was the test of whether Elisha's God could help their master. Their captain has come all this way, and would have gladly participated in a grand ritual. Why not take a chance on doing what the prophet said, and possibly not wasting the trip?

D. Obedience, healing, and faith, 14-15a

14 Then went he down, and dipped himself seven times in Jordan, according to the saying of the man of God: and his flesh came again like unto the flesh of a little child, and he was clean.

15a And he returned to the man of God, he and all his company, and came, and stood before him: and he said, Behold, now I know that there is no God in all the earth, but in Israel:

To Naaman's credit, he listens to the advice of his servants and decides to do what Elisha commanded. Note that this requires an extra dose of humility, since the prophet had not condescended to come out of his house and greet this important personage. Yet, when Naaman arises from the water that seventh time, his skin has become as tender and healthy as that of a child.

Verse 15a shows why this well-told story is allowed to interrupt the narrative of wars and idol worship and alternate purges of idolatry in the books of the Kings. A foreigner has summoned the willingness to obey the God of the Jews. Naaman's healing shows not only that Yahweh is the only true God, but that His love extends to races other than His chosen people. The story therefore becomes a forecast of a day when what Israel has to offer—the Messiah—will be preached to all nations.

Evangelistic Emphasis

Naaman would have jumped through hoops to be cleansed from his leprosy. When the instructions for healing came, they were almost too simple for this great general to grasp. He was told to dip himself in the Jordan River seven times and he would be healed. One can read from the story that Naaman was not really a fan of this method of healing. He thought that the pristine waters of his own country would have been far more medicinal than the dirty Jordan River. There was a happy ending, however. Naaman decided that since he was there, he should take a dip— seven actually. Naaman was healed.

Jesus Christ brings salvation to all who repent of their sins and believe in His love and grace. You would think that Jesus would demand more of us. Perhaps some religious act worthy of canceling our sins would be called for. The scandal of the gospel is that salvation cost Jesus His life, but for you and me it is free. We can't earn it. We don't deserve it. Jesus gave His life for us because He loves us. Do you believe it?

ℰℭ

Memory Selection

And his servants came near, and spake unto him, and said, My father, if the prophet had bid thee do some great thing, wouldest thou not have done it? how much rather then, when he saith to thee, Wash, and be clean? Then went he down, and dipped himself seven times in Jordan, according to the saying of the man of God: and his flesh came again like unto the flesh of a little child, and he was clean.—*2 Kings 5: 13-14*

If it meant your healing, or your soul, or the soul of a loved one; would you do something great? Many of us are organ and tissue donors. We sign the back of our driver's license, so when our end comes our organs can go to another person. (I have told my wife to be sure I have finished using mine before she agrees to give them away.) Our simple act of donation in certain circumstances becomes a great thing that leads to life for others.

Christ wants us to do one simple thing for Him. He wants us to give Him our hearts in faith. A simple act that will save a life—*yours.*

Weekday Problems

Estelle was just a little blue over the news she had heard. The doctor had told here that she only had six months to live. Cancer had spread throughout her body. The doctors told her there was no hope. Estelle shared this news with her pastor as she entered the morning aerobics class at the church. She had ridden her bicycle to church that morning. She told the pastor, with a smile, that a terminal cancer patient had nothing to worry about riding a bike in city traffic.

Laura called the pastor that same day and demanded a visit to her house. The pastor found her in bed attended by her husband. She was home from a "secret surgery." In that surgery the doctor had removed a mass. He told Laura that he got it all and was certain she would make a full recovery. She demanded prayer and daily visits because she was certain that she would be dead in a matter of days. Once outside the room, Laura's husband confessed his anxiety that indeed the tumor had been completely removed, but his wife had convinced herself of her quick demise.

Six months later Laura was dead. Estelle lived for five more years.

* What role does faith, hope, and a positive attitude play in healing?

The Pride that Goes Before a Fall

From pride, vain-glory, and hypocrisy; from envy, hatred, and malice, and all uncharitableness, good Lord, deliver us.—*Book of Common Prayer*

* * * *

And the Devil did grin, for his darling sin
Is pride that apes humility.
　　　　　—*Samuel Taylor Coleridge, in* The Devil's Thoughts

* * * *

There is no greater pride than in seeking to humiliate ourselves beyond measure! And sometimes there is no truer humility than to attempt great works for God.—*Abbe dé Saint-Cyran*

* * * *

A man who thinks he is righteous is not righteous . . . for the reason, primarily, that he is full of spiritual pride, the most deadly form that sin can take.—*D. Elton Trueblood*

* * * *

The pride of dying rich raises the loudest laugh in hell.—*John Foster*

This Lesson in Your Life

Naaman had leprosy. It was a disease the made him an outcast. It was a disease that a strong general should not have, one for which there was no cure. All kinds of social stigmas were attached to this disease. We have some parallels in today's culture. Naaman would do anything to have this disease cured. He secured an introduction to a prophet in Israel who had the power to heal.

One can almost visualize Naaman pulling up to Elisha's front door in his four-wheel-drive SUV chariot. He had a whole convoy in tow. The prophet Elisha didn't bother to come to the front door. He sent his secretary out to tell the great general what he needed to do to be healed. Naaman, who so desperately wanted to be healed, was furious at this turn of events. The general thought that he was worthy of some kind of ceremony or a long, lofty prayer.

It was the simple faith of Naaman's servant that turned the tide for the great general. He pointed out that Naaman was in Israel for healing and he should try to be obedient to the prophet's words. In a simple act of obedience and faith, Naaman dipped himself in the Jordan river seven times.

Have you ever wondered what Naaman thought after coming up the fourth time or the fifth and he still wasn't healed? Do you think his servant had to encourage him back into the water for the sixth and seventh time?

Faith in Christ involves coming to Jesus on His terms, not ours. He invites us to come, just as we are. He invites us to have our lives transformed by His grace. This is not something we can work for nor earn. It is a life we accept on faith. There is no bargaining with Jesus at this point. We can't stop after just a few steps into the faith arena. He demands the whole of our lives in trust, just as He gave His life on the cross. Faith does have that demanding element called obedience.

1. What information is given about Naaman?
Naaman was the commander of the army of Aram (or Syria), and a great man.

2. How did the king of Aram feel about Naaman, and why?
He held Naaman in high favor because the Lord had given a mighty victory to Aram.

3. What was not right in Naaman's life?
Although a mighty warrior, Naaman suffered from leprosy.

4. How did Naaman hear about the possibility of healing?
Naaman's wife had a slave girl who had been captured in a raid on Israel. She told Naaman's wife about the possibilities of a miracle.

5. What did the slave girl tell Naaman's wife?
"If only my lord were with the prophet who is in Samaria. He would cure him of his leprosy."

6. What did Naaman do with this information?
Naaman went to his lord and told him what had been shared by the Israelite girl.

7. What did the king of Aram do?
He sent a letter to the king of Israel, which made the king of Israel responsible for Naaman and his healing.

8. How did the king of Israel respond to the king of Aram's letter regarding Naaman?
The king of Israel read the letter and tore his garments. He complained that he was not God and thus not able to cure this man of his leprosy.

9. When Naaman arrived at Elisha's home, what did the prophet do?
The prophet did nothing. Instead, he sent his servant out with instructions for Naaman.

10. What instructions did Elisha the prophet gave to Naaman in order that he might be healed?
Elisha's message was for Naaman to go and dip himself seven times in the Jordan river and be cleansed.

239

Two Christians have lived very good, and also very healthy lives. They die, and go to heaven. As they are walking along, marveling at the paradise around them, one turns to the other and says "Wow! I never knew heaven was going to be as good as this!"

"Yeah," says the other. "And just think, if we hadn't eaten all that oat bran we could have got here ten years sooner."

The story of Naaman reminds us that God heals powerfully and miraculously. We need to also be reminded that we participate with God in our own healing in some circumstances. Naaman had to put himself in the position where his faith could be exercised. He had to go to the Jordan River. He had to walk down into the water. He had to dip himself in seven times. Not three or four; the prophet told him to do this same act seven times.

We must put ourselves in the right attitude for healing. Taking care of the physical body is caring for the temple of the Holy Spirit. You don't want God's Spirit dwelling in a building whose shutters are falling off, or a building that is bigger than God created it to be! So take care to live a healthy life. Eat right. Get enough sleep. Spend time each day exercising. When you do get sick, see a doctor if necessary.

All of this is participating with God in healing and wholeness.

Lesson 12
Overcoming Uncertainty

John 3:1-16

There was a man of the Pharisees, named Nicodemus, a ruler of the Jews:

2 The same came to Jesus by night, and said unto him, Rabbi, we know that thou art a teacher come from God: for no man can do these miracles that thou doest, except God be with him.

3 Jesus answered and said unto him, Verily, verily, I say unto thee, Except a man be born again, he cannot see the kingdom of God.

4 Nicodemus saith unto him, How can a man be born when he is old? can he enter the second time into his mother's womb, and be born?

5 Jesus answered, Verily, verily, I say unto thee, Except a man be born of water and of the Spirit, he cannot enter into the kingdom of God.

6 That which is born of the flesh is flesh; and that which is born of the Spirit is spirit.

7 Marvel not that I said unto thee, Ye must be born again.

8 The wind bloweth where it listeth, and thou hearest the sound thereof, but canst not tell whence it cometh, and whither it goeth: so is every one that is born of the Spirit.

9 Nicodemus answered and said unto him, How can these things be?

10 Jesus answered and said unto him, Art thou a master of Israel, and knowest not these things?

11 Verily, verily, I say unto thee, We speak that we do know, and testify that we have seen; and ye receive not our witness.

12 If I have told you earthly things, and ye believe not, how shall ye believe, if I tell you of heavenly things?

13 And no man hath ascended up to heaven, but he that came down from heaven, even the Son of man which is in heaven.

14 And as Moses lifted up the serpent in the wilderness, even so must the Son of man be lifted up:

15 That whosoever believeth in him should not perish, but have eternal life.

16 For God so loved the world, that he gave his only begotten Son, that whosoever believeth in him should not perish, but have everlasting life.

Feb. 20

Memory Selection
John 3:5-6
Background Scripture
John 3:1-21
Devotional Reading
John 3:17-21

Some unbelievers think that the Christian life must be dull and boring. After all, how exciting can it be to "follow the rules," "go by the Book," and take orders from a reputed King we never see? On the other hand, many people who have thought it would be more fun to "walk on the wild side" report that a life of waking up with hangovers, being treated for sexually transmitted diseases, and spending time either in jail or trying to avoid it isn't so exciting after all.

The dreary cycles of life without God and the hope for something more has led many to wonder whether they could start over again. This lesson focuses on Jesus' teaching on just that opportunity. He calls it being "born again." It's a compelling part of God's call, "Whosoever will—*come!*"

ഇറ

A leading author once wrote, "What's all this talk about being 'born again'? I was born once, and that's quite enough for me, thank you!" You can begin this session by asking group members how they would respond to such a statement.

Discuss what experiences might lead a person to feel differently from this writer, and to *long* to be born again. What does it mean, really, to be born again? That is, how does it feel, and what difference does it make in a person's outlook on life? How would life *after* being born again be different?

From an unbeliever's viewpoint, why might people say they would *not* be interested in the born-again experience? Have believers misrepresented it, claiming too much or too little for the experience? Note that this lesson is on the origin in Jesus' teaching of being "born again."

Teaching Outline

I. A Seeker Comes to Jesus—1-4
  A. Exceptional Pharisee, 1-2
  B. Facts and Questions, 3-4
II. Spiritual and earthly viewpoints—5-13
  A. Explanation and wonder, 5-6
  B. Who has seen the wind?, 7-8
  C. Inadequate leadership, 9-11
  D. Adequacy of Christ, 12-13
III. Basis of the New Birth—14-16
  A. Moses and Jesus, 14-15
  B. God so loved, 16

Daily Bible Readings

Verse by Verse

I. A Seeker Comes to Jesus—1-4

A. Exceptional Pharisee, 1-2

1 There was a man of the Pharisees, named Nicodemus, a ruler of the Jews:

2 The same came to Jesus by night, and said unto him, Rabbi, we know that thou art a teacher come from God: for no man can do these miracles that thou doest, except God be with him.

That this honest searcher Nicodemus was a Pharisee is a surprise because they were "the strictest sect" of the Jews (Acts 26:5), and Jesus often condemned their teaching as being legalistic and without heart.

Some scholars think the term "Pharisee" comes from a word that means "separate." At any rate, they generally considered themselves above associating with the common people. They studied the Law of Moses intensely, but mainly to apply it in ever more severe ways. Jesus accused them of loving to "show off" their piety to be seen of men (Matt. 6:5). He often lumped them together with the scribes, and pronounced a long list of judgments or "woes" on them (see Matt. 23).

Adding to our surprise is that Nicodemus is also a "ruler of the Jews"—a member of the Sanhedrin, the ruling council that Rome allowed to oversee Jewish religious matters—and the body that will eventually rule that Jesus must die. Furthermore, his uncharacteristic behavior is seen in two other scenes in the Gospels. He counsels against rushing hastily to condemn Jesus (John 7:50), and after Jesus' crucifixion Nicodemus honors Him by accompanying Joseph of Arimathea to the burial site (19:39).

As a "member of the opposition," therefore, Nicodemus seeks Jesus by night to avoid being seen. He is drawn to Jesus because His miracles were compelling evidence that He was a teacher from God—which would have been far from the consensus view among the Pharisees.

B. Facts and Questions, 3-4

3 Jesus answered and said unto him, Verily, verily, I say unto thee, Except a man be born again, he cannot see the kingdom of God.

4 Nicodemus saith unto him, How can a man be born when he is old? can he enter the second time into his mother's womb, and be born?

Why does Jesus begin His conversation with this honest seeker with the topic of the "new birth"? Possibly because the fact that Nicodemus was a "good Pharisee" may have tempted him to think that he could join the Kingdom Jesus preached about if he could just be a little *better* Pharisee. No, Jesus says, entering the Kingdom requires a *break* with traditional views. Pharisaism emphasized the letter of the Law, and external forms of piety, while Jesus emphasized the heart. A change from one to the other requires something as radical as the change from a fetus to a baby—a birth into one world from another. Literal-minded that he is, Nicodemus asks how that could possibly happen to a grown man.

As a variety of translations show, the word for "again" in verse 3 may also be translated "anew" or "from above." Actually, the new birth is both new and "from above," in that it allows sinful people to start over again—and even the "righteous" Nicodemus to turn over a new leaf.

III. Spiritual and earthly viewpoints—5-13

A. Explanation and wonder, 5-6

5 Jesus answered, Verily, verily, I say unto thee, Except a man be born of water and of the Spirit, he cannot enter into the kingdom of God.

6 That which is born of the flesh is flesh; and that which is born of the Spirit is spirit.

Jesus wants Nicodemus to think in spiritual instead of literal terms. A literal birth is "of the flesh," while the new birth is of the Spirit. This can mean either that it is of the *Holy* Spirit, or *spiritually* ("figuratively"). Unless Nicodemus can think in spiritual terms, he cannot grasp the imagery of the new birth.

The term "water" Jesus introduces in verse 5 probably refers to baptism. Some hold that since water is often a symbol of the Holy Spirit, the term refers to the Spirit here; but that would have Jesus saying "You must be born of the Spirit and the Spirit." Others have held that "water" refers to the amniotic fluid of physical birth; but that would have Jesus saying that you must be born physically to be reborn spiritually—which seems too obvious. It is more likely that Jesus is combining the spiritual or inner experience of a change of heart with the outer experience of baptism. This view corresponds with Paul's description of baptism as a burial and a raising to "newness of life" (Rom. 6:4-6).

B. Who has seen the wind? 7-8

7 Marvel not that I said unto thee, Ye must be born again.

8 The wind bloweth where it listeth, and thou hearest the sound thereof, but canst not tell whence it cometh, and whither it goeth: so is every one that is born of the Spirit.

To help the literal-minded, Jesus compares the Force behind the new birth with the wind. It is easy to say that the Spirit doesn't exist because we cannot see Him—but we could also say that about the wind. Just as we can see the *results* of the wind, so we should be able to see the results of a spiritual rebirth in a changed life. (The fact that both "wind" and "Spirit" come from the word *pneuma* does not change Jesus' analogy.)

C. Inadequate leadership, 9-11

9 Nicodemus answered and said

unto him, How can these things be?

10 Jesus answered and said unto him, Art thou a master of Israel, and knowest not these things?

11 Verily, verily, I say unto thee, We speak that we do know, and testify that we have seen; and ye receive not our witness.

Nicodemus is confused by all this "spiritual" talk. Perhaps his background with the Pharisees has made him a "left-brained" thinker, interpreting everything literally. A person simply can't re-enter his mother's womb and be reborn, so how can we speak of being born again? Jesus chides him for thinking so literally, asking how anyone could be a "master" (lit. "teacher") in Israel without confronting the distinction between the flesh and the spirit.

D. Adequacy of Christ, 12-13

12 If I have told you earthly things, and ye believe not, how shall ye believe, if I tell you of heavenly things?

13 And no man hath ascended up to heaven, but he that came down from heaven, even the Son of man which is in heaven.

Jesus' mild rebuke continues, first with the question of how a teacher such as Nicodemus can possibly understand teaching about the Kingdom of heaven if he is still hung up on the difference between physical and spiritual birth. This spiritual or "heavenly" teaching Jesus is imparting could not be delivered except by Him, since no one else has "been there, done that." This implies the

necessity of Nicodemus' believing in Jesus if his night-time visit is to profit him at all.

III. Basis of the New Birth—14-16

A. Moses and Jesus, 14-15

14 And as Moses lifted up the serpent in the wilderness, even so must the Son of man be lifted up:

15 That whosoever believeth in him should not perish, but have eternal life.

Many religions speak of experiences somewhat like the new birth. For example, Buddhism has its "enlightenment." Jesus, however, ties His teaching to biblical religion by comparing Christ with Moses. Just as people were cured of snake-bite by gazing on the bronze serpent Moses lifted up in the Wilderness (see Num. 21:9), so those who trust and obey Jesus, who will be lifted up on the Cross, will be "cured" of sin and have the gift of eternal life.

B. God so loved, 16

16 For God so loved the world, that he gave his only begotten Son, that whosoever believeth in him should not perish, but have everlasting life.

This justly famous verse affirms that the basis of the new birth is love. It is only because God, in love even with sinful humankind, sent Jesus from heaven that it is possible to speak realistically of being born again. The entire experience of spiritual rebirth is encompassed in the word "believeth"—not mere mental assent but holistic commitment to the One whom God sent.

Evangelistic Emphasis

An old "Peanuts" comic strip shows Linus listening carefully as his sister, Lucy, boasts about her religious faith and her potential as an evangelist.

She says to Linus, "I could be a terrific evangelist. Do you know that kid who sits behind me in school? I convinced him that my religion is better than his religion."

Linus asks, "How did you do that?"

Lucy replies, "I hit him with my lunch box."

Nicodemus came to Jesus by night, expecting to have a nice religious discussion. Those are the kinds of things you do in your Sunday school class. No one is offended by a religious discussion and no one is ever changed. Jesus did not want to discuss religion with Nicodemus. The Lord looked directly into his soul and saw the spiritual need he was bringing.

When we try to keep Jesus at arm's length we will always be disappointed with the results. Jesus is interested not in our discussion of religion, but whether or not our souls have been born from above.

℘℥

Memory Selection

Jesus answered, Verily, verily, I say unto thee, Except a man be born of water and of the Spirit, he cannot enter into the kingdom of God. That which is born of the flesh is flesh; and that which is born of the Spirit is spirit.—*John 3: 5-6*

God has no grandchildren.

We can't get into heaven based on what our parents or other relatives have done. We can't get into heaven based on what church we attend. Our transport into eternity comes through a personal relationship with Christ. Jesus was explaining that truth to the Jewish leader Nicodemus.

Your relationship with Christ is not something earned nor inherited. It is given freely by the Lord and received through faith by us. It is a spiritual matter. It is a matter of the heart.

Are you a CHILD of God?

Weekday Problems

Drake was standing in the middle of a covey of furious secretaries. Drake was the new boy in the office. He was affable. He was energetic. He was curious about all aspects of the running of the office. For every problem or perceived problem, Drake had an answer.

Drake was particularly fond of solving computer problems for the secretaries. He had been in rare form on this Friday morning. The secretaries were working on a major project that was due at the end of the day for the big Boss to pack in his luggage and take with him on his business trip.

The secretaries were having some difficulty merging certain parts of the presentation together. Drake asked if he could help. The big boss's secretary wanted to know if Drake knew what he was doing. He assured her that he was proficient in all areas of computer hardware and software. He bragged that he was an expert.

With all the deftness of an expert, in five minutes Drake had managed to crash the whole computer network.

* How are people who are merely curious about religion a hindrance to those really seeking a relationship with Christ?

* How did Jesus use the curiosity of Nicodemus to change his soul?

'It Gives Me Great Pleasure to Introduce . . . '

"And now I'd like to present the funniest, most talented, best-educated, most eloquent speaker, and the man who wrote this introduction for me. . . ."

* * * *

"Ladies and gentlemen, I have the microphone, but I now present to you the loud speaker."

* * * *

Speaker, after his talk: Did you notice how my voice filled the town hall?
Emcee: Yep, in fact I saw several people leave to make room for it.

* * * *

"After a dinner program like this, a speaker is like parsley . . . not really needed."

* * * *

"I think you'll find our speaker's most interesting point is his point of departure."

247

This Lesson in Your Life

Nicodemus came to Jesus at night.

That phrase appears again in a description of Nicodemus. He became known as the one who came to Jesus by night.

Nighttime was the normal time when Rabbis discussed the law. Nicodemus, showing due respect was treating Jesus as a colleague in ministry. He had come to have a polite discussion with this new Rabbi about His interpretation of the law and the miracles He was able to work. The tone was polite. The level of the conversation was superficial, at least when it began.

Jesus listened to the words, but answered the question that was really on Nicodemus' heart.

I wonder how many times we come to church looking for simple answers for our soul's struggles. We want a simple answer that can be quickly applied to a hurt that we are not willing to admit. We are looking for a cure without exploring the systemic root cause of our pain.

Jesus knew that Nicodemus needed more in his life than another theological discussion about the nature and mission of the God's Messiah. Nicodemus needed to have a personal relationship with that Messiah. He needed to experience the new birth.

We might make long lists of what our needs are, but they all boil down to one. We all need a life-changing, sin-forgiving, personal relationship with Jesus, the Son of God.

Until we have that relationship we are in the dark about our real problems and the solution to those problems.

1. How was Nicodemus described?
He was a Pharisee, a leader of the Jews. Jesus further described him as a teacher of Israel.

2. Nicodemus affirmed that Jesus was a teacher come from God. What is the basis for this?
The signs that have been attributed to Jesus attest to His position as a teacher from God.

3. Jesus answered Nicodemus' compliment with what statement about the Kingdom of God?
"No one can see the kingdom of God without being born from above."

4. How are the compliment of Nicodemus and the statement of Jesus related?
There is a play on the word " see" and the word "sign." The play on words is further highlighted by Nicodemus coming to Jesus by night.

5. What is the evidence that Nicodemus does not understand the nature of the new birth?
He asks Jesus "How can anyone be born after having grown old? Can he enter his mother's womb a second time?"

6. How did Jesus say one enters the Kingdom of God?
Jesus said that no one can enter the Kingdom of God without being born of water and of the Spirit.

7. What statement of Jesus contrasts "spirit" with "flesh"?
Jesus told Nicodemus, "that which is born of the flesh is flesh, and that which is born of the Spirit is spirit."

8. With what force of nature does Jesus compare the Spirit?
Jesus talks about the wind. We hear the sound of it, but we don't know where it comes from or where it goes.

9. What was Jesus' question to Nicodemus about his apparent lack of understanding of Jesus' words?
"Are you not a teacher of Israel and yet you do not understand these things?"

10. What is the second image that connects the early part of the conversation with the latter part of the conversation?
Nicodemus calls Jesus a teacher. Jesus questions Nicodemus as a teacher.

A boy and his father were walking along a road when they came across a large stone. The boy said to his father, "Do you think if I use all my strength, I can move this rock?"

His father answered, "If you use all your strength, I am sure you can do it."

The boy began to push the rock. Exerting himself as much as he could, he pushed and pushed. The rock did not move. Discouraged, he said to his father, "You were wrong. I can't do it."

The father placed his arm around the boy's shoulder and said, "No, son, you didn't use all your strength — you didn't ask me to help."

Nicodemus climbed up the steps that night to meet Jesus and knew that his religion required him to be faithful to God in his own strength. The religion of Nicodemus was a self-service kind of religion. It was a time-consuming and high-maintenance religion. It gave little hope and brought little joy.

Jesus promised Nicodemus the new birth. There was nothing Nicodemus could do to earn a new birth. He couldn't work for it. He couldn't achieve it. The new birth came through the power of the Holy Spirit. Nicodemus needed to *experience* the new birth.

Faith in Jesus Christ is not so much something we do. It is something we experience. Have you had that faith experience, yet?

John 4:7-10, 19-26

Τhere cometh a woman of Samaria to draw water: Jesus saith unto her, Give me to drink.

8(For his disciples were gone away unto the city to buy meat.)

9 Then saith the woman of Samaria unto him, How is it that thou, being a Jew, askest drink of me, which am a woman of Samaria? for the Jews have no dealings with the Samaritans.

10 Jesus answered and said unto her, If thou knewest the gift of God, and who it is that saith to thee, Give me to drink; thou wouldest have asked of him, and he would have given thee living water.

19 The woman saith unto him, Sir, I perceive that thou art a prophet.

20 Our fathers worshipped in this mountain; and ye say, that in Jerusalem is the place where men ought to worship.

21 Jesus saith unto her, Woman, believe me, the hour cometh, when ye shall neither in this mountain, nor yet at Jerusalem, worship the Father.

22 Ye worship ye know not what: we know what we worship: for salvation is of the Jews.

23 But the hour cometh, and now is, when the true worshippers shall worship the Father in spirit and in truth: for the Father seeketh such to worship him.

24 God is a Spirit: and they that worship him must worship him in spirit and in truth.

25 The woman saith unto him, I know that Messias cometh, which is called Christ: when he is come, he will tell us all things.

26 Jesus saith unto her, I that speak unto thee am he.

Memory Selection
Galatians 3:28

Background Scripture
John 4:1-42

Devotional Reading
John 4:35-42

Feb. 27

The opening verses of John 4 are good background for the focus of this lesson. Jesus' enemies, the Pharisees, had heard of His success in and around Jerusalem, and would no doubt take steps to stop His work (vs. 1). Since He has not yet completed His mission, Jesus retreats to Galilee. He chooses to go through Samaria instead of going around this area which most Jews would have avoided. The Samaritans were considered "half-breeds" since they were the result of Jewish and non-Jewish settlement after the main body of the 10 northern tribes had been carried away into Assyrian captivity in the 8th-century B.C. They had set up worship centers. other than the Temple in Jerusalem.

Now Jesus deliberately invades this "forbidden" territory to show His disciples that His message is for all people. Racial prejudice is incompatible with life in the Kingdom; and the King is among us!

80CR

The attack by radical Muslims on the U. S. has raised racial issues in new ways. While some Americans still struggled with black-white, brown-white, and black-brown prejudice, suddenly everyone with Arab names was under suspicion.

Introduce this lesson on racial acceptance by asking group members how their thinking was challenged by this attack. Should we exercise greater caution in allowing people of Arab descent to enter the U.S., or does that constitute unacceptable "racial profiling"? Are there Muslim worshipers, or perhaps even a mosque, in or near your community? What can be done now to increase inter-racial acceptance and reach across Arab-American lines?

Teaching Outline

I. Encounter at a Well—7-10
  A. A woman of Samaria, 7-8
  B. Living water, 9-10
II. How It's Been—19-22
  A. Jews vs. Samaritan, 19-20
  B. Salvation is of the Jews, 21-22
III. How It's Going to Be—23-26
  A. Worship in spirit and truth, 23-24
  B. 'I am He!', 25-26

Daily Bible Readings

Mon. Christ Is All and in All
      Colossians 3:11-17
Tue. Jesus in Samaria
      John 4:1-6
Wed. Literal vs. Living Water
      John 4:7-12
Thu. A Woman's Thirst
      John 4:13-18
Fri. 'I Am the Messiah'
      John 4:19-26
Sat. 'Come and See This Man!'
      John 4:27-34
Sun. Many Samaritans Believe
      John 4:35-42

Verse by Verse

I. Encounter at a Well—7-10

A. A woman of Samaria, 7-8

7 There cometh a woman of Samaria to draw water: Jesus saith unto her, Give me to drink.

8 (For his disciples were gone away unto the city to buy meat.)

Jesus, ministering in Judea, has begun to attract even more followers than John the Baptist (4:1). Perhaps because He is not yet ready for a confrontation in Jerusalem that might lead prematurely to His death, he decides to return to His home country around Galilee.

Most Jews would make this trip by circling Samaria to the east, to avoid going through territory that had been a hostile and "unclean" area, for "orthodox" Jews, since foreign gentiles were located there upon the fall of the 10 northern tribes in 722 B.C. Even earlier, Samaritan Jews had established worship centers that competed with Jerusalem. Yet Jesus deliberately goes through the area to begin to tear down this wall of racial and religious prejudice, and He strikes up a conversation with a woman at a well (which local guides say is still identifiable).

B. Living water, 9-10

9 Then saith the woman of Samaria unto him, How is it that thou, being a Jew, askest drink of me, which am a woman of Samaria? for the Jews have no dealings with the Samaritans.

10 Jesus answered and said unto her, If thou knewest the gift of God, and who it is that saith to thee, Give me to drink; thou wouldest have asked of him, and he would have given thee living water.

The woman instantly questions the break with tradition that allows Jesus to speak to a Samaritan, especially a woman. Jesus chooses to answer her question as to why He dares break the taboos by pointing out that if she knew that He was the Messiah, *she* would be the one asking for a favor, and it would be for the living water of eternal life instead of water which could only temporarily slake one's physical thirst. (For evangelistic insights, note that Jesus [1] seizes on a matter of immediate interest to the woman [water]; and [2] indicates that *she* can fill His need for water, thus implying her own dignity and capability instead of treating her as a mere target.)

II. How It's Been—19-22

A. Jews vs. Samaritan, 19-20

19 The woman saith unto him, Sir, I perceive that thou art a prophet.

20 Our fathers worshipped in this mountain; and ye say, that in

Jerusalem is the place where men ought to worship.

Perceiving that Jesus is not just an ordinary traveler, probably from His reference to "living water," and to his being "the gift of God," the woman immediately raises one of their fundamental differences. About 975 B.C., Jeroboam, rebel son of Solomon, set up worship centers in Samaria, at Dan and Bethel, to keep his followers from going to Jerusalem to worship at Solomon's Temple (1 Kings 12:25-30). In light of the way Jesus had delved into the woman's personal life (vss. 16-18), her switching the subject to the age-old argument about the proper place to worship seems to be a way to draw His attention away from her personal issues to a more abstract issue.

B. Salvation is of the Jews, 21-22

21 Jesus saith unto her, Woman, believe me, the hour cometh, when ye shall neither in this mountain, nor yet at Jerusalem, worship the Father.

22 Ye worship ye know not what: we know what we worship: for salvation is of the Jews.

Although the Samaria-Jerusalem split was about to become a moot argument, verse 23 shows that Jesus does not overlook the flagrant sign of opposition to God's Old Covenant plan to consolidate worship at Jerusalem. For all their legalism, it had been Jews, not Samaritans, who had stayed truest to the Law of Moses and to Temple worship.

Yet, as verse 21 indicates, the lo-cation of formal worship is about to cease to be of importance. The kind of worship of which Jesus will approve will occur in the temple of the heart and in the Body of Christ, wherever it is assembled (see Eph. 2:19-22).

III. How It's Going to Be—23-26

A. Worship in spirit and truth, 23-24

23 But the hour cometh, and now is, when the true worshippers shall worship the Father in spirit and in truth: for the Father seeketh such to worship him.

24 God is a Spirit: and they that worship him must worship him in spirit and in truth.

Jesus now elaborates on the radical change in worship He is inaugurating. One of the most fundamental differences will be between the material nature of holy vessels, altars, sacrifices, and buildings under Jewish practices of the day, and the spiritual nature of *the heart* in the Christian worship that will follow the resurrection of Christ. This will have practical as well as theological significance, in that it will facilitate the worship of God wherever Christians go in their missionary efforts, instead of worship being tied to Jerusalem under the less evangelistic Jewish system.

Verse 24 states this distinction in different terms. Under the Jewish system, the emphasis was on doing external things such as sacrificing correctly. The Christian way will emphasize the attitude or spirit of the worshiper, and engage the mind. As

The Message translation says, "Your worship must engage your spirit in the pursuit of truth." This does not mean that every Jew let his mind wander while the priest made the sacrifice he brought to the Temple, or that his prayers were mere formalities. It means that the general requirements of Temple- and priest-centered worship lent themselves to such abuses more than would be allowed in Christian worship. Obviously, in light of the fact that Christians still sometimes worship by rote and let their minds wander, or even plan mischief while going through the motions of worship, all indicate that the problem is not yet totally solved. Jesus is speaking of what *should* happen in worship in the "Age to come." Since God is Spirit, and cannot be confined to a place, we are to strive to approach him with our spirits.

B. 'I am He!', 25-26

25 The woman saith unto him, I know that Messias cometh, which is called Christ: when he is come, he will tell us all things.

26 Jesus saith unto her, I that speak unto thee am he.

The woman is at least theologically sensitive enough to realize that all this talk about worship lends itself to bringing up the topic of "He who comes," the Messiah in Hebrew and Aramaic, the Christ in Greek. Just as she had hoped to use the proper location of worship to move the conversation away from the fact that she was not adhering to the ideal situation of "one man, one woman, for life," perhaps she hoped to get Jesus started on a long discussion of just what Messiah would be like, and when He would appear. Imagine her surprise when Jesus cuts through her musings with the direct statement that the Messiah she referred to as a mere discussion topic was in fact standing before her in person.

Verses 24-30 describe the impact Jesus had on the woman's entire village when she left her water jar and returned to tell them about "a man which told me all things that ever I did," and even ventured to indicate that she believed His claim to be the Messiah. The story remains a model of "cross-cultural" and "cross-gender" communication, with Jesus treating a "mere woman" as a real person, against cultural expectations, and their racial differences as inconsequential.

Later attempts to follow through with the implications of this (then) radical move on Jesus' part met with varied degrees of success. A woman named Phoebe would be referred to as a "servant" or "deacon" of the church (Rom. 16:1), and Paul will affirm that in Christ there is "neither Jew nor Greek, there is neither bond nor free, there is neither male nor female" (Gal. 3:28). Largely, however, the sad truth is that later years found most Christians reverting to male- and white-dominance, and being about as guilty as other groups in allowing such practices to become the rule.

Evangelistic Emphasis

How far will your love reach?

In our human frailty, we often erect barriers to our love. Some of those barriers might be cultural and ethnic. Some of those barriers involve geography and language. We tend to love people who are "like us." We tend to be suspicious of people who are different.

The story of Jesus and the woman at the well is a story that challenges our barriers. Jesus set no limits on His love. He was willing to love and minister to this woman who had never experienced love in her life.

The good news is that God reached down to each of us and in His love and grace has lifted us out of spiritual darkness. We were saved regardless of who we were or what we have done. The challenge of the good news is that we, as the Church, have been called to be that inclusive.

This Sunday as you worship, look at your congregation. Do you see any barriers?

৪১০৪

Memory Selection

There is neither Jew nor Greek, there is neither bond nor free, there is neither male nor female: for ye are all one in Christ Jesus.— *Galatians 3: 28*

Those are radical words from the Apostle Paul. We are all equals in Christ Jesus. There is no upper or lower class Christian. Maybe we would better get a flavor for the verse if it read, "There is neither Christian or Arab, there is neither victim or victor, there is neither male nor female, we are all one in Jesus." If you change some of the words you have a clearer understanding of what Paul was saying. The gospel of Christ transcends all of society's barriers. The gospel of Christ extends, through his love, equality to all participants in the kingdom of God.

What makes this verse a challenge is that it removes all of our prefabricated excuses not to reach out and do ministry in the name of the Lord.

Weekday Problems

How do our judgments get us into trouble?
In 1884, a couple called on the President of Harvard
University, Charles Elliot. They wanted to give money in
memory of their 15-year-old son who had died. The mother
said, "We would like to give a memorial so that other young men might get
an education." The couple looked as though they had meager resources. President Elliot suggested that they give a scholarship in his name. "No, something more substantial than that—perhaps a building or two." Irritated, Elliot
said, "Buildings are very expensive."

The mother asked, "President Elliot, what has this entire university cost?"
Eliot said it was worth several million dollars. She said to her husband, "Let's
go, Leland. I have an idea." Her "idea" was to contribute $26 million to start,
"Leland Stanford University."

When we judge people based on what they are, we err. Jesus has called us
to look at others based on *whose* they are. Everyone you meet belongs to
God. Are you treating His creatures with respect?

* Can you think of ways in which you and/or your church are not thinking
as big as God would want you to think?

The Gender Wars: News from the Front

Any wife with an inferiority complex can cure it by being sick in bed for a
day, while her husband manages the household and the children.

* * * *

He to She: No siree, no wife of mine will ever have to work. I want her to
be able to stay home and clean house and cook and wash and . . . ."
She: (This recording was interrupted by a loud explosion and the breaking of the tape.)

* * * *

Marriage counselor: Do you encourage your wife in her career?
Husband: All the time. I keep telling her she ought to ask for a raise.

* * * *

My wife told our neighbors that 30 years ago she had a close encounter
with a subhuman alien creature from outer space, but she never reported it to
the authorities. Instead, she says she married it.

257

This Lesson in Your Life

The key to understanding this lesson is to see what the lady left behind at the well. The Bible tells us that she "left her jar."

The Samaritan woman was no lady. She would not be invited to be a part of the Junior League. She would not be on the short list of Sunday School candidates. She was terrible at marriage. She had become adept at divorce. She knew lots about rejection. She knew even more about loneliness.

She came to the well at noon to get water. The usual time to come to a well would be early in the morning. She was tired of being shunned by the ladies of the community. She had grown weary of being the object of their stares and the subject of their gossip. Why deal with those gossips? She made the trip at noon when none of the other women would be there.

Her goal was simple: to take care of this daily task, and not have to deal with any of the problems associated with the gossips. Instead of being alone, she met One who probed the very reason for her loneliness. Her encounter with Jesus was so life-changing that she left her jar behind so she could run into town with her news.

"I've met a man who told me everything I have ever done," she said breathlessly. "Could he be the Messiah?" The inference was that not only had Jesus probed into her past, He did so without condemning her. She felt for the first time that her sins had been forgiven. When she found grace, she was willing to be a part of the community. When you have receive love and acceptance from the Lord, you don't have to worry about what anyone else thinks.

What "jar" do you need to leave behind?

GETTING THE FACTS STRAIGHT

1. According to the Bible, one day at noon, Jesus was sitting by a well. What happened there?
A Samaritan woman came to draw water, and Jesus asked her for a drink.

2. What was her response to Jesus' request?
She wanted to know how Jesus as a Jew would ask a drink from a Samaritan.

3. What was the reason given for her surprise that a Jew would ask for a drink?
Jews did not share things in common with Samaritans.

4. What did the woman assume about Jesus' statement concerning the living water?
She may have assumed that the living water came from deep within the well. Since she had no bucket she had no access to the living water.

5. What was the difference between the water from the well and the water that Jesus gives?
The water from the well would only lead to more thirst, while the water that Jesus gives refreshes forever.

6. What promise does Jesus make about the water that He gives?
The water that He gives will become a spring of water gushing up into eternal life.

7. What did the woman say when Jesus told her to get her husband?
She told Jesus that she had no husband.

8. What did Jesus identify as the truth of her marital relationship?
It was true she had no husband. She had had five husbands, and her current companion was not legally married to her.

9. When Jesus shared the truth about her husbands, what was her response?
She left her water jar by the well and ran into town telling everyone about the encounter with Jesus.

10. How did the returning disciples react to Jesus talking with the Samaritan woman?
They were surprised he was talking to a woman. They were doubly surprised he was talking to a woman of Samaria.

In the remarkable story of our text, Jesus crosses four boundaries that have been common bases of prejudice:

(1) He crossed the barrier of *race*. The Samaritans were a mixed race often spurned by traditional Jews because of their intermarriage with gentiles. Jesus transcended this bias by being willing to converse with, and even ask a favor of, this Samaritan.

(2) Jesus surmounted the barrier of *religion*. The Samaritans had established an alternate center of worship that did not recognize Jerusalem, or its Temple, as central to Jewish worship. Jesus did not allow this to obscure His recognition of the Samaritan woman as a person of importance and worth.

(3) Jesus crossed the bounary of *gender*. It was not customary for men to have conversation with women in public. Jesus was willing to ignore this in order to be of help to the Samaritan woman.

(4) *Status* was a fourth barrier surmounted by Jesus. The custom was for women to be of service to men. Although Jesus asked the Samaritan woman for water, He also elevated her status by indicating His willingness to serve her with "living water."

In crossing these barriers of prejudice, Jesus was affirming that all people are equal before God, and that all should treat each other with equal dignity and respect.

Lesson 1

All Have Sinned

Romans 1:16-20; 3:9-20

For I am not ashamed of the gospel of Christ: for it is the power of God unto salvation to every one that believeth; to the Jew first, and also to the Greek.

17 For therein is the righteousness of God revealed from faith to faith: as it is written, The just shall live by faith.

18 For the wrath of God is revealed from heaven against all ungodliness and unrighteousness of men, who hold the truth in unrighteousness;

19 Because that which may be known of God is manifest in them; for God hath shewed it unto them.

20 For the invisible things of him from the creation of the world are clearly seen, being understood by the things that are made, even his eternal power and Godhead; so that they are without excuse:

3:9 What then? are we better than they? No, in no wise: for we have before proved both Jews and Gentiles, that they are all under sin;

10 As it is written, There is none righteous, no, not one:

11 There is none that understandeth, there is none that seeketh after God.

12 They are all gone out of the way, they are together become unprofitable; there is none that doeth good, no, not one.

13 Their throat is an open sepulchre; with their tongues they have used deceit; the poison of asps is under their lips:

14 Whose mouth is full of cursing and bitterness:

15 Their feet are swift to shed blood:

16 Destruction and misery are in their ways:

17 And the way of peace have they not known:

18 There is no fear of God before their eyes.

19 Now we know that what things soever the law saith, it saith to them who are under the law: that every mouth may be stopped, and all the world may become guilty before God.

20 Therefore by the deeds of the law there shall no flesh be justified in his sight: for by the law is the knowledge of sin.

Memory Selection
Romans 3:10

Background Scripture
Romans 1:16-20; 3:9-20

Devotional Reading
Psalm 59:1-5

This lesson has a twin focus: *the fact of sin* and *the way of salvation.* The emphasis on the fact of sin seems both too easy and too hard. It is too easy in the sense that everyone, down deep, knows that he sins. It is too hard in the sense that many people resist responding to this fact, either, by denying that they are sinners or by condemning themselves so thoroughly that they feel unworthy of taking God's way of escape.

The sensitive teacher will be aware of these opposite tendencies. Group members who deny their sinfulness need to be confronted with it, while those who are already burdened with guilt need to be led to the realization that while "all have sinned" (Rom. 3:23), all may come to Christ through the cleansing that is revealed in the gospel.

ഇൻരൂ

Before class, make an outlandish "object lesson" to introduce this session on universal sinfulness. Make a double-sided "sandwich board" sign out of two posters, fastened by tape at the top, like those worn by street-hawkers advertising everything from salvation to sandwiches.

On one poster, write in large letters, SINNER, PREPARE TO MEET THY GOD! On the other, write YOU CAN BE SAVED THROUGH JESUS! Put the signs on over your head, so one hangs over your front and the other down your back. Parade before the group so all can see each side.

After the chuckling subsides, ask, *Which sign is true?* Of course the answer you seek is *Both.* The biblical message is both a judgment against sin and a promise of forgiveness.

Teaching Outline	Daily Bible Readings	
I. The Saving Message—1:16-17	Mon.	No One Is Perfect *Psalm 14:1-6*
A. Revealing God's power, 16	Tue.	Rejecting God *Psalm 10:1-6*
B. The power of faith, 17	Wed.	Who Will Cast Stones? *John 8:1-9*
II. The Need for the Message—1:18-20; 3:9-18	Thu.	The Gospel's Saving Power *Romans 1:16-20*
A. Without excuse, 1:18-20	Fri.	We Are All Sinful *Romans 3:9-14*
B. None are righteous, 3:9-18	Sat.	We Are All Guilty *Roman 3:15-20*
III. The Role of the Law—3:19-20	Sun.	We Have All Sinned *1 John 1:5-10*
A. To show our guilt, 19		
B. Not to save our souls, 20		

Verse by Verse

I. The Saving Message—1:16-17
A. Revealing God's power, 16
16 For I am not ashamed of the gospel of Christ: for it is the power of God unto salvation to every one that believeth; to the Jew first, and also to the Greek.

The apostle Paul had never been to Rome, but longed to go there not only to strengthen and be strengthened by the few Christians in the city (1:11-12) but because, as the center of the Roman Empire, it would make a powerful sounding board for his message. The saying "All roads lead to Rome" was widespread even then, and it was equally true that "all roads lead everywhere else *from* Rome."

By this time in Paul's ministry, his message of salvation by grace through faith, apart from works of the Law, had come under strong criticism. Everywhere he went, "Judaizing teachers" insisted that if Gentiles wanted to come to the Messiah, it had to be through the Law, and must include male circumcision as the Law required. Paul objects, however, that this amounted to "works salvation." In verse 16, he maintains that he is not ashamed of this message of grace—which in fact had been the ruling of a Church council in Jerusalem (Acts 15). Grace was the basis of the gospel,

or good news; and it was Paul's glad task to take that message "to the Jew first," and also to Greeks (or Gentiles) such as those in Rome.

Why "to the Jew first"? Because they were first on God's "adoption list," and it was to them that the Covenant was first given, and the promises that Messiah would come not only for them but for all (see Rom. 9:4). Thus, when Paul was on a missionary trip he always went first to a synagogue, and only then shared his message with the Gentiles. That practice is now explained and reflected on in the book of Romans.

B. The power of faith, 17
17 For therein is the righteousness of God revealed from faith to faith: as it is written, The just shall live by faith.

Although it is clear that "therein" refers to the gospel, it is far from clear what is meant by God's righteousness being revealed in the gospel "from faith to faith." The variety of ways this phrase is translated shows the difficulty. The NIV translators understand it to mean that God's righteousness is obtained not by works but "by faith *from first to last*." It is also possible that Paul is saying that God's righteousness is revealed *from* the faith of the Old Covenant way *to* faith under the New Covenant. In other words, both Jew and Gentile are saved by faith, just as he had said in verse 16, and will say again in many other passages.

II. The Need for the Message—1:18-20; 3:9-18

A. Without excuse, 1:18-20

18 For the wrath of God is revealed from heaven against all ungodliness and unrighteousness of men, who hold the truth in unrighteousness;

19 Because that which may be known of God is manifest in them; for God hath shewed it unto them.

20 For the invisible things of him from the creation of the world are clearly seen, being understood by the things that are made, even his eternal power and Godhead; so that they are without excuse:

It would be natural for the mostly Gentile Christians in Rome to ask if only Jews who reject salvation by faith need the salvation promised by the gospel. Here Paul begins a lengthy argument that shows that Gentiles need the Good News as much as the Jews. Just as the Jews had not kept the "special revelation" of the Law of Moses perfectly, so Gentiles have not kept the laws God had given since creation by "general revelation," through nature.

These "laws" or principles include the fact that creation speaks of a Creator, even though He is "invisible." (It was important for Paul to include this, since some former pagans in the church at Rome may have been idolaters, or worshipers of *visible* gods.) Even without a Holy Book, all people can know that God has not left Himself "without witness, in that he did good, and gave us rain from heaven, and fruitful seasons, filling our hearts with food and gladness" (Act 14:17). Also, the universal fact of *conscience* speaks of a divine Source of morality (2:15).

Note that verse 20 does *not* say that nature, or general revelation, tells Gentiles enough about God to *save* them, but enough to show His "eternal power and divine nature" (NIV). The specifics about salvation come not through nature, but through the good news of Jesus. At any rate, Gentiles had not lived up to "natural law." As a whole they had held what truths they knew about God "unrighteously," not living up to what they understood about Him. Thus, they are "without excuse."

B. None are righteous, 3:9-18

3:9 What then? are we better than they? No, in no wise: for we have before proved both Jews and Gentiles, that they are all under sin;

10 As it is written, There is none righteous, no, not one:

11 There is none that understandeth, there is none that seeketh after God.

12 They are all gone out of the way, they are together become unprofitable; there is none that doeth good, no, not one.

13 Their throat is an open sepulchre; with their tongues they have used deceit; the poison of

asps is under their lips:

14 Whose mouth is full of cursing and bitterness:

15 Their feet are swift to shed blood:

16 Destruction and misery are in their ways:

17 And the way of peace have they not known:

18 There is no fear of God before their eyes.

In much of chapters 1 and 2, Paul had shown that Gentiles or pagans are sinners, and thus need to be saved by the gospel. In 3:1 he had anticipated a Gentile concluding that they are worse sinners than Jews. Now Paul counters this view by asking the rhetorical question, "Are we (Jews) better than they?"—then answering his own question, "No, in no wise!" by citing a string of quotations from Ecclesiastes, Psalms, Proverbs, and Isaiah. In other words, the Jews' Holy Scriptures themselves often charged them with the sins listed here.

In fact, the *idolatry* lapsed Jews, which led to many of the sins Paul lists, was what had prompted God to allow the Jews to be conquered and scattered to the four corners of the earth. The point, as he had "before proved" (or affirmed), is that both Jew *and* Gentile have sinned, and thus both needed to be saved.

III. The Role of the Law—3:19-20

A. To show our guilt, 19

19 Now we know that what things soever the law saith, it saith to them who are under the law:

that every mouth may be stopped, and all the world may become guilty before God.

If the Jews are as guilty of sin as the Gentiles, of what good was the Law? Paul says it served the purpose of *naming* sin, so that "every mouth may be stopped," or so that no one could say they did not know they had sinned. We know not to run a red light only because a law says, as we teach our children, "red says stop." Paul will elaborate on this point in chapter 7, saying "I had not known sin but by the law" (7:7).

B. Not to save our souls, 20

20 Therefore by the deeds of the law there shall no flesh be justified in his sight: for by the law is the knowledge of sin.

Although the Law of Moses was for the express purpose of *defining* sin, it could not *justify* sinners. There is a vast difference between "the knowledge of sin" the Law brought, and the salvation from sin available through Christ. In fact, keeping our eyes on the Law only reminds us of how far short we fall in keeping it: "the law entered that the offence might abound" (5:20).

In short, our text has shown that "The scripture hath concluded all under sin, that the promise by faith of Jesus Christ might be given to them that believe" (Gal. 3:22). Since Jews have broken their Law from Moses, and the Gentiles have failed to keep the laws of nature, they both need the good news that all can be saved by faith, not law-keeping.

Evangelistic Emphasis

There are several times in the gospel of Mark where Jesus does a miracle. He casts out evil spirits in Mark 3. He raises Jairus' daughter from the dead in Mark 5. He heals the deaf and mute man in Mark 7. In each of these cases Jesus said, "Don't tell anybody about this." Yet, "the more he did so, the more they kept talking about it" (Mark 7:36).

Jesus is still doing great things for us today. He is transforming lives, healing hurts, mending families, and saving souls. Jesus instructed us to tell others what He has done and is doing for us, yet we are so hesitant to do so. I wonder if Paul was thinking about people like us when he wrote, "For I am not ashamed of the gospel." Are we ashamed to tell others the good news of the gospel? Are we embarrassed to tell others what Jesus has done for us? We should not be, for the gospel of Jesus Christ is the greatest story ever told. I pray that we will freely claim the gospel as our own and share the good news every opportunity we have to do so.

ഇരു

Memory Selection

As it is written, There is none righteous, no, not one.—*Romans 3:10*

These words of Paul are a hard teaching for us open-minded folks of the 21st century. We want to think of all people as basically good. We tend to say, "There is a little good in the worst of us and a little bad in the best of us." I believe that is true. Yet, in human beings there is that selfish tendency to go our own way. We tend to lean toward those things that are pleasant and easy on us.

Many people, when given the opportunity to do what they want to do in every situation without fear of getting caught or held accountable, will eventually choose that which is self-serving and not God-serving. In our hearts, we know that is true. It is illustrated in the fact that we do not have to teach our children to be bad. No, we have to teach our children how to be good. They can learn to be bad on their own, because the tendency to sin has been in our hearts since the first human beings were created.

Paul wrote, "There is none righteous. . . ." We say this ourselves in another way when we say, "Nobody's perfect."

Weekday Problems

"Don't come here with that 'holier-than-thou' stuff! You're no better than I am," Dimitri huffed. "You think you're something special! Well, you're not!"

Dimitri's words stung Marcus. He hadn't intended to imply that he was any better than anyone else. He was just trying to share with Dimitri what God had done for him. Marcus knew that there was within his own heart a tendency to drift away from God and do things that were not pleasing to God. He knew that he was far from perfect himself.

Yet Marcus also knew that the transforming power of the Holy Spirit had been working in his life since he asked Jesus Christ to be his Savior and Lord. Because the Lord was doing so much in Marcus' life, he wanted to tell others about it. He was not ashamed to admit that his life was worse before Christ and better after he invited Christ in.

*Have you ever had an occasion in which you shared your testimony and it was misunderstood?

*Have you ever been "ashamed of the gospel"? Why do you think that might have been?

Hints of Heaven

To believe in God for me is to feel that there is a God, not a dead one, or a stuffed one, but a living one, who with irresistible force lures us towards more loving.—*Vincent van Gogh*

* * * *

Who . . . has ever seen an idea? . . . Who has ever seen love? . . . Who has ever seen faith? . . . The real things in the world are the invisible spiritual realities. Is it so difficult, then, to believe in God?—*Charles Templeton.*

* * * *

Believe that life is worth living, and your belief will help create the fact.—*William James*

* * * *

Belief consists in accepting the affirmations of the soul; unbelief, in denying them.—*Ralph Waldo Emerson*

This Lesson in Your Life

Once upon a time there was a man in Miami, Florida, who planned to go to Paris, France. He did not want to spend the money necessary to buy an airline ticket, or book passage on an ocean-going vessel. He decided the best way to get from Miami to Paris without expense was to swim.

So, on a Tuesday, he stripped down to his swim trunks, dived into the waters of the Atlantic Ocean, and began to swim. He planned to swim nonstop to Paris alone.

After a few miles of swimming, a huge boat pulled alongside. "Ahoy, swimmer!" came a voice from a bullhorn. "What are you doing?"

"I'm swimming to Paris nonstop," the swimmer shouted back.

"You can't do that!"was the astonished response. "It is humanly impossible to swim across the Atlantic Ocean. Your efforts are futile. We can take you there for free, but you have to get in the boat."

"No, thanks," the swimmer replied. "I would rather do it on my own."

Alas, after eight days in the water, the man became too exhausted to move and he sank beneath the waves.

This is just a story. Yet, it illustrates a point. Some things are humanly impossible. For instance, it is humanly impossible to live a perfect life. Every person has sinned. Every person will sin. Every person needs a Savior.

Paul reminds us in our passage that all have sinned and therefore need the righteousness that only God can provide through faith in Jesus Christ. The man in the story could not get from Miami to Paris without getting in the boat. We cannot get from sinful lives to lives of righteousness without faith in Christ. We must get into and trust the old "Ship of Zion."

GETTING THE FACTS STRAIGHT

1. What is the power of God for salvation?
The gospel message is God's power for salvation.

2. Who can receive salvation?
Salvation is available to everybody, and received by all those who believe.

3. According to Romans 1:18, what is holding back the truth and revealing God's wrath?
God's wrath is being revealed because of humanity's godlessness and wickedness.

4. According to Romans 1:20, could people have seen the eternal power of God and the divine nature of God even before Jesus came?
Yes. Natural revelation through God's creation has revealed His invisible qualities so clearly that humanity has no excuse not to believe in Him.

5. When looking at Romans 3:9, would we conclude that no race of people is inherently better than another race?
Yes. There is no particular race that is more nearly righteous than another. We are all sinners in need of a Savior, regardless of our race or culture.

6. Was Paul unsure about basic human unrighteousness? (Rom. 3:10-18.)
No. Paul is very sure that people have no righteousness of their own.

7. If we stood in a court of law and were judged only by our works of the law and our keeping of the law, what would the verdict be?
We would stand guilty before God (Rom. 3:19). If we were still under the Law of Moses, we would be subject to God's judgment.

8. Can we do enough good works to be declared righteous and be justified in God's sight?
No. Paul says that no one can be justified or declared righteous by deeds of the law (see Rom. 3:20).

9. How then can a person be justified or declared righteous?
Paul said, "The just (or righteous [NIV]) shall live by faith" (1:17). It is only by faith in God's saving power through Jesus Christ and the sanctifying power of the Holy Spirit that a person can be justified and declared righteous.

10. In Romans 3:18, Paul quotes Psalm 36:1. How does the fact that people generally have no fear of God fit in with the other statements about unrighteousness?
The fear of God—that is, awesome reverence for God—is the source of all godliness. (See Gen. 20:11.)

When I was a young boy I was baseball crazy. I played baseball in Mr. Hughes' vacant lot when I grew old enough for the big kids to let me play. I remember my first glove. An older friend gave it to me. It was his glove until he bought himself a new one. He handed his old glove down to me. I was not particularly proud of that glove because it was so old and beat up. But it got me in the games and that was very important to me.

The old, used glove was not my love, though. Every Saturday, while my mom was grocery shopping, I would go down the street to Brewton's Hardware and look at their selection of baseball gloves. I tried each one on. I pounded my fist in the pocket of each. I visualized myself making the game-saving catch in the most important game of the season. It was at the hardward store that I fell in love—with a beautiful, long-fingered, black glove. But I knew it would never be mine. The glove was entirely too expensive for an eight-year-old's pocketbook.

One day my dad came home from work carrying a brown paper bag. "What did you get, Dad?" I asked. He handed me the bag. Inside was that glove I wanted so badly! I could hardly believe it. It was not my birthday. It was not Christmas. My dad just gave me a gift I wanted with all my heart.

You know, there is great joy when we receive something for which we have longed that we have not earned and for which we cannot pay. A gift like that demonstrates the love the giver has for the person who receives.

God has given us a gift for which we can never pay. There is nothing we can do that is good enough to pay God back for our salvation. An equally great truth is that there is nothing we can do that is bad enough to prevent God from offering that gift. All we have to do is accept the gift of salvation joyfully and gratefully.

Then get out there and play ball!

God's Judgment Is Just

Roman 2:1-16

Therefore thou art inexcusable, O man, whosoever thou art that judgest: for wherein thou judgest another, thou condemnest thyself; for thou that judgest doest the same things.

2 But we are sure that the judgment of God is according to truth against them which commit such things.

3 And thinkest thou this, O man, that judgest them which do such things, and doest the same, that thou shalt escape the judgment of God?

4 Or despisest thou the riches of his goodness and forbearance and longsuffering; not knowing that the goodness of God leadeth thee to repentance?

5 But after thy hardness and impenitent heart treasurest up unto thyself wrath against the day of wrath and revelation of the righteous judgment of God;

6 Who will render to every man according to his deeds:

7 To them who by patient continuance in well doing seek for glory and honour and immortality, eternal life:

8 But unto them that are contentious, and do not obey the truth, but obey unrighteousness, indignation and wrath,

9 Tribulation and anguish, upon every soul of man that doeth evil, of the Jew first, and also of the Gentile;

10 But glory, honour, and peace, to every man that worketh good, to the Jew first, and also to the Gentile:

11 For there is no respect of persons with God.

12 For as many as have sinned without law shall also perish without law: and as many as have sinned in the law shall be judged by the law;

13(For not the hearers of the law are just before God, but the doers of the law shall be justified.

14 For when the Gentiles, which have not the law, do by nature the things contained in the law, these, having not the law, are a law unto themselves:

15 Which shew the work of the law written in their hearts, their conscience also bearing witness, and their thoughts the mean while accusing or else excusing one another;)

16 In the day when God shall judge the secrets of men by Jesus Christ according to my gospel.

Memory Selection
Romans 2:16
Background Scripture
Romans 2:16
Devotional Reading
Psalm 50:1-15

The setting of this lesson is Paul's bold admonition for Jews not to judge Gentiles. Since both groups have sinned, both need a Savior. However, the sin of judgmentalism is so widespread that the lesson quickly takes on a mantle that fits all of us, whether the relationship of Jew and Gentile concerns us or not.

Be sure, however, that the lesson doesn't degenerate into an invitation to be so politically correct and broad minded that no one can tell what we believe. Jesus Himself said to "judge for yourselves what is right" (Luke 12:57). Here in Romans, Paul does not call us not to use *discernment,* but not to be harsh and critical of others' motives and attitudes, or even of evil works if our own are not above reproach either. The Jews criticized Gentiles for not keeping God's law, when they failed to keep Moses' Law.

The American system of justice is supposed to *presume innocence until proved guilty.* We are not to judge a person guilty until a legally constituted judge or jury pronounces him so.

Yet ask your group if there are some cases when this tradition is hard to uphold. Does people's previous history cause us to judge them guilty before a jury does? Do we instinctively "rush to judgment" on the basis of whether persons are rich or poor? Of one race or another? Or on their occupation? What other factors can make it hard for a judge or jury to stay committed to the principle of "innocent until proved guilty"? Point out that U.S. legal tradition seems based on the principles Paul teaches in today's lesson.

Teaching Outline	*Daily Bible Readings*

I. Who Is Better than Another?—1-10
  A. God alone is judge, 1-2
  B. God's goodness to all, 3-4
  C. God's judgment, 5-10
    1. *For* goodness, 5-7
    2. *Against* unrighteousness, 8-10
II. Who Is Above the Law?—11-16
  A. Law judges all, 11-13
  B. Gentiles' law, 14-16
	Mon. God the Righteous Judge
	     Psalm 7:6-17
	Tue. God Himself Is Judge
	     Psalm 50:1-15
	Wed. Don't Judge Others
	     Romans 2:1-5
	Thu. God Will Judge All
	     Romans 2:6-11
	Fri. Doers of the Law Justified
	     Romans 2:12-16
	Sat. Do Jews Follow the Law?
	     Romans 2:17-24
	Sun. Real 'Jews' Obey the Law
	     Romans 2:25-29

Verse by Verse

I. Who Is Better than Another?–1-10
A. God alone is judge, 1-2

1 Therefore thou art inexcusable, O man, whosoever thou art that judgest: for wherein thou judgest another, thou condemnest thyself; for thou that judgest doest the same things.

2 But we are sure that the judgment of God is according to truth against them which commit such things.

In 1:18-32, Paul had listed the horrible ways Gentiles had defied God's "natural" law. They were guilty of idolatry, lust and unnatural sexual excess, and a whole laundry list of sins named in 1:29-31. Because the reality of God and His power are "clearly seen" in creation, such Gentile sinners are "without excuse" (1:20). We can almost hear self-righteous Jews cheering Paul on: *Get 'em, Paul! Those Gentiles are wicked beyond belief!*

That judgmental position is exactly where Paul wants the Jews in his audience. For now he will turn the spotlight of God's righteous light on their own sins, to reinforce his general point that "There is none righteous, no, not one" (3:10, a paraphrase of Ps. 14:1). If the latter part of chapter 1 is a powerful indictment

against Gentiles, most of chapter 2 indicts the Jews of being the same kind of law-breakers—only of a different law.

To "judge" in Greek, as in English, can mean to "decide," but also to "condemn'" and Paul uses the term in the latter, harsher sense. This view is supported by his use of a strengthened form of "judge" later in verse 1, a word which literally means to "judge *down*," or to condemn.

In what sense can Paul say that a Jew who at least tried to live right "doest the same things" as the Gentiles—sins as heinous as those listed in chapter 2? In the sense that both the good Jews' "little" sins, of which the best of them were guilty, and the Gentiles' "big" sins, *break God's law* and thus make Jews sinners, too. The pronouncement in verse 2 that God's judgment is "according to truth" is therefore of little comfort to the person who denies his need for grace. God's fair judgment yields the uncomfortable truth that *all* have sinned, and *all* deserve His judgment of spiritual death that is avoided only by the grace of Christ.

B. God's goodness to all, 3-4

3 And thinkest thou this, O man, that judgest them which do such things, and doest the same,

that thou shalt escape the judgment of God?

4 Or despisest thou the riches of his goodness and forbearance and longsuffering; not knowing that the goodness of God leadeth thee to repentance?

Again, we are to read "O man" as addressed particularly to Jews. The scribes and Pharisees especially loved to make even longer lists of how bad the Gentiles were than Paul had made in 1:19-31. In fact, that list no doubt reflects Paul's earlier training as a Pharisee himself (Philip. 3:5). Yet even the best Pharisee had surely had a wrong thought or a base motive, or had *omitted* to do good, which itself is a sin (Matt. 23:23). He must therefore rely on God's grace as much as a Gentile.

In fact, Paul touches here on what John Calvin would later emphasize: Moses' Law pointed to the need for grace. It is therefore the goodness of God that even makes us aware that we need to repent of breaking His law. The implication of Paul's question in the latter part of verse 4 is: *How can you, as a Jew, count on God's goodness to overlook your sins, while not admitting that the same goodness and grace is available to the Gentiles?*

C. God's judgment, 5-10

1. *For* goodness, 5-7

5 But after thy hardness and impenitent heart treasurest up unto thyself wrath against the day of wrath and revelation of the righteous judgment of God;

6 Who will render to every man according to his deeds:

7 To them who by patient continuance in well doing seek for glory and honour and immortality, eternal life:

Here Paul addresses the self-righteous Jews who thought that they not only were "above" Gentiles as the Chosen Race, but also a morally superior people. While making out their lists of the sins of the Gentiles, the rabbis conveniently overlooked the high moral standards among some. The writings of pagans such as Plato, Aristotle, Marcus Aurelius, and Seneca are still quoted for their moral values. For Jews to "judge" them closes the door of grace to themselves, for God will render even-handed justice to all. Here, however, the emphasis is on God's judgment *in favor* of all those, Jew or Greek, whose life-endeavor is "well-doing."

2. *Against* unrighteousness, 8-10

8 But unto them that are contentious, and do not obey the truth, but obey unrighteousness, indignation and wrath,

9 Tribulation and anguish, upon every soul of man that doeth evil, of the Jew first, and also of the Gentile;

Now the sad side of God's judgment is recognized. His same fair-minded and even-handed justice that saves the righteous will condemn the unrighteous. Paul summarizes this unrighteousness under the headings of "contentiousness and disobedience." Verse 9 should actually begin just before the word "indignation," for there God's *response* to deliberate evil begins: indignation, wrath, tribulation and anguish. Then, like a repeated refrain after each verse of a song, such fair judgment will be rendered "to the Jew first, and also to the Gentile." After a brief relisting of the rewards of grace in verse 10, this "both-and-ness" of God is repeated.

II. Who Is Above the Law?—11-16
A. Law judges all, 11-13

11 For there is no respect of persons with God.

12 For as many as have sinned without law shall also perish without law: and as many as have sinned in the law shall be judged by the law;

13(For not the hearers of the law are just before God, but the doers of the law shall be justified.

When Paul uses the term "law" it is not always easy to tell whether he means "the Law of Moses" or simply "law" in general. In the original, the article "the" does not appear in these verses. The King James translators faithfully omit the article in verse 12 to show that the law Gentiles sin against is simply "law" in general, or God's moral law. They *insert* "the" in verse 13 to show their view that Paul means the Law of Moses here. Actually, Paul is stating the universal principle he will elaborate on later: Gentiles break law in general and Jews break *the* Law (of Moses) in particular. Therefore, all are law-breakers, and, without grace,

justly deserve God's punishment.
B. Gentiles' law, 14-16

14 For when the Gentiles, which have not the law, do by nature the things contained in the law, these, having not the law, are a law unto themselves:

15 Which shew the work of the law written in their hearts, their conscience also bearing witness, and their thoughts the mean while accusing or else excusing one another;)

16 In the day when God shall judge the secrets of men by Jesus Christ according to my gospel.

The use of the article "the" does show that Paul now refers to Moses' law. Much of that law consists of universal moral principles—laws of the conscience such as not lying, stealing, and lusting after other people's spouses. If a Gentile who kept this moral law perfectly could be found, he would be justified before God because he kept the law that God wrote on the human heart, or the conscience.

The fact is that "*all* have sinned." The only "saving grace" at Judgment will in fact be Christ's saving grace, implied in Paul's last phrase, "according to my gospel," or the gospel that had been delivered to him (see Gal. 1:11-12). The crux of the passage is that if Jews shut the door of grace to Gentiles for breaking God's moral law, they shut it on themselves because they have broken God's law to them, through Moses. Therefore neither they nor we are to judge others.

Evangelistic Emphasis

Jesus said, "Judge not, that ye be not judged" (Matt. 7:1). Paul is saying the same thing right here in Romans 2. The only one who is qualified to pass judgment on another is Jesus Christ Himself. Why? Because we cannot judge another while we are doing the same things ourselves.

One might argue, "I'm not doing those same things. I'm not cursing, lying, or . . . " (fill in the blank).

While we may not be sinning in the same way, rest assured each of us has enough sin within our own hearts to be convicted of being sinners, too.

We are grateful that Jesus Christ has made a way for us to escape judgment—not by our own merits, but by the merits of His sinless life, atoning death, and miraculous resurrection. We do not have to concern ourselves with judging others. In fact, when we accept Jesus as Savior, we do not have to concern ourselves with our own judgment. Jesus has washed our sins away. When we think about it, would we not agree that we are all sinners saved by grace?

ෂ෬

Memory Selection

In the day when God shall judge the secrets of men by Jesus Christ according to my gospel.—*Romans 2:16*

Jesus knows our hearts. He is not unclear about our motives. He knows what we do and He knows why we are doing the things we are doing. Jesus is not like the judge on the bench in our courtrooms. If a person is clever enough, he can deceive even the most diligent of judges. One could manipulate evidence. One could tell lies convincingly. One could win over the judge with persuasive words. This is possible because even the wisest of judges is unable to see into the human heart.

Jesus, however, knows our hearts. We cannot "fake Jesus off." He will judge our actions, of course. Anyone can judge the things we do that are visible to all. Jesus will also judge our thoughts. He knows even those secret thoughts, those secret things, that no one else knows. Our task is to live our lives in an upright and godly manner. It is our task to live our lives as if Jesus can see everything we do and everything we think. We live our lives as if Jesus sees all . . . because He does.

Weekday Problems

Roger was in church practically every Sunday. He went to an adult Sunday School class as well. He was even in a mid-week small group Bible study that met in Mike's home. Roger probably knew as much Scripture as anyone else his age in the church. Yet, Mike knew Roger was not living by what he knew.

When Roger came over to Mike's house for Bible study, Mike invited him into the kitchen for coffee. "Roger," Mike began, "I consider you my friend. You are a person I care about deeply. That's why I feel compelled to confront you with the fact that I know you are seeing a woman at work who is not your wife. That type of action is not consistent with Christian teaching. If I dare say it, you know better."

Roger blew up. "You are not my judge!" he shouted as he stormed out of the house.

*Should we confront our friends when we know they are participating in sinful behavior?

*Was Mike judging Roger? Explain your view.

Salvos on Sin and Salvation

Long before the Mormons made polygamy illegal, a Mormon with more than one wife dared the renowned Mark Twain to cite a single Bible passage against the practice.

"Easy," said Twain: "No man can serve two masters."

* * * *

An IRS agent called a minister and said, "We're checking to see if one of your church members, Mr. Brown, really gave $1,000 to the church."

"I don't have the records before me," said the minister, "but I can tell you right now that if he didn't, he will!"

* * * *

St. Peter looked at the new arrival skeptically. He had had no advance notice that he was coming to heaven's gates.

"How did you get here?" Peter asked sternly.

"Flu," the man replied.

In this passage of Scripture Paul is giving us some excellent teaching that will help us in our Christian walk. He sets forth principles that govern God's judgment.

First, Paul tells us in verse 2 that God judges according to the truth. We can be comforted by that. Who among us has not set out to do something, guided by the best of intentions and motives, only to have that act go wrong? Maybe our act of good will was taken the wrong way. Maybe the recipient of our kindness misinterpreted our motives. Maybe we did not know all the factors involved in the situation, and what we meant for the good turned out to do harm. Even though some may judge what you did wrongly, God is certainly judging your actions by your motives. God judges our hearts. God judges our sincerity. God judges according to the truth.

There is another facet to God's judging according to the truth that is not so comforting. Because God judges our hearts, our motives, and our intentions according to the truth, it is imperative for us to see that motives are always pure. We must live our lives filled by the sanctifying power of the Holy Spirit in order that our actions and our motives hold up under God's scrutiny.

We can also be assured that God judges according to the light a person has. That is, we will not be held accountable for things that have not been revealed to us. God will not judge the ignorant one harshly. Many of us have wondered, "What is God going to do with those who have never heard the Gospel?" Paul gives us a glimpse here. People will be judged only by what has been revealed to them. However, Paul reminds us, a considerable amount of God's revelation has come to even the heathen through nature and through conscience.

We can rest assured God will judge fairly. His judgment will be full of justice, truth, and righteousness.

STRAIGHT

1. Upon what is God's judgment based?
God's judgment is based on the truth, the whole truth, and nothing but the truth. God judges us with total honesty.

2. Do we have any right to judge other persons even though we are also sinners? Why or why not?
No, we do not have that right. Only God has the right to judge because only God is without sin.

3. What will happen to us if we judge hypocritically?
We will not escape God's judgment. Further, we can be sure that God will judge us righteously. He will not overlook our hypocrisy.

4. According to verse 4, what does God offer us that leads us to repentance?
God offers His kindness to us, to give opportunity for repentance. See also 2 Peter 3:9.

5. What do our stubbornness and unrepentant hearts lead to?
Our stubborn and unrepentant hearts result in God's wrath being stored up against us for the day when His righteous judgment will be revealed.

6. According to verse 7, who will be receiving eternal life?
Eternal life will be given to those who, by persistence in doing good, seek glory, honor, and immortality.

7. What will those who are self-seeking, who reject the truth, and follow evil, receive?
They will be facing God's wrath and His anger.

8. Is it the Jew or the Gentile who will be judged with leniency?
According to verse 11, all persons will be judged by the same standards. God shows no favoritism.

9. According to verse 13, did hearing and knowing the Law make a Jew righteous?
No. Under the dispensation of the Law, only those who obeyed the Law could be declared righteous.

10. Who will judge the secret thoughts of all humans?
Jesus Christ Himself will judge men's secrets. Only He is qualified to judge both thought and deed, for only He is entirely righteous.

There is a story attributed to the late Dr. E. Stanley Jones, who was a missionary to India for many years. It seems Dr. Jones had been invited back to the United States to address a pastors' convention.

Dr. Jones began his remarks politely enough, but very soon he began to enumerate sins into which the American pastors had backslidden . He called the pastors to task for their lack of zeal. He challenged them to be more effective in their work. He chided them in a less than gentle manner for their lack of zeal in winning souls to Christ. Dr. Jones did everything but point fingers and call out names as he bombarded the pastors with warning after warning of God's judgment if they did not return to God's work with more diligence.

As he was descending from the platform after his address, one of the pastor's wives who was in attendance caught him at the bottom step. She had fire in her eyes.

"How dare you, Dr. Jones!" she said. "How dare you speak to these great men of God as you did! You are not their judge. God is their judge. Jesus said a man has no right to judge another!"

"Dear Madam," Dr. Jones replied. "I suppose you are referring to Jesus' words in Matthew 7:1 when you say, "Do not judge, or you too will be judged."

"That is correct," she replied, without softening.

"Please, dear lady," Dr. Jones went on. "Continue reading chapter 7. Jesus also says, 'By their fruit you will recognize them.' You are right when you say I am not their judge. I am simply a fruit inspector."

Paul reminds us that it is not sufficient to hear the law of God. It is not even enough to know God's law. Our task is to obey God as we follow in Christ's footsteps. Then we will not have to worry about judgment. We will not even have to be anxious about fruit inspectors.

We Are Justified By Faith

Romans 5:1-11, 18-21

Therefore being justified by faith, we have peace with God through our Lord Jesus Christ:

2 By whom also we have access by faith into this grace wherein we stand, and rejoice in hope of the glory of God.

3 And not only so, but we glory in tribulations also: knowing that tribulation worketh patience;

4 And patience, experience; and experience, hope:

5 And hope maketh not ashamed; because the love of God is shed abroad in our hearts by the Holy Ghost which is given unto us.

6 For when we were yet without strength, in due time Christ died for the ungodly.

7 For scarcely for a righteous man will one die: yet peradventure for a good man some would even dare to die.

8 But God commendeth his love toward us, in that, while we were yet sinners, Christ died for us.

9 Much more then, being now justified by his blood, we shall be saved from wrath through him.

10 For if, when we were enemies, we were reconciled to God by the death of his Son, much more, being recon-ciled, we shall be saved by his life.

11 And not only so, but we also joy in God through our Lord Jesus Christ, by whom we have now received the atonement.

18 Therefore as by the offence of one judgment came upon all men to condemnation; even so by the righteousness of one the free gift came upon all men unto justification of life.

19 For as by one man's disobedience many were made sinners, so by the obedience of one shall many be made righteous.

20 Moreover the law entered, that the offence might abound. But where sin abounded, grace did much more abound:

21 That as sin hath reigned unto death, even so might grace reign through righteousness unto eternal life by Jesus Christ our Lord.

Memory Selection
Romans 5:11

Background Scripture
Romans 5

Devotional Reading
2 Corinthians 3:4-11

 Paul's letter to the Romans contains the most thorough statement of his theology. In brief, he holds that all who are saved, both Jew and Gentile, are justified by faith, not works. As simple as it sounds, this view raises several questions for which the teacher will want to be prepared. If we are saved by faith, what is the role of works (which Paul also champi-ons; see Rom. 8:13)? Also, if every-one, including Gentiles, is saved by faith, what happened with God's "eternal" covenant to Abraham? Paul had dealt with this question in chap-ter 4, showing that Gentiles are "sons of Abraham" if they have *believed* as strongly as he did.

Now Paul expands on the idea of what it means to be justified by faith—both in our relationship with God, and with each other.

 This lesson on Paul's use of the term *justification* can be introduced by a balance sheet like this one:

ASSETS		DEBTS	
House	$50,000	House	$35,000
Car	20,000	Car	15,000
Cash	2,000	Misc. Debts	25,000
Totals:	**$72,000**		**$75,000**

Note that you owe $3,000 more than you have. Applying the illustration to *salvation,* a works-system would require that we come up with $3,000 worth of works. Paul says that we can't do that because we are spiritually "broke." With no righteousness of our own, God Himself, through Christ, supplies it. The columns can be "justified" only by grace.

Teaching Outline	*Daily Bible Readings*	
I. Peace with God—1-2	Mon.	Justified and Made Heirs *Titus 3:1-7*
II. Glory in Trials—3-5	Tue.	Abounding in Glory *2 Corinthians 3:4-11*
III. Justified while Enemies—6-11	Wed.	Faith Like Abraham's *Romans 4:13-25*
A. Above and beyond duty, 6-8	Thu.	Justified by Faith *Romans 5:1-5*
B. His death and His life, 9-11		
IV. The One and the Many—18-21	Fri.	Christ Died for Sinners *Romans 5:6-11*
A. Adam and Christ, 18-19	Sat.	Christ's Free Gift *Romans 5:12-17*
B. The Law's role, 20-21	Sun.	Grace Abounding *Romans 5:18-21*

Verse by Verse

I. Peace with God—1-2

1 Therefore being justified by faith, we have peace with God through our Lord Jesus Christ:

2 By whom also we have access by faith into this grace wherein we stand, and rejoice in hope of the glory of God.

Beginning the sentence with "Therefore" indicates that Paul is building on his previous argument that God had accepted Abraham *before* he was circumcised (4:10), thus justifying him by faith, not works.

"Therefore," Paul continues, *we*—that is, everyone who is saved, both Jew and Gentile—also are brought into a "peaceful" relationship with God not by works but by faith in the work of Christ on the Cross. Verse 2 makes it clear that Paul is not saying that all we have to do is believe in goodness or justice or "religion" in general, but *in Christ*. We "stand" in the grace that Jesus exhibited by substituting Himself for the sacrifices God had commanded under the Old Covenant. We rejoice in *that* hope, indicating that if we had only works in which to trust there would be no basis for rejoicing—since no one can keep a works-based law perfectly.

II. Glory in Trials—4-5

3 And not only so, but we glory in tribulations also: knowing that tribulation worketh patience;

4 And patience, experience; and experience, hope:

5 And hope maketh not ashamed; because the love of God is shed abroad in our hearts by the Holy Ghost which is given unto us.

Being brought into a right relationship with God doesn't just produce a passive feeling of joy; it leads to the more aggressive attitude of "glorying" in tribulations or trials. Paul seems to say that salvation by grace through faith produces the attitude of "Bring it on! I can do all things through Christ which strengtheneth me" (Phil. 4:13).

Paul develops a list of progressive steps toward victory, all based on faith. With faith, we can progress from tribulation to patience, to experience, to hope—which is a kind of proof that our trust was well-placed, and we need not be ashamed of it. All this is related to the Holy Spirit, which is associated with salvation by grace far more than it appears in the Old Covenant when the emphasis was on the Law. This Spirit-guided confidence in the face of trials is far more realistic when our relationship with God is based on the grace/faith model than it could ever be if we were trusting in our ability to keep the Law.

III. Justified while Enemies—6-11
A. Above and beyond duty, 6-8

6 For when we were yet without strength, in due time Christ died for the ungodly.

7 For scarcely for a righteous man will one die: yet peradventure for a good man some would even dare to die.

8 But God commendeth his love toward us, in that, while we were yet sinners, Christ died for us.

Now Paul supports his argument in favor of the grace/faith system of salvation by noting the *sequence* of man's sin in relation to Christ's sacrificial death on the Cross. In a system of law, we would expect a person to become righteous by keeping the rules, thus convincing God to condescend to send Jesus. Even among human beings, it is not impossible to imagine a person giving his life for a righteous person. In God's case, however, He made the first move, sending His Son not because mankind was righteous but because we were *un*righteous. This argument is a death blow to the idea that we must first keep the rules in order to win God's love.

B. His death and His life, 9-11

9 Much more then, being now justified by his blood, we shall be saved from wrath through him.

10 For if, when we were en-emies, we were reconciled to God by the death of his Son, much more, being reconciled, we shall be saved by his life.

11 And not only so, but we also joy in God through our Lord Jesus Christ, by whom we have now received the atonement.

Instead of being saved from the angry judgment of God against sinners by perfectly keeping the Law, Paul's hope is in being justified, or "counted" righteous (4:3) by trusting in the cleansing blood of Christ. This implies both that the blood of animal sacrifices under the Old Law and the blood of sinners themselves are inadequate to "purchase" salvation. As the Church has long sung, *"What can wash away my sins? / Nothing but the blood of Jesus."*

Paul is not advocating a gloomy, death-oriented faith that only looks backward to the Cross. The spirit of Christians is lifted up by faith in the resurrection of Christ as much as by His death. Again as we sing, *"Because He lives, I can face tomorrow."*

Just as the term "justified" is one of Paul's favorite terms to describe the unearned salvation brought by Christ, so the word "reconciliation" (often translated "atonement") is loaded with significance. It means to be changed and brought into agreement with God's will. Again, this is a change that believers *receive* as something done for us, not one that we achieve by human works.

IV. The One and the Many—18-21
A. Adam and Christ, 18-19

18 Therefore as by the offence of one judgment came upon all men to condemnation; even so by the righteousness of one the free gift came upon all men unto justification of life.

19 For as by one man's disobedience many were made sinners, so by the obedience of one shall many be made righteous.

Paul often sought carefully balanced parallels to illustrate his points. Here and in 1 Corinthians 15 he balances Adam and Christ, comparing and contrasting similarities and differences, especially for any Jews in his audience. The point of comparison here is how both Adam and Christ, though single individuals, influenced masses of people.

On the one hand, Adam's "offence" or sin brought condemnation into the world. Although this is an obvious reference to what is often called "original sin," it does not necessarily mean that everyone is born with the *guilt* of Adam's sin, but with the *consequence*—that is, sin that is ready at hand, beckoning so strongly that in our humanity we become guilty by sinning, not just by being born. The parallel contrast, of course, is Christ's act of atonement, a single act that brought the free gift of justification—again, not to all who are *born* but to all who believe. Verse 19 repeats this parallel in terms of the disobedience of Adam contrasted with the obedience of Christ (to His heavenly Father's will).

B. The Law's role, 20-21

20 Moreover the law entered, that the offence might abound. But where sin abounded, grace did much more abound:

21 That as sin hath reigned unto death, even so might grace reign through righteousness unto eternal life by Jesus Christ our Lord.

Throughout this section, the Law of Moses is never far from Paul's mind, since he addresses a mixed audience of Jews and Gentiles. If Gentiles can be saved by coming to God directly through Christ, without going through Moses and the law of circumcision, what is the role of the Law? One answer that we have previously considered (in 3:20) is that the Law highlighted the ways both Jew and Gentile had offended God. As Paul will illustrate in 7:7, he would not have known lust had the Law not said, "Thou shalt not covet."

Finally the passage closes with another parallel, or compare-and-contrast reference. Just as *sin*, with the result being eternal death, ruled as long as Gentiles and Jews lived in disobedience to their respective laws, so *righteousness* rules now that Christ and His grace have come to our rescue, with its own radically different result: eternal life.

Paul's contrast of Adam and Christ have both cosmic and personal significance. The apostle is saying that step for step, every ill that entered the world through Adam's sin has been matched by Christ's righteousness. The Law could not cure this disease, only grace can.

Evangelistic Emphasis

In my estimation, one of the most comforting verses of the Bible is Romans 5:8—"But God demonstrates his own love for us in this: While we were still sinners, Christ died for us" (NIV). We do not have to be good enough to earn God's love. We do not have to turn over a new leaf before we can be loved by God. We do not have to "get our lives together" before we can be loved by God. God loves us just as we are.

God loves us so much that He sent His Son, Jesus, to die for us on the cross. Jesus loves us so much that He willingly gave His life for us on that cross. We were not worthy of that love. We were sinners. Still, Jesus died on the cross, a perfect sacrifice, that the fine for the sin that was in our lives might be paid in full.

We do not have to be good enough to be worthy of that love. In fact, we *cannot* be good enough. We simply need to accept it. "For while we were still sinners, Christ died for us."

ଅଓଔ

Memory Selection

Therefore being justified by faith, we have peace with God through our Lord Jesus Christ.—*Romans 5:1*

There have been times in my marriage when I have done things that hurt my wife's feelings. I may have done something insensitive. It may have been a thoughtless act. I may have said something that was sharp or sarcastic. Because of my actions, we may have had an argument. After that argument our relationship was strained. We were distant from one another. Things were a little tense around our house for a while. There may not have been any further conflict, but there was no peace.

Eventually, and this has happened every time, one or both of us comes to the other to apologize and ask forgiveness. Forgiveness is extended. The tension that was once there is broken. There is peace in the household again.

Our Lord extends peace like that. When we come to Him in faith, asking forgiveness for the times we offended Him, He always forgives us. The distance that was between us is dissolved. Peace reigns in our hearts again.

Weekday Problems

"Ralph, why don't you come to church with me this Sunday?"Buddy asked.

"Nah," Ralph answered, his eyes avoiding Buddy's. "I don't fit in very well with church people. Besides, I'm kind of afraid what people will say to me or about me."

"People won"t talk about you. They will be glad you came," Buddy countered.

"Buddy, you know what kind of life I've lived. Heck, I still live the kind of life that wouldn't be welcome in church. I've tried Jesus a time or two. It just didn't take. I can't come right now. I'm trying to get my life together. I'm trying to walk the straight and narrow. When I get my life cleaned up, maybe I'll come with you to church."

* Do you agree that Ralph needs to straighten up a little before coming to church? Explain why or why not.

* In light of the text from Romans for our lesson today, what would you say to Ralph right now that might be encouraging to him?

The Age of Television

Some people are confirmed TV addicts. I have a friend who absent-mindedly walked into the room and turn on the radio instead of the TV set, and called 911 saying that he had suddenly gone blind.

* * * *

We've had television ever since I can remember. I've watched it grow from infancy to adultery.

* * * *

An old TV star's show was canceled because of low ratings. One die-hard fan saw him in public, and asked, "Do you answer personally the hundreds of letters that must have come in demanding that they continue your show?"

"Goodness no!" replied the aging star. "I hardly have time to write them."

* * * *

Ace: What's the longest word in the English language?
Grace: "And now a word from our sponsor."

287

This Lesson in Your Life

There have been times in my life when finances were tight—especially while I was in seminary. My wife, two children, and I had to watch our pennies carefully. There was one particular stretch when we were barely getting by. There were absolutely no frills in our lives. Our necessities were met, but nothing more. I remember the day we received a note in the mail from some Christian friends. In the note was a prayer of encouragement . . . and a $100 bill. In the note were words to the effect, "Don't buy anything with this money. Just spend it. We are blessed to be a blessing." We needed to hear some words of encouragement as well as receive some financial encouragement at that specific time.

Today's passage of Scripture reminds me of that day. At just the right time, when we had absolutely no power to help ourselves, much less save ourselves, Christ died for our salvation. Jesus died for us not because He was compelled by some outside force, but because He loves us too much to let us perish in our sins.

Not only did Jesus save us from hell and to heaven, His justifying death brought us back into friendship with God the Father. Our relationship with God is made whole again, reconciled by faith. For those who are in Christ Jesus there is no longer any need to fear what an angry God may do to us. Because we have been justified through faith, there is peace in our hearts. We are no longer separated from God. Instead, we can approach Him as any child would a good Daddy. His grace has also brought us peace and love.

No matter who we have been, no matter what we have done, God's grace through Jesus Christ has provided for us to live in eternal fellowship with Him.

GETTING THE FACTS STRAIGHT

1. What do we gain when we have been justified through faith (Rom. 5:1)?
Peace with God through our Lord Jesus Christ.

2. How can Paul say we now "stand" in grace, or "unmerited favor" (5:2)?
Because grace provides a more solid place to stand than works could not provide.

3. What reasons(s) does Paul give for "rejoicing in suffering" (vs. 3)?
Christians rejoice in suffering because we know that suffering produces perseverance, character, and hope.

4. According to verse 4, who is the channel through whom God pours out His love to us today?
God pours His love into our hearts by the Holy Spirit, whom God has given us.

5. Are human beings intrinsically good enough or spiritually strong enough to work our way into a holy life and into heaven?
No. We needed Jesus to die for our sins and to save us. We need the Holy Spirit to sanctify us. Paul says that we are powerless to save ourselves.

6. It is human nature to want to do something good for those who treat us right. How does God demonstrate that He loves us even though we may not "treat Him right"?
Paul reminds us in verse 8 that "But God demonstrates His own love for us in this: While we were still sinners, Christ died for us."

7. According to verse 9, what awaits those who refuse to accept the justifying grace that is offered by Jesus' death?
Those who have not accepted justification by the blood of Jesus will face God's wrath.

8. How did God make friends out of His enemies, and how does God continue to reconcile those who are hostile to Him?
God reconciles His enemies to Himself through the death of His Son, Jesus. God made the way for us to be His children when Jesus paid the price, the fine, for our sins when He died on the cross.

9. Although sin and condemnation entered the world through Adam, what act of righteousness brought forgiveness and life?
It was the birth, sinless life, atoning death, and bodily resurrection of Jesus.

10. Is it possible to sin so much that God's grace cannot cover the sin?
No. Paul reminds us that "where sin increased, grace increased all the more" (Rom. 5:20, NIV). There is always enough of God's grace to forgive our sins if only we will accept it.

Years ago in England there was a man who worked as a bookkeeper for a good boss. The man had worked for years for the same employer. The shop owner had treated the man well. The man was paid fairly. Working conditions were excellent. The owner paid excellent Christmas bonuses, along with several days off around the holiday for every one of his workers.

Things could not have been better, until the bookkeeper's son fell ill. Doctors were no help. The boy got weaker and weaker. The boy's medical expenses began to take a toll on the bookkeeper's finances. Rather than ask for some financial help to pay the bills, the bookkeeper simply began to "borrow" money from his employer. He fully intended to pay the money back, but the longer the ailment persisted, the deeper in debt the man became.

Eventually the bookkeeper was overcome with guilt at what he was doing. He decided he would confess his transgression and pay all the stolen money back to the shop owner. However, when he began to total up what he had embezzled he realized there was no way he could ever repay it. He also realized there was no way he could face his boss, who had been so good to him.

So one evening after everyone else had left the shop, the bookkeeper produced a bottle of whiskey and a pistol. He fully intended to get drunk enough to erase his inhibitions, then kill himself. He wrote his suicide note, then began to fill himself with enough "liquid courage" to pull the trigger. Alas, he got so drunk he passed out before he could do the deed.

The next morning he awoke, angry at himself for botching the suicide. But as he put the pistol to his head, he looked down at his suicide note. Apparently the shop owner had come back that evening. Now, under the bookkeeper's handwriting of "A great debt! Who can pay it?" was the shop owner's handwriting: "Paid in Full."

Jesus paid our debt. We treated Him badly. We disappointed Him. We ran up "sin debts" for which He was not responsible, and which we could never pay. Yet, Jesus paid our debts completely.

"A great debt! Who can pay it?" Jesus paid it all.

Lesson 4

We Have Victory In Christ!

John 20:1-10; Romans 6:1-8

John 20:1—The first day of the week cometh Mary Magdalene early, when it was yet dark, unto the sepulchre, and seeth the stone taken away from the sepulchre.

2 Then she runneth, and cometh to Simon Peter, and to the other disciple, whom Jesus loved, and saith unto them, They have taken away the Lord out of the sepulchre, and we know not where they have laid him.

3 Peter therefore went forth, and that other disciple, and came to the sepulchre.

4 So they ran both together: and the other disciple did outrun Peter, and came first to the sepulchre.

5 And he stooping down, and looking in, saw the linen clothes lying; yet went he not in.

6 Then cometh Simon Peter following him, and went into the sepulchre, and seeth the linen clothes lie,

7 And the napkin, that was about his head, not lying with the linen clothes, but wrapped together in a place by itself.

8 Then went in also that other disciple, which came first to the sepulchre, and he saw, and believed.

9 For as yet they knew not the scripture, that he must rise again from the dead.

10 Then the disciples went away again unto their own home.

Rom. 6:1—What shall we say then? Shall we continue in sin, that grace may abound?

2 God forbid. How shall we, that are dead to sin, live any longer therein?

3 Know ye not, that so many of us as were baptized into Jesus Christ were baptized into his death?

4 Therefore we are buried with him by baptism into death: that like as Christ was raised up from the dead by the glory of the Father, even so we also should walk in newness of life.

5 For if we have been planted together in the likeness of his death, we shall be also in the likeness of his resurrection:

6 Knowing this, that our old man is crucified with him, that the body of sin might be destroyed, that henceforth we should not serve sin.

7 For he that is dead is freed from sin.

8 Now if we be dead with Christ, we believe that we shall also live with him:

Memory Selection
Romans 6:9

Background Scripture
John 20:1-10; Romans 6:1-14

Devotional Reading
Romans 6:15-23

This session connects the glorious Easter message, taken from the Gospel of John, with its *ethical* implications. It allows the apostle Paul to ask and answer the question, *So if the tomb was empty, how should we then live?*

This real-life application of the message of Easter is from Romans 6. Here Paul connects the ancient form of immersion for baptism with the burial and resurrection of Christ. He insists that the believer's baptism should make as radical a difference in his everyday life as Christ's death and resurrection made in His divine life.

Golgotha changed Jesus from a flesh-and-blood Person to a spiritual Being, who lives and reigns with Christ. Paul challenges believers to let their baptism signal their own spiritual transformation as well.

few days earlier?

On this Easter, invite group members to imagine that they are standing with Christ's disciples as they watched Him die on the Cross. How would their hopes and dreams have been changed by this shocking reversal in the fortunes of the Messiah who had been praised by the crowds when He entered Jerusalem only a

Now announce the glad tidings of Easter: *He is not here! He is risen!* Ask group members how they imagine they might have been changed if they could have seen the empty tomb just after the Lord arose. Would the resurrection have changed their behavior, their attitudes, their relationships? This lesson holds that since Christ's tomb is still empty, since He is still risen, we should continue to live changed lives.

Teaching Outline

I. The Empty Tomb—John 1:1-10
   A. Mary's message, 1-2
   B. Disciples' discovery, 3-10
      1. John's approach, 3-5
      2. What Peter saw, 6-7
      3. Faith and wonder, 8-10
II. The Changed Life—Rom. 6:1-8
   A. Symbolism of baptism, 1-4
   B. The "risen" life, 5-8

Daily Bible Readings

Mon.	Walk in Newness of Life	*Romans 6:1-5*
Tue.	Under Grace, not Law	*Romans 6:6-14*
Wed.	Slaves of Righteousness	*Romans 6:15-23*
Thu.	Jesus Rises to New Life	*Luke 24:1-9*
Fri.	Jesus' Resurrection	*John 20:1-10*
Sat.	Appearance to Mary	*John 20:11-18*
Sun.	Appearance to the Disciples	*John 20:19-23*

Verse by Verse

I. The Empty Tomb—John 20:1-10
A. Mary's message, 1-2
1 The first day of the week cometh Mary Magdalene early, when it was yet dark, unto the sepulchre, and seeth the stone taken away from the sepulchre.
2 Then she runneth, and cometh to Simon Peter, and to the other disciple, whom Jesus loved, and saith unto them, They have taken away the Lord out of the sepulchre, and we know not where they have laid him.

The Gospels mention various women in their accounts of the first discovery of Jesus' empty tomb, according to their own purposes and sources. Although John names only Mary Magdalene, he may imply that others were with her when he quotes her as saying that "*we* know not where they have laid him" (vs. 2).

The disciples waited until "the first day of the week" to avoid desecrating the *seventh* day, the Sabbath, by working. In doing so, they inadvertently fulfilled Jesus' prophecy that He would rise after (parts of) "three days." They could not have known that discovering the resurrection on the first day of the week would have led to the tradition of Christians' assembling on the first

day instead of on the Sabbath.

Most scholars assume that throughout his Gospel it is the author, John, who is "the disciple whom Jesus loves," and that he declines to give his name out of modesty. Mary Magdalene first tells Peter and John of her fear that "they," probably thieves, have stolen Jesus' body. Modern archeologists have discovered a decree from the emperor Claudius, who ruled from A.D. 41-54, that made it a capital offense to destroy a tomb or remove a body from it. It is possible that this anti-grave-robbing trend was afoot even when Jesus was buried. If so, it would give less credibility to the later claim that His body was stolen (Matt. 28:12-13).

B. Disciples' discovery, 3-10
1. John's approach, 3-5
3 Peter therefore went forth, and that other disciple, and came to the sepulchre.
4 So they ran both together: and the other disciple did outrun Peter, and came first to the sepulchre.
5 And he stooping down, and looking in, saw the linen clothes lying; yet went he not in.

Peter and John run to the tomb to verify Mary's report, both because of the personal stake they have in

Jesus as His closest disciples, and perhaps because the culture of the times required males to verify such a report if the matter came to a judicial hearing. Although John outruns Peter in his eagerness and excitement, fear or some other hesitation overtakes him, and he only peers into the gaping hole left by the removal of the great stone that had been rolled in front of the cave-like tomb, to seal it (Mark 15:46).

2. What Peter saw, 6-7

6 Then cometh Simon Peter following him, and went into the sepulchre, and seeth the linen clothes lie,

7 And the napkin, that was about his head, not lying with the linen clothes, but wrapped together in a place by itself.

True to his impetuous nature, Peter casts aside all fear and bursts into the tomb first. There he finds not only the clothes or wrappings that John saw, but a napkin that had been wound about the head of the body when it was buried. It is neatly folded (NIV) and laid separately from the larger wrapping. (To this day, scholars debate whether the famous "Shroud of Turin," which contains the imprint of a bearded man on it, could be the larger grave-cloth the disciples discovered.)

3. Faith and wonder, 8-10

8 Then went in also that other disciple, which came first to the sepulchre, and he saw, and believed.

9 For as yet they knew not the scripture, that he must rise again from the dead.

10 Then the disciples went away again unto their own home.

Entering the tomb after Peter, John sees what Peter saw but adds that it all resulted in at least some level of belief. This probably means that he believed that Jesus was God's Son as never before, rather than believing the entire gospel that He was also the Messiah whom the Jews awaited; for verse 9 indicates considerable reserve in the breadth of John's faith. He had not yet connected his and Peter's discovery with Jesus' prediction that He would rise again on the third day.

III. The Changed Life—Rom. 6:1-14

A. Symbolism of baptism, 1-4

1 What shall we say then? Shall we continue in sin, that grace may abound?

2 God forbid. How shall we, that are dead to sin, live any longer therein?

3 Know ye not, that so many of us as were baptized into Jesus Christ were baptized into his death?

4 Therefore we are buried with him by baptism into death: that like as Christ was raised up from the dead by the glory of the Father, even so we also should walk in newness of life.

The shift from John 20 to Romans 6 is radical in one sense, because it takes us more than 20 years into the future, from the discovery of the empty tomb to the time when Paul wrote to Christians at Rome. In another sense, however, we are still on

294

the same subject: the death and resurrection of Christ. Now, however, Paul is making the case for those who have been transformed from unbelievers to live lives that are as different as life and death—repeating symbolically, in baptism, the death and resurrection of their Lord.

As previous lessons have indicated, Paul has pressed the view that we are saved by grace through faith, not works. Romans 6:1 anticipates the question, If grace covers sin, shall we sin to receive more grace? "By no means!" Paul answers (NIV). Instead, believers should use their baptism as an analogy of their earnest desire to live a life of good works *because* they have been saved, not *in order* to be saved.

Most scholars agree that the earliest form of Christian baptism was a dipping, or immersion; and this conclusion is strengthened by Paul's argument. The believer re-enacts Christ's *burial* when he is lowered into the "watery grave," and His *resurrection* when he is raised from the water. From that point on, just as Jesus lived a new life in a spiritual existence, so the believer is to live "in newness of life" that is no longer characterized by habitual and deliberate sin. This is possible because something was "buried with Christ" in baptism—which will be named in verse 6.

B. The "risen" life, 5-8

5 For if we have been planted together in the likeness of his death, we shall be also in the like- ness of his resurrection:

6 Knowing this, that our old man is crucified with him, that the body of sin might be destroyed, that henceforth we should not serve sin.

7 For he that is dead is freed from sin.

8 Now if we be dead with Christ, we believe that we shall also live with him:

Paul strengthens the analogy of arising from baptism to "newness of life" by using a word that referred to the planting of a seed that would germinate and burst into a plant. In baptism, believers are "planted" like a seed, and the expectation is that what emerges will be a "plant" or life that is spiritual, like Jesus' resurrected life. This is possible because "the old man" was crucified, dead, and buried, as symbolized in baptism.

Just as the Old West developed the saying, "Dead men don't lie," verse 7 states another obvious truth: Dead men don't *sin.* The believer leaves the old man, the "body" of sin, in the grave of baptism, "freeing" him to rise from the water a "new man," ready to walk in the new paths that lead to life eternal. To "live with him" is therefore seen to be *actual,* in this life, as well as *anticipatory,* reflecting life with Christ in heaven.

To summarize, baptism is a *re-enactment* of Christ's own burial and resurrection. To fail to walk a "new life" after baptism is to deny the reality of Christ's own saving death and resurrection.

Evangelistic Emphasis

John tells us that Mary Magdalene was the first one to the tomb on that first Easter morning. She saw that the tomb was empty and she *ran* to tell Peter and John, the disciple Jesus loved. John tells us that he and Peter *ran* to the tomb. John tells us that Mary Magdalene, Simon, and John all three saw the empty tomb, but did not understand exactly what had happened there. Even though their initial interpretation of what occurred in the graveyard was not complete, they were nevertheless excited enough to run to the tomb to see what happened.

When was the last time you were excited enough about something to *run* to tell someone? We know the whole truth about the Resurrection today. Our knowledge is neither incomplete nor confused. We know that the body of Jesus was not stolen. The body of Jesus was brought back to life! That is something to get excited about! That is something we should be telling others. Jesus is alive!

ഇൻ

Memory Selection

Knowing that Christ being raised from the dead dieth no more; death hath no more dominion over him.—*Romans 6:9*

The old song says,

> *I serve a risen Savior.*
> *He's in the world today.*
> *I know that He is living,*
> *Whatever men may say.*

We serve a living Lord. We do not embrace some particular dusty philosophy. We do not adhere to a codified list of rules written by a wise man long ago. We serve a living Savior.

That is why Jesus could truthfully say, "Lo, I am with you always, even unto the end of the world."

Jesus is not dead. He is alive! That is why we can truthfully say that a person can have a personal relationship with Jesus. He is a living being. He was once dead, but is now alive; and He will never die again. He will take us to live with Him one day.

296

Weekday Problems

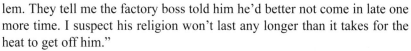

It was Saturday morning and the barber shop was full. "I heard Carter got religion," Bob chuckled. "If anybody needed religion, Carter needed it."

"You know, Carter and his wife are having trouble," Mark contributed. "I hear he has a little drinking problem. They tell me the factory boss told him he'd better not come in late one more time. I suspect his religion won't last any longer than it takes for the heat to get off him."

"Yeah," Bob came back. "The more I watch people, the more I'm convinced people don't change."

Then Jesse waded into the conversation. "You might be right. But I believer Carter's conversion is real. I really believe he is a new man."

"We'll see," Mark answered. "We'll see."

*How does the resurrection of Jesus relate to Carter's situation?

*Do you personally know a person whose life has genuinely changed when they "died to sin"? Tell that person's story, protecting identities if "telling all" might hurt a person's reputation.

Good Sports

There are two kinds of fishermen—those who fish for sport, and those who catch fish.

* * * *

Golfer: Pardon me, but would you mind if I play through? I've just received word that my wife has been taken seriously ill.

* * * *

Talkative hunter: Once while I had stopped for lunch in the jungle, a lion came so close to me that I could feel his breath. What do you think I did?

Bored listener: You turned up your collar!

* * * *

Personnel manager to job applicant: We're looking for a man of vision; a man with drive, determination, and fire; a man who never quits; a man who can inspire others . . . in short, a man who can pull the company's bowling team out of last place!

297

This Lesson in Your Life

I was never a huge fan of the long-ago-canceled television show, "Hee Haw." Still, I remember one of the skits they did. It made a point that has stuck with me till this day.

A man walks into "Doc" Campbell's office with his arm in a sling. "Doc" Campbell takes a look at his arm as he asks the man, "What seems to be the trouble?"

"Doc," the man replies, "I broke my arm in three places."

"Well, for goodness sake," Doc Campbell reacts with alarm. "Stay out of them places!"

I cannot help but think of that when I read Romans 6:2, where Paul writes, "We died to sin; how can we live in it any longer?" (NIV). Living in sin is a bad place to live. It causes undue pain, anxiety, and suffering. Therefore, we should find us another place to live—that is, out of sin.

So many times we see people around us, maybe even ourselves, who want to flirt with sin. They think, "A little sinning is okay. God doesn't expect me to be perfect." Those statements are half true. God does not expect us to be perfect. Yet, sinning, even a little bit of sinning, is not okay in God's eyes.

That is why it is so important to put sin to death in our lives. Don't just *wound* sin severely. For even with severe wounds, sin may come back to life, rise up, and bite us again. No, sin should be put to death in our lives, never to be resuscitated.

As sin is put to death, we then gain life in Christ Jesus. It must be our goal to live a new life, not just a white-washed, cleaned-up version of our old lives. May we become new creatures in Christ Jesus. May we become people in whose hearts sin has been put to death, and Jesus has been allowed to live.

1. According to John, what was Mary Magdalene's reaction when she found Jesus' tomb was empty?
Initially, she thought someone had moved Jesus' body. Apparently she had no thought of a resurrection.

2. Describe the scene inside the tomb as Simon Peter found it.
He saw no body, but only the strips of linen and the burial cloth that had been around Jesus' head.

3. Who were the first two men, apostles, to see the empty tomb?
Simon Peter and John. John got to the tomb first but Peter was first to actually enter.

4. What was John's initial reaction after he entered the empty tomb?
The Scripture reports that John saw and believed. Although he did not understand that what had happened there was according to Scriptural prophecies, he apparently believed that Jesus had risen from the dead.

5. Since God's grace is sufficient to cover any and all sin, is it all right for a person to keep on sinning?
Of course not. Each person has a moral responsibility to God. If we have decided to live for Christ, then we must decide to die to sin.

6. What sacrament do Christian churches practice today that reflects the death and resurrection of Jesus Christ?
Baptism. It symbolizes the fact that we are buried with Christ as we go under the water and we are raised to life with Christ as we emerge.

7. How are we united with Christ in His death?
We die to sin just as Christ did, and we are to live a new life just as Christ came to life again after His deah.

8. When Paul speaks of the "old man" and the "body of sin" in verse 6, what is he talking about?
Paul is referring to our unregenerate self—what we once were. The body is the old self in its pre-Christian state.

9. What does the Bible teach about the person who dies with Christ?
If we die with Christ, then we shall also live with Christ. This refers to our new life in Christ on this earth, as well as our resurrection after death.

10. Verse 9 says that death has no more power over Jesus. Does death still have power over the Christian?
Not really. We all will die a physical death if Jesus does not return before our demise. Yet, because we are dead to sin on this earth, we will be made alive again to God in Christ Jesus.

One of my favorite authors is Max Lucado. In his book, *Six Hours One Friday*, he has three chapters. The titles of the last two chapters speak very eloquently to our passages. The titles are, *My failures are not fatal,* and *My death is not final.*

Our God has made a way for us even after we have messed up horribly. The life of Simon Peter, the apostle, is a living illustration of the fact that our failures are not fatal. You remember when Peter said about Jesus in Matthew 16, "You are the Christ, the Son of the Living God." Jesus was ready to build His Church on Peter's confession. Yet just a few verses later we read that Jesus rebuked Peter, saying, "Get behind me, Satan!" Still, Jesus gave Peter another chance.

In Matthew 14 Peter walked on the water a few steps, but when he began to sink he cried out to Jesus. Did Jesus let Peter drown? No, Jesus pulled Peter to safety, giving him another chance.

Finally, in John 18, on the night Jesus was arrested, Peter denied three times being a disciple of Jesus. Later the risen Lord met with His disciples by the seashore and commissioned Peter to do His work. He gave Peter another chance even after the ultimate betrayal.

Jesus does the same for us. There is no sin so grievous that God's grace cannot forgive it. As we turn to Christ to confess and repent, Jesus is loving and gracious to forgive us, wipe our slates clean, and give us another chance. Our failures are not fatal.

We must also remember that our deaths are not final. You see, the death of Jesus was not the end of His story. Neither is the death of the believer the end of the believer's story. When we die to sin and self on this earth and live for Christ on this earth, we are assured that our death on this earth is not the end. Just as we live with Jesus and walk with Him here, we will also live with Him and walk with Him in heaven.

The tomb of Jesus was and still is empty. That's because He is alive. Our graves may hold our earthly bodies, but we can be sure our spirits live forever with Him in a beautiful place not built by human hands. Praise God!

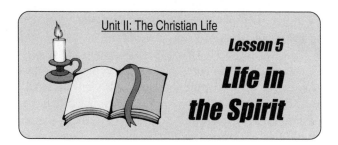

Unit II: The Christian Life

Lesson 5

Life in the Spirit

Romans 8:1-16

April 3

There is therefore now no condemnation to them which are in Christ Jesus, who walk not after the flesh, but after the Spirit.

2 For the law of the Spirit of life in Christ Jesus hath made me free from the law of sin and death.

3 For what the law could not do, in that it was weak through the flesh, God sending his own Son in the likeness of sinful flesh, and for sin, condemned sin in the flesh:

4 That the righteousness of the law might be fulfilled in us, who walk not after the flesh, but after the Spirit.

5 For they that are after the flesh do mind the things of the flesh; but they that are after the Spirit the things of the Spirit.

6 For to be carnally minded is death; but to be spiritually minded is life and peace.

7 Because the carnal mind is enmity against God: for it is not subject to the law of God, neither indeed can be.

8 So then they that are in the flesh cannot please God.

9 But ye are not in the flesh, but in the Spirit, if so be that the Spirit of God dwell in you. Now if any man have not the Spirit of Christ, he is none of his.

10 And if Christ be in you, the body is dead because of sin; but the Spirit is life because of righteousness.

11 But if the Spirit of him that raised up Jesus from the dead dwell in you, he that raised up Christ from the dead shall also quicken your mortal bodies by his Spirit that dwelleth in you.

12 Therefore, brethren, we are debtors, not to the flesh, to live after the flesh.

13 For if ye live after the flesh, ye shall die: but if ye through the Spirit do mortify the deeds of the body, ye shall live.

14 For as many as are led by the Spirit of God, they are the sons of God.

15 For ye have not received the spirit of bondage again to fear; but ye have received the Spirit of adoption, whereby we cry, Abba, Father.

16 The Spirit itself beareth witness with our spirit, that we are the children of God:

Memory Selection
Romans 8:14

Background Scripture
Romans 8:1-17

Devotional Reading
Romans 7:1-6

301

The apostle Paul had a way of knifing through the fog and ambiguity of life and reducing them to walking "in the spirit" or "in the flesh." This lesson invites us to share his view by simplifying our overall *intent* and *purpose*. If our primary aim is to walk in obedience to God's will, we can develop the spiritual life. If we find ourselves habitually seeking exceptions, evading godly responsibilities, and giving in to temptations, Paul would call us "carnal" or fleshly.

The group leader will do well to avoid specific "lists" of what is spiritual and what is carnal. The New Testament leaves much of the "list-making" to individual attitude and intent. This lesson does promise that the intent to be "led of the Spirit" characterizes a child of God, while being content with satisfying fleshly appetites bars our being adopted into His family.

Challenge group members to nail down the elusive concept of what it means to be "spiritual." The term sometimes takes on a super-sweet connotation describing someone " so spiritual he's no earthly good."

Yet in this lesson we are asked to live by the Spirit, to be led by the Spirit, and in general to be "spiritual"

instead of "fleshly." Does this mean every true Christian is sinless? Can the term "spiritual" best be defined by what it *doesn't* mean (syrupy-religious, out of touch with reality, walking with head down and hands folded, etc.)?

Perhaps group members can define the term by recalling people they know who seem to embody spirituality. Amplify on all suggestions that show that real people, not just spirits, can be spiritual.

Teaching Outline	Daily Bible Readings

I. Freedom Is in the Spirit—1-5
   A. Condemnation of the Law, 1-3
   B. Mind over matter, 4-5
 II. Fleshliness Means Death—6-8
 III. If Christ Is in You—9-11
 IV. Adopted Sons of God—12-16
   A. Spirit over flesh, 12-13
   B. The spirit of the adopted, 14-16
	Mon. New Life in the Spirit
	         Romans 7:1-6
	 Tue. Sin Brings Death
	         Romans 7:7-13
	 Wed. The Struggle with Sin
	         Romans 7:14-19
	 Thu. Captive to Sin
	         Romans 7:20-25
	 Fri. The Spirit-Led Life
	         Romans 8:1-5
	 Sat. You Are in the Spirit
	         Romans 8:6-11
	 Sun. Led by the Spirit
	         Romans 8:12-17

Verse by Verse

I. Freedom Is in the Spirit—1-5

A. Condemnation of the Law, 1-3

1 There is therefore now no condemnation to them which are in Christ Jesus, who walk not after the flesh, but after the Spirit.

2 For the law of the Spirit of life in Christ Jesus hath made me free from the law of sin and death.

3 For what the law could not do, in that it was weak through the flesh, God sending his own Son in the likeness of sinful flesh, and for sin, condemned sin in the flesh:

In chapter 7, Paul confessing with moving candor the struggle of anyone who tries to live by law, but is threatened by the compulsions of "the flesh" (see the Daily Bible Readings for Monday through Thursday). Regardless of how highly we esteem God's moral law, for example, we find "a law, that, when I would do good, evil is present with me" (7:21). When we try to overcome a weakness with a weak will, there is a moral stalemate. So in desperation, Paul closed chapter 7 with the anguished question, "Who shall deliver me from the body of this death?" (vs. 24). The glad answer is given in 7:25 and chapter 8: We can triumph over the law and urges of the flesh through the Holy Spirit, which comes not through law but

through the grace of Christ.

Thus Paul can exclaim with relief that there can be "no condemnation" of those who walk in the Spirit, rather than in the flesh. The term "flesh" is used in two ways in these verses. Its most frequent meaning is what the Contemporary English Version translates "selfish desires" (NIV "sinful nature"). In this sense, "flesh" refers not just to body-related lusts such as sexual sins, but to self-centered ungodliness such as envy and strife (specifically included among the "sins of the flesh" in Galatians 5:19-20). Thus the second sense in which "flesh" is used here includes the self-centered pleasure some derive from keeping the law strictly in order to boast about it.

The good news is that Christ's death "in the flesh" became something of a "black hole" that drew all such self-centered fleshliness into itself. When we live in His Spirit, we find freedom both from the oppressiveness of works-salvation and from all other "fleshliness."

B. Mind over matter, 4-5

4 That the righteousness of the law might be fulfilled in us, who walk not after the flesh, but after the Spirit.

5 For they that are after the flesh do mind the things of the

flesh; but they that are after the Spirit the things of the Spirit.

Charges of "antinomianism," or being against all rules, followed Paul after his conversion. Here he reaffirms the necessity of "righteousness," but denies that it can be achieved by law-keeping. Instead, the goal of "being put right" with God is fulfilled by those who walk after the Spirit, not after either the letter of the Law or sinful desires that would ignore all rules.

II. Fleshliness Means Death—6-8

6 For to be carnally minded is death; but to be spiritually minded is life and peace.

7 Because the carnal mind is enmity against God: for it is not subject to the law of God, neither indeed can be.

8 So then they that are in the flesh cannot please God.

To be fleshly minded is death. because God is Spirit, the opposite of flesh. Hence, those who devote themselves either to fleshly pleasures or to fleshly boasting of how well they keep the Law cannot please God.

III. If Christ Is in You—9-11

9 But ye are not in the flesh, but in the Spirit, if so be that the Spirit of God dwell in you. Now if any man have not the Spirit of Christ, he is none of his.

10 And if Christ be in you, the body is dead because of sin; but the Spirit is life because of righteousness.

11 But if the Spirit of him that raised up Jesus from the dead dwell in you, he that raised up Christ from the dead shall also quicken your mortal bodies by his Spirit that dwelleth in you.

Both self-righteousness and sexually-oriented "fleshliness" are so common, yet so opposed to the principle or "law" of the Spirit, that Paul has had to deal with them extensively. In verse 9 he reassures believers that he expects better things of them. They have already indicated a measure of willingness to live after the Spirit. Paul has had to deal with "fleshliness" among them to show the anti-spiritual mindset of Gentiles who deny God and are deliberately immoral (chap. 1), and of Jews who boast of works-salvation but are in fact as immoral as pagans (chap. 2).

Otherwise, those who confess their allegiance to the law of the Spirit, or who have Christ *"in"* them, can feel safe in the assurance that they will "live"—in two senses. In verse 10 Paul assures them that they will triumph over the flesh *in this life*—not by their own willpower but by the power of the Spirit. Then in verse 11 he assures them that the Spirit will "quicken" or make alive their fleshly bodies *after death*, thus equipping them to live in the realm of the spirit, heaven.

Here we can see the continuity in Paul's theology between life in the Spirit on earth and living in the spiritual realm after death. The Holy Spirit, who enables us to triumph over the flesh in this life, is the same Spirit who will change our decaying bodies and reclothe them with spiritual bodies. The Spirit can therefore be considered as a guarantee, "earnest money," or down-payment on eternal life, to be ultimately realized in the Last Day (2 Cor. 5:5).

V. Adopted Sons of God—12-16

A. Spirit over flesh, 12-13

12 Therefore, brethren, we are debtors, not to the flesh, to live after the flesh.

13 For if ye live after the flesh, ye shall die: but if ye through the Spirit do mortify the deeds of the body, ye shall live.

"Debtors" is used here to refer to the principle that "lends" us our life force—the law by which we live. Paul says that this principle is spiritual, not fleshly. Many people in our own day who have lived after the law of pleasure have become addicted or otherwise dependent on a pleasure, only to find that it destroys them. If we really want to live, both in the sense of enjoying "the abundant life" now and life with God in the hereafter, we must "mortify" or put to death the flesh, allowing the Spirit to assert Himself over substance abuse, self-centeredness, sexual immorality, and other forms of "the flesh. (Although the term "mortify" implies that we must make bodily lusts *subject* to the Spirit, it does not call for the practice, as in some cultures, of beating or starving our bodies into submission to the Spirit.)

B. The spirit of the adopted, 14-16

14 For as many as are led by the Spirit of God, they are the sons of God.

15 For ye have not received the spirit of bondage again to fear; but ye have received the Spirit of adoption, whereby we cry, Abba, Father.

16 The Spirit itself beareth witness with our spirit, that we are the children of God:

In context, to be "led by the Spirit of God" is to exercise control over the deeds of the flesh. It is also true that the truly "spiritual" will listen to the voice of God, especially as it comes through His Spirit-inspired Word, but that is not the primary application of being "led by the Spirit" Paul has in mind here.

The main focus of these verses is, instead, the term *adoption*. Many Jews boasted that they had become "sons of God" merely by being born as children of Abraham. In this very letter, Paul is in the process of revising the definition of being a "Jew" or Israelite. "They are not all Israel which are of Israel," he will say in 9:6. Now, under the New Covenant, even Gentiles can be "adopted" into God's family, figuratively becoming an "Israelite." They can even call God by the Aramaic word "Abba," which was an intimate and familiar term such as "Daddy" is to Americans. In contrast to a Jew who might produce a document tracing his lineage back to Abraham, all who follow the law of the Spirit have the Holy Spirit Himself testifying to their own spirits that they are children of God.

305

Evangelistic Emphasis

God gave the Law, specifically the Ten Commandments, in the Old Testament, as a guide or moral compass. It was a good guide, instructing God's people concerning what to do and what not to do in order to live according to God's will and His way.

There is a problem with the Law, however. The Law simply *instructs*. It does not provide a person the power nor the ability to follow it.

God poured out the Holy Spirit on the day of Pentecost. With the Spirit came the power, ability, and the desire to walk according to God's Law. While the Law was condemning, the Spirit is enabling. While the Law was confining, the Spirit is liberating. While the Law instructed concerning sin, the Spirit gives us power over sin.

This power of the Spirit is available to us because God sent Jesus Christ to live for us and die for us. He met the penalty of the Law on our behalf. Now we do not have to be afraid of being condemned by the Law. Jesus received that condemnation for us. All we have to do now is live for Jesus. "There is therefore no condemnation for those who are in Christ Jesus!"

℘℧

Memory Selection

For as many as are led by the Spirit of God, they are the sons of God.— *Romans 8:14*

I had a good dad. There were five children in my family and Dad did his best to be involved in the lives of each. He coached my Little League baseball team. He went to after-school activities in which I was involved. I cannot remember that he ever missed a basketball or football game in which I was playing, home or away. I loved my dad. I listened to him. I wish he were still here to talk to and give me advice. I wanted to please my dad.

God is a good Father. We know that He will not ask us to do anything that will not build our character. He will not lead us into anything that will not benefit us. We know that God wants for us only those things that are for our good.

We demonstrate that we are children of our Heavenly Father, just as we do with good earthly dads—by listening to Him. Children of God follow His counsel. Children of God want to please Him.

Weekday Problems

"Susan, all the girls are going by Stars and Garters for drinks this evening after work. Why don't you come?" Janice asked.

"No, thanks," Susan answered. "I'll probably just head on home. I have lots to do at the house."

"Oh, I forgot," Janice smirked. "You think having a drink or two after work is sinful." Janice drew out the word "sinful" in a very sarcastic manner. "You think you're too good to hang out with the rest of us. There's nothing wrong with a little toddy. You need to loosen up." With that, Janice turned on her heel and was gone.

"Janice is partly right," Susan thought. "I do think drinking is wrong and I don't care if I'm the only one who thinks that." She gathered her purse and went home.

*How might Susan use this opportunity to share her faith with Janice?

*Is Susan trying to live according to the sinful nature or according to the Spirit? Explain.

Teen Times

Tired of teens not talking when the family gathers at the dining table? Try bringing a "speaker" telephone to the table and lifting the receiver. A dial tone is the only guaranteed way to get a teen to talk.

* * * *

Teen answering the phone: No, Judy isn't in just now. This is her blonde-haired, blue-eyed sister, just the right height at 5-foot-3 and weighing about 100 pounds.

* * * *

Why can't life's problems hit us when we're 18 and have all the answers?

* * * *

My teenage daughter is at that stage where she's all skin and phones.

* * * *

Dad to daughter: Here's something that will make you feel really grown up . . . your very own phone bill.

* * * *

Want to recapture your youth? Try cutting off his allowance.

This Lesson in Your Life

Suppose a man is hauled before the judge for driving under the influence of alcohol. The police officer observed the man weaving from side to side on the highway. When the officer pulled him over and gave him a breathalyzer test, the man's blood alcohol level registered well beyond the legal limit. Witnesses testified that the man was driving erratically. He was caught dead to rights. He was obviously guilty.

When the man comes before the judge, the man pleads, "Please, your honor, I have a wife and children to support. If I go to jail I cannot work to feed, shelter, and clothe my family. Please, your honor, I won't do it again. I will never touch another drop of alcohol as long as I live."

The judge believes the man is sincere, and lets him go with only the warning, "If I ever hear of you driving under the influence again, you will certainly go to jail!"

Let's break from the story just a moment. The man is guilty. There is no doubt in anyone's mind about that. Yet, the judge forgave him and let him go free. Suppose the law said the man could have been sent to jail. Did the judge break the law? No, the judge opted to extend mercy.

Now, suppose the man wants to drink again. His desire to drink is overpowering when the man is alone. However, the man knows if he gives in to that desire and gets behind the steering wheel of a car, he will surely go to jail.

So, rather than give in to that overpowering desire to drink, the man gets a friend to accompany him everywhere the man goes when opportunities to drink will arise. Every time the man feels as though he needs a drink, the friend stops him.

In a very simplistic way, that is what God has done for us. We have sinned. The law condemns us. God forgives us. God sends His Holy Spirit, our Friend, to walk with us always to give us the power to live according to God's will and not according to our sinful nature. The Spirit will do that, if we allow Him to control our lives.

STRAIGHT

1. Why is the Christian not condemned under the Law?

Because through Christ Jesus the law of the Spirit of life has set those in Christ free from the law of sin and death. Also, believers no longer live according to their sinful nature, but according to the Spirit.

2. What is the weakness of the Law? What is it that the Law is powerless to do?

Although it can define and condemn sin, it cannot give us the strength to avoid or overcome it. Only the Holy Spirit through Christ Jesus can do that.

3. According to verse 5, how can you tell if a person is a Spirit-filled, Spirit-led Christian or not?

Those who are Spirit-filled live in accordance with the Spirit and have their minds set on what the Spirit desires.

4. What does life lived after the sinful nature (the carnal mind) lead to? What does life lived in the Spirit lead to?

To be carnally minded, or to live according to the sinful nature, is death. To live life controlled by the Spirit of God brings life and peace.

5. Can a person live his life pleasing himself, his sinful nature, and at the same time please God?

No. Those who are in the flesh, living after the sinful nature, cannot please God. We cannot have it both ways.

6. Can the carnal (sinful) mind and the Spirit of God peacefully coexist in a person's soul?

No. Paul says the sinful mind is hostile to God. As God's enemy, the sinful mind resists submitting to God's will.

7. What determines whether we are controlled by the sinful nature or by the Spirit of God?

Whether God's Spirit lives in us. If anyone does not have the Spirit of Christ, that person does not belong to Christ.

8. According to verse 13, what is the difference between life and death?

If we live according to the flesh (sinful nature) we will die. If by the Spirit we put to death the misdeeds of the body, we will live.

9. What privilege is granted to those who are led by the Spirit (vs. 14)?

Those who are led by the Spirit of God are children of God.

10. What is one way we know that we are God's children?

We have received the Spirit of adoption, and that Spirit testifies with our spirit that we are God's children.

309

There is a difference in our lives when we give our lives to Jesus Christ. When we are in Christ and led by the Spirit, our desires change. I remember hearing the testimony of a man who had once been a pretty rough character, but his life changed when he became a Christian. He was married and had children. For a while every Sunday his wife would beg him to go to church with her. He never would. Finally, she quit asking. She would just get up, get herself and the children ready, and go. He usually would go hunting or fishing on Sunday; and there always seemed to be beer along on all the hunting and fishing trips.

Every weekday afternoon after work, he would stop off at a local bar. He would have a couple of beers with his buddies before going home. Sometimes a couple of beers turned into six or eight. When he came home after too many beers, he and his wife would always get into a fight.

One autumn his wife's church was having a revival. She begged him to go with her and the children. In a moment of weakness, he said Yes. Lo and behold, the evangelist seemed to be talking only to him that night. The Holy Spirit convicted him. He found himself walking down the aisle of the church, repenting of his sins, and giving his life to Jesus.

Immediately he quit going to the bar after work. He quit hunting and fishing on Sunday mornings and started going to church with his whole family. Even when he did go hunting or fishing, he quit drinking beer.

About a month after the revival, the man ran into some of his former drinking buddies at the barber shop. One said, "Yep, now that you got religion we don't see much of you anymore. Seems you're doing everything your wife always nagged you to do. It looks like you don't do anything *you* want to do anymore."

The new Christian grinned real big at his friend. "You know, I still do everything I want to do. God just changed my want-to's."

Isn't it great that God plants in the hearts of His children the desire to please Him?

Lesson 6
Salvation In Christ

Romans 10:5-17

For Moses describeth the righteousness which is of the law, That the man which doeth those things shall live by them.

6 But the righteousness which is of faith speaketh on this wise, Say not in thine heart, Who shall ascend into heaven? (that is, to bring Christ down from above:)

7 Or, Who shall descend into the deep? (that is, to bring up Christ again from the dead.)

8 But what saith it? The word is nigh thee, even in thy mouth, and in thy heart: that is, the word of faith, which we preach;

9 That if thou shalt confess with thy mouth the Lord Jesus, and shalt believe in thine heart that God hath raised him from the dead, thou shalt be saved.

10 For with the heart man believeth unto righteousness; and with the mouth confession is made unto salvation.

11 For the scripture saith, Whosoever believeth on him shall not be ashamed.

12 For there is no difference between the Jew and the Greek: for the same Lord over all is rich unto all that call upon him.

13 For whosoever shall call upon the name of the Lord shall be saved.

14 How then shall they call on him in whom they have not believed? and how shall they believe in him of whom they have not heard? and how shall they hear without a preacher?

15 And how shall they preach, except they be sent? as it is written, How beautiful are the feet of them that preach the gospel of peace, and bring glad tidings of good things!

16 But they have not all obeyed the gospel. For Esaias saith, Lord, who hath believed our report?

17 So then faith cometh by hearing, and hearing by the word of God.

Memory Selection
Romans 10:9
Background Scripture
Roman 10:5-21
Devotional Reading
Hebrews 5:5-10

This lesson continues Paul's analysis of salvation by law *vs.* salvation by grace through faith. This was crucial, because as the apostle often worked with churches such as the one at Rome that were usually composed both of Jews who were reluctant to cut themselves loose from the Law of Moses, and Gentiles, who were "strangers to the law" (Eph. 2:12).

Paul's approach here is skillful. He finds the principle of salvation by faith in the Jewish Scriptures themselves, and lifts it up as God's long-range plan. The Law of Moses, he will argue, was given as an interim strategy until the Messiah could come through Abraham's descendants. Now that this momentous event has occurred, "There is no difference between the Jew and the Greek" (Rom. 10:12).

ℰᏩℭᏒ

This lesson can be introduced by summarizing on a writing board the key differences Paul has shown between salvation by the Law of Moses and salvation through Christ:

LAW	GOSPEL
Came through Moses	Came through Christ
Given for Jews	Given for all people
Inadequate sacrifice	Christ is our sacrifice
Can't be kept perfectly	Grace covers imperfections
Defines the sin problem	*Solves* the sin problem

In today's lesson, Paul does not so much oppose these two systems against each other as show that the Gospel or "Faith" system was actually implied in the Law itself. A good Jew can therefore consider Christ's way as a natural outgrowth of the Old Testament, instead of being a foreign intrusion.

Teaching Outline	Daily Bible Readings

I. Law vs. faith—5-8
  A. *Doing . . .* , 5
  B. *vs. Accepting,* 6-8
II. Liberation by faith, 9-13
  A. Confession of faith, 9-10
  B. Calling on the Lord, 11-13
III. Listening to the Word—14-17
  A. The need for proclamation, 14
  B. The need for sending, 15
  C. The solution of faith, 16-17
	Mon. Source of Salvation
	    Hebrews 5:5-10
	Tue. On the Lips, in the Heart
	    Romans 10:1-8
	Wed. Christ Is Lord of All
	    Romans 10:9-13
	Thu. Faith through the Word
	    Romans 10:14-21
	Fri. Israel not Forsaken
	    Romans 11:1-6
	Sat. Gentiles Are Accepted
	    Romans 11:13-18
	Sun. All Grafted Together
	    Romans 11:19-23

Verse by Verse

I. Law vs. faith—5-8
A. *Doing* . . . , 5

5 For Moses describeth the righteousness which is of the law, That the man which doeth those things shall live by them.

Although the Law of Moses called for heartfelt faith as well as obedience, many Jews in Paul's day were emphasizing such works circumcision to the *neglect* of faith. To combat this mistake, Paul goes to the book of Leviticus, with its emphasis on observing the sacrificial system. If only those who "doeth those things" are acceptable to God, what about those who are too ill to offer sacrifices? What about "outsiders" such as Gentiles? What about those who go through the acts the Law required, but whose heart is not in it? What about those who live in societies that prohibit animal sacrifices?

B. *vs. Accepting,* 6-8

6 But the righteousness which is of faith speaketh on this wise, Say not in thine heart, Who shall ascend into heaven? (that is, to bring Christ down from above:)

7 Or, Who shall descend into the deep? (that is, to bring up Christ again from the dead.)

8 But what saith it? The word is nigh thee, even in thy mouth, and in thy heart: that is, the word of faith, which we preach;

In answer to such "What abouts?" as those above, Paul affirms that there is another kind of "righteousness," the righteousness which is *by faith* or trust in Christ as having already fulfilled the Law's requirements for us. He finds another emphasis in the Old Testament: the protest that keeping the endless details of the Law perfectly was too hard to be humanly possible (Deut. 30:12).

Apparently on his authority as an apostle, Paul interprets this passage as a longing for a divine being such as the Messiah ("Christ," from the Greek), who could keep the Law *for* us. But where is this divinity? Various sects and heresies still looked for a Christ-like figure to descend from the heavens. Others speculated that He had descended into Hades after death, failed to emerge, and therefore was still expected to appear from the realms below. Paul, however, affirms that we need not engage in such speculation because Word about the Messiah's having come in Jesus of Nazareth is already "near at hand." He has already descended from heaven, been crucified for our sins, descended for a moment into the netherworld, and then been gloriously resurrected.

For those who have heard this Word preached, the source of salvation is already in the heart. It is a "word of faith," not of works, something that simply requires *acceptance* instead of trying to work our way to heaven. Although this acceptance involves works *in response* to salvation (see Eph. 2:10), the emphasis is on faith, which was not emphasized in the Law.

II. Liberation by faith, 9-13
A. Confession of faith, 9-10

9 That if thou shalt confess with thy mouth the Lord Jesus, and shalt believe in thine heart that God hath raised him from the dead, thou shalt be saved.

10 For with the heart man believeth unto righteousness; and with the mouth confession is made unto salvation.

As it turns out, salvation through grace *does* require something, but it is not a "work of the Law," or of human merit. The requirement is to *confess* (Grk. "agree with") the lordship of Jesus, fully believing that He came and died for our sins, and that God then raised Him from the dead. Obviously this "confession" is not the same as confessing our sins, although that is also required. This confession is an open statement of faith that clearly pronounces our allegiance to Jesus as Lord.

Today, in free societies, this may seem a trivial requirement. In Paul's day, however, it could cost a person his life. This means that the Christian way could not be dismissed as a "free and easy" way to avoid religious commitment, as opposed to the rigors of keeping the Law of Moses. For more than 200 years, waves of persecution would result in the deaths of thousands of "confessing" Christians, depending on the whim of the current ruling Emperor. Confessing could cost one's life.

Verse 10 explains the separate, but connected, roles of belief and confession. Although rooted in the heart, "belief" for Paul meant a responsive faith, not mere "mental assent." Confession is the result of faith overflowing into words. (See Acts 8:36-38 for an example of this faith-confession response to the gospel, which also included baptism.)

B. Calling on the Lord, 11-13

11 For the scripture saith, Whosoever believeth on him shall not be ashamed.

12 For there is no difference between the Jew and the Greek: for the same Lord over all is rich unto all that call upon him.

13 For whosoever shall call upon the name of the Lord shall be saved.

Again Paul turns to the Old Covenant Scriptures to show the continuity between the Law and the Gospel. He cites Isaiah 28:16 (which he has already quoted in 9:33) as a prophecy of the time when people will have opportunity to believe in the Messiah, who will never prove unfaithful. The same prophetic book,

Isaiah, had also predicted the inclusion of the Gentiles (e.g., 49:22); so Paul follows this quotation with the fact that Jew and Gentile are *one* in the invitation to believe in and confess Jesus as Lord.

Once more citing the Old Testament, Paul brings Joel 2:32 alongside Isaiah. This is the passage that was actually lived out by the apostles on the Day of Pentecost in Acts 2, where "calling on the name of the Lord" is shown to include a heartfelt, whole-life response and commitment to Jesus, not the simple presence of His name on the lips.

III. Listening to the Word—14-17
A. The need for proclamation, 14

14 How then shall they call on him in whom they have not believed? and how shall they believe in him of whom they have not heard? and how shall they hear without a preacher?

If what Paul has said is true, Christianity must become a far different faith than Judaism. Since the Law of Moses was primarily for Abraham's descendants, the Jewish faith never became a missionary faith. Here, however, Paul follows the logical consequence of salvation by hearing that Messiah has come in the form of Jesus. That message must be proclaimed to be heard and believed.

B. The need for sending, 15

15 And how shall they preach, except they be sent? as it is written, How beautiful are the feet of them that preach the gospel of peace, and bring glad tidings of good things!

Continuing the logical progression of thought, Paul follows through with the obvious fact that if proclaimers of the faith are necessary, they must be "sent" or supported by communities of faith. This statement reflects Paul's own missionary enterprise, which he hoped would eventually find him in Rome itself, sharing personally with those to whom he now writes (see 15:22-24). He again grounds missions in the Old Testament exclamation about the beauty of sharing God's love with others (from Isa. 52:7). It is significant that, as noted above, the Jews did not respond to such missionary challenges—except for those who accepted Jesus as the Messiah.

C. The solution of faith, 16-17

16 But they have not all obeyed the gospel. For Esaias saith, Lord, who hath believed our report?

17 So then faith cometh by hearing, and hearing by the word of God.

The prophet Isaiah is continually on Paul's lips no doubt because Isaiah was "the Messianic prophet." Here the citation is from Isaiah 53:1, which Christ Himself had quoted in the face of stubborn unbelief (John 12:38). The answer to such unbelief lies only in equally persistent proclamation designed continuously to offer unbelievers the opportunity to come to saving faith by the hearing of the Good News.

Evangelistic Emphasis

"Salvation is free to all, everybody can be saved. Jesus died for the sins of the whole world." True statements, yet not everybody is saved. Salvation does not come to all. Why is that? Because while anyone can be saved, there is still something each person has to do to be saved. Each person has some personal responsibility in his own salvation.

Paul uses words such as *trust*, *believe*, and *confess* to describe our personal response and responsibility to the offer of Jesus Christ for salvation. We must trust that Jesus did what was needed to buy our pardon. We must accept some things in faith even though they cannot be explained in rational, scientific ways. We must be willing to demonstrate our devotion to Christ by our words. By our trusting, our believing, and our confessing, Christ becomes not just *the* Savior, but *our* Savior. By those same methods we convince others of their need for salvation, too.

ഓരു

That if thou shalt confess with thy mouth the Lord Jesus, and shalt believe in thine heart that God hath raised him from the dead, thou shalt be saved.—*Romans 10:9*

Probably the earliest confession of faith in the Christian church was the declaration, "Jesus is Lord." This public profession made it clear that the person was no longer entirely under the domination of Roman rule. Caesar was no longer the guiding force in that person's life. When a person accepted Christ's rule in his heart, Jesus, not Caesar, was his Lord.

The resurrection of Jesus Christ was and still is the bedrock truth of Christian doctrine. The resurrection was the central thrust of apostolic preaching. Christians believe not only that Jesus lived, but that Jesus still lives.

There are not many people who cannot understand this verse. If we confess Jesus publicly and can accept by faith the resurrection of Jesus, we will receive salvation. It is pretty clear, isn't it?

Weekday Problems

The folks at the McDaniel and Long Agency were visiting around the coffee pot the day after they had all attended a co-worker's funeral. The discussion turned to the question, "What happens to a person after he dies?"

"Well, I believe that the soul is eternal," Skye commented. "When a person dies the soul leaves that body and waits until a new baby is born and the soul is gloriously re-cycled."

"That's baloney,!" Pete scoffed. "When a person dies, he just dies. He ceases to exist. The body dies. The mind dies. If there is a soul, the soul dies, too." With that he crossed his arms as thought that was the final word on the subject.

Rebekah was listening to the discussion. She knew what the Bible said about the subject. She swallowed hard and began to speak.

*If you were in Rebekah's position what might you say?

*Would you consider this an opportunity to confess that "Jesus is Lord"? Explain.

Dieters Anonymous

Following its dire warnings about widespread obesity, the government has issued the following diet suggestions:

Breakfast: Crumbs scraped from burnt toast
Boiled-out stains from table cloth
Weak tea

Lunch: 1 bouillon cube in 2 cups dehydrated water
½ doz. poppy seeds
Broiled filet of butterfly
Dessert: 1 doughnut hole

Dinner: 2 oz. prune juice (gargle only)
1 jellyfish skin (small)
Grilled bees' knees and mosquito knuckles
3 eyes from Irish potatoes (diced)
Dessert: Empty plate from chocolate pie (aroma only)

This Lesson in Your Life

Some people believe that Christianity is supposed to be a personal, private, encapsulated religion. Obviously Paul was not one of those people. In this passage Paul uses words such as "confess with your mouth" and "call on the one you believed in" and "preaching." In fact, Paul seems to indicate that one of the proofs of salvation is whether or not one is willing to profess publicly and vocally that "Jesus is Lord."

We hear it now and again. Folks say, "My life is my witness." Certainly a believer's life must be a witness for Jesus Christ. Nowhere in the Scripture is there evidence that the way a person lives is unimportant to God. In fact, Jesus Himself said, "Let your light shine before men, that they may see your good deeds and praise your Father in heaven" (Matt. 5:16).

Yet, there is a problem with letting one's life be one's *total* witness. For there is always the chance that a person will see your good life and say, "What a great person he is." That is not the purpose of letting our lives be our witness. The purpose of letting our lives shine before others is so that they will glorify God. The point is not for people to say, "What a great person she is!" but "What a great God she serves!"

When we confess that Jesus is our Lord, we are giving Him credit for all the good things in our lives, not taking credit for ourselves. When we confess that Jesus is our Lord we are letting others know who is in charge of our lives.

Besides, our goodness never saved anybody. Only the righteousness of Jesus can save. Don't you want to turn people toward Jesus and not toward yourself?

GETTING THE FACTS STRAIGHT

1. What is necessary for a person to be right with God on the basis of the Law?

A person has to fully keep the Law to be right with God on the basis of the Law.

2. What Old Testament passage does Paul cite in Romans 10:6 to explain the nature of righteousness by faith?

Paul cites Deuteronomy 30:13-14 to show that righteousness by faith does not require miraculous feats. In fact, we cannot do the things described.

3. What is the "word" to which Paul refers in verse 8?

The message of righteousness by faith that Paul is preaching.

4. What are two things we must do to be saved?

We must confess verbally that Jesus is Lord and we must believe sincerely that God has, in fact, raised Jesus from the dead.

5. In verse 9, one criteria is something we *do*, while the other is something we *believe*. What might this tell us about salvation?

That both action and belief are important. One is not enough without the other. Our words, deeds, and convictions are closely connected. Salvation involves inward belief as well as outward confession.

6. What quote does Paul use in verse 13 to describe the benefits of those who call upon and trust in the name of the Lord?

Paul quotes Isaiah 28:16: "Whoever believes on Him will not be put to shame" (NKJV).

7. How does Paul remind us that salvation comes the same way to those who grew up with the Law and those who do not know the Law?

He says there is no difference between Jew and Gentile in that regard. Jesus is Lord of all, and richly blesses, those who call on Him.

8. According to verse 13, who is eligible to be saved?

Everyone who calls on the name of the Lord shall be saved.

9. Why is it so important that those who know the gospel willingly share the gospel in word and deed?

Because the lost cannot call on the One they have not believed in; cannot believe in the One of whom they have not heard; and cannot hear unless someone tells them (preaches to them).

10. How does faith come?

Faith comes from hearing the message. The message is heard through the word of Christ (vs. 17).

When our son Bryan was young, he accepted Christ as his Savior. I remember the occasion. My wife, Bryan, and I were coming home from somewhere in our car. A tape by Don Francisco was playing. In the song, Don Francisco was describing the scene where Jesus walked on the water.

Bryan turned to me and said, "I know how Jesus was able to walk on the water."

I recognized this as a teaching moment. I asked, "How was he able to do that, son?"

"Because He had the power," Bryan answered.

I held my breath as I replied, "Would you like to have that power?"

"Yes, sir," he answered.

By now we had pulled into our car port. We sat there in the car and prayed. We confessed and repented and asked for forgiveness and Bryan asked Jesus to come into his life. My wife and I laughed and cried at the same time. It was a glorious time.

Immediately Bryan said, "I'm a Christian now. I have to tell Shanna." So he got on the phone and told his friend about what had happened to him.

Now, this could have been a little boy simply trying to please his parents. But it was more. At the time of this writing, Bryan is 28 years old, and he is still walking with the Lord. He and his wife host and lead Bible studies in their home. They are active in their local church. They are still saved.

When Bryan asked Jesus into his life, even as a child, his first impulse was to tell somebody. He was ready to confess publicly that Jesus was his Lord. Paul says it should work that way with everyone—that confessing publicly that Jesus is Lord is part of our salvation process. I agree with Paul. Don't you?

Lesson 7
Marks of the True Christian

Romans 12:1-2, 9-21

I beseech you therefore, brethren, by the mercies of God, that ye present your bodies a living sacrifice, holy, acceptable unto God, which is your reasonable service.

2 And be not conformed to this world: but be ye transformed by the renewing of your mind, that ye may prove what is that good, and acceptable, and perfect, will of God.

9 Let love be without dissimulation. Abhor that which is evil; cleave to that which is good.

10 Be kindly affectioned one to another with brotherly love; in honour preferring one another;

11 Not slothful in business; fervent in spirit; serving the Lord;

12 Rejoicing in hope; patient in tribulation; continuing instant in prayer;

13 Distributing to the necessity of saints; given to hospitality.

14 Bless them which persecute you: bless, and curse not.

15 Rejoice with them that do rejoice, and weep with them that weep.

16 Be of the same mind one toward another. Mind not high things, but condescend to men of low estate. Be not wise in your own conceits.

17 Recompense to no man evil for evil. Provide things honest in the sight of all men.

18 If it be possible, as much as lieth in you, live peaceably with all men.

19 Dearly beloved, avenge not yourselves, but rather give place unto wrath: for it is written, Vengeance is mine; I will repay, saith the Lord.

20 Therefore if thine enemy hunger, feed him; if he thirst, give him drink: for in so doing thou shalt heap coals of fire on his head.

21 Be not overcome of evil, but overcome evil with good.

April 17

Memory Selection
Romans 12:9-10

Background Scripture
Romans 12:1-21

Devotional Reading
Romans 12:3-8

 Romans 12 marks a clear break in Paul's intense letter to the church at Rome. Up to now he has dealt with crucial doctrinal matters having to do with salvation by grace through faith, as opposed to salvation through law or works. As someone has said, this is the *What?* Of the book of Romans.

Now comes the *So what?* So we are saved by grace, not works: *What*

now? Paul answers this question with a variety of topics in the general arena of "Christian living." This is typical of the apostles' letters: theology first, then practical living. He wants what we do to be grounded in the truth about God, Christ, and salvation.

The focus of this lesson may seem to vary from verse to verse. Actually, the diverse topics are linked by Paul's counsel on how to present our very lives as holy offerings to God.

ಲ೧೪

Lead a discussion on the question, *What difference does grace make?* For 11 intense chapters, the apostle Paul has dwelt on the doctrine of salvation by grace through faith, "not of works, lest any man should boast." Now, in chapter 12, he shows how that doctrine should work itself out in our lives. Those who are saved by grace should then show themselves

to be gracious; those saved by faith should above all others be faithful.

It is clear, therefore, that despite his emphasis on grace, Paul remained concerned about works. Although he has taught strongly against works-salvation, he believes just as strongly that believers should "show their faith by their works" (James 2:18). Thus the charges sometimes leveled against Paul are groundless: he is not "antinomian," or against law; he is concerned not only about theology, but ethics as well.

Teaching Outline

I. A Whole and Holy Sacrifice—1-2

II. How to Respond to Grace—9-21

  A. On love, 9-10

  B. On graciousness, 11-15

  C. On relationships, 16-21

    1. Unity and humility, 16

    2. Attitudes toward enemies, 17-20

    3. Attitude toward evil, 21

Daily Bible Readings

Mon.	Living Instructions *Colossians 4:2-6*
Tue.	A Life Pleasing to God *1 Thessalonians 4:1-12*
Wed.	Hold Fast to the Good *1 Thessalonians 5:12-22*
Thu.	Do What Is Right *2 Thessalonians 3:6-13*
Fri.	Members One of Another *Romans 12:1-5*
Sat.	Marks of the True Christian *Romans 12:6-13*
Sun.	Overcome Evil with Good *Romans 12:14-21*

I. A Whole and Holy Sacrifice—1-2

1 I beseech you therefore, brethren, by the mercies of God, that ye present your bodies a living sacrifice, holy, acceptable unto God, which is your reasonable service.

2 And be not conformed to this world: but be ye transformed by the renewing of your mind, that ye may prove what is that good, and acceptable, and perfect, will of God.

How can Paul, who has written so fervently supporting salvation by grace instead of works, shift into a section on *works* after all? By commending works *because* we have received grace, or "the mercies of God," not to *earn* grace. Paul is following the pattern set by Jesus in the Parable of the Unjust Servant, who was condemned for having been forgiven a debt himself, then being highly unmerciful to those who owed him money (see Matt. 18:23-35). He who has been shown grace should be the first to show grace to others. Paul can therefore never be rightly accused of neglecting *ethics,* and being concerned only with the theology of salvation by grace.

Instead of killing an animal for a sacrifice, those saved by the sacrifice of Christ are to present themselves as *living* sacrifices. The *placement* of the sacrifice mentioned here is crucial. Under the Law, the sacrifice of an animal was thought to *procure* grace or forgiveness. Paul, however, tells Christians who have already received forgiving grace to *then* present their sacrificial life— not to obtain grace but as evidence that they have received it.

The difference in the sacrifice is also crucial. No longer will an animal suffice; it must be the whole self of the person who has received grace. This is a "spiritual" sacrifice (NIV), which the word the KJV translates "reasonable" can also mean. That is, giving our bodies as a sacrifice spiritualizes the animal sacrifices under the Law. The term "spiritual" is also appropriate in balancing the word "bodies," indicating that both body and spirit must be offered as a whole-life, as well as a "holy" life, to God.

The J. B. Phillips translation has an unsurpassed way of stating verse 2a: "Don't let the world around you squeeze you into its own mold." Instead, we are to be transformed by grace in ways that prove that *this* system, not the system of works/ Law, is the perfect will of God. ("The proof is in the pudding.")

II. How to Respond to Grace—9-21
A. On love, 9-10

9 Let love be without dissimulation. Abhor that which is evil; cleave to that which is good.

10 Be kindly affectioned one to another with brotherly love; in honour preferring one another;

Now follows a laundry list of behaviors and attitudes that Paul says should flow into and out of the life of the person who is saved by grace. "Dissimulation" means "hypocrisy," which Paul says must not contaminate *agape*-love. Abhoring the evil and clinging to the good will flow from sincere love.

The attitudes of people saved by grace instead of law should be markedly different in that there is no competition to see who can keep the most rules, or to keep the rules "better." It was this sort of attitude that Jesus condemned among the Pharisees. We are more likely to be "kindly affectioned" toward each other with "brotherly love " (*philadelphia*) if we consider that we are all sinners saved by grace, than if we think some among us are better rule-keepers than others. Instead of trying to outdo each other in law-keeping, the competition should be in trying to be the best at honoring others.

B. On graciousness, 11-15

11 Not slothful in business; fervent in spirit; serving the Lord;

12 Rejoicing in hope; patient in tribulation; continuing instant in prayer;

13 Distributing to the necessity of saints; given to hospitality.

14 Bless them which persecute you: bless, and curse not.

15 Rejoice with them that do rejoice, and weep with them that weep.

There should be no letdown in business ethics simply because we are saved by grace instead of law. The grace-filled person should have a more fervent spirit than those preoccupied with rule-keeping, since grace is so often associated with Spirit (as *works* is associated with *law*). This principle has been sorely tested in our day of "bumper sticker" and "label" religion, when some Christians in business plaster the "ichthus" or fish on their storefront or their ad in the Yellow Pages—then turn out to be as unscrupulous as non-Christians in the quality of service or product they offer.

The general graciousness of Christian communities to those in need would lead to the first hospitals in the ancient world. The idea is that those responding to the needs of others out of the grace that has been shown to them should have a limitless spirit that continues to bless others above and beyond the call of duty; while those whose good deeds are required by law are likely to limit their deeds to those specified by that law.

The gist of verses 14-15 will be repeated, and treated, below.

C. On relationships, 16-21

1. Unity and humility, 16

16 Be of the same mind one toward another. Mind not high things, but condescend to men of

low estate. Be not wise in your own conceits.

Again, a community consisting of those ruled by law is more likely to be afflicted with competition than those who confess that they are all, together, sinners saved by grace. Whatever their status in society, Christians are to "condescend" (NIV "be willing to associate with people of low positions") because *all* have sinned and come short of the glory of God" (Rom. 3:28), and thus all have the same need for grace. It is in such ideas as this that democracy, the great "leveling" movement in the realm of politics, tends to grow out of cultures influenced by Christian teaching.

2. Attitudes toward enemies, 17-20

17 Recompense to no man evil for evil. Provide things honest in the sight of all men.

18 If it be possible, as much as lieth in you, live peaceably with all men.

19 Dearly beloved, avenge not yourselves, but rather give place unto wrath: for it is written, Vengeance is mine; I will repay, saith the Lord.

20 Therefore if thine enemy hunger, feed him; if he thirst, give him drink: for in so doing thou shalt heap coals of fire on his head.

Paul's teaching that we should respond even to our enemies in love recalls Jesus' teaching in the Sermon on the Mount (see Matt. 5:38-48). The quotation limiting vengeance to God is a rough translation of Deuteronomy 32:35, reminding us that the graciousness that is to characterize people saved by grace actually has its roots in the Old Covenant.

In fact, verse 20 quotes almost verbatim Proverbs 25:21. It seems that Paul, after showing the often sharp differences between grace and law in Romans 1–11, is now concerned to show that the behavior expected of Christians is grounded in the spirit of the Law after all. The difference is that godly Christian behavior is not to *achieve* salvation, but *in response* to salvation.

Whether the teaching of Paul and Jesus on how to treat enemies is aimed at personal or social ethics continues to be debated. Some Christians, such as those in the Quaker tradition, hold that loving our enemies precludes going to war, while others hold that Paul and Jesus are aiming at changing individual hearts and not nations, which may or may not be "Christian."

3. Attitude toward evil, 21

21 Be not overcome of evil, but overcome evil with good.

Paul's "last word" here has to do with our entire attitude. If our perspective is shaped only by the daily news of the world, it will sometimes seems that evil will triumph. If we trust in salvation by grace we know that in the end love and grace, not evil, will be shown to be the greater power. The cosmic triumph of the good portrayed in the book of Revelation is balanced here by Paul's vision of small, personal acts of good.

Evangelistic Emphasis

Christians are to be different from the prevailing culture of the world. If we are not careful, the world will mold us into a worldly way of acting, thinking, and being. Soon we could find ourselves no different from worldly, non-Christian people.

Christians are to be transformed. Our Christianity is not something that happens to us one night at a revival meeting. Our Christianity consists of growing more and more nearly into the image of Jesus Christ. We are to be transformed into Christ's image, not conformed into the world's mold.

Additionally, we are to be transforming agents. We are to make a difference in our world around us. Jesus came to bring salvation, and to relieve suffering. His life changed the world. We are to be like Him, giving our lives to transforming ministries as well. If we are not making a difference, maybe Jesus has not made a difference in us.

ഇൗര

Memory Selection

Let love be without dissimulation. Abhor that which is evil; cleave to that which is good. Be kindly affectioned one to another with brotherly love; in honour preferring one another;—*Romans 12:9-10.*

I am shocked at the things that pass for love today. Paul says love must be sincere. I wonder how many people tell another person, "I love you," simply as a ruse to get what they want. How many abusive husbands have used the words "I love you" to get their battered wives to stay with them? How many women have used the words "I love you" to persuade a lousy man to stay with them simply because they wanted access to his money? I wonder how many high school boys have told high school girls "I love you" just to try to convince them to have sex?

Paul's words indicate that insincere love is actually not love at all. Love cannot be used for self-promotion. Love is in action when a person is sincerely seeking the well-being of the beloved over her or his own well-being. Love says, "I want the best for you, not for me." There really is no "me first" in true love.

Weekday Problems

"Bryce, did you hear? Ed just won salesman of the year! He set a company record this year for the number of units sold! Isn't that great?" Chuck was so excited as he shared this news that his voice was several tones higher.

Bryce just smiled a weak smile and nodded, "Sure. That's great, Chuck. We're all so proud of Ed." But Bryce was not proud at all. Ed was Bryce's best friend, but Bryce found himself envious, even jealous, that Ed had been so successful. Bryce had given Ed several good leads on prospective buyers. Now Ed wins the sales award, not Bryce.

About that time Ed stuck his head in Bryce's office. "Hey, buddy. Got a minute? I just had to come by and share the news with my best friend. They gave me the sales award this year. I want to tell you, I could not have done it without you. You helped me so much."

*If their friendship was sincere, should Bryce have expected something in return for his help? Explain.

*What would a loving reaction be from Bryce right now?

The 'Lord Sprayer' and Other Misunderstandings

Children's "true misunderstandings" of adult prayers and other sayings:.

• Give us this steak and daily bread, and forgive us our mattresses.

• Our Father, who art in heaven, how didja know my name?

• Give us this day our jelly bread.

• Lead a snot into temptation ("I thought I was praying for my little sister to get into trouble.")

• He suffered under a bunch of violets ("under Pointius Pilate").

• When my older brother was very young, he always accompanied my mother to the altar when she took communion. Once he whispered, "What does the priest say when he gives you the bread?" He didn't understand what she whispered back, and was shocked to learn, years later, that the priest doesn't say, "Be quiet until you get to your seat."

• I led the pigeons to the flag, and to the republic for Richard Stands.

This Lesson in Your Life

I am convinced that it is easier to *become* a Christian than it is to *be* one. The preacher preaches or a friend testifies. The Holy Spirit begins to move in your heart. Your pulse quickens. Your heart pounds. All of a sudden you find yourself with tears in your eyes, confessing your sins, repenting, and vowing to follow Jesus for the rest of your life. After some moments, the service is over. You have become a Christian. That was the easy part.

Now comes the ironic part, the hard part. In the Christian life, you win the race; then you have to run it. You pass the test, then you have to study for it. You gain the victory, then you have to fight the fight.

We constantly find ourselves wrestling with the old nature in our hearts. Activities and actions down whose paths we formerly walked still know our names, and call out to us at our weakest moment. Things that come out of who we used to be and what we formerly were lie to us, trying to convince us that the way of the Lord is a broad road with a wide gate. In contrast, our faith reminds us that the way of the Lord is a straight and narrow road with a small gate that leads to life.

We constantly find ourselves wrestling with the ways of the world. The world teaches, "Me first." The world teaches, "Do unto others, only do it first." The world teaches, "Look out for number one." Jesus teaches us the way of love, humility, and honoring others.

We read this litany of do's and don'ts in Paul's letter, and we are reminded how different we Christians are supposed to be. Well, maybe I should say, "How different we Christians *are*." For if there is no difference, we have already conformed to the world, instead of being transformed by God's love and grace.

1. According to Romans 12:1, what is the primary motivation for our obedience to God?
A Christian's motivation to obedience is overwhelming gratitude for God's mercy.

2. After reading verse 1, do you think God would rather that we live for Him or die for Him?
God wants us to present ourselves as living sacrifices, not an animal to be slain on the altar. However, one is not ready to live wholly for God until one is ready to die for Him.

3. Why is it so important for us to study and know the Scriptures and to read Christian books?
Studying and knowing the Scriptures and reading Christian books transforms our minds, and helps us avoid adopting the world's standards.

4. What are some ways Paul describes Christian love in verses 9-10?
Love must be sincere. It must be affectionate. It must be like the love that one family member has for another.

5. How is the Christian supposed to handle hope, tribulation (affliction), and prayer (v.12)?
We are to be joyful in hope, patient in affliction, and faithful (continuing instant) in prayer.

6. How are we Christians to react to people who persecute us?
We are to bless them, not curse them.

7. How does Paul describe ways we demonstrate that we are not proud?
When we are willing to associate with people of low position. When we are not conceited.

8. What do verses 17, 19, and 21 teach us about getting back at people who do us wrong?
If someone does us wrong, do not pay that person back with another unkind act. Do not seek revenge. In fact, if someone does evil to us, we are supposed to something good for them. Good will overcome evil.

9. In verse 20 Paul quotes an Old Testament passage, Proverbs 25:21-22. What does this say that we should do for our enemies?
We are to do good for our enemies. The "coals of fire" seems to mean conviction that will lead to them to repentance.

10. Can we always live in peace with others?
Not necessarily. Paul encourages us to live at peace with others as far as we are concerned—that is, do everything we can to live in peace with others.

Wouldn't it be great if we all could live by just these 15 verses in Romans 12? Now, I'm not suggesting that we discard the rest of the Bible. I'm simply saying that the world would be a much better place if every person would commit these 15 verses to memory and covenant to consider these verses as a guide for everyday life.

Our churches would certainly be better if all those who claim the name of Jesus Christ would walk by these few verses. What would our meetings be like if every one sincerely loved each other? What would happen if we all committed to consider the well-being of our Christian sister or brother above our own? Why, half the trouble that arises in churches concerns rights, privileges, and prestige. Someone has not been given her or his place. Someone has been neglected or un-thanked. What would it be like if we determined to love our Christian brothers and sisters as we love our blood kin?

What would it be like if we were always zealous in serving the Lord, joyful in our hope, patient when things went wrong, and faithful in our prayer life? We want the world to live in harmony and peace. How about aiming first for folks who call themselves Christians to live in harmony and peace?

It can be like that. It can happen that we exhibit the behavior that Paul describes. However, it will not happen by accident. It will not happen as long as we refuse to allow our minds to be changed. It will not happen until our mind-set is transformed. It will not happen if we are willing only to be like everybody else.

It can happen, though. It *will* happen when we submit ourselves to the transforming power of the blood of Jesus Christ. It will happen when we allow the Holy Spirit free rein in our hearts.

It can happen. Let it start with you.

Don't Judge One Another

Romans 14:1-13; 15:5-6

Him that is weak in the faith receive ye, but not to doubtful disputations.

2 For one believeth that he may eat all things: another, who is weak, eateth herbs.

3 Let not him that eateth despise him that eateth not; and let not him which eateth not judge him that eateth: for God hath received him.

4 Who art thou that judgest another man's servant? to his own master he standeth or falleth. Yea, he shall be holden up: for God is able to make him stand.

5 One man esteemeth one day above another: another esteemeth every day alike. Let every man be fully persuaded in his own mind.

6 He that regardeth the day, regardeth it unto the Lord; and he that regardeth not the day, to the Lord he doth not regard it. He that eateth, eateth to the Lord, for he giveth God thanks; and he that eateth not, to the Lord he eateth not, and giveth God thanks.

7 For none of us liveth to himself, and no man dieth to himself.

8 For whether we live, we live unto the Lord; and whether we die, we die unto the Lord: whether we live therefore, or die, we are the Lord's.

9 For to this end Christ both died, and rose, and revived, that he might be Lord both of the dead and living.

10 But why dost thou judge thy brother? or why dost thou set at nought thy brother? for we shall all stand before the judgment seat of Christ.

11 For it is written, As I live, saith the Lord, every knee shall bow to me, and every tongue shall confess to God.

12 So then every one of us shall give account of himself to God.

13 Let us not therefore judge one another any more: but judge this rather, that no man put a stumblingblock or an occasion to fall in his brother's way.

Rom 15:5 Now the God of patience and consolation grant you to be likeminded one toward another according to Christ Jesus:

6 That ye may with one mind and one mouth glorify God, even the Father of our Lord Jesus Christ.

Memory Selection
Romans 15:5-6

Background Scripture
Romans 14:1-13; 15:5-6

Devotional Reading
James 4:7-12

The most obvious differences in the membership of the church at Rome were between Jews and Gentiles, who brought drastically different customs with them when they tried to unite in "one body." Beyond that, the Jews among them may have come from several sects such as the Pharisees, Sadducees, and possibly the Zealots. Others would have had their own diversity, from atheism to the worship of several gods.

This lesson focuses on the mutual tolerance that would be required for such people to be welded into a congregation that reflected the unity they shared in all having come to God through Christ. Paul does not advocate compromising the gospel just to "get along." Indeed it is the Good News that God was in Christ that was the basis for their coming together in the first place. Beyond that shared faith, however, he counsels non-judgmentalism—which is still sorely needed among most believers today.

An Edwin Markham poem titled "Outwitted," can start this lesson:

He drew a circle that shut me out—
Heretic, rebel, a thing to flout.
But Love and I had the wit to win:
We drew a circle that took him in!

Ask what kinds of judgmentalism sometimes divides churches today.

Are they usually social cliques, doctrinal divisions, or class-based tensions? What can be done to foster tolerance of diversity? On the other hand, are there limits to the diversity a congregation faithful to Christ should set? Point out that Paul confronts these issues in Roman 14. Note how his teaching echoes that of Jesus in the Sermon on the Mount (Matt. 7:1-5).

Teaching Outline	Daily Bible Readings	
I. The Issue of Religious Diets—1-3	Mon.	Speak No Evil *James 4:7-12*
A. The virtue of acceptance, 1	Tue.	Don't Be Grouchy *James 5:7-12*
B. Diversity of diets, 2-3	Wed.	Don't Judge Each Other *Romans 14:1-6*
II. The Issue of Special Days—4-6		
A. Pleasing the One who matters, 4	Thu.	Accountable to God *Romans 14:7-13*
B. Diversity of days, 5-6	Fri.	Don't Argue Over Food *Romans 14:14-18*
III. The Unity Jesus Creates—7-9		
IV. On Not Judging Each Other'—10-13	Sat.	Don't Be a Stumbling Block *Romans 14:19-23*
V. Having 'One Mind'—15:5-6	Sun.	Live in Harmony *Romans 15:1-6*

Verse by Verse

I. On Religious Diets—1-3
A. The virtue of acceptance, 1

1 Him that is weak in the faith receive ye, but not to doubtful disputations.

In Paul's day, Rome was the crossroads of the world. The infant church there attracted people from a bewildering variety of backgrounds. Amid such diversity, how could they be "one Body"?

The first principle Paul lays down is that newcomers don't have to have perfect knowledge of all details of the faith. Verse 1 seems to counsel an open policy of accepting new members, even though their faith is "weak" or incomplete, as long as they do not try to force their weak views on others, which would inevitably lead to "disputations."

B. Diversity of diets, 2-3

2 For one believeth that he may eat all things: another, who is weak, eateth herbs.

3 Let not him that eateth despise him that eateth not; and let not him which eateth not judge him that eateth: for God hath received him.

Paul deals first with the matter of religious scruples about what to eat. The most obvious example in the Roman church no doubt involved Jewish Christians who still followed Old Testament dietary laws, such as not eating the meat of certain animals (see Lev. 11). Even among Jews there would have been some differences of opinion on how to slaughter "clean" animals according to the rabbis' laws of "kosher." Also, various pagans had their own religiously-ordained diets, such as not eating meat because of the conviction that killing animals killed some divine form of life. Then there was the question (dealt with extensively in 1 Cor. 8) of whether it was right for either Jews or Gentiles to eat meat that had been slaughtered for idolatrous ceremonies.

Paul himself believed that nothing is "unclean of itself" (vs. 14). Yet he urges such "liberals" on that issue not to be judgmental toward "conservatives," and for those with dietary scruples not to judge those who had none. The only "law" on the issue is that there *is* no law.

II. The Issue of Special Days—4-6
A. Pleasing the One who matters, 4

4 Who art thou that judgest another man's servant? to his own master he standeth or falleth. Yea, he shall be holden up: for God is able to make him stand.

Paul pauses for a moment to lay down a principle that applies to both dietary views and observance of days (the next topic). That principle is one of two that are essential in any harmoniously-working group. The one introduced here is the principle of *individualism:* God, not our brothers and sisters in Christ, will judge each of us on our own terms. Even if we are "wrong" in some of our opinions about eating or observing special days, God's grace is able to "make us stand" on the Day of Judgment. (The second principle will be introduced in vs. 7.)

B. Diversity of days, 5-6

5 One man esteemeth one day above another: another esteemeth every day alike. Let every man be fully persuaded in his own mind.

6 He that regardeth the day, regardeth it unto the Lord; and he that regardeth not the day, to the Lord he doth not regard it. He that eateth, eateth to the Lord, for he giveth God thanks; and he that eateth not, to the Lord he eateth not, and giveth God thanks.

Again, traditions from both Judaism and paganism would have affected the issue of observing special days. Prominent among Jews who wanted to cling to their heritage would have been the major feasts of Unleavened Bread or Pentecost, the Feast of Weeks, and the Feast of Tabernacles (see Lev. 23). Furthermore, pagan days (such as those that led to some of the names of our days of the week—Sun-day, Moon-day, Thorsday, etc.—would have been observed by some Gentile Christians.

Paul's permissive counsel is based on the underlying *gratitude* among both observers and non-observers. Those who observe special days thank God for the feast, while those who abstain thank Him for what He has otherwise given them (an early reference, incidentally, to the Christian habit of saying thanks at meals). Why would opinionated people on either side of the issue disturb congregational harmony when both partakers and abstainers are praising God?

III. The Unity Jesus Creates—7-9

7 For none of us liveth to himself, and no man dieth to himself.

8 For whether we live, we live unto the Lord; and whether we die, we die unto the Lord: whether we live therefore, or die, we are the Lord's.

9 For to this end Christ both died, and rose, and revived, that he might be Lord both of the dead and living.

Now the second of Paul's principles of harmony is introduced. While the first (vs. 4) was based on *individualism*, it is balanced here by the paradoxically equal principle of *togetherness*. As the English poet-preacher John Donne would later write, "No man is an island / entire in itself." People in a congregation depend not only on the individual judgment of God but on each other. Ignoring or judging others breaks down this interdependency.

The freedom that Paul and others felt must not be flaunted before those with stricter scruples. A "liberaler-than-thou" attitude is no better than the "holier-than-thou" mindset of those who had more dietary and/or holy day observances than others. Verse 8 emphasizes that both observers and non-observers live and die under the eyes of God, and their hope of salvation lies not in "works" such as religious observances, but in the grace of God through Christ. Therefore none should judge the other.

IV. On Not Judging Each Other— 10-13

10 But why dost thou judge thy brother? or why dost thou set at nought thy brother? for we shall all stand before the judgment seat of Christ.

11 For it is written, As I live, saith the Lord, every knee shall bow to me, and every tongue shall confess to God.

12 So then every one of us shall give account of himself to God.

13 Let us not therefore judge one another any more: but judge this rather, that no man put a stumblingblock or an occasion to fall in his brother's way.

Just as all Christians live and die under the eyes of God, so will all be judged by a gracious God. Again the principles of liberty-in-unity and unity-in-diversity are emphasized. Verse 12 implies that I will not be called into account for your behavior, nor you for mine. If such separate and individual judgment will be exercised by God at Judgment Day, why not benefit *now,* in congregational life, from this positive aspect of individual accountability?

The "stumbling block" principle is often misunderstood. Some think, for example, that they should not eat meat even if a brother or sister is only offended by it. Paul himself said that if eating meat caused a brother to stumble, he would become a vegetarian (1 Cor. 8:13). "Stumbling," however, does not mean merely being offended but going against one's conscience and doing what a brother does, while thinking it is wrong.

V. Having 'One Mind'—15:5-6

5 Now the God of patience and consolation grant you to be likeminded one toward another according to Christ Jesus:

6 That ye may with one mind and one mouth glorify God, even the Father of our Lord Jesus Christ.

Although Paul has more to say in the rest of chapter 14 on the issue of not being judgmental, today's text moves to a summary statement. It is also a "benediction" said over a congregation struggling with diversity. Paul prays that the God of patience might give the church patience, and the God of consolation give each member a spirit that yearns to support each other more than demanding one's rights. Being of "one mind" and praising God with "one mouth" requires two main attitudes, which Paul has put forward as essential for church unity: (1) Not forcing one's opinions on others, on non-essential issues, while (2) Not boasting of one's freedom or deriding those whose consciences place more restrictions on them.

Evangelistic Emphasis

Some people see the Christian walk as a long list of rigid rules that a person must follow. If a person does not strictly follow the rules, that person must not be a Christian. Granted, there are rules the Christian must follow. There are standards of holy living that God requires. There are also standards of conduct and behavior that we humans have set up which God does not require.

Some say we cannot dance and be Christian, while others say it doesn't matter. Some say alcohol consumption is a sin, while others say moderate drinking isn't wrong. Some say long hair or long sleeves or long trousers or hats are required.

I am glad God does not judge us by outward actions. God determines who we are and whether we are following Him by looking at our hearts. God discerns our thoughts, our intent, and our motives. After judgment day there will be dancers and non-dancers and long hair and short hair in heaven and in hell. But there will not be anyone in heaven whose heart is not pure.

₰₯

Memory Selection

Now the God of patience and consolation grant you to be likeminded one toward another according to Christ Jesus: That ye may with one mind and one mouth glorify God, even the Father of our Lord Jesus Christ.—*Romans 15:5-6*

I think it interesting that Paul recognizes God as being the God of patience and consolation. I can only imagine how often we would become exasperated if we had to put up with people like ourselves. I sometimes chuckle at the things that we choose to dispute about. In one church I served, the head usher threatened to quit if I required the ushers to direct people where to kneel at the chancel rail for the Lord's Supper. Needless to say, the pastor and the head usher were not like minded on that issue.

It would be funny if it were not so sad. When we bicker about the unimportant things, we find ourselves unable to come together on the crucial things as well. It is God's desire that we praise Him and glorify Him in complete unity of love and spirit. We do want to please God, don't we?

Weekday Problems

The two ladies were sitting next to each other at the community Thanksgiving service. One lady had her hair cut very short. She wore lots of makeup. Two diamond earrings were in each ear. She obviously enjoyed expensive perfume. Tears were running down her cheeks and onto her pants legs.

The lady next to her had extremely long hair. She wore no makeup at all, not even lip gloss. She wore absolutely no jewelry, except for her watch and a plain wedding band. Her long skirt almost reached the floor. Tears dripped down her cheeks and into her lap.

The pastor was reminding the congregation how good and how pleasant it is when God's children dwell together in unity.

The lady with the long skirt gently took the other lady's hand. Their eyes met, then closed as they bowed their heads in prayer.

*Recall an experience you have had concerning God's people coming together in unity.

*List some things that keep Christians apart that should not be divisive.

Judgments on Judgmentalism

God himself, sir, does not propose to judge man until the end of his days.—*Samuel Johnson*

* * * *

In men whom men condemn as ill
I find so much of goodness still,
In men whom men pronounce divine
I find so much of sin and blot,
I do not dare to draw a line
Between the two, where God has not.
—*Joaquin Miller*

* * * *

Man judges from a partial view,
None ever yet his brother knew;
The Eternal Eye that sees the whole
May better read the darkened soul,
And find, to outward sense denied,
The flower upon its inmost side!
—John Greenleaf Whittier

Early in his ministry, a pastor friend of mine was preaching in a church in eastern Kentucky that had strong roots in the "Holiness" tradition. He had been there only a couple of Sundays when a lady in his church came to meet with him in his office.

"Pastor," she began. "I know you believe in God's Word. And the Word says in 1 Peter 3:3, "Whose adorning let it not be that outward adorning of plaiting the hair, and of wearing of gold, or of putting on of apparel." Yet I noticed that you were wearing an expensive wristwatch. I knew you would want someone to let you know that you should not be wearing any gold."

My friend thanked the woman for coming and showed her the door. He looked at his wristwatch. It was an expensive gold watch that had been given to him as a graduation gift. He also looked at his graduation ring. He prayed, "Lord, I don't want to do anything outside of your will." And with that he took off the watch and the graduation ring.

The next Sunday the same lady caught him after church. "I thought you heard what God's Word said," she remarked.

"Yes, ma'am," he answered. "I took off my watch and my graduation ring."

"But what about *that* ring?" she replied, tapping the plain gold wedding band on his left hand.

He looked at her for a long moment. Then he pulled his watch and his other ring out of his pocket and put them back on.

Paul says, "Accept him whose faith is weak, without passing judgment on disputable matters." There are some matters that we consider vitally important that probably are not important at all to God. Christians must abide by God's standards of moral excellence and ethical purity. To those things we must strictly adhere. Concerning those things that are disputable, let's leave others a little leeway.

1. What are some things today that might fall under the heading of "doubtful disputations"?

Practices that really make no difference in a person's character or are not eternally important.

2. Who does Paul consider "weak"—the person who is or is not strict about following religious dietary laws?

Paul considers the person who follows the dietary laws weak because that person is still trying to gain God's approval through works.

3. What should be the reaction of one who has discovered Christian liberty to the one who is not walking in that freedom?

The one who is walking in liberty should not look down on the one who has not discovered the freedom Christ brings.

4. What should be the attitude of one who still observes stricter external rules to those who do not?

The one who observes the stricter rules should not condemn the one who lives in liberty, for God has accepted that person, too.

5. Is Paul saying that anything is acceptable as long as it is done "unto the Lord?"

Indeed not. He is discussing "disputable" matters (14:1), not fundamental precepts of the faith that apply to everyone.

6. Many Christians consider Sunday, the Christian Sabbath, a sacred day. Is Paul saying this is wrong?

No. Paul is addressing the fact that some Christians put so much emphasis on one day that it seems the other days do not matter. Paul reminds us that every day belongs to the Lord.

7. For whom should we live every day of our lives? How should we react when we are given another day?

We live to the Lord. The Christian is to give thanks to God for every day.

8. Paul says that Jesus Christ is Lord of both the living and the dead. What events proved that for us?

The crucifixion and the resurrection of Jesus, which showed that Jesus is Lord of both the living and the dead.

9. Are the people in our churches and in our communities accountable to the church, to you, or to God?

We all are accountable to God, so there is no need for us to pass judgment upon each other. Each servant is accountable to her or his Master.

10. Why is it so important that Christians live together in unity?

So that we can glorify God with one mind, one heart, and one voice.

The seminary I attended hosts an annual outdoor Christian music festival called "Ichthus." One year, when my son was 10 years old, several Christian "punk" bands attended the festival. Up until I saw Christian punk bands, I had always thought of myself as a fairly progressive guy. I could not relate to Christian punk, but the kids could.

My son and I were walking across the crowded grounds when a member of the punk band, "The 77s," walked by. His hair was halfway down his back. An earring was glistening from his left ear. He wore leather pants and a leather vest. He had on knee-high jackboots with chrome studs up the sides. He had chrome chains draped around his chest and down from his waist. He was a sight!

I punched my young son and pointed, "Bryan, look at that." Wouldn't you know it! At the exact time I pointed and snickered, the young man turned around and looked straight at us. I was so embarrassed. You can imagine my greater shame when the young man walked over to us. He greeted me, but did not strike up a conversation with me. Instead, he knelt down on one knee and spoke to Bryan.

"Hi," he said. "What's your name?"

"Bryan."

"Well, Bryan, would you do something for me?" he asked.

"Yes sir," my good son answered.

"Would you pray for me? Would you pray that God would use me to reach young men and women, boys and girls for Jesus Christ?"

"Yes, sir. I sure will," Bryan replied. With that the young man gave Bryan a 77s pin, and left.

God taught me something that day. He taught me not to be so quick to judge another by externals. A short-haired guy from Louisiana and a long-haired, leather-clad guitar player both had a heart for souls for the Kingdom.

Bryan and I both became 77s fans that day.

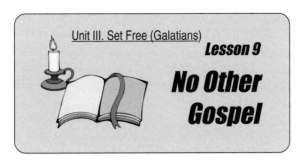

Lesson 9

No Other Gospel

Galatians 1:1-12

aul, an apostle, (not of men, neither by man, but by Jesus Christ, and God the Father, who raised him from the dead;)

2 And all the brethren which are with me, unto the churches of Galatia:

3 Grace be to you and peace from God the Father, and from our Lord Jesus Christ,

4 Who gave himself for our sins, that he might deliver us from this present evil world, according to the will of God and our Father:

5 To whom be glory for ever and ever. Amen.

6 I marvel that ye are so soon removed from him that called you into the grace of Christ unto another gospel:

7 Which is not another; but there be some that trouble you, and would pervert the gospel of Christ.

8 But though we, or an angel from heaven, preach any other gospel unto you than that which we have preached unto you, let him be accursed.

9 As we said before, so say I now again, If any man preach any other gospel unto you than that ye have received, let him be accursed.

10 For do I now persuade men, or God? or do I seek to please men? for if I yet pleased men, I should not be the servant of Christ.

11 But I certify you, brethren, that the gospel which was preached of me is not after man.

12 For I neither received it of man, neither was I taught it, but by the revelation of Jesus Christ.

May 1

Memory Selection
Galatians 1:11

Background Scripture
Galatians 1

Devotional Reading
Acts 13:26-33

This lesson shows the need for the Church to stay faithful to apostolic doctrine. The churches in "Galatia," a Roman province in Asia Minor (now central Turkey), serve as the model for this principle.

Acts 13–14 record the initial work of Paul and Barnabas in this area. Although they had been met with opposition from some Jews, the spiritual soil of Galatia had been well-plowed and sown, and the infant church plantings well-nourished. It is therefore understandable when Paul indicates disappointment and even shock at his discovery that "Judaizing teachers" had since threatened the stability of these congregations. The text for today reflects Paul's attempt to recall them back to the true gospel, after being led astray by false teachers.

Lead a discussion on the *Advantages* and *Disadvantages* of sticking with "old-time religion." Note that this tension faces all who take the original apostolic message seriously, but who realize also that new times raise new issues.

Discussion should include such *Advantages* as *staying grounded and attached to the original Message . . . finding comfort in the familiar . . . not stirring up questions that Scripture doesn't answer . . . keeping historical continuity with the past.*

On the *Disadvantages* side, include entries such as *becoming staid and "stuck" . . . failing to reach new people with different presuppositions . . . falling into irrelevance.* Challenge the group to perceive in this lesson what Paul would insist on keeping, and what he might agree to change.

Teaching Outline	Daily Bible Readings	
I. Opening Shot—1-5	Mon.	Don't Be Led Astray *2 Corinthians 11:1-15*
A. Paul's authority, 1-2		
B. Glory to God!, 3-5	Tue.	Holding All Together *Colossians 1:15-23*
II. Another Gospel?—6-7	Wed.	'We Bring Good News' *Acts 13:26-33*
III. For God or Man?—8-10	Thu.	Set Free by the Gospel *Act 13:34-41*
A. Curse on heresy, 8-9	Fri.	Salvation for All *Acts 13:44-49*
B. Serving man or God?, 10		
IV. Origin of Paul's Message—11-12	Sat.	Stick to the Gospel! *Galatians 1:1-7*
	Sun.	A Curse on Heresy *Galatians 1:8-12*

Verse by Verse

I. Opening Shot—1-5

A. Paul's authority, 1-2

1 Paul, an apostle, (not of men, neither by man, but by Jesus Christ, and God the Father, who raised him from the dead;)

2 And all the brethren which are with me, unto the churches of Galatia:

Since Paul is writing to correct error, he immediately stakes out his claim of authority with a claim to apostleship. The term for "apostle" can refer generally to anyone "sent" on a special mission, and it occasionally refers to persons such as certain "brethren" of Paul sent to the church at Corinth (2 Cor. 8:23). Here, however, Paul means for the term to refer more "officially" to himself, as one "born out of due time" (1 Cor. 15:8), or called after the original 12, plus Matthias, were appointed. He asserts his apostolic authority by showing that he had seen the Lord on the Damascus road, and was otherwise as qualified as the original 12 (see Gal. 1:12–2:13; 1 Cor. 9:1). Additionally, Paul wants to reinforce the authority of this letter by noting that it is "seconded" by faithful brethren who are accompanying him.

The phrase "churches of Galatia" probably refers to the congregations Paul had established in the south Galatian area: Antioch, Iconium, Derbe, and Lystra (Acts 13–14). The area received its name when the Romans imported conquered people from Gaul (later, France), to break up opposition to the Roman military conquests in northwestern Europe in the third-century B.C.

The Gauls had a reputation among some critics for being unstable and flighty; and some scholars attribute the susceptibility to heresy of Christians there to this national character. This is probably an unfeasible generalization, since the false teaching Paul confronts appeals more to Jews than to "Gaul-atians."

B. Glory to God!, 3-5

3 Grace be to you and peace from God the Father, and from our Lord Jesus Christ,

4 Who gave himself for our sins, that he might deliver us from this present evil world, according to the will of God and our Father:

5 To whom be glory for ever and ever. Amen.

Before plunging into the crucial problem of heresy that prompted this letter, Paul prefaces it with a highly appropriate greeting consisting of a prayer for grace and peace, and a word of praise to God. The contents of these verses, however, are more than a formality. They lay a groundwork for Paul's later plea to stay with the fundamentals of the gospel, by reminding his readers from the start that it is in *Christ* that deliverance from sin is to be found.

II. Another Gospel?—6-7

6 I marvel that ye are so soon removed from him that called you into the grace of Christ unto another gospel:

7 Which is not another; but there be some that trouble you, and would pervert the gospel of Christ.

As later lessons will indicate, "Judaizing teachers" constantly followed Paul, trying to bind the Law of Moses on Gentiles. For Paul, this was virtually "another" gospel, as he says in the latter part of verse 6. Here he uses the word *heteros* which can mean something in a totally different class or of a different nature. Then in the first part of verse 7 "another" translates a different Greek word, *allos*, meaning only that the heresy is "somewhat" but not totally different, because there is really only one gospel—which he had first preached to them.

That the teaching "troubling" the Galatians is the familiar "Judaizing" heresy is also indicated by the fact that it followed Paul's true teaching "so soon." This reminds us of the immediate steps Judaizing teachers took in the area to attach requirements such as circumcision from the Mosaic Law to Paul's message of salvation (see Acts 13:45; 15:1).

III. For God or Man?—8-10

A. Curse on heresy, 8-9

8 But though we, or an angel from heaven, preach any other gospel unto you than that which we have preached unto you, let him be accursed.

9 As we said before, so say I now again, If any man preach any other gospel unto you than that ye have received, let him be accursed.

Whether different "in kind" (*heteros*) or in variation on a theme (*allos*), the false teaching ensnaring the Galatians is placed under a surprisingly strong curse that is doubled by repetition. While it is very doubtful that a true "angel from heaven" would distort Paul's original message, his warning is appropriate because Satan can disguise himself as an "angel of light" (2 Cor. 11:14), and could even work miracles to deceive those who do not desire the truth (2 Thess. 2:9-11). Furthermore, worshiping angels seemed to be a part of other forms of heresy that attacked the early Christian communities (see Col. 2:18).

B. Serving man or God?, 10

10 For do I now persuade men, or God? or do I seek to please men? for if I yet pleased men, I should not be the servant of Christ.

"Persuade" probably means "win the approval" (as in the NIV, and its twin phrase "pleased men"). This question also indicates that the

Galatian heresy was Jewish-based, since Paul's own training as a Jew could easily have drawn the criticism that he had forsaken his roots in preaching Christ apart from the Law. He responds to this rhetorical question by saying that he could have had a much easier life had he preached salvation through Moses, thus pleasing the Judaizing teachers. His conversion, however, had been so radical, and he saw so clearly the danger of attaching anything such as circumcision to the simple gospel of salvation by grace through faith, that he could not sacrifice his message for anyone.

IV. Origin of Paul's Message—11-12

11 But I certify you, brethren, that the gospel which was preached of me is not after man.

12 For I neither received it of man, neither was I taught it, but by the revelation of Jesus Christ.

Paul "certifies" that the original message he had preached to the Galatians is sound because it came from God, not man. The claims Paul makes here, and on through chapter 2, are central to the integrity of his claim to be an apostle. One requirement of an apostle was that he had "seen" Jesus; and Paul contends that his vision of the Lord on the road to Damascus qualifies him in that respect (see 1 Cor. 9:1; Acts 22:18).

Beyond that, Paul claims not to have received the message he had preached to the Galatians from other apostles, but by direct "revelation" from Jesus Himself. Part of this rev-elation can be traced to what Paul saw and heard on the Damascus road, when we put together the three accounts of this stunning experience (Acts 9; 22; 26:12ff.). The rest of the revelation from Christ can probably be accounted for during Paul's "Arabian sojourn," which he recounts in verses 17-18. (We need not think of his going far into the Arabian peninsula, since the borders of "Arabia" as a nation extended to within easy traveling distance from Damascus.) In fact, Paul maintains that it was three years before he had contact with Peter, who could conceivably have taught him the gospel (vs. 18).

All this argument for the Galatians to stand firm in the message Paul had originally preached to them sounds too conservative to some Christians, who realize the need to be open to changes in society in order to maintain contact with them, and to preach to them a message that is relevant to their own life and times. Paul, however, had a very similar flexibility to adapting the gospel to different times and cultures. He said that he was willing to adapt himself to Jews and their customs in order to relate to them, or to Greeks in order to speak in terms familiar to them (1 Cor. 9:20-21. What he would *not* adapt, or change, however, was the fundamental truth that both Jew and Greek can be saved by grace, quite apart from the "aid," which was actually an encumbrance, of the Law. That is what is at stake among the Galatians.

Evangelistic Emphasis

Sometimes what at first sounds like good news turns out to be bad news. A good example is what happens to some who have won state lotteries. Receiving a king's ransom in a lump sum payment, they have quit their jobs and begun to live the high life. Then in only a few years, they have blown all their gambling winnings and are in worse shape than they were before their windfall. What seemed to be good news for a time was not good news in the long run.

The gospel of Jesus Christ is about a cross. It is about how He died for our sins. It is about how we gain eternal life by dying to self and living for Jesus. Sometimes folks try to present the gospel in other ways. They try to twist the gospel just a little bit to make it easier for us to handle. Some try to make the gospel more palatable to modern society. If the truth of the good news of Jesus Christ is changed, what is presented as the gospel is really no gospel at all. When we accept the fact that Jesus died for our sins and we decide to allow Him as Savior and Lord of our lives, what starts out as bad news (the death of Jesus), really is good news for us.

℘℃℞

But I certify you, brethren, that the gospel which was preached of me is not after man.—*Galatians 1:11*

I have heard it said, "Opinions are like feet. Most people have them and most of them smell." Almost everybody has an opinion about the Christian faith. Some say Christians are too narrow-minded. Others say true Christianity loves everybody and condemns no one. Some say Christianity is to be exclusive. Others say Christianity is to be entirely inclusive.

Actually, when it comes down to it, what matters is not what anybody thinks, but what God says. Paul reminds the Galatians that the gospel he taught them was not something he had conjured up from within his own mind. The gospel he preached was revealed to him by Jesus Christ Himself.

There is a huge difference between what God says and what humans think. That is why it is so important for us 21st century Christians to read the Bible. It is vital that we study God's Word, for we must be guided not what people think, but what God says.

Weekday Problems

Todd, Greg, and Lisa were early for Sunday School. They had poured themselves a cup of coffee and were sipping on the hot brew. "I was just thinking," Todd said. "How could a loving God send someone to hell? I mean, doesn't the Bible say that God is love?"

"Right," Greg agreed. "My friend, Donnell, lives down the street from me. He is a good guy. He never does anybody any harm. He is a deep thinker, too. He says all good people go to heaven, regardless of whether or not they subscribe to Christianity or to another religion. That makes a lot of sense to me. What do you think, Lisa?"

Lisa sat there for a moment looking up a particular passage of Scripture. When she found it she said, "It doesn't matter that much what we think. Listen to this . . . ."

* What is the final authority on things of the Spirit: what we think or what the Bible says? Explain your answer.

* Do you think we are ducking the issue when we refer to the Bible? Explain.

Back to Basics

- If at first you don't succeed, sky diving is not for you.
- Money can't buy happiness, but it sure makes misery easier to live with.
- Nothing in the known universe travels faster than a bad check.
- People for the Ethical Treatment of Animals (PETA) are said to now be suspicious that research causes cancer in rats.
- The last known rampaging Viking is said to have forgotten the principle that one must pillage *before* burning.
- It may be that your sole purpose in life is simply to serve as a warning to others.
- When feeling woozy, remember a fundamental law of gravity: You cannot fall off of the floor.
- Some claim that the average woman would rather have beauty than brains because the average man can see better than he can think.

This Lesson in Your Life

We want to remember that our New Testament book of Galatians is really a letter. It is a letter from the apostle Paul to the churches of Galatia. Usually in a letter we make some chit-chat at the first of the letter such as "I hope this letter finds you well" and "How's your Momma doing?" Paul also usually does the same sort of thing. Here, however, instead of the customary thanksgiving Paul launches right into the issue that prompts his letter.

Apparently, the Galatians were abandoning their divine call and moving toward some "alternative gospel." This alternative gospel was really not good news at all, but bad news which simply sounded good at first. The Galatians were abandoning the truth for a lie.

We must be careful about that today, too. There is a lot of information out there that some folks are trying to pass off as the gospel of Jesus Christ. I went on the Internet this morning, typed the words "gospel of Jesus Christ" into my search engine and came up with *1.3 million sites* concerning the gospel! Although I certainly did not research every one of the 1,300,000 sites, I suspect that there are not that many authentic ways to look at the gospel of Jesus. Just because someone has written a book about the gospel, or has a website discussing it, does not mean it is the truth.

So, how do we tell? How do we determine who is a just a so-called gospel preacher and who is presenting the true gospel? How do we separate reality from myth?

We read the Book. We read the Bible. We go back to see what Jesus actually taught. We scour Matthew, Mark, Luke, and John to see what Jesus really said and did. We do not simply take some man's opinion about what Jesus said and did as truth. We must go back to the Bible to read what happened in the Acts of the Apostles. We must take seriously what Paul taught in his writings. We must read James and John and Peter. We must discipline ourselves to read the Old Testament as well as the New Testament.

Paul himself said, "All Scripture is God-breathed and is useful for teaching, rebuking, correcting and training in righteousness" (2 Tim 3:16 NIV). We must go back to the Book. Read your Bible.

1. **From whom was Paul sent, and from whom did he get his authority as an apostle?**

Paul was sent by Jesus Christ and God the Father. His authority came from God, not from human beings.

2. **According to verse 4 in Paul's greeting, what did Jesus accomplish on our behalf when He came to earth?**

Jesus gave Himself for our sins to rescue us from the present evil age according to the will of the Father.

3. **What behavior in the Galatians caused Paul to be astonished?**

Paul was shocked because the Galatians were turning away so soon from the gospel he preached and they accepted.

4. **According to verse 6, by what or into what were the Galatians called?**

They were called into the grace of Christ. Paul reminds us in Ephesians 2:8, "For it is by grace you have been saved . . . ."

5. **What is Paul's opinion of the "different gospel" to which the Galatians were turning?**

Paul reminds the Galatians (and us) that the so-called other gospel is actually not the gospel at all.

6. **How sure is Paul that the gospel he preached and the gospel the Galatians accepted is truly the good news of Jesus Christ?**

He says that if he, anybody else, or even an angel from heaven should preach anything different than the gospel Paul originally preached, then that preacher should be eternally condemned.

7. **What were the tactics being used by those turning the Galatians away from the pure gospel?**

They were perverting the gospel, twisting the words. They are also troubling and confusing the Galatian Christians.

8. **Was Paul concerned with what people thought of him?**

Not really. He was not trying to win the approval of other people, but to be pleasing to God as His servant.

9. **Did the gospel Paul preached originate with him? Did he read the gospel message in some great teacher's book?**

No. Paul's message was not something he dreamed up. It was not something he was told or taught by another human being.

10. **Who gave Paul the gospel he preached?**

The gospel Paul preached was given to him by divine revelation from Jesus Christ Himself.

Some years ago Andrae Crouch wrote a song that contains the lines, "Jesus is the answer for the world today. Above Him there's no other. Jesus is the way." Jesus said about Himself, "I am the way, the truth, and the life: no man cometh unto the Father, but by me (John 14:6)." Jesus is all we need to receive eternal life. As a matter of fact, if we try to add anything else to Jesus to gain eternal life, we have added in error. Jesus is the full, perfect, and sufficient sacrifice for our sins.

Sometimes we think we have to do more. We think we might have to help Jesus out a little bit. Sometimes we begin to think that Jesus' sacrificial life and death were not really enough to cover all our sins. That's when we find ourselves wrapped up in "religion." That's when we begin to try to work our way into God's good graces. We find ourselves toiling under our own strength to earn our right to be called God's children. We discover we are working our fingers to the bone to gain the Kingdom of God, and all we have to show for it is bony fingers. It cannot be done.

Jesus is *the* way, not *a* way. I am not the one saying that, Jesus is. It is by His grace we have been saved. Peter says it in Acts 14:11, "We believe it is through the grace of our Lord Jesus that we are saved." Paul says it twice in Ephesians 2: "It is by grace you have been saved (2:5, 8)." Paul says it again in 2 Timothy 1:9. We do not earn salvation. We cannot earn it. God does it for us through Jesus Christ. All we need to do is have faith in Him.

Nothing we can do is good enough to earn our way into the Kingdom of God. There is nothing we can do that is so bad that God's grace cannot reach us.

You see, "Jesus paid it all. All to Him I owe. Sin had left a crimson stain. He washed it white as snow."

That's good news!

Lesson 10
All Saved By Faith

Galatians 2:15–3:5

e who are Jews by nature, and not sinners of the Gentiles,

16 Knowing that a man is not justified by the works of the law, but by the faith of Jesus Christ, even we have believed in Jesus Christ, that we might be justified by the faith of Christ, and not by the works of the law: for by the works of the law shall no flesh be justified.

17 But if, while we seek to be justified by Christ, we ourselves also are found sinners, is therefore Christ the minister of sin? God forbid.

18 For if I build again the things which I destroyed, I make myself a transgressor.

19 For I through the law am dead to the law, that I might live unto God.

20 I am crucified with Christ: nevertheless I live; yet not I, but Christ liveth in me: and the life which I now live in the flesh I live by the faith of the Son of God, who loved me, and gave himself for me.

21 I do not frustrate the grace of God: for if righteousness come by the law, then Christ is dead in vain.

3:1 O foolish Galatians, who hath bewitched you, that ye should not obey the truth, before whose eyes Jesus Christ hath been evidently set forth, crucified among you?

2 This only would I learn of you, Received ye the Spirit by the works of the law, or by the hearing of faith?

3 Are ye so foolish? having begun in the Spirit, are ye now made perfect by the flesh?

4 Have ye suffered so many things in vain? if it be yet in vain.

5 He therefore that ministereth to you the Spirit, and worketh miracles among you, doeth he it by the works of the law, or by the hearing of faith?

May 8

Memory Selection
Galatians 2:20

Background Scripture
Galatians 2:15–3:5

Devotional Reading
Galatians 3:6-14

 In the previous lesson, the apostle Paul vigorously opposed a heresy which had arisen in the churches of Galatia, in central Asia Minor (now Turkey). Several clues to the nature of that false teaching indicated that it held that people could come to Christ only by coming through Moses and the Law, including circumcision.

This lesson clearly names this false doctrine salvation by works as opposed to grace. Paul goes into detail about the consequences, for both Jew and Gentile, of clinging to this religion of the Jewish past instead of moving into the New Covenant. He argues that any attempt to be justified by keeping rules voids the work of Christ, and makes His death on the Cross useless or "vain."

ဆာ၈

This parable of salvation by grace can introduce this lesson. A struggling young artist won a contract to paint a huge mural on the wall of a great art museum. He was paid $10,000 "up front." Unfortunately, he was stricken almost immediately with an illness that confined him to bed. He ran a high fever, and in his delirium he had visions of being dismissed, disgraced—and $10,000 in debt.

By the time he was well, the deadline had passed. Going to look at the wall, he found to his joy that a master artist had stepped in for him and completed the vast mural. The wall was aglow with a masterpiece of vivid colors and graceful lines.

The young artist's reaction was to turn to the wall opposite the magnificent new mural, and to start to work painting as never before.

How is this story like salvation by grace? How is it different?

Teaching Outline	Daily Bible Readings

I. Don't Misuse the Law—2:15-18
  A. The Law's inadequacy, 15-16
  B. 'Righteous' sinners, 17-18
II. Death and Life—19-21
  A. Dying to the Law, 19
  B. Living through the Cross, 20-21
III. Don't be foolish—3:1-5
  A. You experienced Christ crucified, 1-4
  B. The Spirit worked wonders, 5
	Mon. Righteousness Through Faith
	       Romans 3:21-26
	Tue. Grace Through Christ
	       1 Corinthians 1:3-9
	Wed. Fullness of Life
	       Colossians 2:6-14
	Thu. Good News for All
	       Galatians 2:5-10
	Fri. Salvation by Faith
	       Galatians 2:15-21
	Sat. Law or Faith:
	       Galatians 3:1-5
	Sun. Fulfilled Promise
	       Galatians 3:6-14

Verse by Verse

I. Don't Misuse the Law—2:15-18
A. The Law's inadequacy, 15-16

15 We who are Jews by nature, and not sinners of the Gentiles,

16 Knowing that a man is not justified by the works of the law, but by the faith of Jesus Christ, even we have believed in Jesus Christ, that we might be justified by the faith of Christ, and not by the works of the law: for by the works of the law shall no flesh be justified.

Beginning this passage with "We" indicates that as a Jew himself, Paul can identify with the Jews of the Galatians churches. Although the Judaism of the day included some Gentile "proselytes," Paul was a Jew "by nature"—born into the faith, "the son of a Pharisee" (Acts 23:6). Although they could be arrogant, and feel that they were superior in holiness, many Pharisees opposed the Christian movement for fear that relaxing the Law would cause their faith to generate into immorality.

The problem with this view is that the Law which Paul's opponents want to impose on Gentiles cannot "justify" anyone, or make them righteous. Even Abraham, Paul argues, was justified by faith, being accepted by God *before* he was circumcised

(Rom. 4:9-12; Gal. 3:6-9). This is parallel to the fact that people are "put right" or justified now by "the faith of Jesus Christ . . . and not by the works of the law."

B. 'Righteous' sinners, 17-18

17 But if, while we seek to be justified by Christ, we ourselves also are found sinners, is therefore Christ the minister of sin? God forbid.

18 For if I build again the things which I destroyed, I make myself a transgressor.

Now Paul asks the Judaizing teachers about their personal relationship both with God and with the churches among whom they are working. If they try to be justified by Christ, while clinging at the same time to a Law that cannot justify anyone, they "are found [to be] sinners." It is as though they are trying to smother the fires of sin with a blanket that has been soaked in gasoline!

Or, in the metaphor suggested by verse 18, these false teachers are trying to build a safe house out of the materials of a "building" that has been shown to be *un*safe—the Law. In doing so, they are going about trying to save people while themselves transgressing God's will. This not only makes the would be "saviors" sinful; in linking Christ to the Law, they imply that His way is inadequate and therefore make Him appear to be a sinful minister!

It is important to remember that such pronouncements of the Law's insufficiency do not mean that it was a mistake, in its own context. Judaism was not invented by men, but instituted by God. Thus Paul can say that "the law is holy, and the commandment holy, and just, and good" (Rom. 7:12). It was an important and essential part of God's plan *in its time.* What makes the Law "wrong" now is to cling to it when God Himself, through Christ, had "nailed it to the Cross" (Col. 2:14).

II. Death and Life—19-21
A. Dying to the Law, 19

19 For I through the law am dead to the law, that I might live unto God.

The principle here is well illustrated by the story of a "reform" movement among some American Christians in the 19ᵗʰ century. They found themselves in a separatist denomination that denied fellowship to any Christian who did not follow their own narrow set of rules. In their study of Scriptures, they saw that this was not what Jesus intended, so they withdrew from their denomination and established a new one. Shortly thereafter they realized that they had only repeated their earlier mistake, under new rules. So they came together and wrote a new "constitution" that they called their "Last Will and Testament." In it they affirmed their intention to blend into the Body of Christ at large, and that their former separatist constitution was "dead."

In essence, the Judaizing teachers Paul faces had made a similar error to the one confessed by this group of people. They were trying to enforce a "constitution" or Law that had *itself* predicted that it would be replaced by a New Covenant (Jer. 31:31). They were trying to resurrect and live by a code to which they had "died" in the death of Christ. Their work would have resulted in a Jewish-Christian people instead of a people whose confidence in salvation was in Christ alone, not in "Christ-plus-Moses" or Christ-plus-anyone else.

B. Living through the Cross, 20-21

20 I am crucified with Christ: nevertheless I live; yet not I, but Christ liveth in me: and the life which I now live in the flesh I live by the faith of the Son of God, who loved me, and gave himself for me.

21 I do not frustrate the grace of God: for if righteousness come by the law, then Christ is dead in vain.

The Judaizing teachers were right in thinking that no one can live without a code of conduct. It was not enough to be "dead" to the Law of Moses; they must then "put on Christ," or confess allegiance to His code of grace instead of Moses' code of Law. Not only had Moses' Law been nailed to the Cross; so had the self-will of Christ's followers. Christians are those who have been buried with Christ to rise to walk in newness of life (Rom. 6:3-4). Now they are bound to God not by Law but by love—for Him who gave Himself for them.

Verse 21 shows the folly of trying to make people into "Jewish-Christians." If Moses and his Law is enough, Christ need not have died; and to impose the Law "frustrates" God's purpose in the Cross. If the Cross had not been necessary, then the Crucifixion stands as the world's greatest injustice—the cruel death of a righteous man. The fact is that the Cross delivers to the world what no law could—the atonement won by the Son of God dying for the sins of the world. Trying to blend this simple but profound truth with any add-on means of being saved is a sign that the Cross is considered inadequate.

III. Don't be foolish—3:1-5

A. You experienced Christ crucified, 1-4

1 O foolish Galatians, who hath bewitched you, that ye should not obey the truth, before whose eyes Jesus Christ hath been evidently set forth, crucified among you?

2 This only would I learn of you, Received ye the Spirit by the works of the law, or by the hearing of faith?

3 Are ye so foolish? having begun in the Spirit, are ye now made perfect by the flesh?

4 Have ye suffered so many things in vain? if it be yet in vain.

The problem in the Galatian churches is not to be laid at the feet of the false teachers alone. Those who listen to them have the responsibility not to be "bewitched" or taken in by their false doctrine. Rank-and-file Christians are held responsible on two grounds.

First, the Galatians had personally experienced Christ-crucified, not Christ-plus-Moses. This might refer to the sacrificial ministry of Christian preachers who had actually given their lives for the faith (the implication being, Why would anyone doubt the truth of their message if they were willing to die for it?). More likely, it simply refers to Paul's initial preaching of Christ-crucified.

Furthermore, verses 2-4 indicate that Paul knew that the Galatians had suffered persecution for embracing the Good News. Was the zealous willingness to be that committed prompted by hearing the Law, or the proclamation of the Spirit of freedom in Christ?

B. The Spirit worked wonders, 5

5 He therefore that ministereth to you the Spirit, and worketh miracles among you, doeth he it by the works of the law, or by the hearing of faith?

The second reason the Galatians are called "foolish" is that it had not been the proclamation of the Law but of Christ that had produced among them the works of the Holy Spirit. According to verse 5, these works included various miracles that accompanied the preaching of Christ-crucified. They saw no such miracles accompanying the teaching of the Judaizing teachers.

Evangelistic Emphasis

Wow! Maybe we should get the message of verse 16 that a person cannot be justified by observing the Law. Paul says that three times in one verse.

It sounds like the old country preacher who preached with great power and results. He was asked what was the secret to his effectiveness. He replied, "I tell 'em what I'm gonna tell 'em. Then I tell 'em. Then I tell 'em what I told 'em."

That's what Paul does here. He says it in so many ways that there can be no doubt that a person is not justified by the works of the Law.

There is the temptation still today to try to earn God's favor. There is the temptation to try to do works that are good enough, righteous enough, or plenteous enough to make up for the sin in our hearts. It cannot be done.

The only way the sin in our lives and in our hearts can be erased is by the grace of God working through our faith. We just cannot do enough. We must rely on what Jesus has done.

&)(&

Memory Selection

I am crucified with Christ: nevertheless I live; yet not I, but Christ liveth in me: and the life which I now live in the flesh I live by the faith of the Son of God, who loved me, and gave himself for me.—*Galatians 2:20*

Paul had tried the way of the law. He was a Pharisee of Pharisees. Under the Law he was blameless. Yet, he suddenly recognized himself as still a sinner, and abandoned the way of the Law to cast himself on the mercy of God. So great was the change, so dramatic was the shift, that the only way Paul could describe it was to say that he had been crucified with Christ. The man he used to be was dead. The living power that was within him now was the living Christ Himself.

This is the same scenario that is played out in every Christian today. We recognize that we cannot overcome sin by the Law and certainly not by our own strength. Thus, we turn to Christ. We die to ourselves and live for Christ. Christ lives in us by faith—the Christ who loves us enough that He gave his life for us.

Weekday Problems

"Preacher, I quit. I've had enough of it. I'm tired. I quit!" Martha was obviously agitated.

"Quit what, Martha?" Pastor Richards asked.

"Everything!" Martha replied. "I'm quitting everything. I work around this church all the time. I'm up here every day. Nobody else does anything. I can't take it anymore. I quit."

Pastor Richards spoke softly to Martha. "Martha, you do a lot, but it's not true that nobody else does anything. You can quit if you would like. God does not want you worn to a frazzle. He does not expect you to do everything."

"Oh, yes He does," Martha snapped back. "Oh, yes He does."

*How would you counsel Martha concerning God's expectations of her?

*Do you think Martha might have a distorted view of God's grace working through faith? Explain your answer.

He and She

He: Do you love me, dear?
She: Of course I do!
He: Enough to live on my income?
She: Of course . . . if you'll get another for yourself, too.
* * * *

He: Do you love me, dear?
She: Of course I love you.
He: Enough to die for me?
She: No . . . mine is an undying love.
* * * *

He: I must go! But how can I leave thee?
She: Well, by train, plane, taxi, your own car . . . .
* * * *

He: Will you marry me, dear?
She: No, but I'll always admire your good taste.

357

This Lesson in Your Life

I have been a Christian since I was in college. Even at that time I sought God's will for my life. When I was about to graduate from pharmacy school I had three excellent job offers. Each one had some great advantages. In one job I would be starting my own pharmacy with two Christian partners. That sounded good. In another I would be working back in my home town as a relief pharmacist among four local drug stores. That would be great. The third offer would pay me more money than either of the others.

I could not decide which one I should take. I wanted to choose the job that God wanted me to choose. I wanted the job in which I would fulfill God's will and find significance in my work.

My wife and I prayed and sought God's will. It seemed our prayers were not getting past the ceiling. God seemed to be silent. Then, one morning when I was in the bathroom shaving, God spoke to me. I did not actually hear an audible voice. Maybe it would be more accurate to say God impressed these words upon me.

God said, "David, in your life from here on you only have to make one decision. And that is, to let Me make all the decisions." That was a revelation to me. Of course, let God make the decision. I prayed right then, "God, I give it all to you. I trust your decision."

Within a week's time the men who wanted to put me in business called. Their store had burned to the ground; so that door was closed. Then a pharmacist from my home town called. Two of the pharmacists backed out of the deal. That door closed, too. Then the big-paying chain simply withdrew their offer. A door slammed again. All the options I had weighed so carefully were no longer open.

Then, I received out of the clear blue sky an offer from Eckerd Drugs, which I took. I worked in that same spot for 10 years until I resigned to go to seminary. I loved my 10 years with Eckerd.

We become Christians by faith alone. Also, the Christian life is more enjoyable when we live by faith.

1. Can a Jew by birth be saved by the Law while a Gentile sinner is saved by grace through faith?

No. Everyone who is saved, Jew or Greek, male or female, slave or free, is saved by grace through faith.

2. The dictionary defines "justified" as "being shown to be just, righteous, etc; and "free from blame." Why can't a person be justified by the Law?

The Law is *shows* blame, rather than releasing us from it. When we measure our lives by the Law, we see how much blame and guilt we have.

3. Paul says that we can only be justified by faith in Jesus Christ. How does faith in Jesus relieve us from blame?

Jesus took our blame upon Himself when He was executed for the sins of the whole world. One who was blameless took our guilt upon Himself that we may no longer bear that guilt. We must accept that fact by faith.

4. In verse 17 Paul asks, "Does Christ promote sin?" or "Is Jesus a minister of sin?" How would you answer that question?

I would answer as Paul did: "God forbid!" or "Absolutely not!" The fact that Jesus saves us by grace instead of Law does not mean that He dismisses us from the need for holy living.

5. In verse 18 how does Paul describe one way a person proves she/he is a lawbreaker?

We prove we are lawbreakers when we try to rebuild that which was destroyed—that is, when we try to earn salvation through the Law, which Jesus fulfilled on the Cross.

6. In verse 20 what is the strong metaphor Paul uses to describe the fact that he no longer lives according to the Law?

Paul says he has been crucified with Christ. His life before, that of a Pharisee trying to gain righteousness by the Law alone, is dead and gone.

7. To whom or for whom did Paul live his life after his conversion?

Paul lived his life for Christ, instead of for the Law.

8. What is Paul's question concerning the idea that a person could be good enough to be declared righteous by following the Law scrupulously?

He concludes that Christ would have died for nothing.

9. If righteousness could be obtained by following the Law, then who would be responsible for our righteousness?

If we could be righteous on our own, then salvation would by our own effort.

10. Do we receive the Holy Spirit by being good enough, or by faith?

We receive the Holy Spirit by faith, not because are good enough.

There is a story about a young woman who was brought up in the church. Her parents taught her to be good. She was polite. She always did what she was told. She dedicated her life to Jesus at a young age.

She grew up, graduated from college, got a job, and began living on her own. She wanted so much to live for God. She read her Bible and prayed every day. Her goal was to be the person God wanted her to be. However, there were things that continued to pop up in her life that did not glorify God. She wrestled with those things, and those things wrestled with her.

She wanted so much to be rid of those things once and for all. To remind herself, she cut some six-inch tall letters out of red construction paper and taped them to her mirror so she would see them first thing every morning. The letters said, "Let God."

She prayed diligently every night, but it seemed every morning those same things were waiting for her. "Maybe I'm not working hard enough at this," she reasoned. So she doubled her Bible reading and prayer time. Still, those things plagued her.

One night as she prayed she told God, "Lord, I am at the end of my rope. I think I've done everything I can. I don't know what to do anymore. I give up." The next morning she woke up and looked at her mirror as she always did. This morning things were different. The *d* had fallen off. Now, instead of the red letters reading, "Let God," the message read simply, "Let Go."

"Thank you, Lord," she whispered in prayer.

"Let go." Paul wrote, "I can do all things through Christ which strengtheneth me." He did not write, "Christ can do all things through me." If you find yourself this week trying to work things our by your own effort, it may be time for you to "Let go and let God."

The Purpose Of the Law

Galatians 3:19-29; 4:4-7

Wherefore then serveth the law? It was added because of transgressions, till the seed should come to whom the promise was made; and it was ordained by angels in the hand of a mediator.

20 Now a mediator is not a mediator of one, but God is one.

21 Is the law then against the promises of God? God forbid: for if there had been a law given which could have given life, verily righteousness should have been by the law.

22 But the scripture hath concluded all under sin, that the promise by faith of Jesus Christ might be given to them that believe.

23 But before faith came, we were kept under the law, shut up unto the faith which should afterwards be revealed.

24 Wherefore the law was our schoolmaster to bring us unto Christ, that we might be justified by faith.

25 But after that faith is come, we are no longer under a schoolmaster.

26 For ye are all the children of God by faith in Christ Jesus.

27 For as many of you as have been baptized into Christ have put on Christ.

28 There is neither Jew nor Greek, there is neither bond nor free, there is neither male nor female: for ye are all one in Christ Jesus.

29 And if ye be Christ's, then are ye Abraham's seed, and heirs according to the promise.

4:4 But when the fulness of the time was come, God sent forth his Son, made of a woman, made under the law,

5 To redeem them that were under the law, that we might receive the adoption of sons.

6 And because ye are sons, God hath sent forth the Spirit of his Son into your hearts, crying, Abba, Father.

7 Wherefore thou art no more a servant, but a son; and if a son, then an heir of God through Christ.

May 15

Memory Selection
Galatians 4:4-6
Background Scripture
Galatians 3:19–4:7
Devotional Reading
Romans 3:27-31

In this lesson, the apostle Paul explains in detail his insistence that we are justified by grace through faith, and not Law. He repeats his previous emphasis on the "faith" system, and also asks and answers the question: *If the Law doesn't save us, why did God give it to Moses?*

Many believers still struggle with the role of the Law, and of works.

When the realization that we are sinners strikes us, it is natural for us to want to *do* something about it. At first glance, the faith-grace system seems too easy, although it really is a life-long challenge. Some people seem to need the Law so they can "tick off" points of obedience and be reassured of their faithfulness. For all these reasons, and more, Paul's explanations here remain highly pertinent to our own life-situations.

Challenge your group to put themselves in the place of Jewish Christians whom Paul tells not to rely on the Law for salvation. Ask whether there are any advantages to the law-works system, over the grace-faith basis of salvation.

Paul will mention two good uses of the Law in this passage: (1) It was added to give people a foretaste of how to deal with sin (Gal. 3:19); and (2) just as clear rules are easier for children to follow than shapeless good will, the Law helped mature people for living under grace (3:24). The Law also acts as a moral compass to keep us "on track," and reassured that "we are on God' side."

Despite such positive aspects of salvation by Law, Paul opposes it as a basis for salvation, insisting on our maturing to the point where we follow Christ out of love, not law.

Teaching Outline	*Daily Bible Readings*
I. Highlighter of Sin—3:19-22 　A. Defining transgressions, 19 　B. One Law, One God, 20-22 II. Preparation for Grace—3:23-29 　A. Law as prep school, 23-24 　B. Graduation day!, 25 　C. One 'graduating class,' 26-29 III. Education for Adoption—4:4-7 　A. Redeemed slaves, 4-5 　B. Beloved children, 6-7	Mon.　God's Law Is Perfect 　　　*Psalm 19:7-14* Tue.　Understanding the Law 　　　*1 Timothy 1:3-11* Wed.　Jesus Fulfills the Law 　　　*Matthew 5:17-22* Thu.　Law Upheld by Faith 　　　*Romans 3:27-31* Fri.　Why the Law? 　　　*Galatians 3:19-23* Sat.　Our Disciplinarian 　　　*Galatians 3:24-29* Sun.　Heirs, No Longer Slaves 　　　*Galatians 4:1-7*

Verse by Verse

I. Highlighter of Sin—3:19-22

A. Defining transgressions, 19

19 Wherefore then serveth the law? It was added because of transgressions, till the seed should come to whom the promise was made; and it was ordained by angels in the hand of a mediator.

If, as Paul has been teaching, the Law cannot save us, of what use is it? The first answer Paul gives here is that the Law was added "because of" transgressions. This can hardly mean that Moses' Law was added to "fix" the problem of sin, since in both Romans and Galatians Paul argues over and over that in fact the Law could *not* fix the sin problem. The New English Bible's translation is therefore to be preferred: the law "was added to make wrongdoing a legal offence." This is in harmony with verse 22 (see below), and with other statements made by Paul: "By the law is the knowledge of sin" (Rom. 3:20), and "I had not known sin, but by the law" (Rom 7:7).

However this is to be understood, nothing could be clearer than that the Law was temporary, given "until the seed [Christ] would come." (In verse 16 Paul had emphasized that "seed" is singular in these quotations, referring to the Messiah.)

The last line in verse 19 appar-

ently reflects the belief among many Jews in Paul's day that angels had a prominent place in administering the Law of Moses. An angel whom the Israelites in the Wilderness were to obey had been announced in Exodus 23:20-21. Through the years, angels had become more prominent in Jewish tradition (so much so that Paul will have to warn against worshiping angels—see Col. 2:18).

B. One Law, One God, 20-22

20 Now a mediator is not a mediator of one, but God is one.

21 Is the law then against the promises of God? God forbid: for if there had been a law given which could have given life, verily righteousness should have been by the law.

22 But the scripture hath concluded all under sin, that the promise by faith of Jesus Christ might be given to them that believe.

Paul refers briefly to the fact that while viewing Moses as a "mediator" was in one sense true, since the Law came through Him on Sinai, he could not be considered *divine* because of the strict Jewish doctrine of monotheism. Paul probably wants, in this statement, to leave room for *Christ* as the divine Mediator who is really required, since He is at once God and man.

363

Paul's main point here, however, is to show that the fact that the Law can only show sin to be "exceeding sinful" (Rom. 7:13), rather than being able to provide salvation, does not go against God's promises. This is because He promised that a coming Messiah, not the Law, would be mankind's Savior. A system of rules cannot save us; it can only show how badly we *need* to be saved.

II. Preparation for Grace—3:23-29

A. Law as prep school, 23-24

23 But before faith came, we were kept under the law, shut up unto the faith which should afterwards be revealed.

24 Wherefore the law was our schoolmaster to bring us unto Christ, that we might be justified by faith.

Now Paul shows a second reason for the Law. Before giving that reason, he notes briefly that until Jesus came with salvation by grace, some might almost consider the Law as a "jailer" that actually *prevents* our receiving grace. Paul places a more positive face on the Law, by referring to it, in Greek, as a *paidagogos* (KJV "schoolmaster"). This word referred to a servant, often an educated Greek slave, in a well-to-do person's household, whose primary task was to escort the children of the household to and from school, and, once having brought them home, to continue their supervision and education in specific ways dictated by the master of the house.

The easiest way to translate this word is "pedagogue," which simply means "teacher" or "tutor" (ASV).To many English-speakers, however, "pedagog" is a somewhat "high-falutin'" word, so various translations struggle to give it the proper meaning—"strict governess," *J. B. Phillips;* "schoolmaster," KJV. Someone has even suggested "school bus," while the NIV tries to avoid the problem by omitting the title and describing the *function:* "the law was put in charge to lead us to Christ."

Paul's primary point is that this definition of the Law is *temporarily instructive.* It served a necessary purpose in the evolution of salvation history, but to try to preserve it after we have "graduated" to the next level of education is a failed attempt to cling to the past. After graduating to the "faith level" of high school, why would anyone want to go back to the "works curriculum" of grade school? After being freed from needing a tutor, why return to one?

B. Graduation day!, 25

25 But after that faith is come, we are no longer under a schoolmaster.

Paul says plainly that the work of the Law, the temporary "pedagogue" or tutor, has been completed. This does not mean that the eternal moral principles contained *in* the Law are to be abandoned (all the Ten Commandments except "Remember the Sabbath" are repeated as a part of the New Covenant). However, no one keeps the moral part of the Law perfectly, so even that element of the

Mosaic system lacks the saving power of forgiving grace and the cleansing blood of Jesus.

C. One 'graduating class,' 26-29

26 For ye are all the children of God by faith in Christ Jesus.

27 For as many of you as have been baptized into Christ have put on Christ.

28 There is neither Jew nor Greek, there is neither bond nor free, there is neither male nor female: for ye are all one in Christ Jesus.

29 And if ye be Christ's, then are ye Abraham's seed, and heirs according to the promise.

Bringing his various arguments to a beautiful conclusion, Paul beckons us to the ideal that baptism into Christ is the sign that all Christians, Jew and Gentile, have left behind the "primary" stages of their salvation-education. They have all "graduated" together *"by faith,"* putting behind not only the Jew-Gentile distinction but the master-slave and male-female "ordering" of society also. All the saved are on the same level: heirs of Abraham, partakers of God's promise to him (see, e.g., Gen. 12:2-3).

Unfortunately, in many circles it remains for this promise, so freely offered, to be fully accepted. Racial and gender discrimination continue to be stubbornly clung to as examples of the Fall, instead of arenas that exhibit Redemption.

III. Education for Adoption—4:4-7

A. Redeemed slaves, 4-5

4 But when the fulness of the time was come, God sent forth his Son, made of a woman, made under the law,

5 To redeem them that were under the law, that we might receive the adoption of sons.

The twofold nature of Christ, both human and divine, is underscored in verse 4. He is both the divine Son, and born of woman. His role was *not* to force the Law of Moses on Gentiles, but to *redeem* both Jew and Gentile. This part of Paul's teaching "concluding all under sin" so that He could save all, was particularly galling to Jews who considered their strict keeping of the rules to be salvation enough.

B. Beloved children, 6-7

6 And because ye are sons, God hath sent forth the Spirit of his Son into your hearts, crying, Abba, Father.

7 Wherefore thou art no more a servant, but a son; and if a son, then an heir of God through Christ.

Leaving his tone of rebuke, Paul presents the gospel as positively as possible, inviting both Jew and Gentile to accept the Spirit's gracious call to be adopted into God's family. Everyone can "graduate" from being a slave to being a *child,* and everyone who does so has the privilege of addressing the Father as "Daddy," which is an approximate equivalent of the Aramaic word "Abba." Becoming members of the family of grace also makes us co-heirs with Christ of the promises of God to Abraham.

Evangelistic Emphasis

Paul opens this passage with a question, "What is the purpose of the Law?" The Law was given for the purpose of transgressions. What he means is, where there is no law there is no sin. A person cannot be condemned for doing wrong if there is no standard to let that person know she/he is doing wrong. The function of the Law is to define sin.

While the Law can and does define sin, it cannot do anything about *curing* sin. The Law is like a doctor who is an expert diagnostician, but is a lousy practitioner who knows nothing about medication or surgery to clear up the problem he just diagnosed.

God did not leave us in that kind of predicament. The Law shows us where we are doing wrong. The Law diagnoses our sin. Jesus is the cure. Jesus gives us forgiveness of our sins. Jesus declares us not guilty. Jesus, by the power of His Holy Spirit, enables us to overcome sin in our lives. We are no longer prisoners to sin. We are free from the power of sin because of the power of the Spirit of Christ.

ഇൗരു

Memory Selection

But when the fulness of time was come, God sent forth his Son, made of a woman, made under the law, to redeem them that were under the law, that we might receive the adoption of sons. And because ye are sons, God hath sent forth the Spirit of his Son into your hearts, crying Abba, Father.—*(Galatians 4:4-6)*

Loving children act like loving children. It really does not matter whether that child was conceived and brought into the world by the people the child calls Mom and Dad or whether the child was adopted. Loving children act like loving children.

This applies to the spiritual realm as well. One might say that we are not really God's "blood kin." We were not conceived by the Holy Spirit and born of the virgin Mary. Yet those of us who have been born again are just as much God's children as Jesus Himself. We have been adopted into the family. Our heavenly Father loves us so much that He was willing to adopt us as His own. We love Him so much we call Him "Father."

Weekday Problems

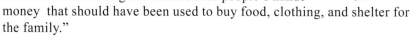

"Brother John, is it a sin to gamble?" Frank asked.

Brother John thought a minute. "Frank," he replied, "it is wrong to gamble. Gambling has led to many broken homes. Gambling has taken out of people's hands money that should have been used to buy food, clothing, and shelter for the family."

"Yeah, I know all that," Frank countered. "But is gambling a *sin*? Will a person go to hell for gambling? Where in the Bible does it say gambling is a sin?"

"Frank, I cannot quote chapter and verse that teach against gambling. But, listen—if you are asking that question, then you must not be sure it is something God would approve of. And if you are wondering if God approves, why would you want to do something God might not like?"

*If we are children of God, wouldn't we want to please God, rather than displease Him?

*Sin is anything that separates us from God. Is sin limited only to those things specifically listed by the Law? Explain your answer.

The Weigh of Life

Q: Why are fat men usually so good-natured?
A: Because it takes so long for them to get mad clear through.

* * * *

Putting on weight is the penalty for exceeding the feed limit.

* * * *

Q (at the health club): And what is your weight, madam?
A: I weigh a hundred-and-plenty.

* * * *

Enraged large woman, struck by car: You ran me down! Why couldn't you have swerved one way or the other?
Embarrassed motorist: Because I did not think I had enough gas.

* * * *

He's living 'way beyond his seams.

This Lesson in Your Life

I love the game of basketball. I love to play the game. I love to watch the game. When I was younger, I even loved to practice. I wonder how many hours of my life I have spent on the basketball court. I do not *have* to play. I *get* to play.

There is something about basketball that really gets to me, though. I do not like to play with someone who does not follow the rules. For instance, a guy dribbles the basketball then picks it up. He cannot shoot it. He cannot find anybody to whom to pass it, so he begins to dribble again.

"That's double dribbling! You can't do that!" I shout. "It's against the rules!"

"I don't play by the rules," my opponent shouts back as he makes a basket.

To tell the truth, I don't play with folks like that. I play with people who play by the rules. The rules are there not to punish the ignorant, but to make the game more enjoyable for those who love to play.

We have rules in life that we must follow. Some people think the rules don't apply to them. Some simply refuse to conduct their lives by the rules. Some are simply ignorant of the rules and do not care to learn. Some think the rules are too restrictive or are punitive. I disagree. The rules are there to make life more enjoyable for all, if everybody will follow the rules.

God is our heavenly Father. He has given us some rules to live by. He loves us; and He did not give us the rules to make puppets out of us. He gave us the rules to improve our lives.

That is not very different from loving earthly parents. We love our children beyond measure. Having rules for them to follow as they grow up doesn't mean that we love them less, but that we love them enough to require healthy behavior of them.

1. What was one purpose of the Law, according to Galatians 3:19?

The Law was given because of transgressions. That is, to instruct us between right and wrong in God's eyes. The purpose of the Law was to define sin.

2. Who was the seed to whom the promise was made?

The "seed" was Jesus Christ.

3. What is the function of a mediator?

A mediator is called in to help settle a disagreement or to help negotiate an agreement between at least two parties.

4. Can the Law make us righteous?

No, the Law can only show us that which makes us *un*righteous, and instruct us to avoid those things. The Law has no power to impart righteousness to us. If it did, righteousness would come by the Law.

5. According to verse 23, before faith came what was our predicament?

Before faith came, we were prisoners of sin, locked up by the Law until faith could be revealed.

6. Why was the Law put in charge before Jesus came to the earth?

The Law was put in charge to lead us to Christ. Without the Law we would not know that we need a Savior.

7. How do we become true children of God?

We become children of God through faith in Jesus Christ.

8. What metaphor does Paul use in verse 27 to describe what happens to the believer at baptism?

Paul describes baptism as a person clothing himself with Christ. As we are baptized, we "wrap ourselves up" in Jesus Christ.

9. How does Paul remind us that unity in Christ Jesus transcends ethnic, social, and gender distinctions?

Paul reminds us that in God's eyes there is neither Jew nor Greek, slave nor free, male nor female. When we are born again we all become one in God's family.

10. What does it mean to be a son or daughter of God?

By adoption, the justified believer becomes a son or daughter of God. We become heirs in God's family, with all the attendant rights and privileges that come with that.

One of the saddest stories in the Bible is contained in the story which we call the Prodigal Son. No, the sad part is not the young son leaving his loving father. It is not the grief the father must have felt over his younger son's rejection. I believe the saddest part of that story is the plight of the older son.

The younger son comes home after a period of wild living. The father decides to throw a party, a feast, celebrating the return of the son who was lost. The father goes to get the older son to come in.

Hear the words of Luke 16: 28-31 (NIV): *"The older brother became angry and refused to go in. So his father went out and pleaded with hm. But he answered his father, 'Look! All these years I've been slaving for you and never disobeyed your orders. Yet you never gave me even a young goat so I could celebrate with my friends. But when this son of yours who has squandered your property with prostitutes comes home, you kill the fattened calf for him!'*

"'My son,' the father said, 'you are always with me, and everything I have is yours.'"

Did you notice? The older brother viewed himself as a slave in his own father's house, when, in fact, everything the father had was already his.

Paul is reminding us in our passage today, that we are not slaves to our Father, God. Though sometimes God's rules may seem restrictive, the fact always remains that God makes available to His children all the riches, power, and strength which are at His disposal. Instead of being slaves, we are God's children! We now enjoy all the rights and privileges that go along with being children of the King. Because we are God's children, we are also His heirs. To quote the father in the Prodigal Son story, "You are always with me, and everything I have is yours." Thank you, God.

Lesson 12
Christian Freedom

Galatians 5:1-15

Stand fast therefore in the liberty wherewith Christ hath made us free, and be not entangled again with the yoke of bondage.

2 Behold, I Paul say unto you, that if ye be circumcised, Christ shall profit you nothing.

3 For I testify again to every man that is circumcised, that he is a debtor to do the whole law.

4 Christ is become of no effect unto you, whosoever of you are justified by the law; ye are fallen from grace.

5 For we through the Spirit wait for the hope of righteousness by faith.

6 For in Jesus Christ neither circumcision availeth anything, nor uncircumcision; but faith which worketh by love.

7 Ye did run well; who did hinder you that ye should not obey the truth?

8 This persuasion cometh not of him that calleth you.

9 A little leaven leaveneth the whole lump.

10 I have confidence in you through the Lord, that ye will be none otherwise minded: but he that troubleth you shall bear his judgment, whosoever he be.

11 And I, brethren, if I yet preach circumcision, why do I yet suffer persecution? then is the offence of the cross ceased.

12 I would they were even cut off which trouble you.

13 For, brethren, ye have been called unto liberty; only use not liberty for an occasion to the flesh, but by love serve one another.

14 For all the law is fulfilled in one word, even in this; Thou shalt love thy neighbour as thyself.

15 But if ye bite and devour one another, take heed that ye be not consumed one of another.

May 22

Memory Selection
Galatians 5:13

Background Scripture
Galatians 5:1-15

Devotional Reading
1 Peter 2:11-17

The apostle Paul has delved deep into his training as a Pharisee and student of the Old Covenant Scriptures to affirm the doctrine of salvation by grace through faith, not through the works of the Law. Now he approaches this issue, which has caused particular contention among the churches of Galatia, from a more practical standpoint.

His focus here shows his concern not only that the Galatians affirm their freedom from the Law, but that they use that freedom in a positive way. He did not want his teaching to be interpreted as "antinomianism," or being against all rules. He wanted people not only to "talk the talk" about salvation by grace, but to "walk the walk" which that message made possible. It would only harm the cause for those freed from the Law then to come under the bondage of the flesh.

ഇൗരു

Remind group members of the one most commonly known identifying mark of "Jewishness" in the ancient world: *circumcision.* This was so prominent a distinction that Jews as a body were often referred to as "the circumcision" (Rom. 4:9).

Then ask the group how they would hope *they* would be recognized, as a faithful church. Ask them to suggest brief, pithy "mission statements," perhaps drawing from statements on your church bulletin or other material. Point out that in a fast-paced world many people will have only one "glimpse" of the church. What do we want that glimpse to tell them about who we are? Note that after making tentative suggestions as to a church "motto," they may want to remain open to one that Paul suggests in Gal. 3:13b— *"By love serve one another".*

Teaching Outline	Daily Bible Readings	
I. Stand Fast in Freedom!—1	Mon.	Truth Will Make You Free *John 8:31-38*
II. Circumcision as a Sign—2-6	Tue.	Live as Free People *1 Peter 2:11-17*
A. Slippery slope, 2-3		
B. Ineffective mark, 4-6	Wed.	Free in Christ *1 Corinthians 7:17-24*
III. Hoping Against Hope—7-12	Thu.	Out of Bondage *Hebrews 2:14-18*
A. Warning: false leaven, 7-9		
B. Warning: false teachers, 10-12	Fri.	Christ Has Set Us Free *Galatians 5:1-5*
IV. Responsibility of Freedom—13-15	Sat.	Faith Works through love *Galatians 5:6-10*
A. Liberty vs. the flesh, 13		
B. Summary of the system, 14-15	Sun.	Love Neighbor as Self *Galatians 5:11-15*

Verse by Verse

I. Stand Fast in Freedom!—1

1 Stand fast therefore in the liberty wherewith Christ hath made us free, and be not entangled again with the yoke of bondage.

Paul has just argued, from the story of Isaac, son of promise, and Ishamael, son of Hagar by "natural" law, that "promise" trumps "law" for those who claim to be true heirs of the Abrahamic promise. Now he draws the conclusion that those who choose to be saved by faith, or children of promise, are liberated from the limitation of mere natural law, as well as from the Law of Moses; and that they should stand fast in that freedom instead of submitting to attempts by Judaizing teachers to impose the Law on them.

II. Circumcision as a Sign—2-6

A. Slippery slope, 2-3

2 Behold, I Paul say unto you, that if ye be circumcised, Christ shall profit you nothing.

3 For I testify again to every man that is circumcised, that he is a debtor to do the whole law.

The apostle is not saying here that every male child who is circumcised for health reasons loses the promise of salvation through Christ. He *is* warning against circumcision being performed as a *religious* ritual that

supposedly marked a person as a part of God's family. The pro-circumcision argument was at first strong in the early Church not only because of Judaizing teachers but because Jesus Himself had been circumcised (Luke 2:21), since He was born "under the law" (Gal. 4:4). Of course this argument could not rightly be used to support Gentile circumcision.

Yet circumcision was so central for distinguishing Jews as "the people of God" that it stood for the willingness to submit to the entire Law of Moses. Because of this "slippery slope" principle, Paul strongly warns that being circumcised for religious reasons would make believers indebted to keep the whole Law, and forfeit their freedom in Christ.

B. Ineffective mark, 4-6

4 Christ is become of no effect unto you, whosoever of you are justified by the law; ye are fallen from grace.

5 For we through the Spirit wait for the hope of righteousness by faith.

6 For in Jesus Christ neither circumcision availeth anything, nor uncircumcision; but faith which worketh by love.

If circumcision were to open the

door to the whole system of (supposed) salvation by the Law of Moses, then it would be a clear repudiation of salvation by grace. It is partly due to his stand against the Law-element, which won over almost all of the early churches, that the subsequent history of Jews and Christians divided so sharply.

Verse 5 shows another of the appeals of circumcision: to the legalistic mind it was a definite mark that clearly designated a person as already belonging to the saved. On the other hand, the grace-faith system was based on *trust* that when Christ returns He will take the saved with Him to heaven. A Judaizing teacher could be expected to make the most of what he would call the "uncertainty" of salvation for anyone without the visible mark of circumcision. The fact is, the grace of God accepted by faith, is a much surer place to stand, because it depends on *Christ's* righteousness, rather than on unsuccessful attempts to keep the Law.

Verse 6 seems to be a softening of Paul's dogmatic statement in verse 4 that being ritually circumcised separates the believer from Christ. Perhaps he wants to make this more neutral statement to show just how irrelevant such rituals or "works" are. Just as he forbids the Jewish Christian to boast in his circumcision, neither does he want the Church to be further divided by Gentiles boasting that they had *not* been circumcised. The real "mark" of the true believer is *faith that works by love.*

III. Hoping Against Hope—7-12
A. Warning: false leaven, 7-9

7 Ye did run well; who did hinder you that ye should not obey the truth?

8 This persuasion cometh not of him that calleth you.

9 A little leaven leaveneth the whole lump.

The Galatian Christians had "run well" because their first exposure to the gospel was not contaminated with the later efforts of Judaizing teachers to impose the Law of Moses on them. It is not that they should not "obey" anything, but that they should obey the original call to truth and freedom in Christ which Paul and others had extended to them. The question "Who did hinder you?" may mean that Paul actually did not know the names of those who followed him with a message of works-salvation (as is indicated in verse 10, below), or it may simply be a rhetorical question, with the answer being "Judaizing teachers." The one thing that Paul does know is that works-salvation was not the message of Christ, who is ultimately the One who calls us to salvation.

Like the "slippery slope" argument in verse 3, Paul warns in verse 9 that to submit to "a little" Law is to take a short step on the long journey toward bondage, and the impossible burden of the entire Law. (Compare Jesus' use of the "bad leaven" metaphor in Matthew 16:6, 11-12.)

B. Warning: false teachers, 10-12

10 I have confidence in you

through the Lord, that ye will be none otherwise minded: but he that troubleth you shall bear his judgment, whosoever he be.

11 And I, brethren, if I yet preach circumcision, why do I yet suffer persecution? then is the offence of the cross ceased.

For all of Paul's stern and vigorous warning, he now expresses confidence that the Galatian Christians will make the decision for salvation by grace. If this occurs, then the judgment or condemnation that might have fallen on them for rejecting Christ's pure grace would fall on the false teacher(s) among them instead.

Verse 11 sounds as though some of Paul's critics claimed that he inconsistently preached circumcision when it seemed convenient. If so, they must have misconstrued such events as when Paul had Timothy circumcised because his mother was a Jew (Acts 16:1-3).

12 I would they were even cut off which trouble you.

Paul is so exasperated by the inroads of the pro-circumcision party among the Galatians that he makes the earthy exclamation that he wishes they would "circumcise" themselves off from the rest of the Body of Christ so they would no longer trouble it.

IV. Responsibility of Freedom— 13-15

A. Liberty vs. the flesh, 13

13 For, brethren, ye have been called unto liberty; only use not liberty for an occasion to the flesh, but by love serve one another.

Paul has warned those who have been approached by "Judaizing teachers" that they are freed from the law of circumcision. Now he asserts that this does not mean that they are free from all moral obligations. There is an unfortunate tendency for people whose heart longs to be disobedient anyway to take liberty to mean license. Such people might take Paul's ruling against requiring the law of circumcision to mean he is against all rules, and is teaching that freedom in Christ means that they need not be subject to any laws at all. Actually, they are free to live under the "law" of service.

B. Summary of the system, 14-15

14 For all the law is fulfilled in one word, even in this; Thou shalt love thy neighbour as thyself.

15 But if ye bite and devour one another, take heed that ye be not consumed one of another.

Finally, Paul hopes to put the issue of circumcision to rest by quoting from the Law itself: "Thou shalt love they neighbor as thyself" was even cited from Leviticus 19:18 by Jesus, when He summarized the Law (Matt. 19:19). This "core value," however, could not be kept as long as such arguments as those pressed on them by Judaizing teachers continued to divide the Church. How ironic it would be if the pressure to conform to circumcision as a sign for God's true followers would result in their disintegration.

Evangelistic Emphasis

Many people these days see the Christian faith as extremely harsh. The image they have is the one the media has developed for them. Christianity is portrayed as a list of rigid rules that lead to narrow mindedness and a lifestyle that is out of touch with the rest of society. In reality, nothing could be farther from the truth. Of course, Christianity teaches certain moral and ethical standards, and they are certainly higher standards than those of the world. However, the list of rules and commandments is not nearly as long as folk make it out to be. In fact, the list seems long because we continue to discover ways to go against God's Law. If we practiced only one rule, Paul says, and worked that out to its fullest, we would have enough rules.

The rule? "Love your neighbor as yourself." If every person would put the other person's well-being above her or his own well-being, life on this earth would improve dramatically. If each of us would consider the other person rather than looking out for ourselves first and foremost, life would be better for us all. Isn't today a good day to love our neighbors as ourselves?

ৰূওজ

Memory Selection

For, brethren, ye have been called unto liberty; only use not liberty for any occasion to the flesh, but by love serve one another.—*Galatians 5:13*

I have heard the old saying, "One man's freedom stops where another man's freedom begins." That statement rings true. If my idea of a relaxing evening is to play my electric guitar as loud as the amplifier can be turned up, and my wife's idea of a relaxing evening is reading a good book in undisturbed quietness, then, obviously, we cannot both enjoy a relaxing evening in the same room at the same time. We are not completely free to do what we want. We must always consider the other person.

In the same sense, although we are free in Christ Jesus, we must not use that freedom to do anything we may want. Sometimes, what the sin nature within us wants is diametrically opposed to what God wants for us. We are free, but we must consider first what God wants us to do and be.

Weekday Problems

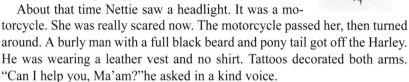

Nettie did not know what to do. The engine of her car had quit. She could not get it started again. She was on an out-of-the-way country road where her cell phone would not work. It was getting dark. She was scared.

About that time Nettie saw a headlight. It was a motorcycle. She was really scared now. The motorcycle passed her, then turned around. A burly man with a full black beard and pony tail got off the Harley. He was wearing a leather vest and no shirt. Tattoos decorated both arms. "Can I help you, Ma'am?" he asked in a kind voice.

Nettie reluctantly said, "Yes, please help me get my car started." He worked for a moment and got the car going.

"Praise the Lord," he said, "that was easy."

"Are you a Christian?" Nettie asked.

"Yes, ma'am," he answered. "I minister to bikers all over the state. God has given me great success in leading many to Christ."

*Would it be better for the man to wear a suit and tie to minister? Explain your answer.

*Does one need to look a certain way to be a Christian? Explain.

The Lack-Luster Side of Law

The infallible way of inducing a sense of wrong-doing is by making laws.—*William Bolitho*

* * * *

The Jews ruin themselves at their Passover; the Moors at their marriages; and the Christians in their lawsuits.—*Spanish proverb*

* * * *

These written laws are just like spiders' webs; the small and feeble may be caught and entangled in them, but the rich and mighty force through and despise them.—*Anacharsis*

* * * *

To go to law is for two persons to kindle a fire at their own cost, to warm others and singe themselves to cinders; and because they cannot agree as to what is truth and equity, they will both agree to unplume themselves that others may be decorated with their feathers.—*Owen Feltham*

This Lesson in Your Life

Going to church does not make you a Christian any more than watching a football game on television makes you a pro football player. I know that is a harsh statement to make, but I believe it to be true. Of course, folks ought to go to church. They should listen to the pastor. Folks ought to pray, and to read their Bibles. Still, those things, in and of themselves, do not a Christian make.

It is a pity that some folks have hinged eternity on such a misconception. There are those who believe that if they go to church every Sunday morning and evening and attend every mid-week service they will be okay with the Lord. There are those who are convinced that if they say the Lord's Prayer so many times it will erase sin. Others are convinced that if they put enough time in serving at the church's soup kitchen they are automatically Christians. Some believe that if they send an e-mailed prayer to enough people it will prove their love for Jesus Christ.

I hope you are not one of those people. If we read Galatians carefully, we will discover that religious rituals and other external signs do not grant us entry into the Christian faith. Those things do not earn our entry into the Kingdom of God. Outer rituals, such as circumcision, have no particular benefit for disciples of Jesus Christ. We cannot do enough to obligate God to accept us. What makes the difference is faith working through love.

When we love Jesus we will go to church to worship. When we love Christ we will serve Him by serving others. When we love Him we will want to pray and read our Bibles.

Yet even when we do our "duty" we do not obligate God to love us. He loves us already. He has made a way for us already by grace through faith.

We can do what we want to do while we love God with all our hearts. However, the longer we love and serve God, the more we discover that what we want to do becomes what He wants us to do.

1. When Paul speaks of the "yoke of bondage" in verse 1, to what is he referring?

The yoke of bondage refers to strict adherence to the Law. Christians are no longer under the Law but under grace.

2. What was the evidence to which Paul refers that shows the Galatians were trying to turn away from grace and back to adherence to the Law?

The act of circumcision, which was required under the Law of Moses.

3. According to verse 4, why was circumcision such a big deal in a negative way?

Because if a man felt the need to be circumcised to be saved (justified) then he must feel that the grace of God through Jesus and the Holy Spirit were not sufficient.

4. Does our righteousness come from what we do? Can we work our way into righteousness?

No. Verse 5 tells us that by faith we eagerly wait for righteousness, which comes through the Holy Spirit.

5. Must modern Christian males avoid circumcision to demonstrate their reliance on the grace of God?

No. Paul reminds us that neither circumcision nor uncircumcision matters when one is in Christ Jesus.

6. What counts the most in the Christian walk, according to verse 6?

What counts most is faith expressing itself through love.

7. In verse 9, what does Paul mean when he says, "A little leaven leaveneth the whole lump?"

He is reminding the Galatians that it does not take long for sin or false teaching to work its way throughout the whole Christian community.

8. In Christ we are free from strict adherence to the Law. What warning does Paul give us concerning that freedom?

We are not to use our freedom to indulge in the sinful nature, or the flesh.

9. Paul says the entire law of relationships is wrapped up in one command. What is that command?

Love your neighbor as yourself.

10. What will happen in a church where the members are constantly back-biting?

Paul says if that continues, the church will be destroyed. It would be consumed, eaten up by one another.

The Galatians were turning back to works of the Law. They were turning away from grace. They began to think that their salvation depended somehow on human achievement. They had been convinced that the grace of God working through Jesus Christ was not enough. They must have reasoned that God's grace needed something added to it to be effective. It does not work that way.

The person who accepts the way of grace simply throws himself and his sin upon the mercy of God. There is no penance one could do to make up for sin. There is no ritual that will take away sin. The only way sin is removed is by our confession, our repentance, and the washing of forgiveness that comes from the blood of Jesus Christ shed on Calvary's cross. We do not need to do anything extra. Jesus did it all. We must simply accept God's grace.

It is the grace of God, not the works of the Law, that brings salvation. Yet, good works follow, or are the result of, salvation. We are free, yes. We are free from the law of sin and death. However, we are now bound in another sense. We are bound by our love to serve one another.

A young man in our community came to saving faith a year ago. This young man was a hard-living fellow. He was fond of alcohol and drugs. His marriage had fallen apart. Suffice it to say that he was far from the Lord. Basically, he was doing whatever he wanted to do when he wanted to do it.

Since he came to Christ he has been telling everybody who will listen (and some who will not listen) about Jesus. He has gone to our state prison to witness. He goes to a different church just about every weekend to tell folks about Jesus. His heart has turned from selfish to selfless. Once he was bound by sin. Now he is bound by love to love others as much as he once loved himself.

Living Our Covenant with One Another

Galatians 5:22–6:10

ut the fruit of the Spirit is love, joy, peace, long-suffering, gentleness, goodness, faith,

23 Meekness, temperance: against such there is no law.

24 And they that are Christ's have crucified the flesh with the affections and lusts.

25 If we live in the Spirit, let us also walk in the Spirit.

26 Let us not be desirous of vain glory, provoking one another, envying one another.

6:1 Brethren, if a man be overtaken in a fault, ye which are spiritual, restore such an one in the spirit of meekness; considering thyself, lest thou also be tempted.

2 Bear ye one another's burdens, and so fulfil the law of Christ.

3 For if a man think himself to be something, when he is nothing, he deceiveth himself.

4 But let every man prove his own work, and then shall he have rejoicing in himself alone, and not in another.

5 For every man shall bear his own burden.

6 Let him that is taught in the word communicate unto him that teacheth in all good things.

7 Be not deceived; God is not mocked: for whatsoever a man soweth, that shall he also reap.

8 For he that soweth to his flesh shall of the flesh reap corruption; but he that soweth to the Spirit shall of the Spirit reap life everlasting.

9 And let us not be weary in well doing: for in due season we shall reap, if we faint not.

10 As we have therefore opportunity, let us do good unto all men, especially unto them who are of the household of faith.

Memory Selection
Galatians 6:2
Background Scripture
Galatians 5:22–6:10
Devotional Readings
1 John 3:14-23

May 29

Paul has now completed his often complicated arguments in support of salvation by grace through faith, as opposed to salvation by Law. That is the *"What"* of most of the letter to the Galatians. Now comes the *"So what?"* As he did in Romans, Paul deals first with theology, then with ethics. He wants us to walk the walk for the right reasons.

The focus on this section is doing the right deeds *because* of what God did for us through Jesus Christ, not *in order to earn* the gift of salvation. Chapter 5 consists of the "fruit of the Spirit," which are listed in contrast to the "works of the flesh" in verses 16-21. The emphasis here is on living out the New Covenant in morality and love.

ෆ෮ය

This lesson can be effectively introduced by connecting the "fruit of the Spirit" in Galatians 5:22-23 with the "works of the flesh" in verses 19-21. Ask group members to compare and contrast these two famous lists as you write them on a writing board. Head the two lists like this:

Works of the Flesh	**Fruit of the Spirit**
(Gal. 5:19-21)	*(Gal. 5:22-23*

Note this paradox: Paul expects those who are saved by grace to avoid, and to do, the same works as those that "Judaizing teachers" require of their followers who think they can be saved by works. Explain that the difference is in motives: People saved by grace do good works *because* they have been saved, while the works-law group do them *in order* to be saved. Ask whether this difference is worth emphasizing, or if the *reason* for good works is irrelevant as long as they are performed.

Teaching Outline	**Daily Bible Readings**
I. Fruit of the Spirit—5:22-26	Mon. A Tree and Its Fruit *Matthew 7:15-20*
A. Specific fruits, 22-23	Tue. Christ Is Among Us *Matthew 18:15-20*
B. Walking in the Spirit, 24-26	Wed. Be Rich in Good Works *1 Timothy 6:11-19*
II. Covenant of the Spirit—6:1-10	Thu. Love One Another *1 John 3:18-24*
A. Concern for others, 1-2	Fri. The Fruit of the Spirit *Galatians 5:22-26*
B. Concern for self, 3-5	Sat. Bear One Another's Burdens *Galatians 6:1-5*
C. Sowing and reaping, 6-9	Sun. Work for the Good of All *Galatians 6:6-10*
D. Opportunities to do good, 10	

Verse by Verse

I. Fruit of the Spirit—5:22-26
A. Specific fruits, 22-23

22 But the fruit of the Spirit is love, joy, peace, longsuffering, gentleness, goodness, faith,

23 Meekness, temperance: against such there is no law.

Both the works of the flesh (vss. 19-21) and the fruit of the Spirit, here, grow out of Paul's previous teaching that we are saved by grace, not Law. He continues to be concerned that his emphasis on grace not be misinterpreted as meaning that believers can be careless about good works. If they engage in the "works of the flesh" they are as guilty as those who try to earn their salvation by good works. If they are saved by the Spirit, rather than Law, it would be unthinkable for them not to allow the fruit of the Spirit to bloom.

Love here is *agape,* the willing of the best for others, regardless of sentiment or our personal stake in what they do.

Joy indicates that believers are not to become so embroiled in the faith-works controversy, or any other, that they forget to be happy.

Peace is to be sought at all cost except compromising the basics of the gospel, which are headed by salvation by grace.

Longsuffering means "patience" (as in the NIV).

Gentleness, which comes from a word for "usefulness," refers to usefulness in the manner in which we treat others, giving the term a practical edge.

Goodness is an all-encompassing term for right living.

Faith (NIV "faithfulness") refers to "putting shoe-leather" to belief.

Meekness (NIV "gentleness") implies humility in dealing with others, rather than insisting on one's own way.

Temperance means "self-control" (as in the NIV).

Paul can say that "there is no law" against these fruits of the Spirit because they are traits that should not have to be commanded of those who are saved by grace. Instead, they should flow *out* of a person's heart and life with the same graciousness as that in which God, through His Spirit, allowed them to flow *in.*

B. Walking in the Spirit, 24-26

24 And they that are Christ's have crucified the flesh with the affections and lusts.

25 If we live in the Spirit, let us also walk in the Spirit.

26 Let us not be desirous of vain glory, provoking one another, envying one another.

The basic reason why the "works of the flesh" of verses 19-21 should not have to be forbidden by the Law to those who have been saved by grace is that the "old man" that would have lusted after the flesh has been "slain"—nailed to the Cross. The whole attitude or spirit has been changed to the degree that the saved allow the *Holy* Spirit to raise the "new man" out of the watery grave of baptism to walk in newness of life (Rom. 6:3-4). This is what prompts Paul to refer to the Spirit in verse 25.

It is important to note just what kind of sins are included in those works of "the flesh" that have hopefully been cancelled by the work of the Spirit. Usually the term "flesh" is taken to refer to sexual sins. Although they are included in the term, verse 26 also includes "vainglory" (or conceit) and envy in the category of "the flesh." This also suggests why the flesh and *law* are so often seen in the same context. Those who assume that rule-keeping is the basis of salvation inevitably begin to compete with each other and are critical of those who keep fewer laws. In Paul's lexicon, this is just as "fleshly" as adultery or fornication. (Note that "envying" is one of the works of the flesh—vs. 21.)

II. Covenant of the Spirit—6:1-10
A. Concern for others, 1-2

1 Brethren, if a man be overtaken in a fault, ye which are spiritual, restore such an one in the spirit of meekness; considering thyself, lest thou also be tempted.

2 Bear ye one another's burdens, and so fulfil the law of Christ.

One of the risks of Paul's break with the Mosaic Law, which he considered to be a Covenant of Works, is that believers might lose the sense of *peoplehood* that bound the Jews together as one nation, despite factions within the whole. In this passage, the apostle urges a level of concern for brothers and sisters of the New Covenant that would keep them bound even more closely together.

The first "mark" of this New Covenant togetherness is the practice of *mutual accountability.* A believer who is failing to walk in the Spirit is to be spoken to with respect, and restored to the faith instead of being summarily shunned. This is to be done with the "meekness" that was listed as a fruit of the Spirit (5:23), with the one speaking to a back-sliding brother or sister remembering that he is also subject to weaknesses.

Verse 2 will be deliberately posed as a paradox in an opposite-but-equal balance with verse 5. Unlike much of our own society, when members of the same fellowship often don't want to know details about each other's lives, we are to bear each other's burdens—apparently, in this context, supporting them in their struggle against temptation. Yet believers must admit that in the past, peering into each other's lives was often done judgmentally. This was illustrated vividly by Nathaniel Hawthorne's classic story, *The Scarlet Letter.* A woman who was an adulteress was merely shunned by a self-righteous majority, who should have tried to help her bear her burden.

B. Concern for self, 3-5

3 For if a man think himself to be something, when he is nothing, he deceiveth himself.

4 But let every man prove his own work, and then shall he have rejoicing in himself alone, and not in another.

5 For every man shall bear his own burden.

Concern for others must be balanced by concern for self to avoid the hypocrisy of "helping" a brother or sister overcome a sin, when we ourselves are guilty of the same sin or others just as bad. It is self-deceptive for us to appoint ourself as the caretaker of others' souls without confessing that we are also in need of care, and of forgiveness. Only when we "prove our own work" (NIV "test [our] own actions") by self-examination, confession, and repentance, are we qualified to help others face their own shortcomings. This is what leads to the paradox between verses 2 and 5. Only the one who has confessed his own sin and delivered it to Jesus can help others bear their burdens and shortcomings.

C. Sowing and reaping, 6-9

6 Let him that is taught in the word communicate unto him that teacheth in all good things.

7 Be not deceived; God is not mocked: for whatsoever a man soweth, that shall he also reap.

8 For he that soweth to his flesh shall of the flesh reap corruption; but he that soweth to the Spirit shall of the Spirit reap life everlasting.

9 And let us not be weary in well doing: for in due season we shall reap, if we faint not.

A part of living under the New Covenant is providing God's people with sound teaching and encouragement. The term for "communicate" also means to "have fellowship." It is sometimes used in the sense of financial support, as when Paul thanked the Philippians for their "fellowship in the gospel" (Philip. 1:5). Here, then, Paul speaks of helping to support a teacher or preacher as a part both of sowing good seeds as deeds, and in building up the community of faith.

Paul adds that such good works as supporting faithful teachers will be rewarded by a good "harvest,"just as sowing evil deeds will result in destruction. Grace can cancel this "law of the harvest" when we seek it penitently, but stubborn, willful sin assures a harvest of destruction.

D. Opportunities to do good, 10

10 As we have therefore opportunity, let us do good unto all men, especially unto them who are of the household of faith.

In a summary statement, the apostle holds up the goal of constantly seeking opportunities for good deeds as proof of faith. Our first obligation here is to fellow-Christians, although many other examples show that the early Christians engaged in helping anyone in need. This, too, is a "fruit of the Spirit."

Evangelistic Emphasis

It has been said that the army of the Lord, the Church, is the only army that shoots its wounded. While we may smile at that pithy saying, it points to a grave mistake. Paul encourages us to restore the one who is caught in sin. There is none among us who has not sinned. I suspect that there are few among the Christian faith who are not still dealing in some fashion with sin or a sin in their lives. Most of us commit sin. Most of us know how to keep that sin hidden.

I pray that when a person in your church and my church stumbles and falls, we are there to help that person back to her or his feet. I pray that we do everything we can to encourage that person to try again to walk in God's way.

We must not ignore those who stumble, for when we pretend it did not happen we are hindering the opportunity for repentance and forgiveness. We pick up the one who has fallen, dust him off, accept his repentance as genuine, and walk with him again along the way. That's what the church does. It's a hospital to heal the sin-sick soul.

Memory Selection

Bear ye one another's burdens, and so fulfill the law of Christ.— Galatians 6:2

Paul has been writing in the whole Galatian letter that we must not depend upon the works of the Law. He has told us that following the Law will not lead us to righteousness. He has told us that God's grace is enough. Grace is strong where the Law is weak.

Now, Paul is telling us to fulfill the Law—not the Law of Moses but the Law of Christ. The Law of Christ to which he refers is the law of love. Jesus said in John 13:34, "A new commandment I give unto you, That ye love one another; as I have loved you, that ye also love one another." We still "go by the law," if we mean the law of Christ.

The British singing group, "The Hollies," put out a song years ago with the title, "He Ain't Heavy. He's My Brother." I do not know if any in the group had ever read the Scriptures, but somebody wrote a very scriptural song. We bear one another's burdens, and in doing so we fulfill the law of Christ. We are compelled not by threat of punishment, but by love.

Weekday Problems

Marcus was reading his Bible when he came to the passage on "the fruit of the Spirit." He read about love, joy, peace, patience . . . ."

"Hmm. *Patience*," Marcus chuckled, as he thought. "Patience is something I need more of. I don't think even God could be patient with some of the people I work with. Ralph just makes the same mistakes over and over again. I tell him and I tell him and it just seems to do no good. And Susan! She just seems to move from crisis to crisis. She hasn't caught on yet that she brings those crises upon herself. And she goes to my Sunday School class! I have to listen to it on Sunday, too!

"And oh my! There's Brad—he's the worst. He is always coming to me with stupid questions. I know he is doing that just to see how much time he can waste to keep from working."

Marcus could feel his stress level rising. He read again, *Love, joy, peace, patience.* "Lord," Marcus prayed, "I understand what you are trying to tell me. Please be patient with me."

*Do you deal with problem people who require extra patience? Explain.

*The fruit of the Spirit should be evident in every Christian's life. Take time to memorize the list, praying that the fruit of the Spirit will be seen in you.

~~Martial~~ Marital Arts

Ah, the month of June is approaching . . . when thousands of men will take some young woman as their awful wedded wife.

* * * *

Ike: I'm a man of few words.
Mike: I'm married, too.

* * * *

Infuriated by her husband's laziness, his wife was on a tirade. "When he dies, I won't bury him, I'll have him cremated," she raved. "Then I'll put his ashes in an hour-glass. He never did a lick of work while he was alive, but I'll have him working for me keeping time after he's gone."

* * * *

Jack: Why are you cutting out that newspaper article?
Mack: It's about a man who shot his wife for going through his pockets, and I'm going to stick this article in my pocket.

This Lesson in Your Life

In John's Gospel, chapter 15, Jesus is discussing the relationship among the Father, Christians, and Jesus Himself. Jesus says that He is the vine, God the Father is the vine dresser, and we are the branches of the vine. Jesus also warns that the vine dresser "cuts off every branch in me that bears no fruit, while every branch that does bear fruit he prunes so that it will be even more fruitful. This is to my Father's glory, that you bear much fruit, showing yourselves to be my disciples (John 15:2, 8, NIV)."

We know these statements are true, because Jesus Himself said them. Therefore, it would be prudent for us Christians to be fruit bearers. We bear fruit so that we will not be cut off from the vine. We bear fruit to bring glory to God while showing ourselves to be disciples.

What is fruit? First, we know that plants produce fruit after their own kind. Apple trees produce apples. Blackberry bushes produce blackberries. Thus, we could reason that Christian disciples should produce more disciples of Jesus. So we must. That is fruit bearing. Did not Jesus tell us in the verse we call the Great Commission to "Go therefore and make disciples of all nations, baptizing them in the name of the Father and of the Son and of the Holy Spirit"? (Matt. 28:19, NRSV). We must bear fruit—that is, make other disciples—or we are in jeopardy of being cut off from the vine.

There is another type of fruit the Christian must bear as well. We must the fruit of the Spirit. We must display in our lives the character of Christ. When we are born again, the Spirit is born within us. As we mature as Christians the fruit of the Spirit becomes more and more evident. We begin to act more nearly like Jesus. The fruit is "love, joy, peace, longsuffering (or patience), gentleness, goodness, faith (or faithfulness), meekness , temperance (or self-control)." If this fruit does not grow in our lives, if the character of Jesus is not evident in our lives, we are also in jeopardy of being cut off from the vine.

We must do everything in our power to let the fruit of new disciples and the fruit of the Holy Spirit grow in our lives. We do not want to be cut off from the vine!

STRAIGHT

1. List the fruit of the Spirit in Galatians 5:22-23.

According to the KJV they are love, joy, peace, longsuffering, gentleness, goodness, faith, meekness, and temperance. The NIV lists them as love, joy, peace, patience, kindness, goodness, faithfulness, gentleness, and self-control.

2. According to Galatians 5:24, what must happen to the sinful nature in those who belong to Christ?

The sinful nature (the flesh) must be crucified along with its passions and desires.

3. The Christian must be born again of the Spirit. However, what does Paul say is needed next (5:25)?

Those who are born of the Spirit must live by the Spirit and be guided by the Spirit.

4. What should Christians do when they see a fellow-believer living in sin?

Those who are spiritual should restore gently the one who has fallen.

5. Galatians 6:2 tells us one way to fulfill the law of Christ. What is it?

We fulfill the law of Christ when we bear one another's burdens.

6. What does Paul tell us in 6:3 about spiritual pride?

If anyone thinks he is something when he is nothing, he only deceives himself. A sense of self-importance would make it difficult for such a person to bear another's burdens.

7. Does bearing another's burdens mean that we are always to let others carry the load for us?

No. We are to carry our own load when we are able. Every person has a task in the Body of Christ. Each must function in her or his own role.

8. Paul explains the spiritual law of sowing and reaping in Galatians 6:7-8. What is that spiritual law?

We cannot mock God. The one who sows to please his sinful nature shall reap destruction from that nature. The one who sows to please the Spirit shall from the Spirit reap eternal life.

9. We must not give up on the Christian walk nor in Christian service, no matter how hard it gets. Why?

We must not get tired and quit doing good, for at the proper time we will reap a harvest if we do not give up.

10. How often are we to work for the good of all humanity?

Whenever we have an opportunity, we are to do good to all people, especially to those who belong to the family of believers.

Football season has just begun as I am writing this. If you think about it, the team sport of football and life as a Christian in community have a lot in common.

In football, no one player can win a game by himself. The players must work as a team. If one player falls, other players must take up the slack or the whole team suffers. In the Christian faith, if one person falls into sin, the whole church suffers until that one has been restored into the fellowship with repentance and forgiveness.

In football, if one player thinks he can do everything by himself, he is soon brought to his senses. I remember one time when the quarterback on our team thought he was the greatest player since Bart Starr. We decided to let some of those big defensive linemen through to get at this quarterback just once. After he got out from under the pile of tacklers and spit the grass out of his mouth, he was a lot more humble and willing to acknowledge the contribution of his offensive line. In the church there are those with more visible positions that receive adulation. Still it takes those working behind the scenes, especially in prayer, to make the church a "winning team."

I also believe the weight room in football has a lot in common with the "prayer closet." Lifting weights is never done on the football field. The crowd never cheers while the players are working out on the weights. Yet, time in the weight room pays off on the field. When you meet an opponent on the football field, most often the stronger man wins. Our prayer closet is also the same. As we spend in prayer and in fellowship with God, we are getting stronger. When the battle comes, we are prepared and strong enough to defeat the enemy.

In football and in the Christian life, we are called to look out for one another. We are also called to fulfill our own responsibilities. Like football, the Christian walk is a team effort.

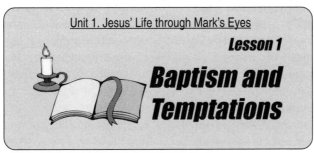

Unit 1. Jesus' Life through Mark's Eyes

Lesson 1

Baptism and Temptations

Mark 1:1-13

The beginning of the gospel of Jesus Christ, the Son of God;

2 As it is written in the prophets, Behold, I send my messenger before thy face, which shall prepare thy way before thee.

3 The voice of one crying in the wilderness, Prepare ye the way of the Lord, make his paths straight.

4 John did baptize in the wilderness, and preach the baptism of repentance for the remission of sins.

5 And there went out unto him all the land of Judaea, and they of Jerusalem, and were all baptized of him in the river of Jordan, confessing their sins.

6 And John was clothed with camel's hair, and with a girdle of a skin about his loins; and he did eat locusts and wild honey;

7 And preached, saying, There cometh one mightier than I after me, the latchet of whose shoes I am not worthy to stoop down and unloose.

8 I indeed have baptized you with water: but he shall baptize you with the Holy Ghost.

9 And it came to pass in those days, that Jesus came from Nazareth of Galilee, and was baptized of John in Jordan.

10 And straightway coming up out of the water, he saw the heavens opened, and the Spirit like a dove descending upon him:

11 And there came a voice from heaven, saying, Thou art my beloved Son, in whom I am well pleased.

12 And immediately the Spirit driveth him into the wilderness.

13 And he was there in the wilderness forty days, tempted of Satan; and was with the wild beasts; and the angels ministered unto him.

Memory Selection
Mark 1:11

Background Scripture
Mark 1:1-13

Devotional Reading
Matthew 12:17-21

This lesson is typical of the Gospel of Mark's direct and powerful style. It focuses on the dynamic leadership required for introducing the Messianic Age. The lesson has a wealth of information for leaders in today's Church, as well as for the congregations whom they lead.

The first leader Mark presents is John the Baptist, who is charged with preparing the way of the Lord (1:3). "Winding down" the Old Covenant

age was demanding as well as rewarding (as is all church leadership). Then Mark introduces us to the ministry and leadership of the Messiah Himself. Perhaps since Mark writes toward the Roman reader's interest in power and action, he bypasses stories of Jesus' birth, as in the other Gospels, and plunges immediately into the Messianic ministry.

The old . . . the new . . . challenges . . . temptations—a remarkably accurate description of the work church leaders face today!

ഇരു

You can introduce this lesson by challenging your group to role-play the work of John the Baptist. Suggest that you will play the "audience" to whom John speaks, while group members throw out sentences that John might have used in preparing the way for the Messiah.

They may use sentences from the

Bible itself: *Prepare the way of the Lord!* (Mark 1:3) . . . *I'm not worthy even to unlatch the straps of the sandals of the One who is coming after me!* (vs. 7) . . . *The Kingdom of God is at hand!* (vs. 15a) . . . *Repent, and believe the gospel!* (15b). Or, they may choose to imagine phrases John might have used. The point is to put ourselves in the historical context of the lesson, experiencing the excitement moving from the Old Law to the New.

Teaching Outline	Daily Bible Readings	
I. John the Baptist's Work—1-8	Mon.	'You Are My Son' *Psalm 2:7-12*
A. The gospel's beginning, 1	Tue.	Baptism for Repentance *Mark 1:4-8*
B. John's message, 2-3	Wed.	The Baptist's Message *Matthew 3:7-12*
C. Preparing for Jesus, 4-6	Thu.	Jesus Is Baptized *Matthew 3:13-17*
D. Comparing two ministries, 7-8	Fri.	Jesus Is Baptized and Tested *Mark 1:9-13*
II. Jesus Begins His Work—9-13	Sat.	'Here Is My Servant' *Matthew 12:17-21*
A. Jesus' baptism, 9-11	Sun.	Tempted by Satan *Matthew 4:1-11*
B. The Great Temptation, 12-13		

Verse by Verse

I. John the Baptist's Work—1-8

A. The gospel's beginning, 1

1 The beginning of the gospel of Jesus Christ, the Son of God;

Matthew and Luke begin their accounts of the life and ministry of Jesus with the accounts of His birth. Perhaps Mark omits this part of the good news because he writes for Roman readers who were interested in action narratives, and the supernatural. Thus Mark plunges directly into the dynamic story of a wild-looking, desert-dwelling figure and his blunt message for people to prepare for the supernatural Son of God.

The word for "beginning" gives us our word "archaic," but there is no hint of Mark's message being "out-dated." The term indicates that Mark is going back to the roots of what would grow into the Messianic Age.

B. John's message, 2-3

2 As it is written in the prophets, Behold, I send my messenger before thy face, which shall prepare thy way before thee.

3 The voice of one crying in the wilderness, Prepare ye the way of the Lord, make his paths straight.

Sticking to his theme of prophetic fulfillment, Mark affirms that the story of Jesus fulfills the prophecy in Malachi 3:1 that God would send a messenger to prepare the way for the Messiah. **John is not only that messenger; he is, figuratively, the prophet Elijah returned—again in fulfillment of prophecy (Mal. 4:5-6; Matt. 11:14).**

In verse 3, Mark shows that John the Baptist's ministry was rooted in the prophet Isaiah, who was considered to be "the Messianic prophet" because of his many predictions of His coming. He quotes from Isaiah 40:3, which calls for people to "make straight in the desert a highway for our God." Citing this text indicates John's (and Mark's) belief in the deity of Christ. To "make his paths straight" recalls the days when workers would straighten roads and level them out for a gala procession of a deity or king into a city. Here is a call for the people to welcome the Messiah by putting their lives "straight" or in order, as the next verse also emphasizes.

C. Preparing for Jesus, 4-6

4 John did baptize in the wilderness, and preach the baptism of repentance for the remission of sins.

5 And there went out unto him all the land of Judaea, and they of

393

Jerusalem, and were all baptized of him in the river of Jordan, confessing their sins.

6 And John was clothed with camel's hair, and with a girdle of a skin about his loins; and he did eat locusts and wild honey;

John's message shows that the way to "make a straight path" for the coming King is to turn from sin. One Jewish tradition even held that Messiah would not come until masses of His people reformed. John apparently focused more on the individual necessity of changing one's heart to make a safe haven for the Messiah.

Ceremonial washings or baptisms had been practiced in various groups, both pagan and Jewish. What was new about John's call was a symbolic cleansing with the immediate appearance of the Messiah in mind. Although the confession of sin no doubt pointed to its eventual removal in the blood of Christ, Acts 19:1-6 shows that John's baptism was temporary, eventually giving way to baptism in the name of Jesus.

John's rough clothing and wilderness lifestyle were no doubt to remind the people that he came "in the spirit and power" of Elijah (Luke 1:17), who had a similar life-style.

D. Comparing two ministries, 7-8

7 And preached, saying, There cometh one mightier than I after me, the latchet of whose shoes I am not worthy to stoop down and unloose.

8 I indeed have baptized you with water: but he shall baptize you with the Holy Ghost.

Although the "unworthiness" John professes is readily understandable in light of the superior worth of the Holy One who succeeded him, John's mission as a "forerunner" for God's own Son had its own worthiness. Although its limitations were a part of God's plans, it is a tribute to John that he understood and submitted to his role.

The baptism of the Holy Spirit (vs. 8) has been variously understood as baptism that induces charismatic gifts (see Acts 19:1-6), and baptism that is accompanied by the Spirit's authority and indwelling (see vs. 10, below, and Acts 2:38).

II. Jesus' Begins His Work—9-16

A. Jesus' baptism, 9-11

9 And it came to pass in those days, that Jesus came from Nazareth of Galilee, and was baptized of John in Jordan.

10 And straightway coming up out of the water, he saw the heavens opened, and the Spirit like a dove descending upon him:

11 And there came a voice from heaven, saying, Thou art my beloved Son, in whom I am well pleased.

The baptism of Jesus signals Mark's turn from the ministry of John to focus on the work of the Messiah Himself. Luke has a single sentence describing the silent ministry during Jesus' childhood: He "increased in wisdom and stature, and in favor with God and man" (Luke 2:52). No doubt Mark understands baptism as having a significance beyond an empty ritual or rite of passage. It was sufficiently important in Jesus' life that the Holy Spirit accompanies it in the form of a dove (a symbol that has endured through the centuries with the aid of Christian art).

Matthew recalls John's humility and even protest at baptizing the One he said should actually be baptizing him, since Jesus has no sins to confess (Matt. 3:14; see Heb. 4:15). Jesus, however, insists on submitting to John's baptism, no doubt to identify with those who will follow His example and undergo this sign of cleansing as a sign also of being born into a new life (John 3:3-5).

Some scholars see a marked difference between the Spirit's voice being directed to Jesus here, proclaiming His Sonship, and Matthew's version of Jesus' baptism in which the voice seems directed to the gathered observers (Matt. 3:17). "Adoptionists" draw from this that Jesus was only adopted as God's Son at His baptism, when He had to be told about His status. It is more in accord with the whole New Testament record to view Jesus as being the divine Son "eternally," before creation (see John 1:1, 14; Col. 1:15-16; Heb. 1:1-2).

B. The Great Temptation, 12-13

12 And immediately the Spirit driveth him into the wilderness.

13 And he was there in the wilderness forty days, tempted of Satan; and was with the wild beasts; and the angels ministered unto him.

Mark gives only a tantalizing summary of the awesome account of Jesus being tempted in the wilderness by Satan. The story is packed with significance in many areas. (1) It places Jesus along with Old Testament prophets such as Moses and Elijah, who found in the desert the sustenance and strength required to return and plunge into the hectic life of people and their problems. (There may also be some significance in the "40 days" as a parallel to the 40 years when Moses led the Israelites through a similar wilderness, thus hinting that Jesus is "a new Moses.")

(2) The wilderness experience, like his baptism, shows Jesus' willingness to identify with those He came to serve and save. It was a necessary part of equipping Himself to understand the various temptations that mere humans go through. Matthew (4:1-11) describes Jesus' experience in more detail, showing that these temptations were of a physical, mental, and spiritual nature, forecasting the endurance tests Christ's followers have to endure as well.

(3) Although Jesus, because of His divine and pre-existent nature, knew the demonic world very well, portraying His direct confrontation with Satan reassures His followers that, insidious though evil is, it can be overcome. Also, Jesus' strategy of quoting Scripture ("It is written . . .") is shown to be a necessary and sufficient weapon in overcoming temptation, and the account therefore lives as a "handbook" showing Christians how to triumph in similar situations.

Evangelistic Emphasis

Did you ever open a carbonated beverage that has been shaken? The resulting geyser is similar to the effect of opening the Gospel of Mark. "The beginning of the Gospel of Jesus Christ, the Son of God," Mark boldly proclaims—and the lid is off. Out gushes almost all of the significant themes of his Gospel, and almost all that one needs to know in a lifetime of discipleship. In Mark's opening account of the ministry of John the Baptist, Mark introduces us to Jesus as the Christ, the only true Son of God. He plants in our hearts the need for repentance, confession and baptism. He makes us hungry for the blessing of the pouring out of the Holy Spirit and the gracious forgiveness of our sins. He cautions us about the reality of the wilderness through which we travel as we come to the Savior and how Satan will use our wilderness time to test our resolve and commitment. Finally he dares suggest that we can become children of God and announces that the kingdom of God has come near.

If we ever wonder where to begin in proclaiming the Good News, Mark bids us take the lid of off his gospel. If we ever become weary in our Christian walk, the explosive beginning of Mark can be just the energy we need to regain the excitement of our first love.

ᔓᘒ

Memory Selection

And there came a voice from heaven, saying, Thou art my beloved Son, in whom I am well pleased.—*Mark 1:11*

Jesus' baptism was different from ours. When Jesus was coming up out of the waters of the Jordan River, the sky was suddenly ripped open and the Holy Spirit descended visibly as a dove. The voice of God thundered the proclamation that Jesus was unique. There had never been a being like Him before, and there would never be one like Him again—nor has there ever been another baptism like this one.

Of course, our baptism was much like the baptism of Jesus. Oh, there was no tearing apart of the skies as the water dripped from our body. No dove flew from heaven. No audible voice thundered from above. But the Holy Spirit did descend and God did speak. As Paul tells us in Galatians 4:5,6, the proclamation is much the same as on that day at the Jordan. Because we too have been obedient to His will, God has claimed us as His children, and the Spirit sent into our hearts cries, "Abba! Father!"

Weekday Problems

"Come in," John responded to the knock on his study door. Then Jeff was standing at his desk, his face streaked with tears. This was much the same way the two had met just last week. Jeff had come to the church in deep despair, confessing his sinful life and pleading with John to help him give his life to the Lord. The joy that Jeff discovered in his conversion was as deep and real as any John had ever witnessed. Now, however, John could see that the despair had returned. In a torrent of words, Jeff said that his conversion had not worked. The old temptations were back, and some were stronger than ever. What had he done wrong? Now it was time for *John* to feel convicted. He had not told Jeff the whole story. Together, they sat down and read the opening of the Gospel of Mark. "What happened to Jesus immediately after His baptism?" John asked.

Jeff nodded knowingly. "Temptation," the young man replied. "It looks like Satan takes such a commitment to the Lord seriously, doesn't he? I guess he wants to know if I really mean it."

* Why do our commitments to the Lord get Satan's attention?

The Wilderness of Temptation

A driver tucked this note under the windshield wiper of his car: "I've circled the block for 20 minutes. I'm late for an appointment and if I don't park here I'll lose my job. 'Forgive us our trespasses.'"

When he came back, he found a parking ticket and this note: "I've been on this beat for 20 years, and if I don't give you a ticket, I'll lose my job. 'Lead us not into temptation.'"

* * * *

The sermon went on and on, until one parishioner was tempted to get up and leave. However, he gave in to a lesser temptation when the preacher said earnestly, "What more, my friends, can I say?"

Said the restless listener, "How about 'Amen'?"

* * * *

The man had listened patiently, but with some exasperation, to the feminist speaker who put down all home-makers and held up "professional women" as the only acceptable kind in today's world. Finally he gave in to the temptation to stand up and ask, "What other kind of women are there—amateurs?"

This Lesson in Your Life

If we read Mark's account of John the Baptist only as an historical footnote to the story of Jesus, we are missing out on the continuing ministry of this remarkable prophet. John was sent ahead of Jesus to proclaim the coming of the Messiah and to cry out, "Prepare the way of the Lord." This message was vital to the people of John's day—because Jesus was coming. This message is vital to us today—because Jesus is coming again. John's message to the people of his day was to prepare for the coming of the Lord through repentance. His message for us today remains, "Repent." John was sent to prepare the hearts of the religious people of his day—the people of God's own nation. His message today is still aimed at the hearts of those of us who wear the name of God.

In view of the imminent coming of Jesus, all God's people are called to repent. We must repent of the assumption that we have already repented . . . and of living only in comparison to others—judging ourselves to be better than some. We must repent of the spiritually powerless lives we are often content to lead. We must repent of our attitudes toward others—both within and without the Kingdom of God. We must repent of our belief that our world will never change.

Each time we go out to see Jesus, we pass through the wilderness where John is preaching. There we encounter this strange man clothed with camel's hair, wearing a leather belt around his waist, eating locusts and wild honey. As we look around for Jesus, John holds up a mirror before us and invites us to look there first—and to repent. Repentance is the beginning of the Good news every time we hear it.

1. Which Old Testament prophet described the mission of John the Baptist?
The prophet Isaiah prophesied concerning John's mission (Mark 1:2; Isaiah 40:3).

2. What did John preach in the wilderness?
John preached the baptism of repentance for the remission of sins (Mark 1:4).

3. What did the people do as they were baptized in the Jordan River?
They confessed their sins. (Mark 1:5)

4. How did Mark describe John's appearance?
He was clothed with camel's hair, with a leather belt around his waist, and he ate locusts and wild honey (Mark 1:6).

5. How did John compare himself to Jesus?
John said he was not worthy to untie Jesus' sandals and that while he baptized with water, Jesus would baptize with the Holy Spirit (Mark 1:8).

6. What did Jesus see when He was baptized?
When Jesus was coming up out of the water, He saw the heavens torn apart and the Spirit descending on Him like a dove (Mark 1:10).

7. What did God say to Jesus when He was baptized?
God said, "Thou art my beloved Son, in whom I am well pleased." (Mark 1:11).

8. What compelled Jesus to go into the wilderness immediately after His baptism?
The Spirit drove Him out into the wilderness (Mark 1:12).

9. What hardships did Jesus face in the wilderness?
He was in the wilderness 40 days, tempted by Satan, and He was with the wild beasts (Mark 1:13).

10. Who ministered to Jesus in the wilderness?
Angels ministered to Him (Mark 1:13).

In 1980, a New Yorker named Allen Bridge advertised a telephone number that he called "The Apology Line." The intent of the phone line was simple. Bridge wanted to provide a number for people to call to express their regret for things they had said and done. When he first opened the line, he was not sure anyone would take advantage of it, but the response was overwhelming. For years, people called to relate stories from their past. Many of the stories were about events that were decades old. Some called about trivial slights and offenses. Others called to confess more serious wrongs—even murder. Bridge concluded that the need for us to confess, to admit the truth about ourselves, is basic to our nature.

When the people from Judea and Jerusalem came to John to be baptized in the Jordan River, they confessed their sins; but this was not the first time that confession had been encouraged as a way to spiritual health. God's Word has always said that freedom is found in finally telling the truth—and not just telling it to anyone, but laying it fully before the Lord. David, the great man of God, once wrote,

> While I kept silence, my body wasted away through my groaning all day long . . . then I acknowledged my sin to you, and I did not hide my iniquity; I said, 'I will confess my transgressions to the Lord,' and you forgave the guilt of my sin" (Psalm 32:2-5 NRSV).

No wonder David could begin his psalm by shouting, "Happy are those whose transgression is forgiven, whose sin is covered!"

If at any point in our journey, we find ourselves in the wilderness, a good question to ask ourselves is, "Am I hiding anything?" While we often fear that bringing our shame into the light of God will result in condemnation, the Good News is that just the opposite is true. The light of God's grace removes the guilt of confessed wrongs.

Lesson 2

Healed to Wholeness

Mark 2:1-12

And again he entered into Capernaum, after some days; and it was noised that he was in the house.

2 And straightway many were gathered together, insomuch that there was no room to receive them, no, not so much as about the door: and he preached the word unto them.

3 And they come unto him, bringing one sick of the palsy, which was borne of four.

4 And when they could not come nigh unto him for the press, they uncovered the roof where he was: and when they had broken it up, they let down the bed wherein the sick of the palsy lay.

5 When Jesus saw their faith, he said unto the sick of the palsy, Son, thy sins be forgiven thee.

6 But there were certain of the scribes sitting there, and reasoning in their hearts,

7 Why doth this man thus speak blasphemies? who can forgive sins but God only?

8 And immediately when Jesus perceived in his spirit that they so reasoned within themselves, he said unto them, Why reason ye these things in your hearts?

9 Whether is it easier to say to the sick of the palsy, Thy sins be forgiven thee; or to say, Arise, and take up thy bed, and walk?

10 But that ye may know that the Son of man hath power on earth to forgive sins, (he saith to the sick of the palsy,)

11 I say unto thee, Arise, and take up thy bed, and go thy way into thine house.

12 And immediately he arose, took up the bed, and went forth before them all; insomuch that they were all amazed, and glorified God, saying, We never saw it on this fashion.

Memory Selection
Mark 2:11

Background Scripture
Mark 2:1-12; 3:1-6; 8:1-10

Devotional Reading
Mark 7:31-37

401

This lesson, from early in Jesus' earthly ministry, focuses on His twin abilities to heal the body and the soul. Some people, even in modern times, assume that any sickness is the direct result of sin. Although Scripture sometimes shows such a connection, it is far from "automatic." In the sense that all sickness is related to the Fall, there is certainly a connection; but it is not immediate or direct, for, as Jesus taught, rain—or the lack of it—falls on the just and the unjust (Matt. 5:45; see also John 9:1-3).

In this story, Jesus forgives the sins of the man He heals, but He does not say that sin caused the man's illness. He pronounces the man forgiven in order to show His power over the unseen world of sin, while His power over the visible world of sickness was fresh on His critics' minds.

೮ಌ

the same Lord who healed the body also has the power to heal the soul.

Note that there is less controversy over healing the soul because it occurs in the unseen realm of the heart. Of course we may see the *results* of the forgiveness of sins, but, unlike the healing of the body, God's work of grace in healing the soul is largely hidden. However much we trust modern medicine to heal the body, we are challenged to trust Jesus to do this unseen work of curing the soul.

This lesson can be introduced by a discussion of how your group members feel about "faith healing." While the teacher should accept all comments and opinions, since they grow out of experience and/or conviction, the main point to draw from this discussion is the fact that whether or not physical healing occurs today as it did in Bible times,

Teaching Outline	Daily Bible Readings

I. Authority to Forgive—1-5
  A. Ministry at Capernaum, 1-2
  B. Faith of friends, 3-4
  C. Forgiveness pronounced, 5
II. Enemies' Questions—6-9
  A. Only God can forgive, 6-7
  B. Which is easier? 8-9
III. Authority to Heal—10-12
	Mon. Healing a Demoniac
	        Mark 5:1-13
	Tue. Doing All Well
	        Mark 7:31-37
	Wed. How Much Do We Have?
	        Mark 8:1-5
	Thu. Four Thousand Are Fed
	        Mark 8:6-10
	Fri. 'Stretch Out Your Hand'
	        Mark 3:1-6
	Sat. 'Your Sins Are Forgiven'
	        Mark 2:1-5
	Sun. 'I Say to You, Stand Up!'
	        Mark 2:6-12

Verse by Verse

I. Authority to Forgive—1-5
A. Ministry at Capernaum, 1-2

1 And again he entered into Capernaum, after some days; and it was noised that he was in the house.

2 And straightway many were gathered together, insomuch that there was no room to receive them, no, not so much as about the door: and he preached the word unto them.

Jesus is teaching in a house in Capernaum, a city on the northwest edge of the Sea of Galilee which He has made his temporary home base. Capernaum was important enough to have its own Roman tax office (Matt. 9:9), and a contingency of Roman soldiers stationed there, with their own centurion (Luke 7:2). Archeological excavations have unearthed the ruins of a synagogue dating from the third or fourth century A.D., and possibly built on the foundation of a previous synagogue which could have been the very one where Jesus healed a man with a withered hand (Mark 3:1).

Now, however, Jesus is in a private home. Although it is not certain that He is even conducting a teaching session, and even though it is early in His ministry, He has begun to attract so many hearers (1:45) that the place is packed beyond capacity, and no one else can get in through the door. Jesus cannot turn away those who seek to learn more about this One who is rumored to be the Messiah Himself. Also, the work of John the Baptist, as well as some false Messiahs (see Acts 5:36-37), has made the "Messianic fever" run high among the Jews.

B. Faith of friends, 3-4

3 And they come unto him, bringing one sick of the palsy, which was borne of four.

4 And when they could not come nigh unto him for the press, they uncovered the roof where he was: and when they had broken it up, they let down the bed wherein the sick of the palsy lay.

These friends of the man with the "palsy" (paralysis) were not deterred by the crowd, but simply climbed atop the one-story house and uncovered the "tiling" (Luke 5:19)—actually digging through the mud-and-thatch roofing material to make a hole big enough to let their paralyzed friend down into the house on a home-made gurney.

B. Forgiveness pronounced, 5

5 When Jesus saw their faith, he said unto the sick of the palsy, Son, thy sins be forgiven thee.

Although the Jews (as well as most people of that day) generally assumed that if a person were sick or poor or otherwise "unblessed," it was a sign that he had offended God. Even today, it is common for people who suffer a tragedy to wonder what they did wrong. Occasionally, as in the man at the pool of Bethesda, Jesus indicates that God may send illness as a corrective measure (John 5:14). However, He also warned that this is purely God's choice, and that we are not to assume a direct connection between sin and sickness (see John 9:1-3); and He makes no such connection in this case. Here, perhaps Jesus accommodates the common belief that sickness was a sign of sin, in order to prepare the crowd for His demonstration of authority over both body and spirit.

Some modern healers say they cannot do their work unless the sick person believes; and even non-religious health care workers affirm the power of belief to facilitate healing. In Jesus' case, however, the faith is sometimes in the person to be healed, sometimes in the healer, but here in the friends of the healer. In other words, Jesus is sovereign over ailments in general, and can therefore utilize the means of healing He chooses. Here, perhaps He wants to teach us a lesson on the importance of His followers' tending to their friends in faith. At any rate, He is so impressed by the lengths the crippled man's friends went to that He immediately tends to him.

No doubt word of Jesus' healing powers had been one reason the house was full. Surprisingly, however, Jesus goes to work first on the man's soul instead of his body. This bold exercise of His power over the inner man creates the opportunity to demonstrate His trustworthiness when He exercises power over the body.

II. Enemies' Questions—6-9
A. Only God can forgive, 6-7

6 But there were certain of the scribes sitting there, and reasoning in their hearts,

7 Why doth this man thus speak blasphemies? who can forgive sins but God only?

We can imagine startled gasps from the crowd, especially from the keepers of Jewish orthodoxy who knew very well that only God could forgive sins. Priests under the Old Covenant could pronounce forgiveness, but they had no divine authority actually to remove guilt.

The scribes, who were among Jesus' strongest critics, were not only literate in the law of the land, and thus sought out as attorneys are today; they were especially well-read in the Jewish Law, which impinged at every hand on civil law. They are so prejudiced that they pronounce Jesus guilty of blasphemy before He can tend to the man's body, which was the reason his friends had brought him. They have walked directly into Jesus' trap. Perceiving their mindset, He takes another bold step.

B. Which is easier? 8-9

8 And immediately when Jesus perceived in his spirit that they so reasoned within themselves, he said unto them, Why reason ye these things in your hearts?

9 Whether is it easier to say to the sick of the palsy, Thy sins be forgiven thee; or to say, Arise, and take up thy bed, and walk?

Being divinely able to look into His critics' hearts, Jesus proceeds to give them reason to believe in Him, if they choose. Since forgiving the man's sins resulted in no outward sign or proof that the words "worked," Jesus heals the man's paralyzed body to provide that visible sign. He leaves it to the onlookers themselves to bridge by faith the gap between spiritual and physical healing. This is typical of His respect for others' integrity. He will not force faith. Healings and other miracles are not full "proof" of His divinity; they are evidence of it for those who are not too prejudiced to accept it.

III. Authority to Heal—10-12

10 But that ye may know that the Son of man hath power on earth to forgive sins, (he saith to the sick of the palsy,)

11 I say unto thee, Arise, and take up thy bed, and go thy way into thine house.

12 And immediately he arose, took up the bed, and went forth before them all; insomuch that they were all amazed, and glorified God, saying, We never saw it on this fashion.

Imagine the surprise of the crowd when they see the man let down through the roof on his bed, roll it up and walk out with it! Although verse 12 says that "all" were amazed and glorified God, Jesus' critics are no doubt not included in the crowd's general reaction.

No passage illustrates better the Gospel of Mark's style of writing, which is full of dynamic pointers to Jesus' supernatural power. "Son of man," the title Jesus preferred to use Himself, derives from the books of Daniel and Ezekiel, where it describes a being of just the sort of supernatural power that appealed to a Roman reader. It was also susceptible to the more "humble" or human interpretation, leaving it open for Jesus also to be the Lamb of God who would be sacrificed for the sins of the world. This dual interpretation is possibly why Jesus preferred the title when He spoke of Himself.

Most of the crowd are "amazed" (another of Mark's favorite words in describe the reactions to Jesus' work) at what they saw, thus inviting faith also in the healing of the man's sins, which they could not see. The fact is that if we believe that creation represents the supernatural appearance of matter out of nothing (Heb. 11:3), it is not a giant step to accepting the Bible's claim that the Creator's Son could "create" wholeness in both body and mind.

Evangelistic Emphasis

We know the story. Some people were bringing a paralyzed man to lay before Jesus, but because of the large crowd gathered around Jesus in the house, they could not reach him. Then they climbed up on the roof, and . . . we know the rest of the story.

Have you ever wondered what those people's relationship to the paralyzed man was? Were they relatives? Were they friends? Was he a stranger they encountered begging on the side of the road? Any of these scenarios is possible, but the most important thing is that they had faith that Jesus could help the man. Did the paralyzed man have faith, too? We cannot answer that question with certainty, but we do know that it was the faith of those who brought the man that moved Jesus to action.

Do you ever see others who need to be laid before Jesus for healing and forgiveness? Certainly we can invite them to come worship with us at the feet of Jesus. We can ask them to meet Jesus in the written Word. Sometimes, however, because of their paralysis, the only way to bring them to Jesus is to lift them up and carry them to the Lord in prayer.

Let us be assured that Jesus honors such faith of friends, and, like the friends in the story, we leave the rest up to Him.

ഇറദ്ധ

Memory Selection

I say unto thee, Arise, and take up thy bed, and go thy way into thine house.—*Mark 2:11*

Jesus spoke these words to a man who had only moments before been lost in his sins as well as physically disabled. Through the faith and dedication of others, he was placed before Jesus and had received both forgiveness and healing. Now it was the man's turn to respond. Having received such blessings, he was called to go and live fully the life so graciously returned to him.

Jesus continues to speak these words to each person who experiences His forgiveness and his healing. The way to express gratitude to God for a life returned to us is to live it fully. The way to bear witness to the great power of Jesus is to live that restored life before others who may yet be skeptical of Jesus' power. When the man in the story stood up, took up his bed and went out, all those who saw him were amazed and glorified God. Lord, may our friends and neighbors do the same as we walk daily among them.

Weekday Problems

Michael was a dedicated Christian who knew his Bible well, and he delighted in discussing it with others. Rarely did he come away from such sessions—which usually ended up as confrontations—without the feeling that his interpretations were more accurate. He particularly liked to challenge others on how they had experienced the power of Jesus in their lives. Without fully realizing it, Michael had formed a strong opinion of how Jesus operates in the world today, and when the testimonies of others challenged his perspective, he would dismiss their claims with a few well-chosen scriptures.

One day, in the midst of such a discussion, Michael's "opponent" stopped him cold by asking, "Are you saying that you don't think Jesus *would* do that, or that you don't think Jesus *could* do that?" Suddenly, Michael realized that he had drawn his own boundaries around the power of Jesus. To his chagrin, he recognized the foolishness of ever saying, "Jesus can't. . . ."

* How can we be faithful both to our understanding of the Word of God and to the power of Jesus?

The Amazement Continues

Seems it strange that thou shoudst live forever? Is it less strange that thou shouldst live at all?—*Edward Young*

* * * *

Miracles and truth are necessary, because it is necessary to convince the entire man, in body and soul.—*Blaise Pascal*

* * * *

I have never seen a greater monster or miracle in the world than myself.—*Michael Eyquem de Montaigne*

* * * *

(In answer to a question on why he believed in miracles:)—Because I see them every day in the changed lives of men and women who are saved and lifted through faith in the power of the living Christ.—*Henry Drummond*

* * * *

Every moment of this strange and lovely life from dawn to dusk, is a miracle. Somewhere, always, a rose is opening its petals to the dawn . . . a flower is fading in the dusk. [All] are gathered, sooner or later, into the solitary fragrance that is God. Faintly, elusively, that fragrance lingers over all of us.—*Beverley Nichols*

This Lesson in Your Life

Statisticians tell us that the average person living in a city today might see more people in one day than the average person living in the Middle Ages saw in a lifetime. The sheer number of people we encounter each day leaves little time for reflection on how we view each individual. However, in the blur of faces rushing past us on the sidewalk, in the mall, or on the highway, our attention is immediately drawn to some. We pause when we see a friend or acquaintance or someone famous, and we also tend to notice the person who is facing particular challenges—one who is walking with the aid of crutches or riding in a wheelchair. Seeing a person facing physical disabilities evokes our compassion. If it were possible for us to help restore that person to physical wholeness and health, most people would do it.

The men who brought the paralytic to Jesus shared this universal human response. Whether the invalid was a close friend or a man they had just met, they were doing something to help. The special thing about what they did is that they believed Jesus was the one who could provide the answer. Evidently they had heard that this man from Nazareth had remarkable healing powers. After going to extreme measures to lay the man before Jesus, were they surprised to hear him offer forgiveness before physical healing? The others who were watching the scene certainly were. In first addressing the paralyzed man's sinful state, Jesus had made his point.

We all have needs that eclipse our physical struggles. While others saw only a man in need of a restored body, Jesus saw a man in need of the grace of God. We are all moved to compassion by the needs of others. How strongly is our compassion stirred by their spiritual needs? In the blur of faces rushing past us, do we see them?

1. Where was Jesus teaching when the man with palsy was brought to Him?

He was teaching in a house in Capernaum (Mark 2:1). (Note: Many believe this was Peter's house, the ruins of which can still be seen today.)

2. What did the men carrying the invalid man do when they could not get into the house where Jesus was?

They carried the man to the roof where they broke through the roof and lowered the man in front of Jesus (Mark 2:4).

3. Whose faith impressed Jesus?

Jesus was impressed with the faith of the men who had brought the palsied man to him (Mark 2:5).

4. What was the first thing Jesus said to the man with palsy?

Jesus said, "Son, thy sins be forgiven thee" (Mark 2:5).

5. Who was offended by Jesus' proclamation of forgiveness, and why were they offended?

The scribes were offended because they believed Jesus was blaspheming by assuming the power of forgiveness that belongs to God only (Mark 2:6,7).

6. How did Jesus know what the scribes were thinking?

Jesus perceived it in His spirit (Mark 2:8).

7. What answer did Jesus give the scribes?

He asked them if it was any easier to heal the man's palsy than to forgive his sins (Mark 2:9).

8. What did Jesus' healing of the man's palsy prove?

By healing the man's body, Jesus proved He also had the power to heal his soul, or forgive the man's sins (Mark 2:10).

9. What did Jesus tell the healed man to do?

Jesus told him to "stand up, take your mat and go to your home" (Mark 2:11 NRSV).

10. How did the crowd in the house react when the man stood up and walked?

They were amazed, and they glorified God (Mark 2:12).

A few years ago I received in the mail a brochure about a seminar. The subject of the seminar intrigued me, and the featured speaker was a man I had long wanted to hear and meet. The seminar was expensive, and the flight would be almost across the nation, but I decided that attending the seminar would be worth the effort and money. As the date for my departure approached, my schedule got crazy. I considered canceling, but I would lose most of the money I had invested. I arrived in the unfamiliar city at midnight, got in my rental car, and promptly got lost in the downtown area. It was 3 a.m. before I finally settled into the motel room.

The next morning there was more bad news. The main speaker had an emergency in his family and was unable to participate. Also, I had misinterpreted the topic of the seminar. It was not what I had come to hear. Yet, after all these seemingly negative factors, the end result was that it turned out to be the best seminar I had ever attended.

How wonderful it is when our expectations do not limit our blessings. The man who was brought to Jesus on the stretcher obviously hoped for healing. We do not know how long he had suffered paralysis, but any length of time is too long. The faith and the fidelity of the four who carried the paralyzed man were amazing. Overcoming all obstacles, they brought him before Jesus to be healed as they hoped and expected. What a blessing that Jesus was not limited by their expectations. They encountered God that day—but in a surprising way.

We, too, must leave ourselves open to God's surprises. Although we plan, we hope, and we expect—most of all we trust in a God who can see our greater needs and surprise us with opportunities we had yet to consider. The greatest service these four men did for the paralyzed man was to lay him before the Lord and let the Lord decide what He would do. We are wise to do the same for ourselves.

Lesson 3
The Trials and Opposition

Mark 14:53-65; 15:1-3

And they led Jesus away to the high priest: and with him were assembled all the chief priests and the elders and the scribes.

54 And Peter followed him afar off, even into the palace of the high priest: and he sat with the servants, and warmed himself at the fire.

55 And the chief priests and all the council sought for witness against Jesus to put him to death; and found none.

56 For many bare false witness against him, but their witness agreed not together.

57 And there arose certain, and bare false witness against him, saying,

58 We heard him say, I will destroy this temple that is made with hands, and within three days I will build another made without hands.

59 But neither so did their witness agree together.

60 And the high priest stood up in the midst, and asked Jesus, saying, Answerest thou nothing? what is it which these witness against thee?

61 But he held his peace, and answered nothing. Again the high priest asked him, and said unto him, Art thou the Christ, the Son of the Blessed?

62 And Jesus said, I am: and ye shall see the Son of man sitting on the right hand of power, and coming in the clouds of heaven.

63 Then the high priest rent his clothes, and saith, What need we any further witnesses?

64 Ye have heard the blasphemy: what think ye? And they all condemned him to be guilty of death.

65 And some began to spit on him, and to cover his face, and to buffet him, and to say unto him, Prophesy: and the servants did strike him with the palms of their hands.

15:1 And straightway in the morning the chief priests held a consultation with the elders and scribes and the whole council, and bound Jesus, and carried him away, and delivered him to Pilate.

2 And Pilate asked him, Art thou the King of the Jews? And he answering said unto him, Thou sayest it.

3 And the chief priests accused him of many things: but he answered nothing.

Memory Selection
Mark 14:55

Background Scripture
Mark 14:53-65; 15:1-5

Devotional Reading
Mark 14:17-21

411

Jesus, now about age 33, had led an exemplary life, keeping the Law of Moses "without sin" (Heb. 4:15). Yet He is now brought before the courts on serious charges. Although His death was by the foreknowledge and will of God, this lesson focuses on the human designs that weighed against Him, and who was behind it.

The text implicates both Jews and Romans. Jesus is arrested and brought to appear before both the Jewish high priest and the Roman provincial ruler, Pilate. Unfortunately, some modern Christians focus only the role of the Jews in the death of Christ, leading to unwarranted anti-Semitism. Not only were the Gentile Romans also involved; the sins of every race on earth actually brought Jesus to the "kangaroo courts" that led to His death. There is plenty of blame to share with all mankind.

ഇൻ

Pose the question, *Who was guilty of bringing the guiltless Jesus to trial?* At various times in history, the Jewish people have been singled out as especially to blame. Countless "pogroms" or persecutions were capped by the horror of the Holocaust, perpetrated by Nazi Germany. Guide the discussion so that it includes also the Roman ruler, Pontius Pilate, since the death sentence required Roman approval. Later the text says that Pilate disagreed with the Jewish ruling that Jesus was worthy of death, but went along with it under political pressure. Point out that the real "guilty party" in Christ's false arraignments and trials consists of sinful people, of all races and religions. The Jews cannot be singled out as objects of special scorn.

Teaching Outline	Daily Bible Readings		
I. Traitor at the Trial—53-54	Mon.	Peter's Denial Predicted *Mark 14:26-31*	
II. Search for Witnesses—55-59	Tue.	Jesus Betrayed by Judas *Mark 14:43-50*	
A. Inconsistent testimony, 55-56	Wed.	False Testimony Given *Mark 14:53-59*	
B. Commitment of perjury, 57-59	Thu.	Jesus Is Condemned *Mark 14:60-65*	
III. Questioning Jesus—60-62			
A. Direct question, 60-61	Fri.	Peter Denies Jesus *Mark 14:66-72*	
B. Direct answer, 62	Sat.	Jesus Before Pilate *Mark 15:1-5*	
IV. Condemnation of Christ—63-65			
V. Christ Before Pilate—15:1-3	Sun.	Jesus Given Up to Die *Mark 15:6-15*	

Verse by Verse

I. Traitor at the Trial—53-54

53 And they led Jesus away to the high priest: and with him were assembled all the chief priests and the elders and the scribes.

54 And Peter followed him afar off, even into the palace of the high priest: and he sat with the servants, and warmed himself at the fire.

The apostle Peter, who had quickly protested he would never deny His Lord (14:29), is just as quick to decline to stay close to Jesus after He is arrested. The expectations that Jesus would be a warlike Messiah were simply too firmly entrenched in the disciples' minds to allow them to understand what Jesus had said plainly: His mission was to die. Now that this plan was beginning to take shape, they have no will to follow a dying Messiah.

From 14:27ff. we have been told that these events occurred at night, showing one of the many illegalities in the hearings and trials Jesus endured. A hearing on an offense such as blasphemy, which might yield a death sentence, was to be held only in the daytime, then the night was supposed to pass before sentencing.

Matthew (26:57) adds that the high priest to whom Jesus is led was Caiphas. John's Gospel also involves Annas as another high priest. Ironically, the Romans had deposed Annas from the official high priest's office about 15 years earlier, for sentencing a person to death in direct disobedience to Roman law. Perhaps Caiphas involves Annas out of courtesy, either because Annas was his father-in-law, or because Annas may not have abdicated all of his duties.

One of the duties of the high priest was to preside over the Sanhedrin, the Jewish ruling council. Since it was Caiphas who had said that it might be well for one person to die than for a general Messianic uprising to cost the lives of many (John 11:50), he obviously cannot be an impartial judge.

II. Quest for Witnesses—55-59
A. Inconsistent testimony, 55-56

55 And the chief priests and all the council sought for witness against Jesus to put him to death; and found none.

56 For many bare false witness against him, but their witness agreed not together.

To give at least the appearance of going by the Law of Moses, Jesus' prosecutors sought multiple witnesses against Jesus (see Deut. 19:15). Although they "suborned perjury," or sought witnesses who would lie, they failed to instruct them adequately in order to get their stories straight; so their various testimonies did not agree with each other.

B. Commitment of perjury, 57-59

57 And there arose certain, and bare false witness against him, saying,

58 We heard him say, I will destroy this temple that is made with hands, and within three days I will build another made without hands.

59 But neither so did their witness agree together.

Finally the authorities find witnesses who can agree on one bit of testimony, although they deliberately misinterpret what Jesus had said about destroying "this temple." John 2:21 says plainly that Jesus was predicting that the "temple" of His body, which housed His soul, would be destroyed, then "rebuilt" or raised. Of course the true meaning of what Jesus had said does not matter to witnesses who are bought, and even these disagree on details.

III. Questioning Jesus—60-62
A. Direct question, 60-61

60 And the high priest stood up in the midst, and asked Jesus, saying, Answerest thou nothing? what is it which these witness against thee?

61 But he held his peace, and answered nothing. Again the high priest asked him, and said unto him, Art thou the Christ, the Son of the Blessed?

As "chairman" of the Sanhedrin, the high priest had the power to in-terrogate Jesus, but he can do so only by overlooking the fact that the witnesses could not agree what Jesus had actually said. Roman authorities had placed the Jews in charge of maintaining the sanctity of the Temple. By choosing a literal interpretation of Jesus' words, Caiphas could perhaps win a death sentence from the Romans—a step that Rome had reserved for itself.

Since Jesus chooses not to explain what He had meant by the "destroy this temple" saying, Caiphas takes another tack. If he can get Jesus to admit to being the Christ (Heb. mesheach, Messiah), and the divine Son of God, then the charge of blasphemy will be secured.

B. Direct answer, 62

62 And Jesus said, I am: and ye shall see the Son of man sitting on the right hand of power, and coming in the clouds of heaven.

Other Gospels quote Jesus admitting that He is the Messiah in less direct terms ("Thou sayest," as in 15:2). Mark, however, quotes an unambiguous confession, making the charge of blasphemy inevitable. In the books of Daniel and Ezekiel, where the title "Son of man" seems to have originated, he is a divine figure seen in the clouds; so in confessing that He is that Son, Jesus goes on to use Old Testament language of judgment to include Caiphas.

IV. Condemnation of Christ—63-65

63 Then the high priest rent his clothes, and saith, What need we any further witnesses?

64 Ye have heard the blasphemy: what think ye? And they all condemned him to be guilty of death.

65 And some began to spit on him, and to cover his face, and to buffet him, and to say unto him, Prophesy: and the servants did strike him with the palms of their hands.

Although Jesus has cast a mild threat in His prediction that He will come and judge Caiphas the judge, the high priest surely over-acts, no doubt for its calculated effect. Although the rest of the "judge and jury" team agree with the charge of blasphemy, their call for Jesus' death is another illegal part of these trials and hearings, since, as noted above, only Rome could exact the death penalty.

V. Christ Before Pilate—15:1-3

1 And straightway in the morning the chief priests held a consultation with the elders and scribes and the whole council, and bound Jesus, and carried him away, and delivered him to Pilate.

2 And Pilate asked him, Art thou the King of the Jews? And he answering said unto him, Thou sayest it.

3 And the chief priests accused him of many things: but he answered nothing.

The Jewish Sanhedrin may have been putting on at least the appearance of "going by the Book," in reassembling the next morning and reaffirming their judgment that since Jesus had been found guilty of blasphemy He would need to be re-manded to Pontius Pilate, governor of the Roman province of Judea. Luke (23:2) records their report to Pilate, carefully changed to say that Jesus claimed to be a king, not the Messiah. This changed the charge from a matter of Jewish religion, with which Rome did not want to be bothered, to sedition or treason. Although Rome was concerned about anyone who claimed he belonged on the throne instead of Caesar, it is hard to imagine that Pilate seriously thought that the bedraggled figure before him, who had lost all His supporters, could actually be planning to overthrow the government.

Still, since King Herod was on the throne, Pilate sends Jesus to him as a matter of courtesy (see Luke 23:11-16). Pilate may also have hoped that Herod would pronounce the death sentence for him, but after a brief interview Herod returned Jesus to Pilate.

The rest of the account records one last attempt on Pilate's part to spare Jesus' life. Since he cannot believe the charges brought against Him deserve the death penalty, he offers to release Him, in accordance with the custom at Passover (vs. 6). By then, however, the Jewish authorities have swayed the crowds, and they demand the release of a murderer and insurrectionist named Barabbas, instead. Bowing to the clamoring crowd instead of following his conscience, Pilate releases Jesus to the Sanhedrin, in effect authorizing His crucifixion.

Evangelistic Emphasis

As the trial of Jesus began, the priests and their followers made false accusations about Him, but Jesus responded to none of these. When He was asked directly if he were "the Christ, the Son of the Blessed," He did speak, and what He gave them was the multi-layered answer, "I am." Students of the Old Testament recognize these words. More than simply an affirmative reply, Jesus was identifying himself with the very God who once named Himself before Moses as "I AM." In these words (which were actually one word in Jesus' tongue), Jesus made the most basic statement of revelation. He was God incarnate.

The most basic element of faith is to accept that Jesus truly is the "I AM." Jesus offered no immediate evidence to validate this claim. Instead, He pointed toward the future when His statement would be verified—when all would acknowledge His true identity. It is interesting that there is still no present proof. There is only faith. To embrace these words in this present age of faith is to align ourselves with the One before whom every knee shall bow and every tongue confess. It is that very faith that asssures us of salvation in the great day of revelation.

ഇറ

Memory Selection

And the chief priests and all the council sought for witness against Jesus to put him to death; and found none.—*Mark 14:55*

It's intriguing how the priests and the council sought to do injustice by just means. Isn't it amazing that they could blindly persist in pursuing a course of violent evil only if they could wrap it in the appearance of goodness and fairness? The fact that they could find no justification to put Jesus to death did not cause them to rethink their course of action. What was about to happen had been determined. All that remained to be done was the packaging.

Though we cannot say what we would have done had we faced Jesus in that room, we do know that we often follow the same path as Jesus' accusers when we seek to justify our own acts of retribution and vengeance. How easy it is for us to lash out against someone because "he had it coming." How blind we can become when we clothe our acts of punishment and retribution with noble motives. We cannot change what happened in the house of the high priest 2000 years ago, but we can learn from it.

Weekday Problems

Lauren kept telling herself that the fact she did not like Christine had nothing to do with the situation. True, she felt that Christine undermined her relationship with the supervisor, and that she never missed an opportunity publicly to point out any mistake that Lauren had made. But all that was irrelevant now. Some money was missing from petty cash, and one of Lauren's friends had mentioned that she suspected Christine.

"Of course," Lauren had immediately thought, "it all makes sense to me." She began building her case against Christine. Christine had a key to the petty cash drawer, and she had stayed at her desk while all the others had gone to lunch yesterday. Soon Lauren had convinced herself and several other employees that Christine was indeed guilty. Although she knew that they did not have enough evidence to take to the supervisor, Lauren was satisfied that at least her co-workers could finally see Christine for who she really was.

* Can we rightly allow jealousies and personal feelings to cloud our judgment about someone?

* What would be a better way for Lauren to deal with her relationship with Christine?

'Again the Story Is Told'

Pilate, Pilate, wash your hands,
    Cry "What is Truth?" again.
None asks or cares, these wiser days,
    Nor fears so small a stain.
Peter, Peter, save your skin,
    Then, futile, weep your shame.
No one will notice. After all
    We have done the same.
Judas, Judas, hang yourself.
    How many times is this?
The Lesson's yet to learn. We still
    Betray Him with a kiss.
Jesus, Jesus, nailed on high,
    Christ Whom the nations praise,
Which is the Cross that tore thee most—
    Golgotha's or today's?

—Ada Jackson

This Lesson in Your Life

When we read the account of Jesus' trial before the priests and His appearance before Pilate, a part of us calls out for Him to defend Himself—to give full explanation of who He is—to demonstrate his power for all to see and be amazed. We know, of course, that there are many reasons why He did not do this. On one level, we can recognize, as did He, that a defense would accomplish nothing at this point. The minds of those before whom he stood were set. Also, His response to this situation had been prophesied centuries before by Isaiah: "He was oppressed, and he was afflicted, yet he did not open his mouth; like a lamb that is led to the slaughter, and like a sheep that before its shearers is silent, so he did not open his mouth" (Isa. 53:7 NRSV).

Another reason Jesus did not speak was that He knew His time had come. This was the very reason He was on the earth. Though the authorities were under the impression that they were in power, Jesus knew the truth. As He Himself had said, "I lay down my life in order to take it up again. No one takes it from me, but I lay it down of my own accord." (John 10:17,18 NRSV).

All this leads us to the most basic reason of all—His love for us. As Jesus stood before His accusers, He held each one of us in His heart. As they condemned Him, spat on Him, and hit Him, it was His love for each of us that held back His wrath. Each false accusation was endured by Jesus so that the true accusations against us might be nullified. Each blow that was struck was to remove the punishment that we each deserve. The sentence of death was accepted so that our sentence might be repealed. Jesus refused to defend Himself in that powerless court so we would never be called to defend ourselves before the one true Judge in eternity.

The Scripture records that Pilate marveled when Jesus refused to answer. Pilate marveled because he could not understand why. We understand why—and we marvel, too.

GETTING THE FACTS STRAIGHT

1. Before whom was Jesus first led away to be tried?
Jesus was taken to the high priest and with Him were assembled all the chief priests and the elders and the scribes (Mark 14:53).

2. According to Mark, which one of Jesus' disciples followed Him to the palace of the high priest?
It was Peter who followed from afar and sat with the servants and warmed himself at the fire (14:54).

3. What showed that the witnesses against Jesus were not credible?
The fact that they could not agree in their testimony (14:56).

4. What specific accusation about the Temple was made against Jesus?
The false witnesses testified that Jesus had said He would destroy the Temple, and build another in three days (14:58).

5. To what direct question by the high priest did Jesus respond?
He responded to the question, "Art thou the Christ, the son of the Blessed?" (14:62).

6. Based on Jesus' affirmative reply to this question, what charge was brought against Him?
The high priest accused Jesus of blasphemy (14:64).

7. What was the verdict of the entire group?
They found Jesus to be guilty of blasphemy and condemned Him to die (14:64).

8. How did Jesus' accusers mock and abuse Him?
They spat on Him. They covered His face and hit Him, then demanded that He prophesy who struck Him (14:65).

9. To whom did the chief priests deliver Jesus?
In the morning they bound Him and carried him to Pilate (15:1).

10. At what did Pilate marvel concerning Jesus?
Pilate marveled that Jesus did not attempt to answer His accusers (15:5).

We can all understand how someone might bend or break a principle when faced with a life and death situation. The impulse to survive and to avoid suffering and pain runs strong within us—strong enough at times for us to abandon beliefs. While we can understand how this can happen, we do not honor those who give in. We remember few of the names of those who abandoned their principles. The ones we remember are those who stood fast.

We remember Dietrich Bonhoeffer who had the opportunity to remain in New York and enjoy the safety afforded him by his teaching position in the United States. Bonhoeffer, however, could not remain silent about the abuses he knew were occurring in his native Germany. In 1940, he returned to his country to work against the Nazis and their oppression. His decision eventually resulted in his arrest and—only days before the liberation of the death camps—his execution.

We remember the Norwegian Eivind Berggrav who was ordered to silence his criticism of the Nazi occupation of his county. When he continued to speak out, he was persecuted. Finally, the soldiers arrived to arrest him, and as he was marched away he quoted from Scripture, "Have no fear of them, nor be troubled, but in your hearts reverence Christ as Lord" (1 Pet. 3:15).

For a Christian, the greatest example of standing fast in the face of persecution is Jesus before His accusers. As we wonder at His strength of will, we should not forget that only a few hours before He lay before God in the Garden of Gethsemane begging that another way be found. If we are to find the strength to stand—as did our Lord and Bonhoeffer and Berggrav—the beginning point is to lay all our fears honestly before God. To pretend we do not have such fears is to be vulnerable to their power when fears become reality.

Lesson 4
The Triumph

Mark 16:1-8, 12-15

And when the sabbath was past, Mary Magdalene, and Mary the mother of James, and Salome, had bought sweet spices, that they might come and anoint him.

2 And very early in the morning the first day of the week, they came unto the sepulchre at the rising of the sun.

3 And they said among themselves, Who shall roll us away the stone from the door of the sepulchre?

4 And when they looked, they saw that the stone was rolled away: for it was very great.

5 And entering into the sepulchre, they saw a young man sitting on the right side, clothed in a long white garment; and they were affrighted.

6 And he saith unto them, Be not affrighted: Ye seek Jesus of Nazareth, which was crucified: he is risen; he is not here: behold the place where they laid him.

7 But go your way, tell his disciples and Peter that he goeth before you into Galilee: there shall ye see him, as he said unto you.

8 And they went out quickly, and fled from the sepulchre; for they trembled and were amazed: neither said they any thing to any man; for they were afraid.

12 After that he appeared in another form unto two of them, as they walked, and went into the country.

13 And they went and told it unto the residue: neither believed they them.

14 Afterward he appeared unto the eleven as they sat at meat, and upbraided them with their unbelief and hardness of heart, because they believed not them which had seen him after he was risen.

15 And he said unto them, Go ye into all the world, and preach the gospel to every creature.

Memory Selection
Mark 16:6

Background Scripture
Mark 16

Devotional Reading
Matthew 28:16-20

It might be considered too commonplace to say that the focus of this lesson is "the gospel"; yet this "good news" is precisely the content not only of the text before us but the note on which Mark wanted to end his account of the life and teachings of Jesus. "He is risen; he is not here" (vs. 6) is the triumphant note toward which all the preceding narrative has pointed.

Yet it is a mistake to sound this news out so triumphantly that we overlook the frank way Mark also records the uncertainty with which those who first heard the news of the empty tomb took this "good news." The situation here at the end of Mark's Gospel is very much like many believers' view of the end of life. They believe, while asking God to help their unbelief (Mark 9:24). While the sensitive teacher will entertain any doubts group members may have, faith calls us to act on the announcment of the empty tomb despite our never having seen one.

Invite group members to play "the devil's advocate" by questioning the resurrection, then deal with each question. Following are objections to be prepared for, followed by suggested answers. *We have never seen a resurrection.* ("We walk by faith, not by sight.") *Jesus' body was stolen.* (By whom? The tomb was guarded so Jesus' disciples could not steal it, and His enemies certainly did not want it to be missing.) *The resurrection accounts in the four Gospels differ.* (But not in the essential message: "He is risen!") *Christ's followers invented the story.* (Why would they give their lives for something they knew to be a lie?)

While accepting the questions of sincere seekers, it is also important that believers be ready to give reasons for their hope (1 Pet. 3:15).

Teaching Outline	Daily Bible Readings	
	Mon.	Jesus' Tomb Is Sealed *Matthew 27:62-66*
I. Grim Task—1-3	Tue.	'He Is Not Here!' *Matthew 28:1-6b*
II. Glad Discovery—4-6	Wed.	'He Has Been Raised' *Mark 16:1-8*
III. 'Go and Tell'—7-8	Thu.	Appearance to the Women *Matthew 28:6c-10*
IV. Giving Evidence—12-14	Fri.	Appearance to Others *Mark 16:9-13*
V. Great Commission—15	Sat.	'I Am with You Always' *Matthew 28:16-20*
	Sun.	'Go into All the World' *Mark 16:14-20*

Verse by Verse

I. Grim Task—1-3

1 And when the sabbath was past, Mary Magdalene, and Mary the mother of James, and Salome, had bought sweet spices, that they might come and anoint him.

2 And very early in the morning the first day of the week, they came unto the sepulchre at the rising of the sun.

3 And they said among themselves, Who shall roll us away the stone from the door of the sepulchre?

The Gospels make more than might be expected of the burial of Jesus. Could it not be assumed that a person who was crucified would be buried? Not if, as the enemies of Jesus feared, His disciples might spirit away the body in order to produce an empty tomb to fulfill His predictions; and not if Jesus were only a spirit, as would later be taught by gnostics, and did not really have a body to bury. Perhaps to counter such tales, both the New Covenant Scriptures and the earliest Christian creeds emphasize that Jesus was "crucified, dead, and buried" (see 1 Cor. 15:3-5). Obviously a burial was also an essential preface to the doctrine and reality of His resurrection.

With the exception of Jacob (Gen. 50:2-3, 26), Israelites only washed and packed the body of the deceased with spices (Acts 9:37} instead of using the method of embalming invented by the Egyptians some 2,000 years earlier. Two "secret" disciples, Joseph of Arimathea and Nicodemus, had already packed Jesus' body with 100 pounds of myrrh and aloe, wrapping them with the body as was the Jewish custom (John 19:38-40). Yet these women, who had been among Jesus' closest public followers and had tended to His needs in life, were not about to be denied the opportunity of tending to Him also in death.

They waited until the first day of the week to avoid breaking the Jewish law against working on the Sabbath. They did not, however, have the ways or means to roll back the great stone that had been used to "seal" the tomb-like cave. In addition to the problem of its size, the round stone would have been allowed to roll down an inclined track that allowed gravity to add to its great weight.

II. Glad Discovery—4-6

4 And when they looked, they saw that the stone was rolled away: for it was very great.

5 And entering into the sepulchre, they saw a young man sitting on the right side, clothed in a long white garment; and they were affrighted.

6 And he saith unto them, Be not affrighted: Ye seek Jesus of Nazareth, which was crucified: he is risen; he is not here: behold the place where they laid him.

Although their physical problem was solved by the miraculous removal of the stone, the women now had an emotional problem: fright! Other Gospels call the young man who appeared to the women an angel, who seeks to reassure the women that no one has stolen Jesus' body. Matthew (28:2) says that an earthquake accompanied the appearance of the angel, apparently causing the stone to be dislodged.

Note that the first being to announce the gospel, the good news of the death, burial, and resurrection of Jesus is an angel; and the first audience to hear the stunning news, "He is risen!" are women. The young man or angel invites the women to inspect the tomb so they can be certain He is not hiding there. His words, designed to calm their fears, echo down through the centuries and resonate in the hearts of believers: we need not be afraid of death either, because it only introduces another chapter of life.

III. 'Go and Tell'—7-8

7 But go your way, tell his disciples and Peter that he goeth before you into Galilee: there shall ye see him, as he said unto you.

8 And they went out quickly, and fled from the sepulchre; for they trembled and were amazed: neither said they any thing to any man; for they were afraid.

To tell the women to report the good news to "his disciples and Peter" indicates that Peter is becoming a special leader among them (although this will not guard him from error, according to Galatians 2:11-12). Mark only hints at what John will report as an important post-resurrection appearance of Jesus in Galilee (see John 21). "As he said" represents Mark's typical way of abbreviating, declining to quote Jesus' entire statement directing the women to tell the disciples to go to Galilee and wait for him there (Matt. 28:10). Not only have women been the first to witness the empty tomb; the angel now commissions them as the first "evangelists." However, they prove to be too frightened to tell anyone immediately.

Although "amazement" is one of Mark's frequent words used to call attention to the supernatural impact of Jesus' deeds and words, it is also a subtle way of lending credibility to Jesus' resurrection. Neither the women nor the other disciples were expecting such an event, having utterly failed to understand His teaching on both the necessity of His dying and on His resurrection after (parts of) three days. Their amazement shows that they could not likely invent the story. They are told to go tell the rest of the disciples, perhaps because in Jewish culture the testimony of women was often not taken seriously. They are so stunned, however, that they cannot at first repeat what they had seen to any one.

The earliest manuscripts of Mark's Gospel end here. Yet the ending is so abrupt that many scholars believe that what follows (verses 9-20), or variations of those verses, were a part of the original manuscript which was somehow lost. Others hold that early Church leaders gave the Gospel a better-rounded ending by adding material from the other Gospels or other sources.

IV. Giving Evidence—12-14

12 After that he appeared in another form unto two of them, as they walked, and went into the country.

13 And they went and told it unto the residue: neither believed they them.

14 Afterward he appeared unto the eleven as they sat at meat, and upbraided them with their unbelief and hardness of heart, because they believed not them which had seen him after he was risen.

Saying that Jesus "appeared in another form" seems to describe the "Walk to Emmaus" account in Luke 24:13ff. Again showing his love for condensing stories, Mark only makes a quick reference to an event that the Gospel of Luke expands on a great deal.

Although the disciples who walked with Jesus to Emmaus eventually concluded that the "stranger" was Jesus, Mark is more concerned to emphasize the initial unbelief both of those disciples and "the eleven." The incident when Jesus appeared to them while eating no doubt refers to the event in John 20:19ff. John portrays Jesus as speaking peace to the fearful and anxious disciples, while Mark here includes the sterner note of Jesus upbraiding those who did not believe the report of disciples who had previously seen Him. There is an echo here of Jesus' encounter with Thomas, who would not believe until he had actually touched the risen Christ. Jesus' answer is for all who would come after Jesus' departure into heaven: "Blessed are they who have not seen, and yet have believed" (John 20:29).

V. Great Commission—15

15 And he said unto them, Go ye into all the world, and preach the gospel to every creature.

This ending of Mark closes with the "Great Commission," in what is perhaps an echo of Matthew 28:18-20. Jesus has fully allowed for the initial shock of His disciples, and given them time to recover their faith that He was not a mere spirit, but had truly arisen from the grave. It is time to stop dwelling on their doubts, to begin to emphasize what they have seen and heard with their own eyes, and to proclaim this good news to all the world. Modern Christians owe their own faith to the faithfulness of these dedicated disciples in responding to Jesus' challenge.

Evangelistic Emphasis

We have no empirical proof that Jesus was raised from the dead. What we have are stories—stories told by eyewitnesses who claim to have seen the empty tomb, heard the voice of the messenger, and encountered the resurrected Jesus Himself. We have no scientific data to corroborate these stories. We cannot even ask the witnesses questions. All we have is their stories—their stories plus our own hearts. It is in our hearts that these stories ring true, for our hearts have told us all along that there is more to life—more to us—than the few years we have in this world.

This is the same thing that the Apostle Paul told the people of Athens when he said, "God is not far from each one of us, for in him we live and move and have our being." (Acts 17.28). We cannot explain our awareness of God, and we cannot fully explain why we believe the stories of Jesus' resurrection—but our hearts tell us the stories are true. Just as the first disciples found meaning and life when they encountered the risen Lord, we, too, find life when He comes to us in these stories— when He comes to us in our hearts.

ഇൗൽ

Memory Selection

And he saith unto them, Be not affrighted: Ye seek Jesus of Nazareth, which was crucified: he is risen; he is not here: behold the place where they laid him.—*Mark 16.6*

In almost every biblical account of human beings witnessing a mighty work of the Lord, it is necessary for the first words spoken to be words of comfort. The women who discovered the empty tomb were frightened and confused. The presence of the young man in the white robe added to their fears. Their world had been turned upside down just two days ago when the one they believed to be the Messiah had been crucified. Now their last connection to Him—His lifeless body—was gone, too. We wonder if the words, "He is risen," even registered with them as they stood in the tomb. They obviously had not understood when Jesus Himself had told them of His approaching death and resurrection in the final days before that Friday. Were they hearing it now?

We are good at building up expectations, and surprises can rock our world. Surprises frighten us, and the resurrection of Jesus was God's greatest surprise of all. Can we dare to enter the tomb with the women and be frightened with them? Perhaps it is only in such fear that we can hear the words of comfort and good news. "Don't be frightened. He is risen."

426

Weekday Problems

Francisco slowly dialed the number, but before the phone rang he hung it up. He sat thinking for a moment, and then picked the receiver up again and this time made the call. "Bob," he began when his friend answered, "I'm not going to be able to go with you this evening . . . Yeah, I'm sorry, too . . . No, nothing is wrong. I've just got some reports I need to finish before morning . . . Sure, give me a call some other time." Francisco felt guilty as he hung up the phone. He had lied. He had no reports that were due. The truth was he was afraid. He was afraid to go downtown and work in the church's homeless shelter with Bob. It wasn't that he feared for his safety. His fear was much deeper than that. He was afraid that he would have little to offer in terms of comfort and support to those who were in such desperate need. He had tried it once, and a man had asked him for some spiritual guidance. Francisco had felt like such a failure. He didn't want to feel that way again.

* What could Francisco have done rather than avoid this opportunity to serve?

* What opportunities to serve others frighten you?

Small but Sporty

Ken: *Pretty small sports car you have there, isn't it?*
Ben: *Oh it has its advantages. When the carburetor floods all I have to do is put it over my shoulder and burp it.*

* * * *

The older gentleman was getting up shakily after being knocked down by a St. Bernard dog chasing a cat at a busy intersection. No sooner did he regain his feet when a small sports car careened around the corner and knocked him down again.

"Are you OK?" asked a by-stander, helping him up again. "That was a huge dog!"

"Well," said the man, "the dog didn't hurt me much, but that tin can tied to his tail nearly killed me."

* * * *

A man returned to his sports car and found a fender crushed. A note was attached, which read: The people who saw me sideswipe your car are also watching me write this note. No doubt they think I'm leaving you my name, address, and insurance company so you can contact me. They're partly right. I AM leaving.

This Lessonn in Your Life

The Gospel of Mark is special in the way it presents the disciples of Jesus as real human beings—complete with their failures and their misunderstandings. Back in the first chapter, Peter and his companions felt compelled to track down Jesus when He sought solitude to pray. They scolded Him for not realizing that everyone wanted to know where He was (Mark 1:35-37). Later, they were annoyed when Jesus was able to sleep through what they perceived as a life-threatening storm on the sea (4:35ff.). The disciples were incredulous when Jesus, walking through a pressing crowd, stopped and asked who had touched Him (5:24-34). They saw no possibilities when Jesus told them that they should feed a crowd of 5,000 men along with their wives and children (6.30-44). To make matters worse, only a few days later they had no idea how they were going to feed a crowd of only 4,000! (8.1-10). With all this background, perhaps we should not be shocked when the women at the tomb could not bring themselves to follow the instructions of the angel. "Go," the angel said, "go tell his disciples and Peter that He is going ahead of you to Galilee." The women, Scripture tell us, "said nothing to anyone, for they were afraid."

The word "gospel" means "good news." How can the mistakes and failures of Jesus' first disciples be good news to us? The good news comes as we follow the disciples through the book of Acts and learn of their great faithfulness and courage. The good news comes as the women do find the strength to tell of the resurrection and proclaim that death and sin had been defeated. The good news comes when we realize the many ways we have misunderstood and doubted the ability of Jesus to act in a situation—yet he acts anyway—and we learn. To be a disciple is to be a learner. The first disciples learned in many ways—often through their mistakes. So do we. And as Jesus was their patient teacher, so he remains with us.

GETTING THE FACTS STRAIGHT

1. Why did the three women wait until Sunday morning to visit the tomb of Jesus?

They had to wait until the Sabbath (Saturday) had passed (Mark 16:1).

2. Who were the three women who went to the tomb?

Mary Magdalene, Mary the mother of James, and Salome went to visit the tomb (16:1).

3. Why did they go to the tomb?

They took sweet spices to anoint the body of Jesus (16:1).

4. What problem were they discussing on their way to the tomb?

They did not know who they would find to roll away the stone from the door of the tomb (16:3).

5. Who did they find in the open tomb?

They saw a young man sitting on the right side, clothed in a long white garment (16:5).

6. What great announcement did the young man make to the women?

He told them that Jesus had risen and that He was not there (16:6).

7. Whom were the women instructed to tell about the resurrection?

The young man told the women to go tell the disciples and Peter (16:7).

8. Where were the disciples to go to meet Jesus?

The disciples were to go to Galilee and there they would see Him (16:7).

9. What did the women do when they left the tomb?

They went out quickly and fled. They said nothing to anyone because they were afraid (16:8).

10. When Jesus appeared to the disciples, what commission did He give them?

Jesus told the disciples to go into all the world and preach the gospel to every creature (16:15).

When I was a boy, I enjoyed listening to a religious station that broadcast from a border town in Mexico. The station claimed to be the world's most powerful radio station. The late evening schedule was a mixture of gospel songs and sermons from preachers across the country. The music was especially intriguing to me. It was not the polished music of commercial radio, but soulful songs recorded with primitive equipment.

One song in particular was a favorite of mine. It was titled, "White Rags in the Ol' Apple Tree." The song told the story of a man recently released from prison. In his final letter home before his release, he had written that he would understand if his family never wanted to see him again. He told them that he would be riding on the bus on a certain day, and if the family wanted him to stop, they were to tie a white rag in the ol' apple tree in front of the house. Of course, when he neared the house, what he saw was hundreds of white rags tied in the branches of the tree. Many will recognize this story as one that was adapted in later years to become the song, "Tie a Yellow Ribbon 'Round the Old Oak Tree." The yellow ribbon has now become the universal symbol of welcome—especially for servicemen returning from duty.

In a sense there is a yellow ribbon in the story told in Mark Chapter 16. It is included in the message the angel gave to the women. He did not just say, "Go tell all the disciples." He added specifically, "Go tell Peter." If any disciple would need to hear that a resurrected Jesus still wanted him, it would have been Peter. Peter was the one who had denied Him—not once but three times. Peter was the one who had cursed and said he never knew Jesus. Jesus knew he needed a special word. He knew he need a ribbon of welcome. He sent it to his beloved disciple.

430

Lesson 5

The Beatitudes

Matthew 5:1-16

And seeing the multitudes, he went up into a mountain: and when he was set, his disciples came unto him:

2 And he opened his mouth, and taught them, saying,

3 Blessed are the poor in spirit: for theirs is the kingdom of heaven.

4 Blessed are they that mourn: for they shall be comforted.

5 Blessed are the meek: for they shall inherit the earth.

6 Blessed are they which do hunger and thirst after righteousness: for they shall be filled.

7 Blessed are the merciful: for they shall obtain mercy.

8 Blessed are the pure in heart: for they shall see God.

9 Blessed are the peacemakers: for they shall be called the children of God.

10 Blessed are they which are persecuted for righteousness' sake: for theirs is the kingdom of heaven.

11 Blessed are ye, when men shall revile you, and persecute you, and shall say all manner of evil against you falsely, for my sake.

12 Rejoice, and be exceeding glad: for great is your reward in heaven: for so persecuted they the prophets which were before you.

13 Ye are the salt of the earth: but if the salt have lost his savour, wherewith shall it be salted? it is thenceforth good for nothing, but to be cast out, and to be trodden under foot of men.

14 Ye are the light of the world. A city that is set on an hill cannot be hid.

15 Neither do men light a candle, and put it under a bushel, but on a candlestick; and it giveth light unto all that are in the house.

16 Let your light so shine before men, that they may see your good works, and glorify your Father which is in heaven.

Memory Selection
Matthew 5:6

Background Scripture
Matthew 5:1-16

Devotional Reading
Luke 6:17-23

Many Americans seem to be on an endless quest for "peace of mind," a desire to discover true meaning in life. Thousands of people regularly stream to gurus atop mountains in India, to the forests of the northwest, rented hotel ballrooms in Flordia, and retreat centers in a California desert, exploring the latest technique of self-discovery, fulfillment, and happiness.

This lesson focuses on Jesus' "Beatitudes." The fact that each one begins with the term "Blessed," from a word also widely translated "happy," places this teaching in a similar category as the teachings which entice so many to travel so far seeking happiness. There is, however, a fundamental difference. The happiness of which Jesus speaks is related to "the kingdom of heaven." This lesson endeavors to bring out that difference.

ഇറ.

What do people want or need most to be fulfilled or happy? One of the best-known lists in our time has been the late psychologist Abraham Maslow's "Hierarchy of Needs." This lesson can be introduced by discussing his formula. In the "Maslow Pyramid" below, the most basic need is at the bottom, and

assumes that most people will satisfy that need before ascending to the next. How valid do group members find it? How do these needs compare with the Beatitudes?

Teaching Outline	Daily Bible Readings

Teaching Outline	Daily Bible Readings
I. A New Moses?—1-2	Mon. On Discipleship *Luke 6:17-23*
II. The Way Up Is Down—3-4	Tue. On the Christian Life *Matthew 5:1-8*
III. What's Most Important?—5-6	Wed. Being True Disciples *Matthew 5:9-16*
IV. What Attitudes Are Best?—7-9	Thu. Love Your Enemies *Matthew 5:43-48*
V. What About Criticism?—10-12	Fri. Be Merciful *Luke 6:32-36*
VI. On Being Different—13-16	Sat. Don't Be Judgmental *Matthew 7:1-5*
A. Salt of the earth, 13	Sun. More on Judging Others *Luke 6:37-42*
B. Light in the darkness, 14-16	

Verse by Verse

I. The Setting—1-2

1 And seeing the multitudes, he went up into a mountain: and when he was set, his disciples came unto him:

2 And he opened his mouth, and taught them, saying,

Some students of Matthew's Gospel have wondered if Jesus goes up on a mountain to give this famous teaching as a deliberate gesture to present Himself as a new Moses, who also "went up into a mountain," Sinai, then delivered his own famous summary of the Law, the Ten Commandments. It has been suggested that Matthew, whose Gospel seems to be especially directed at Jewish readers, is deliberately showing that Jesus is supplanting Moses as the giver of a new law—one that deals more than the Old Law did with personal and inner issues such as the need of the heart to experience true "blessedness." Whether or not these parallels are intentional, we are drawn to the scene in response to the Messianic prophet Isaiah's call: "Come ye, and let us go up to the mountain of the Lord . . . and he will teach us of his ways" (Isa. 2:3).

Further to the scene's setting, it is significant that Jesus "sat down" (NIV) to deliver this famous teaching.

Unlike most teachers today, the rabbis so customarily sat down to teach that it became a sign for the audience to quiet down and pay close attention. What was said from the "teaching chair" was considered of grave importance (compare the Roman Catholic view of the special significance of the Pope's teaching when he speaks ex cathedra, or "from the chair"). Thus, as Jesus delivers this teaching, Matthew wants us to give to Him the special respect Jews gave to a beloved rabbi.

II. The Way Up Is Down—3-4

3 Blessed are the poor in spirit: for theirs is the kingdom of heaven.

4 Blessed are they that mourn: for they shall be comforted.

Some modern versions translated "blessed" as "happy." While the original word can mean that, it seems superficial in this context. The term is probably closer to the Hebrew *shalom*, meaning wholeness, peace and joy.

To understand the Beatitudes we must first consider them in their original setting, looking for what Jesus wanted His original hearers, probably Jews, to understand by this "profoundly simple" teaching.

For example, these first two Beatitudes were originally a blessing or benediction on Jews who were disheartened and reduced to mourning by the current state of Jewry; for only they, not those who happily ignored how far the Jews are from "kingdom living," can appreciate that the Kingdom of God is about to break through in the form of Jesus the King's presence and teaching.

If we make the mistake of taking these sayings first as what has been called "be happy attitudes" aimed at our personal feelings today, Jesus is advising us to be sad (or, in Luke 6:20, "poor") because of some inherent value in sadness or poverty. Jesus' point is that only when we realize our spiritual poverty are we ready to accept God's spiritual riches through Christ, thus "actualizing" the kingdom of God in our own lives.

III. What's Most Important?—5-6

5 Blessed are the meek: for they shall inherit the earth.

6 Blessed are they which do hunger and thirst after righteousness: for they shall be filled.

Again, note how "meekness" applied to Kingdom-living in Jesus' day. He is not recommending a spineless, "milktoast" character, but the more aggressive attitude required for a Jew to turn the other cheek, walk the second mile, and give both coat and cloak to an oppressive Roman who was taking advantage of his "superior power" (see vss. 39-42). The power to live with such humility is far greater than the supposed power of a sword-carrying Roman soldier. If that was true for a Jew, then a secondary application teaches us that those with such attitudes will "inherit the earth," or be rewarded with all the riches of Christ the King's spiritual Kingdom.

A similar point can be made about hungering and thirsting for righteousness. As in most of these sayings, Jesus stands "common sense" values on their head. The fact is that only those who are hungry for God can ever by filled by Him. The Kingdom is shut to those who think they have "arrived" spiritually and are already full of God.

IV. What Attitudes Are Best?—7-9

7 Blessed are the merciful: for they shall obtain mercy.

8 Blessed are the pure in heart: for they shall see God.

9 Blessed are the peacemakers: for they shall be called the children of God.

Being merciful, pure in heart (or single-mindedly trying to keep the mind turned toward God), and working for peace, are character traits that are typically despised by the real "movers and shakers" of this world. Jesus, however, is recommending character traits that are valued in another world—the Kingdom of God. Whether we are open to this teaching depends on what "kingdom" we want to live in. We should not expect to be fulfilled by the values of the world.

V. What About Criticism?—10-12

10 Blessed are they which are persecuted for righteousness' sake: for theirs is the kingdom of

heaven.

11 Blessed are ye, when men shall revile you, and persecute you, and shall say all manner of evil against you falsely, for my sake.

12 Rejoice, and be exceeding glad: for great is your reward in heaven: for so persecuted they the prophets which were before you.

Again, it is clear that this sermon was directed toward those whose longing for the breaking in of God's kingdom had so far been thwarted, both by oppression from without and by a low state of commitment from within the People of God. Their efforts at reform had been met with persecution, reviling, and false charges. Some politically-motivated Jews dismissed these Kingdom-seekers as "too spiritual for any earthly good."

Jesus has a pointed word of encouragement for such people. They can rejoice that they are in the good company of the prophets who preceded them. They can be satisfied that their goal is not to live forever, or without discomfort, but to live after Kingdom principles.

VI. On Being Different—13-16
A. Salt of the earth, 13

13 Ye are the salt of the earth: but if the salt have lost his savour, wherewith shall it be salted? it is thenceforth good for nothing, but to be cast out, and to be trodden under foot of men.

As is often noted in comments on this verse, salt was the universal preservative in a day that lacked refrigeration and chemical preservatives. When it had served its purpose and lost its "tang," it was often poured on pathways as a kind of "soft paving." Jesus' saying is designed to give heart to those whose commitment to Kingdom-values had done far more than they realized to "preserve" the world. If they gave up their determination to "season" the world with their Kingdom-living, "wherewith will it be seasoned?"

B. Light in the darkness, 14-16

14 Ye are the light of the world. A city that is set on an hill cannot be hid.

15 Neither do men light a candle, and put it under a bushel, but on a candlestick; and it giveth light unto all that are in the house.

16 Let your light so shine before men, that they may see your good works, and glorify your Father which is in heaven.

Turning the metaphor from salt to light, Jesus holds up Kingdom-seeking people as the light necessary if a world stumbling in darkness is ever to find its way to God. If Kingdom citizens grow weary of holding up their light, their fate will not just be a personal tragedy; the world will no longer have a light by which to see God and glorify Him.

To summarize, the Beatitudes are not mere handy adages for personal happiness. They have a theological and a social edge to them, and are designed to help others see the value not just of feeling good but of living as citizens of the Kingdom of God.

Evangelistic Emphasis

In The Beatitudes, Jesus makes a list of people who are not normally considered "winners" and pronounces them blessed. This world rarely rewards the poor in spirit, the mourners, the meek, or those who are hungry for justice. Success usually goes to the aggressors—not to those who dispense mercy, seek purity, or promote peace. The good news Jesus brought is that within the Kingdom of God—in contrast to this world—these are the very people who find fulfillment and blessing. The Gospel of Jesus turns this world upside down. The first shall be last and the last shall be first. The proud are humbled and the lowly are lifted up. The poor receive the kingdom, and the meek inherit the earth.

As we seek to spread the Gospel, we cannot say that Jesus did not tell us who would hear the word as good news. If we seek to bring the blessing of the kingdom into the lives of our neighbors, we know whom to look for. In The Beatitudes, Jesus has given us at least a beginning point in our quest for those who will listen—those who will be blessed.

ɛɔႷૹ

Memory Selection

Blessed are they which do hunger and thirst after righteousness: for they shall be filled.— Matthew 5:6

What happens when you are hungry? Although I have never known true hunger, I do know that when my body signals me it is time to eat, all other interests tend to fade into the background. There are times when that hunger is focused. Someone might mention a food, or I might see an ad on television that sends me on a quest for a particular food to satisfy my desire. One thing is sure—hunger is difficult to ignore.

Some among us hunger for righteousness. They are horrified by the injustices around them and by the suffering they witness. They long for the time that God's goodness and fairness will be experienced completely. The good news is that in the Kingdom of God, those who hunger for God's righteousness will be completely filled. The promise of that blessing is sufficient to drive us to keep searching for that particular food—and to encourage others who are hungry to look with us.

Weekday Problems

Allison had to admit that her feelings were hurt. At the end of the morning service, the pastor had recognized several members of the congregation who had recently volunteered extra time in some of the church's ministries. Of course, Allison did not expect to receive public notice for the things she did, but she was surprised that she had not been included in the list. Just a few weeks ago she had stayed up half the night baking cookies for Vacation Bible School. And she was teaching the four-year-old Sunday school class for the third straight year because no one else would do it. How long had she served as Fellowship Chairwoman for the Tuesday Ladies Bible Study? As she drove home from church that morning, Allison thought that it might be time for her to take a break from her activities. Maybe then people would appreciate how much work was involved. Maybe then they would remember to say Thanks.

* According to Jesus, who is to receive the glory for our good works?

* What might need to change in our lives for us to be pleased with this arrangement?

On Self-Centered Beatitudes

"In his "Christmas Oratorio" W. H. Auden satirizes the self-centered trend of so many current religious attitudes in the following prayer:

"'O God, put away justice and truth, for we cannot understand them and we do not want them. Eternity would bore us dreadfully. Leave thy heavens and come down to our earth of water-clocks and hedges. Become our uncle. Look after Baby, amuse Grandfather, . . . help Willie with his homework, introduce Muriel to a handsome naval officer. Be interesting and weak like us, and we will love you as we love ourselves.'

"The cult of the happiness seekers would reduce God to a Santa Claus who comes down our chimneys to fill our stockings with our desires. In the midst of the popular man-centered effort to make God our ally rather than our sovereign, this book explores the charter of the higher happiness, as given in the Beatitudes."

—Ralph W. Sockman, in his Foreword
to *The Higher Happiness*

This Lesson in Your Life

Once a large crowd gathered at the foot of a mountain. They had been slaves in the land of Egypt. In their misery and pain, they had cried out to the Lord for deliverance, and the God of their fathers had sent them Moses. Now Moses was telling them to prepare themselves to hear the voice of this God. As they stood in fear and awe, amid thunder and lightning, a thick cloud descended upon the mountain, and they heard the blast of a trumpet so loud that even the strongest among them trembled. The mountain was enshrouded in smoke and the ground shook. Then the voice—the voice of God, "I am the Lord your God, who brought you out of the land of Egypt, out of the house of slavery . . . ." The people listened to the blessing, and they listened to the responsibilities of being God's people that followed.

Several hundred years later, God's Son ascended a mountain. There was no thunder or lightning or fire, but a crowd of people gathered around Him. "Blessed are the poor in spirit," He said. "Blessed are those who mourn. Blessed are the meek. Blessed are those who hunger and thirst for righteousness." In awe, the people listened—for these were the ones whom society had left behind. They were the poor, the sad, the powerless and the hungry. Jesus spoke the word of His father as He pronounced the blessing of the kingdom and as He spoke of the responsibilities of living in the kingdom.

The question for us is, "Will we listen?" For us, there is no thunder or smoke or earthquake. For the most part, we are not the disenfranchised of this earth. Can we hear the word of blessing and the call to responsibility? We can if we are aware enough to realize that we, too, have been freed from slavery. We will listen when we see that in so many ways we remain poor in spirit and powerless. When we pause to face our griefs and our hungers, we hear the word of God's blessing with eager ears and with awe and trembling. Then, and only then, will we gladly hear, too, the calling of the Father to responsible living in His Kingdom.

1. When Jesus saw the multitude of people following Him, what did He do?

He went up on a mountain and sat down to teach them (Matt. 5:1,2).

2. In the beginning of his Sermon on the Mount, Jesus pronounced blessings on several groups of people. How many of these groups can you name?

Jesus blessed the poor in spirit, those who mourn, the meek, those who hunger and thirst for righteousness, the merciful, the pure in heart, the peacemakers, and those who are persecuted for righteousness' sake (5:3-10).

3. Who will be called children of God?

Jesus said that peacemakers will be called the children of God (5:9).

4. Who will inherit the earth?

The meek will inherit the earth (5:5).

5. According to Jesus, why are those who are reviled and persecuted and spoken against falsely for His sake able to rejoice?

They can rejoice because their reward in heaven is great (5:11,12).

6. Who serve as examples to believers as people who were mistreated in the name of God?

The prophets were persecuted in these same ways (5:12).

7. To what two essential elements of life did Jesus compare His disciples?

Jesus said His disciples were the salt of the earth and the light of the world (5:13,14).

8. What would make salt useless?

Salt becomes useless when it loses its savor (saltiness or taste, 5:13).

9. What defeats the purpose of light?

The purpose of light is defeated if it is hidden (5:14).

10. When people see the light of the good works of Jesus' disciples, what is their response?

They who see the good works of Jesus' disciples will glorify the Father in heaven (5:16).

Have you ever been asked to bring a "white elephant gift" to a party? To us, such an invitation means that we should bring a gift that is amusing and worthless—but harmless. But the original white elephants were anything but harmless. Years ago in Southeast Asia, an albino elephant was considered a sacred animal and the property of the king. White elephants, by decree, could do no work. If one of the king's subjects offended him, he would present the offender with the gift of a white elephant. Having an elephant that could not work and produce income but did eat with an elephantine appetite would soon reduce its owner to ruin. So, the original white elephant was actually a curse disguised as a blessing. It was called a gift, but it was really a burden.

Jesus began his Sermon on the Mount by pronouncing wonderful blessings in the lives of people. For centuries, God's people had heard the promise of blessings and favor found in Isaiah 61. Now, in the person of Jesus, the fulfillment of these blessings is announced. This is why the word of Jesus is gospel—good news. "Congratulations," Jesus is saying, "you will receive what was promised."

Do we still read these words of Jesus as blessing? Do we rush past the blessing and transform His words in exhortations? "If you wish to be blessed," we say, "then you must become poor in spirit. If you desire blessing, you must learn to mourn." If we are not careful, we present these marvelous blessings as white elephants—burdens to be born rather than words of deliverance. Let Jesus' words uplift you today. In the list of blessings we call "beatitudes," surely there is at least one that touches your life. Surely there is a word of blessing to you. Though you may have suffered loss or loneliness or frustration in this world, the blessing of the Kingdom is yours. Though you may hunger for unfound justice and long for peace in an aggressive society, the blessing is yours. This is good news.

Lesson 6

Practice of Piety

Matthew 6:1-13

$\mathfrak{T}$ ake heed that ye do not your alms before men, to be seen of them: otherwise ye have no reward of your Father which is in heaven.

2 Therefore when thou doest thine alms, do not sound a trumpet before thee, as the hypocrites do in the synagogues and in the streets, that they may have glory of men. Verily I say unto you, They have their reward.

3 But when thou doest alms, let not thy left hand know what thy right hand doeth:

4 That thine alms may be in secret: and thy Father which seeth in secret himself shall reward thee openly.

5 And when thou prayest, thou shalt not be as the hypocrites are: for they love to pray standing in the synagogues and in the corners of the streets, that they may be seen of men. Verily I say unto you, They have their reward.

6 But thou, when thou prayest, enter into thy closet, and when thou hast shut thy door, pray to thy Father which is in secret; and thy Father which seeth in secret shall reward thee openly.

7 But when ye pray, use not vain repetitions, as the heathen do: for they think that they shall be heard for their much speaking.

8 Be not ye therefore like unto them: for your Father knoweth what things ye have need of, before ye ask him.

9 After this manner therefore pray ye: Our Father which art in heaven, Hallowed be thy name.

10 Thy kingdom come. Thy will be done in earth, as it is in heaven.

11 Give us this day our daily bread.

12 And forgive us our debts, as we forgive our debtors.

13 And lead us not into temptation, but deliver us from evil: For thine is the kingdom, and the power, and the glory, for ever. Amen.

14 For if ye forgive men their trespasses, your heavenly Father will also forgive you:

July 10

Memory Selection
Matthew 6:1

Background Scripture
Matthew 6:1-18

Devotional Readings
Luke 11:5-13

441

Religious acts usually have two dimensions—the public and the private. Those who pray publicly may bless those who hear them while at the same time speaking directly to God. Although this lesson focuses on the priority of the inner, private dimension, this does not mean that Jesus condemned all public expressions of piety. He observed public feast days such as Passover. He allowed a public demonstration on Palm Sunday when He entered Jerusalem in what was virtually a parade atmosphere.

What Jesus condemns in today's text deals with the *motive* for public piety. It must not be for the purpose of impressing other people, but directed God-ward. It must be sincere, and heart-felt. The lesson also includes the famous "Lord's Prayer" or "Model Prayer."

&)C&

Invite discussion of the pros and cons of prayer at public school events, and the display of religious icons such as the Ten Commandments or manger scenes on public property. Of course all viewpoints are to be treated with respect.

Raise such questions as (1) Does freedom of speech include public prayers, or infringe on the rights of people of different religions? (2) Is our country, and by extension its schools and other public institutions, "Christian"? (3) Does a religious monument on public property, paid for by taxes, unfairly suggest the support of those who do not agree with its religious message? (4) Do such prayers and/or monuments violate the principle of "separation of church and state," and is this principle actually valid anyway? (5) Do public prayers encourage insincere religion or piety "for show"?

Teaching Outline	Daily Bible Readings

I. Motives for Giving—1-4
  A. Approval from others, 1-2
  B. Privately, for God, 3-4
II. Motives for Praying—5-8
  A. Different rewards, 5-6
  B. Virtue of brevity, 7-8
III. Model Prayer—9-14
  A. Addressing God, 9
  B. Surrender of the will, 10
  C. Petition, 11
  D. Forgiveness, 12
  E. Kingdom-power over evil, 13
	Mon. Importance of Prayer
	James 5:13-18
	Tue. Faith and Prayer
	Mark 11:20-25
	Wed. God Answers Prayer
	Matthew 7:7-11
	Thu. Perseverance in Prayer
	Luke 11:5-13
	Fri. Almsgiving and Prayer
	Matthew 6:1-8
	Sat. The Lord's Prayer
	Matthew 6:9-15
	Sun. Fasting and Treasures
	Matthew 6:16-21

Verse by Verse

I. Motives for Giving—1-4

A. Approval from others, 1-2

1 Take heed that ye do not your alms before men, to be seen of them: otherwise ye have no reward of your Father which is in heaven.

2 Therefore when thou doest thine alms, do not sound a trumpet before thee, as the hypocrites do in the synagogues and in the streets, that they may have glory of men. Verily I say unto you, They have their reward.

Jesus' teaching on being outwardly religious focuses on alms-giving, prayer, and fasting (vs. 16), since contemporary Jewish practice had virtually reduced "righteousness" to these three forms of piety.

The Law of Moses required Jews to help the poor (Deut. 15:11). Later rabbis had followed the universal human tendency to equate such good works as alms-giving with *earning* God's approval. This tendency was so strong that even here in verse 1 the KJV translates "righteousness" by "alms," as though they are the same.

Since the scribes and Pharisees wanted to be considered righteous, they made much of their alms-giving. Generous contributors were often called to the front of a synagogue assembly to be honored; and Jesus

warns that if this is the motive for giving, the giver's reward will be limited to the applause of the people. ("They have their reward."). There is no record of alms-giving being literally accompanied by trumpets, but it makes a vivid exaggeration to underline Jesus' point: Alms-giving is for the poor and for the glory of God, not for the alms-giver.

B. Privately, for God, 3-4

3 But when thou doest alms, let not thy left hand know what thy right hand doeth:

4 That thine alms may be in secret: and thy Father which seeth in secret himself shall reward thee openly.

One "hand" stands both for one's own sense of self-approval and for other people, while the other stands for the act of giving. There is to be no connection between helping others on the one hand and basking in the congratulations of self or others, on the other. "Openly," therefore, must mean "generously" or "freely," or perhaps the approval that will be made public only at Judgment Day.

II. Motives for Praying—5-8

A. Different rewards, 5-6

5 And when thou prayest, thou shalt not be as the hypocrites are:

443

for they love to pray standing in the synagogues and in the corners of the streets, that they may be seen of men. Verily I say unto you, They have their reward.

6 But thou, when thou prayest, enter into thy closet, and when thou hast shut thy door, pray to thy Father which is in secret; and thy Father which seeth in secret shall reward thee openly.

Prayer is to be treated as private as alms-giving. That this does not prohibit all public prayers is seen by such incidents as Lydia's "prayer group," in Acts 16:13. This admonition is another radical over-statement for the deliberate purpose of emphasizing that God can hear private prayer as well as public. As in the case of alms-giving, what is prohibited is praying "to be seen of men."

The word for "hypocrite" also referred to an actor, one who was skilled at "playing a part." Jesus is condemning not only insincere prayers, but those that are "performed" for people as the audience, instead of God.

B. Virtue of brevity, 7-8

7 But when ye pray, use not vain repetitions, as the heathen do: for they think that they shall be heard for their much speaking.

8 Be not ye therefore like unto them: for your Father knoweth what things ye have need of, before ye ask him.

The prayers of many pagans consisted of rote chants and phrases whose real meaning had been lost long ago (compare the Buddhist "prayer-wheel"). It is natural to think that if prayer "works," then much prayer works more. The warning here is twofold: Christian prayer is to be heart-felt instead of "vain" (or empty); and its effectiveness cannot be measured by its length, since God already knows our needs. This doesn't mean that we should not pray aloud at all; we need to hear ourselves pray partly to help us discern our priorities.

III. Model Prayer—9-14

A. Addressing God, 9

9 After this manner therefore pray ye: Our Father which art in heaven, Hallowed be thy name.

Having taught us how not to pray, Jesus now tells us how we should pray, in phrases that have become a part of virtually every Christian tradition. Ironically, the merely "liturgical" use of what is usually called "the Lord's Prayer" violates Jesus' teaching about not praying "in vain." Jesus probably intended for the elements of this prayer to be remembered, and to become incorporated in principle in Christian prayers, rather than for it to be remembered and recited word-for-word. Yet the condemnation of its "formal" use by those from non-liturgical traditions ignores the fact that it can be recited with heart-felt fervency.

Jesus first reminds us that God is to be addressed with respect and honor. Since He is in heaven and we are on earth, our words should be respectful and few (Eccles. 5:2). To "hallow" God's name is to "sanctify" it, or treat it as holy. It was about this time that Jews began to treat God's personal name, Yahweh, as so holy that they would not pronounce it (leading to the modern English practice among many conservative Jews merely to hint at God's name, writing it as G-d, or using an indirect name such as "The Blessed").

B. Surrender of the will, 10

10 Thy kingdom come. Thy will be done in earth, as it is in heaven.

Since Jesus is the King, there is a sense in which His Kingdom came when He did. We do not merely look for its coming at the end of time, since early converts were said to be translated into the Kingdom (Col. 1:13). In another sense, however, it is always appropriate to pray that the Kingdom come to a fuller extent, both in the form of social justice throughout the world and in taking root more fully in our own hearts.

C. Petition, 11

11 Give us this day our daily bread.

Again, as a loving Father God knows we need food daily; yet we express our dependence on Him when we ask for it specifically. The original language hints at our need to ask only for what we need in the short term, "day by day," rather than asking for life-long security.

D. Forgiveness, 12

12 And forgive us our debts, as we forgive our debtors.

14 For if ye forgive men their trespasses, your heavenly Father will also forgive you:

"Debts" means "what we owe"; and Jesus chooses a word that the rabbis used to describe the accumulation of sins between man and God. They formed a mountain that Jesus says is to be "prayed away." There are several conditions for this to occur, such as faith and obedience; but Jesus chooses a condition that relates directly to our own forgiveness: forgiving others. This is explained, after skipping a verse, not as a "work" of forgiveness that earns our own forgiveness, but simply as a matter of fairness: We have no right to ask God to remove the mountain of debt between ourselves and Him if we are content to leave one between ourselves and others.

E. Kingdom-power over evil, 13

13 And lead us not into temptation, but deliver us from evil: For thine is the kingdom, and the power, and the glory, for ever. Amen.

To ask God not to lead us into temptation does not imply that He would. It is a negative way to state the positive idea that the world is a "mine field," and that we need God's aid in avoiding them.

The last word in this model prayer is a word of praise. To ascribe to God these majestic phrases is not, as one modern critic has said, to give God "excessive metaphysical compliments." God knows His "place" very well. It is rather our need, not God's, that makes it appropriate to end our prayers with such reminders of His majesty and power.

Evangelistic Emphasis

In the prayer Jesus taught His disciples to pray, He included the phrase, "Forgive us our debts as we forgive our debtors." When we give our hearts to God, we are well aware of our need for forgiveness, but Jesus pushes us beyond seeking forgiveness for ourselves to becoming forgivers as well. As if the prayer did not make this point strongly enough, Jesus quickly adds that if we do not learn to forgive others our own forgiveness is in jeopardy.

There are many reasons Jesus was insistent that we learn to forgive others, but one of the most meaningful is that in forgiving others we learn how difficult it can be to give grace. Each time we are called upon to forgive someone who has wronged us, we face once again the realization that forgiveness can be painful. It can hurt to let go of our wounded feelings and our outrage at the injustice we have suffered. Jesus calls on us to use those times to remind ourselves of how much our own forgiveness cost God. Our forgiveness hung His Son on a cross. Are we willing to suffer in order to pass this gift of grace on to others? As we wrestle with our own feelings, let us be lost in praise to God for His willingness to pay the price to forgive us.

೫ℭ೫

Memory Selection

Take heed that ye do not your alms before men, to be seen of them: otherwise ye have no reward of your Father which is in heaven.—*Matthew 6:1*

Once there was a man who went from house to house in a poor rural area offering to buy the junk out of people's attics and barns. He would knock on the door and ask the occupants if they needed a little extra cash in return for getting rid of some of their clutter. He found many takers, and those who sold to him were usually satisfied because they had done some cleaning and received money in return.

Of course, the man was a knowledgeable antique dealer. Much of the "junk" he bought for only a few dollars ended up with hefty price tags in his shop in the city. He became a wealthy man because many unsuspecting people did not know the value of their goods and settled for far too little.

Today's memory verse warns us that we can seek the wrong reward. If we do acts of kindness so that others will think well of us, then we do receive the payment we were wanting. However, we forfeit a much greater reward. It is up to us to decide the marketplace for any good deeds we might be privileged to do, and, thanks to Jesus, we know their true value.

Weekday Problems

During one of his daily devotional times, Ray was convicted by Jesus' admonition in Matthew 6:4 to do acts of kindness "in secret." Throughout the day, he considered ways he could obey this Word from the Lord. He could send an anonymous donation to a charity or to the church, but even then, if he wanted the tax benefit, he would need a receipt—so someone would have to know. He considered many possibilities, only to be frustrated at how difficult it would be to do something totally in secret. Finally, as he was leaving his office, he stumbled upon his opportunity. He walked past a car with a parking ticket on the window. He recognized the car as belonging to one of his co-workers. Quickly, he removed the ticket, placed the required amount in the envelope and deposited it in the ticket box down the street. Mission accomplished. In the days that followed, he was surprised at how difficult it was not to mention to the co-worker what he had done for her. He was convicted again by how strong the need to be thanked and appreciated is.

* Was it necessary for Ray to go to this extreme to keep Jesus' word?

* Can you find a way to do something kind and remain totally anonymous?

Prayers from the Mouths of Babes

Dear God . . .

I went to this wedding, and they kissed right there in church. Is that OK?

Who draws those lines around the countries?

It rained every day during our vacation, and my dad said some things about You that people are not supposed to say. I hope you will not hurt him. Your friend (but I'm not going to give my name).

Please send me a pony. I never asked for anything before. You can look it up.

If we come back as someone else, please don't let me be Jennifer because I just hate her.

I want to be like my daddy when I get big, only not with so much hair all over, OK?

My brothers told me about being born, but it doesn't sound right. They are just kidding, aren't they?

If You watch me at church on Sunday, I'll show You my new shoes.

This Lesson in Your Life

Most of us can recite the Lord's Prayer by heart. This model prayer of Jesus has become part of our spiritual language that is utilized by disciples daily. This is what Jesus intended it to be. Our problem is that familiarity with the prayer can hinder our appropriation of the power it contains. We must dedicate ourselves to meditating on these words so that they always remain fresh and vibrant as we say them.

One way we can do this is by taking the statements of the prayer and turning them into questions. In this way, the prayer becomes not only a time for us to talk to God but also a time for us to listen. Below are listed some possible questions based on the Lord's Prayer. Try asking these questions, leaving time for God to bring His answers to you. See if this is not yet one more way this prayer can live within you.

* As the perfect Father, what do you want to make possible in my life that I, your child, cannot see or imagine?

* What do you want to make holy (or whole) in my life today?

* How can your Kingdom come through me today?

* What are my Gethsemanes, where I need to say, "Thy will be done"?

* What nourishment (physical and spiritual) do I need today?

* For what do I need to be forgiven, and with whom do I need to be reconciled?

* From what do I need to be protected today?

* How can I give you the glory in my life today?

This beautiful prayer is a gift directly from God. Seek all the ways it can bless your life.

STRAIGHT

1. What does Jesus say is a wrong motive for giving alms?

Jesus warned us not to give alms in order to be seen by other people (Matt. 6:1).

2. What reward is given to those who want others to know of the alms they give?

Their only reward is the very recognition by others. They have no reward in heaven (6.1:2).

3. What did Jesus say that the Father who sees in secret would do for those who give secretly?

Jesus said that the Father would openly reward such secret gifts (6:4).

4. Where did Jesus urge us to pray?

Jesus told us to go into our closet and shut the door to pray to God in secret (6:5,6).

5. What does Jesus say to warn us not to let our prayers become only a ritual?

Jesus warned us not to let our prayers be vain repetitions (6:7).

6. According to Jesus, what does God already know before we pray?

Jesus said that the Father already knows the things we need before we pray (6:8).

7. Where is God's will completely followed?

God's will is totally done in heaven (6:10).

8. In praying for provisions, how far in advance are we to look?

Jesus said we should pray for daily bread (6:11).

9. We are to ask for God to forgive us in the same manner as we do what?

We should ask God only to forgive us in the same way we forgive others (6:12).

10. From what should we seek constant deliverance?

We must pray to be delivered from temptation and from evil (6:13).

In the Los Angeles riots that followed the arrest of Rodney King, millions of television viewers watched in horror as a group of men dragged Reginald Denny from his truck and beat him severely. The scene came to represent the senseless nature of all violence—whether it be the initial offense or the retaliation. Weeks later, another event involving these same people did not receive such wide coverage. Once Mr. Denny had recovered from his injuries, he met with his attackers and shook their hands. He stated that he forgave them for what had happened. A local news team recorded this meeting, and at the end of the news item, the reporter added, "It is said that Mr. Denny is suffering from brain damage."

In our society that encourages victims to seek justice and punishment, the grace of forgiveness does not make sense. With the possibility of large sums of money as recompense or the desire for vengeance and punishment so strong, an offer of a hand of forgiveness can seem strange and naïve. Some can explain such an action only as "brain damage." Reginald Denny would explain it differently. He would tell of One who, "When he was abused, he did not return abuse; when he suffered, he did not threaten; but he entrusted himself to the one who judges justly" (1 Peter 2:23 NRSV). This is the same One who, when suffering for all the wrongs of humankind, said, "Father, forgive them; for they do not know what they are doing" (Luke 23:34 NRSV).

Mr. Denny's story is a reminder of both the power and the surprise that forgiveness still brings to our lives. As we seek to follow the example of the Master, we not only obey Him; we bring His power to bear on those around us.

Father, teach us to forgive as You have forgiven us.

The Purpose of the Parables

Matthew 13:9-17

ho hath ears to hear, let him hear.

10 And the disciples came, and said unto him, Why speakest thou unto them in parables?

11 He answered and said unto them, Because it is given unto you to know the mysteries of the kingdom of heaven, but to them it is not given.

12 For whosoever hath, to him shall be given, and he shall have more abundance: but whosoever hath not, from him shall be taken away even that he hath.

13 Therefore speak I to them in parables: because they seeing see not; and hearing they hear not, neither do they understand.

14 And in them is fulfilled the prophecy of Esaias, which saith, By hearing ye shall hear, and shall not understand; and seeing ye shall see, and shall not perceive:

15 For this people's heart is waxed gross, and their ears are dull of hearing, and their eyes they have closed; lest at any time they should see with their eyes, and hear with their ears, and should understand with their heart, and should be converted, and I should heal them.

16 But blessed are your eyes, for they see: and your ears, for they hear.

17 For verily I say unto you, That many prophets and righteous men have desired to see those things which ye see, and have not seen them; and to hear those things which ye hear, and have not heard them.

July 17

Memory Selection
Matthew 13:9

Background Scripture
Matthew 13:1-23

Devotional Reading
Mark 4:10-20

This lesson focuses on one of the most famous and distinctive methods of Jesus' teaching: the parables. In the next lesson a particular parable will be considered; but in this session we look at the important reason why Jesus used this "story-telling" approach, and the kind of mindset that is required to understand them.

Many Christians have grown up believing the parables to be nice and simple stories used to make Jesus' teaching clearer. With the proper attitude that isn't far off the mark. What we do not always hear, however, is that Jesus used parables to confuse people whose hearts were not attuned to Him, and who did not really want to understand. This places a crucial obligation on the reader: if we "have ears to hear," we can understand. But those who have closed ears and a closed heart will go away from sitting at the feet of the Master Teacher wondering what He really meant.

Tell your group of the literal-minded editor who, reading Shakespeare, wanted to changed the bard's statement that here are *"books in the running brooks, [and] sermons in stone."* The editor wanted to change the line to read *"There are sermons in books and stones in the running brooks."*

Note that had this change been allowed to stand, the metaphorical or figurative aspect of Shakespeare's writing would have been lost. In a similar way, we must approach the parables of Jesus with a certain mindset. We must *want* to understand Jesus, and use our "right brain" to understand His figurative speech.

Teaching Outline	Daily Bible Readings	
I. Disciples with a Gift—9-12	Mon.	Truth in a Parable *Psalm 78:1-7*
A. Good question, 9-10	Tue.	Looking and Listening *Isaiah 6:1-10*
B. Starting point needed, 11-12	Wed.	Parable of the Sower *Mark 4:1-9*
II. Dulled Senses—13-15	Thu.	Purpose of Parables *Mark 4:10-20*
A. On seeing and hearing, 13	Fri.	Those with Ears, Listen! *Matthew 13:1-9*
B. Ominous prophecy, 14-15	Sat.	Blessed Eyes and Ears *Matthew 13:10-17*
III. Disciples with a Blessing—16-17	Sun.	Parable Explained *Matthew 13:18-23*

Verse by Verse

I. Disciples with a Gift—9-12

A. Good question, 9-10

9 Who hath ears to hear, let him hear.

10 And the disciples came, and said unto him, Why speakest thou unto them in parables?

Although Jesus was not the first great teacher to teach with stories or parables , He certainly emphasized them more than anyone else, and for more than one reason, as we shall see.

The term "parable" is from the Greek word *parabole*, with para meaning "alongside" and *bole* from a word for "throw." In other words a parable is a story that "throws" an idea "alongside" a person, instead of hitting him squarely in the face with it. It is therefore a form of teaching that is ideally suited for a teacher such as Jesus, who wants His followers to "connect" with Him in their hearts, seeing how His teaching applies to their lives instead of just having a superficial knowledge of what was said. This "depth-perception" and intimate application requires the hearer to "reach out" to the idea of the parable that was thrown "alongside" him and catch it. He must be an active participant in the learning process instead of

a passive listener. For the teaching to accomplish its purpose, the hearer must literally "get it."

Another helpful aspect of teaching by parable is that its story form invites hearers to see themselves in it. A skillfully told story is like a play in which the audience is invited up on the stage and allowed to stand with one or another of the characters with whom they identify. A parable therefore allows listeners who want to involve themselves in the story to do so. They are not forced to "put themselves in the place" of one of the characters, but the opportunity is theirs.

For example, in the Parable of the Sower (or "the Soils," as it has also been called), a hearer may listen to Jesus describe the "stony soil" which lacks the depth of soil needed for the seed to take root, and see his own superficial commitment in this picture (see vss. 5, 20). The word picture may cause him to remove the hard places from his heart and to give the seed of the Word greater depth of soil in which to take root.

B. Starting point needed, 11-12

11 He answered and said unto them, Because it is given unto you

**to know the mysteries of the king-
dom of heaven, but to them it is
not given.**

**12 For whosoever hath, to him
shall be given, and he shall have
more abundance: but whosoever
hath not, from him shall be taken
away even that he hath.**

At first glance, Jesus' answer may
seem elitist, showing favoritism to
the disciples as though they have received the ability to understand the
parables while others have been ar-
bitrarily turned away. A second look
reveals that the reason the disciples
have been given something others
don't have is because they wanted
to understand the mysteries of the
Kingdom, while others did not.

This point of view places an awesome responsibility on anyone who
hears Jesus' teaching. If we give
Him some indication of our desire
to understand His will, He will increase that desire so that we can learn
more and more, and go deeper and
deeper into His "mysteries." On the
other hand, if we aren't really very
interested in what He has to say (perhaps fearing that it might change our
life), then even what little interest allowed us to hear Him in the first
place will be taken away.

God respects our will, our freedom of choice, too much to force us
to understand Jesus' teaching. Further, Jesus wants disciples who joyfully choose to understand and follow Him, not reluctant followers
who would really rather be doing
something else. Thus it should come

as no surprise that Paul warned that
God will send a "powerful delusion"
to those who lack a love for the truth,
"so that they will believe the lie" (2
Thess. 2:10-11, NIV).

II. Dulled Senses—13-15
A. On seeing and hearing, 13

**13 Therefore speak I to them in
parables: because they seeing see
not; and hearing they hear not,
neither do they understand.**

Although Jesus answers the disciples' question with a certain direct-
ness, even the answer has something
of the nature of a parable, since it
requires effort to "get it." There is a
certain veiled quality to the words,
"they seeing see not; and hearing
they hear not." Again, however, a
second look and a little thought reveals a truth that we instinctively
know: it is possible to see someone
we know without recognizing him,
and to hear words that are muffled
and jumbled so that we cannot make
sense out of them.

Jesus is saying that He speaks in
parables to see if we want to understand them enough to take this second glance. If we don't, we are acting like the child who hears Mom
say something, but doesn't understand it; and fearing that it's something he doesn't want to understand
(such as "Take out the trash" or
"Clean your room"), he closes the
door to his room so he won't understand what she said.

B. Ominous prophecy, 14-15

**14 And in them is fulfilled the
prophecy of Esaias, which saith,**

By hearing ye shall hear, and shall not understand; and seeing ye shall see, and shall not perceive:

15 For this people's heart is waxed gross, and their ears are dull of hearing, and their eyes they have closed; lest at any time they should see with their eyes, and hear with their ears, and should understand with their heart, and should be converted, and I should heal them.

Now Jesus quotes the prophet Isaiah, who was called to reform the Jews in the eighth-century B.C.—a time when many lusted after idol worship instead of serving the Lord. God does not ask Isaiah to go out and debate an issue that should have been settled at the Exodus, when the true God, with outstretched arm, brought them out of Egyptian captivity. If idols are what Israel wants, idols are what they will get. Neither Isaiah nor God can help them if they have closed their eyes and ears and hearts to the message. For those who choose to say "Yes" to idols and "No" to Yahweh, God will further stop up their eyes, ears, and hearts. Again, the awesome responsibility of choice, of asking ourselves what we would do with salvation if it were offered, is painfully clear. At this point, we do not face the "Gentle Jesus, meek and mild" of childhood prayers. We face a God who sternly requires us to want Him before He opens our eyes and ears and hearts to receive His teaching.

III. Disciples with a Blessing—16-17

16 But blessed are your eyes, for they see: and your ears, for they hear.

17 For verily I say unto you, That many prophets and righteous men have desired to see those things which ye see, and have not seen them; and to hear those things which ye hear, and have not heard them.

Finally Jesus has worked His way through the surprisingly blunt warnings that if we don't "give Him something to work with" He will encourage us in our deafness, blindness, and hardness of heart. Now he turns to His disciples, who have given up all to follow Him. They are not like those Jews who chose idols over Yahweh, of whom Isaiah spoke. Again, therefore, He is not showing favoritism by blessing their eyes and ears, for they have already given them to Him.

Yet verse 17 does show the privileged position of the disciples, not because of their own righteousness but because, in God's timing, they live at the great moment of truth that faithful prophets and righteous people in the past had looked forward to for so many centuries: the days of the Messiah. They cannot enter into the Kingdom without His grace, much of which is explained in the parables; but He promises to extend His grace only to those who show their desire for it, and their interest in having that "Aha!" experience that shows not only that they "get it," but that they *long* to.

Evangelistic Emphasis

Jesus' teaching in this scripture sounds harsh to our ears. He says that He speaks in parables so that some will understand and others will not. Wouldn't Jesus want everyone to understand his teachings? The answer to that question is a resounding, "Yes," but Jesus knows the reality of the human heart. The position of this passage between the telling of the Parable of the Sower and Jesus' explanation of that parable is not accidental. The Parable of the Sower deals with the reality that some hearts are receptive to the word and others are not.

This is good information for Christians who desire to be evangelistic. Many times we work up our courage to share God's word with another individual only to have those efforts rejected. We can interpret such times as failures on our part. Jesus is gracious in revealing the truth of the matter to us. Like the prophet Ezekiel, we are responsible only for spreading the word (Ezek. 33:1-9) . We cannot control the reception to that word. What we can do is focus on the reality that there is fertile soil to be planted. There are hearts just waiting for us to share what has been given to us. While we puzzle at Jesus' words that some will hear and not understand, we can rejoice that there are those whose hearts will produce a hundredfold. Anyone with ears, listen.

ഉറ

Memory Selection

Who hath ears to hear, let him hear.— *Matthew 13:9*

This exhortation comes at the conclusion of Jesus' telling of the Parable of the Sower. Most people readily understand this story. It is one of the most transparent of all Jesus' parables. Much like our response to the Parable of the Prodigal Son, we immediately relate to the truth Jesus is teaching. The different soils represent the various conditions of the human heart. The seed is the word of God that grows into a bountiful harvest in the fertile soil of the receptive heart. We are all aware that there are hearts that are too full of the world's cares and troubles to receive God's word.

So we understand what Jesus is saying. Now, by adding the words of our memory verse, we are called upon to bear the responsibility of that understanding. Jesus calls on those who hear to truly *listen* to His Word. When we hear and understand, we have no excuse not to act upon that understanding. Our problem is not the same as those who have no ears to hear. Our ears call us to faithfulness.

Weekday Problems

Every time Blake drove into the church parking lot he felt the burden. This was a good church that had accomplished much within the community, but it was a church removed from its neighborhood. When the church had been built several decades ago, most of its members lived within a few blocks of the building. Over the years, the members had become more prosperous and moved to the newer suburbs, and the surrounding neighborhood had fallen on hard times. Like Blake, most church members now drove long distances to worship together, and their interests were tied to the areas in which they lived. Blake could not understand why they did not see the need to minister to those who lived so near the building. He had proposed many ideas such as block parties, a church fair, and summer programs for the neighborhood children, but no one had followed up on any of these. He was disappointed that someone would not step forward and take the leadership. Couldn't they see the need? Couldn't they hear the neighbors' cries for help?

* What is the responsibility that comes with seeing and hearing?

* Do you see a need that "someone" should address?

Get It?

Red: Did you mark that place where the fishing was good, so we can find it next time?

Ted: Yep. I put an X on the side of the boat.

Red: You nut! What if we bring another boat next time?

* * * *

A farmer bought a chain saw from a logger who told him that he would guarantee that he could cut down 15 trees a day with it. A week later, an unhappy farmer returned, saying the saw must be faulty. "It would cut down only a couple of trees a day, and I want my money back," he said.

The logger took the saw to check it out, pulled the start rope, and it immediately went Bzzzzzzzzzzzzzzzzzz.

"Hey!" said the farmer. "What's that noise?

* * * *

Val: That's a funny looking dog. Why does he have such a flat nose?

Hal: I broke him from chasing moving cars.

This Lesson in Your Life

I have often heard people say that they wished they could have lived during the time that Jesus was on the earth as a man. They usually are referring to how great it would have been to witness His miracles firsthand or to hear Him present the Sermon on the Mount. Sometimes they are curious about what He looked like. Some have questions they wish they could have asked Him. Personally, I am grateful that I was not there. A part of me fears that I might find myself comfortable among the Pharisees or among those who doubted Jesus' message. What a blessing it is to have the perspective that comes in looking back over the whole of Jesus' earthly ministry—not to mention the benefit of having an inspired record of the apostles' actions and writings that followed. We are those who have all the advantages.

In our text, Jesus told his disciples, "Blessed are your eyes, for they see, and your ears, for they hear. Truly I tell you, many prophets and righteous people longed to see what you see, but did not see it, and to hear what you hear, but did not hear it" (Matt. 13:16,17). Wow! We think of men like Isaiah and Jeremiah who were God's faithful spokesmen, yet, according to Jesus' words, we know more of the full will of God than they did.

Peter was emphatic about the same point in his letter,: "It was revealed to them that they were serving not themselves but you, in regard to the things that have now been announced to you through those who brought you good news by the Holy Spirit sent from heaven—things into which angels long to look!" (1 Pet. 1:12).

What a blessing to live in a time in which the mystery of God is revealed to our eyes and ears. What a blessing—and what a responsibility: to respond with obedience to that which we are privileged to know.

1. What is the responsibility of those who have ears to hear?

Jesus said that those who have ears to hear should hear (listen to, or heed—Matt. 13:9).

2. After Jesus told the Parable of the Sower, what question did His disciples ask?

They asked Jesus why He spoke in parables (13:10).

3. In the economy of the Kingdom, who receives "more"?

Jesus said that those who have (the desire to understand) will be given more (understanding; 13:11).

4. What will happen to those who have "little" in the kingdom?

Jesus said that what they do have will be taken from them (13:11).

5. What reason did Jesus give for speaking in parables?

So His message would be hidden from those to whom it was "not given" to understand it, because of their lack of desire (13:11).

6. What prophet did Jesus quote about ears that cannot hear and eyes that cannot see?

Jesus quoted the prophet Isaiah (6:9-10; 13:14-15).

7. What causes people not to see and hear the word of God?

Jesus quotes Isaiah as saying that the problem is their hearts have grown dull and they have shut their eyes (13:15).

8. According to Isaiah, what will God do if the people understand with their heart and turn to Him?

God will heal them (13:15).

9. What blessing did the disciples have?

They were blessed because their eyes could see and their ears could hear (13:16).

10. Who had desired to witness the things the disciples were seeing and hearing?

Jesus said that many prophets and righteous people had desired to hear and see these things (13:17).

In a small city in West Texas, one man had eyes to see and ears to hear. As he looked around, he saw people with needs and Christians with means to meet those needs. Others told him that the situation was hopeless—the need was too great and resources were too meager. Some even told him that there were plenty of places for people to find help, and those who were need were just too lazy to help themselves. This man saw things differently. Perhaps it was because of what he heard. He heard the words of Jesus, "Whoever has two coats must share with anyone who has none; and whoever has food must do likewise" (Luke 3:11).

This man heard words like those of Basil the Great, "The bread that is spoiling in your house belongs to the hungry. The shoes that are mildewing under your bed belong to those who have none. The clothes stored away in your closet belong to those who are naked. The money depreciating in your treasury belongs to the poor." He was amazed at how many others seemed not to hear these words, but he could not forget them.

Finally, he found a few others with eyes and ears and began collecting goods to help those in need. The church allowed them to store their goods for a while, but as the clothes and food spilled out into the church foyer the church leaders insisted something else be done. The man noticed that a local beer distributor had built a new warehouse and was trying to lease the old one. He made an impassioned plea, and from corporate headquarters the decision was made to lease the facility at a reduced rate. No one else had seen that possibility. When the beer company decided to dispose of the property, they gave the ministry an opportunity to purchase it. A ministry that gives away all its resources has little to offer. Another decision was made. The property was sold to the ministry for one dollar. No one else had heard of such a thing.

In a small West Texas city there is now a building stocked with goods for the poor. Daily, people in need come through its doors and receive goods, grace, and mercy. All this is because one man could see and hear.

What do you see? Have you heard anything lately?

The Unforgiving Servant

Matthew 18:21-35

Then came Peter to him, and said, Lord, how oft shall my brother sin against me, and I forgive him? till seven times?

22 Jesus saith unto him, I say not unto thee, Until seven times: but, Until seventy times seven.

23 Therefore is the kingdom of heaven likened unto a certain king, which would take account of his servants.

24 And when he had begun to reckon, one was brought unto him, which owed him ten thousand talents.

25 But forasmuch as he had not to pay, his lord commanded him to be sold, and his wife, and children, and all that he had, and payment to be made.

26 The servant therefore fell down, and worshipped him, saying, Lord, have patience with me, and I will pay thee all.

27 Then the lord of that servant was moved with compassion, and loosed him, and forgave him the debt.

28 But the same servant went out, and found one of his fellowservants, which owed him an hundred pence: and he laid hands on him, and took him by the throat, saying, Pay me that thou owest.

29 And his fellowservant fell down at his feet, and besought him, saying, Have patience with me, and I will pay thee all.

30 And he would not: but went and cast him into prison, till he should pay the debt.

31 So when his fellowservants saw what was done, they were very sorry, and came and told unto their lord all that was done.

32 Then his lord, after that he had called him, said unto him, O thou wicked servant, I forgave thee all that debt, because thou desiredst me:

33 Shouldest not thou also have had compassion on thy fellowservant, even as I had pity on thee?

34 And his lord was wroth, and delivered him to the tormentors, till he should pay all that was due unto him.

35 So likewise shall my heavenly Father do also unto you, if ye from your hearts forgive not every one his brother their trespasses.

July 24

Memory Selection
Matthew 18:27

Background Scripture
Matthew 18:21-35

Devotional Reading
2 Corinthians 2:5-11

In the movie "Pay It Forward," actor Kevin Spacey plays a junior high school teacher who challenges his students on the first day of school to do something that, if it were to spread, could change the world. They were to help three people, on the condition that each person they helped would "pay it forward," or show their appreciation by helping three more people, who would then repeat the process.

Today's lesson focuses on the principle of forgiveness in Jesus' story, or parable, about a king who forgave a servant a great debt. The problem is that the servant does not "pay it forward." Instead of showing his gratitude by forgiving his own debtor, he has him thrown in "debtor's prison." Not only does this halt the spread of a forgiving spirit; the king revokes his forgiveness and has his servant thrown in jail. How can group members apply the point of the parable in their own lives?

ಜಾಲ

Explain that the key to interpreting parables is finding a single, central point, and identifying who the key figures in the story stand for.

On a writing board, list the three main characters and lead a discussion of who they stand for. Possible answers are listed below.

The King—Anyone who has lent money to someone . . . Anyone in a privileged position or a position of power and authority.

The first servant—All who have sinned against God . . . ourselves . . . anyone who has benefited from the graciousness of another.

The second servant—Anyone who has offended us . . . anyone who has benefited from our position or favor . . . an actual debtor who owes money.

Conclusion—The main point of this parable is . . . *(complete at end of class).*

Teaching Outline	Daily Bible Reading

I. Forgiveness Unlimited—21-22
 II. Forgiving King—23-27
    A. Operating by law, 23-25
    B. Operating by grace, 26-27
 III. Unforgiving Servant—28-30
 IV. Facing Consequences, 31-35
    A. Debtor reported, 31
    A. Debt reinstated, 32-34
    B. Universal application, 35
	Mon. God Forgives Our Sin
	      Daniel 9:4-10
	 Tue. Blessed Are the Forgiven
	      Psalm 32:1-5
	 Wed. God Is a Forgiving God
	      Psalm 86:1-7
	 Thu. The Faith to Forgive
	      Luke 17:1-5
	 Fri. Forgive the Offender
	      2 Corinthians 2:5-11
	 Sat. About Forgiveness
	      Matthew 18:21-27
	 Sun. The Unforgiving Servant
	      Matthew 18:28-35

Verse by Verse

I. Forgiveness Unlimited—21-22

21 Then came Peter to him, and said, Lord, how oft shall my brother sin against me, and I forgive him? till seven times?

22 Jesus saith unto him, I say not unto thee, Until seven times: but, Until seventy times seven.

Matthew places this parable in a setting that is all too realistic in the modern church. In verse 15 Jesus has laid down the proactive principle of going to a brother who sins against us, instead of stewing silently and harboring a grudge. This gives the parable that follows a very practical edge for citizens of the Kingdom.

Peter seems to approach Jesus with a question formed out of his background in the Law of Moses. Legalistically-minded people seek limits, numbers, and finite rules. The prophet Amos had a formula for the limits of God's patience: "For three transgressions . . . and for four . . ." (1:3, 6, 9, etc.). Although this was no doubt a figurative saying, it is easy for such people to make it literal in their search for numbers, rules, and limits. Peter probably thinks he is being generous in suggesting he might forgive a brother

not once or twice, but seven times.

Among the Jews, the number seven stood for infinity, eternity, the completeness of time. "Seven times seven" (or, in some manuscripts "seventy times seven") therefore indicates that there is no limit to the number of times we are to forgive others.

II. Forgiving King—23-27

A. Operating by law, 23-25

23 Therefore is the kingdom of heaven likened unto a certain king, which would take account of his servants.

4 And when he had begun to reckon, one was brought unto him, which owed him ten thousand talents.

25 But forasmuch as he had not to pay, his lord commanded him to be sold, and his wife, and children, and all that he had, and payment to be made.

The Parable of the Unforgiving Servant is given to illustrate the attitude of infinite forgiveness Jesus has just taught. Linking "a certain king" to "the kingdom of heaven" no doubt means that we are to take the king as representing God, and the man who owed the 10,000 talents as representing any of His servants—especially ourselves.

Because rates of exchange vary so much, we can get a better idea of how much this servant owed the king by noting that a talent was a weight of silver worth about 6,000 denarii, and that a denarius was an ordinary day's wages (20:2, NIV). The servant therefore owed the king 60,000 days' work, or more than 160 years' time! The point is not that this is just a huge amount, but that it is an impossible amount ever to work off or repay.

By now, we as hearers of such a parable are to have put ourselves into the story, identifying with the servant. We simply cannot "make up" for the way we have sinned against God. We all owe "the king" a debt we can never pay.

B. Operating by grace, 26-27

26 The servant therefore fell down, and worshipped him, saying, Lord, have patience with me, and I will pay thee all.

27 Then the lord of that servant was moved with compassion, and loosed him, and forgave him the debt.

The repentance noted in Luke's version (17:4) is illustrated in the servant's fervent reaction. Lacking the ability to pay anything near what he owes, he can only beg for mercy—just as repentance is required of the believer since he has nothing else to offer in payment for his debt of sin.

Emotions such as the compassion attributed to the king are described in Greek by a word that also refers to the bowels or other organs. It is the emotion ascribed to Jesus when He "had compassion on the multitudes" (Matt. 9:36), and implies that He (and the king in our parable) hurt for hurting people "from the insides out." No doubt this usage can be traced to the view among many ancient people that the literal heart, liver, spleen, or another organ was actually the seat of the emotions.

This heart-felt compassion caused the king literally to "loosen" the servant from his tie to the huge debt. Both "loosed" and "forgave" are used elsewhere for the forgiveness not just of a monetary debt but of sin; so those who were listening to Jesus could immediately sigh with relief that God, as the king, is doing for us what we cannot do for ourselves. As the chorus goes: "He paid a debt He did not owe / I owed a debt I could not pay . . . ."

III. Unforgiving Servant—28-30

28 But the same servant went out, and found one of his fellowservants, which owed him an hundred pence: and he laid hands on him, and took him by the throat, saying, Pay me that thou owest.

29 And his fellowservant fell down at his feet, and besought him, saying, Have patience with me, and I will pay thee all.

30 And he would not: but went and cast him into prison, till he should pay the debt.

"The rest of the story" belies the forgiven servant's gratitude. He immediately goes to a fellow-servant who owes him a paltry 100 denarii (KJV "pence")—a debt that could have been settled relatively easily with just over three months' work. Instead of "paying forward" (see the "Focus" section) and passing along to his fellow-servant the mercy the king had shown him, the first servant irately has his debtor arrested and thrown into debtor's prison.

IV. Facing Consequences, 31-35
A. Debtor reported, 31

31 So when his fellowservants saw what was done, they were very sorry, and came and told unto their lord all that was done.

Since not every element of a parable has a significant point to make, this verse may simply be inserted to move the story forward to the king's reaction. On the other hand, some interpreters see in the report brought by the fellowservants the principle of church discipline, such as that referred to in 18:17 (see also the case of the man living in adultery, 1 Cor. 5).

B. Debt Reinstated, 32-34

32 Then his lord, after that he had called him, said unto him, O thou wicked servant, I forgave thee all that debt, because thou desiredst me:

33 Shouldest not thou also have had compassion on thy fellow-servant, even as I had pity on thee?

34 And his lord was wroth, and delivered him to the tormentors, till he should pay all that was due unto him.

At this point Jesus' story illustrates the principle stated in the Sermon on the Mount: "If ye forgive not men their trespasses, neither will our Father forgive your trespasses." Although the king is angry, he renders a penalty that is no more than the first debtor originally would have incurred: he is cast into the prison that was his just due. His fate reminds us of the way the Persian official Haman wound up being hanged on the very gallows he had built for his Jewish enemy Mordecai, in the book of Esther. The phrase "till he should pay all . . ." does not imply a temporary confinement, since the man's debt was infinite. It is merely a way of saying "forever" (cp. Matt. 24:50-51).

C. Universal application, 35

35 So likewise shall my heavenly Father do also unto you, if ye from your hearts forgive not every one his brother their trespasses.

As in most parables, this one is followed by a concluding "moral to the story." It affirms the principle that those who receive grace must be gracious. This does not mean that forgiving others is a "law" by which we earn our salvation. It is an indication of whether the spirit of grace God has shown us has permeated our character to the extent that we can "pay it forward." An unforgiving spirit betrays a human impossibility, not a divine short-coming: those who cannot forgive betray their inability to accept forgiveness themselves.

Evangelistic Emphasis

Suppose the story in this lesson actually began with Matthew 18:28. If we read only the story of a servant who insisted that a fellow servant pay a debt, we would find that situation justifiable and normal. All of us expect debts to be paid. It is the opening of the story that renders this second scene both unthinkable and horrible. How can a man who has experienced forgiveness at the level of the first servant—forgiveness for a debt so large it could never be repaid in several lifetimes—even consider asking for payment of any debt owed him?

This unforgettable story that Jesus told his disciples captures the whole of evangelism. Certainly it gives us a story to tell—a story of a Master who, out of His mercy and at considerable personal expense to Himself, has cancelled our debt. More than that, however, it gives us a story to *live*. Each time we endure a wrong or a hurt in the name of our gracious Lord and do not seek to avenge the wrong, the gospel rings true in our own heart and speaks clearly to those around us. Saint Francis once said that we should always preach the gospel—and, when necessary, use words. If we truly extend the same grace to others that God has poured out upon us, we spread the Good News each day of our lives.

෨෮ඏ

Memory Selection

Then the lord of that servant was moved with compassion, and loosed him, and forgave him the debt.—*Matthew 18:27*

This verse is the key verse of Jesus' Parable of the Unforgiving Servant. Unless we pause here and pray over these words, the remainder of the parable will have little effect in our lives.

Jesus chooses three verbs to describe the master's actions. They are translated *moved with compassion, setting free,* and *forgiving.* We know this story well enough to realize that the "master" in the story is none other than God Himself, and the "servant" in the hopeless situation is each one of us. Have we really come to believe that our Master is one who is moved with compassion for us? Do we really believe that He desires to set us free? Do we live each day as those who have been completely forgiven? If we yet harbor the idea that our Master will eventually demand payment from us, we will continue in our ways of demanding that any debt or wrong owed us be repaid as well. But if this verse has become truth for us, it will show immediately in every action and reaction of every relationship we have. This is the key.

Weekday Problems

Ann had a lot of options to choose from, and she delighted in turning over the possibilities in her mind. She knew her husband Jim like a book, and she was sure that she could pick just the right course of action to make her point with him. After all, he deserved it.

She had told Jim repeatedly how she felt about his coming home late from work on the one night of the week she had her club meeting. Tuesday evenings were her only break from her duties of wife and mother, and Jim seemed always to have some excuse for not making it home on time. She knew he would come in sheepishly and apologize once again. Maybe a sharp reply this time. Maybe the silent treatment again. Maybe she could stay out a little late herself and let him worry about her for a change. All these had been effective before. After all, she needed to teach him a lesson in consideration.

* What do you think Jim's reaction might be to Ann's planned revenge?

* What other options are available to Ann?

Further to Forgiveness

The small boy, saying the Lord's Prayer at bedtime, prayed, "And forgive us our debts as we forgive those who are dead against us."

* * * *

Everyone should have a special cemetery lot in which to bury the faults of friends, loved ones, and enemies alike.

* * * *

Only the brave know how to forgive; it is the most refined and generous pitch of virtue that human nature can arrive at. A coward never forgave; it is not in his nature.—Laurence Sterne

* * * *

We may think that holding a grudge places boundaries around one who sins against us, as though throwing him in jail. The fact is that those who cannot forgive find that they are the ones who are imprisoned.—Anonymous

This Lesson in Your Life

The Old Testament story of Jacob and Esau provides an excellent contrast to Jesus' Parable of the Unforgiving Servant. Throughout the first part of his life, Jacob schemed and plotted to steal the blessing and birthright that belonged to Esau. With the help of his mother Rebekah, he finally succeeded in deceiving not only his brother but also his father Isaac. The result of his plan was probably not as he had imagined it. With blessing and birthright in hand, Jacob was forced to leave home and make a new life for himself. Years later, having prospered through the grace and protection of God, Jacob faced the prospect of returning to meet the brother he had so grievously offended. It was then that he realized that in his effort to gain power and control over his brother, he had actually handed these over to Esau. His whole future rested in Esau's reactions. Could he appease his angry brother? Could he ever make things right? He knew that Esau was the one who controlled his destiny.

Committing a wrong against another—whether that other is God or a fellow human being—gives control of the situation over to that person. From that moment on, a portion of our own peace and security is under the other's control. Will that other one seek revenge? Can that other one forgive? Jesus' answer is that God has chosen the way of forgiveness and mercy, but we might not be so fortunate with the others we have offended.

Of course, the real power of Jesus' story is that it asks us how we are doing when we are the ones who have been wronged. Has our experience with God's mercy been effective in leading us to realize the blessing of healing we can bring to a relationship? Are we so overjoyed in the freedom we have found that we want to share that same wonderful experience with another?

When Jacob and Esau met, Esau blessed his brother because he said that he did not need to seek vengeance on Jacob. "I have enough, my brother; keep what you have for yourself," Esau said (Gen. 33:9). Jesus asks us if, in light of the marvelous grace of God toward us, we can say the same.

GETTING THE FACTS STRAIGHT

1. In Jesus' parable, Peter seemed to think that a person would be gracious in forgiving someone how many times, and what was Jesus' response?
Peter wondered if we should be willing to forgive someone up to seven times; but Jesus suggested 70 times seven (Matt. 18:21, 22).

2. How much did the first servant owe the king, in Jesus' parable?
The servant owed 10,000 talents (18:24; scholars tell us that this amount was several times what an average person could expect to earn in a lifetime).

3. What was the king's first verdict against the servant?
The king ordered that the servant, his wife and children, and all his possessions be sold to pay the debt (18:25).

4. How did the servant respond to this judgment?
The servant fell down, worshiped the king, and promised full repayment (18:26).

5. Why did the king forgive the debt?
The king forgave the debt because he was moved with compassion (18:27).

6. How much did the fellow servant owe the first servant?
The second servant owed the first servant 100 pence (pennies; 18:28).

7. How did the second servant respond to the first?
The second servant begged for patience, in the same way the first servant had begged the king (18:29).

8. What was the first servant's judgment against his fellow servant?
He had him cast into prison until he paid the debt (18:30).

9. Who reported the servant's actions to the king?
The other fellow servants, who were sorry for what was done (18:31).

10. What was the fate of the first servant?
The king delivered him to the "torturers" (NRSV) until he should pay all that was due (18:34).

In his novel *Love in the Time of Cholera,* Gabriel Garcia Marquez tells the story of a couple that had been married 30 years. The doctor and his wife had settled into a comfortable daily routine of life. He rose early each morning, bathed, dressed and went to work. One morning, while he was dressing, the doctor said, "I've been bathing for almost a week without any soap." Replacing the soap was a part of the wife's routine. Her husband's comment hit the woman hard.

"Three days ago I checked the soap," she thought to herself.
"It was three days, not a week," she indignantly told her husband. "I've bathed every day, and there has always been soap." The argument escalated from that point until the doctor moved into his intern's quarters for three months.

Marquez comments, "He was not ready to come back as long as she refused to admit there had been no soap in the bathroom, and she was not prepared to have him back until he recognized that he had consciously lied to her." During this three-month period, the couple found opportunities to evoke many other trivial quarrels, and they became amazed at how what they had once thought such a contented marriage had actually been so miserable. Finally, one night, the doctor could not bear to leave the house. He fell onto his bed and said, "Let me stay. There was soap."

Marquez concludes, "Even when they were old and placid, they were careful about bringing up the issue of soap, for the barely healed wounds could bleed easily again."

So it goes when we are prepared to defend our rights and expectations more than we are prepared to forgive. Jesus' parable emphasizes the example, the quantity, and the quality of God's forgiveness that has blessed our lives. It also highlights the inhumane response of failing to pass that forgiveness on to others. Gabriel Garcia Marquez's story is amusing, but too true to be funny. Such is the misery we bring—not only to our Father—but to ourselves when we fail to understand the point of this parable on forgiveness.

Final Accounting

Matthew 25:31-46

Hen the Son of man shall come in his glory, and all the holy angels with him, then shall he sit upon the throne of his glory:

32 And before him shall be gathered all nations: and he shall separate them one from another, as a shepherd divideth his sheep from the goats:

33 And he shall set the sheep on his right hand, but the goats on the left.

34 Then shall the King say unto them on his right hand, Come, ye blessed of my Father, inherit the kingdom prepared for you from the foundation of the world:

35 For I was an hungred, and ye gave me meat: I was thirsty, and ye gave me drink: I was a stranger, and ye took me in:

36 Naked, and ye clothed me: I was sick, and ye visited me: I was in prison, and ye came unto me.

37 Then shall the righteous answer him, saying, Lord, when saw we thee an hungred, and fed thee? or thirsty, and gave thee drink?

38 When saw we thee a stranger, and took thee in? or naked, and clothed thee?

39 Or when saw we thee sick, or in prison, and came unto thee?

40 And the King shall answer and say unto them, Verily I say unto you, Inasmuch as ye have done it unto one of the least of these my brethren, ye have done it unto me.

41 Then shall he say also unto them on the left hand, Depart from me, ye cursed, into everlasting fire, prepared for the devil and his angels:

42 For I was an hungred, and ye gave me no meat: I was thirsty, and ye gave me no drink:

43 I was a stranger, and ye took me not in: naked, and ye clothed me not: sick, and in prison, and ye visited me not.

44 Then shall they also answer him, saying, Lord, when saw we thee an hungred, or athirst, or a stranger, or naked, or sick, or in prison, and did not minister unto thee?

45 Then shall he answer them, saying, Verily I say unto you, Inasmuch as ye did it not to one of the least of these, ye did it not to me.

46 And these shall go away into everlasting punishment: but the righteous into life eternal.

July 31

Memory Selection
Matthew 25:40

Background Scripture
Matthew 25:31-46

Devotional Reading
Luke 6:27-31

This lesson focuses on the Last Judgment, and one of the factors in the decision of where people will spend eternity—heaven or hell. Jesus has already taught on factors such as being ready for His Second Coming (Matt. 24–25:13), and on the faithful use of gifts He has given us (The Parable of the Talents, 25:14-30).

The factor Jesus emphasizes here is whether we have cared for the needy. The focus is therefore more on *doing* the faith than on *theorizing* about it, or tidying up our doctrine and theology into neat packages. The bottom line here is *What did you do for the least, the lost, and the last?*

Yet there is an important theological point that distinguishes the Church from other benevolent groups. We are to help the needy because Christ dwells in them; and what we do for them we do for Him.

ഔാ

Challenge your group to hammer out a mission statement for your church. (No fair looking on the church bulletin and copying one that may be written there!) Ask such questions as What should the church be about? How is it different, say, from the local Lions' Club? How should the funds given to the church be spent?

Note that through the ages churches have been involved mainly in proclaiming the Good News, promoting harmonious fellowship among members, and ministering to the needy. An adequate mission statement should refer in some way to each of these three arenas.

Lead into today's lesson by noting that it emphasizes our responsibility to feed the hungry, accept the stranger, clothe the naked, and minister to those in prison. Allow the text to be a test to how faithfully your congregation is fulfilling this mission.

Teaching Outline	**Daily Bible Readings**	
I. The Great Divorce—31-33	Mon.	The Call to Do Good *Psalm 14*
A. The Second Coming, 31	Tue.	Don't Withhold the Good *Proverbs 3:27-33*
B. The great gathering, 32-33	Wed.	The Golden Rule *Luke 6:27-31*
II. Addressing the Sheep—34-40		
A. Approval for ministry, 34-36	Thu.	Be Good and Generous *1 Timothy 6:13-19*
B. Christ in the needy, 37-40	Fri.	Help Each Other *1 John 3:11-17*
III. Confronting the Goats—41-46		
A. Judgment for neglect, 41-43	Sat.	'You Did It to Me' *Matthew 25:31-40*
B. On not seeing Jesus, 44-45		
C. Final sentencing, 46	Sun.	'You Did It Not to Me' *Matthew 25:41-46*

Verse by Verse

I. The Great Divorce—31-33
A. The Second Coming, 31

31 When the Son of man shall come in his glory, and all the holy angels with him, then shall he sit upon the throne of his glory:

The earliest known Christian creeds affirm the belief that Christ will come "to judge the quick ('the living') and the dead." Many early Christians expected this "second coming" to occur within their lifetime. When they were disappointed, some skeptics doubted "the promise of His coming" (2 Pet. 3:4), but believers were reassured that "one day is with the Lord as a thousand years, and a thousand years as one day" (3:8). Furthermore, Jesus Himself warned that no one knew when this great event would occur, and that the Christian's duty is therefore to live as though Christ might come today, or to "watch" (Mark 13:31-32).

B. The great gathering, 32-33

32 And before him shall be gathered all nations: and he shall separate them one from another, as a shepherd divideth his sheep from the goats:

33 And he shall set the sheep on his right hand, but the goats on the left.

This scene serves to alert us to the fact that language about the Second Coming or the end-time is necessarily figurative, to some extent. For example, the saying that "every eye shall see him" (Rev. 1:7) does not take into consideration the curvature of the earth, and the impossibility of a person standing at the rear of a crowd consisting of everyone who has ever lived. Our language is limited by space and time; and since Jesus' Second Coming will occur at the end of time, Bible words used to describe it "jar the language." This does not mean that the Second Coming is not "real," but that it takes symbolic language to describe it. However we understand the language, there will come a time beyond time when Christ will return and judge "the quick and the dead."

The reasons for sheep and "the right hand" being considered positive, and goats and "the left hand" negative, are lost in antiquity. Some speculate that sheep are presented in a good light because they are docile and meek, while goats are over-sexed and ill-tempered. Also, long-standing discrimination has considered left-handed people awkward. (English has adopted the French word *gauche* to mean ill-mannered

473

or clumsy, while it means both that and left-handed in French.) To sit at a king's "right hand" was considered a sign of greater honor than sitting at the left.

II. Addressing the Sheep—34-40
A. Approval for ministry, 34-36

34 Then shall the King say unto them on his right hand, Come, ye blessed of my Father, inherit the kingdom prepared for you from the foundation of the world:

35 For I was an hungered, and ye gave me meat: I was thirsty, and ye gave me drink: I was a stranger, and ye took me in:

36 Naked, and ye clothed me: I was sick, and ye visited me: I was in prison, and ye came unto me.

For Christian faith to be valid, it must be put into practice. Inherent in the fact that Jesus' ministry included meeting human needs is the response of His followers to "go and do likewise." The good works listed here are not intended to be a complete list: feeding the hungry, giving drink to the thirsty, showing hospitality to the stranger, clothing the naked, and bringing hope to those who are imprisoned stand for any other human need so widely experienced in the world.

The fact that judgment—heaven or hell—depend on these good works does not mean that we "earn" salvation. Jesus is teaching His disciples—those who have already responded to His grace and been saved by faith. The question now, as in the title of a book several years ago is

"What do you do after you say Amen?" The services of worship conducted by Christian churches, the private devotion of Christians, and the study of sound doctrine make the Church unique as an organization; but such activities are "necessary but not sufficient." All such exercises are focused on the love of God, and to stop the process of following Him at the point of mere mental activity is to cut others off from seeing that love in the lives of His followers.

B. Christ in the needy, 37-40

37 Then shall the righteous answer him, saying, Lord, when saw we thee an hungered, and fed thee? or thirsty, and gave thee drink?

38 When saw we thee a stranger, and took thee in? or naked, and clothed thee?

39 Or when saw we thee sick, or in prison, and came unto thee?

40 And the King shall answer and say unto them, Verily I say unto you, Inasmuch as ye have done it unto one of the least of these my brethren, ye have done it unto me.

These verses show that doing good to those in need is not a self-conscious effort to prove our salvation by good works, but a natural response. Those who have been touched by love should instinctively reach out to touch others. The "sheep" do not recall ever doing good to Jesus Himself, so He has to remind them that He dwells in every needy person in a special sense. If the saved are to understand that salvation consists of the victorious "Christ in you, the hope of glory" (Col. 1:27), all people are to understand that the needy Christ dwells in them as well.

This concept should prevent "benevolence" from being condescending, and from communicating the idea of the givers as "do-gooders" who have no needs themselves. They are to see in the needy not a "have-not" to be "treated" by the "haves," but as persons who are to respected because they are made in God's image, and embody Christ.

III. Confronting the Goats—41-46
A. Judgment for neglect, 41-43

41 Then shall he say also unto them on the left hand, Depart from me, ye cursed, into everlasting fire, prepared for the devil and his angels:

42 For I was an hungred, and ye gave me no meat: I was thirsty, and ye gave me no drink:

43 I was a stranger, and ye took me not in: naked, and ye clothed me not: sick, and in prison, and ye visited me not.

Why does Jesus find it necessary to repeat in opposite or negative form what He has just said positively? Perhaps because we are more likely to commit the sin of omission and fail to do good than we are to commit sins overtly. Thus we are not only told that living eternally with God depends on doing good; we are also reminded that failing to do good seals our eternal destiny apart from God.

B. On not seeing Jesus, 44-45

44 Then shall they also answer him, saying, Lord, when saw we thee an hungred, or athirst, or a stranger, or naked, or sick, or in prison, and did not minister unto thee?

45 Then shall he answer them, saying, Verily I say unto you, Inasmuch as ye did it not to one of the least of these, ye did it not to me.

Unfortunately it is a universal human tendency to "see Christ," or representatives of Him, in those who make a good appearance, seeming to need little or nothing. Jesus' saying here challenges us to reverse that tendency by seeing Him in the needy. A similar idea is taught in Hebrews 13:2, where we are taught to "be not forgetful to entertain strangers: for thereby some have entertained angels unawares." The concept grew in Christian story-telling through the centuries, with Jesus appearing to believers in the guise of a beggars or other needy strangers as a test to see if believers will recognize the truth that Jesus lays down in these verses.

C. Final sentencing, 46

46 And these shall go away into everlasting punishment: but the righteous into life eternal.

Jesus now foresees the pronouncement of final judgment on the sheep and the goats, depending on how they have responded to human needs in His name. Up to now we have been challenged to "choose ye this day whom you will serve." At the Last Judgment, the opportunity for choice is gone, and our eternal doom or salvation is sealed.

Evangelistic Emphasis

I have sometimes made the comment that I am an NFL linebacker trapped in a preacher's body. We all have dreams and goals we wish we could have achieved, but there comes a time when we must face the reality that we do not have the abilities or resources to do certain things.

What a blessing it is to know that the call of our Lord is not a call to an unattainable goal. When Jesus calls us to His service, He calls us to a way of life well within the grasp of each one of us. He calls us simply to look behind us—to look back and see those who have less than we have—and to share the bounty he has given us.

This is a call to turn our heads— for our natural inclination is to look ahead with envy or frustration toward those who have more than we have. But the voice of Jesus says, "Turn." Whether the need we see be physical, emotional or spiritual, we have all the resources we are called to use. What a blessing to know we can do it—if we will just turn around.

&⟩⟨&

Memory Selection

And the King shall answer and say unto them, Verily I say unto you, Inasmuch as ye have done it unto one of the least of these my brethren, ye have done it unto me.—*Matthew 25:40*

A mother saw her young son busily drawing on a piece of paper. "What are you drawing?" she asked. Without looking up, the boy replied, "A picture of Jesus." The mother was pleased. She peeked over the boy's shoulder to get a glimpse of his interpretation of Jesus. "Don't look yet, Mom," the boy said. "Sorry," she apologized. Finally the picture was done, and the boy proudly presented it to his mother. Expecting to find a crude drawing of a man with long hair and a beard, she was surprised to discover a picture of a round-faced man wearing glasses. "How sweet," she said. "He looks a little like Grandpa." The boy smiled with satisfaction. "I think Grandpa looks a lot like Jesus," he said.

Have we learned the simple lesson that we can find the face of Jesus in everyone we encounter? If we take the time to look, we can find a way to minister to all—and in doing so we will be surprised to find Jesus with glasses and false teeth and tattoos and . . . .

Weekday Problems

Dan Anderson pulled his car into his designated parking place, threw open the door, and walked quickly toward the building. "Good morning," the secretary said.

"I'll get back to you on that," Dan said dryly.

"Mr. Anderson," the secretary called, as he tried to escape into his office.

"Yes?" He hoped she would pick up on his annoyed tone.

"Mr. Anderson, we're taking up a collection for Bill."

"Bill? Who's Bill?"

The secretary could not hide her surprise at his reply. "Bill is the janitor for this area of the building. He's cleaned our offices for six years."

"Oh," Dan said, his mind already shifting to the presentation he would make in the next few minutes.

"His son passed away yesterday," the secretary continued, "so we thought we might help out."

"Sure. O.K.," Dan muttered. He dug in his pocket and pulled out a twenty.

"Thanks," she replied. Then she added, "Bill's a great guy. You ought to get to know him."

Dan did not respond. His first thought was "Who has time?" His second thought was Matthew 25:40. Six years? Had he walked past Bill for that long?

The Good, the Bad, and the Judgment

The preacher was waxing eloquent on the topic of Judgment Day. "There will be thunder and lightning, floods and earthquakes!" he roared.

Wide-eyed, an eight-year-old boy whispered to his mother: "Does that mean I'll get out school?"

* * * *

An injured motorist, picked up unconscious after a wreck, was being carried to a nearby service station. Suddenly he regained consciousness and started kicking and squirming to be released. Turns out the first thing he saw was the station's Shell sign, and someone was standing in front of the S.

* * * *

"How can you believe in God?" scoffed the atheist. "What about that story of Jonah and the whale?"

"I don't know," said the believer, "but when I get to heaven I'll ask him."

"Yeah?" sneered the unbeliever. "And what if he's not there?"

"Then you ask him," replied the believer.

This Lesson in Your Life

The story of the Great Judgment is one of the heaviest passages in all scripture. The words of the great King, "Depart from me, you cursed, into everlasting fire, prepared for the devil and his angels," cut directly to our hearts. Once this story is heard, it is never forgotten. Its ominous tone is intentional, and the warning it gives should be taken very seriously.

There is, however, another side to the story—a lighter side. We can't help but smile when we read about the naïve sheep—those who served the Lord without even realizing that they were being faithful. We hear their amazed question, "Lord, when did we see you hungry and fed you or thirsty and gave you a drink?" We quickly translate this into the lesson that we should be aware of all who are in need around us because they are Jesus to us. This is a good lesson—a worthy lesson. Were they serving others to serve Jesus? They were simply serving because that is who they were—or rather—who they had become.

In the midst of the exhortations of this story, we should also hear a sweet word of promises fulfilled. Passages such as 2 Corinthians 5:17 come to mind: "If any man be in Christ, he is a new creation." Think of Ephesians 3:20, "Now unto him that is able to do exceeding abundantly above all that we ask or think, according to the power that worketh within us." And then there is Philippians 2:13: "For it is God which worketh in you both to will and to do his good pleasure."

We can think of many more such words. Truly, one of the greatest blessings of the gospel is that God not only redeems us, but He also reclaims and regenerates us to do the work He has appointed. If we have truly given Him our hearts, we rest in these promises. Won't it be wonderful to stand before Him and hear of the things He has done through our weak and feeble efforts? The glory and the praise is His.

1. Who will accompany the Son of Man when He comes in his glory?
The holy angels will be with Him when He sits on the throne of His glory (Matt. 25:31).

2. Who will be called before the throne of glory?
All nations will be gathered before Him (25:32).

3. To what is the dividing of the nations into two groups compared?
He will separate them one from another as a shepherd divides his sheep from the goats (25:32).

4. Where does the King place the two groups once they are separated?
He sets the sheep on His right hand and the goats on his left (25:33).

5. In this teaching, by what standards will the nations will be judged?
They will be judged according to their ministry to those in need (25:35-40).

6. Were the righteous aware that they were serving Jesus when they ministered to those in need?
No. They asked the Lord when they saw Him in need (25:37,38).

7. What are the areas of need in which the King says the righteous served Him?
They served him when He was hungry, thirsty, a stranger, naked, sick, and in prison (25:35.36).

8. What is the punishment for the wicked, and for whom was it prepared?
The punishment is everlasting fire prepared for the devil and his angels (25:41).

9. Did the wicked overlook the Lord intentionally?
No. They claimed they did not recognize Him (25:44).

10. What is the reward for the righteous?
The righteous enter into life eternal (25:46).

I had heard the story before, but I didn't stop him from telling it again. It was too good a story. "Have I ever told you about ol' Joey Sloan?" the man we called "Coach" said on the phone.

I pretended to try to remember the name. "You know, Coach, I think you've mentioned him to me before. Wasn't he the kid you convinced to play quarterback for you in the '50s, and he turned out to be All-State?"

The old coach smiled. "Yeah, but that's not the best part. Did you know that he made a football coach himself and holds the state record for the most wins at one high school?"

"I think you've said something about that." He smiled again. "But that's not the best part," he said.

"Tell me the best part," I prompted.

The elderly man sat down and collected his thoughts. This story had to be told well because of its importance. I studied his face while he drifted back in time. I had tremendous respect for this good Christian man. He had taught many boys to play sports, but even more importantly, he had helped many boys become men. The past few years had been difficult for him, with failing health and several tragic events in his family. A lesser man would have been broken, but Coach, even in these final years, was a strong man.

Finally he began to speak. "The best part is that right after he started coaching he called me up one night. We talked for a long time about the old days when he was playing ball, and about coaching strategies for his team. I thought he was about to hang up when he said what he had really called to say." I knew what Joey had said, but I was touched once again as I saw the Coach's eyes moisten with tears as he prepared to tell it again. "He said, 'Coach, I want you to know I'm a Christian now.' I told him, 'Joey, that's the greatest thing you've ever done.' I asked him if the girl he had married had led him to Christ. He said she had helped—but then he told me something that's the best thing anyone ever said to me. He said, 'Coach, it was you who showed me Jesus.' Well, I just started crying. I told him that I didn't know what he was talking about because I had never talked about my faith to him. Joey said I didn't have to talk about it. I just showed it."

With that, the story was over. Coach could never continue once he said that. "Coach," I said, "that's the way it is when Christ lives in you. Sometimes you don't even know when He's using you to reach others."

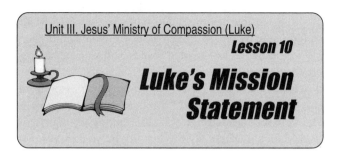

Unit III. Jesus' Ministry of Compassion (Luke)

Lesson 10

Luke's Mission Statement

Luke 4:16-24, 28-30

nd he came to Nazareth, where he had been brought up: and, as his custom was, he went into the synagogue on the sabbath day, and stood up for to read.

17 And there was delivered unto him the book of the prophet Esaias. And when he had opened the book, he found the place where it was written,

18 The Spirit of the Lord is upon me, because he hath anointed me to preach the gospel to the poor; he hath sent me to heal the brokenhearted, to preach deliverance to the captives, and recovering of sight to the blind, to set at liberty them that are bruised,

19 To preach the acceptable year of the Lord.

20 And he closed the book, and he gave it again to the minister, and sat down. And the eyes of all them that were in the synagogue were fastened on him.

21 And he began to say unto them, This day is this scripture fulfilled in your ears.

22 And all bare him witness, and wondered at the gracious words which proceeded out of his mouth. And they said, Is not this Joseph's son?

23 And he said unto them, Ye will surely say unto me this proverb, Physician, heal thyself: whatsoever we have heard done in Capernaum, do also here in thy country.

24 And he said, Verily I say unto you, No prophet is accepted in his own country.

28 And all they in the synagogue, when they heard these things, were filled with wrath,

29 And rose up, and thrust him out of the city, and led him unto the brow of the hill whereon their city was built, that they might cast him down headlong.

30 But he passing through the midst of them went his way,

Aug. 7

Memory Selection
Luke 4:18

Background Scripture
Luke 4:14-30

Devotional Reading
Matthew 13:54-58

In our series of lessons on the life and teachings of Jesus from the synoptic Gospels (Matt.–Luke) we come now to samplings from Luke. We have noted Matthew's concern to present Jesus to the Jews, and Mark's dynamic style that may have appealed to Roman readers. Luke is thought to have been intended to circulate among Greeks. Written in more polished Greek than the other Gospels, it presents Jesus as the Ideal Man, emphasizes His social and humanitarian concerns (particularly for women and the poor), and tends to the logical order and sources of his material.

In this first lesson from Luke, the humanitarian aspect of Jesus' mission shines through with brilliant clarity. In His very first sermon at His hometown synagogue in Nazareth, He says boldly that He has come especially to meet the needs of the poor and the broken-hearted. Luke's "mission statement" is one that is sorely needed in the Church today.

&)CR

Working singly or in groups, challenge your class to imagine that they are Jesus' "press agent," and to come up with a one-sentence "mission statement" that might be suitable for His first appearance before His hometown congregation in Nazareth. You may want to call on the help of business persons or others in the class who have had experience with "mission statements." Note how they help clarify for both the public and the firm's employees the main business they intend to be about. Ask, Out of all that Jesus said and did, how would you summarize His primary goals and purposes in a single sentence?

After time for reflection, call on several of the groups or members to share what they have written. See if the group can reach consensus on an adequate statement.

Teaching Outline

I. Jesus Arises to Speak—16-19
A. His habit of worship, 16
B. Preaching from Isaiah, 17-19
II. Applying the Scripture, 20-21
III. Initial Reaction, 22-24
A. 'Gracious words,' 22
B. Doubt dawns, 23-24
IV. Eventual Anger, 28-30

Daily Bible Readings

Mon.	Year of the Lord's Favor *Leviticus 25:8-12*
Tue.	Elijah Revives a Youth *1 Kings 17:17-24*
Wed.	Jesus Rejected in Nazareth *Matthew 13:54-58*
Thu.	Teaching in His Hometown *Mark 6:1-6*
Fri.	Reading from Isaiah *Luke 4:14-19*
Sat.	Fulfillment of Prophecy *Luke 4:20-24*
Sun.	Rage in the Synagogue *Luke 4:25-30*

Verse by Verse

I. Jesus Arises to Speak—16-19
A. His habit of worship, 16

16 And he came to Nazareth, where he had been brought up: and, as his custom was, he went into the synagogue on the sabbath day, and stood up for to read.

Although this is the first time we are told that Jesus visited His hometown synagogue, we know that this is not the beginning of His ministry. Verse 14 notes that after "the Great Temptation" Jesus gained fame for His work around the Sea of Galilee.

B. Preaching from Isaiah, 17-19

17 And there was delivered unto him the book of the prophet Esaias. And when he had opened the book, he found the place where it was written,

18 The Spirit of the Lord is upon me, because he hath anointed me to preach the gospel to the poor; he hath sent me to heal the brokenhearted, to preach deliverance to the captives, and recovering of sight to the blind, to set at liberty them that are bruised,

19 To preach the acceptable year of the Lord.

This glimpse of a synagogue service is the earliest that has survived.

From Acts 13:14-15 we also know a typical service included a reading from "the Law," or the first five books of the Old Covenant Scriptures, and that visitors were often invited to speak. Synagogues were a product of the Dispersion, when Jews were scattered throughout the known world and their Temple at Jersualem was destroyed. They were centers not only of worship but instruction. No doubt Jesus' fame in the region prompted the rulers of the synagogue to invite Him to speak.

"As his custom was" indicated Jesus' faithfulness to Jewish worship traditions. Although He would become known as a revolutionary, He had no interest in discarding institutions that fostered the truth. In fact for years many Jewish-Christians continued to attend Sabbath services at the local synagogue while meeting also on the first day of the week for Christian worship.

The "book" was actually a scroll, since the "codex," a book with leaves or pages as we know it, was only beginning to be experimented with at about this time, and it was not until the 4th century that it became widely used. It seems that Jesus did not choose the text (Isa. 61:1), but that it was "given" to Him. If so, the Holy Spirit must have guided the person who selected it, since it so aptly describes the mission of the Reader who stood before the congregation.

Of all the Messianic prophecies, a passage about the deliverance of the poor, the brokenhearted, the captives, the blind, and the bruised is significant in their combined focus on the needy. Although it almost seems that the list omits the spiritually needy, or sinners, the term "brokenhearted" no doubt includes at least those who are ready to turn from their sin.

"The acceptable year of the Lord" seems to echo the description of the Year of Jubilee, which occurred every 50th year (Lev. 25:8ff.). This was supposed to be a time to let land revert to its original owners, release slaves, mourn one's sins, and celebrate God's forgiveness; but there is no evidence that the Jews observed it regularly. Jesus seems to use the marvelous gifts He brought as a kind of figurative "jubilee."

II. Applying the Scripture, 20-21

20 And he closed the book, and he gave it again to the minister, and sat down. And the eyes of all them that were in the synagogue were fastened on him.

21 And he began to say unto them, This day is this scripture fulfilled in your ears.

Jesus closed the book (NIV "rolled up the scroll") and sat down, assuming the usual posture of a rabbi about to deliver a sermon or teaching. Luke heightens the drama of the scene by noting that all eyes were fastened on Jesus—and little wonder, since the young man they had known for years as the son of Joseph the Carpenter had applied a Messianic text to Himself. Jesus then removes all doubt of this application by saying clearly that He was the embodiment of what Isaiah had predicted. It would be hard to overstate the potential impact this claim might have had. Yet it seems to have been taken with relative calm—no doubt an example of the "ordinariness of the familiar."

III. Initial Reaction, 22-24
A. 'Gracious words,' 22

22 And all bare him witness, and wondered at the gracious words which proceeded out of his mouth. And they said, Is not this Joseph's son?

At first Jesus' hearers seem to have heard Him with an element of pride, as though their reaction was "Isn't it good that Joseph's son turned out to be such a nice Jewish boy . . . and such a good speaker!" The phrase "gracious words" means literally "words of grace," and can refer either to the content of what Jesus had said or the eloquent way in which He said them. It is hard to square this initial positive reaction with what follows.

B. Doubt dawns, 23-24

23 And he said unto them, Ye will surely say unto me this proverb, Physician, heal thyself: whatsoever we have heard done in Capernaum, do also here in thy country.

24 And he said, Verily I say unto you, No prophet is accepted in his own country.

Although the proverb Jesus used is a natural enough axiom, it is not known from other sources. The turning of the scene from positive to negative may suggest that some who needed healing were present, and the people wondered why this hometown boy who, they had heard, worked miracles in and around Capernaum, did not apply his magic here at home.

Mark (6:1-5) provides more detail for helping us understand the shift from admiration to hostility. At first there is "astonishment" that a home-grown boy could have the miraculous gifts and wisdom that had been reported. Astonishment, however, is not faith; and Mark adds that Jesus "could there do no mighty work, save that he laid his hands upon a few sick folk, and healed them. And he marveled because of their unbelief" (vss. 4-5).

IV. Eventual Anger, 28-30

28 And all they in the synagogue, when they heard these things, were filled with wrath,

29 And rose up, and thrust him out of the city, and led him unto the brow of the hill whereon their city was built, that they might cast him down headlong.

30 But he passing through the midst of them went his way,

"These things" which the congregation heard must refer to Jesus' proverb about "No prophet is accepted in his own country." The audience may also have reflected further on how Jesus had applied Isaiah's Messianic prophecy to Himself, and decided that it was blasphemous for one of their own, and him only a carpenter's son, to make such claims. Most would have expected Messiah to come in the clouds, or with a mighty army. The principle "miracle" they looked for from Messiah was that he would drive out the hated Romans, not concern himself with the wounded and broken-hearted, imprisoned and poor.

Amazingly, the same crowd of people who admired Jesus' "gracious words" now turn on Him and hustle Him out of the synagogue to a nearby hill where they intended to show their displeasure by hurling Him to His death. Here we have "proper church folk" about to murder a guest speaker in direct disobedience to Roman law. The scene reflects a pattern seen more than once: the crowds that should have praised Jesus for delivering the man with a "Legion" of spirits begged Him to leave . . . and the crowd that threw a parade for Jesus on Palm Sunday soon turned into a snarling mob clamoring for His death on the Cross.

Yet the rather sensational, if criminal, way the text ends must not cause the modern Christian to forget Jesus' telling words in verse 18. The level of faithfulness of any church can be gauged by how they reflect the mission of Jesus to those who are poor and needy.

Evangelistic Emphasis

We in the church like to think of ourselves as "God's chosen people." We even have scriptures to legitimize this claim (cf. 1 Pet. 1:2; 2:9; Col. 3:12). Reminding ourselves that we have been chosen by God is comforting and reassuring. It can also be dangerous. It becomes dangerous when we begin to think that we have God all to ourselves and that His attention is and should be directed primarily to us. It is dangerous when we feel that God's purpose is to meet our every perceived need.

It is dangerous when we think that we should be first in line for God's blessings. In the text for today, Jesus offends some of God's chosen people when He points out to them that even though there were great needs among their ancestors, God chose to bless some outsiders. Hearing again the stories of the feeding of the widow at Zarephath and the healing of Naaman the Syrian made the chosen so angry that they tried to kill Jesus. How do we feel about God's mercy to those outside the chosen? Do we celebrate the love He shows them? Do we celebrate it enough to cooperate with Him in bringing it to bear on their lives?

ഈറ

Memory Selection

The Spirit of the Lord is upon me, because he hath anointed me to preach the gospel to the poor; he hath sent me to heal the brokenhearted, to preach deliverance to the captives, and recovering of sight to the blind, to set a liberty them that are bruised.— *Luke 4:18*

I am a list maker. If I want to make sure that my time is well organized and the necessary tasks are accomplished, I have to stop and make a list. I have found this practice helpful at my job and for chores around the house. It is a good spiritual discipline as well. If I just assume I will give attention to the important aspects of my spiritual walk, I can find myself wasting time and ignoring pressing matters.

In this verse, Jesus presents a list of his tasks. He says that the Spirit of the Lord has anointed Him to do these things. It is an impressive list—a list that touches our hearts. The question is, Are any of these items on our list, too? While we cannot claim for ourselves the same authority that Jesus had to accomplish these things, we have been made His ambassadors—and He has promised to go with us as we work. So, what's on our list to do?

486

Weekday Problems

Jeff sat in the prayer group trying to control his emotions. He had been joined the group after losing his job. He had long believed in the power of prayer, and his fear and despair had driven him to be faithful in taking his problems to God. For the first few weeks, he had been encouraged as the other members prayed for him and as he heard their testimonies of answered prayers.

This particular morning, however, was tough. One of the other men who had been out of work for only a month reported that he had found a new job. As the group celebrated and offered praise for God's provision, Jeff found himself growing resentful. Hadn't he been faithful in his prayers? Why had God chosen to ignore him? Evidently, Jeff was not able to hide his reaction. After the meeting, a couple of the men walked to the car with him and asked him how he was feeling. Jeff told them exactly how he felt and what he was thinking. Their response surprised him. They said that he should tell God exactly how he felt. One said, "Jeff, God is big enough to take your anger, and He will delight in your honesty before him."

* Have you ever been disappointed with God?

* What do you do with such disappointments? (Read Psalm 13.)

Fooled Again

Newsboy: Extra! Extra! Read all about it—two men swindled!

Customer: I'll take a paper . . . but say! The story says only one man was swindled!

Newsboy: Extra! Extra! Read all about it—three men swindled!

* * * *

Man on the street: Here's $5 if you can tell me the score of tonight's hockey game before it starts. I can make more than that on a bet.

Fortune teller, closing eyes while pocketing the $5: Tonight, the score will be 0 – 0 before the game starts.

* * * *

Renter: I can't pay the rent this month.

Landlord: But you said that last month!

Renter: And I kept my word, too, didn't I?

* * * *

Glen: Why do doctors and nurses wear masks?

Ben: So if someone makes a mistake, no one will know who did it.

This Lesson in Your Life

In Luke's Gospel, Jesus chose his hometown of Nazareth to make His big announcement. Hometown crowds can be rough. As He stood up in the synagogue that day, He was facing friends, neighbors and relatives who brought with them the full gamut of emotions—from pride and excitement to jealousy and suspicion. Jesus certainly did not back away from the situation. He read the passage from Isaiah that describes the role of God's Messiah, and then He made a statement that shook the entire crowd—even His most fervent supporters. "Today," he said, "this scripture has been fulfilled in your hearing."

"Today" is one of the themes of Jesus' ministry. Later in the Gospel, He will preach, "The kingdom of God is at hand." Out of all of Jesus' words, there is none more important than "today." This word breaks through to a people who are attracted to yesterday and enticed by tomorrow. For the Jewish people in that synagogue audience, there was no sweeter thought than a return to the days of yesterday when King David sat on the throne and the nation of Israel was powerful. Jesus challenged their perception of yesterday with His stories of Elijah and Elisha. We don't like to have our idealized past questioned. Of course, if there is a rival to the glory of yesterday, it is found in tomorrow. We are excited that some day things will be as they should be again. We believe it will happen. For Jesus' audience, God's Messiah was definitely coming—tomorrow—not today.

Alongside this passage from Luke we should place at least two other scriptures: "Jesus Christ the same yesterday, and today, and forever" (Heb. 13:8) and "Now is the accepted time; behold, now is the day of salvation" (2 Cor. 6:2). Jesus' announcement of "today" should not become our yesterday, nor should we set it aside for tomorrow. Like Jesus, our theme is "today."

STRAIGHT

1. **What was the reaction to Jesus when He returned to Galilee following his temptation in the wilderness?**
His fame spread throughout the region, and He was honored for his teaching in the synagogues (Luke 4:14,15).

2. **What was Jesus' hometown?**
He was brought up in Nazareth (4:16).

3. **What scripture did Jesus read in the synagogue at Nazareth?**
He read from the prophet Isaiah (4:17; in our Bibles it is Isaiah 61:1,2).

4. **How did the people initially respond to Jesus' message?**
They wondered at His gracious words and said, "Is not this Joseph's son?" (4:22).

5. **What did Jesus know that the people of His hometown were expecting?**
They wanted Him to work the miracles they had heard He did in Capernaum (4:23).

6. **What is Jesus' famous statement about a prophet in His hometown?**
"Verily I say unto you, No prophet is accepted in his own country" (4:24).

7. **What two Old Testament prophets did Jesus include in his lesson?**
Jesus told stories about Elijah and Elisha (4:25-27).

8. **What was the reaction of the crowd when Jesus spoke of the prophets?**
They were filled with wrath (4:28).

9. **How did the crowd try to kill Jesus?**
They led Him to the brow of the hill on which their city was built and tried to cast Him off (4:29).

10. **How did Jesus escape the crowd?**
He somehow passed through their midst and went on His way (4:30).

It was 2:00 a.m., and the camp director was making one more inspection of the grounds. This had been his most difficult camp session ever. One group of high school boys had arrived with the intent of breaking as many rules as possible. He had seriously considered sending them home, but he felt that he should at least try to make some progress with them first. The leader of the group was Jake. The director knew that Jake came from a strong Christian family, but the boy seemed to have no interest in spiritual matters. He had already decided that if Jake caused one more problem he would have to leave camp.

Just as the director reached his cabin, he saw shadows moving along the tree line. He clicked on his flashlight and was not surprised by the faces he discovered. "This is just too much," he thought as he yelled for the boys to stop. "Jake is history." The director stormed toward the boys, who now stood casually waiting for him. He walked directly up to Jake and unleashed his anger. He had never talked to one of his campers this way, but it was 2:00 a.m. and it was Jake. For several minutes, the director listed all of Jake's offenses. Then he began his dissertation on how miserable Jake was making him and the rest of the staff and campers. Finally, he paused to take a breath.

"You finished?" Jake asked. The question caught the director off guard. Suddenly he realized that he had gone too far in his verbal assault.

"Just go to your cabin," he muttered to the boys.

"Not yet," Jake replied. The director felt his anger rekindling, but before he could explode once again Jake continued. "I was just out looking for you because I want to be baptized."

"You what?" the director said, shaking his head. "I want to be baptized," Jake repeated.

"Now?" the director asked. "Yes, and I want you to do it. Will you?"

Of course the director could say nothing but "Yes, I will." And he did.

The camp director says he thinks back to that day often. In fact, every time he is tempted to give up on someone, he thinks of Jake. Earlier that night, he thought it would be a long time before Jake ever changed. He learned that it can always be today.

490

Girl Restored, Woman Healed

Luke 8:40-56

And it came to pass, that, when Jesus was returned, the people gladly received him: for they were all waiting for him.

41 And, behold, there came a man named Jairus, and he was a ruler of the synagogue: and he fell down at Jesus' feet, and besought him that he would come into his house:

42 For he had one only daughter, about twelve years of age, and she lay a dying. But as he went the people thronged him.

43 And a woman having an issue of blood twelve years, which had spent all her living upon physicians, neither could be healed of any,

44 Came behind him, and touched the border of his garment: and immediately her issue of blood stanched.

45 And Jesus said, Who touched me? When all denied, Peter and they that were with him said, Master, the multitude throng thee and press thee, and sayest thou, Who touched me?

46 And Jesus said, Somebody hath touched me: for I perceive that virtue is gone out of me.

47 And when the woman saw that she was not hid, she came trembling, and falling down before him, she declared unto him before all the people for what cause she had touched him and how she was healed immediately.

48 And he said unto her, Daughter, be of good comfort: thy faith hath made thee whole; go in peace.

49 While he yet spake, there cometh one from the ruler of the synagogue's house, saying to him, Thy daughter is dead; trouble not the Master.

50 But when Jesus heard it, he answered him, saying, Fear not: believe only, and she shall be made whole.

51 And when he came into the house, he suffered no man to go in, save Peter, and James, and John, and the father and the mother of the maiden.

52 And all wept, and bewailed her: but he said, Weep not; she is not dead, but sleepeth.

53 And they laughed him to scorn, knowing that she was dead.

54 And he put them all out, and took her by the hand, and called, saying, Maid, arise.

55 And her spirit came again, and she arose straightway: and he commanded to give her meat.

56 And her parents were astonished: but he charged them that they should tell no man what was done.

Aug. 14

Memory Selection
Luke 8:48

Background Scripture
Luke 8:40-56

Devotional Reading
Matthew 9:18-26

This lesson selects two healing miracles of Jesus— one of a young girl and the other of a woman—that focus on Luke's apparent interest in showing that women are an integral part of the Kingdom. Luke the Greek physician was the only Gospel writer who was not a Jew; and the Greeks had a long, if uneven, history of experimenting with women's equality.

The emphasis here, however, is not on gender but on Christ's miraculous power and compassion. Note that the text starts with the young girl, whose story is interrupted in verses 43-48 by a woman with an uncontrolled menstrual flow. At the teacher's discretion, the story of the young girl can be presented without interruption by omitting verse 43-48, then returning to those verses and dealing separately with that account.

ഇരുള

This lesson can be introduced by inviting group members to share experiences of God's healing presence in their lives. Some may have stories that are apparently miraculous, with healing apparently accomplished only by prayer. Others may tell how a combination of modern science and medicine accomplished a healing. Point out that God can work both through, and "around," scientific methods, and that even when people have been healed without prayer, medicines and medical skills can also be attributed to Him.

Be sensitive in such a discussion to those who have lost loved ones despite prayers and/or medical treatment. People died in spite of prayer even in the days of Jesus and His apostles, and the area remains in the province of God's sovereignty rather than being in the control of man.

Teaching Outline	Daily Bible Readings
I. Girl on Her Deathbed—40-42	Mon. A Servant Is Healed *Luke 7:1-10*
II. Woman in Desperation—43-48	Tue. One Restored, One Healed *Matthew 9:18-26*
A. Faith in a touch, 43-44	Wed. Two Blind Men See *Matthew 9:27-31*
B. Feeling the power, 45-46	Thu. Hemorrhaging Healed *Mark 5:24b-34*
C. Faith brings health, 47-48	Fri. Girl Restored to Life *Mark 5:35-43*
III. In God's Good Time—49-56	Sat. Sick Woman Healed *Luke 8:40-48*
A. Is it too late?, 49-50	Sun. Jairus' Daughter Restored *Luke 8:49-56*
B. Private meeting, 51-53	
C. 'Maid, arise!', 54-56	

Verse by Verse

I. Girl on Her Deathbed—40-42

40 And it came to pass, that, when Jesus was returned, the people gladly received him: for they were all waiting for him.

41 And, behold, there came a man named Jairus, and he was a ruler of the synagogue: and he fell down at Jesus' feet, and besought him that he would come into his house:

42 For he had one only daughter, about twelve years of age, and she lay a dying. But as he went the people thronged him.

Jesus had been ministering in "the country of the Gadarenes" (8:26), east of Galilee, and apparently returns now to His home base of Capernaum. As mentioned in a previous lesson, modern archeologists have uncovered a synagogue there built on the foundations of a previous structure that could well have been the synagogue of which Jairus was "ruler." As such, he would have been its administrator, and in charge of choosing men who would read Scripture, offer prayer, and preach or teach. While we may doubt that he was a follower of Jesus, he would have heard reports of His healing powers since Jesus made His headquarters in Capernaum when He was in the area.

II. Woman in Desperation—43-48
A. Faith in a touch, 43-44

43 And a woman having an issue of blood twelve years, which had spent all her living upon physicians, neither could be healed of any,

44 Came behind him, and touched the border of his garment: and immediately her issue of blood stanched.

All three synoptic Gospels interrupt the story of Jairus' daughter with that of this woman. The postponment of the girl's healing can teach us that God's sovereign work of healing is on His own time, as a lesson against being discouraged when our own pleas in behalf of loved ones seem unanswered or delayed.

Ancient records of Jewish methods of healing unstanched menstrual flow leave little wonder that the woman had spent all her livelihood seeking healing. Treatments included the application of a variety of herbs and spices, having the patient drink a potion of Persian onions boiled in wine, and even having someone jump from behind her to frighten her out of her ailment, like the hiccups. The crowds are so dense that the woman cannot reach Jesus to speak to Him personally. Her own only hope is to touch his garment with the hope that some of His power clings to it.

B. Feeling the power, 45-46

45 And Jesus said, Who touched me? When all denied, Peter and they that were with him said, Master, the multitude throng thee and press thee, and sayest thou, Who touched me?

46 And Jesus said, Somebody hath touched me: for I perceive that virtue is gone out of me.

The first reaction of a modern reader may be that it is superstitious to suppose that healing power can be attached to a material object. In Jesus' case, however, this seems to be true since it is said that He felt "virtue" (Grk. dynamis, lit. "power") leave His body at the woman's touch. (See also Acts 19:11-12, where healing power apparently adhered to cloths that had been in the apostle Paul's possession.) Although God nowhere promises that the "natural" and "supernatural" worlds will interact the same way in all ages, it is also possible that Jesus only accommodates Himself to the view of the woman, and asks "Who touched me?" for her own benefit so she can be singled out in the crowd for the real healing power, which was faith.

C. Faith brings health, 47-48

47 And when the woman saw that she was not hid, she came trembling, and falling down before him, she declared unto him before all the people for what cause she had touched him and how she was healed immediately.

48 And he said unto her, Daughter, be of good comfort: thy faith hath made thee whole; go in peace.

This must have been a temporarily embarrassing moment. As a woman, this "daughter" of Israel was not supposed to speak out in public, and she no doubt would rather that the sexual nature of her ailment not be broadcast. Yet the demonstration both of her equality with men and the power of Jesus over her sickness made it worth it for Jesus to coax her to go public with her needs.

III. In God's Good Time—49-56
A. Is it too late?, 49-50

49 While he yet spake, there cometh one from the ruler of the synagogue's house, saying to him, Thy daughter is dead; trouble not the Master.

50 But when Jesus heard it, he answered him, saying, Fear not: believe only, and she shall be made whole.

The delay caused by the woman with the hemorrhage has, to human eyes, cost the life of Jairus' daughter. We can imagine Jairus' frustration as he waits impatiently to lead Jesus to his home, only to hear from a friend helping tend to her that the little girl has died. This time the faith Jesus asks for is obviously not from the one in need of healing, but, like the friends of the paralyzed man in Mark 2, from those who love her. We can only imagine the stress Jairus must feel: he is being asked to believe that this One whose wonders he has only heard about, but not experienced, actually has power to do something for his daughter even though she is dead. Yet in some ways, faith that is tested and stretched is the only kind of faith that is worth the name.

B. Private meeting, 51-53

51 And when he came into the house, he suffered no man to go in, save Peter, and James, and John, and the father and the mother of the maiden.

52 And all wept, and bewailed her: but he said, Weep not; she is not dead, but sleepeth.

53 And they laughed him to scorn, knowing that she was dead.

Jesus' exhibits exquisite sensitivity in His concern for both the woman with the menstrual flow and for this little girl and her family. The woman needed to assert herself publicly and to have her faith bolstered, so Jesus called for her to make herself known before healing her. Jairus and his family, however, need a quiet room and intimacy; so Jesus does just the opposite, asking all but his innermost circle of disciples to leave the room.

Matthew (9:23-24) explains that those who laughed at Jesus in scorn at His suggestion that the girl is only asleep were the professional mourners normally hired by Jewish families as a part of the ritual of grieving. The minstrels had already begun to play their dirges, and they would lose a "gig" if there turns out to be no funeral!

As in our own day, the Jews often sought euphemisms to avoid saying that someone actually died (passed away, went on, left us, etc.). Jesus accommodates Himself to this practice, partly because He knows that her sleep of death is about to be reversed. At any rate, for those in the path of Jesus' love and care, death is little more than sleep.

C. 'Maid, arise!', 54-60

54 And he put them all out, and took her by the hand, and called, saying, Maid, arise.

55 And her spirit came again, and she arose straightway: and he commanded to give her meat.

56 And her parents were astonished: but he charged them that they should tell no man what was done.

Mark (5:41) preserves Jesus' words, "Maid arise" in Aramaic ("Talitha cumi"), one of the clues we have of Jesus' native tongue. Luke, writing to Greeks, does not bother to include a phrase that would have been as strange to them as it is to us. The King James often translates the word for "food" as "meat"; the verse doesn't really specify what kind of food was given to the little girl.

The miracle story concludes with another command not to tell about it. Commonly called "the Messianic secret," it is generally explained by the supposition that this early in His ministry Jesus does not want word of His miracles to draw mobs, and to risk the resulting intrusion of Roman political power to cut short His work. Just as in the case of stopping on His way to heal Jairus' daughter, the sovereign Lord has His own time table.

Evangelistic Emphasis

My guess is that Jairus, a successful man of social standing, had never fallen at the feet of another person and begged for anything. What could possibly move him to do such a thing? I would also think that a woman who had hemorrhaged for 12 years would have stayed away from the crush of huge crowds, fearing injury or total exhaustion. What could possibly convince her to push her way through—perhaps even crawling on her hands and knees—just to touch the hem of a man's clothes?

Obviously the answer to both questions is faith. Jairus believed Jesus could help his dying daughter, and the woman believed that Jesus could and would heal her. However, behind their faith was desperation. They both had exhausted all other options. They both knew that there was no other answer. Desperation can push people beyond decorum and beyond fear. The good news is that Jesus responds to desperation. He knows that He is truly the last resort, and He is not offended when we treat Him as such. The real tragedy is when we arrive at the point of desperation and, out of pride or fear, refuse to approach the only One who can offer hope. Desperate? You are in the right place.

☜☞

Memory Selection

And he said unto her, "Daughter, be of good comfort: thy faith hath made thee whole; go in peace."—*Luke 8:48*

When Jesus pronounced this blessing on the woman who had been gravely ill for 12 years, He chose his words carefully. Rather than simply declaring her healed, He used a word that can mean so much more. In essence, Jesus said, "Your faith has saved you." More than simply granting her a few more years of physical health, Jesus blessed her for eternity because of her absolute trust in Him. While others—even Jesus' own disciples—were puzzled by Jesus' ability to distinguish a touch of faith amid the jostling of the crowd, this woman placed no such limits on His power.

We might wonder how many others who were within arm's length of Jesus had needs that were not met because they did not have the faith to reach out to Him. Perhaps they thought that Jesus would not care about their particular struggle or need. Years later, Paul praised "Him who by the power at work within us is able to accomplish abundantly far more than all we can ask or imagine" (Eph. 3:20). The woman in the crowd has taught us not to put boundaries on the power of Jesus in our lives.

Weekday Problems

Cheryl had grown up in a strong Christian family, but when she married Don she had drifted away from the church. At first she had felt guilty, but Don's lack of interest in church and their busy schedules worked together to convince her she really did not need to be involved. Now, after several stormy years of marriage, Cheryl found herself single once again.

As she grieved over her failed relationship, one of her first thoughts was to return to church. She mentioned this to several of her friends, and she was surprised to hear them tell her that they did not think church was the answer for her. Some of them told her stories of how churches had judged and rejected divorced people—especially divorced women. Others told her she needed to get more active socially and meet a good man. Cheryl was confused and discouraged. She had grown up thinking that church was a loving place that provided comfort and healing for broken people. Her heart still told her to *try*—even though her friends told her it would be a waste of time.

   * What do the stories in today's text have to say about acting faithfully even when others might discourage us?

How Love 'Naturally' Works

The "miracles" in Scripture are often thought to be divine contradictions of the natural laws of God. I believe, instead, that they are illustrations of how God "naturally" works. They pack into one moment all the potential of a universe created to operate by love.

When Jesus healed a person, He was not performing a trick of magic, and it was not understood by those who knew Him as a violation of the way the world "really" operates. His healing touch was the opening of a tiny window into the fact that "the universe is friendly"; that the truly "normal" way things work is *for* people, not *against* them.

Believe the miracles in the Bible not because they show how odd Jesus could make the world work. Believe them because they show how glorious a world we will enjoy when the truly odd and ruinous parts of our world run out of their ability to hurt and maim, leaving only love in their place.

—Anonymous

This Lesson in Your Life

How long is 12 years? Your answer to this question might depend on your age. The older we get, the shorter a span of 12 years can seem. Your answer might also depend on the events of those 12 years. How long is 12 years to a person who has suffered from a serious illness for that length of time? To say that someone has been sick for 12 years is the comment on how long that time can be. Our opinion of the length of 12 years changes, though, when we hear of a 12-year-old child who has contracted a life-threatening illness. Our question then is why someone who has lived such a short time is faced with death.

A common thread in the two stories that are intertwined in our text today is the mention of the span of 12 years. In one story, a little girl of 12 is dying. In the other, a woman has suffered for 12 years. In both stories, the span of 12 years heightens the sense of desperation felt by those who were there and felt by those of us who read their stories. We can understand why a woman so ill for so long would crawl through the crush of a large crowd in hope of finding healing. We can also relate to the desperation of the father—a man of importance and structure—who would humble himself by falling on the ground and begging for the life of his young daughter. Both of these were desperate enough to overcome any obstacles of discouragement and pride to get to the one person who could help.

These stories define faith. Faith is not easily discouraged. Faith grows from the desperation of realizing there is only one source of true help. Faith is not too proud to beg. Faith can endure mockery. Faith can be misunderstood and judged by those who have no faith, but faith presses on. Faith saves.

1. Who was Jairus?
Jairus was a ruler of the synagogue in Capernaum (Luke 8:41).

2. What did Jairus do before Jesus, and for what did he ask?
Jairus fell down at Jesus' feet and begged Him to come to his house to heal his 12-year-old daughter, who was dying (8:41-42).

3. Why was the woman who had been ill for 12 years also financially ruined?
She had spent all her living on physicians who were unable to heal her (8:43).

4. What did the woman do to be healed by Jesus?
She came behind Him and touched the border of His garment (8:44).

5. What was the attitude of the disciples when Jesus asked who in the crowd had touched Him?
They were skeptical that Jesus could feel one touch while such a large crowd was pressing against Him (8:45).

6. To what did the woman testify before all the people?
She declared why she had touched Jesus and how she had been healed immediately (8:47).

7. What message did Jairus receive while Jesus was speaking with the woman?
One from his household came to him and told him his daughter had died (8:49).

8. What did Jesus say in response to this message?
Jesus told Jairus, "Fear not, believe only, and she shall be made whole" (8:50).

9. How did the people in Jairus' house respond when Jesus said that the girl was not dead but only sleeping?
They laughed Him to scorn because they knew she was dead (8:53).

10. What instructions did Jesus give to Jairus and his wife after He raised their daughter?
He told them to give her food, and not to tell anyone what had been done (8:56).

The story is told of a man named George Muller who was convicted to begin praying for five of his friends who had never named the name of the Lord. After several months of prayer for these friends, George was discouraged that he had not noticed any change in them. Just as he was tempted to give up his prayer, one of the friends came to the Lord. George was greatly encouraged and rejoiced over the man's decision. He also recommitted to his prayers. Ten years would pass before two of the others would come to faith. It was 25 years before the fourth gave his heart to the Lord. The fifth, however, continued to show no interest, but George persisted. He continued to be faithful in his prayers for this remaining friend until his death. In all, George had prayed for this one man for 52 years. Soon after Muller's funeral, the last friend was saved.

The two stories in the text for today are stories of faithful persistence. They raise the question of how determined we are in our faith. What things can discourage us? Will circumstances or other's lack of faith deter us? Will our own pride get in the way? And how long is long enough to persist in our petitions? How long have you prayed for something or someone specifically before giving up?

The disciples of Jesus saw no value in simply touching Him. The friends of Jairus saw no need to continue asking for Jesus' help once the little girl had died. The suffering woman, on the other hand, pressed on. Jairus and his wife continued to believe. Let us follow their examples—and the example of the faithful George Muller—as we judge a lifetime of faithfulness to be our calling.

Lesson 12

The Good Samaritan

nd, behold, a certain lawyer stood up, and tempted him, saying, Master, what shall I do to inherit eternal life?

26 He said unto him, What is written in the law? how readest thou?

27 And he answering said, Thou shalt love the Lord thy God with all thy heart, and with all thy soul, and with all thy strength, and with all thy mind; and thy neighbour as thyself.

28 And he said unto him, Thou hast answered right: this do, and thou shalt live.

29 But he, willing to justify himself, said unto Jesus, And who is my neighbour?

30 And Jesus answering said, A certain man went down from Jerusalem to Jericho, and fell among thieves, which stripped him of his raiment, and wounded him, and departed, leaving him half dead.

31 And by chance there came down a certain priest that way: and when he saw him, he passed by on the other side.

32 And likewise a Levite, when he was at the place, came and looked on him, and passed by on the other side.

33 But a certain Samaritan, as he journeyed, came where he was: and when he saw him, he had compassion on him,

34 And went to him, and bound up his wounds, pouring in oil and wine, and set him on his own beast, and brought him to an inn, and took care of him.

35 And on the morrow when he departed, he took out two pence, and gave them to the host, and said unto him, Take care of him; and whatsoever thou spendest more, when I come again, I will repay thee.

36 Which now of these three, thinkest thou, was neighbour unto him that fell among the thieves?

37 And he said, He that shewed mercy on him. Then said Jesus unto him, Go, and do thou likewise.

Memory Selection
Luke 10:27

Background Scripture
Luke 10:25-37

Devotional Reading
Matthew 22:34-40

Aug. 21

501

This famous parable challenges us to examine the boundaries of our care and concern for other people. All of us no doubt had rather be around some people than others. While Jesus does not deny that family and friends may rightly claim more of our concern than strangers, He asks about our willingness to cross traditional lines of prejudice to help a stranger in need.

Our Lord tells this story not just in response to the question "Who is my neighbor?" (vs. 29), but "What shall I do to inherit eternal life?" (vs. 25). The lawyer who asks the question lived under the Law of Moses, so Jesus' answer is not in terms of salvation by grace through faith. Still, the parable does not teach salvation merely by works, but works that flow out of love (vs. 27)—showing that even the Old Covenant was based not on works of merit but on sharing with others the love first given by God.

ംൻഝ

Use a word-association exercise to introduce the lesson. On a writing board, write the word *neighbor*, and draw out first-impression, "top-of-the-head" responses from the group that show what they think of first when they hear that term.

Some may think first of the family next door, or across the street. Since most will anticipate that the parable will broaden their definition, they may think of terms such as anyone who is in need, or those whose need is within their ability to meet.

Does anyone mention a terrorist or a Middle-Easterner? Note that Jesus tells this story to nudge us to the edge of our comfort zone of "neighborliness." The parable is a kind of test to see how far we are able to reach in extending to others the love God has shown us.

Teaching Outline	**Daily Bible Readings**
I. A Test for Jesus, 25-29	Mon. The Great Commandment *Deuteronomy 6:1-9*
A. A lawyer's question, 25-26	Tue. 'Love Your Neighbor' *Leviticus 19:11-18*
B. Love in the law, 27-28	Wed. The Greatest Commandment *Matthew 22:34-40*
C. 'Who is my neighbor?, 29	Thu. The First Commandment *Mark 12:28-34*
II. A Story in Response, 30-35	Fri. Love Your Neighbor *Luke 10:25-29*
A. Introduction, 30	Sat. The Good Samaritan *Luke 10:30-37*
B. Two failures as neighbors, 31-32	Sun. Love Fulfills the Law *Romans 13:8-14*
C. A Samaritan as neighbor, 33-35	
III. Applying the Parable, 36-37	

Verse by Verse

I. A Test for Jesus, 25-29

A. A lawyer's question, 25-26

25 And, behold, a certain lawyer stood up, and tempted him, saying, Master, what shall I do to inherit eternal life?

26 He said unto him, What is written in the law? how readest thou?

The Parable of the Good Samaritan is unique to Luke. It reflects both the Greek physician's humanitarian and cosmopolitan spirit, showing that national and racial prejudice have no place in the Kingdom.

A "lawyer" among the Jews referred to a man who was trained in the interpretation of the Law of Moses, although he might also interface as an attorney with the law of the land since the Jewish Law touched on secular life at so many points. This lawyer was no doubt allied with Jesus' critics, since his aim was to "tempt" or test Jesus rather than to gain understanding.

This question was debated by the rabbis, in an ongoing attempt to find a single answer in the mass of Jewish Scripture and tradition. Since the question dealt with inheriting "eternal life," the lawyer's sentiment would have been with the Pharisees instead of the Sadducees, since they did not believe in a resurrection (Matt. 22:23). As a wise teacher, Jesus turns the question back to the questioner, to draw him into helping find the answer.

B. Love in the law, 27-28

27 And he answering said, Thou shalt love the Lord thy God with all thy heart, and with all thy soul, and with all thy strength, and with all thy mind; and thy neighbour as thyself.

28 And he said unto him, Thou hast answered right: this do, and thou shalt live.

Since this conversation takes place before the Cross, Jesus could hardly have given the same answer the apostle Paul would give: both He and the Lawyer still lived under the Law. Yet the lawyer's wise summary represents a bridge between Moses and Christ, works and grace. It shows that even with all its detailed commandments, the Law of Moses was based on love (see Lev. 19:18).

This is essentially the same summary of the Law that Jesus Himself gives in Matthew 23:36-40, so Jesus commends the lawyer for his insight. It is "simply profound" in its depth and breadth, pointing explicitly to the virtue of loving God and neighbor, and implicitly to the need for self-respect or loving ourselves.

C. 'Who is my neighbor?, 29

29 But he, willing to justify himself, said unto Jesus, And who is my neighbour?

Jesus' questioner must have been surprised to hear Jesus' commendation. He was not really seeking an answer, but a way either to trap Jesus or to place himself in a "justified" light, showing that he had already done all that Jesus might say he should do. Yet, after the manner of the rabbis, who loved to argue endlessly, the lawyer seizes on the opportunity to debate a fine definition of "neighbor"; so he presses further.

II. A Story in Response, 30-35

A. Introduction, 30

30 And Jesus answering said, A certain man went down from Jerusalem to Jericho, and fell among thieves, which stripped him of his raiment, and wounded him, and departed, leaving him half dead.

The Parable of the Good Samaritan provides a classic illustration of the way Jesus used stories to provide various opportunities for the hearers to identify with the story's characters. The lawyer must have immediately begun to wonder which character Jesus intends to represent him.

Given the context, "A certain man" is to be understood as a Jew. Although Jericho was only some 17 miles from Jerusalem, the road descended 3,000 feet as it twisted through treacherous hills that gave thieves plenty of places to hide and to set ambushes. Although we are not told that the man was robbed, the fact that his attackers were thieves implies that they not only stripped him of his clothes but his money as well.

B. Two failures as neighbors, 31-32

31 And by chance there came down a certain priest that way: and when he saw him, he passed by on the other side.

32 And likewise a Levite, when he was at the place, came and looked on him, and passed by on the other side.

Priests were charged with various duties in the Temple, having been carefully instructed on just how to offer the right sacrifices in the right way, and even tending to some instructional duties. In order to preserve their purity in offering sacrifices for others, priests could not touch dead bodies. Since the traveler had been left "half dead," he was probably unconscious; and looking over at him the priest could not be sure whether he was dead or alive. He chose to "play it safe," placing the ritual requirements of the Law over the possibility that the man might still be alive.

Both "priests" and "Levites" were descended from Levi, son of Aaron, the first high priest. By Jesus' day, however, Levites generally were assigned more menial duties than priests, such as the upkeep of the Temple. They also, however, were responsible for certain aspects of worship such as arranging for the music required for certain services (see 2

Chron. 29:25-26). Thus the Levite too felt that he could not risk being "defiled" by touching a dead body.

C. A Samaritan as neighbor, 33-35

33 But a certain Samaritan, as he journeyed, came where he was: and when he saw him, he had compassion on him,

34 And went to him, and bound up his wounds, pouring in oil and wine, and set him on his own beast, and brought him to an inn, and took care of him.

35 And on the morrow when he departed, he took out two pence, and gave them to the host, and said unto him, Take care of him; and whatsoever thou spendest more, when I come again, I will repay thee.

The Samaritans lived in middle Palestine, between Jerusalem and Galilee. A "proper" Jew had no dealings with them (John 4:9), because, as the descendants of foreigners brought in to intermarry with Israelites some seven centuries earlier, they were "half-breed" Jews. They were also still tainted with the sin of dividing from Judah some eight centuries earlier, and becoming a separate kingdom with a separate place of worship (see the interesting interchange between Jesus and the woman at the well of Samaria, John 4:9, 22).

Despite this history of tension and prejudice between the two groups, it is the Samaritan who stops to tend the wounded traveler. He administers oil and wine, common "first aid" treatment for wounds, places the wounded man on his own donkey, and completes the journey to Jericho where he finds an inn that will keep him. Estimates of how long the two pence he gives the inn-keeper would have paid for his upkeep range from one to two months.

III. Applying the Parable, 36-37

36 Which now of these three, thinkest thou, was neighbour unto him that fell among the thieves?

37 And he said, He that shewed mercy on him. Then said Jesus unto him, Go, and do thou likewise.

When we think of this parable, we usually assume that Jesus has answered the lawyer's question, "Who is my neighbor?" by portraying the Samaritan as the person toward whom we should overcome our prejudice, and extend help. A closer look, however, shows that Jesus actually answers the question To whom am I neighbor? The position of the Samaritan as helper instead of the one who needs help actually elevates him to an even higher position than that which we usually assume. A "mixed breed" man, who would have had every reason to disdain to assist a Jew who hated him, swallows his pride and proves to be the neighbor in the story.

Jesus' last word, "Go, and do thou likewise" shows that it is by expanding our comfort zones and helping even those who hate us that we not only prove to be a neighbor, but that we fulfill "the royal law," the law of love, that underlies both the Law of Moses and the rule of Christ.

Evangelistic Emphasis

The Parable of the Good Samaritan is one of the best known stories in the Bible. While the main point of the story is obvious, we do have some questions about some of the details. For example, the priest and the Levite pass by the man in need. Ever wonder why? Jesus does not answer this question. We can only think of the excuses they might have given. Maybe they were too busy to stop. Perhaps they were frightened that the robbers might still be in the area. In their minds, they might have thought was some kind of trap. A more cynical motive might be that they felt they could get away with not stopping since no one else was around to see them. Of course, it could be that they just did not care about the man's predicament, but we find that reason to be disturbing. Surely there was something else that blocked out their human response of compassion.

Every day we pass someone in need. Though they may be physically healthy, they are emotionally beaten or spiritually devastated. Yet we pass by. Ever wonder why?

Memory Selection

And he answering said, Thou shalt love the Lord thy God with all thy heart, and with all thy soul, and with all thy strength, and with all they mind; and thy neighbor as thyself.—*Luke 10:27*

These words were not spoken by Jesus but by the lawyer who was questioning Jesus. The man had asked what he must do to inherit eternal life, and Jesus had in turn asked him to answer his own question. Surprisingly, the man knew the correct answer. Was he only trying to test Jesus to see if Jesus knew the right answer, too? Or was he hoping that Jesus knew another answer that was not as demanding as this one? The lawyer's second question ("And who is my neighbor?") seems to indicate that he was having difficulty believing he could do what the Scripture commanded.

The author G. K. Chesterton once wrote, "It isn't that the Christian life has been tried and found wanting, it's that it's been found difficult and left untried." This exchange between the lawyer and Jesus cautions us against using our questions to delay our response to what we already know and understand. Love the Lord. Love our neighbor. These easily grasped concepts call for a lifetime of humble response.

506

Weekday Problems

It was Saturday morning, and Ed and Joe were once again driving to the golf course as they had for many years. When the light turned red, Joe sighed impatiently and pulled the car to a stop. Next to them—near the passenger window—stood a disheveled man holding a sign: *Hungry. Disabled. Please Help. Jesus Loves You.* Ed reached for his wallet.

"What are you doing?" Joe snorted.

"I'm going to give the man some money," Ed replied.

"Why?" Joe asked obviously irritated by the events. "That man probably makes more money that we do with his scam. There are plenty of agencies to help him. You're just helping him abuse the system and rip people off."

Ed held the five-dollar bill in his hand. "But Jesus said we should help anyone in need."

"Well," Joe replied, "he didn't mean giving handouts to people like that."

* Who do you think is right—Ed or Joe?

* Is the man standing on the corner truly in need? In need of what? How can you help?

Ups and Downs of Ministers

A group of ministers were returning from a church convention in a plane that suddenly flew into a storm. The flight attendant stepped into the cabin and assured the pilot that all was well. "We have 13 ministers on board," she said.

"Well," said the pilot, "that's reassuring, but I'd rather have four good engines than 13 ministers."

* * * *

Minister: Don't disturb me for awhile, dear. I'll be into my devotional.

Wife: OK, dear. Shall I wake you up when you've finished?

* * * *

The famous preacher Henry Ward Beecher once received a letter with one word written on it: **Fool**. The next Sunday he read the letter from the pulpit and said, "I receive many letters from people who forget to sign their names, but this is the first time I've received one from someone who signed his name but forgot to write the letter."

This Lesson in Your Life

The teacher assigns a 20-page paper that lists 10 resources. Invariably, someone will raise a hand and ask, "What if the paper is only 19-1/2 pages? Will that be enough?"

"No," the teacher replies, "a 20-page paper means just that. Twenty pages with 10 resources. Do it."

Another hand goes up. "Will you count off if it's late?"

"Yes," the answer comes, "20 pages, 10 resources, due on December 3rd."

"Will you take it on the 4th?"

Anyone who has ever sat in a classroom will recognize this conversation. There is something within us that drives us to test boundaries. This was true for the lawyer questioning Jesus in Luke Chapter 10. The two had agreed that loving our neighbors was a part of God's plan, but the lawyer had to ask the question, "How far does that go? How big is the neighborhood?"

Jesus' parable of the Good Samaritan is the answer to where the boundaries fall in our neighborhood. Two characters in the story—the priest and the Levite—had definite boundaries, and the injured man beside the road did not lie within them. The third man—a Samaritan who was a victim of boundaries himself—evidently had a much larger neighborhood. What allowed him to include this beaten, naked stranger within his circle of concern?

Perhaps the answer lies in how we perceive our resources. We often draw boundaries because we do not think we have enough of something to go around—and enough to have some left for ourselves. Jesus and the lawyer were discussing the resource of love. Another way of asking the lawyer's question is, "Do I have enough love to be able to share it with just anyone I come across? Do I have enough love to share it with someone who will not return it?" Paul tells us in Romans 5:5 that God pours his love into our hearts through the Holy Spirit. Surely, we, above all people, are confident that we can share our love with anyone. We never have to fret that the love we give might be wasted or even undeserved. After all, our supply is endless.

1. What question did the lawyer pose to Jesus in order to test Him?

The lawyer asked, "Master, what shall I do to inherit eternal life?" (Luke 10:25).

2. What two Old Testament passages did the lawyer quote in response to his own question?

The lawyer quoted Deuteronomy 6:5 and Leviticus 19:18.

3. Did Jesus agree with the lawyer's answer to His question?

Yes. Jesus said, "You have answered right. Do this, and you shall live" (Luke 10:28).

4. Why did the lawyer continue to question Jesus after the answer was given?

The lawyer was trying to justify himself (10:29).

5. In Jesus' story, what happened to the man traveling from Jerusalem to Jericho?

The man fell among thieves and was stripped, beaten and left half dead (10:30).

6. Who saw the man, but decided not to help him?

Two men passed him by—a priest and a Levite (10:31,32).

7. What is surprising about the man who did decide to help the wounded man?

The one who stopped to help was a Samaritan (10:33), and Jewish people of Jesus' day would have no interaction with Samaritans (cf. John 4:9).

8. What actions did the Samaritan perform to help the man?

He treated his wounds, took him to an inn, and cared for him through the night (10:34).

9. When the Samaritan had to leave, what provision did he make for the wounded man?

The Samaritan paid the innkeeper in advance and promised to pay any other expenses incurred when he made his return trip (10:35).

10. What point did Jesus make at the end of the parable?

Jesus led the lawyer to understand that any person who shows mercy on another understands what it means to be a neighbor (10:36-37).

In Robert James Waller's novel *The Bridges of Madison County,* a love story is told as a flashback. As the novel begins, a family is gathered for the funeral of Francesca, who had asked that she be cremated and her ashes be scattered from the local covered bridge. In order to explain this request, she leaves her journal to her two adult children—because she wanted them to know her story. Through the journal, Francisca's children learn that when they were teenagers, Francisca had met a dashing, creative photographer with whom she had a four-day affair.

The photographer had wanted to take her away from the rural life with all its drabness and stress of everyday family life, but Francisca had made a different choice. While the photographer had thought he was asking Francisca to act out of love, Francisca decided that she would act out of true love. "I could not do that to my husband," she tells the photographer. She chose to honor the love to which she was committed, and she wanted her children to know how much she loved them. She wanted her children to know what true love is all about.

When Jesus tells the story of the Good Samaritan, he wants us all to know what true love is all about. When we understand that real love does not grow from feelings but rather feelings follow true love, then his command to "Go, do this," makes sense. Though our culture tries to teach us that we cannot control whom we love, Jesus begs to differ. Because God has chosen to love us, we do have the ability to choose to love others. When we think of the story in this way, this simple, familiar parable becomes much more than a reminder to help strangers on the road.

This story defines how we will choose to live—especially among those to whom we have dared to say the words, "I love you."

Lesson 13

Humility and Commitment

Luke 14:7-11, 15-24

nd he put forth a parable to those which were bidden, when he marked how they chose out the chief rooms; saying unto them,

8 When thou art bidden of any man to a wedding, sit not down in the highest room; lest a more honourable man than thou be bidden of him;

9 And he that bade thee and him come and say to thee, Give this man place; and thou begin with shame to take the lowest room.

10 But when thou art bidden, go and sit down in the lowest room; that when he that bade thee cometh, he may say unto thee, Friend, go up higher: then shalt thou have worship in the presence of them that sit at meat with thee.

11 For whosoever exalteth himself shall be abased; and he that humbleth himself shall be exalted.

15 And when one of them that sat at meat with him heard these things, he said unto him, Blessed is he that shall eat bread in the kingdom of God.

16 Then said he unto him, A certain man made a great supper, and bade many:

17 And sent his servant at supper time to say to them that were bidden, Come; for all things are now ready.

18 And they all with one consent began to make excuse. The first said unto him, I have bought a piece of ground,

and I must needs go and see it: I pray thee have me excused.

19 And another said, I have bought five yoke of oxen, and I go to prove them: I pray thee have me excused.

20 And another said, I have married a wife, and therefore I cannot come.

21 So that servant came, and shewed his lord these things. Then the master of the house being angry said to his servant, Go out quickly into the streets and lanes of the city, and bring in hither the poor, and the maimed, and the halt, and the blind.

22 And the servant said, Lord, it is done as thou hast commanded, and yet there is room.

23 And the lord said unto the servant, Go out into the highways and hedges, and compel them to come in, that my house may be filled.

24 For I say unto you, That none of those men which were bidden shall taste of my supper.

Memory Selection
Luke 14:23

Background Scripture
Luke 14:7-24

Devotional Reading
1 Peter 5:3-10

Aug. 28

511

Jesus often compared the Kingdom of God with a great feast, now often called "the Messianic banquet." This lesson presents two scenes in which this theme of "feasting" is prominent.

Although two different aspects of the Messianic banquet are presented here, they have in common the idea that serving God is like receiving an invitation to a party! This triggers at least two different responses among many people. Some ask Who else will be there, and How can I upstage them?, while others (guys?) ask, Do I have to go?

The first part of the lesson affirms that we don't need to compete with others for prominence at the banquet. There is room for all, and since everyone is invited we are advised to have a humble spirit about being there. The second "feast" lesson is about the importance of commitment, of showing up at the banquet. If we don't, we can be sure others will take our place!

Lead into this lesson by asking group members to share their thoughts when they receive an invitation to a party. Responses might include *What shall I wear? . . . Who else will be there? . . . Is it important that I attend? . . . If I don't, what will people say about me?*

Note that the ideal reason for hosting a party or a banquet is so that guests can have a good time being together. Jesus' frequent use of the feast as a symbol of the Kingdom of God grows out of His desire for all people to know this joy. Although many of His people, the Jews, had an exclusive view of the Kingdom, Jesus taught that the Messianic banquet is for all, that there should be no competition for the host's favor, and that since the feast is hosted by the King Himself, it's something we don't want to miss.

Teaching Outline	**Daily Bible Readings**

I. Seeking Prominence—7-11
  A. The shame of demotion, 8-9
  B. The honor of promotion, 10-11
II. Giving Excuses—15-24
  A. 'All things are ready!', 15-17
  B. Distractions and excuses, 18-20
  C. Filling empty seats, 21-24
	Mon. Bear with One Another
	        Ephesians 4:1-6
	Tue. Imitate Christ's Humility
	        Philippians 2:1-8
	Wed. Be Clothed in Humility
	        1 Peter 5:3-10
	Thu. The Wedding Banquet
	        Matthew 22:1-10
	Fri. Jesus Heals a Man
	        Luke 14:1-6
	Sat. Humility and Hospitality
	        Luke 14:7-14
	Sun. The Great Feast
	        Luke 14:15-24

Verse by Verse

I. Seeking Prominence—7-11
A. The shame of demotion, 7-9

7 And he put forth a parable to those which were bidden, when he marked how they chose out the chief rooms; saying unto them,

8 When thou art bidden of any man to a wedding, sit not down in the highest room; lest a more honourable man than thou be bidden of him;

9 And he that bade thee and him come and say to thee, Give this man place; and thou begin with shame to take the lowest room.

Reading ahead to verse 12, we learn that Jesus and others had been invited to a banquet; so the lessons he draws here are not technically a parable, but were drawn from an actual event. In verses 7-11 He uses this event to draw lessons on humility, while in verses 12-14 the lesson is on the virtue of inclusiveness over exclusiveness when inviting guests.

Jesus uses the imagery of a feast or banquet at least four times in His teaching. This theme would have grown naturally out of the importance of feast days in the Jewish faith. Before the destruction of Jerusalem in A.D. 70, adult male Jews were expected to attend at least one

of four great annual events in Jerusalem—the feast of Passover (or Unleavened Bread), Atonement, Pentecost (or Weeks) and Tabernacles (or Booths). These great gatherings were supplemented by many other less important feasts. It was out of these glad times of fellowship and feasting that the concept of the "Messianic banquet" as the culmination of the Kingdom of God grew.

Verse 7 pictures several low tables with pillows on which to recline, and invited guests competing for the "chief rooms" (NIV "places of honor"), or places closest to the host. Since not everyone could sit at the host's table, special reservations were often made for prominent people.

B. The honor of promotion, 10-11

10 But when thou art bidden, go and sit down in the lowest room; that when he that bade thee cometh, he may say unto thee, Friend, go up higher: then shalt thou have worship in the presence of them that sit at meat with thee.

11 For whosoever exalteth himself shall be abased; and he that humbleth himself shall be exalted.

Common sense can see how much

better it would be to be asked to move up to the "head table" than down to a lower place. Unless the host signals a guest to come up immediately and join him, Jesus advises that it's better to take a lower seat. Then, if the host has reserved a higher place for you, rising to go take that seat will bring "worship" (*doxa*, lit. "glory" or honor) from the other guests.

The adage in verse 11 that Jesus adds to this common-sense picture shows that glory is not something to be sought in this life after all. The imagery here transforms the actual banquet to which Jesus was invited to the Messsianic feast in the future; and Jesus shows how to be invited to the "chief seat" not at a mere party but in the kingdom of God. That method, He says, is to take a place of lowly service in this life.

This is the same lesson Jesus taught when He realized that His closest disciples were walking along and arguing with each other about who would be "the greatest" in the Kingdom. He told them that he who would be the greatest there must be the lowliest servant here. (Note that the saying in verse 11 is repeated in 18:14.

Although the most obvious application of this truth is at the level of personal humility, we may wonder if it also has overtones of the Jewish "competition" with the Gentiles. We recall the serious debate even after Jesus' death and resurrection on whether Gentiles were even to have a place at the Messianic Banquet without an "invitation" through the Law of Moses (leading to the Jerusalem conference in Acts 15). The fact that the Gentile question arises in the next "feast parable" makes it at least possible that Jesus is also saying to Jews that they should take the lower seats lest they be supplanted in dishonor by the inclusion of Gentiles in the higher seats, next to the Host.

II. Giving Excuses—15-24
A. 'All things are ready!', 15-17

15 And when one of them that sat at meat with him heard these things, he said unto him, Blessed is he that shall eat bread in the kingdom of God.

16 Then said he unto him, A certain man made a great supper, and bade many:

17 And sent his servant at supper time to say to them that were bidden, Come; for all things are now ready.

One of Jesus' companions overheard Him comment on the importance of inviting the poor and disadvantaged to such feasts, and made the very good observation that those were truly blessed who were invited to the Messianic Banquet, the grandest feast of all. That prompts the following parable, with the "certain man" standing for God Himself. "Those who were bidden" probably represent the Jews, God's chosen race, to whom the Messiah was sent to invite to His great feast. Although Jesus' companion did not know it, since the Messiah is here, the feast was ready!

B. Distractions and excuses, 18-20

18 And they all with one consent began to make excuse. The first said unto him, I have bought a piece of ground, and I must needs go and see it: I pray thee have me excused.

19 And another said, I have bought five yoke of oxen, and I go to prove them: I pray thee have me excused.

20 And another said, I have married a wife, and therefore I cannot come.

None of these reasons given for being unable to come to the feast are unacceptable activities in themselves. Buying land and oxen, and getting married, are all worthy activities—until they come between a person and accepting an invitation to the Messianic banquet. Actually, all these are transparent excuses, rather than reasons. For example, who would buy a piece of land without looking at it first, or a yoke of oxen without first "trying them out" (NIV)? As for marriage, a newlywed should surely pay attention to his spouse, but even a new wife deserves an occasional break! The point, of course, is that none of these invited guests really want to come to the banquet. The consistent resistance of most Jews to the invitation extended by their own Messiah makes it likely that they are represented in this parable by those who are making the flimsy excuses.

C. Filling empty seats, 21-24

21 So that servant came, and shewed his lord these things. Then the master of the house being angry said to his servant, Go out quickly into the streets and lanes of the city, and bring in hither the poor, and the maimed, and the halt, and the blind.

22 And the servant said, Lord, it is done as thou hast commanded, and yet there is room.

23 And the lord said unto the servant, Go out into the highways and hedges, and compel them to come in, that my house may be filled.

24 For I say unto you, That none of those men which were bidden shall taste of my supper.

This description of the "substitute guests" also suggests the Jew-Gentile comparison in the parable. Since those for whom the banquet was originally planned turn down their invitations, the host seeks replacements among the lowest and most socially unacceptable people—a good description of the Gentiles, in the eyes of the Jews. These "socially unacceptable" people also, by design, fit the description of inclusiveness Jesus had given in verses 12-14.

The parable emphasizes the importance of commitment. The only requirement to attend the Messianic Banquet is caring about it enough to accept the invitation. Verse 24 indicates that those who cannot bring themselves even to do that will not be given a later chance.

Evangelistic Emphasis

Have you ever worked up the courage finally to invite a friend to church only to have that person make several excuses about why he or she cannot go? It can be an uncomfortable situation. Usually the reasons have to do with being busy with other things: *I'm going out of town... We promised to visit my mother on Sunday.* If we listen closely to what is being said, what we hear is people who are finding their fulfillment and life in other places. They see no need for church or regular religious involvement. The end result is that we might become discouraged in asking.

We might think that no one is interested. Jesus' parable of the Great Supper reminds us that this is not true. There are many who have yet to hear that they are truly welcome at the table of the Lord. The parable encourages us to look with new eyes—to look beyond those whom we think should be receptive to the call—to look for those we have overlooked—to look for those who will rejoice when invited. Of course, such an approach might take us places we have yet to go.

෨)෬

And the lord said unto the servant, Go out into the highways and hedges, and compel them to come in, that my house may be filled.—*Luke 14:23*

This short sentence from Jesus' parable corrects several of our mistaken assumptions about God. While it may be easy for us to lapse into thinking that He is primarily an exacting God of judgment and exclusion, Jesus' parable tells us that God is determined that He will have a full house to celebrate with Him. He anticipates a joyous feast with a huge crowd, and He is willing to search for those who will respond to His invitation—even compelling them to accept.

This means that God does not easily give up on us. We may find ourselves in the highways and hedges of life thinking that we are of little value to the Master. It is easy for us to imagine that we are not among those in whom God would find pleasure and enjoyment. Jesus says that kind of thinking is wrong. Who we have been and where we have been is not a factor in gaining entrance to the feast. All that is necessary is to hear the invitation of God's servant and to respond in joy.

516

Weekday Problems

Margaret sat in the Bible classroom looking around in dismay. This was the reason she had considered not even coming to class today. Since moving to this city and becoming a member of this church, she had tried numerous ways to form a circle of friends.

From where Margaret sat she could see three people she had invited to her home for dinner, yet she had not received one invitation in return. What was up with these people? Didn't they at least have good manners? Margaret was so upset she did not hear the teacher give the Scripture reference for the day's lesson. "When you give a luncheon or a dinner," the teacher began to read, "do not invite your friends . . . ."

Margaret was transfixed. It was as if her mind was being read. "If you do," the teacher continued, "they may invite you back and so you will be repaid."

"Well, wasn't that the idea?" Margaret thought. The rest of the passage presented a different idea. Margaret left that day with a new mission.

* From the remainder of today's text, what do you think Margaret's new plan was?

* Where could Margaret find guests for her next dinner party?

Point of View

Your Problem		My Situation
When you get angry, it's because you are ill-tempered.	___	It just happens that my nerves are bothering me.
When you don't like someone, it's because you are prejudiced.	___	I happen to be a good judge of human nature.
When you compliment someone, you're using flattery.	___	I'm a natural-born encourager.
When you take a long time to do a job, it's because you're slow.	___	When I take a long time, it's a sign I believe in quality workmanship.
When you spend your paycheck in 24 hours, you're a spendthrift.	___	When I spend it all, it's because I'm just a generous person.
When you stay in bed until 11, you're a lazy goldbrick.	___	When I sleep late, it's because I am totally exhausted.

This Lesson in Your Life

The lesson for today includes three short parables of Jesus. The three have in common the theme of eating, but each one teaches a different lesson. From the final story (Luke 14:16-24), we learn of God's determined and persistent grace. In the second parable (14:12-14), we are challenged to abandon our usual pattern of giving with the expectation of receiving in return. Both of these stories strike a chord with us.

The first story, however, can be easily dismissed as not relevant to our lives. Few of us would dare attend a formal banquet and presume to seat ourselves at the head table without being invited to do so. Surely we possess enough social grace to avoid such a faux pas. The question, however, is do we apply this same grace to all areas of our lives? What are the ways in which we do seek to sit in the place of honor? This is cause for serious self-examination. Perhaps some more questions are in order:

* How do I respond when a co-worker is recognized and I am not?

* Do I ever practice the subtle art of name-dropping?

* Do I ever stop to consider what others might think when I am selecting a new car or new clothes?

* Do I ever steer a conversation in a direction that will allow me to mention an accomplishment or event of which I am proud?

* Do I ever take the opportunity to mention a negative quality or trait of another person?

There are many ways we can attempt to "work ourselves up to the choicest seats." Jesus' exhortation to avoid such embarrassments continues to be wise instruction even to those of us who have learned more sophisticated ways of arranging the seating.

1. What prompted Jesus to tell a parable about humbling oneself?
Jesus observed that the guests at the dinner were choosing to sit in the choicest seats (Luke 14:7).

2. What is the danger of seeking out the place of honor?
You can be embarrassed when you are asked to take a more lowly position (14:9).

3. What is the danger of inviting only friends, family, or wealthy people to one's home?
They may return the invitation, and you will be repaid (14:12).

4. To whom should a disciple of Jesus try to minister?
Jesus encourages us to provide for those who cannot repay us: the poor, the maimed, the lame, and the blind (14:13).

5. What statement made by a guest at the dinner Jesus was attending prompted Jesus to tell the Parable of the Great Supper?
A guest said, "Blessed is he that shall eat bread in the kingdom of God" (14:15).

6. In Jesus' Parable of the Great Supper, what did the invited guests do when the feast was ready?
They began to make excuses to avoid attending the feast (14:18-20).

7. Who were summoned to the feast when the invited guests declined?
The servant was to go into the streets and lanes of the city and bring in the poor, the maimed, the lame and the blind (14:21).

8. What was the problem after these guests were invited?
The servant reported that there was more room available (14:22).

9. How did the master address this problem?
He sent the servant to the highways and hedges to compel people to come in so that his house would be filled (14:23).

10. What was the fate of the original guests who had received invitations?
None of them were allowed to partake of the master's supper (14:24).

Bob was glad to let the migrant workers use his barn to hold their end-of-the season party. Through the years, the orchard owner had come to know many of them well, and counted them among his friends. In appreciation for his generosity, the workers had invited Bob to share in the festivities. He and his wife Sherry were having a great time watching the celebration of another year's work well done. "Mr. James," one of the workers said to Bob, "we would like for you to draw the name for the lottery."

"Lottery?" he asked.

"Yes sir," came the reply. "Every year at our party we all buy tickets for $50. The family who wins gets the money for a visit back home." Bob was deeply touched. He knew what that kind of money meant to these hard working people.

"I'd be honored," Bob said.

"There's one more thing," the man said. "We're taking up a collection to buy a ticket for Rosa." Bob knew Rosa. Her husband had been killed in a tragic auto accident early in the season, and the crew had continued caring for her and her small children throughout the fall.

"Let me just pay for it," Bob offered.

"Thanks, but no," the man said. "We all want to do it."

A few moments later Miguel, the crew leader, stood on a box and got the crowd's attention. "Friends," he said, "it's time for the drawing. Mr. James will draw the winning name." The workers applauded Bob warmly as he made his way toward the basket filled with folded strips of paper. He stood looking down at the tangled slips—wishing he could pick out Rosa's. He even said a quick prayer as he plunged his hand into the basket.

"And the winner is . . . " he said dramatically, " . . . the winner is . . . *Rosa!*" The crowd erupted into cheers. Bob could hardly believe his eyes. He looked again at the paper strip. Yes, it had Rosa's name. He saw the young woman dissolve into tears, clutching her children to her. The rest of the evening was filled with joy. It was as if every family had won the state lottery.

Later that night, Bob was helping with the clean-up. He picked up the basket to empty its contents into the trash can. On a whim, he plucked another paper from the stack and read the name. "Rosa." He chose another. "Rosa." All the slips read, "Rosa." Each family had written the young widow's name on their treasured slip of paper. It was their gift—to one who had nothing to give in return.